Course Nielsen-HandlerTaking Sides: Clashing
Views in American Foreign Policy 6e

JUN 0 3 2013

The McGraw-Hill Companies

http://create.mcgraw-hill.com

ISBN-10: 1121824579   ISBN-13: 9781121824577

Contents

Credits

Preface

On October 9, 2009, shortly after taking office, President Barack Obama was awarded the Nobel Peace Prize. The Norwegian Nobel Committee said they selected him because of his "efforts to strengthen international diplomacy and cooperation between peoples . . . . and [to] create a new climate in international politics [in which] multilateral diplomacy has regained a central position." They further stated that his "diplomacy is founded in the concept that those who are to lead the world must do so on the basis of values and attitudes that are shared by the majority of the world's population" (The Nobel Peace Prize, 2009). At the time he received this award, the foreign policy challenges facing President Obama included wars in Iraq and Afghanistan, Iran's nuclear program, troubled relations with Russia, and concerns over the size of the U.S. trade deficit with China. As he addressed these challenges—and others that followed, such as the Arab Spring and the European debt crisis—did President Obama succeed in fulfilling the hopes of the Nobel Committee by changing the direction of U.S. foreign policy? The answer to this question has been the subject of a vigorous debate.

In foreign policy, there are elements of continuity between presidential administrations as well as opportunities to change direction. As of this writing, the United States is about to select its next president. However, it is not clear—other than in tone or rhetoric—how different the foreign policy of another Obama Administration would be from that of an administration led by his Republican challenger, Governor Mitt Romney. By thinking critically about the issues discussed in this book, readers can gain a better appreciation of the constraints facing policymakers that may help to explain continuity as well as change.

This volume seeks to engage students in some of the most significant foreign policy debates taking place in the United States today. It is structured in a pro–con format and each issue centers on a question that is answered by YES and NO selections. Of course, most of these questions have more than two answers, and students should seek to explore these possibilities by reading the framing sections that surround each set of articles and in subsequent class discussions. In approaching these debates, it is critical to recognize that it is possible to have reasoned arguments with people who hold different views. In addition, it is important that analysts and policymakers—as well as students—seek multiple and competing perspectives to test and improve their understandings. This approach, known as intellectual pluralism, recognizes that no single theory can explain all the challenges in American foreign policy. Instead, it is valuable for both practitioners and students to consider a variety of viewpoints when analyzing American foreign policy choices and thinking about the way ahead.

This collection consists of 17 issue questions and 34 answer articles. The *Introduction* provides additional ways of thinking about the analysis of important foreign policy challenges. The Issue questions are grouped into six units—*The United States and its Place in the International System; National Security Issues; Regional and Bilateral Relations; U.S. Economic Concerns; The United States and International Rules, Norms, Laws, and Institutions;* and *Domestic Influences on U.S. Foreign Policy.* Each *Issue Introduction* has been expanded (from the previous edition of this book and other Taking Sides books) to include more information and appreciation for the context of the debate. Each *Issue Introduction* also includes a section on key *Learning Outcomes*, which lists the specific information that students should take out of each issue. The *Exploring the Issue* section that follows the pro–con articles presents critical thinking questions to guide student reflection. This section also includes an *Is There Common Ground?* commentary that explores whether contrasting viewpoints can be reconciled. Finally, the *Additional Resources* section provides sources for further information on the topic and specific articles cited in the *Issue Introduction.*

All 34 articles in this sixth edition are new to *Taking Sides: Clashing Views in American Foreign Policy.* Additionally, this edition has added an entirely new unit. Unit 6 is about *Domestic Influences on U.S. Foreign Policy* and explores the relevance of Congress and the power of the president in making important decisions relating to U.S. foreign policy. This new edition also includes recent essays on subjects that include multilateralism, defense spending, foreign aid, state building in Afghanistan, aid to Pakistan, dependence on foreign oil, the International Criminal Court, and the circumstances governing U.S. military intervention abroad.

An *Instructor's Resource Guide with Test Questions* is available through the publisher for instructors using Taking Sides in the classroom. Also available is a general guidebook, *Using Taking Sides in the Classroom,* which offers suggestions for adapting the pro–con approach in any classroom setting. An online version of *Using Taking Sides in the Classroom* and a correspondence service for Taking Sides adopters can be found at www.mhhe.com/cls. *Taking Sides: Clashing Views in American Foreign Policy,* 6th edition, is only one title in the Taking Sides series. If you are interested in seeing the table of contents for any of the other titles, please visit the Taking Sides website at www.mhhe.com/cls.

Acknowledgments

We co-editors are indebted to our colleagues at the United States Military Academy who were instrumental in helping us produce this volume by contributing their expertise on the issues covered. We would like to especially acknowledge the work of Brian Babcock-Lumish, Jordan Becker, Ruth Beitler, Heidi Brockmann, Dean Dudley, Jim Golby, John Hagen, Liesl Himmelberger, Paul Larson, Ruth Mower, Irvin Oliver Jr., William Parsons, Robert Person, Sukhdev Purewal, Mike Rosol, Phil Salter, William Taylor, Heidi Urben, and Tom Walsh. We would also like to thank Jill Meloy and the McGraw-Hill team for their efforts to produce this book.

Suzanne C. Nielsen
United States Military Academy

Scott P. Handler
United States Military Academy

Editors

Suzanne C. Nielsen, a colonel in the U.S. Army, is an associate professor and the director of the International Relations Program at the United States Military Academy at West Point, New York. Responsible for an academic major and associated electives, as well as a core course taught to every cadet, she teaches courses in international relations theory and national security. Her research interests include change in military organizations, civil–military relations, and cyber as a national security challenge. Her dissertation, *Preparing for War: The Dynamics of Peacetime Military Reform*, won the American Political Science Association's Lasswell Award for the best dissertation in the field of public policy in 2002 and 2003. Her books include *American National Security*, 6th edition, which she co-authored, and *American Civil-Military Relations: The Soldier and the State in a New Era*, which she co-edited, both released by Johns Hopkins University Press in 2009.

Scott P. Handler, a major in the U.S. Army, is an assistant professor of international relations at West Point. He has served as an executive officer of the international relations and comparative politics programs, the course director for the core course in international relations taken by all cadets, and the director of the international relations and comparative politics thesis programs. He has taught classes on international relations, national security strategy, and cyber strategy and policy. He is the editor of *International Politics: Classic and Contemporary Readings*, released by CQ Press in 2012.

Issue Researchers

Brian Babcock-Lumish is a military intelligence officer in the U.S. Army and an assistant professor of international relations at West Point.

Jordan Becker is a foreign area officer in the U.S. Army and an instructor of international relations at West Point.

Ruth Margolies Beitler is a professor of comparative politics at West Point.

Heidi Brockmann is a military intelligence officer in the U.S. Army and an assistant professor of American politics at West Point.

Dean Dudley is an associate professor of economics at West Point.

Andrew Gallo is an infantry officer in the U.S. Army and a former assistant professor of American politics at West Point.

Jim Golby is an army strategist in the U.S. Army and an assistant professor of American politics at West Point.

John Hagen is an air force officer and an assistant professor of international relations at West Point.

Liesl Himmelberger is an army strategist in the U.S. Army and an instructor of economics at West Point.

Paul Larson is an infantry officer in the U.S. Army and a former assistant professor of international relations at West Point.

Ruth Mower is an engineer officer in the U.S. Army and an instructor of international relations and comparative politics at West Point.

Irvin Oliver Jr. is an army strategist in the U.S. Army and a former assistant professor of international relations and comparative politics at West Point.

William Parsons is an infantry officer in the U.S. Army and an assistant professor of international relations at West Point.

Robert Person is an assistant professor of international relations and comparative politics at West Point.

Sukhdev Purewal is a foreign area officer in the U.S. Army and a former assistant professor of comparative politics at West Point.

Mike Rosol is a cavalry officer in the U.S. Army and an instructor of international relations at West Point.

Philip Salter served as the chair for national intelligence studies and visiting professor of international relations at West Point from 2010 to 2012.

William Taylor is a strategic intelligence officer in the U.S. Army and a former assistant professor of American politics at West Point.

Heidi A. Urben is a military intelligence officer in the U.S. Army and an assistant professor of American politics at West Point.

Tom Walsh is a foreign service officer in the U.S. Department of State currently assigned as a visiting professor of international relations at West Point.

Academic Advisory Board Members

Correlation Guide

The *Taking Sides* series presents current issues in a debate-style format designed to stimulate student interest and develop critical thinking skills. Each issue is thoughtfully framed with an issue summary, learning outcomes, an issue introduction, and a section on exploring the issue. The pro and con essays—selected for their liveliness and substance—represent the arguments of leading scholars and commentators in their fields.

Taking Sides: Clashing Views in American Foreign Policy, 6/e is an easy-to-use reader that presents issues on important topics such as *security issues, regional and bilateral relations,* and *economic and environmental issues.* For more information on *Taking Sides* and other *McGraw-Hill Contemporary Learning Series* titles, visit www.mhhe.com/cls.

This convenient guide matches the issues in **Taking Sides: American Foreign Policy, 6/e** with the corresponding chapters in one of our best-selling McGraw-Hill Political Science textbooks by Boyer.

TAKING SIDES: American Foreign Policy, 6/e	Global Politics, 1/e by Boyer et al
Should the United States Seek a Leadership Role in International Affairs?	**Chapter 2:** Interpreting Power: A Levels-of-Analysis Approach
Should Promoting Democracy Abroad Be a Top U.S. Priority?	**Chapter 3:** Nations, States, and Identity
Is a Multilateral Approach to International Affairs in the Best Interest of the United States?	**Chapter 2:** Interpreting Power: A Levels-of-Analysis Approach
Should U.S. Defense Spending Be Reduced Dramatically?	**Chapter 6:** Pursuing Security
Does Spending on Foreign Aid Further U.S. National Interests?	**Chapter 6:** Pursuing Security **Chapter 11:** Human Rights: A Tool for Preserving and Enhancing Human Dignity
Should the United States Continue a Strategy of State Building in Afghanistan?	**Chapter 5:** International Organizations: Global and Regional Governance **Chapter 7:** Conflict and Conflict Management
Should the United States Use Military Force to Prevent Iran from Developing a Nuclear Weapon?	**Chapter 6:** Pursuing Security **Chapter 7:** Conflict and Conflict Management
Is a Rising China a Threat to U.S. National Security?	**Chapter 6:** Pursuing Security
Should the United States Play the Leading Role in Revitalizing the Israeli–Palestinian Peace Process?	**Chapter 7:** Conflict and Conflict Management
Should the United States Cut Foreign Aid to Pakistan?	**Chapter 7:** Conflict and Conflict Management
Is Free Trade Good for the United States?	**Chapter 9:** Global Political Economy—Protecting Wealth in the Dominant System **Chapter 10:** Global Political Economy—Searching for Equity in the Dependent System
Should the United States Eliminate Its Dependence on Foreign Oil?	**Chapter 12:** Global Political Ecology
Should the United States Join the International Criminal Court?	**Chapter 8:** International Law and Transitional Justice
Should the United States Intervene Militarily in the Absence of a Direct Threat to U.S. National Interests?	**Chapter 8:** International Law and Transitional Justice
Are U.S. Diplomatic Efforts Needed to Create a Binding International Climate Change Treaty?	**Chapter 12:** Global Political Ecology
Is Congress Still Relevant in U.S. Foreign Policy Making?	**Chapter 1:** Thinking about Global Politics
Does the President Have Too Much Power in Decision Making About the Use of American Military Power Abroad?	**Chapter 1:** Thinking about Global Politics **Chapter 4:** Globalization: Politics from Above and Below

Topic Guide

Selected, Edited, and with Issue Framing Material by:
Suzanne Nielsen, *U.S. Military Academy*
and
Scott Handler, *U.S. Military Academy*

Afghanistan

Does Spending on Foreign Aid Further U.S. National Interests?
Should the United States Continue a Strategy of State Building in Afghanistan?
Should the United States Cut Foreign Aid to Pakistan?

Alliances

Should the United States Seek a Leadership Role in International Affairs?
Is a Multilateral Approach to International Affairs in the Best Interest of the United States?

American Exceptionalism

Should the United States Seek a Leadership Role in International Affairs?
Should Promoting Democracy Abroad Be a Top U.S. Priority?
Is a Multilateral Approach to International Affairs in the Best Interest of the United States?

China

Should Promoting Democracy Abroad Be a Top U.S. Priority?
Is a Rising China a Threat to U.S. National Security?
Is Free Trade Good for the United States?

Climate Change

Should the United States Eliminate Its Dependence on Foreign Oil?
Are U.S. Diplomatic Efforts Needed to Create a Binding International Climate Change Treaty?

Congress

Should U.S. Defense Spending Be Reduced Dramatically?
Does Spending on Foreign Aid Further U.S. National Interests?
Should the United States Cut Foreign Aid to Pakistan?
Is Congress Still Relevant in U.S. Foreign Policy making?
Does the President Have Too Much Power in Decision Making About the Use of American Military Power Abroad?

Constitution (United States)

Is Congress Still Relevant in U.S. Foreign Policy Making?
Does the President Have Too Much Power in Decision Making About the Use of American Military Power Abroad?

Defense

Should U.S. Defense Spending Be Reduced Dramatically?
Should the United States Continue a Strategy of State Building in Afghanistan?
Should the United States Use Military Force to Prevent Iran from Developing a Nuclear Weapon?
Is a Rising China a Threat to U.S. National Security?
Should the United States Intervene Militarily in the Absence of a Direct Threat to U.S. National Interests?
Is Congress Still Relevant in U.S. Foreign Policy Making?
Does the President Have Too Much Power in Decision Making About the Use of American Military Power Abroad?

Democratization

Should Promoting Democracy Abroad Be a Top U.S. Priority?
Should the United States Continue a Strategy of State Building in Afghanistan?

Development

Does Spending on Foreign Aid Further U.S. National Interests?
Should the United States Continue a Strategy of State Building in Afghanistan?
Should the United States Cut Foreign Aid to Pakistan?
Are U.S. Diplomatic Efforts Needed to Create a Binding International Climate Change Treaty?

Diplomacy

Should the United States Seek a Leadership Role in International Affairs?
Is a Multilateral Approach to International Affairs in the Best Interest of the United States?
Does Spending on Foreign Aid Further U.S. National Interests?
Should the United States Play the Leading Role in Revitalizing the Israeli–Palestinian Peace Process?
Should the United States Cut Foreign Aid to Pakistan?
Should the United States Join the International Criminal Court?
Are U.S. Diplomatic Efforts Needed to Create a Binding International Climate Change Treaty?

Domestic Politics

Should U.S. Defense Spending Be Reduced Dramatically?
Does Spending on Foreign Aid Further U.S. National Interests?
Is Free Trade Good for the United States?
Is Congress Still Relevant in U.S. Foreign Policy Making?
Does the President Have Too Much Power in Decision Making About the Use of American Military Power Abroad?

Economics

Should U.S. Defense Spending Be Reduced Dramatically?
Does Spending on Foreign Aid Further U.S. National Interests?
Should the United States Cut Foreign Aid to Pakistan?
Is Free Trade Good for the United States?
Should the United States Eliminate Its Dependence on Foreign Oil?

Energy

Should the United States Eliminate Its Dependence on Foreign Oil?
Are U.S. Diplomatic Efforts Needed to Create a Binding International Climate Change Treaty?

Environment

Should the United States Eliminate Its Dependence on Foreign Oil?
Are U.S. Diplomatic Efforts Needed to Create a Binding International Climate Change Treaty?

Foreign Aid

Should Promoting Democracy Abroad Be a Top U.S. Priority?
Does Spending on Foreign Aid Further U.S. National Interests?
Should the United States Cut Foreign Aid to Pakistan?

Globalization

Should the United States Seek a Leadership Role in International Affairs?
Should Promoting Democracy Abroad Be a Top U.S. Priority?
Is a Multilateral Approach to International Affairs in the Best Interest of the United States?
Is Free Trade Good for the United States?
Are U.S. Diplomatic Efforts Needed to Create a Binding International Climate Change Treaty?

(Continued)

Human Rights

Should Promoting Democracy Abroad be a Top U.S. Priority?
Does Spending on Foreign Aid Further U.S. National Interests?
Should the United States Continue a Strategy of State Building in Afghanistan?
Should the United States Join the International Criminal Court?
Should the United States Intervene Militarily in the Absence of a Direct Threat to U.S. National Interests?

Humanitarian Intervention

Should the United States Intervene Militarily in the Absence of a Direct Threat to U.S. National Interests?

International Criminal Court

Should the United States Seek a Leadership Role in International Affairs?
Is a Multilateral Approach to International Affairs in the Best Interest of the United States?
Should the United States Join the International Criminal Court?

International Institutions

Should the United States Seek a Leadership Role in International Affairs?
Is a Multilateral Approach to International Affairs in the Best Interest of the United States?
Should the United States Join the International Criminal Court?
Are U.S. Diplomatic Efforts Needed to Create a Binding International Climate Change Treaty?

International Law

Is a Multilateral Approach to International Affairs in the Best Interest of the United States?
Should the United States Join the International Criminal Court?
Are U.S. Diplomatic Efforts Needed to Create a Binding International Climate Change Treaty?

International Relations

Should the United States Seek a Leadership Role in International Affairs?
Should Promoting Democracy Abroad Be a Top U.S. Priority?
Is a Multilateral Approach to International Affairs in the Best Interest of the United States?
Is a Rising China a Threat to U.S. National Security?
Is Free Trade Good for the United States?
Are U.S. Diplomatic Efforts Needed to Create a Binding International Climate Change Treaty?

Iran

Should the United States Use Military Force to Prevent Iran from Developing a Nuclear Weapon?

Israel

Should the United States Play the Leading Role in Revitalizing the Israeli–Palestinian Peace Process?

Middle East

Should Promoting Democracy Abroad Be a Top U.S. Priority?
Should the United States Use Military Force to Prevent Iran from Developing a Nuclear Weapon?
Should the United States Play the Leading Role in Revitalizing the Israeli–Palestinian Peace Process?

Military

Should U.S. Defense Spending Be Reduced Dramatically?
Should the United States Continue a Strategy of State Building in Afghanistan?
Should the United States Use Military Force to Prevent Iran from Developing a Nuclear Weapon?
Should the United States Intervene Militarily in the Absence of a Direct Threat to U.S. National Interests?
Does the President Have Too Much Power in Decision Making About the Use of American Military Power Abroad?

Pakistan

Should Promoting Democracy Abroad Be a Top U.S. Priority?
Does Spending on Foreign Aid Further U.S. National Interests?
Should the United States Cut Foreign Aid to Pakistan?

Palestine

Should the United States Play the Leading Role in Revitalizing the Israeli–Palestinian Peace Process?

Peace

Should the United States Seek a Leadership Role in International Affairs?
Should Promoting Democracy Abroad Be a Top U.S. Priority?
Is a Multilateral Approach to International Affairs in the Best Interest of the United States?
Should the United States Continue a Strategy of State Building in Afghanistan?
Should the United States Play the Leading Role in Revitalizing the Israeli–Palestinian Peace Process?

President (United States)

Is Congress Still Relevant in U.S. Foreign Policy Making?
Does the President Have Too Much Power in Decision Making About the Use of American Military Power Abroad?

Terrorism

Should Promoting Democracy Abroad Be a Top U.S. Priority?
Does Spending on Foreign Aid Further U.S. National Interests?
Should the United States Continue a Strategy of State Building in Afghanistan?
Should the United States Cut Foreign Aid to Pakistan?

Trade

Should the United States Seek a Leadership Role in International Affairs?
Is a Multilateral Approach to International Affairs in the Best Interest of the United States?
Is Free Trade Good for the United States?
Should the United States Eliminate Its Dependence on Foreign Oil?

War

Should the United States Continue a Strategy of State Building in Afghanistan?
Should the United States Use Military Force to Prevent Iran from Developing a Nuclear Weapon?
Should the United States Intervene Militarily in the Absence of a Direct Threat to U.S. National Interests?
Does the President Have Too Much Power in Decision Making About the Use of American Military Power Abroad?

Introduction

In his farewell address in 1796, President George Washington famously argued that it "is our true policy to steer clear of permanent alliances with any portion of the foreign world." While he advocated the promotion of U.S. commercial interests abroad, Washington was concerned that political allegiances to foreign countries could become a threat to democracy at home. Having weathered controversy during his presidency stemming from his efforts to avoid entanglement in wars involving great powers in Europe, he went on to explain: "With me a predominant motive has been to endeavor to gain time to our country to settle and mature its yet recent institutions, and to progress without interruption to that degree of strength and consistency which is necessary to give it, humanly speaking, the command of its own fortunes." If the United States maintained unity at home and was prudent in its public affairs, Washington foresaw the day when Americans would be free to "choose peace or war, as [their] interest, guided by justice, shall counsel" (Washington, 1796).

Looking back on these remarks from the perspective of the twenty-first century, it is easy to identify what has changed. The United States no longer has political institutions facing their first tests; the framework established by the U.S. Constitution has survived more than 200 years of practice. And the United States is no longer weak relative to great powers abroad; instead, it is often identified as the one country in the world possessing such a disproportionate concentration of power that it is labeled a "superpower." As Washington hoped would one day be the case, the United States now has the capability to chart its own course. One thing that has not changed, however, is the existence of a lively debate over the role the United States should play in international affairs. The number of dimensions along which this debate can take place begins to reveal the complexities and uncertainties associated with American foreign policymaking.

Foreign Policy and the National Interest

When thinking about foreign policy, a useful place to start is with the concept of national interest. In essence, American foreign policies are choices made by the U.S. government about what to do beyond the country's borders to serve U.S. interests. Therefore, a useful first step for foreign policymakers as they look at particular opportunities or threats is to ask themselves what U.S. interests are at stake. In generic terms, these interests are easy to identify, and include physical security, economic prosperity, and the preservation of the system of government that enables the American way of life. Nevertheless, even

if these general interests are widely embraced in principle, as soon as one evaluates them in the context of particular cases, there is plenty of room for contention over what they mean and what promoting them should actually entail. The promotion of economic prosperity provides one easy example. While both Republicans and Democrats in the United States would seek to promote the strength and vitality of the American economy, they are likely to differ about the extent and nature of appropriate government involvement. These fundamental differences in perspective carry over into the realm of foreign policy.

As illuminated by the issues in this volume, there are at least four important sources of debate with regard to the relationship between U.S. national interests and foreign policy choice. First, scholars, pundits, and policymakers may disagree over whether a particular U.S. interest is at stake in a particular policy choice. A good example of this is the issue *Should the United States Continue a Strategy of State Building in Afghanistan?* in this volume, which looks at whether it is in the national interest of the United States to pursue a policy of state building in Afghanistan. Ever since the terrorist attacks against the United States on September 11, 2001, it has been an important goal of U.S. policymakers to combat terrorist groups in order to prevent a repeat of the events of that terrible day. Is this U.S. interest in protecting its physical security against acts of terrorism being served by the state-building efforts undertaken by the United States and its international partners in Afghanistan? Some argue that the prevention of future, large-scale acts of terrorism that are resourced and coordinated from within Afghanistan requires the development of an Afghan government capable of maintaining order within its borders and meeting the needs of its people. Others argue that U.S. physical security is not at stake because it is possible to prevent a repeat of 9/11 through less expensive and more targeted policies that do not aim to achieve the infeasible objective of creating an Afghan state. In sum, while all may agree that combating terrorism is a good thing, there is disagreement over whether state building efforts in Afghanistan will contribute to this end.

As a second potential source of debate, policymakers may agree that important national interests of the United States are at stake in a particular situation and disagree on how they may best be served. An excellent example of this is the issue in this book, *Is Rising China a Threat to U.S. National Security?* which examines the implications of the reemergence of China as a great power in Asia. There is wide agreement among policymakers and national security analysts that the rise of China has important implications for U.S. economic and security interests. However, that does not mean that there is agreement over the best way for the United States to respond to this dynamic. The different perspectives presented here contrast sharply with one another, with one side arguing that the United States should view China's rise as a security threat and seek to slow the growth of the Chinese economy, while the other argues that China's rise need not be seen as menacing as long as China continues to embrace the international institutions that provide a framework for peaceful economic competition among states. Even though there is agreement that important U.S. interests are at stake in the reemergence of China as a great power, the differences between the two sides' policy recommendations could not be starker.

A third possible area of disagreement about the relationship between U.S. national interests and foreign policy choice arises when there is more than one U.S. interest involved—and this is almost always the case. In this situation, there is a clear need to prioritize interests, particularly if the national interests have incompatible policy implications. A good example of this is in the issue *Should U.S. Defense Spending Be Reduced Dramatically?* in this volume that examines the appropriate scale of U.S. defense spending. One issue that is at stake is the physical security of the United States, since the core mission of the Department of Defense is to defend the country against external threats. However, this debate also has implications for economic prosperity, since the U.S. government has accumulated a significant deficit and sound fiscal management is important to the health and continued growth of the U.S. economy.

Even if observers on all sides of the defense budget debate agree that both economic prosperity and physical security are at stake, they may disagree on the right policy response. On the one hand, it is possible to argue that the defense budget is not the most significant contributor to deficit spending and that cutting defense spending too dramatically could create risks that might bring even greater economic costs over the longer term. On the other hand, those on the opposite side of this issue tend to point out that the defense budget is the single largest category of discretionary spending in the federal budget and then argue that the defense budget needs to be reduced as part of any effort to address the fiscal deficit. Many who hold this latter view also assert that such cuts would not pose grave risks to the physical security of the United States. When more than one national interest is at stake, choices will often have to be made over which deserves priority and how they ought to be balanced.

As a fourth and final area for debate, there are differing views over the extent to which the United States ought to serve its values in its actions abroad, as well as its material interests. Some argue that this is a false distinction, in that U.S. values are so intertwined with the country's conception of its interests that these two ideas are inseparable. Nevertheless, in some cases, it seems clear that the U.S. material interests at stake are slight and the primary drivers of foreign policy are nonmaterial concerns. An example in this volume is the issue *Should the United States*

Intervene Militarily in the Absence of a Direct Threat to U.S. National Interests? which focuses on U.S. involvement in the international coalition that intervened militarily in Libya in 2011. Many of those who supported U.S. military intervention in this case argued that it represented an important reflection of U.S. ideals since the United States refused to stand by as a brutal government threatened to inflict mass murder on its citizens. Some of those who opposed this military intervention, on the other hand, believed that it represented an unaffordable international activism and an unwise allocation of U.S. military power that ought to be husbanded to protect against more vital U.S. national security concerns. Those in the latter camp would argue that since the military capabilities of the United States will always be limited, their use should be confined to situations in which the material interests of the United States are at stake.

The debate over the extent to which the United States should actively promote its values abroad goes back to the earliest days of the Republic. The basic values of the United States—as expressed in documents such as the Declaration of Independence—are stated in universal terms:

> We hold these truths to be self-evident, that all men are created equal, that they are endowed by their Creator with certain unalienable Rights, that among these are Life, Liberty and the pursuit of Happiness.—That to secure these rights, Governments are instituted among Men, deriving their just powers from the consent of the governed,—That whenever any Form of Government becomes destructive of these ends, it is the Right of the People to alter or to abolish it, and to institute new Government, laying its foundation on such principles and organizing its powers in such form, as to them shall seem most likely to affect their Safety and Happiness. (1776)

However, even those who embrace the universal validity of U.S. values tend to recognize that the United States lacks the means to foster them everywhere in the world at all times; indeed, the initiation of such an undertaking could undercut democracy at home. As articulated by the sixth President of the United States, John Quincy Adams, before he assumed that office: "Wherever the standard of freedom has been or shall be unfurled, there will [America's] heart, her benedictions, and her prayers be. But she does not go abroad in search of monsters to destroy" (1821). If the United States cannot act to promote its values abroad in all situations, should the country avoid adopting an inconsistent approach and act abroad only when its material interests are at stake? Or are there instances when the threats to U.S. values are so severe—such as a case in which genocide appears imminent—that the United States should still act, even if it does so in an inconsistent manner?

These questions are not easily subject to final resolution. In practice, presidents often make the case for their foreign policies based on appeals to both U.S. interests and values. A famous example is President Woodrow Wilson's explanation that U.S. involvement in World War I was necessary to make the world "safe for democracy" (1917). As an argument that U.S. involvement in the war was necessary to assure the physical protection of the United States and the preservation of its way of life, this was a claim that the war served U.S. interests. However, given that the war would make the world safe for all democracies, it would also further U.S. values on a global scale.

After World War II, Republican Chairman of the Senate Foreign Relations Committee Senator Arthur Vandenburg explained his collaboration with Democratic President Harry Truman on foreign policy with his famous declaration that "politics stop at the water's edge" (1947). In the current era, when partisanship can often seem to create stark divides, this advocacy of bipartisanship in U.S. foreign policy may sound particularly welcome. However, the ideal articulated by Vandenberg can never be true in the strictest sense. At stake in U.S. foreign policy are fundamental questions about how U.S. national interests should be defined and how they may best be served. It is natural that political leaders in the United States will hold differing interpretations on these important questions, as a matter of personal conviction as well as political interest. Therefore, politics cannot be separated from foreign policy choice, which is not necessarily a bad thing. In fact, it is consistent with the democratic deliberation that the founders intended to foster. And public debate may be critical to generating the public support that may be necessary to sustain a foreign policy over the long run.

The Contributions of Different Disciplinary Perspectives

In addition to differing interpretations of the national interest, debates about foreign policymaking can take place along many additional dimensions as well. One way to identify these dimensions is to recognize the wide array of academic disciplines that offer expertise that is relevant to foreign policymakers, to include some such as physics and geology that may not immediately come to mind. The findings of scientists from a variety of disciplines within the physical sciences, for example, are critically important in informing foreign policy choice relating the issue *Are U.S. Diplomatic Efforts Needed to Create a Binding International Climate Change Treaty?* in this volume, which is about global climate change. Though there is an emerging global scientific consensus that climate change is occurring and that human activity has played a role in causing this change, there are still those who dispute the scientific evidence. As long as there are influential voices that challenge the existence of the phenomenon itself, it will be all the more difficult to gain consensus about the foreign policies that are needed to address this intrinsically transnational challenge.

A second issue that provides a great example of the value of technical disciplines to foreign policy relates to the prospects for an international treaty governing the activities of states in cyberspace. Cybersecurity is an issue of increasing importance, as countries such as the United States have come to depend on cyberspace as a place to make and store wealth, as a venue for the delivery of essential services, and for important national security functions. It is not possible to make sound policy—either domestic or foreign—with regard to cyberspace without a solid technical understanding that draws on the expertise of computer scientists, mathematicians, electrical engineers, and other technology experts. Though some policies may seem reasonable on the surface, the physical or logical structure of cyberspace may render them infeasible.

While basic questions about the physical world—and even the virtual world—are at stake in some foreign policy choices, almost all foreign policies would benefit from being informed by history and the social science disciplines of international relations, comparative politics, American politics, and economics. Turning first to history, foreign policymakers almost never have an opportunity to start from a clean slate. Instead, they must be aware of the following: the history of the foreign country or countries involved; the history of that region of the world; and the history of U.S. foreign relations as they pertain to the issue area; and to the country or countries of concern. Even new presidential administrations will inherit past policies that they need to take into account.

Though there are numerous possible examples from the issues within this volume of the importance of history, a particularly pertinent one is the issue *Should the United States Use Military Force to Prevent Iran from Developing a Nuclear Weapon?* which examines whether the United States should use force to prevent Iran from developing a nuclear weapon. All the categories of historical considerations listed above are highly relevant in determining the appropriate way ahead. Iran's history is germane to assessments as to whether the regime will ultimately decide to build nuclear weapons. An understanding of the history of relations between Iran and its neighbors is important in estimating what the expected effects of a U.S. military strike would be. With regard to the issue area, the success or wisdom of past U.S. counter proliferation efforts are pertinent to this choice. And finally, the United States has had problematic relations with the current Iranian regime since its founding. This troubled history of U.S.–Iranian relations increases the difficulty of creating a productive, problem-solving dialogue between the two countries. In sum, the context created by all of these histories is relevant to estimations about what policy will work as well as whether, all things considered, adopting that policy will be in the best interest of the United States.

Another discipline of obvious relevance to foreign policymaking is international relations. Two fundamental areas of inquiry for international relations scholars relate to patterns of conflict and cooperation among states in the international system and the sources of state foreign policy behavior. Scholars working in the discipline draw on schools of thought and more refined theories to describe, explain, or predict events and developments in international affairs. These theories generally have policy-relevant implications. A helpful example from within this volume is the issue *Should the United States Seek a Leadership Role in International Affairs?* which explores whether the United States should assume a leadership role in international affairs. The two sides of the debate differ on fundamental assumptions of international relations theory—such as the primary driver of state behavior—and therefore come up with different propositions about the impact of U.S. leadership on the behavior of other states. As a result, these two perspectives come to dramatically different conclusions as to whether efforts to play a leadership role are in the best interest of the United States.

In addition to international relations, the discipline of comparative politics offers valuable insights to foreign policymakers. Though there is some overlap between the disciplines of international relations and comparative politics, scholars of international relations generally focus on the level of the international system, while scholars of comparative politics examine phenomena and dynamics internal to states. Some comparativists tend to focus on functional concerns—like the conditions under which democratization is likely to be successful—across many states and regions, where others tend to focus on particular regions or countries of primary interest. While the perspective of a comparative politics scholar would be useful in informing all the debates in this book, a particularly valuable example may be the issue *Should the United States Continue a Strategy of State Building in Afghanistan?* which examines the appropriate role of the United States in the Israeli–Palestinian peace process. A scholar of comparative politics would point out the importance of understanding the factors within the parties to the conflict that affect their behavior, to include political institutions, political party structure, political participation, and culture, that will impact the likely success of any way ahead.

In addition to international relations and comparative politics, a third and indispensable field of political science that explores questions relevant to foreign policy making is American politics. As discussed in the previous section, ultimately U.S. foreign policy will be produced through a political process within the United States. Therefore, the nature of U.S. government institutions—to include the three branches of the federal government—will be important, as will the process through which policy is made. Given the pluralism inherent in the U.S. political system, also significant will be political mobilization, political participation, the electoral cycle, and the voting behavior of U.S. citizens.

In this volume, a good example of the importance of insights from American politics in examining U.S. foreign policymaking is the issue titled *Is Congress Still Relevant in*

U.S. Foreign Policymaking? which examines the relevance of Congress in the making of U.S. foreign policy. As the issue highlights, there are some Congressional prerogatives—such as the authority to declare war—that seem to have grown less significant over time. However, there are other areas of foreign policymaking that remain heavily influenced by the power of Congress to control the purse, to make laws, and to exercise oversight. This issue helpfully reveals the importance of distinctions, careful analysis, and evidence. Congress is more influential in some aspects of American foreign policymaking than in others.

A final social science of significance to foreign policymakers is economics. There are two ways that economic considerations may be of fundamental importance. First, the funds that the federal government draws upon to execute all of its functions—to include foreign policy—are drawn from a budget whose size will be shaped by the health and vitality of the U.S. economy as a whole. Therefore, economic considerations shape the resources available to foreign policymakers. Second, a country's foreign economic relations can have a significant impact on a country's prosperity and wealth. Though the United States is less dependent on trade than many countries that have smaller internal markets, international commercial exchange remains important to many U.S. corporations.

In this volume, the importance of economic considerations in American foreign policy is particularly evident in the issue *Is Free Trade Good for the United States?* which looks at whether free trade is good for the United States. Since World War II, a fundamental purpose of U.S. foreign policy has been to foster a liberal, international economic order characterized by free trade. However, whether a policy supporting free trade remains in the best interest of the United States is the subject of some debate, and both sides use economic arguments to reinforce their positions. Assessing the relative validity of these arguments—as opposed to their political appeal—requires the application of economic expertise.

As is evident in the above discussion, a large number of academic disciplines offer insights that are relevant to foreign policymakers. These disciplinary perspectives also constitute dimensions along which debates about American foreign policy can take place. In addition to divergent views about U.S. national interests, disagreements about foreign policy may stem from differences in each of the following: interpretations of scientific evidence about the physical world; knowledge of and interpretation of the relevant history surrounding a particular situation; assumptions about the dynamics that drive state behavior on the international stage; the political dynamics or other internal characteristics of foreign states; the feasibility or appropriateness of a policy given the characteristics of the U.S. government; and assessments of the impact of policies on the U.S. economy. In order for debates along any of these dimensions to be constructive, it is useful for both sides to be clear about their assumptions, the definitions of the concepts they are using, the causal logic implied by their arguments, and the evidence that they are bringing to bear. Without clarity on these points, participants in important debates may simply talk past one another without really revealing the key areas of disagreement. The participants in discussions that lack precision on these points also have less prospect of finding common ground.

Why Foreign Policy Matters Today

The United States today exists in an increasingly globalized world in which the significance of state borders is decreasing. Enabled by advances in transportation, communication, and the choices of governments, international trade is growing, capital is increasingly free to move across borders, and multinational corporations are increasingly transnational in nature. The world today is also an environment in which ideas flow more easily across borders, and developments within particular states more immediately become known to a global audience. It is an international environment of great possibility, and also one that creates new political, social, economic, and security challenges. In this globalized world, it is increasingly difficult to argue persuasively that foreign policy should be a matter for a select, elite group of power brokers and experts. Instead, given that foreign policy has the potential to affect the daily lives of American citizens, members of the general public should seek to become and remain informed so that they can hold the government accountable for its choices.

A decade after the terrorist attacks of September 11, 2001, and the two wars that followed, the United States faces important questions about its future course in international affairs. Do the economic and fiscal challenges faced by the United States imply that a relative withdrawal would be appropriate, or that greater engagement is essential? Should the United States continue to support the international system of institutions that played such an integral role in creating after World War II—to include those that seek to promote economic development, encourage free trade, ensure currency stability, and foster international peace and security—or is it time to pass the mantle of leadership to others? These are just two of the critical questions for policymakers today. The quality of the answers to them would likely benefit from vigorous public debate.

References

Adams, John Quincy, 1821, as quoted in "A Short History of the Department of State: The Expansionist Years, 1823-1867," U.S. Department of State. Available at: http://history.state.gov/departmenthistory/short-history/expansion.

"Declaration of Independence," 1776. Available at: www.archives.gov/exhibits/charters/declaration_transcript.html.

Vandenburg, Arthur, 1947, as quoted in "Arthur Vandenberg: A Featured Biography," U.S. Senate. Available at: www.senate.gov/artandhistory/history/common/generic/Featured_Bio_Vandenberg.htm.

Washington, George. "Washington's Farewell Address," 1796. Available at: http://avalon.law.yale.edu/18th_century/washing.asp.

Wilson, Woodrow, 1917, as cited in "28. Woodrow Wilson, 1913-1921," The White House. Available at: www.whitehouse.gov/about/presidents/woodrowwilson.

Suzanne C. Nielsen
United States Military Academy

Scott P. Handler
United States Military Academy

Unit I

UNIT

The United States and Its Place in the International System

*A*t its founding in the late eighteenth century, the United States was a minor power in the international system dominated by great powers such as Britain, France, the Ottoman Empire, Russia, and Prussia. It was a multipolar world, meaning that three or more great powers existed who vied with one another through shifting alliances and war. Despite this contemporary reality, however, a few of the founding fathers envisioned that the United States would one day become a great power—a vision that ultimately came to fruition in the twentieth century. After World War II, the international system shifted to a bipolar world with just two outsized great powers—known as superpowers—as the United States and the Soviet Union balanced one another and maintained rival spheres of influence. Following the collapse of the Soviet Union in 1991, the United States became the sole superpower in a unipolar world. Since then, U.S. foreign policymakers have sought to interpret what this position requires. Should the United States focus narrowly on its own national interests? Or should the United States seek to lead by promoting free trade, democracy, and peace and security worldwide? While there are times when these two visions point to the same foreign policies, there are others when they appear to clash.

As the twenty-first century unfolds, the rise of countries such as China, India, and Brazil causes some to wonder whether a return to multipolarity is imminent or whether a new form of nonpolarity will take form. In either case, it is clear that the relative power advantage of the United States over other great powers will decrease over time. The issues presented here explore the U.S. leadership in this context.

Selected, Edited, and with Issue Framing Material by:
Suzanne Nielsen, *U.S. Military Academy*
and
Scott Handler, *U.S. Military Academy*

ISSUE

Should the United States Seek a Leadership Role in International Affairs?

YES: **Robert Kagan**, from "Why the World Needs America," *The Wall Street Journal* (February 2012)

NO: **Stephen Walt**, from "The End of the American Era," *The National Interest* (November/December 2011)

Learning Outcomes

After reading this issue, you should be able to:

• Evaluate the feasibility of U.S. international leadership given the rise of new powers.
• Evaluate the role of domestic economic constraints on U.S. leadership ability.
• Discuss the potential structure of the international system without U.S. leadership.
• Evaluate whether U.S. leadership is beneficial or harmful to U.S. security.
• Discuss the normative moral and ethical concerns associated with U.S. leadership.

ISSUE SUMMARY

YES: Robert Kagan, a senior fellow at the Brookings Institute, argues that the United States must continue to exercise assertive leadership to preserve a liberal international order in which free markets and democracy can thrive. An American retreat from leadership will undermine this order and contribute to a more unstable, chaotic, and warlike international system.

NO: Stephen Walt, Robert and Renee Belfer professor of international relations at Harvard University's Kennedy School of Government, argues that it is not in the best interest of the United States to seek to exercise a global primacy that is increasingly beyond America's means. Instead, the United States should disengage from commitments in Europe and the Middle East, forcing its allies in these regions to take a more active role in providing for their own defense.

Across political parties, the call for American global leadership is common in domestic discourse about foreign policy. There was little new in President Barack Obama's 2012 State of the Union address when he claimed, " . . . anyone who tells you that America is in decline or that our influence has waned, doesn't know what they are talking about . . . America remains the one indispensable nation in world affairs . . ." (Obama, 2012). President Bill Clinton and his Secretary of State, Madeleine Albright, frequently used the same "indispensible nation" language, as did President George W. Bush in 2006, claiming that "the only alternative to American leadership is a dramatically more dangerous and anxious world" (Bush, 2006). However, numerous scholars and policymakers have called into question these assumptions about the necessity, desirability, and even possibility of American global leadership.

Advocates and skeptics disagree over three key claims about U.S. global leadership. Proponents argue, first, that

due to its economic and military power, the United States is uniquely capable to lead in international affairs. Second, they hold that the United States must take on this leadership role in order to maintain American national interests and security. Third, the United States, as the world's most powerful liberal democracy, has an ethical and moral obligation to lead. Critics dispute each of these claims. First, they argue that the United States is declining in relative power to the rest of the world and cannot afford to continue an aggressive leadership role. Second, they claim that such a role is not in the U.S. national interest; global leadership is both costly and likely to provoke adverse reactions. Finally, they point to the fact that states face different moral dilemmas than individuals in the international system, and leaders have a greater moral obligation to preserve the state's own survival.

At the end of the Cold War, journalist Charles Krauthammer famously argued that the United States stood in a "unipolar moment" (Krauthammer, 1990/1991). As the single great superpower in the world with no peer competitors—a position no state had held in two millennia—it could do much to remake the international system for the better if it only had the will to act. Advocates of U.S. leadership do not think that moment has passed. In 2008, political scientists Stephen Brooks and William Wohlforth predicted that U.S. unipolarity would last as long as 20 years. This period, they argued, offers a golden window for "using American leverage to reshape international institutions, standards of legitimacy and economic globalization" (Brooks and Wohlforth, 2008).

Leadership advocates differ regarding whether the United States should lead multilaterally or unilaterally—through international institutions or through military force—but lead it must. These advocates distrust the capabilities of international institutions, focusing instead on the material capabilities of the United States. Further, they argue that with the right policies, the United States can maintain its predominant status nearly indefinitely (Krauthammer, 1990/1991).

Other advocates of leadership who draw on the tradition of neoliberal institutionalism expect a decline in U.S. power relative to competitors and see greater value in abiding by the rules, norms, and decision-making procedures of international institutions. Indeed, they argue that the potential for American decline provides the imperative for the United States to lead in shaping international institutions today in a way that will serve long-term U.S. interests. Political scientist John Ikenberry, for example, claims that the United States can "lead through rules," creating the type of international system that is mutually beneficial to it and to rising powers like China and India. In the process, the United States can ensure a lasting, open, liberal order that favors free markets and liberal democracy, even after future U.S. decline (Ikenberry, 2011). Thus, although Krauthammer and Ikenberry might disagree about how the United States ought to apply its power, both agree on the need for strong leadership.

Critics of U.S. activism argue that recent attempts at global leadership have proven counterproductive to U.S. security. In a harsh critique of the current and past two administrations, international relations scholar John Mearsheimer argues that all three pursued leadership through a strategy of "global dominance." Mearsheimer argues that the United States sought to maintain U.S. primacy and to spread democracy worldwide. While these might seem like admirable goals to many Americans, Mearsheimer contends, ".. . . this grand strategy is 'imperial' at its core." He claims that pursuit of these goals produced quagmire wars with little reward, loss of international respect and prestige, and massive increases in military spending in a country already plagued with debt and financial woes. By squandering resources and power in pursuit of global leadership, the United States left itself less capable of dealing with more important security threats such as the rise of China, nuclear proliferation, and terrorism (Mearsheimer, 2011).

Aggressive leadership also risks triggering efforts by other states to contain U.S. power. Political scientist Robert Pape has argued that aggressive U.S. policy leads other states to perceive the United States as a threat, and causes them to "soft balance"—the use of diplomatic and economic power, rather than military power—against the United States (Pape, 2005). Paradoxically, by taking a more humble international role, the United States may increase its influence and power on the most essential issues, while a more ambitious use of U.S. power will lead to an unproductive diffusion of resources and international resistance to U.S. objectives.

In addition to the political, economic, and strategic arguments about whether or not the United States should seek a leadership role in international affairs, there is a parallel normative debate taking place. Supporters of U.S. leadership argue that the United States has a moral obligation to lead since it is the only state capable of preserving an international order that supports democracy and economic freedom. Applying a logic that "to whom much is given, much is expected," political philosopher Jean Bethke Elshtain has argued that the United States has not only a right but also a moral responsibility to lead the world in the use of military force against unjust aggression and terrorism in order to establish a just peace, even if such leadership entails difficult, long-term state building projects (Elshtain, 2004).

Some critics make normative arguments as well, but focus on ethical problems related to the domestic effect of global leadership. Christopher Layne argues that attempts at world leadership require political leaders to justify international intervention through an "exaggeration of threats" and compel "U.S. policy makers . . . to overstate the dangers to American interests to mobilize domestic support for their policies" (1997). As historian and retired army officer Andrew Bacevich has argued, an aggressive foreign policy can also lead to a militarized state and conflict between far-reaching international objectives on one hand and domestic civil rights and transparent government on the other (Bacevich, 2006, 2016). These issues raise serious concerns about the compatibility of republican government and global leadership.

In answering YES to whether the United States ought to pursue a leadership role in world affairs, historian Robert Kagan argues that American leadership is essential if the United States is to maintain an international system that values liberal democracy, open markets, free trade, and relative stability. Kagan holds that the current international system is both a creation of the United States and dependent on continued U.S. power and leadership. Kagan rejects the idea that other states could replace the United States in enforcing the current system, as well as the idea that international institutions could sustain the current order without a United States that was willing to provide enforcement capabilities. Worst of all, Kagan believes that a decline in the U.S. power or leadership could lead to a multipolar system, which he argues would be inherently more warlike and unstable. Ultimately, the choice to lead is the choice to preserve economic and political freedom, stability, and democracy around the world.

In the NO selection, Harvard political scientist Stephen Walt recognizes the leadership role that the United States played in the post–World War II period and the tremendous benefits gained through American dominance as a world power in the international system. However, Walt argues that the international system has fundamentally changed. The United States is still likely to remain the most powerful country in the world, but a group of strong second-tier powers will limit the ability of the United States to lead in specific key regions. Further, significant economic constraints will further limit U.S. global capabilities. Walt suggests a grand strategy of "offshore balancing" that focuses on the use of regional powers by a great power to balance against the rise of potentially hostile powers within the region. He argues such a policy would ensure that no single state could gain regional dominance while facilitating the sharing of the costs with U.S. allies.

YES ⬅

Robert Kagan

Why the World Needs America

History shows that world orders, including our own, are transient. They rise and fall, and the institutions they erect, the beliefs and "norms" that guide them, the economic systems they support—they rise and fall, too. The downfall of the Roman Empire brought an end not just to Roman rule but to Roman government and law and to an entire economic system stretching from Northern Europe to North Africa. Culture, the arts, even progress in science and technology, were set back for centuries.

Modern history has followed a similar pattern. After the Napoleonic Wars of the early 19th century, British control of the seas and the balance of great powers on the European continent provided relative security and stability. Prosperity grew, personal freedoms expanded, and the world was knit more closely together by revolutions in commerce and communication.

With the outbreak of World War I, the age of settled peace and advancing liberalism—of European civilization approaching its pinnacle—collapsed into an age of hyper-nationalism, despotism and economic calamity. The once-promising spread of democracy and liberalism halted and then reversed course, leaving a handful of outnumbered and besieged democracies living nervously in the shadow of fascist and totalitarian neighbors. The collapse of the British and European orders in the 20th century did not produce a new dark age—though if Nazi Germany and imperial Japan had prevailed, it might have—but the horrific conflict that it produced was, in its own way, just as devastating. If the U.S. is unable to maintain its hegemony on the high seas, would other nations fill in the gaps?

Would the end of the present American-dominated order have less dire consequences? A surprising number of American intellectuals, politicians and policy makers greet the prospect with equanimity. There is a general sense that the end of the era of American pre-eminence, if and when it comes, need not mean the end of the present international order, with its widespread freedom, unprecedented global prosperity (even amid the current economic crisis) and absence of war among the great powers. American power may diminish, the political scientist G. John Ikenberry argues, but "the underlying foundations of the liberal international order will survive and thrive." The commentator Fareed Zakaria believes that even as the balance shifts against the U.S., rising powers like China "will continue to live within the framework of the current international system." And there are elements across the political spectrum—Republicans who call for retrenchment, Democrats who put their faith in international law and institutions—who don't imagine that a "post-American world" would look very different from the American world.

If all of this sounds too good to be true, it is. The present world order was largely shaped by American power and reflects American interests and preferences. If the balance of power shifts in the direction of other nations, the world order will change to suit their interests and preferences. Nor can we assume that all the great powers in a post-American world would agree on the benefits of preserving the present order, or have the capacity to preserve it, even if they wanted to.

Take the issue of democracy. For several decades, the balance of power in the world has favored democratic governments. In a genuinely post-American world, the balance would shift toward the great-power autocracies. Both Beijing and Moscow already protect dictators like Syria's Bashar al-Assad. If they gain greater relative influence in the future, we will see fewer democratic transitions and more autocrats hanging on to power. The balance in a new, multipolar world might be more favorable to democracy if some of the rising democracies—Brazil, India, Turkey, South Africa—picked up the slack from a declining U.S. Yet not all of them have the desire or the capacity to do it.

What about the economic order of free markets and free trade? People assume that China and other rising powers that have benefited so much from the present system would have a stake in preserving it. They wouldn't kill the goose that lays the golden eggs.

Unfortunately, they might not be able to help themselves. The creation and survival of a liberal economic order has depended, historically, on great powers that are both willing and able to support open trade and free markets, often with naval power. If a declining America is unable to maintain its long-standing hegemony on the high seas, would other nations take on the burdens and the expense of sustaining navies to fill in the gaps?

Even if they did, would this produce an open global commons—or rising tension? China and India are building bigger navies, but the result so far has been greater competition, not greater security. As Mohan Malik has noted in this newspaper, their "maritime rivalry could spill into the open in a decade or two," when India deploys an aircraft carrier in the Pacific Ocean and China deploys one in the Indian Ocean. The move from American-dominated oceans to collective policing by several great powers could be a recipe for competition and conflict rather than for a liberal economic order.

And do the Chinese really value an open economic system? The Chinese economy soon may become the largest in the world, but it will be far from the richest. Its size is a product of the country's enormous population, but in per capita terms, China remains relatively poor. The U.S., Germany and Japan have a per capita GDP of over $40,000. China's is a little over $4,000, putting it at the same level as Angola, Algeria and Belize. Even if optimistic forecasts are correct, China's per capita GDP by 2030 would still only be half that of the U.S., putting it roughly where Slovenia and Greece are today.

As Arvind Subramanian and other economists have pointed out, this will make for a historically unique situation. In the past, the largest and most dominant economies in the world have also been the richest. Nations whose peoples are such obvious winners in a relatively unfettered economic system have less temptation to pursue protectionist measures and have more of an incentive to keep the system open. China's leaders, presiding over a poorer and still developing country, may prove less willing to open their economy. They have already begun closing some sectors to foreign competition and are likely to close others in the future. Even optimists like Mr. Subramanian believe that the liberal economic order will require "some insurance" against a scenario in which "China exercises its dominance by either reversing its previous policies or failing to open areas of the economy that are now highly protected." American economic dominance has been welcomed by much of the world because, like the mobster Hyman Roth in "The Godfather," the U.S. has always made money for its partners. Chinese economic dominance may get a different reception.

Another problem is that China's form of capitalism is heavily dominated by the state, with the ultimate goal of preserving the rule of the Communist Party. Unlike the eras of British and American pre-eminence, when the leading economic powers were dominated largely by private individuals or companies, China's system is more like the mercantilist arrangements of previous centuries. The government amasses wealth in order to secure its continued rule and to pay for armies and navies to compete with other great powers.

Although the Chinese have been beneficiaries of an open international economic order, they could end up undermining it simply because, as an autocratic society, their priority is to preserve the state's control of wealth and the power that it brings. They might kill the goose that lays the golden eggs because they can't figure out how to keep both it and themselves alive.

Finally, what about the long peace that has held among the great powers for the better part of six decades? Would it survive in a post-American world?

Most commentators who welcome this scenario imagine that American predominance would be replaced by some kind of multipolar harmony. But multipolar systems have historically been neither particularly stable nor particularly peaceful. Rough parity among powerful nations is a source of uncertainty that leads to miscalculation. Conflicts erupt as a result of fluctuations in the delicate power equation.

War among the great powers was a common, if not constant, occurrence in the long periods of multipolarity from the 16th to the 18th centuries, culminating in the series of enormously destructive Europe-wide wars that followed the French Revolution and ended with Napoleon's defeat in 1815. The 19th century was notable for two stretches of great-power peace of roughly four decades each, punctuated by major conflicts. The Crimean War (1853–1856) was a mini-world war involving well over a million Russian, French, British and Turkish troops, as well as forces from nine other nations; it produced almost a half-million dead combatants and many more wounded. In the Franco-Prussian War (1870–1871), the two nations together fielded close to two million troops, of whom nearly a half-million were killed or wounded.

The peace that followed these conflicts was characterized by increasing tension and competition, numerous war scares and massive increases in armaments on both land and sea. Its climax was World War I, the most destructive and deadly conflict that mankind had known up to that point. As the political scientist Robert W. Tucker has observed, "Such stability and moderation as the balance brought rested ultimately on the threat or use of force. War remained the essential means for maintaining the balance of power."

There is little reason to believe that a return to multipolarity in the 21st century would bring greater peace and stability than it has in the past. The era of American predominance has shown that there is no better recipe for great-power peace than certainty about who holds the upper hand.

President Bill Clinton left office believing that the key task for America was to "create the world we would like to live in when we are no longer the world's only superpower," to prepare for "a time when we would have to share the stage." It is an eminently sensible-sounding proposal. But can it be done? For particularly in matters of security, the rules and institutions of international order rarely survive the decline of the nations that erected them. They are like scaffolding around a building: They don't hold the building up; the building holds them up.

Many foreign-policy experts see the present international order as the inevitable result of human progress, a combination of advancing science and technology, an increasingly global economy, strengthening international institutions, evolving "norms" of international behavior and the gradual but inevitable triumph of liberal democracy over other forms of government—forces of change that transcend the actions of men and nations.

Americans certainly like to believe that our preferred order survives because it is right and just—not only for us but for everyone. We assume that the triumph of democracy is the triumph of a better idea, and the victory of market capitalism is the victory of a better system, and that both are irreversible. That is why Francis Fukuyama's thesis about "the end of history" was so attractive at the end of the Cold War and retains its appeal even now, after it has been discredited by events. The idea of inevitable evolution means that there is no requirement to impose a decent order. It will merely happen.

But international order is not an evolution; it is an imposition. It is the domination of one vision over others—in America's case, the domination of free-market and democratic principles, together with an international system that supports them. The present order will last only as long as those who favor it and benefit from it retain the will and capacity to defend it.

There was nothing inevitable about the world that was created after World War II. No divine providence or unfolding Hegelian dialectic required the triumph of democracy and capitalism, and there is no guarantee that their success will outlast the powerful nations that have fought for them. Democratic progress and liberal economics have been and can be reversed and undone. The ancient democracies of Greece and the republics of Rome and Venice all fell to more powerful forces or through their own failings. The evolving liberal economic order of Europe collapsed in the 1920s and 1930s. The better idea doesn't have to win just because it is a better idea. It requires great powers to champion it.

If and when American power declines, the institutions and norms that American power has supported will decline, too. Or more likely, if history is a guide, they may collapse altogether as we make a transition to another kind of world order, or to disorder. We may discover then that the U.S. was essential to keeping the present world order together and that the alternative to American power was not peace and harmony but chaos and catastrophe—which is what the world looked like right before the American order came into being.

Robert Kagan is a senior fellow in foreign policy at the Brookings Institution. He serves as a member of State Department's Foreign Affairs Policy Board, writes a monthly column for the *Washington Post,* and is a contributing editor at both the *Weekly Standard* and *The New Republic.*

Stephen Walt    **NO**

The End of the American Era

The United States has been the dominant world power since 1945, and U.S. leaders have long sought to preserve that privileged position. They understood, as did most Americans, that primacy brought important benefits. It made other states less likely to threaten America or its vital interests directly. By dampening great-power competition and giving Washington the capacity to shape regional balances of power, primacy contributed to a more tranquil international environment. That tranquility fostered global prosperity; investors and traders operate with greater confidence when there is less danger of war. Primacy also gave the United States the ability to work for positive ends: promoting human rights and slowing the spread of weapons of mass destruction. It may be lonely at the top, but Americans have found the view compelling.

When a state stands alone at the pinnacle of power, however, there is nowhere to go but down. And so Americans have repeatedly worried about the possibility of decline—even when the prospect was remote . . .

Yet for all the ink that has been spilled on the durability of American primacy, the protagonists have mostly asked the wrong question. The issue has never been whether the United States was about to imitate Britain's fall from the ranks of the great powers or suffer some other form of catastrophic decline. The real question was always whether what one might term the "American Era" was nearing its end. Specifically, might the United States remain the strongest global power but be unable to exercise the same influence it once enjoyed? If that is the case—and I believe it is—then Washington must devise a grand strategy that acknowledges this new reality but still uses Americas enduring assets to advance the national interest.

The American Era began immediately after World War II . . . International-relations scholars commonly speak of this moment as a transition from a multipolar to a bipolar world, but Cold War bipolarity was decidedly lopsided from the start.

In 1945, for example, the U.S. economy produced roughly half of gross world product, and the United States was a major creditor nation with a positive trade balance. It had the world's largest navy and air force, an industrial base second to none, sole possession of atomic weapons and a globe-circling array of military bases. . . . Washington also enjoyed considerable goodwill in most of the developed and developing world.

Most importantly, the United States was in a remarkably favorable geopolitical position. There were no other great powers in the Western Hemisphere, so Americans did not have to worry about foreign invasion. Our Soviet rival had a much smaller and less efficient economy. Its military might, concentrated on ground forces, never approached the global reach of U.S. power projection capabilities. The other major power centers were all located on or near the Eurasian landmass—close to the Soviet Union and far from the United States—which made even former rivals like Germany and Japan eager for U.S. protection from the Russian bear. Thus, as the Cold War proceeded, the United States amassed a strong and loyal set of allies while the USSR led an alliance of comparatively weak and reluctant partners. In short, even before the Soviet Union collapsed, America's overall position was about as favorable as any great power's in modern history.

What did the United States do with these impressive advantages? In the decades after World War II, it created and led a political, security and economic order in virtually every part of the globe, except for the sphere that was directly controlled by the Soviet Union and its Communist clients. Not only did the United States bring most of the world into institutions that were largely made in America (the UN, the World Bank, the IMF, and the General Agreement on Tariffs and Trade), for decades it retained the dominant influence in these arrangements.

In Europe, the Marshall Plan revitalized local economies, covert U.S. intervention helped ensure that Communist parties did not gain power, and NATO secured the peace and deterred Soviet military pressure. . . . The United States built an equally durable security order in Asia. . . . In the Middle East, Washington helped establish and defend Israel but also forged close security ties with Saudi Arabia, Jordan, the shah of Iran and several smaller Gulf states. America continued to exercise a position of hegemony in the Western Hemisphere, using various tools to oust leftist governments in Guatemala, the Dominican Republic, Chile and Nicaragua. In Africa, not seen as a vital arena, America did just enough to ensure that its modest interests there were protected.

To be sure, the United States did not exert total control over events in the various regional orders it created. . . . But the United States retained enormous influence in each of these regions, especially on major issues.

Furthermore, although the U.S. position was sometimes challenged—the loss in Vietnam being the most obvious example—America's overall standing was never in danger. . . . Beijing formed a tacit partnership with Washington. Moreover, China eventually abandoned Marxism-Leninism as a governing ideology, forswore world revolution and voluntarily entered the structure of institutions that the United States had previously created. Similarly, Tehran became an adversary once the clerical regime took over, but America's overall position in the Middle East was not shaken. Oil continued to flow out of the Persian Gulf, Israel became increasingly secure and prosperous, and key Soviet allies like Egypt eventually abandoned Moscow and sided with the United States. Despite occasional setbacks, the essential features of the American Era remained firmly in place.

Needless to say, it is highly unusual for a country with only 5 percent of the world's population to be able to organize favorable political, economic and security orders in almost every corner of the globe and to sustain them for decades. Yet that is in fact what the United States did from 1945 to 1990. And it did so while enjoying a half century of economic growth that was nearly unmatched in modern history.

And then the Soviet empire collapsed, leaving the United States as the sole superpower in a unipolar world. According to former national-security adviser Brent Scowcroft, the United States found itself "standing alone at the height of power. It was, it is, an unparalleled situation in history, one which presents us with the rarest opportunity to shape the world." And so it tried, bringing most of the Warsaw Pact into NATO and encouraging the spread of market economies and democratic institutions throughout the former Communist world. It was a triumphal moment—the apogee of the American Era—but the celebratory fireworks blinded us to the trends and pitfalls that brought that era to an end.

The past two decades have witnessed the emergence of new power centers in several key regions. The most obvious example is China, whose explosive economic growth is undoubtedly the most significant geopolitical development in decades. The United States has been the world's largest economy since roughly 1900, but China is likely to overtake America in total economic output no later than 2025. Beijing's military budget is rising by roughly 10 percent per year, and it is likely to convert even more of its wealth into military assets in the future. If China is like all previous great powers—including the United States—its definition of "vital" interests will grow as its power increases—and it will try to use its growing muscle to protect an expanding sphere of influence. Given its dependence on raw-material imports (especially energy) and export-led growth, prudent Chinese leaders will want to make sure that no one is in a position to deny them access to the resources and markets on which their future prosperity and political stability depend.

This situation will encourage Beijing to challenge the current U.S. role in Asia. Such ambitions should not be hard for Americans to understand, given that the United States has sought to exclude outside powers from its own neighborhood ever since the Monroe Doctrine. By a similar logic, China is bound to feel uneasy if Washington maintains a network of Asian alliances and a sizable military presence in East Asia and the Indian Ocean. Over time, Beijing will try to convince other Asian states to abandon ties with America, and Washington will almost certainly resist these efforts. An intense security competition will follow.

The security arrangements that defined the American Era are also being undermined by the rise of several key regional powers, most notably India, Turkey and Brazil. Each of these states has achieved impressive economic growth over the past decade, and each has become more willing to chart its own course independent of Washington's wishes. None of them are on the verge of becoming true global powers—Brazil's GDP is still less than one-sixth that of the United States, and India and Turkey's economies are even smaller—but each has become increasingly influential within its own region. This gradual diffusion of power is also seen in the recent expansion of the G-8 into the so-called G-20, a tacit recognition that the global institutions created after World War II are increasingly obsolete and in need of reform.

Each of these new regional powers is a democracy, which means that its leaders pay close attention to public opinion. As a result, the United States can no longer rely on cozy relations with privileged elites or military juntas. When only 10–15 percent of Turkish citizens have a "favorable" view of America, it becomes easier to understand why Ankara refused to let Washington use its territory to attack Iraq in 2003 and why Turkey has curtailed its previously close ties with Israel despite repeated U.S. efforts to heal the rift. Anti-Americanism is less prevalent in Brazil and India, but their democratically elected leaders are hardly deferential to Washington either.

The rise of new powers is bringing the short-lived "unipolar moment" to an end, and the result will be either a bipolar Sino-American rivalry or a multipolar system containing several unequal great powers. The United States is likely to remain the strongest, but its overall lead has shrunk—and it is shrinking further still.

Of course, the twin debacles in Iraq and Afghanistan only served to accelerate the waning of American dominance and underscore the limits of U.S. power. The Iraq War alone will carry a price tag of more than $3 trillion once all the costs are counted, and the end result is likely to be an unstable quasi democracy that is openly hostile to Israel and at least partly aligned with Iran. Indeed, Tehran has been the main beneficiary of this ill-conceived adventure, which is surely not what the Bush administration had in mind when it dragged the country to war.

The long Afghan campaign is even more likely to end badly, even if U.S. leaders eventually try to spin it as some sort of victory. The Obama administration finally got Osama bin Laden, but the long and costly attempt to eliminate the Taliban and build a Western-style state in

Afghanistan has failed. . . . In either scenario, Kabul's fate will ultimately be determined by the Afghans once the United States and its dwindling set of allies leave. And if failure in Afghanistan [weren't] enough, U.S. involvement in Central Asia has undermined relations with nuclear armed Pakistan and reinforced virulent anti-Americanism in that troubled country. If victory is defined as achieving your main objectives and ending a war with your security and prosperity enhanced, then both of these conflicts must be counted as expensive defeats.

But the Iraq and Afghan wars were not simply costly self-inflicted wounds; they were also eloquent demonstrations of the limits of military power. There was never much doubt that the United States could topple relatively weak and/or unpopular governments—as it has in Panama, Afghanistan, Iraq and, most recently, Libya—but the wars in Iraq and Afghanistan showed that unmatched power-projection capabilities were of little use in constructing effective political orders once the offending leadership was removed. In places where local identities remain strong and foreign interference is not welcome for long, even a global superpower like the United States has trouble obtaining desirable political results.

Nowhere is this clearer than in the greater Middle East, which has been the main focus of U.S. strategy since the USSR broke apart. Not only did the Arab Spring catch Washington by surprise, but the U.S. response further revealed its diminished capacity to shape events in its favor. After briefly trying to shore up the Mubarak regime, the Obama administration realigned itself with the forces challenging the existing regional order. The president gave a typically eloquent speech endorsing change, but nobody in the region paid much attention. Indeed, with the partial exception of Libya, U.S. influence over the entire process has been modest at best. Obama was unable to stop Saudi Arabia from sending troops to Bahrain—where Riyadh helped to quell demands for reform—or to convince Syrian leader Bashar al-Assad to step down. U.S. leverage in the post-Mubarak political process in Egypt and the simmering conflict in Yemen is equally ephemeral. . . .

America's declining influence is also revealed by its repeated failure to resolve the Israeli–Palestinian dispute. It has been nearly twenty years since the signing of the Oslo accords in September 1993, and the United States has had a monopoly on the "peace process" ever since that hopeful day. Yet its efforts have been a complete failure, proving beyond doubt that Washington is incapable of acting as an effective and evenhanded mediator.

Taken together, these events herald a sharp decline in America's ability to shape the global order. And the recent series of economic setbacks will place even more significant limits on America's ability to maintain an ambitious international role. The Bush administration inherited a rare budget surplus in 2001 but proceeded to cut federal taxes significantly and fight two costly wars. The predictable result was a soaring budget deficit and a rapid increase in federal debt, problems compounded by the financial crisis of 2007–09. The latter disaster required a massive federal bailout of the financial industry and a major stimulus package, leading to a short-term budget shortfall in 2009 of some $1.6 trillion (roughly 13 percent of GDP). The United States has been in the economic doldrums ever since, and there is scant hope of a rapid return to vigorous growth. These factors help explain Standard & Poor's U.S. government credit rating downgrade in August amid new fears of a "double-dip" recession.

The Congressional Budget Office projects persistent U.S. budget deficits for the next twenty-five years—even under its optimistic "baseline" scenario—and it warns of plausible alternatives in which total federal debt would exceed 100 percent of GDP by 2023 and 190 percent of GDP by 2035. State and local governments are hurting too, which means less money for roads, bridges, schools, law enforcement and the other collective goods that help maintain a healthy society.

The financial meltdown also undermined an important element of America's "soft power," namely, its reputation for competence and probity in economic policy. . . . Other states have reason to disregard Washington's advice and to pursue economic strategies of their own making. The days when America could drive the international economic agenda are over, which helps explain why it has been seventeen years since the Uruguay Round, the last successful multilateral trade negotiation.

The bottom line is clear and unavoidable: the United States simply won't have the resources to devote to international affairs that it had in the past. When the president of the staunchly internationalist Council on Foreign Relations is penning articles decrying "American Profligacy" and calling for retrenchment, you know that America's global role is in flux. Nor can the United States expect its traditional allies to pick up the slack voluntarily, given that economic conditions are even worse in Europe and Japan.

The era when the United States could create and lead a political, economic and security order in virtually every part of the world is coming to an end. Which raises the obvious question: What should we do about it?

The twilight of the American Era arrived sooner than it should have because U.S. leaders made a number of costly mistakes. But past errors need not lead to a further erosion of America's position if we learn the right lessons and make timely adjustments.

Above all, Washington needs to set clear priorities and to adopt a hardheaded and unsentimental approach to preserving our most important interests. When U.S. primacy was at its peak, American leaders could indulge altruistic whims. They didn't have to think clearly about strategy because there was an enormous margin for error; things were likely to work out even if Washington made lots of mistakes. But when budgets are tight, problems have multiplied and other powers are less deferential, it's important to invest U.S. power wisely. As former secretary of defense Robert Gates put it: "We need to be honest with the president, with the Congress, with the American people . . . a smaller military, no matter how superb, will be able to go fewer places and be able to do fewer things." The chief lesson, he emphasized, was the need for "conscious choices" about our missions and means. Instead of trying to be the "indispensable nation" nearly everywhere, the United States will need to figure out how to be the decisive power in the places that matter.

For starters, we should remember what the U.S. military is good for and what it is good at doing. American forces are very good at preventing major conventional aggression, or reversing it when it happens. . . .

By contrast, the U.S. military is not good at running other countries, particularly in cultures that are radically different from our own, where history has left them acutely hostile to foreign interference, and when there are deep ethnic divisions and few democratic traditions. The United States can still topple minor-league dictators, but it has no great aptitude for creating stable and effective political orders afterward.

It follows that the United States should eschew its present fascination with nation building and counterinsurgency and return to a grand strategy that some (myself included) have labeled offshore balancing.[1] Offshore balancing seeks to maintain benevolent hegemony in the Western Hemisphere and to maintain a balance of power among the strong states of Eurasia and of the oil-rich Persian Gulf. At present, these are the only areas that are worth sending U.S. soldiers to fight and die in.

Instead of seeking to dominate these regions directly, however, our first recourse should be to have local allies uphold the balance of power, out of their own self-interest. Rather than letting them free ride on us, we should free ride on them as much as we can, intervening with ground and air forces only when a single power threatens to dominate some critical region. For an offshore balancer, the greatest success lies in getting somebody else to handle some pesky problem, not in eagerly shouldering that burden oneself.

To be more specific: offshore balancing would call for removing virtually all U.S. troops from Europe, while remaining formally committed to NATO. Europe is wealthy, secure, democratic and peaceful, and it faces no security problems that it cannot handle on its own. (The combined defense spending of NATO's European members is roughly five times greater than Russia's, which is the only conceivable conventional military threat the Continent might face.) Forcing NATO's European members to take the lead in the recent Libyan war was a good first step, because the United States will never get its continental allies to bear more of the burden if it insists on doing most of the work itself. Indeed, by playing hard to get on occasion, Washington would encourage others to do more to win our support, instead of resenting or rebelling against the self-appointed "indispensable nation."

In the decades ahead, the United States should shift its main strategic attention to Asia, both because its economic importance is rising rapidly and because China is the only potential peer competitor that we face. The bad news is that China could become a more formidable rival than the Soviet Union ever was: its economy is likely to be larger than ours (a situation the United States has not faced since the nineteenth century); and, unlike the old, largely autarkic Soviet Union, modern China depends on overseas trade and resources and will be more inclined to project power abroad.

The good news is that China's rising status is already ringing alarm bells in Asia. The more Beijing throws its weight around, the more other Asian states will be looking to us for help. Given the distances involved and the familiar dilemmas of collective action, however, leading a balancing coalition in Asia will be far more difficult than it was in Cold War Europe. U.S. officials will have to walk a fine line between doing too much (which would allow allies to free ride) and doing too little (which might lead some states to hedge toward China). To succeed, Washington will have to keep air and naval forces deployed in the region, pay close attention to the evolving military and political environment there, and devote more time and effort to managing a large and potentially fractious coalition of Asian partners.

Perhaps most importantly, offshore balancing prescribes a very different approach to the greater Middle East. And prior to 1991, in fact, that's exactly what we did. The United States had a strategic interest in the oil there and a moral commitment to defending Israel, but until 1968 it mostly passed the buck to London. After Britain withdrew, Washington relied on regional allies such as Iran, Saudi Arabia and Israel to counter Soviet clients like Egypt and Syria . . . it deployed U.S. ground and air forces only when the balance of power broke down completely, as it did when Iraq seized Kuwait. This strategy was not perfect, perhaps, but it preserved key U.S. interests at minimal cost for over four decades.

Unfortunately, the United States abandoned offshore balancing after 1991. It first tried "dual containment," in effect confronting two states—Iran and Iraq—that also hated each other, instead of using each to check the other as it had in the past. This strategy—undertaken, as the National Iranian American Council's Trita Parsi and Brookings' Kenneth Pollack suggest, in good part to reassure Israel—forced the United States to keep thousands of troops in Saudi Arabia, sparking Osama bin Laden's ire and helping fuel the rise of al-Qaeda. The Bush administration compounded this error after 9/11 by adopting the even more foolish strategy of "regional transformation." Together with the "special relationship" with Israel, these ill-conceived approaches deepened anti-Americanism in the Middle East and gave states like Iran more reason to consider acquiring a nuclear deterrent. It is no great mystery why Obama's eloquent speeches did nothing to restore America's image in the region; people there want new U.S. policies, not just more empty rhetoric.

One can only imagine how much policy makers in Beijing have enjoyed watching the United States bog itself down in these costly quagmires. Fortunately, there is an obvious solution: return to offshore balancing. The United States should get out of Iraq and Afghanistan as quickly as possible, treat Israel like a normal country instead of backing it unconditionally, and rely on local Middle Eastern, European and Asian allies to maintain the peace—with our help when necessary.

Don't get me wrong. The United States is not finished as a major power. Nor is it destined to become just one of several equals in a future multipolar world. To the contrary, the United States still has the world's strongest military, and the U.S. economy remains diverse and technologically advanced. China's economy may soon be larger in absolute terms, but its per capita income will be far smaller, which means its government will have less surplus to devote to expanding its reach (including of the military variety). American expenditures on higher education and industrial research and development still dwarf those of other countries, the dollar remains the world's reserve currency and many states continue to clamor for U.S. protection.

Furthermore, long-term projections of U.S. latent power are reassuring. Populations in Russia, Japan and most European countries are declining and aging, which will limit their economic potential in the decades ahead. China's median age is also rising rapidly (an unintended consequence of the one-child policy), and this will be a powerful drag on its economic vitality. By contrast, U.S. population growth is high compared with the rest of the developed world, and U.S. median age will be lower than any of the other serious players.

Indeed, in some ways America's strategic position is actually more favorable than it used to be, which is why its bloated military budget is something of a mystery. In 1986, for example, the United States and its allies controlled about 49 percent of global military expenditures while our various adversaries combined for some 42 percent. Today, the United States and its allies are responsible for nearly 70 percent of military spending; all our adversaries put together total less than 15 percent. Barring additional self-inflicted wounds, the United States is not going to fall from the ranks of the great powers at any point in the next few decades. Whether the future world is unipolar, bipolar or multipolar, Washington is going to be one of those poles—and almost certainly the strongest of them.

And so, the biggest challenge the United States faces today is not a looming great power rival; it is the triple whammy of accumulated debt, eroding infrastructure and a sluggish economy. The only way to have the world's most capable military forces both now and into the future is to have the world's most advanced economy, and that means having better schools, the best universities, a scientific establishment that is second to none, and a national infrastructure that enhances productivity and dazzles those who visit from abroad. These things all cost money, of course, but they would do far more to safeguard our long-term security than spending a lot of blood and treasure determining who should run Afghanistan, Kosovo, South Sudan, Libya, Yemen or any number of other strategic backwaters.

The twilight of the American Era is not an occasion to mourn or a time to cast blame. The period when the United States could manage the politics, economics and security arrangements for nearly the entire globe was never destined to endure forever, and its passing need not herald a new age of rising threats and economic hardship if we make intelligent adjustments.

Instead of looking backward with nostalgia, Americans should see the end of the American Era as an opportunity to rebalance our international burdens and focus on our domestic imperatives. Instead of building new Bagrams in faraway places of little consequence, it is time to devote more attention to that "shining city on a hill" of which our leaders often speak, but which still remains to be built.

Note

1 On "offshore balancing," see Christopher Layne, "From Preponderance to Offshore Balancing: America's Future Grand Strategy," International Security 22, no. 1 (1997); John J. Mearsheimer, The Tragedy of Great Power Politics (New York: W. W. Norton, 2001); and Stephen M. Walt, Taming American Power: The Global Response to U.S. Primacy (New York: W. W. Norton, 2005), chap. 5.

STEPHEN M. WALT is the Robert and Renée Belfer Professor of International Affairs at the Harvard Kennedy School of Government. He writes a blog for *Foreign Policy,* where he serves on the editorial board.

EXPLORING THE ISSUE

Should the United States Seek a Leadership Role in International Affairs?

Critical Thinking and Reflection

1. Given the number of rising powers in the world, will U.S. leadership remain a possibility in the future? How will a more powerful China, India, Turkey, or Brazil affect the ability of the United States to exert global influence?
2. How do economic constraints affect the ability of the United States to maintain a global leadership role? Is holding a position of global leadership worth the cost in terms of increasing the national debt? Is global leadership worth the funds that would be diverted from education, roads, and other essential infrastructure? Conversely, if no other state or institution will preserve an open economic order, would the United States suffer even greater economic losses if it gave up its leadership role?
3. While Kagan argues that international institutions are weak without U.S. support, and Walt offers little place for them, scholars of institutions including G. John Ikenberry and Robert Keohane have suggested that once created, institutions can preserve an open economic and political order. Should the United States pursue leadership through international institutions? Could it establish a series of "constitutional" international rules that will last well after U.S. decline?
4. What are the ethical concerns related to U.S. leadership? Has its past record of accomplishment been solid, or has it fallen short as a global leader in moral terms? Does the United States have an obligation to preserve a liberal international order, support the spread of democracy, and stop mass killings and genocide? Is force an effective tool to achieve these objectives? What negative domestic costs do republican forms of government incur when they take on global leadership roles?

Is There Common Ground?

Few scholars or policymakers on either side of this issue deny that the United States will occupy a unique place in the world well into the future. Even as other states rise, it will still take years for any of them to acquire the economic and military might of the United States. While it is arguable whether or not the United States maintains a unique moral position in the world, there is little doubt that the United States has and will continue to have unique military, economic, and political positions. A total withdrawal of American global leadership does not seem a feasible possibility in the near term.

At the same time, those who argue that the United States should pursue global leadership must remain aware of the natural tendency of powerful states to overestimate their own virtues. Great powers must understand that efforts to increase their own security will cause others to feel more vulnerable, and even if the great power thinks it is not a threat to others states, the other states may actually feel threatened. Superpower status may lead to foolish and overaggressive long-term decisions made possible by lack of short-term accountability. Further, the United States must balance international commitments against domestic obligations. The United States has learned from the wars in Iraq and Afghanistan that its actions will not be universally welcomed as just, that the utility of force has limits, and that there is a heavy domestic cost associated with some forms of leadership.

The use of international institutions as a venue in which to exercise leadership may offer some middle ground to the positions presented in this debate. This, of course, depends on the utility of international institutions themselves, a utility that both authors doubt. In the end, this question of whether or not the United States should seek a global leadership role will not go away as long as the United States remains a major world power. Even if the United States adopts a strategy of offshore balancing rather than global dominance, the United States will maintain a different role in the international system from the roles assigned to second- or third-tier powers. At the same time, while the United States will likely remain a great power long into the future, domestic constraints may force a reconsideration of the appropriateness of American leadership.

Additional Resources

Bacevich, Andrew. *The New American Militarism: How Americans are Seduced by War*. New York: Oxford University Press, 2006.

Bacevich, Andrew. *Washington Rules: America's Path to Permanent War*. New York: Henry Holt, 2010.

Historian and retired U.S. Army officer Andrew Bacevich argues that American foreign policy over the last 50 years has undermined transparent republican government and created an endless iteration of wars. He argues that the supposed imperative for "global leadership," which he largely rejects, is likely to propagate this pattern long into the future.

Brooks, Stephen G., and William C. Wohlforth. *World Out of Balance: International Relations and the Challenge of American Primacy.* Princeton, NJ: Princeton University Press, 2008.

Political scientists Stephen Brooks and William Wohlforth argue that the United States will maintain its hegemonic status well into the future. They discount the likelihood of balancing against the United States and provide a realist justification for U.S. leadership through both direct application of power and international institutions.

Bush, George. W. "State of the Union Address— January 31, 2006." Retrieved April 2012, from http://georgewbush-whitehouse.archives.gov/stateoftheunion/2006/

Elshtain, J. Bethke. *Just War Against Terror: The Burden of American Power in a Violent World.* New York: Basic Books, 2004.

Political theorist Jean Elshtain argues that American power comes with the moral burden of global leadership, which may include the use of force against terrorist and violent oppression.

Gholz, Eugene, Daryl G. Press, and Harvey M. Sapolsky. "Come Home, America: The Strategy of Restraint in the Face of Temptation." *International Security* 21, no. 4 (1997): 4–48.

Ikenberry, G. John. *Liberal Leviathan: The Origins, Crisis, and Transformation of the American World Order.* Princeton, NJ: Princeton University Press, 2011.

A leading neo-liberal institutionalist, G. John Ikenberry acknowledges the likely decline of the United States in relative power. For Ikenberry, this is all the more reason that the United States should lead through international institutions. By institutionalizing rules favorable to an open, liberal world order, he holds that the United States can maintain that order long after its power declines.

Kagan, Robert. *The World America Made.* New York: Alfred A. Knopf, 2012.

This is Robert Kagan's book-length treatment of the arguments in the short *Wall Street Journal* article presented here.

Krauthammer, Charles. "The Unipolar Moment." *Foreign Affairs* 70, no. 1, (1990/1991): 23–33.

Layne, Christopher. "From Preponderance to Offshore Balancing: America's Future Grand Strategy." *International Security* 22, no. 1 (2007): 86–124.

Christopher Layne provides perhaps the most complete theoretical explanation of the grand strategy of offshore balancing advocated by Stephen Walt.

Mearsheimer, John. J. "Imperial by Design." *The National Interest* (January/February 2011): 16–34.

A scholar of the realist tradition John Mearsheimer provides a harsh critique of U.S. attempts at global leadership in the administrations of Presidents Bill Clinton, George W. Bush, and Barack Obama. He argues that their strategies have actually undermined American security and, like Walt, he argues for a more restrained policy of offshore balancing.

Pape, Robert. "Soft Balancing Against the United States." *International Security* 30, no. 1 (2005): 7–45.

Powers, Samantha. *A Problem from Hell: America in the Age of Genocide.* New York: Harper Collins, 2007.

Internet References . . .

President Obama's State of the Union Address

President Barack Obama, "State of the Union Address— January 24, 2012."

www.whitehouse.gov/the-press-office/2012/01/24/ remarks-president-state-union-address

Selected, Edited, and with Issue Framing Material by:
Suzanne Nielsen, *U.S. Military Academy*
and
Scott Handler, *U.S. Military Academy*

ISSUE

Should Promoting Democracy Abroad Be a Top U.S. Priority?

YES: Michael McFaul, from *Democracy and American National Interests* (New York: Rowman & Littlefield, 2010)

NO: Dimitri K. Simes, from "America's Imperial Dilemma," *Foreign Affairs* (November/December 2003)

Learning Outcomes

After reading this issue, you should be able to:

- Discuss the relationship between democracy and peace.
- Explain the potential benefits to the United States of having a greater number of democracies in the world.
- Discuss the advantages and disadvantages of various approaches to democracy promotion, including the use of military force.
- Understand arguments against American promotion of democracy in other countries.
- Describe the costs, challenges, and risks associated with democracy promotion.

ISSUE SUMMARY

YES: Michael McFaul, professor of political science at Stanford University and U.S. Ambassador to Russia, argues that American security, economic, and moral interests have been served by the spread of democracy throughout the globe. McFaul makes a comprehensive case that American foreign policy should continue to prioritize democracy promotion to counter threats emanating from autocratic regimes and to gain the security and economic benefits that flow from close relationships with fellow democracies.

NO: Dimitri K. Simes, president of the Center for the National Interest and publisher of *The National Interest*, argues that America's efforts to impose its utopian democratic vision on the rest of the world severely harm the country's long-term interests. Contending that America's dangerous imperial overreach threatens its exercise of power, Simes concludes that a return to a pragmatic and realistic foreign policy—one without democracy promotion—is the only way to maintain America's ability to lead in the world.

The question of whether spreading democracy around the world enhances U.S. national security has become hotly contested in the post–Cold War era. While most believe that a world with more stable democracies would be the safer world, the idea that the United States should take an active role in promoting democracy enjoys no such consensus. There is a broad range of viewpoints on the subject, ranging from those who advocate active democracy promotion—with military force if necessary—to those who reject such efforts as ineffective, wasteful, and even potentially dangerous to U.S. national security interests.

The foundation of the argument in favor of placing democracy promotion as a top U.S. foreign policy priority is the observation that no two liberal democracies have fought a war against each other. This phenomenon, known as the "democratic peace," is in fact a very old concept with philosophical roots in the work of Immanuel Kant. Kant's famous 1798 essay, "Perpetual Peace: A Philosophical Sketch," was in many respects a proposal for achieving an enduring peace among states. In this essay, Kant argued that "The Civil Constitution of Every State Should Be Republican," asserting that a country whose government was based on the principles of representation and division of power would be cautious in going to war (Kant, 2006). If these republican states were to gather in a "federation of free states," this arrangement would further guarantee the freedom and sovereignty of all.

Kant's principles echo in the writings of the early twentieth-century's great liberal democratic standard bearer, President Woodrow Wilson. In his famous "Fourteen

Points" speech, delivered to Congress in January 1918, he laid out the tenets that would govern a peaceful international order based on the principles of freedom, liberty, justice, and equality (Wilson, 1918). Indeed, one might argue that Wilson was the first U.S. president to advocate the promotion of liberal democracy as a foreign policy objective. In his view the key to American security lay in the political transformation of the rest of the world (McFaul, 2010).

Building on the philosophical foundations provided by Kant and Wilson, political scientists continue to explore the precise mechanisms that lead to peaceful relations among liberal democracies (Russett, 2001). Two main schools of thought have developed. The first argues that democratic culture holds the key. Democratic states extend their expectations of nonviolent dispute resolution and compromise to fellow democracies because these other states also share these same norms (Russett, 1993). The second argues the structure and institutions of democracy—institutions such as separation of powers, representative government, elite accountability and turnover through elections, transparency, and a free press—make the march to war in democracies a slow, messy process with many veto points (Russett, 1993). This slow process creates additional time to resolve disputes through negotiation and bargaining rather than violence. Though the two explanations for the democratic peace—the cultural/normative model and the structural/institutional model—are analytically distinct, it is hard to verify empirically which version best explains reality. In fact, it is likely that the two mechanisms operate simultaneously in mutually reinforcing ways.

Regardless of *how* the democratic peace operates, the existence of this peace has clear and important implications for U.S. national security: if democracies do not go to war with other democracies, then a greater number of democracies in the world means fewer potential enemies. Based on this logic, democracy promoters argue that the United States would be better off with more democratic countries in the world. What is less clear is how the United States should promote democratization in foreign countries and what means are acceptable in doing so.

One school of thought that held particularly strong sway in U.S. foreign policy circles during the early years of the twenty-first century is neoconservatism. According to its proponents, "the spread of democracy is not just an end but a means, an indispensable means for securing American interests" (Krauthammer, 2004). Arguing that the spread of democracy enhances American security and power, neoconservatives blend elements of realism and liberalism to arrive at a clear policy conclusion: the United States must take an active role in spreading democracy around the world through a variety of means—including military force when necessary. In order to prevent overextension, neoconservative thinkers such as Charles Krauthammer argue that the priority of effort must go to areas that are strategically important to the United States.

An even more expansive view was offered by President George W. Bush in his second inaugural address. In this speech, he argued that: "The best hope for peace in our world is the expansion of freedom in all the world . . . So it is the policy of the United States to seek and support the growth of democratic movements and institutions in every nation and culture, with the ultimate goal of ending tyranny in the world" (Bush, 2005).

The idea that actively spreading democracy should be a central goal of U.S. foreign policy also has numerous critics. Scholars and policymakers from the realist tradition in international relations have mounted the most forceful challenge. Realists see interstate relations as being driven by an eternal competition for power and security that is inherent in an anarchic international system (Mearsheimer, 2001). Some realists question the very existence of the democratic peace, arguing that the post–World War II peace among democracies was driven by the common existential threat posed by the Soviet Union rather than the characteristics of democracy (Farber and Gowa, 1995). But even realists who do accept the idea of the democratic peace see the endless pursuit of utopian ideals, such as democracy promotion, across the globe as costly and ineffective. Even worse, American efforts to democratize other countries risk producing an anti-American backlash that will harm national security.

Other political science research has suggested that while mature, stable democracies may not fight wars with one another, new (potentially weak) democracies and states undergoing transitions to democracy are actually *more* likely to fight wars than stable democracies or stable autocracies (Mansfield and Snyder, 1995). Thus, realists argue, democratization may actually increase the risk of domestic and international conflict in the short- to medium-term, resulting in messy quagmires.

Other criticisms of democracy promotion question either the priority it receives or the means that are best employed in its service. As an example of the former, former U.S. State Department Director of Policy Planning Richard Haass argues:

> It is . . . neither desirable nor practical to make democracy promotion a foreign policy doctrine. Too many pressing threats in which the lives of millions hang in the balance . . . will not be solved by the emergence of democracy. Promoting democracy is and should be one foreign policy goal, but it cannot be the only or dominant objective. When it comes to relations with Russia or China, other national security interests must normally take precedence over concerns about how they choose to govern themselves. (Haass, 2005)

With regard to the issue of means, some reject the use of force. As Francis Fukuyama argued in a 2005 address to the Foreign Policy Association, "Forcible regime change really creates as many problems as it solves because you are the primary agent that is pushing change . . . [U]nless the local people think they own the democracy that they are creating, it creates a lot of problems" (2005). Less costly but potentially more effective means of democracy promotion include, according to Fukuyama, election monitoring, rhetorical and financial support for independent media, and support for civil society groups.

A final powerful critique of U.S. democracy promotion suggests that particular counties are not suited to democracy, especially when imposed from the outside. Just as a seed planted in barren soil will fail to take root and grow, so too will democracy struggle to survive in places where the conditions are not suitable for its success. One condition that seems strongly correlated with successful democratization is a country's level of economic development. While countries at every level of development have democratized, countries that are well off seem better able to sustain democratic forms of government over time. One finding shows, for example, that no democracy with a real per capita income greater than $6,000 has returned to authoritarian rule (Przeworski et al., 2000). In addition to poverty, less-developed countries are often characterized by a weak state, high levels of corruption, low levels of education, and ethnic and other social cleavages.

Scholars of democratization have also identified culture as an important factor that influences the probability of democratic survival (Fukuyama, 2005). While such arguments risk being overly deterministic, it would be equally problematic to argue that the history, norms, identities, and ideas that constitute political culture play no role in shaping political regimes. Critics of American efforts to promote democracy in the Middle East often point to elements within Islamic political culture as evidence of a worldview that is inhospitable to democracy. Similar arguments have been made about supposed authoritarian values in some East Asian countries. The links between culture and democracy (or authoritarianism) are hotly contested, highly controversial, and problematic on many levels. However, the argument that some

cultures are not suited for democracy remains a common and powerful weapon in the arsenal of those who criticize U.S. democracy promotion in these societies.

Given the above, it is apparent that there is a vigorous debate and wide range of views on the question of whether democracy promotion should be a top foreign policy priority for the United States. Some put the global spread of democracy at the very core of American national security interests and are ready to use any means necessary to achieve that end. Others argue for the importance of promoting democracy but disagree over the appropriateness and effectiveness of various means. Still others question whether the United States should engage in any sort of democracy promotion abroad given the costs, challenges, and risks of such a strategy. This debate over U.S. democracy promotion seems likely to continue for many years to come.

The YES and NO selections by the current Ambassador to Russia, Michael McFaul, and the publisher of *The National Interest*, Dimitri K. Simes, capture this debate. In *Advancing Democracy Abroad*, McFaul argues that the greatest threats faced by the United States come from autocratic regimes. In order to ensure American security, the United States must continue to promote democracy abroad. In addition to bolstering U.S. national security, democracy promotion efforts will promote American economic interests and serve U.S. values.

Simes, in "America's Imperial Dilemma," argues that such views about democracy promotion are not just naïve, they are dangerous. Trying to dominate the political systems and behavior of others is just another form of empire, no matter how benign its proponents believe such efforts to be. History has shown that empires generate opposition that ultimately harms their long-term interests. Therefore, the United States should follow a more pragmatic foreign policy in order to best safeguard U.S. national interests and enable the United States to retain a leadership role in international affairs.

YES

Michael McFaul

Democracy and American National Interests

. . . The history of the last 200 years, but especially the last 80 years, shows that American security, economic, and moral interests have been enhanced by the expansion of democracy abroad, while reliance on realpolitik frameworks as a guide for foreign policy has produced some short-term gains but many long-term setbacks for American national interests. The remainder of this chapter explains why, by looking at (1) the dangers of autocratic foes; (2) the tenuous benefits of autocratic allies; (3) the long-term security advantages from alliances with democracies; (4) the security benefits of democratization; (5) the security threats from democratic breakdown; (6) the economic dividends of democratic expansion; and (7) the positive reputational gains of supporting democracy abroad. These factors all point to America's security and economic interests being enhanced by the advance of democracy around the world.

Autocratic Enemies

Every foreign enemy of the United States has been a dictatorship. Autocracies, not democracies, have attacked and threatened the United States. The consolidation of democratic regimes in states ruled by formerly anti-American, autocratic regimes has transformed such countries from enemies into allies of the United States. Over the last two centuries, the advance of democracy abroad has made Americans safer at home. . . .

After the Cold War

Since the end of the Cold War, America's enemies have continued to be drawn from the ranks of autocratic regimes and antidemocratic movements. In the 1990s, no state directly threatened the United States, but American security interests in peace and stability in Europe were threatened by Serbia's autocratic ruler, Slobodan Milošević, who wreaked havoc in the Balkans through war with his neighbors and ethnic cleansing in Kosovo. Milošević never threatened American security directly, but his wars did undermine security in the backyard of America's closest European allies. Consequently, American armed forces eventually became involved in the Balkan wars, including

a major peacekeeping operation in Bosnia-Herzegovina and a NATO bombing campaign against Serbia in the spring of 1999 to stop Milošević's forced expulsion of ethnic Albanians from Kosovo. Today, American troops remain in Bosnia-Herzegovina and Kosovo.

In September 1994, the United States led a U.N.-sanctioned military intervention called Operation Uphold Democracy to overthrow a dictatorship in Haiti. Again, the Haitian military junta did not represent a direct threat to American national security, but the regime's policies did constitute an assault on American values and a possible economic burden from tens of thousands of Haitians seeking refuge in the United States. American military interventions in Panama and Somalia were likewise not in response to direct threats to the United States, but both regimes were non-democracies.

In the 1990s, Iran, North Korea, Afghanistan, Iraq, Cuba, and Libya did not have the military capacity to threaten the United States directly. Nonetheless, relations that had been tense and confrontational with these countries during the Cold War remained so in the decade that followed. The only common feature among all these countries is autocracy. Certainly it is not the power capabilities of these countries that led American leaders—Democratic and Republican alike—to consider them threats to the United States. . . .

To deter impoverished North Korea, the United States has maintained more than 35 thousand troops in South Korea for over half a century, while also supplying South Korea with billions of dollars in military and economic assistance. To contain Iran, the U.S. has supplied billions of dollars in military equipment and deployed the U.S. Navy in the Persian Gulf. Iran's annual military budget is less than one-eighth that of the United States. To counter future ballistic missile threats from North Korea and Iran, American military planners have spent billions of dollars to develop national and theater ballistic missile defense systems. These asymmetric responses by American foreign policymakers to relatively minor military powers can only be explained if regime type in Iran and North Korea is part of the threat analysis.

After September 11, the Bush administration calculated wrongly that the future military threat from autocratic Iraq was so great that the United States had to intervene preemptively to overthrow Saddam Hussein's dictatorship. An assessment of threats based only on the balance of military power between Iraq and the United States would have produced a different conclusion. Think, however, of the other counterfactual: Had Iraq been ruled by a democratic regime, no amount of intelligence about Iraq's secret nuclear weapons program would have convinced the American people to support a preemptive war.

U.S. policy toward Cuba can likewise be explained only with reference to Fidel Castro's dictatorship. Cuba has virtually no military capacity to threaten the United States, and yet, for more than four decades, president after president—Democrats and Republicans alike—[has] maintained a sanctions regime against this island country, to the detriment of American economic interests.

The People's Republic of China has lingered somewhere between friend and foe of the United States since the end of the Cold War. China's current military capacity and potential for even greater military might create the possibility of serious confrontation with the United States, yet China's regime type also plays a direct role in exacerbating Sino-American tensions. Despite the enormous amount of trade and investment traffic between China and the United States, American leaders continue to support Taiwan's security, both by selling military hardware and by maintaining a deliberately vague commitment to defending the island against attack from the mainland. This American support began when an autocratic regime ruled Taiwan, but has continued in part because Taiwan made the transition to democracy in 2000. Taiwanese leaders and diplomats constantly stress the democratic values they share with the United States as a central reason for close military cooperation. If mainland China were to become a democracy, then the case for defending Taiwanese sovereignty would be weakened.

The current successful management of American–Chinese relations underscores the important observation that conflicts between democracies and autocracies are not inevitable. The Bush administration's casting of China as a "stakeholder" in the international system—that is, a force for the status quo rather than a revisionist power—produced stabilizing results. Nonetheless, there is no question that managing China's rise will remain a central concern of American presidents for the next century. For the past 15 years, China has increased military spending steadily and gradually, a pattern that suggests China is seeking to counter if not challenge American military might. American concern about this military buildup is driven in large measure by the nature of the Chinese regime. A rising democratic China would be less threatening.

In the 1990s, non-governmental movements dedicated to nondemocratic ideologies also posed threats to the United States and its allies. . . . Al Qaeda espouses a set of beliefs antithetical to democracy, which Osama bin Laden and his followers associate with the evil West. In their quest to push the United States out of the Middle East, bin Laden and his followers attacked the United States numerous times in the 1990s, culminating in the

horrendous terrorist attacks on American soil on September 11, 2001. Once again, the United States is at war with a transnational, ideologically motivated enemy whose core beliefs are anti-democratic, anti-liberal, and therefore anti-American.

Political organizations that use terrorism as a weapon do not all embrace the same antidemocratic political objectives as Al Qaeda. Hezbollah in Lebanon has participated in elections and followed the rule of law at times, while also pursuing a parallel terrorist campaign against Israel and justifying extra-constitutional acts within Lebanon when convenient. Hamas has followed a similar dual track strategy in the Palestinian Authority. Most absurdly, Hamas participated in and won the January 2006 parliamentary elections, then executed a coup d'etat to seize power in Gaza the following year. Neither Hamas nor Hezbollah can be considered democratic organizations or part of democratic governments. Both are adversaries of the United States and its democratic allies in the Middle East.

Autocratic Allies: Short-Term Necessities and Long-Term Liabilities

All enemies of the United States have been and are autocracies, but not all autocracies have been or are enemies of the United States. As just discussed, the United States has benefitted from a variety of alliances through the years with monarchists (in France during the American Revolution), and autocrats (in Russia during World War I and the Soviet Union during World War II). Autocratic allies, however, have posed three major national security problems for American leaders: sustainability, consistency, and cost.

Regarding sustainability, most autocratic regimes have no predictable or legitimate way to hand over power, meaning that transitions from one leader to the next can be precarious. Generally, though not always, democracies make leadership transitions more predictable. Even more problematic, autocrats often struggle to stay in power. In the face of societal unrest, autocrats typically resort to additional repression to hold onto power, a response that sidelines moderates and strengthens extremists, be they communists, fascists, or Islamic fundamentalists. These explosive situations often end in revolution, civil war, or state collapse, outcomes that almost never serve American interests. The fall of several autocratic allies, including Chiang Kai-shek in China, Fulgencio Batista in Cuba, the Shah in Iran, and Anastasio Somoza in Nicaragua all produced new autocratic regimes hostile to American interests. In these cases, new extremists came to power and blamed the United States for propping up the *ancien régime* they had just toppled.

Second, autocratic leaders can change their allegiances quickly. Because they do not answer to parliaments or voters, they can move much faster and in much more unpredictable ways to reverse their international orientation. Stalin terminated cooperation with the western allies quickly after the end of the World War II, rejecting U.S. economic assistance offered through the Marshall Plan even though the Soviet economy at the time was in desperate need of such aid. Egyptian leader Gamal Adbul Nasser flip-flopped repeatedly in his relations with the United States before finally deciding to cast his lot with the Soviet Union. Saddam Hussein was eager to cooperate with the United States during his war with Iran from 1980 to 1988, but quickly and easily abandoned his American allies when he decided to invade Kuwait in 1990. . . . Even strains in U.S.-Saudi relations underscore the difficulties of relying on autocrats as enduring and reliable allies. American and Saudi leaders share interests in trading energy resources and containing Iranian influence, but also struggle to manage major disagreements over the Israeli-Palestinian conflict, non-governmental Saudi assistance for fundamentalist religious movements, or more recently the lack of Saudi support for the Shia-dominated government in Iraq. And Saudi Arabia has remained a major supplier of anti-American terrorists not only for the September 11 attacks, but in Iraq as well. American relations with Pakistan have followed a similar topsy-turvy course of cordial relations followed by tenser phases, though it could not be argued that relations are better when democratic governments are in power in Pakistan and worse during periods of autocratic government. It goes without saying, however, that Pakistan has not always acted as a reliable ally of the United States. Support for the Taliban from Pakistan's Inter-Services Intelligence or ISI (their equivalent of the CIA) and the country's continued reluctance to move aggressively against Al Qaeda camps inside Pakistan underscore just how problematic such alliances can be.

A third problem in working closely with autocratic allies is the cost Americans have to incur. Realist thinkers often argue that balancing against threats and supporting other countries to balance against American enemies (called by scholars "offshore balancing") amount to a less costly strategy for pursuing American national security interests compared to promotion of democratic change. Yet maintaining balances of power favorable to the U.S. through the engagement of autocratic allies is an extremely expensive and inexact policy. During the Cold War, in addition to American spending on its own military forces, autocratic allies extracted tremendous military and economic subsidies from the United States as a price for maintaining their allegiance to the international anti-communist coalition. Maintaining regional balances of power between autocratic regimes or between autocratic and democratic regimes also proved costly in both financial and human terms. To maintain a balance of power in the Middle East, the United States has supplied billions of dollars in military and economic aid to both Israel and Egypt. American efforts at tweaking the balance of power between Iraq and Iran not only resulted in the death of more than one million Iraqi and Iranian soldiers in the Iran–Iraq war. but ultimately resulted in regimes hostile to the United States in both countries. In Asia, the U.S.

strategy of balancing Soviet and Chinese power by supporting autocratic allies in Vietnam and Korea proved very costly in American lives and resources. There may have been no other options; for example, had the United States not defended autocratic South Korea against North Korean aggression, a democratic South Korea may never have emerged. But to assume that the embrace of autocratic allies to balance against autocratic enemies is always a more efficient means for pursuing U.S. security interests is also wrong. The short-term benefits of embracing autocratic allies are almost always overshadowed by the long-term costs. . . .

Enduring Democratic Allies

Not every democracy in the world was or is a close ally of the United States, but no democracy in the world has been or is an American enemy. And all of America's most enduring allies have been and remain democracies. . . .

In the aftermath of the Soviet collapse and the disappearance of a common enemy, some predicted that ties developed among Western (and Asian) democracies during the Cold War would weaken and would be replaced by multi-polar competition among these former allies. According to this realist analysis, the new multiple powers in Europe and the international system would be compelled to balance against each other by forming shifting alliances akin to the Concert of Europe in the nineteenth century. To date, however, none of this predicted behavior among the great powers in Europe or among the democracies in the world has occurred: no arms races, spiraling threats, or even trade wars. Nor has balancing occurred between the United States and Europe. The democratic countries that composed the core of the alliance to contain communism have continued to cooperate to address common security threats, while democracies outside this Cold War alliance system—most notably India—have moved closer to the United States. Relations between states in this democratic core have been driven by a different dynamic than balance-of-power politics. Despite realist predictions of its demise, the NATO military alliance has persevered and expanded, enlarging and protecting the democratic community of states in Europe.

The American decision to invade Iraq placed a serious strain on the democratic community of states, since several important democracies, including France and Germany, vehemently objected to the war. When these divisions crystallized in the spring of 2003, some predicted a return to balance of power politics in Europe, with France and Germany siding with Russia as one new constellation, and the United States, Great Britain, and Poland providing the backbone of an opposing axis. This new power configuration never coalesced. Instead, relations between the democracies started to improve well before the war was over and even while President Bush was still in office. As newly elected French president Nikolas Sarkozy perceptively stated upon his arrival in the U.S. for a meeting with

Bush in August 2007, "Do we agree on everything? No. . . . Even within families there are disagreements, but we are still the same family."

The United States has also maintained close military and economic ties with the one democracy in the Middle East, Israel. Common Judeo-Christian values, American sympathy for the plight of the Jews during World War II, and a large Jewish population in the United States have helped to fortify this special American relationship with Israel, a bond that would probably persist even if Israel were a dictatorship. Nonetheless, Israel's unique status as the only liberal democracy in the region provides an added reason for close ties, and one that U.S. leaders frequently invoke as a justification for the deep American commitment to Israeli security. That traditional realist thinkers have questioned the utility of this alliance and cannot explain this close bilateral relationship using traditional metrics of state power suggests that the regime type in both the United States and Israel is critical in explaining this unique alliance. . . .

Security Benefits from Democratic Change

Perhaps the most compelling evidence that democracy's advance serves American national interests comes from those countries that have changed from autocratic to democratic regimes. In every case, the country in transition has developed better relations with the United States after consolidating democracy.

World War II Enemies to Allies

As autocracies, Germany, Japan, and Italy were enemies of the United States. As democracies, all three have developed into important American allies. Immediately after World War II, these three countries were occupied; their governments did not choose to ally with the United States. With time, all three countries put in place democratic institutions and in parallel gained greater sovereignty. As sovereign, democratic countries, Germany, Japan, and Italy all sought to maintain deep military ties with the United States. To be sure, these three countries sided with the United States in part as a response to the communist threat, compelling some to argue that the driving force behind these alliances was a common enemy. But why were they all threatened by communism in the first place? It is because they were democracies. Moreover, these alliance relationships persisted well after the collapse of communism and the disintegration of the Soviet Union.

After communism's demise in Europe, transitions to democracy in East Central Europe, southern Europe, and the Baltic states also produced security benefits for the United States. Poland, the Czech Republic, and Hungary all joined NATO at the first opportunity in 1999, and seven more countries in the region joined in the second wave of

enlargement in 2004. Every new liberal democracy in the region has decided to seek NATO membership. Initially, the benefits of NATO expansion seemed to accrue only to the new members, which were eager to counter a perceived Russian threat. NATO also provided a multilateral bridge for these new members as they pursued European Union membership. With time, however, the security benefits to the United States have grown. East European members of NATO were most vocal in supporting the American-led war in Iraq, including a famous "letter of eight" signed by three East Central European leaders in support of Bush and in opposition to "Western" or "old" European resistance to the military intervention. At varying levels and for different periods of time, several new American allies in Europe, including Albania, Bulgaria, Croatia, the Czech Republic, Estonia, Hungary, Latvia, Lithuania, Poland, Romania, Slovakia, and Slovenia, provided troops in Afghanistan and Iraq. In 2006, Poland agreed to expand its forces fighting under NATO command in Afghanistan to one thousand, making Poland one of the largest contributors to the mission. Some of these new allies, including Slovenia and Hungary, also have supplied troops to the peacekeeping mission in Kosovo. The Czech Republic and Poland agreed to participate in a ballistic missile defense system aimed at thwarting a future threat from Iran. Romania and Bulgaria have agreed to provide territory for new NATO bases.

Soviet Transformation

American national security benefited from democratic transformation in East Central and Southern Europe only because of regime change inside the Soviet Union started by Mikhail Gorbachev. . . . [T]he Soviet Union's collapse in 1991 was not inevitable, but occurred because Gorbachev initiated a process of political change, which then spun out of his control.

This political change within the Soviet Union ended the Cold War, which in turn had a profoundly positive impact on U.S. national security. Speaking to the British parliament in 1982, President Reagan argued that

> there are new threats now to our freedom, indeed to our very existence, that other generations could never have even imagined. There is first the threat of global war. No president, no congress, no prime minister, no parliament can spend a day entirely free of this threat.

Reagan was referring to the threat of war between the West and the Soviet Union. By the summer of 1991, President Bush was not spending much time worrying about world war with the Soviets. The specter of a nuclear holocaust faded, even if Russia maintained the ability to obliterate the United States overnight. The international contest to contain communism in far away places such as Angola or Nicaragua ended. Threats to American allies in Europe subsided. . . .

In the 1990s, radical political and economic change in Russia produced leaders, political forces, and economic interest groups that identified with and benefited from liberal ideas, specifically democratic and market practices at home and integration into Western institutions abroad. Russia's new leaders also rejected communist and fascist ideologies, building instead economic institutions (including first and foremost, private property rights) and to a lesser extent political institutions designed to constrain illiberal, anti-democratic forces. This new regime dramatically diluted the threat from Russia to the United States, to the point that leaders in Washington and Moscow began to refer to each other as strategic partners and friends. It was not Russia's military decline that lessened the threat to the United States, but rather internal democratic change. . . .

Toppling the Taliban Regime in Afghanistan

In the 1990s, an autocratic regime in Afghanistan emerged as an unlikely threat to American national security. Using traditional military and economic measures, Afghanistan did not rank as a major power in the international system. Instead, the threat to the United States came from the nature of the Taliban regime, which wholeheartedly embraced illiberal, totalitarian ideas and established an ideological alliance with another anti-democratic force, Al Qaeda. The Taliban regime offered Al Qaeda logistical support and a territorial base, which in turn aided Al Qaeda's terrorist activities abroad, including the attacks on the United States on September 11, 2001.

By eliminating a base of operations for a major American enemy, the American-led military effort to destroy the Taliban regime in Afghanistan following the September 11 attacks produced immediate security benefits for the United States and its allies. Both the Taliban and Al Qaeda remain threats to American national security, but they are lesser threats because they no longer control a nation-state—a valuable asset for plotting, preparing, and launching terrorist attacks. Even in this weak, peripheral country, the nature of the regime governing Afghanistan produced a profound and direct effect on American national security interests. Whether Afghanistan emerges once again as a threat to American national security will depend heavily on what kind of regime eventually takes hold there.

Deepening Alliances after Democratization

During the Cold War, some American strategists argued that the United States had to defend autocratic allies who helped the United States pursue vital national interests, including containing communism, providing energy resources, protecting trade routes, or securing American investments. In these countries, so the argument went, the process of democratization would bring to power communist forces, which would turn against the United States and undermine democracy. A very similar argument is made about the threat of anti-American, anti-democratic Islamists coming to power through elections in the Middle East.

However, transitions from autocracy to democracy in Chile, Portugal, South Africa, and South Korea, as well as Argentina, Brazil, Indonesia, Spain, and Taiwan, did not damage American strategic interests as predicted. Instead the transitions served to consolidate deeper, more lasting relationships with the new democratic regimes in these countries. New democracies often face threats from autocratic regimes in their neighborhoods, making them more likely to become allies of the United States. Fears of pro-American autocrats giving way to anti-American democrats have been largely unfounded.

Threats from the Failure to Consolidate Democracy

The collapse of autocracy does not always lead to democracy. . . . In the past 50 years, the failure of democracy to replace fallen autocracies in Iraq, Cuba, Vietnam, Nicaragua, Iran, Afghanistan, and Uzbekistan has created threats to American national security. Three of America's most recent and serious security threats—from Iraq, Iran, and Afghanistan—are byproducts of Cold War decisions to befriend and support autocrats in the struggle against communist enemies (perceived or otherwise) which were then replaced by autocracies even more hostile to American national interests.

In the case of Iran, America's involvement in disrupting democratic change generated more direct threats to its national security, albeit delayed. In August 1953, a CIA covert operation codenamed Ajax helped to topple Prime Minister Mossadeq from power and replaced him with the Shah. Not all of Mossadeq's methods of wielding power were democratic, but his ouster in a coup orchestrated by the United States and Great Britain sealed his legacy as a democrat and nationalist toppled by "anti-democratic" imperial powers. After the removal of Mossadeq, the Shah of Iran remained a reliable U.S. ally for nearly four decades. But his eventual fall from power ushered in one of the most anti-American regimes in the world. During the Iranian revolution in 1979, U.S. support for the 1953 coup against Mossadeq served as a rallying cry for anti-American forces in Iran among both leftist leaders and the clergy.

In Afghanistan, as already discussed, the collapse of communist dictatorship from 1989 to 1992 did not lead to a democratic or stable form of government, which eventually allowed the Taliban to seize power by 1996. Whether or not democracy had any chance of taking hold in Afghanistan after the fall of communism is difficult to know. What is clear is that the United States dramatically reduced support to and engagement with the new Afghan government once it came to power in 1992. Before the war against the Soviet occupation in the 1980s, according to Ahmed Rashid, "Islamists barely had a base in Afghan society." They gained a foothold only because Pakistan channeled American funds to the most extremist parties in the anti-Soviet coalition. The Pashtun-based Taliban came to power not because all of Afghanistan embraced their totalitarian interpretation of Islam, but because they offered a Pashtun alternative both to the Tajik-Uzbek dominated government that controlled Kabul after the fall of the communist regime in 1992, and the anarchic warlords who prevailed under the Rabbanni government between 1992 and 1996. The negative consequences for U.S. national security of this failed democratic transition were profound.

Democracy's failure to take hold in Iraq also resulted in direct threats to American security interests. Again, as in Afghanistan, it is not clear that democracy ever had a chance in the wake of the American-led military invasion that toppled Saddam Hussein's regime. Democracy's failure in Iraq stimulated civil war between Sunni and Shia groups, which in turn pulled American forces back into combat within the country. The absence of a legitimate democratic regime also helped to compel disaffected Iraqi Sunnis to ally with Al Qaeda and other anti-American, anti-democratic transnational movements. Beginning in 2005, new participation in a political process—the so-called Sunni Awakening—helped to quell violence in the Sunni regions of Iraq. In combination with an American spike in military forces in 2007, the Awakening helped to reduce threats to Americans based in Iraq and to weaken transnational movements like Al Qaeda that also threatened Americans in Iraq and around the world. . . .

Economic Benefits of Democratic Expansion

In addition to making Americans more secure, the expansion of democracy abroad also has made Americans richer. Most obviously, the transformation of autocratic foes into democratic allies has reduced the need for military spending—the famous "guns and butter" trade-off. As John Owen IV has observed, "The near absence of wars among mature liberal democracies . . . means that democratic states need not prepare for war against one another. This allows them to invest in resources elsewhere that might have been used on such preparations. . . .

In addition to reducing the pressure on government spending for defense purposes, the transformation of former foes into new allies opens new markets for trade and investment for American firms. Democratic states trade more openly and to a greater extent than non-democracies. New democracies tend to reduce trade barriers, especially in developing countries endowed with cheap labor, as the majorities in these countries seek the benefits of trade with the developed world. . . .

Finally, as discussed before, democratization often facilitates the strengthening of checks on executive power, more transparent government, and in the long run, stronger legal institutions. All of these components of a liberal democracy in turn create positive conditions for foreign investment and trade, including American trade and investment in new democracies. Autocrats can nationalize foreign companies, demand bribes from foreign investors, and treat domestic economic actors more favorably than foreign entities to a much greater extent than can democratic leaders.

The Benefits of a Moral Foreign Policy

American support for democratic change abroad aligns the United States with the preferences of the vast majority of people around the world. As discussed in the previous chapter, public opinion surveys of people throughout the world show that solid majorities in every country support democracy. When Americans argue instead that the U.S. should support autocrats in the name of "stability," whose preferences does that serve? Whose stability? It is obviously not the preferences or stability of a majority of people living under these autocracies. And that raises the question of which policy is more imperial: one that supports the aspirations of a people, or one that shores up the power of a dictator who is willing to serve the interests of the global hegemon in return for the survival of his autocracy? As we have seen, democracies do not commit genocide, do not generate refugees, and do not permit wide-scale famines, so by supporting democratic change abroad, the United States also will be supporting a more ethical and just foreign policy.

The direct security and economic benefits of such a moral foreign policy are hard to measure. Famines, genocide, and state collapse often end up costing the United States financially, and have even pulled the U.S. into conflict, as in Somalia and Haiti in the 1990s. Investing in democratic government in other countries today can be thought of as helping to prevent more costly interventions in the future.

Less directly but more importantly over the long haul, a more moral U.S. foreign policy increases America's standing in the world, which in turn increases American leverage on all issues of international politics, including those with more direct consequences for U.S. national security and prosperity. Especially after the United States emerged as a world power, other countries were willing to accept American leadership because of a genuine belief in the American commitment to "doing good" in the world. American leaders were allowed to take the lead in building international institutions that benefited American security and prosperity in part because the United States was the most powerful country in the free world, but also because other leaders trusted the United States as a moral force for good. Conversely, U.S. foreign policies that have undermined American commitment to democracy—by supporting autocrats, undermining democratically-elected leaders, or ignoring international human rights norms—have weakened American influence and standing more generally regarding international affairs.

Finally, Americans—foreign policymakers and citizens alike—may gain some sense of satisfaction by seeing their country do the right thing, or stand on the right side of history. Although impossible to measure, the feeling of pride or contentment with one's country's international standing must register as a benefit to the American people.

MICHAEL MCFAUL is a professor of political science at Stanford University, who is currently serving as the U.S. Ambassador to Russia. Previously, he was a special assistant to the President and senior director of Russian and Eurasian affairs on the U.S. National Security Staff.

Dimitri K. Simes

 **NO**

America's Imperial Dilemma

The Reluctant Empire

ANY REALISTIC DISCUSSION of U.S. foreign policy must begin with the recognition that, notwithstanding Americans' views and preferences, most of the world sees the United States as a nascent imperial power. Some nations support the United States precisely because of this, viewing it as a benign liberal empire that can protect them against ambitious regional powers. Others resent it because it stands in the way of their goals. Still others acquiesce to U.S. imperial predominance as a fact of life that cannot be changed and must be accepted.

It is understandable why supporters of the Bush administration's foreign policy balk at any mention of the "e" word. Many past empires were given a bad name not just by their opponents, from national liberation movements to Marxists, but also by their conduct; Nazi Germany and the Soviet Union were the ugliest manifestations. The United States, on the other hand, is said to seek benign influence rather than domination. Its political culture and even its institutional design mitigate against its acting as an effective imperial power. These arguments are not without merit. Still, they reflect more a reluctance to associate American foreign policy with negative imperial stereotypes than a reasoned appreciation of how earlier empires emerged and functioned.

Although empires, like democracies, have taken vastly different forms through history, they have several features in common. First, empires exercise great authority over large and varied territories populated by diverse ethnic groups, cultures, and religions. They rely on a broad range of tools and incentives to maintain this dominance: political persuasion, economic advantage, and cultural influence where possible; coercion and force when necessary. Empires generally expect neighboring states and dependencies to accept their power and accommodate to it. This often contributes to a sense that the imperial power itself need not play by the same rules as ordinary states and that it has unique responsibilities and rights.

Second, empires, more often than not, have emerged spontaneously rather than through a master plan. They frequently evolve as if following the laws of physics; an initial success generates momentum, which is subsequently maintained by inertia. Each new advance creates opportunities and challenges that extend the empire's definition of its interests far beyond its original form.

Ancient Athens, for example, began as the leader of a victorious alliance that defeated the Persians. But it quickly evolved into an empire, against the will of many of its former partners. Thucydides, one of the fathers of realism, describes the Athenian perspective thus: "We did not gain this empire by force. . . . It was the actual course of events which first compelled us to increase our power to its present extent: fear of Persia was our chief motive, though afterwards we thought, too, of our own honor and our own interest."

Third, empires do not always have sovereignty over their domains. This was certainly the case with Athens. It was also the case in the early period of the Roman Empire, when Rome sought domination rather than direct control over its dependencies. Although some continental European empires, such as Austria-Hungary and tsarist Russia, did establish sovereignty within their territories, other modern empires were less formal, comfortable with enough preponderance to accomplish their political and economic objectives. The Soviet empire, for example, attempted to dominate rather than directly control territories outside of its borders after Stalin's death.

Finally, despite the unpleasant present-day connotations, the imperial experience has not been uniformly negative. Some former empires were agents of change and progress and had generally good intentions vis-à-vis their subjects. The United Kingdom was a prime example of this type, approaching its empire not only with a desire to promote development, but with a self-sacrificing willingness to spend its resources toward that end. . . .

Whether or not the United States now views itself as an empire, for many foreigners it increasingly looks, walks, and talks like one, and they respond to Washington accordingly. There is certainly no reason for American policymakers to refer to the United States as such in public pronouncements, but an understanding of America as an evolving, if reluctant, modern empire is an important analytic tool with profound consequences that American leaders should understand.

Empires cannot escape the laws of history. One of the most salient of these laws is that empires generate opposition to their rule, ranging from strategic realignment among states to terrorism within them. Another is that empires have never been cost free and that the level of opposition to them depends on the costs that the imperial power is willing to shoulder. Both imperial Britain and imperial Rome spent a good deal of time and money

Simes, Dimitri K. From *Foreign Affairs*, November/December 2003, pp. 91–102. Copyright © 2003 by Council on Foreign Relations, Inc. Reprinted by permission of Foreign Affairs. www.ForeignAffairs.com

quelling unrest and promoting loyalty within their territories. Finally, imperial powers often alter their preimperial forms of government and ways of life. Rome, for example, lost its republican government when it chose to don the imperial mantle. And although the United Kingdom chose democracy over the demands of maintaining its empire, it accumulated substantial immigrant populations from its former colonies, with significant political and economic consequences.

Utopian Urges

An empire that displays weakness and is not taken seriously is an empire in trouble. Being perceived as capricious or imperious, however, is also dangerous. This problem has often occurred when an imperial power insists on imposing a particular vision on the world. How many twentieth-century tragedies were caused, directly or indirectly, in this way? Destiny and choice have made the United States the dominant power in the world today, yet many U.S. policymakers—both Republican and Democrat—have failed to learn from past mistakes. The pursuit of their universal democratic utopia, as attractive as it may seem, is damaging vital U.S. interests and is increasingly coming into conflict with the United States' founding principle of "no taxation without representation."

In the past, a pragmatic foreign policy establishment at home and powerful constraints abroad restrained the United States' messianic instincts. This establishment was built largely around business leaders and lawyers who, although they shared American idealism and a strong sense of the national interest, were cautious and flexible in applying their beliefs to international politics. The Vietnam debacle discredited and divided this group, however, and later demographic and social trends diversified and democratized it. By the 1990s, the pragmatic component in the new foreign policy elite had declined in influence. Instead, powerful but too often reckless single-issue groups and nongovernmental organizations—which aspired to shape policy without having responsibility for its consequences—came to the fore, as did emotional but poorly explained television images.

As a result, American foreign policy moved away from its generally high-minded but interest-based roots to espouse a form of global social engineering. Two illusions facilitated this process: that international crusading can be done cheaply and that those who oppose the United States are motivated by a blanket hatred for American freedom and power, rather than by self-interested objections to specific American actions. These assumptions are simply not accurate, however. A recent major global survey by the Pew Research Center for the People and the Press reveals that those who hold unfavorable views of the United States generally support democratic ideals.

As pragmatism waned, the disintegration of the Soviet Union removed the principal external constraint on U.S. international behavior. The United States' unchallenged military, economic, and political superiority facilitated the view that it could do almost anything it wanted to do in the international arena. In this environment, a new utopian vision was born, the notion that the United States is both entitled and obliged to promote democracy wherever it can—by force if necessary. This idea was enthusiastically promoted in Washington by a de facto alliance of aggressive Wilsonians and neoconservatives, whose apparent belief that the United States cannot settle for anything less than permanent worldwide revolution has more in common with Trotsky than with the legacy of America's forefathers or even the muscular but pragmatic idealism of Theodore Roosevelt.

Typically, the pursuit of moralistic projects has undermined not only American interests but also American values. Double standards and deception, or at least considerable self-deception, have become all too common. For example, U.S. politicians who opposed the International Criminal Court—out of legitimate concern for American sovereignty and fear of politically motivated prosecutions of American soldiers—were simultaneously pressuring the newly democratic Yugoslavia to send its citizens to international war crimes tribunals. Others persuaded the Clinton administration to ignore the UN arms embargo in Bosnia but expressed outrage when other nations violated international sanctions. U.S. politicians across the spectrum have also applied double standards in their approach to foreign campaign contributions: appalled at the notion of another country contributing to the Republicans or Democrats, while insisting that the United States has a duty to fund various foreign political parties, regardless of foreign local laws. . . .

Empire's New Clothes

Although September 11 was a wake-up call to American leaders about the dangers of terrorism, too many seem to have drawn the wrong policy conclusions. The principal problem is the mistaken belief that democracy is a talisman for all the world's ills, including terrorism, and that the United States has a responsibility to promote democratic government wherever in the world it is lacking.

The flaw in this approach is not with democracy per se. Liberal democracy with civil society, the rule of law, minority rights, and free but regulated markets is undoubtedly the most humane and efficient way to organize modern society. National Security Adviser Condoleezza Rice is right to point out that suggesting certain people are not interested in freedom or are not ready for democracy's responsibilities is deeply condescending.

It is also condescending, however, to claim that America has the right to impose democracy on other nations and cultures, regardless of their circumstances and preferences. From the Roman Empire to the British Empire, civilization brought on the tips of swords or bayonets has never inspired lasting gratitude. Why should precision weapons be any more effective? As Winston

Churchill said, "democracy is the worst form of government except for all those other forms that have been tried from time to time." Treating democracy as a divine revelation—and Washington as its prophet and global enforcer—simply does not square with the historical record of this form of government, nor with the geopolitical realities of the modern world.

Advocates of the militant promotion of democracy have advanced a variety of questionable arguments to explain why imposing democracy it is not just a moral imperative but an essential practical goal for the United States. One of the most pervasive of these arguments is that democracy will prevent terrorism, since, in the words of former Congressman Newt Gingrich, "the advance of freedom is the surest strategy to undermine the appeal of terror in the world." Recent history suggests otherwise. Even setting aside Islamist terrorists in the United States, how can one explain homegrown terrorists such as radical environmentalists, the Weathermen in the 1960s and 1970s, or Eric Rudolph, recently charged with the Atlanta Olympics bombing? And what about the Irish Republican Army in Northern Ireland or Basque terrorism in democratic Spain?

Another favorite argument is that democracies do not fight one another. But this claim also collapses under scrutiny. If one is willing to consider states democratic by the standards of their time, then there have been several wars between democracies in the past: between Athens and Syracuse, Rome and Carthage, Cromwell's England and the Dutch, and Victorian Britain and South Africa. Moreover, two wars on American soil—the War of 1812 against the United Kingdom and the Civil War itself—were essentially fought between democracies. The reason there were fewer such disputes in the twentieth century was partly because the democracies were united in their struggle against Nazism and communism. With these common enemies gone, however, it is by no means certain that democracies will remain in pacific union. In the Middle East, for example, where popular antisemitic and anti-American feelings abound, democracy could actually increase the probability of conflict between Arab countries and Israel or the United States.

Those who dismiss the idea of conflict between democracies often reject the notion of multipolarity because, in the words of National Security Adviser Rice, "it is a theory of rivalry, of competing interests—and at its worst—competing values." But this position ignores the legitimacy of others' perspectives and would alienate even pro-American democracies if it were to become a principle of U.S. foreign policy. The debate over Iraq demonstrated how little is required for democracies like the United States and France to discover one another's imperfections. Some Russian observers already see recent U.S. administrations as resembling the Soviet Union in their determination to impose homegrown views on others and in their allegedly "Brezhnevite" approach to national sovereignty.

Even if democracy could prevent conflict, it would not guarantee American leadership or even broad support for the United States. In the war against Iraq, for example, democracy was an obstacle to Turkey's support and reinforced, rather than weakened, anti-American policies in France and Germany. On the other hand, the lack of democracy in Egypt, Saudi Arabia, Jordan, and Pakistan allowed those governments to cooperate with the United States, despite hostile public opinion.

Just as democratic nations are not always prepared to support the United States, authoritarian ones sometimes are, including on the crucial issues of our time, such as nonproliferation and terrorism. Driving away such nations—from China to Saudi Arabia—could seriously jeopardize American interests. Obtaining international support for the recent war in Iraq could have been easier if the United States had done a better job in cultivating key partners and regional players.

Breaking the Bonds

THE UNITED STATES must be willing to use force, unilaterally if necessary, to protect its security and that of its allies, but it is time for a hardheaded assessment of American interests to play a greater role in Washington's foreign policy calculus. American-led and American-financed military interventions for humanitarian ends should in the future be reserved for clear-cut cases of genocide, as took place in the Holocaust, Cambodia in the 1970s and 1980s, and Rwanda in 1994. Otherwise, the United States should engage in humanitarian interventions only with a UN mandate (unlike Kosovo) and, more important, in the certain knowledge that other nations are committed to providing substantial resources.

The Bush administration is correct to argue that the United States should be prepared to do what it takes—including engaging in preemptive action—to pursue terrorists and their sponsors, particularly those seeking weapons of mass destruction. But selective wars of "liberation" are likely to alienate crucial allies. And building constructive relationships with key players, including China and Russia and (as distasteful as it may be to some) Germany and France, is key to success in the war against terrorism and the struggle against WMD proliferation. Thus, although decisive—even ruthless—use of force is appropriate when there is a credible threat, it is important that the United States not use force as a routine instrument of nation building.

Take Iraq. Saddam Hussein's checkered record on WMD his persistent bullying of neighboring states, his continued violation of UN Security Council resolutions, his support for terrorists, and his attempt to assassinate a former U.S. president revealed him to be a major threat to American interests. Three administrations in a row could not resolve this problem through diplomatic processes. This stalemate justified the U.S.-led invasion last spring. Yet turning Iraq into another American protectorate is less easy to justify, especially when the United States does not possess an international mandate that would increase its legitimacy and defray the mounting costs. Iraq is, predictably, becoming more of a burden than a prize, and the Bush administration would do well to find a formula through which the United States can cede principal responsibility for reconstruction efforts to international organizations while maintaining military control. Acquiring additional burdens by engaging in new wars of liberation is the last thing the United States needs. Even if the U.S. economy improves, such adventures could overwhelm the federal budget, forcing the United States to choose between Roman exploitation—which sowed the seeds of that empire's destruction—and British imperial overstretch—which led to retreat.

The Bush administration's aggressive promotion of democracy also has worrying implications for American interests. As a rule, democratic advancement should be accomplished through the power of example and positive inducement. It is a self-evident fact that being friends with America brings numerous advantages and that the United States prefers to associate with other democracies. This should be incentive enough. Meanwhile, formal unilateral sanctions, which are usually more irritating than punishing, should not be applied as a matter of routine simply to demonstrate U.S. disapproval.

As the indisputable center of power in the world, the United States both benefits from a bandwagon effect and suffers from inevitable foreign backlash. Recent international debates over the U.S. intervention in Iraq demonstrate that although other countries are not prepared to give Washington carte blanche, most are willing to go a long way to accommodate American preferences. American leaders need not shy away from displaying U.S. power assertively, but they must let go of the pretension that the United States is the ultimate font of global wisdom.

Similarly, U.S. leaders must recognize that although rabid anti-American sentiments held in parts of the Muslim world are wholly unjustified, they are partly fueled by a perception of the United States as Israel's uncritical protector. This is not to say that the administration should abandon a staunch ally, nor pressure Israel into fighting terrorism in an unassertive manner. But ending American support for nonessential and provocative Israeli policies—such as its new settlement activity or its refusal to dismantle existing illegal outposts—could have a significant effect on how the United States is viewed in the Muslim world and would probably reduce the appeal of al Qaeda and other extremist groups.

Finally, the United States must address one of its greatest potential vulnerabilities: the combination of empire and immigration. As James Kurth, professor of political science at Swarthmore College, writes, "the conjunction of American empire (America expanding into the world) and American immigration (the world coming into America) has made the very idea of the American national interest problematic. There is a causal connection between empire and immigration, and the two are now coming together as a dynamic duo to utterly transform our world."

It has become increasingly difficult for state and federal agencies to take the tough measures required to regain control over immigration, which has outpaced the absorptive capacity of American society and institutions and is overwhelming the government's ability to enforce crucial immigration laws. No one knows when the United States will reach the point when Balkanization becomes an inevitability. But it is clear from America's current political environment—where single-issue interest groups and true believers in various causes are increasingly able to shape the national agenda—that this point is not very far away. Taking the necessary steps to stop the creeping invasion by illegal immigrants will be controversial and costly. But it is becoming increasingly vital.

Those who criticize the Bush administration for introducing a heavy-handed and unilateral foreign policy miss the mark. There is considerably more continuity between Clinton's interventionism and the current administration's foreign policy than meets the eye. Although candidate George W. Bush said that the United States should be a humble nation and warned against nation building, powerful domestic interests and the shock of September 11 put U.S. foreign policy back onto the track of dangerous imperial overreach: a "one size fits all" approach to democracy promotion fomented under Clinton. A new approach is badly needed, one that exercises power in a determined yet realistic and responsible way—keeping a close eye on American interests and values—but is not bashful about U.S. global supremacy. Only then will the United States be able to take maximum advantage of its power, without being bogged down in expensive and dangerous secondary pursuits that diminish its ability to lead.

DIMITRI K. SIMES is the president and CEO of the Center for the National Interest and publisher of its foreign policy bi-monthly magazine, *The National Interest*.

EXPLORING THE ISSUE

Should Promoting Democracy Abroad Be a Top U.S. Priority?

Critical Thinking and Reflection

1. Would the United States be better off in a world in which more countries had democratic forms of government? Why or why not?
2. Should the United States form alliances with authoritarian governments if these alliances serve U.S. national security interests? Are there disadvantages as well as advantages to such relationships?
3. What are the most serious risks created by efforts to promote democracy in foreign countries? Are there ways to mitigate these risks while still supporting democratization abroad?
4. When formulating foreign policy, should U.S. policymakers focus only on the national security interests of the United States, or should they also take into account the well-being of citizens of other countries who live under oppressive regimes?
5. Does the United States have a moral obligation to spread the ideals of freedom, equality, and liberty to the citizens of other countries? Justify your answer.
6. What is the most compelling argument in favor of democracy promotion as a top U.S. foreign policy priority? What is the most compelling argument against such a priority? Which side do you find more convincing? What contemporary or historical cases, if any, inform your views about this question?

Is There Common Ground?

As the introduction to this issue revealed, there is a wide array of views on whether democracy promotion is an appropriate U.S. foreign policy priority. At the extremes, there is little room for agreement. The view that the United States should use any means necessary, including force, to promote democracy is difficult to reconcile with the view that democracy promotion in other countries is most often ineffective and can be positively harmful to U.S. national interests.

It is interesting to note that advocates of these diametrically opposed positions, as well as those who advocate policies that fall somewhere between these alternatives, often make their case based on what is best in terms of U.S. national security. One side argues that promoting democracy throughout the world will make the United States more secure. The other side argues that these efforts may in fact make the United States less secure because they will waste resources and because of the anti-American backlash they could produce. Furthermore, critics suggest that too strong a focus on democracy promotion as a foreign policy goal will prevent American policymakers from pursuing key national security interests through cooperation with authoritarian regimes.

Though it takes some effort to discern common ground, it is possible to argue it exists around the notion that a world that included more stable, liberal democratic countries would be a desirable one. Even thinkers from the realist tradition of international relations, who argue that types of government and societal factors are not as

significant as international imperatives in guiding foreign policy behavior, would not necessarily argue that the spread of democracy is harmful. Even here, though, much rests on the terms "stable" and "liberal" as qualifiers for the form of democracy being discussed. While a mature democracy may indeed be less inclined to war—at least with fellow democracies—violence all too often accompanies the process of political transition as legitimacy is contested and political competition is not moderated by a stable rule of law. The existence of a stable rule of law is also an important part of what it means for a state to be liberal, along with limited government, checks and balances among governmental institutions, competitive elections, and the protection of individual rights.

A second place to look for some common ground is suggested—somewhat surprisingly—by John Mearsheimer, a realist and professor of political science at the University of Chicago. In *The Tragedy of Great Power Politics*, he acknowledges that while survival is the number one goal of great powers, states do pursue nonsecurity goals as well. Many realists would classify democracy promotion as such a nonsecurity goal. On such goals, Mearsheimer writes, "states can pursue them as long as the requisite behavior does not conflict with balance-of-power logic, which is often the case. Indeed, the pursuit of these non-security goals sometimes complements the hunt for relative power" (Mearsheimer, 2001). In other words, some realists would concede that democracy promotion is an acceptable activity as long as it does not harm the underlying relative power of the country promoting democracy. At best, such efforts might enhance the state's prestige or at least be a power-neutral activity. Though most realists would question the utility of expending resources on a goal that does nothing to enhance the country's relative power, this thin slice of turf appears to be one where supporters and critics of democracy promotion can find common ground.

Additional Resources

Farber, Henry, and Joanne Gowa. "Polities and Peace." *International Security* 20, no. 2 (1995): 123–146.

Kant, Immanuel. "Perpetual Peace: A Philosophical Sketch." In *Toward Perpetual Peace and Other Writings on Politics, Peace, and History*. Ed. Pauline Kleingold. New Haven, CT: Yale University Press, 2006.

Considered a philosophical foundation of the liberal tradition of contemporary international relations theory, Kant argues that countries with a certain form of political structure—what he labels "republican" states—are more likely to coexist peacefully with each other than other forms of government.

Mansfield, Edward, and Jack Snyder. "Democratization and War." *Foreign Affairs* 74, no. 3 (1995): 79–97.

Mearsheimer, John. *The Tragedy of Great Power Politics*. New York: Norton, 2001.

In this book, Professor John Mearsheimer of the University of Chicago lays out his argument that the actions of great powers in international affairs are—and should be—dominated by a balance-of-power logic as states pursue the only security goal that really matters: survival.

Odom, William, and Robert Dujarric. *America's Inadvertent Empire*. New Haven, CT: Yale University Press, 2004.

Przeworski, Adam, Michal Alvarez, Jose Cheibub, and Fernando Limongi. *Democracy and Development: Political Institutions and Well-Being in the World, 1950–1990*. Cambridge: Cambridge University Press, 2000.

This analyzes the conditions under which democracies emerge, survive, and revert back to authoritarianism. Using 40 years of statistical data, the authors carefully establish the link between a country's level of economic development and the chances of successful democratization.

Rachman, Gideon. "Democracy: The Case for Opportunistic Idealism." *The Washington Quarterly* 32, no. 1 (2009): 119–127.

Windsor, Jennifer. "Advancing the Freedom Agenda: Time of a Recalibration?" *The Washington Quarterly* 29, no. 3 (2006): 21–34.

Internet References . . .

President George W. Bush's Second Inaugural Address

This speech, commonly known as the "freedom speech," articulates a clear justification for making the spread of freedom and democracy in the world a core U.S. foreign policy goal. It was delivered against the backdrop of the ongoing wars in Iraq and Afghanistan. In these wars, the promotion of democracy in the Middle East became a central justification for U.S. involvement.

www.nytimes.com/2005/01/20/politics/20BUSH-TEXT.html?_r=0

"Do We Really Know How to Promote Democracy?" Address to the Foreign Policy Association, May 24, 2005

This speech by scholar Francis Fukuyama, available online, offers a balanced analysis of the many challenges associated with democracy promotion, as well as a critique of the use of military means to spread democracy abroad. Fukuyama also discusses the internal conditions that make democratization efforts more likely to succeed.

www.fpa.org/usr_doc/Francis_Fukuyama.pdf

Democratic Realism: An American Foreign Policy for a Unipolar World

In this piece Charles Krauthammer, a leading figure in the neoconservative movement, lays out the argument for the assertive versions of democracy promotion known as "democratic realism" and "democratic globalism." His argument, originally delivered as lecture to the American Enterprise Institute, prompted a strong response by Francis Fukuyama in the summer 2004 issue of *The National Interest*, followed by an equally robust rebuttal by Krauthammer in the fall 2004 issue of the same journal.

www.aei.org/book/foreign-and-defense-policy/democratic-realism/

The Fourteen Points

Woodrow Wilson's address to U.S. Congress, January 8, 1918, "The Fourteen Points."

avalon.law.yale.edu/20th_century/wilson14.asp

Selected, Edited, and with Issue Framing Material by:
Suzanne Nielsen, *U.S. Military Academy*
and
Scott Handler, *U.S. Military Academy*

ISSUE

Is a Multilateral Approach to International Affairs in the Best Interest of the United States?

YES: Barack Obama, from "Remarks by the President of the United States to the United Nations General Assembly, September 23, 2009," *The White House* (September 24, 2009)

NO: Robert J. Lieber, from "America in Decline? It's a Matter of Choices, Not Fate," *World Affairs Journal* (September/October 2012)

Learning Outcomes

After reading this issue, you should be able to:

- Understand the global position of the United States at the end of the Cold War.
- Discuss how the global position of the United States has changed in the first decade of the twenty-first century.
- Appreciate the sources of constraints on America's ability to exercise power in the world.
- Explain why some argue that the United States can best further its national interests by exercising power in a multilateral manner and why others are convinced that a unilateral approach is better. Which of these two perspectives is most convincing and why?

ISSUE SUMMARY

YES: Barack Obama, the president of the United States, argues for a "new era of engagement based on mutual interest and mutual respect." In asserting that "no nation can or should try to dominate another nation," he seeks to distance his foreign policy from the previous administration's perceived unilateralism.

NO: Robert Lieber, a professor of government and international affairs at Georgetown University, argues that President Obama's "extended hand" to American adversaries has met the harsh realities of international politics. Lieber argues that America remains an indispensable power and guarantor against aggression in the world, and external factors will not change this. American decline, if it were to happen, would only occur from America's own making.

Soon after the fall of the Berlin Wall in November 1989, commentators began to discuss America's "unipolar moment," which was one reflection of a dramatic change that was then underway in the structure of the international system (Krauthammer, 1990). During the more than 40 years of Cold War confrontation between the United States and the Soviet Union that followed World War II, analysts and policymakers became accustomed to thinking of the world as bipolar. It was dominated by two great powers—or poles—that dwarfed all others in material capabilities and influence to such a degree that the term "superpower" came into existence to describe these two states. When the Soviet Union ceased to exist in December 1991, the United States stood by itself as the world's lone remaining superpower. Scholars and other members of the foreign policy community who had spent careers thinking about the dynamics of a bipolar world had a fundamentally new situation to ponder. What would be the dynamics of this new unipolar world—a situation that was arguably unique in modern history?

Security studies scholars came to widely differing conclusions as they examined this question. Some predicted that a unipolar world would be unstable for several reasons. First, any situation of unipolarity was likely to be transitory because differing rates of economic growth would lead other states to catch up over time. Second, and even more importantly, because the unipolar state was not disciplined by the need to carefully manage the balance of power, it would behave in a capricious fashion that would actually hasten its own decline (Waltz, 1997). It would dissipate its own power in unwise ventures and provoke coalitions of other states to form against it. Other scholars were more optimistic, believing that a dominant United States would be able to take actions that would foster international stability and peace (Wohlforth, 1999).

These differing interpretations of the characteristics of a unipolar world have different policy implications. Implicit in propositions about relative decline are usually arguments for restraint in American foreign policy. One approach to restraint, which involves a greater embrace of unilateralism, is to advocate that the United States engage in costly foreign policy ventures only when its vital national interests are at stake. Other states, and other regions around the world, bear primary responsibility for their own security and should also pay the costs. An alternative approach is to embrace multilateralism even more fully. Advocates of this approach often point to the wisdom of U.S. policymakers in the immediate post–World War II era who played a vital role in founding the United Nations and a system of institutions to foster economic openness, trade, and development worldwide. In addition to fostering a peaceful, stable, and open international system, these institutions could help to spread the associated costs. Today, these institutions could play a similarly important role in the management of a relative U.S. decline. If the United States continues to shape these international institutions through active involvement, the logic goes, it can continue to help to preserve an international order that is conducive to U.S. interests and values at a manageable cost (Ikenberry, 1998).

Concerns that the United States might provoke other states to form coalitions against it are also subject to competing policy prescriptions which can also be characterized as relatively unilateral or more multilateral in character. Similar to the above, one unilateral approach would entail a greater withdrawal from international affairs. As an example, while a lesser military presence in Eastern Europe might be a source of concern to U.S. allies, it might also be less likely to provoke Russia to balance against the United States. An alternative approach is again to embrace multilateralism even more fully. Multilateral arrangements are the result of consensus-building and tend to provide greater legitimacy to international action. As a result, this argument suggests, U.S. activities abroad that are taken within a multilateral framework are less likely to provoke balancing behavior.

In the early 1990s, an embrace of multilateralism seemed to dominate U.S. policymaking circles as the end of the Cold War ushered in optimism about the possibilities for state cooperation on questions of international peace and security. Some believed that the United Nations and its Security Council, for example, would no longer be blocked from taking action by an inevitable veto by one of the two superpowers who were usually on the opposite sides of important questions. This was reflected in the national security policies adopted in the administrations of President George H.W. Bush and President Bill Clinton. While both administrations conducted U.S. military operations abroad, for example, these military interventions came only after the United States had obtained some form of international endorsement and participation.

Even as multilateral approaches seemed most common in the current practice of U.S. foreign policy, a competing school of thought was gaining an important following in some foreign policy circles in the United States. This perspective, known as neoconservativism, starts from the assumption that the United States is an exceptional country—in terms of both its material capabilities and its values—and that this exceptionalism gives the United States a unique role in international affairs. The United States has an obligation to put its power at the service of its values, and to exercise this power abroad in accordance with its own judgment. While multilateralism is not necessarily a bad approach in all circumstances, the United States should not let itself be constrained by its requirements; international institutions, particularly those such as the United Nation in which states guilty of massive human rights violations sometimes gain positions of responsibility, are particularly suspect. Adherents of this school of thought advocate a less restrained application of American military and economic power in order to take advantage of the "unipolar moment" (Cheney, 1993).

When the United States was attacked by Al Qaeda on September 11, 2001, the unilateral exercise of American power envisioned by neoconservatives seemed subject to few constraints. The administration of President George W. Bush, which included several influential neoconservatives, recognized the value of alliances and institutions when they supported American interests, but stressed America's preparedness to "go it alone" if necessary. In many ways, the U.S. invasion of Iraq in 2003 was a case study in unilateralism, seeming to represent an almost direct rejection of the multilateralism that had characterized the U.S. military interventions of the preceding decade. In the run up to the war, the United States chose to disregard the views of France and Germany, traditional U.S. allies, who opposed an invasion. The breach was relatively open, as the French voiced their opposition at the United Nations Security Council (de Villepin, 2003). Instead, the United States embarked on the war in Iraq with small contributions from most members of an ad hoc "coalition of the willing," ultimately forging efforts to earn the support of many of America's traditional allies and to gain consensus in the United Nations.

Looking forward, it is not entirely clear whether U.S. foreign policy will be characterized more by unilateralism or by multilateralism in the coming decades. Some analysts have argued that the balance began to shift back to the latter even in the second term of President George W. Bush (Layne, 2006). His successor, President Barack Obama, has emphasized that multilateral approaches to important foreign policy challenges will best serve U.S. interests and values (Obama, 2009). However, even the multilateralism of the Obama administration has seen numerous exceptions. The most famous example of this is probably the raid that resulted in the death of Al Qaeda leader Osama bin Laden in May 2011. Even though this raid was executed on Pakistani soil, the United States took action without informing the government of Pakistan in advance. As a whole, the continuing efforts against Al Qaeda in the Obama administration represent a weave of multilateral and unilateral efforts.

Throughout the history of American foreign policy, thinkers and policymakers of various ideological stripes have advanced arguments for and against unilateralism and multilateralism. This debate is likely to continue, since both approaches have advantages and disadvantages. Unilateral actions may be undertaken more quickly and with greater flexibility. However, they generally have less international legitimacy and do not foster the sharing of costs. Multilateral approaches, on the other hand, may take longer to initiate and coordination and consensus requirements are likely to reduce agility. However, they carry greater legitimacy and facilitate burden sharing.

Taking a stand on this question, during his first speech before the United Nations General Assembly in September 2009, President Obama answers YES to the question of whether a multilateral approach to foreign policy is in the best interest of the United States. Attempting to signal a change from what many saw as the unilateralism of the prior administration, he lays out a vision of a more multilateral U.S. foreign policy. He also speaks of a cooperative bargain in which all nations share both rights and responsibilities as part of the international community.

Robert Lieber's NO article directly argues that the president's foreign policy based on the multilateral vision he outlined in 2009 has met the harsh realities of the international system. The United States cannot lead from behind or naively try to underemphasize the distinction between allies and adversaries in order to ensure international stability. The United States is an indispensable state that can help prevent aggression better than any international institution or alliance. No other nation or alliance will cause America's decline, rather the only likely way for decline to occur would be of America's own making and choice.

YES    **Barack Obama**

Remarks by the President of the United States to the United Nations General Assembly, September 23, 2009

. . . I took office at a time when many around the world had come to view America with skepticism and distrust. Part of this was due to misperceptions and misinformation about my country. Part of this was due to opposition to specific policies, and a belief that on certain critical issues, America has acted unilaterally, without regard for the interests of others. And this has fed an almost reflexive anti-Americanism, which too often has served as an excuse for collective inaction.

Now, like all of you, my responsibility is to act in the interest of my nation and my people, and I will never apologize for defending those interests. But it is my deeply held belief that in the year 2009—more than at any point in human history—the interests of nations and peoples are shared. The religious convictions that we hold in our hearts can forge new bonds among people, or they can tear us apart. The technology we harness can light the path to peace, or forever darken it. The energy we use can sustain our planet, or destroy it. What happens to the hope of a single child—anywhere—can enrich our world, or impoverish it.

In this hall, we come from many places, but we share a common future. No longer do we have the luxury of indulging our differences to the exclusion of the work that we must do together. I have carried this message from London to Ankara; from Port of Spain to Moscow; from Accra to Cairo; and it is what I will speak about today— because the time has come for the world to move in a new direction. We must embrace a new era of engagement based on mutual interest and mutual respect, and our work must begin now.

We know the future will be forged by deeds and not simply words. Speeches alone will not solve our problems— it will take persistent action. For those who question the character and cause of my nation, I ask you to look at the concrete actions we have taken in just nine months.

On my first day in office, I prohibited—without exception or equivocation—the use of torture by the United States of America. . . . I ordered the prison at Guantanamo Bay closed, and we are doing the hard work of forging a framework to combat extremism within the rule of law. Every nation must know: America will live its values, and we will lead by example.

We have set a clear and focused goal: to work with all members of this body to disrupt, dismantle, and defeat al Qaeda and its extremist allies—a network that has killed thousands of people of many faiths and nations, and that plotted to blow up this very building. In Afghanistan and Pakistan, we and many nations here are helping these governments develop the capacity to take the lead in this effort, while working to advance opportunity and security for their people.

In Iraq, we are responsibly ending a war. We have removed American combat brigades from Iraqi cities, and set a deadline of next August to remove all our combat brigades from Iraqi territory. And I have made clear that we will help Iraqis transition to full responsibility for their future, and keep our commitment to remove all American troops by the end of 2011.

I have outlined a comprehensive agenda to seek the goal of a world without nuclear weapons. In Moscow, the United States and Russia announced that we would pursue substantial reductions in our strategic warheads and launchers. At the Conference on Disarmament, we agreed on a work plan to negotiate an end to the production of fissile materials for nuclear weapons. And this week, my Secretary of State will become the first senior American representative to the annual Members Conference of the Comprehensive Test Ban Treaty.

Upon taking office, I appointed a Special Envoy for Middle East Peace, and America has worked steadily and aggressively to advance the cause of two states—Israel and Palestine—in which peace and security take root, and the rights of both Israelis and Palestinians are respected.

To confront climate change, we have invested $80 billion in clean energy. We have substantially increased our fuel-efficiency standards. We have provided new incentives for conservation, launched an energy partnership across the Americas, and moved from a bystander to a leader in international climate negotiations.

To overcome an economic crisis that touches every corner of the world, we worked with the G20 nations to forge a coordinated international response of over $2 trillion in stimulus to bring the global economy back from the brink. We mobilized resources that helped prevent the crisis from spreading further to developing countries. And we joined with others to launch a $20 billion

Obama, Barack. From *Remarks by the President to the United Nations General Assembly,* September 23, 2009.

global food security initiative that will lend a hand to those who need it most, and help them build their own capacity.

We've also re-engaged the United Nations. We have paid our bills. We have joined the Human Rights Council. . . . We have signed the Convention of the Rights of Persons with Disabilities. We have fully embraced the Millennium Development Goals. And we address our priorities here, in this institution—for instance, through the Security Council meeting that I will chair tomorrow on nuclear non-proliferation and disarmament, and through the issues that I will discuss today.

This is what we have already done. But this is just a beginning. Some of our actions have yielded progress. Some have laid the groundwork for progress in the future. But make no mistake: This cannot solely be America's endeavor. Those who used to chastise America for acting alone in the world cannot now stand by and wait for America to solve the world's problems alone. We have sought—in word and deed—a new era of engagement with the world. And now is the time for all of us to take our share of responsibility for a global response to global challenges.

Now, if we are honest with ourselves, we need to admit that we are not living up to that responsibility. Consider the course that we're on if we fail to confront the status quo: Extremists sowing terror in pockets of the world; protracted conflicts that grind on and on; genocide; mass atrocities; more nations with nuclear weapons; melting ice caps and ravaged populations; persistent poverty and pandemic disease. I say this not to sow fear, but to state a fact: The magnitude of our challenges has yet to be met by the measure of our actions.

This body was founded on the belief that the nations of the world could solve their problems together. Franklin Roosevelt, who died before he could see his vision for this institution become a reality, put it this way—and I quote: "The structure of world peace cannot be the work of one man, or one party, or one nation. . . . It cannot be a peace of large nations—or of small nations. It must be a peace which rests on the cooperative effort of the whole world."

The cooperative effort of the whole world. Those words ring even more true today, when it is not simply peace, but our very health and prosperity that we hold in common. Yet we also know that this body is made up of sovereign states. And sadly, but not surprisingly, this body has often become a forum for sowing discord instead of forging common ground; a venue for playing politics and exploiting grievances rather than solving problems. After all, it is easy to walk up to this podium and point figures—point fingers and stoke divisions. Nothing is easier than blaming others for our troubles, and absolving ourselves of responsibility for our choices and our actions. Anybody can do that. Responsibility and leadership in the 21st century demand more.

In an era when our destiny is shared, power is no longer a zero-sum game. No one nation can or should try to dominate another nation. No world order that elevates one nation or group of people over another will succeed. No balance of power among nations will hold. The traditional divisions between nations of the South and the North make no sense in an interconnected world; nor do alignments of nations rooted in the cleavages of a long-gone Cold War.

The time has come to realize that the old habits, the old arguments, are irrelevant to the challenges faced by our people. They lead nations to act in opposition to the very goals that they claim to pursue—and to vote, often in this body, against the interests of their own people. They build up walls between us and the future that our people seek, and the time has come for those walls to come down. Together, we must build new coalitions that bridge old divides—coalitions of different faiths and creeds; of north and south, east, west, black, white, and brown.

The choice is ours. We can be remembered as a generation that chose to drag the arguments of the 20th century into the 21st; that put off hard choices, refused to look ahead, failed to keep pace because we defined ourselves by what we were against instead of what we were for. Or we can be a generation that chooses to see the shoreline beyond the rough waters ahead; that comes together to serve the common interests of human beings, and finally gives meaning to the promise embedded in the name given to this institution: the United Nations.

That is the future America wants—a future of peace and prosperity that we can only reach if we recognize that all nations have rights, but all nations have responsibilities as well. That is the bargain that makes this work. That must be the guiding principle of international cooperation.

Today, let me put forward four pillars that I believe are fundamental to the future that we want for our children: non-proliferation and disarmament; the promotion of peace and security; the preservation of our planet; and a global economy that advances opportunity for all people.

First, we must stop the spread of nuclear weapons, and seek the goal of a world without them.

This institution was founded at the dawn of the atomic age, in part because man's capacity to kill had to be contained. For decades, we averted disaster, even under the shadow of a superpower stand-off. But today, the threat of proliferation is growing in scope and complexity. If we fail to act, we will invite nuclear arms races in every region, and the prospect of wars and acts of terror on a scale that we can hardly imagine.

A fragile consensus stands in the way of this frightening outcome, and that is the basic bargain that shapes the Nuclear Non-Proliferation Treaty. It says that all nations have the right to peaceful nuclear energy; that nations with nuclear weapons have a responsibility to move toward disarmament; and those without them have the responsibility to forsake them. The next 12 months could be pivotal in determining whether this compact will be strengthened or will slowly dissolve.

America intends to keep our end of the bargain. We will pursue a new agreement with Russia to substantially reduce our strategic warheads and launchers. We will move forward with ratification of the Test Ban Treaty, and work with others to bring the treaty into force so that nuclear testing is permanently prohibited. We will complete a Nuclear Posture Review that opens the door to deeper cuts and reduces the role of nuclear weapons. And we will call upon countries to begin negotiations in January on a treaty to end the production of fissile material for weapons.

I will also host a summit next April that reaffirms each nation's responsibility to secure nuclear material on its territory, and to help those who can't—because we must never allow a single nuclear device to fall into the hands of a violent extremist. And we will work to strengthen the institutions and initiatives that combat nuclear smuggling and theft.

All of this must support efforts to strengthen the NPT. Those nations that refuse to live up to their obligations must face consequences. Let me be clear, this is not about singling out individual nations—it is about standing up for the rights of all nations that do live up to their responsibilities. Because a world in which IAEA inspections are avoided and the United Nation's demands are ignored will leave all people less safe, and all nations less secure.

In their actions to date, the governments of North Korea and Iran threaten to take us down this dangerous slope. We respect their rights as members of the community of nations. I've said before and I will repeat, I am committed to diplomacy that opens a path to greater prosperity and more secure peace for both nations if they live up to their obligations.

But if the governments of Iran and North Korea choose to ignore international standards; if they put the pursuit of nuclear weapons ahead of regional stability and the security and opportunity of their own people; if they are oblivious to the dangers of escalating nuclear arms races in both East Asia and the Middle East—then they must be held accountable. The world must stand together to demonstrate that international law is not an empty promise, and that treaties will be enforced. We must insist that the future does not belong to fear.

That brings me to the second pillar for our future: the pursuit of peace.

The United Nations was born of the belief that the people of the world can live their lives, raise their families, and resolve their differences peacefully. And yet we know that in too many parts of the world, this ideal remains an abstraction—a distant dream. We can either accept that outcome as inevitable, and tolerate constant and crippling conflict, or we can recognize that the yearning for peace is universal, and reassert our resolve to end conflicts around the world.

That effort must begin with an unshakeable determination that the murder of innocent men, women and children will never be tolerated. On this, no one can be—there can be no dispute. The violent extremists who promote conflict by distorting faith have discredited and isolated themselves. They offer nothing but hatred and destruction. In confronting them, America will forge lasting partnerships to target terrorists, share intelligence, and coordinate law enforcement and protect our people. We will permit no safe haven for al Qaeda to launch attacks from Afghanistan or any other nation. We will stand by our friends on the front lines, as we and many nations will do in pledging support for the Pakistani people tomorrow. And we will pursue positive engagement that builds bridges among faiths, and new partnerships for opportunity.

Our efforts to promote peace, however, cannot be limited to defeating violent extremists. For the most powerful weapon in our arsenal is the hope of human beings—the belief that the future belongs to those who would build and not destroy; the confidence that conflicts can end and a new day can begin.

And that is why we will support—we will strengthen our support for effective peacekeeping, while energizing our efforts to prevent conflicts before they take hold. We will pursue a lasting peace in Sudan through support for the people of Darfur and the implementation of the Comprehensive Peace Agreement, so that we secure the peace that the Sudanese people deserve. . . . And in countries ravaged by violence—from Haiti to Congo to East Timor—we will work with the U.N. and other partners to support an enduring peace.

I will also continue to seek a just and lasting peace between Israel, Palestine, and the Arab world. . . . We will continue to work on that issue. Yesterday, I had a constructive meeting with Prime Minister Netanyahu and President Abbas. We have made some progress. Palestinians have strengthened their efforts on security. Israelis have facilitated greater freedom of movement for the Palestinians. As a result of these efforts on both sides, the economy in the West Bank has begun to grow. But more progress is needed. We continue to call on Palestinians to end incitement against Israel, and we continue to emphasize that America does not accept the legitimacy of continued Israeli settlements. . . .

The time has come—the time has come to re-launch negotiations without preconditions that address the permanent status issues: security for Israelis and Palestinians, borders, refugees, and Jerusalem. And the goal is clear: Two states living side by side in peace and security—a Jewish state of Israel, with true security for all Israelis; and a viable, independent Palestinian state with contiguous territory that ends the occupation that began in 1967, and realizes the potential of the Palestinian people. . . .

As we pursue this goal, we will also pursue peace between Israel and Lebanon, Israel and Syria, and a broader peace between Israel and its many neighbors. In pursuit of that goal, we will develop regional initiatives with multilateral participation, alongside bilateral negotiations.

Now, I am not naïve. I know this will be difficult. But all of us—not just the Israelis and the Palestinians, but all of us—must decide whether we are serious about peace, or whether we will only lend it lip service. To break the old patterns, to break the cycle of insecurity and despair, all of us must say publicly what we would acknowledge in private. The United States does Israel no favors when we fail to couple an unwavering commitment to its security with an insistence that Israel respect the legitimate claims and rights of the Palestinians. . . . And—and nations within this body do the Palestinians no favors when they choose vitriolic attacks against Israel over constructive willingness to recognize Israel's legitimacy and its right to exist in peace and security. . . .

We must remember that the greatest price of this conflict is not paid by us. It's not paid by politicians. It's paid by the Israeli girl in Sderot who closes her eyes in fear that a rocket will take her life in the middle of the night. It's paid for by the Palestinian boy in Gaza who has no clean water and no country to call his own. These are all God's children. And after all the politics and all the posturing, this is about the right of every human being to live with dignity and security. That is a lesson embedded in the three great faiths that call one small slice of Earth the Holy Land. And that is why, even though there will be setbacks and false starts and tough days, I will not waver in my pursuit of peace. . . .

Third, we must recognize that in the 21st century, there will be no peace unless we take responsibility for the preservation of our planet. And I thank the Secretary General for hosting the subject of climate change yesterday.

The danger posed by climate change cannot be denied. Our responsibility to meet it must not be deferred. If we continue down our current course, every member of this Assembly will see irreversible changes within their borders. Our efforts to end conflicts will be eclipsed by wars over refugees and resources. Development will be devastated by drought and famine. Land that human beings have lived on for millennia will disappear. Future generations will look back and wonder why we refused to act; why we failed to pass on—why we failed to pass on an environment that was worthy of our inheritance.

And that is why the days when America dragged its feet on this issue are over. We will move forward with investments to transform our energy economy, while providing incentives to make clean energy the profitable kind of energy. We will press ahead with deep cuts in emissions to reach the goals that we set for 2020, and eventually 2050. We will continue to promote renewable energy and efficiency, and share new technologies with countries around the world. And we will seize every opportunity for progress to address this threat in a cooperative effort with the entire world.

And those wealthy nations that did so much damage to the environment in the 20th century must accept our obligation to lead. But responsibility does not end there. While we must acknowledge the need for differentiated responses, any effort to curb carbon emissions must include the fast-growing carbon emitters who can do more to reduce their air pollution without inhibiting growth. And any effort that fails to help the poorest nations both

adapt to the problems that climate change have already wrought and help them travel a path of clean development simply will not work.

It's hard to change something as fundamental as how we use energy. I know that. It's even harder to do so in the midst of a global recession. Certainly, it will be tempting to sit back and wait for others to move first. But we cannot make this journey unless we all move forward together. As we head into Copenhagen, let us resolve to focus on what each of us can do for the sake of our common future.

And this leads me to the final pillar that must fortify our future: a global economy that advances opportunity for all people.

The world is still recovering from the worst economic crisis since the Great Depression. In America, we see the engine of growth beginning to churn, and yet many still struggle to find a job or pay their bills. Across the globe, we find promising signs, but little certainty about what lies ahead. And far too many people in far too many places live through the daily crises that challenge our humanity—the despair of an empty stomach; the thirst brought on by dwindling water supplies; the injustice of a child dying from a treatable disease; or a mother losing her life as she gives birth.

In Pittsburgh, we will work with the world's largest economies to chart a course for growth that is balanced and sustained. That means vigilance to ensure that we do not let up until our people are back to work. That means taking steps to rekindle demand so that global recovery can be sustained. And that means setting new rules of the road and strengthening regulation for all financial centers, so that we put an end to the greed and the excess and the abuse that led us into this disaster, and prevent a crisis like this from ever happening again.

At a time of such interdependence, we have a moral and pragmatic interest, however, in broader questions of development—the questions of development that existed even before this crisis happened. And so America will continue our historic effort to help people feed themselves. We have set aside $63 billion to carry forward the fight against HIV/AIDS, to end deaths from tuberculosis and malaria, to eradicate polio, and to strengthen public health systems. We are joining with other countries to contribute H1N1 vaccines to the World Health Organization. We will integrate more economies into a system of global trade. We will support the Millennium Development Goals, and approach next year's summit with a global plan to make them a reality. And we will set our sights on the eradication of extreme poverty in our time.

Now is the time for all of us to do our part. Growth will not be sustained or shared unless all nations embrace their responsibilities. And that means that wealthy nations must open their markets to more goods and extend a hand to those with less, while reforming international institutions to give more nations a greater voice. And developing nations must root out the corruption that is an obstacle to progress—for opportunity cannot thrive where individuals are oppressed and business have to pay bribes. That is why we support honest police and independent judges; civil society and a vibrant private sector. Our goal is simple: a global economy in which growth is sustained, and opportunity is available to all.

Now, the changes that I've spoken about today will not be easy to make. And they will not be realized simply by leaders like us coming together in forums like this, as useful as that may be. For as in any assembly of members, real change can only come through the people we represent. That is why we must do the hard work to lay the groundwork for progress in our own capitals. That's where we will build the consensus to end conflicts and to harness technology for peaceful purposes, to change the way we use energy, and to promote growth that can be sustained and shared.

I believe that the people of the world want this future for their children. And that is why we must champion those principles which ensure that governments reflect the will of the people. These principles cannot be afterthoughts—democracy and human rights are essential to achieving each of the goals that I've discussed today, because governments of the people and by the people are more likely to act in the broader interests of their own people, rather than narrow interests of those in power.

The test of our leadership will not be the degree to which we feed the fears and old hatreds of our people. True leadership will not be measured by the ability to muzzle dissent, or to intimidate and harass political opponents at home. The people of the world want change. They will not long tolerate those who are on the wrong side of history.

This Assembly's Charter commits each of us—and I quote—"to reaffirm faith in fundamental human rights, in the dignity and worth of the human person, in the equal rights of men and women." Among those rights is the freedom to speak your mind and worship as you please; the promise of equality of the races, and the opportunity for women and girls to pursue their own potential; the ability of citizens to have a say in how you are governed, and to have confidence in the administration of justice. For just as no nation should be forced to accept the tyranny of another nation, no individual should be forced to accept the tyranny of their own people. . . .

As an African American, I will never forget that I would not be here today without the steady pursuit of a more perfect union in my country. And that guides my belief that no matter how dark the day may seem, transformative change can be forged by those who choose to side with justice. And I pledge that America will always stand with those who stand up for their dignity and their rights—for the student who seeks to learn; the voter who demands to be heard; the innocent who longs to be free; the oppressed who yearns to be equal.

Democracy cannot be imposed on any nation from the outside. Each society must search for its own path, and no path is perfect. Each country will pursue a path rooted in the culture of its people and in its past traditions. And I admit that America has too often been selective in its promotion of democracy. But that does not weaken our commitment; it only reinforces it. There are basic principles that are universal; there are certain truths which are self-evident—and the United States of America will never waver in our efforts to stand up for the right of people everywhere to determine their own destiny. . . .

Sixty-five years ago, a weary Franklin Roosevelt spoke to the American people in his fourth and final inaugural address. After years of war, he sought to sum up the lessons that could be drawn from the terrible suffering, the enormous sacrifice that had taken place. "We have learned," he said, "to be citizens of the world, members of the human community."

The United Nations was built by men and women like Roosevelt from every corner of the world—from Africa and Asia, from Europe to the Americas. These architects of international cooperation had an idealism that was anything but naïve—it was rooted in the hard-earned lessons of war; rooted in the wisdom that nations could advance their interests by acting together instead of splitting apart.

Now it falls to us—for this institution will be what we make of it. The United Nations does extraordinary good around the world—feeding the hungry, caring for the sick, mending places that have been broken. But it also struggles to enforce its will, and to live up to the ideals of its founding.

I believe that those imperfections are not a reason to walk away from this institution—they are a calling to redouble our efforts. The United Nations can either be a place where we bicker about outdated grievances, or forge common ground; a place where we focus on what drives us apart, or what brings us together; a place where we indulge tyranny, or a source of moral authority. In short, the United Nations can be an institution that is disconnected from what matters in the lives of our citizens, or it can be an indispensable factor in advancing the interests of the people we serve.

We have reached a pivotal moment. The United States stands ready to begin a new chapter of international cooperation—one that recognizes the rights and responsibilities of all nations. And so, with confidence in our cause, and with a commitment to our values, we call on all nations to join us in building the future that our people so richly deserve. . . .

President **BARACK OBAMA** is the 44th president of the United States.

Robert J. Lieber    **NO**

America in Decline? It's a Matter of Choices, Not Fate

The notion of American decline, although now pervasive, is not entirely new. Current concerns need to be seen against a history of pessimistic assessments, as for example during the Great Depression, the post–Vietnam War era, and again in the late 1980s when fears of Japanese primacy and the rise of the European Union as a world power were widely held. Once again the United States needs to overcome serious problems, but much of the thinking and writing about the American future reflects a stubborn undervaluation of the country's resilience, fundamental strengths, and ability to overcome adversity.

Ironically, while much of the current focus has been on the impact of financial and economic crises, a lagging recovery, serious problems of debt and deficit, and competition with a dynamic and rising China, the United States actually continues to possess far greater material strengths than commonly assumed. In any case, decline is not destined by some ineluctable cycle of history. Instead, America's future is a matter of will and willpower, in the sense of crucial choices to be made about policy and strategy. Willpower in particular involves leadership and well-informed decision-making. If the right choices are made in the years ahead, the robustness of American society coupled with its unique capacities for adaptation and adjustment should once again prove decisive.

Despite a lagging recovery from the worst financial and real estate crises in eighty years, the United States still accounts for some twenty-one percent of world GDP (based on market exchange rates, the IMF's preferred indicator for international comparisons). The rate is only modestly lower than its twenty-six percent of 1980 and, as of 2012, is twice the size of China's.

These figures not only reflect limited erosion in the relative standing of the United States compared to that of other countries, but also attest to America's status as the world's largest economy by a substantial margin. Moreover, America's GDP per capita is more than eight times greater than China's. In addition, the United States has the deepest capital markets, benefits from the dollar's role as the world's predominant reserve currency, and, despite a large trade deficit, is the world's third largest exporter of goods and services, as well as the largest importer.

Additional factors underpin the American advantage, including enormous natural resources and a vast land area far less densely populated than the territory of its major competitors. It is the third largest producer of oil after Saudi Arabia and Russia, and thanks to dramatic advances in technology it is experiencing a renaissance in the production of shale gas and tight oil. In addition, it is one of the world's leading agricultural producers. It enjoys a higher fertility rate among women than any other major country except India, it remains by far the most popular destination for immigrants, and it continues to benefit from a growing population and work force.

While other countries seek to develop their own high-tech sectors, Silicon Valley remains unique—a world center for flourishing clusters of technological innovation and development. In addition, the United States remains well positioned to advance in cutting-edge areas of technology, including medicine, biotechnology, gene therapy, nanotechnology, and clean energy.

Nonmaterial factors are also central to America's strength. The society's resilience and adaptability are unusual for a large country, as are its economic competitiveness and entrepreneurship. The United States, thanks to its unmatched research universities, enrolls a higher proportion of the world's international students than any other country, with some two-thirds of graduate students who study abroad doing so in the United States.

Democracy, the rule of law, liberty, and popular sovereignty constitute fundamental strengths. There is no doubt that the democratic process is often messy and raucous, but it makes the political system responsive to a huge and heterogeneous public. It is well to keep in mind that America's main peer competitor, China, lacks these vital features. There, the gap between rulers and the ruled could become increasingly untenable for a wealthier, more educated population with access to information and social media and increasingly aware of its own lack of political and civil liberties, not to mention the absence of accountability on the part of those who control political power. Indeed, China may be experiencing as many as one hundred and eighty thousand political, civil, or labor disturbances per year, and without major changes, which the current leadership is unlikely to countenance, social unrest will only continue to grow . . .

Lieber, Robert J. From *World Affairs*, September/October 2012. Copyright © 2012 by © 2010 World Affairs Institute and American Peace Society. This essay is adapted from: *Power and Willpower in the American Future: Why the United States Is Not Destined to Decline* by Robert J. Lieber (Cambridge University Press, 2012). Reprinted by permission of World Affairs Institute. www.WorldAffairsJournal.org

Almost every deliberation about foreign policy sooner or later gives rise to calls for the US to renew or enhance its reliance on international institutions and multilateralism as the preferred means for addressing problems and threats. However, while the world may now be more multipolar, it is arguably less multilateral. The number and relevance of actors and chessboards on which world politics, economics, and conflict play out has increased, but there is little sign that the world is becoming better able to manage or mitigate these disputes. This deficit is evident in the shortcomings of international and regional institutions and sometimes reckless behavior of rising powers. Nonetheless, some liberal internationalist thinkers remain insistent that the US must trade its own unilateral power for the empowerment of new forms of collaboration and global governance.

Yet evidence for the viability of these emerging forms of cooperation is not easy to discern. The BRICS (Brazil, Russia, India, China, South Africa) and others mostly have been conspicuous in their reluctance to cooperate. This has been apparent not only in Libya, despite UN authorization of all "necessary action" to protect civilians, but in other realms as well. These include human rights, humanitarian intervention, ethnic cleansing, the environment, enforcement of nuclear nonproliferation agreements, the rule of law, free trade regimes, and even in China's deliberate undervaluation of the yuan in direct contravention of IMF and WTO rules to which Beijing is supposedly bound.

Given these international realities, America's strengths constitute a crucial element of stability. Despite a degree of erosion in its relative power compared to a generation ago, the United States remains the world's principal provider of collective goods. Other nations are no more able to take on this role than are the international organizations with their frequently inadequate and often lamentable performance in responding to common problems.

The evolution of the Obama administration's foreign policy provides some evidence of these realities. Barack Obama came to office in January 2009 committed to offering America's adversaries an "extended hand." The idea seemed to be that if only the new president could assure adversaries and allies that he—and thus America—meant well, threats or problems could be mitigated or overcome altogether.

In practice, however, emphasis on interdependence, good intentions, and the belief that "the interests of nations and peoples are shared" did not go very far with Vladimir Putin, Mahmoud Ahmadinejad, Bashar al-Assad, or Hugo Chávez. In a quest to bridge differences, the Obama administration at times underemphasized the distinction between adversaries and allies. For example, Obama's June 2009 Cairo speech suggested that the thorny problems of the Middle East had their origin in the West and downplayed local responsibility for social and economic stagnation, authoritarianism, corruption, and repression. By the end of the following year, the shortcomings of this view would become obvious with the eruption of the Arab Spring.

International institutions, alliances, and balances of power have important uses, but none are by themselves a sufficient substitute for America's unique role. The consequence of a major retrenchment or outright disengagement by the United States would be a serious weakening in the current world order, which liberal internationalists seek to expand, as well as greater threats to our own national security that realist advocates of withdrawal from international responsibility claim to prioritize. Ironically, the centrality of the US role may be better appreciated abroad than here at home. In the same Gallup survey that found the United States by far the most popular destination for would-be foreign migrants, respondents in more than one hundred countries expressed much higher approval of US leadership than for six other major powers, including, in order, Germany, France, Japan, the UK, China, and Russia.

The American role remains—in the oft-used word—indispensable. With its hard-power resources, it is the ultimate guarantor against aggressive and nihilistic movements and regimes. But no foreign policy can be sustained if it lacks sufficient backing. Preserving a solid domestic base of support remains the sine qua non for sustaining a leading world role. This includes the interplay of material and ideational elements. The material dimension requires a strong and dynamic economy at home, as well as the requisite technological and military strength. Essential foreign commitments need to be maintained while avoiding overextension. The ideational component entails leadership and the appreciation and expression of American interests, security, and national purpose. This requires not only the effective use of traditional diplomacy, but public diplomacy as well. Information-age ideas about the world as a global village (as in the Clinton era) or focus on social media (as during the Obama presidency) are all well and good, but they do not provide effective substitutes for focused and well-conceived programs to convey American values and purpose at home as well as abroad.

Absent some extraordinary "black swan" event, America's history and fundamental strengths are likely to be a more reliable guide to its future than the pessimistic assessments that currently dominate the national dialogue. This is not to disparage the thoughtful articulations of concern that have appeared during the past decade, but to note again that even some of the most astute observers have underestimated both the resilience and sense of purpose of the United States. Moreover, public and elite reactions to the September 11th attacks and, nearly a decade later, the expressions of national satisfaction in the killing of Osama bin Laden suggest the reservoirs of national solidarity that exist, whatever the dysfunctional elements of partisanship and animosity in national political life.

Crisis can be a stimulus to change as well as a warning sign of potential failure, and it is often the case that major problems are not grappled with effectively until they become acute. The debt, deficit, and entitlement issues that currently cloud the American future could well fit this pattern. These problems are by no means insurmountable, despite the formidable political obstacles standing in the way of their resolution. In foreign affairs, the dangers from nuclear proliferation and terrorism are serious, and the rise of regional powers makes it more difficult for the United States to gain agreement on approaches to common problems. Other than China, however, there is no real peer competitor on the horizon.

Our staying power is in our own hands. Whether we maintain it is not a matter of large historical forces beyond our control, but a question of choices, policies, and resolve.

ROBERT J. LIEBER is a professor of government and international affairs at Georgetown University. He has served as a foreign policy adviser to several presidential campaigns and a consultant to the State Department and for National Intelligence Estimates.

EXPLORING THE ISSUE

Is a Multilateral Approach to International Affairs in the Best Interest of the United States?

Critical Thinking and Reflection

1. Should the United States unilaterally assume the burdens of international peace and security or should it share those burdens multilaterally? Explain. What, if anything, can the United States do to prevent other states from free-riding on American efforts, whether unilateral or multilateral?
2. Will an effective multilateral foreign policy provide the United States with greater legitimacy as it pursues American interests around the globe? Explain your answer.
3. What external factors could lead to America's decline as a unipolar power in the international system? What domestic factors could lead to America's decline as a unipolar power in the international system? What interaction may occur between international and domestic factors that could lead to America's decline as a unipolar power?
4. What would a unilateral U.S. approach to prevent Iran from obtaining a nuclear weapon look like? What would a multilateral approach look like?

Is There Common Ground?

In the twenty-first century, the United States no longer faces threats solely from state actors but also must respond to a variety of transnational threats such as terrorism, infectious disease epidemics, global warming, food insecurity, organized crime, and the proliferation of weapons of mass destruction. The borderless nature of these challenges, as well as the fact that other states share them, leads to a natural focus on multilateralism. Collaborative approaches are necessary in order to develop foreign policy approaches appropriate to important aspects of the international environment of this century.

As briefly discussed in the introduction, after World War II the United States took the opportunity provided by its great relative power to help build an international order based on multilateral economic and security agreements. Immediately following the Cold War, the United States sought to strengthen and expand these institutions while building new ones. Some of the seemingly contradictory U.S. behavior over the past decade with respect to multilateralism may best be seen as efforts by the United States to maintain its power position in a new era, even as other countries such as China, Russia, India, and Brazil continue to grow. So, for example, the United States has championed the World Trade Organization while failing to join and sign the International Criminal Court and the United Nations Convention on the Law of the Sea. If in fact the two are in some tension, it may be worth considering whether it is more important over the long run for the United States to preserve its relative power or more important that it preserve the web of international institutions and the resulting rule-governed order it helped to create.

As President Barack Obama has noted, the United States boasts unique capabilities that will require it to, at times, take the lead on combined actions with other countries to address different global challenges. But these capabilities should not require the United States to assume sole responsibility for all international security problems. While the United States remains the world's leading power, it should carefully consider the costs of assuming an excessive portion of the global security burden.

Additional Resources

Brooks, Stephen and William Wohlforth. "American Primacy in Perspective." *Foreign Affairs* 81, no. 4 (2002): 20–33.

Although the United States is by far the most powerful state in the world, there are a number of problems that the United States cannot solve on its own. Stephen Brooks and William Wohlforth explore whether primacy necessarily implies unilateralism.

Cheney, Richard. *Defense Strategy for the 1990s: The Regional Defense Strategy.* Washington, DC: Department of Defense, 1993.

Chua, Amy. *Day of Empire: How Hyperpowers Rise to Global Dominance and Why They Fall.* New York: Doubleday, 2008.

This historical discussion of the rise and fall of "hyperpowers" suggests that American power may already be overextended. Amy Chua also discusses why it may be in America's interest to retreat from its go-it-alone approach and promote a new multilateralism in both domestic and foreign affairs.

Haass, Richard. "The Age of Nonpolarity." *Foreign Affairs* 87, no. 3 (2008): 44–56.

Richard Haass argues that the principal characteristic of twenty-first century international relations is turning out to be nonpolarity: a world dominated not by one or two or even several states but rather by dozens of actors possessing and exercising various kinds of power.

Ikenberry, G. John. "Institutions, Strategic Restraint, and the Persistence of American Postwar Order." *International Security* 23, no. 3 (1998): 43–78.

Ikenberry, G. John. *America Unrivaled*. Ithaca: Cornell University Press, 2002.

The author discusses American dominance of the global system at the dawn of the twenty-first century and its implications for political thought.

Ikenberry, G. John, Michael Mastanduno, and William Wohlforth, eds. *International Relations Theory and the Consequences of Unipolarity*. Cambridge: Cambridge University Press, 2011.

This collection of essays attempts to understand the implications of a unipolar system for traditional international relations theory.

Judt, Tony. *Postwar: A History of Europe since 1945*. London: Penguin, 2005.

This history of Europe provides background on the rise of the United States as a global power and the reaction of European states to that rise.

Keohane, Robert. *After Hegemony: Cooperation and Discord in the World Political Economy*. Princeton, NJ: Princeton University Press, 1984.

Krauthammer, Charles. "The Unipolar Moment." *Foreign Affairs* 70, no. 1 (1990/1991): 23–33.

Krauthammer, Charles. "The Unipolar Moment Revisited." *The National Interest*, Winter (2002/2003): 5–17.

Charles Krauthammer's original and updated discussions on unipolarity and how the United States should approach it.

Layne, Christopher. "The Unipolar Illusion Revisited." *International Security* 31, no. 2 (2006): 7–41.

In this critique of Charles Krauthammer's "The Unipolar Moment," Christopher Layne argues for a restrained approach to the use of American power.

Lipset, Seymour Martin. *American Exceptionalism: A Double-Edged Sword*. New York: W.W. Norton & Company, 1996.

Posen, Barry. "Command of the Commons: The Military Foundation of US Hegemony." *International Security* 28, no. 1 (2003): 5–46.

Barry Posen suggests that while American preeminence will last for some time, a strategy of selective engagement might be more appropriate than one that involves the pursuit of primacy.

Schweller, Randall. "The Problem of International Order Revisited: A Review Essay." *International Security* 26, no. 1 (2001): 161–186.

Randall Schweller supports G. John Ikenberry's arguments about the importance of restraint on the part of victorious powers after a way, but critiques Ikenberry's emphasis on the importance of institutions.

Waltz, Kenneth N. "Evaluating Theories." *American Political Science Review* 91, no. 4 (1997): 913–917.

Wohlforth, William. "The Stability of a Unipolar World." *International Security* 24, no. 1 (1999): 5–41.

William Wohlforth argues that a dominant unipole, like the United States at the end of the twentieth century, is likely to preserve stability rather than engender rivalry in the international system, because most potential rivals will see the costs of confrontation as outweighing the benefits of checking the power of the unipole.

Internet Reference . . .

France in the United Kingdom

This piece, "Speech to the United Nations Security Council" by Dominique de Villepin, is available at the below website.

www.ambafrance-uk.org/Speech-by-M-Dominique-de-Villepin,4917

Unit II

UNIT

National Security Issues

*M*any important foreign policy questions touch on issues of national security. Protecting national security entails not just the physical defense of a population and territory but also the preservation of a particular way of life. In the context of the United States, this includes protecting the vision set out in the Declaration of the Independence and safeguarding the system of governance laid out in the Constitution. While most Americans would agree on these fundamental goals, how they may be best served is a question that raises debates along a variety of dimensions—to include everything from whether a particular use of force is justified, to detailed budget questions about the relative value of particular investments.

Some fundamental questions associated with national security policy are touched on in the issues presented here. Given that the makers of national security policy will always have to allocate limited resources against potentially unlimited goals, will it better serve U.S. security interests to buy a strong military, to provide aid to foster economic development, to give aid to build foreign partnerships, or to reduce spending on all foreign and defense-related programs in order to balance the budget or make needed domestic investments? These questions are inextricably tied up with varying estimates about what types of policies will be effective. The trade-offs are not easy to calculate, and uncertainties about the cost, effectiveness, and relative value of different policies are likely to persist.

Selected, Edited, and with Issue Framing Material by:
Suzanne Nielsen, *U.S. Military Academy*
and
Scott Handler, *U.S. Military Academy*

ISSUE

Should U.S. Defense Spending Be Reduced Dramatically?

YES: Gordon Adams, from *Strategic and Fiscal Discipline: The Defense Budget and America's Fiscal Crisis* (July 2011)

NO: Robert M. Gates, from *Defense Spending* (May 2011)

Learning Outcomes

After reading this issue, you should be able to:

- Understand why defense spending cuts are controversial and politically charged.
- Describe how national strategy affects decisions about military spending.
- Evaluate various approaches to defense budget cuts.
- Explain potential consequences of declining resources in military spending categories.
- Assess arguments for and against significant cuts in defense spending.

ISSUE SUMMARY

YES: Gordon Adams, a professor of international relations at American University and a fellow at the Stimson Center, supports deep reductions in U.S. defense spending. Adams argues that the primary threat to American national security is an increasing federal deficit. The Department of Defense, which will remain generations ahead of international competitors despite declining resources, needs to be guided by strategic and fiscal disciplines that have been lacking in the past decade.

NO: Robert M. Gates, former U.S. Secretary of Defense, warns against deep defense budget cuts in weapons' modernization, citing a dangerously marginal increase in military capability over the last decade. Gates also explains that a smaller force will be less capable of addressing major global crises, which may negatively affect U.S. national security.

The United States faces growing federal deficits if additional revenue is not generated or government spending is not constrained. The national debt in 2012 was $15.7 trillion and increasing. Although most Americans and their elected representatives would likely agree that ballooning deficits are problematic and a potential economic crisis should be averted if possible, solutions are elusive. Budgeting is a highly political process in which conflicting interests are the norm.

Today, both mandatory and discretionary spending categories of the federal budget are subject to growing scrutiny. The term "mandatory spending" refers to expenditures that are dictated and disbursed by law and includes programs such as Medicare, Medicaid, and Social Security. Beneficiaries automatically receive payments if they meet statutory eligibility requirements. The term "discretionary spending" refers to the portion of the budget dedicated to the government's chosen priorities each year and negotiated by the President and Congress. The defense budget consumes the largest single share of discretionary federal spending, giving debates about its size added significance.

The United States budgeted $680 billion for defense in fiscal year 2010, comprising about 20 percent of the total federal budget. Looked at in another way, the defense budget equates to approximately $2,200 per person per year in the United States. It is nearly 15 times the 2010 budget for the Department of Education and more than twice the gross domestic product of Greece. The budget provides pay and medical care to about 1.5 million active duty personnel, maintains 11 aircraft carrier groups, funds research into hypersonic laser weapons, and constructs housing for military families. Given its enormous size, at stake in the defense budget are not just the national defense needs of the United States, but also significant trade-offs among possible government investments toward various social purposes and the politics of distribution.

The size of the defense budget is a source of constant discussion and disagreement among government decision makers. Most government officials, including many affiliated with the Department of Defense, would agree that some defense spending cuts are necessary to confront the larger problem of growing federal debt. But there is no consensus on how, when, or where these cuts should occur. Some policymakers favor a so-called "salami slice" approach, which would cut a relatively equal proportion of spending from all segments of the military budget. This strategy may create an impression of fairness across the entire military bureaucracy, but some critics argue that asking organizations to perform the same missions with fewer resources will reduce operational capacity and jeopardize military readiness. Another common strategy to reduce military budgets is to apply cuts to one or several particular spending categories, such as military pay, health care, or weapons' acquisition. There are also possible pitfalls with these approaches, however, which may not adequately balance current operational readiness and future needs. All cuts will involve some tradeoffs. Should the United States buy fewer tanks or airplanes? Should the nation maintain a larger navy and a smaller army? Should the country reduce spending on research and development, relying instead on current technology to defeat potential enemies? Should government-provided health care cover fewer medical procedures for military families? The answers to these questions are rarely clear or uncontested—particularly among elected leaders in the legislature who are ultimately responsible for allocating the nation's resources.

In addition to different judgments about the appropriate size and composition of the defense budget, even casual discussions of military spending are confounded by measurement difficulties. The amount of money the United States budgets for defense is more than any other nation in the world, but is currently only about 4.7 percent of the U.S. Gross Domestic Product. The Department of Defense plans its budget over 6 years (the only government agency to do so), so spending reductions in some areas may not be realized until several years later. Further, some reductions may translate to declining growth rather than net monetary spending decreases. The defense budget is highly intricate, and arguments both for and against spending cuts may use its inherent complexity to appear more convincing.

Each year, Congress reviews the president's budget request, including the amount estimated for defense. Implementing spending cuts is often a difficult and sensitive political process. Each defense program is manufactured in one or several congressional districts, meaning spending reductions generally result in fewer jobs and decreased revenue for local economies. Legislators usually oppose measures that close local production lines, even if the military favors the budget adjustment, as occurred most recently with Air Force C-130 aircraft and the army's high-mobility multipurpose wheeled vehicles. In both cases, lawmakers appropriated funding for additional equipment even though the services' proposed budgets called for decreased spending.

While local political interests may influence defense spending choices, there is also a case for caution about defense cuts based on the needs of the U.S. defense industrial base. Some advocates of stable or increased spending argue that it will only become more expensive to regenerate industrial production once skilled labor is let go and technical production facilities are shuttered. Defense manufacturers often take this position and provide information to members of Congress that may influence decision making as the president's budget request is reviewed.

Even before the budget is submitted to Congress, political considerations abound as military leaders translate the nation's strategic documents into finite resource allocations. The national security strategy, generally issued by presidents every 4 years, describes the most prominent threats to the United States and the method by which the United States will confront them. The Department of Defense receives the national security strategy and attempts to translate goals such as "promoting a just and sustainable international order" into a specific number of fighter jets, submarines, and missiles. This is an imprecise and subjective practice, subject to interpretation and disagreement by those who both support and oppose defense spending cuts.

The subjective nature of deciding exactly what is required to defeat the nation's threats is readily apparent in the YES and NO selections. Both authors agree that spending cuts are inevitable and necessary, but differ greatly in their approach to allocating defense resources. In Gordon Adams's testimony before the Committee on the Budget in the House of Representatives, defense spending cuts are described as a remedy to an even greater threat to national security: economic instability. He welcomes the opportunity to review current defense spending priorities and recommends that the United States divest itself from several expensive and unnecessary military skill sets, including nation building and counterinsurgency. Arguing that the United States currently possesses the technology to outpace its nearest competitors well into the future, Dr. Adams advocates reducing research and development spending and insists that the defense budget must sustain real cuts, not simply reduced growth over time. He makes the case that the United States has never enjoyed a more secure place in the international system and that the nearest peer competitor, China, has not provided sufficient evidence of a military buildup or threat that would justify current force levels.

In a speech to the American Enterprise Institute, former Secretary of Defense Robert Gates maintains that although the defense budget is not the cause of current U.S. fiscal challenges, increases in defense spending are not necessary or desirable. He disagrees, however, with Dr. Adams that deep spending cuts are an effective method for prioritizing defense programs, arguing instead that prioritization has already occurred inside the Pentagon. Secretary Gates opposes the salami-slice approach to budget reductions and supports targeted cuts, to include those that reduce administrative and logistical costs. He agrees with Adams that these particular areas should be scrutinized closely but expresses doubt that sufficient savings can be collected. In sharp contrast with Adams, Gates strongly advocates further investment in modernizing fighter jets, ships, and ballistic submarines, and highlights the importance of recapitalizing equipment worn out by over a decade of war in Iraq and Afghanistan. He argues that the United States has a special responsibility to help foster international peace and security, and that this is not a responsibility that the United States can afford to ignore.

YES

Gordon Adams

Strategic and Fiscal Discipline: The Defense Budget and America's Fiscal Crisis

Chairman Ryan, Ranking Member Van Hollen, and Members of the Committee, thank you for the invitation to appear today on the critical and timely subject of our national security budget.

As you search for avenues to deal with our continuing fiscal crisis, it is important to keep in mind that a solution can only be found if everything is on the table, including national security spending. The underlying theme of my testimony today is that our defense budget is not only part of our fiscal dilemma; it can and should be part of the solution as well. We are at a critical juncture in defense planning and budgeting at which international conditions make it possible and timely to rethink how we use our military as part of our toolkit for international engagement.

The Defense Department has not faced strategic or budgetary discipline for more than a decade. Our military budget has more than doubled in the past decade, consuming 55% of our entire discretionary costs. Last year it reaching a level in constant dollars unprecedented since the end of World War II. And the missions we have asked the military to perform have grown virtually without end.

Such discipline is now both possible and necessary. In the long term, strategy and resources—human and fiscal—have always been linked. As Bernard Brodie, one of America's great strategic thinkers, put it more than fifty years ago: "Strategy wears a dollar sign."[1]

A disciplined approach to both will produce budgetary savings and ensure that our military capabilities and global leadership remain powerful and well focused on core missions. This means making choices linked to a realistic assessment of risks, defining missions better connected to a more coherent strategy, and doing so within constrained resources.

My testimony draws on work we have done at the Stimson Center's project on budgeting for foreign affairs and defense, including consulting with the Bipartisan Policy Center's Rivlin-Domenici Debt Panel, as well as my more than thirty years experience in policy research and government service in the area of national security planning and budgeting.[2] It is based on several key principles:

- Our central national security crisis today is our looming federal debt and annual deficits. All ingredients of national spending and revenues must be on the table for our deficits to be brought under control and our debt to be stabilized. A budgetary solution is achievable only if it is balanced, with every element of federal spending and revenues playing a part.
- A defense "build down" is already under way. Defense budgets are primed to decline, as they generally do at the end of combat deployments and with changes in the international environment, and will do so gradually over the next decade. In my judgment, the starting point for budgetary discipline is the FY2011 appropriation for the base defense budget—$529 billion. The slope of this build down will be gradual, implemented over a number of years, and it should be linked to a coherent set of strategic, mission, and program choices.
- Much deeper reductions than those proposed by the administration are possible, likely, and can be executed with little or no risk to American national security if properly planned. The twelve-year, $400 billion reduction that President Obama announced in April is a very small step in that direction; it could be accomplished while continuing to provide growth with inflation to the defense budget. Deeper cuts are possible and likely. The Simpson-Bowles Fiscal Commission, the Bipartisan Policy Center's Rivlin-Domenici Panel, and the Sustainable Defense Task Force have all endorsed reductions between $500 billion and a trillion dollars over the next ten years. Even those can be accomplished successfully, representing something like 6–13% of the currently projected defense resources.
- The key to a successful build down will be linking strategic and mission discipline to this need for fiscal discipline. This means setting mission priorities for the military. In a *Foreign Affairs* article earlier this year, we recommended focusing on combating Al Qaeda's organization and cybersecurity as the most critical missions and divesting from counter-insurgency and nation-building.[3]
- The strategic, mission, and fiscal discipline I recommend creates little risk for our national security. Indeed, priority-setting might enhance both our security and our global leadership. Even with such reductions, the US military would continue to be decades ahead of any other military in capacity and technology, with the only capacity to fly, sail, and deploy ground force on a global basis and the only global capability for communications, logistics, transportation, and intelligence on the planet.

Understanding the Trend: Defense Budgets in Context

It is not my intent here to analyze the risks that unprecedented US debt and continuous high deficits pose for the US economy and our global role. But it is important to underline that our economic strength is as critical or more for our future security as the level of our defense spending. As Admiral Mike Mullen, Chairman of the Joint Chiefs of Staff, put it, "the single-biggest threat to our national security is our debt."[4]

Today's fiscal problems require perspective. Many attribute our crisis to continuing growth in particular parts of the federal budget, especially mandatory entitlements, and there is no doubt that entitlement spending has grown at a great pace, driven largely by health care costs (which have had their own impact on defense health care costs). Yet it is an overstatement to say that entitlements alone are responsible for our recent deficits. A recent analysis by the Center on Budget and Policy Priorities shows that the deficits of the past decade, as well as those forecast for the next ten years, are primarily the result of the 2001 tax cuts, rapid growth in defense spending, and declining revenues resulting from the economic recession.[5]

Assigning blame for our federal debt and deficit crisis is less important, though, than understanding that defense budget reductions will play a role in getting it under control. It will not be the first time defense savings have been found, or that they have played such a role. In fact, this build down follows three previous ones: the end of the Korean and Vietnam wars, and the Cold War. As OMB Associate Director for National Security and International Affairs from 1993–97, I had direct experience of the last such build down, and it is both instructive and reassuring. The pace was modest, the cuts were real, and the forces that remained were capable.

The chart above tracks this build down. The median annual reduction was 2.54%, real but gradual, the margin

by which this Congress reduced the FY2011 appropriation for the Department of Homeland Security (2%). Reductions at this pace should not lead to sharp changes in strategy. Near-term savings opportunities could include streamlining our "tooth-to-tail" ratio which, at eighty-four support and administrative troops for every sixteen combat personnel, is the highest among industrial powers.[6] Another option would be to consolidate headquarters infrastructure, especially combatant commands, which according to the Defense Business Board have now grown to ten organizations with 98,000 military and civilian staff and a total budget in FY2010 of $16.5 billion.[7] And, even more immediately, Congress could collect the $100 billion from Secretary Gates' recent efficiency scrub, all of which was left with the military services to re-spend.

Budget reductions paced gradually over several years would provide fiscal discipline and an important contribution to deficit reduction. Over time, such a build down would produce real change in the defense budget. The 2.5% annual reductions shrank the Pentagon's budget by 36% in FY1998 relative to FY1985, or $206 billion in constant dollar savings that year alone. Change at this pace allows time to rethink strategy and mission. Over the thirteen years in the last build down, the Pentagon reduced active-duty troops from 2.2 million to 1.47 million, defense civilian employment from 1.11 million to 747,000, and procurement spending by two-thirds. The force that emerged was able to help bring peace to the Balkans in the 1990s, topple the Taliban in 2001, and overrun the Iraqi military in 2003.

This build down was managed by Presidents Reagan, George H.W. Bush, and Clinton working in a bipartisan manner with seven Congresses. Much of it was accomplished under the leadership of Secretary of Defense Dick Cheney and Joint Chiefs Chairman Colin Powell. To some extent, this bipartisan process is again under way; the FY2011 base (i.e., non-war) Pentagon appropriations of

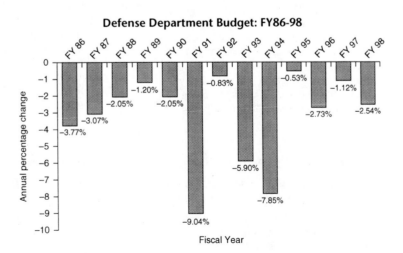

Defense Department Budget: FY86-98

Source: DOD FY12 Green Book: Table 6-8

$528.9 billion effectively froze the FY2010 amount, marking a shift away from endless growth and creating a starting point for a sustained process of budgetary discipline.

Targets for Budget Discipline and Steps along the Way

Congress needs to continue this process. Cuts mean a lower funding level than the previous year, not a slow-down in projected budget growth. A lower level of budget growth does not contribute to deficit reduction; it only slows the pace at which defense is deficit-funded. As long as defense budgets grow, the discipline the Pentagon needs is not being provided.

Secretary Robert Gates claimed that he had cut the defense budget but he only slowed its growth. Some of what he "cut" was overstated. Most prominently, he claimed that his FY2010 weapons system terminations cut $330 billion from future spending. Those savings were gross, however, not net. They included terminating the F-22 and the C-17, though neither was in DOD's long-term budget plans. And Gates routinely did not net out the investment in follow-on programs to replace the ones he terminated, including Army combat vehicles and Marine Corps amphibious landing vehicles. The Gates defense budgets continued to grow—2.9% in FY2010, despite the terminations—and were planned to push even higher over the FYDP.

Congress also has conflated defense growth with budget-wide cuts. The $20 billion cut in the administration's FY2011 base defense budget request was, nonetheless, "approximately $5 billion above last year" for defense.[8]

Congress should use "current services" as its baseline, starting with the FY2011 base defense appropriation. The experience in the Reagan-Bush-Clinton period showed it is possible to manage a gradual budget reduction pace, and the FY2012 request should be the first one to sustain such discipline. The administration's $553 billion base budget request is already overtaken by events. Were it appropriated, as the House Armed Services Committee authorized, it would represent $24 billion (5%) in growth over FY2011. This is unrealistic. Even the President acknowledged it on April 14, seeking a minimum of $400 billion in reductions from his own projections over the next 12 years and using the FY2011 appropriation as the baseline. Similarly, the

House Appropriations Committee reduced the FY2012 request by $8.9 billion, but that still leaves a 3% increase and makes no contribution to deficit reduction.

The President's proposed $400 billion in reductions from the plan should be treated as a "ceiling" for defense, the most the Department might expect to receive. The Defense Department could provide those savings and more from current budget projections and still maintain budget growth at the rate of inflation. This level of build down does not require a change in strategy, despite the "strategic review" Secretary Gates began (see table below).

Indeed, deeper, real cuts are clearly both possible and responsible. The President's Simpson-Bowles debt panel, the Bipartisan Policy Center's Domenici-Rivlin Debt Panel, and the Sustainable Defense Task Force sponsored by Representatives Barney Frank (D-MA) and Ron Paul (R-TX) all proposed more substantial reductions ranging between $500 billion and $1 trillion over ten years. Most interestingly, working different paths, although with some consultation, these panels found common priorities for defense discipline: the size of the force, hardware investment decisions, personnel policies, and management efficiency.

Some of these recommendations are already subject to congressional action. This is an important, if minimal, step. The cost of the military health care program has more than doubled since FY2001, from $24 billion to $52.5 billion, and the Pentagon projects it to continue growing at disproportionate annual rates of 3% to 5% through 2016. Working-age military retirees and their dependents were expected to pay approximately 27% of program costs when TRICARE was established in 1995 but have not seen any cost increase since then. Medical inflation and policy changes thus narrowed their cost sharing to approximately 11%. The fee increase being considered would increase costs for single members by $2.50 a month, from $230 to $260 per year, and for members with families by $5 a month, from $460 to $520 a year. The Defense Department would save $340 million next year if the fee is increased, and indexing that fee to Medicare inflation would accelerate savings in later years.[9]

Congress also appears ready to support the Pentagon's request to terminate two programs targeted by the independent defense savings panels, the Marines' Expeditionary Fighting Vehicle (EFV) and the Army's Medium Extended Air Defense System (MEADS). Both programs needed such budgetary discipline. The Government

Defense Department Budget Authority: Current Plan and Obama Administration Alternatives

Fiscal Year	2012	2013	2014	2015	2016	2017	2018	2019	2020	2021	2022	2023	Total: FY12-23
FY2012 Plan	553.00	570.70	586.40	598.20	610.60	621.60	632.80	644.10	655.70	667.50	679.52	691.75	7511.86
FY2012 Planned Growth Rate		0.03	0.03	0.02	0.02	0.02	0.02	0.02	0.02	0.02	0.02	0.02	
GDP Chained Price Index	0.014	0.016	0.017	0.017	0.017	0.018	0.018	0.018	0.018	0.018	0.018	0.018	
Real Freeze in FY2012 Adjustment	536.30	544.89	554.15	563.57	573.15	583.47	593.97	604.66	615.54	626.62	637.90	649.39	7083.61
Reduction from '12 Budget	16.70	25.81	32.25	34.63	37.45	38.13	38.83	39.44	40.16	40.88	41.61	42.36	428.25

Defense Savings Options: A Comparison

	End Strength Reductions	Investments	Personnel	Overhead
Simpson-Bowles	50K overseas stationing	Cancel V-22 Osprey Cancel Expeditionary Fighting Vehicle Halve USAF/USN F-35 & cut USMC F-35 Reduce Research & Development (10%) Cancel Navy sea-basing Cancel Army tactical vehicles and radios Reduce "Minor" procurement (22%)	Modernize health care cost sharing Freeze civilian pay (3 years) Freeze military pay (3 years)	Pocket "Gates efficiency" savings Double Gates' contracting-out cuts Substitute 62K civilians for 88K troops performing commercial activities Reduce maintenance at bases & facilities Consolidate commissaries with Service exchanges Integrate children into local schools
Rivlin-Domenici/Stimson Center	92K COIN ground forces 80K overseas stationing 100K "infrastructure"	Cancel V-22 Osprey Cancel Expeditionary Fighting Vehicle Cancel F-35 Joint Strike Fighter Reduce Research & Development (19%) Reduce "Minor" procurement (19%) Prioritize Missile Defense (ballistic & cruise) Defer VA-class submarines Streamline intelligence activities	Modernize health care cost sharing Freeze civilian pay (2 years) Freeze military pay (2 years; Stimson plan) Reform retirement structure	Pocket "Gates efficiency" savings
Sustainable Defense Task Force	92K COIN ground forces 50K overseas stationing	Cancel V-22 Osprey Cancel Expeditionary Fighting Vehicle Cancel F-35 Joint Strike Fighter Reduce Research & Development ($5B/yr) Curtail ballistic missile defense Reorganize USN to 230 ship fleet Retire 2 aircraft carriers Retire 4 USN/USAF fighter wings Reduce nuclear arsenal & cut bomber leg of Triad Delay KC-X Tanker	Modernize health care cost sharing Recalibrate military compensation relative to civilian pay	Scale recruiting costs to force reduction Streamline depots, commissaries, exchanges Scale command, support, and infrastructure costs to overall cuts

*Simpson/Bowles and Rivlin/Domenici options are illustrative only. Both commissions' formal recommendations targeted only a savings number.

Accountability Office reported that EFV costs per unit grew by 170% since 2000, to $24 million, and that the vehicle's design and schedule were in doubt.[10] Meanwhile, no amphibious landing of the sort that would justify EFV has been executed under combat circumstances since the Korean War's 1950 Battle of Inchon. MEADS, also on the block, duplicates the ongoing PAC-3 update to theater missile defenses and has long been a low priority for the Army.

Consensus among these panels can provide further guidance for the Congress. Additional savings could come from slowing and terminating parts of the F-35 Joint Strike Fighter program and from reducing end strength as we withdraw from Iraq and Afghanistan.

Linking Fiscal and Strategic Discipline

Returning defense budgets to the peacetime levels more typical of the past 40 years, as proposed by the fiscal panels, raises the more fundamental question of strategy. Budgets discipline strategy and strategic (and mission) choices can discipline budgets. Such discipline has been noticeably absent over the past ten years. The Domenici-Rivlin panel moved in this direction and it is also the focus of our article, based on the panel's work, in the January/February 2011 edition of *Foreign Affairs*.[11] In contrast to the Quadrennial Defense Review of 2010 and, very likely, the current strategic review, this approach would set meaningful priorities among military missions, calculate acceptable levels of risk, and tailor the force within budget constraints. Priority would go to military missions that are probable, consequential, achievable and appropriate.

In our judgment, the United States has never been as secure as it is today. Despite the rhetoric about an increasingly dangerous world, the US faces no existential threat and substantial choice about the international commitments it makes. Confronting Al Qaeda's central network is an important priority. Defending against cyber attack also is significant, though the US needs to be cautious that it does not stimulate an even greater threat though our own offensive investments and to ensure that we work with the international community to control the challenge we face. The quality, rather than the quantity, of our defense investment against these two challenges is what matters. As the bin Laden mission demonstrated, special operators are the most effective capability to deal with the terrorist threat, combined with international action, financial tools, and law enforcement. A large ground force is not the right instrument.

Large-scale conventional combat, a capability that deters adversaries, and some level of sea lane patrol to provide presence are next-level priorities. But, again, the end of the Cold War has brought unprecedented levels of security to the US. Large scale conventional war is less likely and the US is gradually slimming its nuclear deterrent to reflect the much lower level of nuclear threat it now faces. Neither of these missions justifies continued growth in defense spending.

Still, as Secretary Gates pointed out in May 2008, military services with lesser roles in current wars chronically plan around "Next-War-Itis," a fixation on potential future conflicts that would feature them more prominently and thus inflate their budgets well beyond demand. China is the scenario on which this planning focuses, especially for the Air Force, Navy, and advocates of programs that are aimed at ensuring US "access" to the Pacific theater.

There is no doubt that China is a rising power and is making substantial investments in its defense capabilities, but some perspective is needed here. China's military investment is, according to the most informed sources, one-seventh of ours. Chinese capabilities at sea and in the air are minimal compared to those of the US and will take decades to catch up, a goal reachable only if the US stops investing in defense. Moreover, there is little indication that China seeks a military confrontation with the US and no grounds at all for viewing the relationship as one driven by fundamental ideological hostility. We must be careful to avoid the contradiction of viewing China as a country with intentions but no capability for confrontation while considering ourselves as a power with capabilities but no intention for confrontation. There is ample room here for a long-term strategy that maintains our military power and presence in the Pacific region, avoids an arms race, and engages China on the diplomatic, economic, and

financial levels. Indeed, the Chinese may be looking for the US to get its fiscal house in order, which is in the interests of both powers.

The prospect of a major conventional confrontation elsewhere is minimal. North Korea's military is numerically impressive but would be confronted by a substantially different South Korean military than that which existed in 1950. The US role in such a confrontation would be significantly lower, limited to sea and air power. Pacific strategy more broadly can and should be one of nuclear deterrence, air support, and naval presence. The prospect of a long-term conventional conflict with Iran is also low. Iran's vast size, to say nothing of the public hostility to any US presence, makes anything more than air strikes or Special Forces operations unlikely. And for all the rhetoric and concern about Pakistan, the likelihood of a major US ground presence in that country is near zero for the same reason.

It is hard to find another case where a sizeable US conventional ground presence is likely any time in the near future. It is appropriate to hedge against a conventional ground conflict or the use of naval and air power, but a smaller US force and budget would be ample to cope with this risk. Today the US already has the most dominant global conventional capability on the planet, providing a significant hedge against such challenges, and we would continue to have such a capability even should the budget go down as it did in the 1990s.

The most cited danger is also the most recent addition to US military missions: fragile states, insurgencies, nation-building, and post-conflict reconstruction. Here we are at substantial risk of learning the "wrong" lessons from Iraq and Afghanistan. The US was not dealing with state fragility in either country. We consciously pursued a strategy of regime change using conventional combat forces in both cases. Once the occupying power, we faced an insurgency our invasion helped stimulate. The internal capacity to govern and provide for balanced development disappeared partly because we "disappeared" it.

Basing future policy on this model is a dangerous but lesser-known case of the "Next-War-Itis" Secretary Gates warned about. It is far from clear that the US military is or will be in demand for large-scale invasion, regime removal, occupation, nation-building, or fighting insurgents. These missions have had their day, our success has been less than stunning, and, thus, they deserve a low priority. Future conflict resolution, conflict prevention, and support for governance and development are civilian missions for the US, in concert with international partners, not the future of the US military.

Reviewing defense missions in this way would lead to tough, strategy-driven choices on personnel and investment—the areas that the Pentagon most seeks to protect from budgetary scrutiny. US ground forces have grown by 92,000 soldiers and Marines since 2007, in large part linked to the rotation requirements of long counterinsurgency and nation-building campaigns in Iraq and Afghanistan.

Our proposed priorities could reverse that growth. If the likelihood of conventional confrontation is as we see it, our Asian and especially European allies are sufficiently secure to permit a drawdown of the 80,000 US forces permanently stationed overseas. And if the tasks facing US military forces are less than we have given them over the past ten years, the defense infrastructure could shrink as well, eliminating another 100,000 uniformed positions from the half-million service members that the Pentagon classifies as working in overhead positions and not deployed.[12] Taken together, these end strength reductions could be phased in over five years, providing significant savings but retaining a globally operational military capability.

Mission prioritization can also inform investment choices. Our current air dominance suggests that continuing current fighter-jet programs rather than building a new F-35 may be adequate. Slowing the rate at which we buy new Virginia-class attack submarines also may be sufficient given our global dominance, and lowering our current investment in missile defenses may be better tailored to the real missile threat. Ultimately, the defense savings proposed by the independent debt panels would lead to this kind of strategic rethink. Yet these panels would also retain a dominant global military force, and their savings are achievable through modest, incremental steps over a period of years, long enough to accommodate discussion and implementation of a changed strategy.

Enduring Security of the United States

All of these strategy and mission thoughts are, for now, suggestive. We are currently working, with the support of the Peter G. Peterson Foundation, on a more detailed review of military mission priorities and the forces and costs associated with resetting them. Making choices in this way would do what the 2010 Quadrennial Defense Review failed to do and what the ongoing strategy review is unlikely to do: constrain the defense budget to a strategy that prioritizes missions, deliberately manages risk, and accepts the resource discipline reality advised so long ago by Bernard Brodie.

A broad approach to strategic and fiscal discipline in defense helps provide a sound footing for federal finances and the economy while also improving our security. It is possible while retaining the most superior global military capability history has ever seen. The United States would continue to be the only country able to patrol the world's oceans, deploy hundreds of thousands of ground forces to any point on the globe, and dominate the global airspace with superior combat fighters, long-range bombers, and unmanned aircraft. At roughly 60,000, US special operations forces alone would be larger than the militaries of more than half the world's countries. More broadly, the United States' entire post-reform active duty force would exceed the forces of any other country except for China and India. Supporting this overwhelming force, the US

would retain the world's only global military transportation, communications, logistics, and intelligence capabilities. And, even with a trillion-dollar reduction over ten years, an unsurpassed defense budget would enable this force. For perspective, our FY2009 military research and development spending alone exceeded China's entire defense budget.

Admiral Mullen has underlined the importance of returning this budgetary discipline to the Defense Department. As he acknowledged in a budget press briefing on January 6th of this year, "the defense budget has basically doubled in the last decade. And my own experience here is in that doubling, we've lost our ability to prioritize, to make hard decisions, to do tough analysis, to make trades."[13] He is precisely right.

Congress and the administration now have the opportunity to improve our national security at a reduced cost, while ensuring a balanced package of deficit reduction. The experience of the Reagan-Bush-Clinton exercise shows how meaningful that modest defense budget reduction, implemented gradually, can be. When the next generation of policymakers looks back on the era of restraint under way today, they will see that matching fiscal and strategic discipline led to a bipartisan defense program that responsibly and soberly saved as much as a trillion dollars from the coming decade of defense spending while ensuring that the US continues to play a leading role on the world stage.

Notes

1. Bernard Brodie. Strategy in the Missile Age. (Princeton: Princeton University Press, 1959). p. 358.

2. Stimson project work is publicly available at (www.stimson.org/programs/budgeting-for-foreign-affairs-and-defense/) and blog (http://thewillandthewallet.org/). See also Gordon Adams and Cindy Williams. Buying National Security: How America Plans and Pays for its Global Role and Safety at Home. (New York: Routledge, 2010).

3. Gordon Adams and Matthew Leatherman. "A Leaner and Meaner Defense: How to Cut the Pentagon's Budget while Improving Its Performance," Foreign Affairs (Jan/Feb 2011).

4. Admiral Mike Mullen. Chairman of the Joint Chiefs of Staff, Detroit Marriott at the Renaissance Center, Detroit, Michigan. 26 August 2010.

5. Kathy A. Ruffing and James R. Horney. "Economic Downturn and Bush Policies Continue to Drive Large Projected Deficit," Center on Budget and Policy Priorities, 20 May 2011. At www.cbpp.org/files/5-10-llbud.pdf.

6. Scott Gebicke and Samuel Magid. "Lessons from around the world: Benchmarking performance in defense," McKinsey, Spring 2010. Exhibit 3.

7. Arnold Punaro. "Reducing Overhead and Improving Business Operations," Defense Business Board, 22 July 2010. Slide 30.

8. See http://republicans.appropriations.house.gov/_files/41211 SummaryFinalFY2011CR.pdf. Congress was able to grow the defense appropriation while also freezing the Pentagon's base budget, referred to earlier, because of savings from the military construction appropriation resulting from the wind-down of the 2005 BRAC process.

9. Robert Hale. "FY2012 Budget Briefing," 14 February 2011. www.defense.gov/transcripts/transcript.aspx?transcriptid=4770. For the history of TRICARE cost sharing, see "Report of the Tenth Quadrennial Review of Military Compensation: Volume II," Department of Defense, July 2008. p. 46.

10. "Assessment of Selected Weapons Programs," Government Accountability Office, 29 March 2011. http://www.gao.gov/assets/590/589695.pdf

11. Gordon Adams and Matthew Leatherman. "A Leaner and Meaner Defense: How to Cut the Pentagon's Budget while Improving Its Performance," *Foreign Affairs* (Jan/Feb 2011).

12. Arnold Punaro. "Reducing Overhead and Improving Business Operations," Defense Business Board briefing, 22 July 2010. Slide 23.

13. Admiral Mike Mullen. Chairman of the Joint Chiefs of Staff, Pentagon, Arlington, Virginia. 6 January 2011.

GORDON ADAMS is Professor of International Relations at the School of International Service, American University, in Washington, D.C. He is also a Distinguished Fellow at the Stimson Center.

Robert M. Gates    **NO**

Defense Spending

Thank you Arthur, and thanks for that introduction. And my thanks to the American Enterprise Institute for hosting this event on relatively short notice. In many ways it is appropriate that AEI be the setting for my last major policy speech in Washington. The recent history of this institution and some of its more prominent figures is inextricably tied to the war in Iraq, the conflict that pulled me out of private life and back into the public arena nearly four and a half years ago.

As you know, and as Arthur just said, I am in the final weeks of the greatest privilege of my professional life, serving as America's 22nd Secretary of Defense. Most of my time and attention in this post has been dominated by America's two major post-9/11 conflicts—each marked by swift, exhilarating victories against odious regimes followed by grinding, protracted counter-insurgency and counter-terrorism campaigns.

In the course of doing everything I could to turn things around first in Iraq, then in Afghanistan, from the early months I ran up against institutional obstacles in the Pentagon—cultural, procedural, ideological—to getting done what needed to get done on behalf of those fighting the wars we are in. Whether it was outpatient care for the wounded, armored troop transport, medevac, ramping up intelligence, surveillance and reconnaissance support, or any number of urgent battlefield needs.

It became evident over time that changing the momentum of these conflicts—and increasing the odds of military success in the future—would also require fundamentally re-shaping the priorities of the Pentagon and the uniformed services and reforming the way they did business: How weapons were chosen, developed and produced, how troops and their families were cared for, how leaders were promoted and held accountable—and, related to all of the above, where money was spent (or misspent as the case may be).

It is the health and future of the military as an institution—an institution confronted with complex and evolving array of threats abroad while adjusting to an era of debt and austerity at home—that I would like to discuss with you today before taking some questions.

I'll start with America's fiscal situation and how it relates to defense. It is no secret that the United States faces a serious fiscal predicament that could turn into a crisis—of credit, of confidence, of our position in the world—if not addressed soon. On April 13th, President Obama announced his framework for tackling these challenges. As part of that deficit reduction effort, he set a goal of holding the growth in base national security spending slightly below inflation for the next 12 years, which would save about $400 billion, the preponderance of which would come from the Department of Defense.

The President's directive—as well as a number of other proposals such as Simpson-Bowles that could cut defense by up to $1.2 trillion—have stirred a debate in some quarters about the size, use, and cost of our military, and by extension, the appropriate role of the United States in the world.

For starters, I have long believed—and I still do—that the defense budget, however large it may be, is not the cause of this country's fiscal woes. However, as matter of simple arithmetic and political reality, the Department of Defense must be at least part of the solution.

There is an important body of opinion—including, I suspect many people in this room—that would disagree. This view holds that not only should current defense spending levels be maintained, but if anything, they should be increased. That the reason we face tough choices and trade-offs with respect to military programs is because the top-line isn't big enough. As an old Cold Warrior known for most of my career as a national security hardliner, I understand this perspective. Defense expenditures are currently a lower share of GDP than most of the last half century, and a much lower percentage than during previous major wars. When President Eisenhower warned of the "Military Industrial Complex" in 1961, defense consumed more than half the federal budget, and the portion of the nation's economic output devoted to the military was about 9 percent. By comparison, this year's base defense budget of $530 billion—the highest since World War II adjusted for inflation—represents less than 15 percent of all federal spending and equates to roughly three and a half percent of GDP—a number that climbs to about 4 and a half percent when the war costs in Iraq and Afghanistan are included.

But, as I am fond of saying, we live in the real world. Absent a catastrophic international conflict or new existential threat, we are not likely to return to Cold War levels of defense expenditures, at least as a share of national wealth anytime soon. Nor do I believe we need to.

First, the world is different. Our primary adversary then was a comparably armed super power, bristling with millions of troops, tens of thousands of tanks, and

Gates, Robert. From a speech delivered to the American Enterprise Institute on May 24, 2011.

thousands of advanced combat aircraft—not to mention a vast arsenal of nuclear weapons—that was poised to over-run Western Europe and could directly threaten our allies and interests around the globe. I know—as head analyst at CIA I signed off on the studies of Soviet military power. The threats and potential adversaries America faces today and down the road are dangerous and daunting—for their complexity, variety and unpredictability. But as a matter of national survival, they do not approach the scale of the Soviet military threat that provided the political and strategic rationale for defense expenditures that consumed a significant portion of our economy.

Second, we're not going to see a return to Cold War-level defense budgets, at least as a share of GDP, because America is different: Our economy, our demographics, and our fiscal predicament—whether measured in the size of debt and deficits, ratios of retirees to workers, or the share of the federal budget consumed by entitlements. The money and political support simply aren't there.

Seeing the bleak fiscal outlook ahead, I have for the past two years sought to prepare our defense institutions—accustomed to the post 9/11 decade's worth of "no questions asked" funding requests—for the inevitable flattening and eventual decrease of the defense budget. This entailed creating as much "head room" as possible under the existing defense top line to protect the size and fighting strength—the core capabilities—of the U.S. military.

The first stage, beginning in Spring 2009, dealt with procurement—the weapons the military buys or plans to buy in the future. We cancelled or curtailed modernization programs that were egregiously over-budget, behind schedule, dependent on unproven technology, supplied a niche requirement that could be met in other ways, or that simply did not pass the common sense test: A $200 billion future combat system for the Army that, a decade after IEDS and EFPs began to kill or maim thousands of our troops, was based on lightweight, flat-bottomed vehicles that relied on near-perfect information awareness to detect the enemy before he could strike. Or a missile defense program that called for a fleet of laser-bearing 747s circling slowly inside enemy air space to get off a shot at a missile right after launch.

All told, over the past two years, more than 30 programs were cancelled, capped, or ended that, if pursued to completion, would have cost more than $300 billion. At the same time, we made new investments in higher priorities related to the current wars and, in some cases, re-started efforts that filled a genuine military need for the future—such as a follow-on bomber for the Air Force, the Army's Ground Combat Vehicle, and a new Marine amphibious tractor. We also invested in new technologies and capabilities to address emerging sophisticated threats. But our new starts and new investments are on a far more realistic footing that relies on proven technology and can be produced on time and on budget.

This process also forced the Pentagon's leadership to confront this vexing and disturbing reality: since 9/11, a near-doubling of the Pentagon's modernization accounts—more than $700 billion over 10 years in new spending on procurement, research and development—has resulted in relatively modest gains in actual military capability. In fact, most of the significant new capabilities that have come online over the past decade were largely paid for outside the base budget, via supplemental war requests. In particular, larger ground forces and specialized battlefield equipment such as MRAPs, body armor, and other gear.

Reversing an unsustainable course—where more and more money is consumed by fewer and fewer platforms that take longer and longer to build—meant reforming the acquisition process and the department's buying culture. The goal is that any new weapons system should meet benchmarks for cost, schedule and performance while minimizing "requirements creep"—the kind of indiscipline that leads to $25 million howitzers, $500 million helicopters, $2 billion bombers, and $7 billion submarines.

There is another factor to consider. The Reagan build-up of the 1980s fielded a new generation of weapons platforms that continue to be the mainstay of the force today—the M1 tank, Bradley Fighting Vehicle, Apache and Black Hawk helicopters, Burke guided missile destroyers, F-15 fighters, and much more. In contrast, the 1990s represented basically a procurement holiday, except for important developments in precision munitions and UAVs. And, as I mentioned earlier, the post 9/11 defense spending surge resulted in relatively little new recapitalization of the force.

The current inventory is getting old and worn down from Iraq and Afghanistan. Some equipment can be refurbished with life-extension programs, but there is no getting around the fact that others must be replaced. Most of these Reagan-era platforms are still best in class relative to the rest of the world, so with the important exception of air superiority fighters and other high-end systems, pursuing costly, leap-ahead improvements in technology and capability is not necessarily required. Our guiding principle going forward must be to develop technology and field weapons that are affordable, versatile, and relevant to the most likely and lethal threats in the decades to come, not just more expensive and exotic versions of what we had in the past.

I revisit this history because it leads to an important point for the future: when it comes to our military modernization accounts, the proverbial "low hanging fruit"—those weapons and other programs considered most questionable—have not only been plucked, they have been stomped on and crushed. What remains are much-needed capabilities—relating to air superiority and mobility, long-range strike, nuclear deterrence, maritime access, space and cyber warfare, ground forces, intelligence, surveillance and reconnaissance—that our nation's civilian and military leadership deem absolutely critical. For example:

- We must build a new tanker. The ones we have are twice as old as many of the pilots flying them;

- We must field a next generation strike fighter—the F-35—and at a cost that permits large enough numbers to replace the current fighter inventory and maintain a healthy margin of superiority over the Russians and Chinese;
- We must build more ships—in recent years, the size of the Navy fleet has sunk to the lowest number since before World War II, and will get smaller as more Reagan-era vessels reach the end of their service life;
- We must recapitalize the ground forces—the Army and Marines—whose combat vehicles and helicopters are worn down after a decade of war; and
- At some point we must replace our ballistic missile submarines—a program that illustrates the modernization dilemmas we face.

Over the past two years, a dedicated effort by DoD acquisitions experts to reduce requirements and costs brought down the projected price tag of these new boomers by $2 billion each. But that still leaves us with a projected cost of $5 billion per sub—and we're planning to build 12 of them, presenting some serious issues for the Navy's shipbuilding budget down the road.

So as we move forward, unless our country's political leadership envisions a dramatically diminished global security role for the United States, it is vitally important to protect the military modernization accounts—in absolute terms, and as a share of the defense budget.

But sustaining this "tooth" part of the budget—the weapons and the soldiers, sailors, airmen and Marines who use them—is increasingly difficult given the massive growth of other components of the defense budget, the "tail" if you will—operations, maintenance, pay and benefits, and other forms of overhead. America's defense enterprise has consumed ever higher level of resources as a matter of routine just to maintain, staff, and administer itself—the other key reason that major increases in the total base defense budget since 2001 have led to relatively modest increases in usable military capabilities.

As a result, starting last spring, we began to take a hard look at the department's overhead costs, in particular the massive administrative and support bureaucracies—within the military services, and across the defense department as a whole. The purpose was to carve out more budget "headroom" that could be allocated to force structure and modernization.

The results of these efforts were, frankly, mixed. The military services, in my view, successfully leaned forward and found nearly $100 billion in efficiency savings—by closing facilities, combining headquarters, reducing energy costs, and much more—over five years and allocated those funds to make new priority investments and deal with higher than projected expenses. Across the department as a whole, we were able to save another $54 billion through freezing civilian staff and pay levels, eliminating one 4-star command and downgrading two others, eliminating or down-grading more than 350 generals,

admirals, and civilian executive positions, reducing reliance on contractors, getting rid of unnecessary reports and studies, and more.

Then there was the effort to pare down the overhead costs of DoD components outside the military services—in particular, the Office of Secretary of Defense, the Joint Staff, the defense agencies and field activities, plus the major regional and functional military headquarters—referred to as Combatant Commands—apart from Iraq and Afghanistan.

With respect to these components, known internally as the 4th Estate, the efficiencies experience was something akin to an Easter egg hunt. My staff and I learned that it was nearly impossible to get accurate information and answers to questions such as "how much money did you spend" and "how many people do you have?" For example, when I launched the efficiencies effort in August 2010 we projected the savings from closing Joint Forces Command to be about $250 million. That number doubled over the next four months as more details trickled in out about how this organization was funded and staffed from dozens of sources across the department.

Overall, the 4th Estate savings were disappointing—less than a billion dollars in annual projected savings from a group of organizations that consume at least $64 billion a year by our latest estimate. I believe we can and should do much better. There are still too many headquarters, offices, and agencies employing too many high ranking personnel and contractors consuming too many resources relative to real military missions and measurable results.

The efficiencies project also showed that the current apparatus for managing people and money across the DoD enterprise is woefully inadequate. The agencies, field activities, joint headquarters, and support staff functions of the department operate as a semi-feudal system—an amalgam of fiefdoms without centralized mechanisms to allocate resources, track expenditures, and measure results relative to the department's overall priorities.

I have always believed inspired leadership can overcome deficient organization charts. But in this case, it may be time to consider new governance structures and arrangements. Here, the Congress has been ahead of the Department by pushing us to establish a centralized structure led by a Chief Management Officer.

So I believe there are more savings possible by culling more overhead and better accounting for, and thus better managing, the funds and people we have. But one thing is quite clear. These efficiencies efforts will not come close to meeting the budget targets laid out by the president, much less other, higher targets being bandied about. Some perspective is important. What's being proposed by the President is nothing close to the dramatic cuts of the past. For example, defense spending in constant dollars declined by roughly a third between 1985 and 1998. What's being considered today, assuming all $400 billion comes from DoD over 12 years, corresponds to a projected reduction of about 5 percent in constant dollars—or slightly less than keeping pace with inflation.

Nonetheless, meeting this savings target will require real cuts—given the escalating costs of so many parts of the defense budget—and, as a result, real choices. I am determined that we not repeat the mistakes of the past, where the budget targets were met mostly by taking a percentage off the top of everything, the simplest and most politically expedient approach both inside the Pentagon and outside of it. That kind of "salami-slicing" approach preserves overhead and maintains force structure on paper, but results in a hollowing-out of the force from a lack of proper training, maintenance and equipment—and manpower. That's what happened in the 1970s—a disastrous period for our military—and to a lesser extent during the late 1990s.

That is why I launched a comprehensive review last week to ensure that future spending decisions are focused on priorities, strategy and risks, and are not simply a math and accounting exercise. In the end, this process must be about identifying options for the President and the Congress, to ensure that the nation consciously acknowledges and accepts additional risk in exchange for reduced investment in its military.

Part of this analysis will entail going places that have been avoided by politicians in the past. Taking on some of these issues could entail:

- Re-examining military compensation levels in light of the fact that—apart from the U.S. Army during the worst years of Iraq—all the services have consistently exceeded their recruiting and retention goals;
- It could mean taking a look at the rigid, one-size-fits-all approach to retirement, pay and pensions left over from the last century. A more tiered and targeted system—one that weights compensation towards the most high demand and dangerous specialties—could bring down costs while attracting and retaining the high quality personnel we need; and
- It will require doing something about spiraling health care costs—and in particular the health insurance benefit for working age retirees whose fees are one-tenth those of federal civil servants, and have not been raised since 1995.

But, above all, if we are to avoid a hollowing effect, this process will need to address force structure—the military's fighting formations such as Army brigades, Marine expeditionary units, Air Force wings, Navy ships and supporting aviation assets. The overarching goal will be to preserve a U.S. military capable of meeting crucial national security priorities even if fiscal pressure requires reductions in that force's size. I've said repeatedly that I'd rather have a smaller, superbly capable military then a larger, hollow, less capable one. However, we need to be honest with the president, with the congress, with the American people, indeed with ourselves, about what those consequences are: That a smaller military, no matter how superb, will be able to go fewer places and be able to do fewer things.

For example, the assumption behind most of our military planning ever since the end of the Cold War has been that the U.S. must be able to fight two major regional wars at the same time. One might conclude that the odds of that contingency are sufficiently low, or that any eruption of conflicts would happen one after the other, not simultaneously. What are the implications of that with respect to force structure, and what are the risks? One can assume certain things won't happen on account of their apparent low probability. But the enemy always has a vote.

These are the kinds of scenarios we need to consider, the kinds of discussions we need to have. If we are going to reduce the resources and the size of the U.S. military, people need to make conscious choices about what the implications are for the security of the country, as well as for the variety of military operations we have around the world if lower priority missions are scaled back or eliminated. They need to understand what it could mean for a smaller pool of troops and their families if America is forced into a protracted land war again—yes, the kind no defense secretary should recommend anytime soon, but one we may not be able to avoid. To shirk this discussion of risks and consequences—and the hard decisions that must follow—I would regard as managerial cowardice.

In closing, while I have spent a good deal of time on programmatic particulars, the tough choices ahead are really about the kind of role the American people—accustomed to unquestioned military dominance for the past two decades—want their country to play in the world.

Since I entered government 45 years ago, I've shifted my views and changed my mind on a good many things as circumstances, new information, or logic dictated. But I have yet to see evidence that would dissuade me from this fundamental belief: that America does have a special position and set of responsibilities on this planet. I share Winston Churchill's belief that "the price of greatness is responsibility . . . [and] the people of the United States cannot escape world responsibility." This status provides enormous benefits—for allies, partners, and others abroad to be sure, but in the final analysis the greatest beneficiaries are the American people, in terms of our security, our prosperity, and our freedom.

I know that after a decade of conflict, the American people are tired of war. But there is no doubt in my mind that the continued strength and global reach of the American military will remain the greatest deterrent against aggression, and the most effective means of preserving peace in the 21st century, as it was in the 20th.

Robert Gates is the Chancellor of The College of William and Mary. His experience in the U.S. government includes service as the Secretary of Defense and Director of Central Intelligence.

EXPLORING THE ISSUE

Should U.S. Defense Spending Be Reduced Dramatically?

Critical Thinking and Reflection

1. How should resources be allocated to defense spending? What strategic framework should be used to determine U.S. national security priorities?
2. Should defense spending be cut proportionally across all spending categories, or should the Department of Defense employ targeted cuts for specific items? What are the advantages and disadvantages of each approach?
3. How do the political stakeholders in the U.S. democratic system of government either hinder or promote responsible decision making regarding defense spending?
4. Are there categories of defense spending that should be protected from spending cuts? Are there particular functions or weapons that should be eliminated? Why? Can the opposing argument be made? Which is more compelling?
5. What shapes Americans' opinions on defense spending? Will defense spending cuts reflect the will of the American people?

Is There Common Ground?

In all likelihood, defense spending will decline from the levels seen in the decade after the terrorist attacks on the United States on September 11, 2001, and the subsequent U.S. military activism abroad. Most people agree that because of current economic challenges, the United States must become more fiscally responsible. This includes reducing government spending and, due to its significant size relative to the overall budget, defense spending cannot be exempt. But it is unclear precisely which combination of priorities and politics will dictate the scale and composition of the coming defense budget cuts.

Though specific choices will be shaped by many contingent factors, to include the interests and lobbying power of defense companies, the constituency service interests of members of Congress, and the perspectives and interests of the military services, the need for a guiding strategy is embraced by most defense policy experts. As Dr. Adams and Secretary Gates both point out, defense spending must be linked to the national security strategy of the United States. It does not make much sense to ask "how much is enough" with regard to defense spending without asking what purposes national security decision makers want the U.S. armed forces to be capable of serving. What missions must the U.S. military be able to accomplish? How will the military accomplish these missions? How much will it cost to ensure that the military is ready and capable of achieving operational success at an acceptable level of risk? Knowing how and under what conditions the military will be employed to counter future threats should inform decisions about resource allocation. Unfortunately, it is not easy to measure with precision the relative utility of different forms of military spending, and it is not always possible to predict the nature of future

military commitments in advance. These uncertainties add complexity to national strategic planning and leave ample room for principled debate.

Additional Resources

Fenno, Richard. *The Power of the Purse: Appropriations Politics in Congress.* Boston, MA: Little, Brown and Company, 1966.

Fenno provides a detailed description of the interaction between members of Congress and the federal bureaucracy. The book examines congressional decision making in committees, highlighting the most influential political factors that capture members' attention.

Sapolsky, Harvey, Eugene Gholz, and Caitlin Talmadge. *US Defense Politics: The Origins of Security Policy.* New York: Routledge, 2009.

This book includes a detailed description of how the defense budgeting process works inside the Pentagon, where many of the decisions about resources are made before the budget request reaches Congress.

Schick, Allen. *The Federal Budget: Politics, Policy, Process.* Washington, DC: The Brookings Institution, 2000.

Schick's account of the budgeting process is a complete description of budgeting mechanics across the government. Relevant defense examples are provided, along with roles of budgeting stakeholders.

Wildavsky, Aaron. *The Politics of the Budgetary Process.* 3rd ed. Boston, MA: Little, Brown and Company, 1979.

Wildavsky discusses the political context of federal budgeting, including special considerations for defense budgeting, in this approachable and understandable description of the budgeting process.

Internet References . . .

The White House

The most current national strategic guidance is available online from the White House website. This document informs many resource allocation decisions and describes the threats to our national security.

http://www.whitehouse.gov/sites/default/files/rss_viewer/national_security_strategy.pdf

U.S. Department of Defense

This document articulates the Department of Defense view on appropriate priorities for the U.S. military, with a focus on challenges that extend beyond recent U.S. wars in Iraq and Afghanistan.

http://www.defense.gov/news/Defense_Strategic_Guidance.pdf

Selected, Edited, and with Issue Framing Material by:
Suzanne Nielsen, *U.S. Military Academy*
and
Scott Handler, *U.S. Military Academy*

ISSUE

Does Spending on Foreign Aid Further U.S. National Interests?

YES: Rajiv Shah, from *FY 2013 Budget Request* (March 2012)

NO: James M. Roberts, from *Congress Should Reduce the Deficit—Not Increase Funding from American Taxpayers for U.N.-Designed Foreign Aid Programs That Will Not Work* (July 2010)

Learning Outcomes
After reading this issue, you should be able to: • Understand the goals and objectives of U.S. foreign aid.   • Explain the argument that U.S. foreign aid is important to American national security.   • Understand the arguments for and against greater U.S. investment in foreign aid.   • Discuss the possible short-term and long-term impacts of U.S. government aid on developing countries.   • Explain the ongoing debate over the efficacy of official development assistance.

ISSUE SUMMARY

YES: In his testimony before the Senate Foreign Relations Committee, U.S. Agency for International Development (USAID) Administrator Dr. Rajiv Shah highlights the contributions USAID has made to fighting hunger and disease and strengthening education programs in developing countries. Shah argues that these foreign-aid programs advance U.S. interests by combating the factors that fuel violent extremism, while expanding U.S. trade opportunities.

NO: James M. Roberts, a research fellow with The Heritage Foundation and former Foreign Service Officer in the U.S. Department of State, argues that foreign aid often does more harm than good. In target countries, foreign aid can discourage private investment and benefit corrupt elites. In addition, money spent on aid contributes to the U.S. budget deficit. This sets a bad example at a time when the United States should be serving as a sound fiscal role model for developing countries.

The use of foreign aid to promote U.S. interests and values abroad is a poorly understood and contentious aspect of American foreign policy. As evidence that it is poorly understood, many Americans believe that foreign aid accounts for 20 percent of the federal budget, which is around 30 times the actual figure (Sachs, 2005). In addition, it is also not always appreciated that the objectives of various aid programs differ widely, with some intended to strengthen U.S. national security, others to serve U.S. commercial interests, and still others to further humanitarian goals (Tarnoff and Lawson, 2011). Only a small proportion of the overall U.S. aid budget goes to programs that have the promotion of economic development in poor countries as their primary purpose (Sachs, 2005).

The fact that not all U.S. foreign aid specifically targets economic development is sometimes lost in discussions about its success at achieving that aim. Many

U.S. aid programs during the Cold War, for example, were directed at strategic goals; they were primarily intended to promote U.S. power and influence at the expense of the Soviet Union. If these programs fostered economic development in recipient countries, that was an indirect benefit and not their primary purpose. The effectiveness of a particular aid program is best assessed in light of that program's objective.

In addition to being poorly understood, foreign aid is also contentious for a variety of reasons. First of all, the use of taxpayer dollars for aid intrinsically comes with opportunity costs. Dollars that are spent abroad are not spent at home—a simple fact that may be of growing importance in the present era of fiscal austerity. A second concern may be over whether international burden sharing is equitable. Does such a thing as a "fair share" exist and, if it does, is that what the United States is contributing? It is possible to argue that the United States is both generous and stingy in its provision of official development assistance (ODA), with ODA defined as "as the sum of grants and sub-market-rate loans made to developing countries to promote economic development and welfare" (Sachs, 2005). In terms of aggregate amounts, the United States is the single largest donor. In 2009, the United States spent $28.8 billion, which is approximately one-quarter of the ODA provided by the 29 wealthy countries that are part of the Organization for Economic Cooperation and Development (Tarnoff and Lawson, 2011). At the same time, the United States ranks third from the bottom among these countries in terms of the percentage of its gross national income (GNI) it devotes to aid. In 2009, the United States gave only one-fifth of 1 percent of its GNI in official development assistance abroad (Tarnoff and Lawson, 2011).

In addition to the amounts of aid that are appropriate, evaluations of effectiveness are also contentious. In historical terms, the Marshall Plan stands out as an example of success. Intended to help the countries of Europe rebuild after World War II, this large U.S. investment in aid had strategic, economic, and humanitarian purposes. The Marshall Plan was intended to better enable the democratic governments of Western Europe to stand firm against the Soviet Union and indigenous communist groups—and meet the basic needs of their populations—as these countries returned to the status of valued trading partners of the United States. Another oft-cited example of success, in terms of its alleviation of human suffering in the immediate aftermath of a catastrophe, is the U.S. provision of aid to Indonesia after a devastating ysunami in 2004. Even among critics of development assistance, this type of aid, known as disaster relief, generally retains support.

However, the fostering of sustainable development in the world's poorest countries is not an easy undertaking, and there is no settled body of scholarship that lays out what works and what does not. In fact, some critics of development assistance argue that development assistance has the potential to do more harm than good in recipient countries. For one thing, it can further line the pockets of corrupt political leaders in countries where accountability is weak. These elites can also divert the aid to strengthen institutions such as the military or police that can be used for domestic repression. Finally, some aid programs simply may not be effective in achieving the goals of economic growth and sustainable development. Prominent critic of development assistance William Easterly looks to Africa to make this case by pointing out that after receiving $568 billion of aid over 43 years, Africa remains trapped in economic stagnation (Easterly, 2005).

In response to these criticisms, proponents of development assistance argue that the condemnations are too broad. In a survey of studies on the relationship between foreign aid and growth, for example, current Chief Economist of USAID Steven Radelet finds that "aid has been successful in some countries but not others" (Radelet, 2006).

He goes on to argue that research is still needed on the conditions under which certain types of programs are likely to be effective.

An important recent innovation in the provision of U.S. aid is the Millennium Challenge Corporation (MCC), a government aid agency created in 2004. The MCC evaluates developing states based on their good governance practices and then selects countries that seem poised for economic growth. The MCC offers aid agreements called "compacts" to these states; the states that accept these compacts then become primarily responsible for developing their own strategies and for administering the resulting programs in a transparent manner. Arguing for the value of this effort, Secretary of State Hillary Clinton states: "Because of MCC's approach, developing countries are becoming self-sufficient, stronger, and more secure. They are adopting policies and practices that make them smart places to invest, trade, and do business." Going on to suggest that such efforts also serve U.S. commercial interests, she continues: "Let there be no mistake about it: The growth of the developing world presents a major economic opportunity for American workers and businesses today and into the future" (Millennium Challenge Corporation, 2012). While initiatives such as this hold promise, alone they are not a complete solution. Strategic interests remain likely to drive many foreign-aid decisions, and some of the world's least developed countries—arguably, those most sorely in need—may not be able to meet the criteria to become eligible for MCC compacts.

The importance of foreign aid as an instrument of U.S. foreign policy grew after the terrorist attacks on the United States on September 11, 2011. In addition to responding directly against the Al Qaeda terrorist organization, policymakers sought ways to attack the root causes of international terrorism. As pointed out in a report for Congress, "In 2002, a National Security Strategy for the first time established global development, a primary objective of U.S. foreign aid, as a third pillar of U.S. national security, along with defense and diplomacy" (Tarnoff and Lawson, 2011). The has reaffirmed the supposition from President Bush's National Security Strategy that development assistance is a key element of the overall strategy to address violent extremism. Not only would contributions to economic development create a more positive image of the United States abroad, they would also help to foster good governance and give people in developing countries a sense that a better future was within their reach.

The two sets of testimony to Congress presented in this section wade into this debate. In answering YES to whether foreign aid furthers U.S. national interests, USAID Administrator Rajiv Shah argues that for a relatively small outlay of American taxpayer dollars, foreign assistance brings far-reaching benefits. Shah proceeds to highlight a number of foreign-aid initiatives in the Middle East, Central Asia, and the Horn of Africa that promote economic reforms and support emerging democracies. At the end of the day, these programs do not simply combat famine, drought, and disease; they also fight the conditions that enable violent extremism.

In advocating the NO position, James Roberts from the Heritage Foundation argues that the United States should stop funding United Nations development assistance programs because they do not accomplish their objectives. In the case of Africa, for example, he contends that aid usually ends up benefiting corrupt elites, discouraging private investment, and driving poverty rates higher. Foreign aid that is not accompanied by programs that build good governance and fight systemic corruption is simply a waste of money. Instead of spending federal revenue on aid abroad, Roberts suggests that the United States could make a greater contribution by eliminating this unproductive spending from its budget. Even though this would make only a negligible contribution in reducing the U.S. federal deficit, it would at least better enable the United States to serve as a sound fiscal role model for developing countries.

YES

Rajiv Shah

Testimony by USAID Administrator Dr. Rajiv Shah Before the Senate Committee on Foreign Relations on the FY 2013 Budget Request

Thank you Chairman Cardin, Ranking Member Lugar, and members of the Committee. I am honored to join you to discuss the President's fiscal year 2013 budget request for USAID.

Two years ago, President Obama and Secretary Clinton called for elevating development as a key part of America's national security and foreign policy. Through both the Presidential Policy Directive on Global Development and the Quadrennial Diplomacy and Development Review, they made the case that the work USAID's development experts do around the globe was just as vital to America's global engagement as that of our military and diplomats.

The President's FY 2013 budget request enables USAID to meet the development challenges of our time. It allows us to respond to the dramatic political transformations in the Middle East and North Africa. It helps us focus on our national security priorities in frontline states like Afghanistan, Iraq and Pakistan. And it strengthens economic prosperity, both at home and abroad.

This budget also allows us to transform the way we do development. It helps countries feed, treat and educate their people while strengthening their capacity to own those responsibilities for themselves. It helps our development partners increase stability and counter violent extremism. It supports those who struggle for self-determination and democracy and empowers women and girls. And it helps channel development assistance in new directions—towards private sector engagement, scientific research and innovative technologies.

I want to highlight how the investments we make in foreign assistance help our country respond to our current challenges, while delivering results that shape a safer and more prosperous future.

Efficiency, Trade Offs and USAID Forward

While foreign assistance represents less than one percent of our budget, we are committed to improving our efficiency and maximizing the value of every dollar. Ameri-

can households around the country are tightening their belts and making difficult tradeoffs. So must we.

Even as we face new challenges around the world, our budget represents a slight reduction from fiscal year 2012.

We've prioritized, focused and concentrated our investments across every portfolio. In global health, we propose to close out programs in Peru and Mexico as those countries take greater responsibility for the care of their own people.

We've eliminated Feed the Future programs in Kosovo, Serbia and Ukraine and reduced support to Europe, Eurasia, and Central Asia by $113 million to reflect shifting global priorities and progress over time by some countries towards market-based democracy.

And we're keeping our staffing and overall administrative costs at current levels, even in the midst of a major reform effort. It is through that effort that I spoke about last year—USAID Forward—that we've been able to deliver more effective and efficient results with our current staffing profile and operating budget.

Our budget prioritizes our USAID Forward suite of reforms.

That funding allows us to invest in innovative scientific research and new technologies. Last year, our support of the AIDS vaccine research through PEPFAR led to the isolation of 17 novel antibodies that may hold the key to fighting the pandemic. And we're working with local scientists at the Kenyan Agricultural Research Institutes to develop new drought-resistant seed varieties of sorghum, millet and beans, as well as a vitamin-A rich orange-fleshed sweet potato.

It helps us conduct evaluations so we know which of our development efforts are effective and which we need to scale back. The American Evaluation Association recently cited our evaluation policy as a model other federal agencies should follow.

It allows us to partner more effectively with faith-based organizations and private companies. In fact, the OECD recognized USAID as the best among peers in driving private sector partnerships and investment.

And through our procurement reform efforts, among the most far-reaching and ambitious across the federal

Shah, Rajiv. U.S. Senate, March 6, 2012.

government, we are aggressively seeking new ways to work with host country partners instead of through more costly consultants and contractors. This effort will make our investments more sustainable and hasten our exit from countries, while cutting costs.

For instance, in Afghanistan, we invested directly in the country's Ministry of Health instead of third parties. As a result, we were able to save more than $6 million.

That investment also strengthened the Afghan health ministry, which has expanded access to basic health services from nine percent of the country to 64 percent. Last year, we discovered the true power of those investments; Afghanistan has had the largest gains in life expectancy and largest drops in maternal and child mortality of any country over the last ten years.

In Senegal, we are working with the government—instead of foreign construction firms—to build middle schools at a cost of just $200,000 each. That helps strengthen the government's ability to educate its people, but it is also significantly more cost effective than enlisting a contractor.

When we do invest money in partner governments, we do so with great care. Our Agency has worked incredibly hard to develop assessments that make sure the money we invest in foreign governments is not lost due to poor financial management or corruption.

With your continued support of this effort, we can expand our investments in local systems while building the level of oversight, accountability and transparency that working with a new and more diverse set of partners requires.

The Working Capital Fund we've requested would give us a critical tool in that effort. The Fund would align USAID's acquisition and assistance to USAID's program funding levels through a fee-for-service model, so that our oversight and stewardship are in line with our program and funding responsibilities. The result will be improved procurement planning, more cost effective awards, and better oversight of contracts and grants.

Supporting Strategic Priorities and Strengthening National Security

We will continue to support the growth of democracies around the world, especially in the Middle East and North Africa where the transformative events of the Arab Spring are bringing down autocratic regimes and expanding freedom.

State and USAID have requested $770 million for a new Middle East and North Africa Incentive Fund to respond to the historical changes taking place across the region. The Fund will incentivize long-term economic, political and trade reforms-key pillars of stability-by supporting governments that demonstrate a commitment to undergo meaningful change and empower their people. State and USAID will continue to play a major role in helping the people of this region determine their own future.

In Iraq, Afghanistan and Pakistan, USAID continues to work closely with interagency partners including the State and Defense departments, to move towards long-term stability, promote economic growth and support democratic reforms. Civilians are now in the lead in Iraq, helping that country emerge as a stable, sovereign, democratic partner. Our economic assistance seeks to expand economic opportunity and improve the quality of life throughout the country, with a particular focus on health, education and private sector development. With time, Iraq's domestic revenue will continue to take the place of our assistance.

In Afghanistan, we've done work to deliver results despite incredibly difficult circumstances. We established our Accountable Assistance for Afghanistan-or A3-initiative to reduce subcontracting layers, tighten financial controls, enhance project oversight and improve partner vetting. And with consistent feedback from Congress we are focusing on foundational investments in economic growth, reconciliation and reintegration and capacity building, as well as to support progress in governance, rule of law, counternarcotics, agriculture, health and education. We continue to focus on the sustainability of these investments so they ultimately become fiscally viable within the Afghan Government's own budget.

In Pakistan, our relationship is challenging and complex, but it is also critical. Our assistance continues to strengthen democratic institutions and foster stability during a difficult time. Crucial to those efforts are the efforts we make to provide electricity. Over the last two years, we've added as many as 1,000 megawatts to Pakistan's grid, providing power to 7 million households. We've also trained more than 70,000 businesswomen in finance and management and constructed 215 kilometers of new road in South Waziristan, expanding critical access to markets.

The Global Health Initiative

Thanks in large part to the bipartisan support we've had for investments in global health, we're on track to provide life-saving assistance to more people than ever before. Although this year's request of $7.9 billion for the Global Health Initiative is lower than FY 2012 levels, falling costs, increased investments by partner governments, and efficiencies we've generated by integrating efforts and strengthening health systems will empower us to reach even more people.

That includes PEPFAR, which will provide life-saving drugs to those around the world afflicted with HIV and expand prevention efforts in those countries where the pandemic continues to grow. We can expand access to treatment and lift a death sentence for six million people in total without additional funds.

We're also increasingly providing treatment for pregnant mothers with HIV/AIDS so we can ensure their children are born healthy. And because of breakthrough research released last year, we know that putting people on treatment actually helps prevention efforts—treatment is prevention. All of these efforts are accelerating progress towards President Obama's call for an AIDS-free generation.

Our request also includes $619 million for the President's Malaria Initiative, an effective way to fight child mortality. In country after country, we've shown that if we can increase the use of cheap bed nets and anti-malarial treatments, we can cut child death—from any cause, not just malaria—by as much as 30 percent. In Ethiopia, the drop in child mortality has been 50 percent.

Last year, we commissioned an external, independent evaluation of the Presidential Malaria Initiative's performances. That report praised the Initiative's effective leadership for providing "excellent and creative program management."

And we will continue to fund critical efforts in maternal and child health, voluntary family planning, nutrition, tuberculosis and neglected tropical diseases-cost-effective interventions that mean the difference between life and death.

Feed The Future

Last year, the worst drought in 60 years put more than 13.3 million people in the Horn of Africa at risk. Thanks to the humanitarian response led by the United States—and the investments we made in the past to build resilience against crises just like these—millions were spared from the worst effects of the drought.

But as is well known, providing food aid in a time of crisis is seven to 10 times more costly than investing in better seeds, irrigation and fertilizers. If we can improve the productivity of poor farmers in partner countries, we can help them move beyond the need for food aid. And we can prevent the violence and insecurity that so often accompanies food shortages.

That's why we are requesting $1 billion to continue funding for Feed the Future, President Obama's landmark food security initiative. These investments will help countries develop their own agricultural economies, helping them grow and trade their way out of hunger and poverty, rather than relying on food aid.

The investments we're making are focused on country-owned strategies that can lift smallholder farmers—the majority of whom are women—out of poverty and into the productive economy. All told, the resources we're committing to Feed the Future will help millions of people break out of the ranks of the hungry and impoverished and improve the nutrition of millions of children.

We're also leveraging our dollars at every opportunity, partnering with countries that are investing in their own agricultural potential and helping companies like Walmart, General Mills and PepsiCo bring poor farmers into their supply chain.

These investments are working.

In Haiti—where we continue to make great strides thanks to strong congressional support—we piloted a program designed to increase rice yields in the areas surrounding Port-au-Prince. Even while using fewer seeds and less water and fertilizer, Haitian farmers saw their yields increase by almost 190 percent. The farmers also cut 10 days off their normal harvest and increased profit per acre. Today that program is being expanded to reach farmers throughout the country. These results complement our work to cut cholera deaths to below the international standard. And we worked with the Gates Foundation to help nearly 800,000 Haitians gain access to banking services through their mobile phones.

And in Kenya, Feed the Future has helped over 90,000 dairy farmers—more than a third of whom are women—increase their total income by a combined $14 million last year. This effort is critical, since we know that sustainable agricultural development will only be possible when women and men enjoy the same access to credit, land and new technologies.

Overall, since we began the initiative in 2008, our 20 target countries have increased their total agricultural production by an average of 5.8 percent. That's over eight times higher than the global average increase of 0.7 percent.

Building Resilience

We all know that a changing climate will hit poor countries hardest. Our programs are aimed at building resilience among the poorest of those populations.

By investing in adaptation efforts, we can help nations cope with these drastic changes. By investing in clean energy, we can help give countries new, efficient ways to expand and grow their economies. And by investing in sustainable landscapes, we can protect and grow rainforests and landscapes that sequester carbon and stop the spread of deserts and droughts.

That work goes hand in hand with our efforts to expand access to clean water to people hit hard by drought. In 2010 alone, those efforts helped more than 1.35 million people get access to clean water and 2 million people access to sanitation facilities. Increasingly, we're working with countries to build water infrastructure and with communities to build rain catchments and wells to sustainably provide clean water. We're currently in the process of finalizing a strategy for our water work designed to focus and concentrate the impact of our work in this crucial area.

Strengthening Education

Last year, we made some critical decisions about how we strengthen global education. Since 1995, USAID's top recipients have increased primary school enrollment by 15 percent. But even as record numbers of children enter classrooms, we have seen their quality of learning sharply drop. In some countries, 80 percent of schoolchildren can't read a single word at the end of second grade. That's not education; it's daycare.

The strategy we released last year will make sure that our assistance is focused on concrete, tangible outcomes like literacy. By 2015, we will help improve the reading skills of 100 million children.

Conclusion

Thanks to these smart investments, every American can be proud that their tax dollars go towards fighting hunger and easing suffering from famine and drought, expanding freedom for the oppressed and giving children the chance to live and thrive no matter where they're born.

But we shouldn't lose sight that these investments aren't just from the American people—as USAID's motto says—they're for the American people. By fighting hunger and disease, we fight the despair that can fuel violent extremism and conflict. By investing in growth and prosperity, we create stronger trade partners for our country's exports.

And above all, by extending freedom, opportunity and dignity to people throughout the world, we express our core American values and demonstrate American leadership.

Thank you.

RAJIV SHAH is the Administrator of the U.S. Agency for International Development. Prior to this appointment, he was Chief Scientist and Under Secretary of Agriculture for Research, Education, and Economics.

James M. Roberts

 **NO**

Congress Should Reduce the Deficit—Not Increase Funding from American Taxpayers for U.N.-Designed Foreign Aid Programs That Will Not Work

My name is Jim Roberts. I am the Research Fellow for Economic Freedom and Growth in the Center for International Trade and Economics at The Heritage Foundation. Prior to joining Heritage in 2007, I served for 25 years as a Foreign Service Officer with the U.S. Department of State and worked on a variety of development assistance issues in a number of developing countries. The views I express in this testimony are my own, and should not be construed as representing any official position of The Heritage Foundation.

Congress should reject approval of future taxpayer-funded U.S. government official development assistance (ODA) programs that are designed to achieve the U.N.'s Millennium Development Goals (MDGs). I should note at the outset that I do not include emergency and humanitarian assistance in my critique of ODA, such as when the United States responds to earthquakes, floods, and other natural disasters by sending help to victims around the world.

The Declaration adopted at the U.N. Millennium Summit in 2000 addressed a wide range of problems related to peace, security, and development. No one disputes the desirability of reducing poverty, hunger and infant mortality, increasing access to safe drinking water, improving education, reversing the spread of HIV/AIDS, or protecting the environment. There is significant disagreement, however, about the proper methodology to achieve those goals.

The familiar call for the U.S. and other Organisation for Economic Cooperation and Development (OECD) member countries to commit 0.7 percent of gross domestic product (GDP) as official development assistance, first made nearly 40 years ago in a General Assembly resolution and reaffirmed many times since, has been repeated so often that people have forgotten that there is no verifiable evidence that ODA is effective—in any amount.

In my opinion, these U.N. development assistance programs will fail to achieve their objectives. If Congress continues to fund them, the only certainty is that they will further enrich corrupt elites in developing countries and they will provide continuing employment for the cadre of development assistance bureaucrats and other professionals who are advancing them.

Increasingly, experts in the developing world such as Dambisa Moyo of Zambia, author of *Dead Aid: Why Aid is Not Working and How There is a Better Way for Africa*, are voicing opposition to ODA. They know from firsthand experience that 50+ years of foreign aid from developed countries to Africa and elsewhere in the developing world has strengthened corrupt elites, encouraged a morally corrosive culture of corruption, discouraged private foreign and domestic investment, and actually caused poverty rates to rise due to higher levels of non-productive government spending and the welfare-dependency mindset it encourages.

One has only to drive 50 or so miles beyond the Beltway in any direction to see that the massive government "stimulus" spending in the U.S. in recent years, while a boon to public sector unions, has utterly failed to help the average American to achieve his or her own set of "MDGs" (and the U.S. is one of the most economically free nations on earth). So why should anyone expect U.S. government deficit-financed development assistance programs that emphasize welfare-state redistribution solutions to be any more successful in other countries?

This is especially true at a time of unthinkably large U.S. deficits. Analysts at The Heritage Foundation recently reported that the Obama Administration's "FY 2010 Mid-Year Review" projects this year's budget deficit at $1.471 trillion, or 10 percent of the entire U.S. economy. That is the largest nominal deficit in American history and, as a percentage of the economy, it's the largest deficit since World War II. By 2020 the President's budget includes deficits that never fall below $698 billion and leaves our children with $18.5 trillion in debt.

As Swedish development economist Fredrik Segerfeldt argues in a forthcoming book entitled *First, Do No Harm* on the failure of foreign aid to lift people out of poverty over the last 50 years, despite decades of efforts and the expenditure of $1.65 trillion dollars by OECD donor countries, the problems in those countries simply cannot be solved by foreign aid. Only economic growth can rescue the poor and extremely poor, and that growth cannot be generated by statist development assistance programs that center on an ever-expanding welfare state and redistribution schemes.

Roberts, James M. U.S. House of Representatives, July 27, 2010.

Segerfeldt points out that in 1962 the GDP per capita in East Asia and Sub-Saharan Africa was roughly the same. By 2005, the poverty rate in East Asia had been dramatically reduced while in Sub-Saharan Africa it was more or less unchanged. The difference? China, South Korea, the so-called Asian Tigers, and other countries in East Asia generally did not follow the Western development assistance model, preferring to stimulate growth through investing and exporting. Meanwhile countries in Sub-Saharan Africa became increasingly dependent for larger and larger shares of their GDP on ODA flows from OECD donor countries.

The development assistance lobby in OECD countries, however, pushes the MDGs and downplays extensive evidence that growth, not aid, provides the exit from the poverty trap. For evidence, look no further than the U.N. Millennium Declaration, which the U.N. Development Programme purports to be the gold standard of development assistance policy prescriptions. It does not contain a single reference to economic growth. That absence is all the more remarkable given that the stated top priority of ODA is poverty reduction. Yet without economic growth, countries will lack the resources necessary to improve the lives of their citizens.

The MDGs are designed in part to build better institutions and, indeed, they are the key. But they cannot be fixed with a few good governance and anti-corruption programs administered by expatriate development professionals. Only fundamental changes in a country's culture and political philosophy by its own citizens can accomplish the necessary changes.

It is not just the formal institutions of a government in developing countries, but the informal customs governing day-to-day business transactions, that must be reformed. And that can be accomplished only by the people living there. If a country's culture and practices are steeped in corruption, no amount of aid will overcome it. In fact, as Segerfeldt notes, official development assistance over a long period actually degrades these formal and informal institutions, allowing corrupt regimes to hang onto power for long periods through manipulation, military intimidation, patronage, and pay-offs.

It seems that around the world more decisions are made by government leaders to insinuate themselves and their bureaucracies as a partner, financier, or outright owner of formerly private corporations and enterprises, sometimes in joint ventures with labor unions. Often this insidious and growing "crony capitalism" is patterned after European corporatist-style industrial policies, hailed by their statist supporters as the "public–private" wave of the future. Yet these public–private partnerships are generally counterproductive. Despite their high-minded titles under the rubric of "Corporate Social Responsibility" they often end up nourishing a culture of cronyism.

It is instructive to study the countries where the MDGs have actually been realized most fully in the history of the world—the developed countries with high levels of economic freedom and low levels of corruption.

Why? Because those countries have the cultural and political institutions necessary for success that enshrine rule of law, secure private property rights, limit government, and keep taxes as low as possible. These are the policies and practices by which countries can bolster free markets and entrepreneurship, democratic governance, political stability, and prosperity.

According to The Heritage Foundation/*Wall Street Journal's* 2010 *Index of Economic Freedom*, the countries with greater improvements in economic freedom achieved much higher reductions in poverty.

Although the current and requested level of U.S. ODA is vastly more than it should be, the reality is that cutting $30 billion or $40 billion or $50 billion in foreign aid spending from the federal budget would not do much to reduce the U.S. deficit. But it should be done, since it is one of thousands of budget cuts that will be required to restore our country to long-term financial health. In my view, the only role for official U.S. government assistance should be "One Government" programs to achieve short-term U.S. national security objectives that are designed and implemented by fully integrated U.S. military and civilian agency teams.

And what of the $100+ billion per year in total ODA from developed countries? It is a paltry sum compared to the annual level of remittances, private capital investment, and trade flows in a world economy that is increasingly market-oriented and globalized. These private flows are the real source of economic growth and development. So I urge that ODA from all OECD countries be ended, too. Because ODA is not solving the problem of poverty in the world—it is actually blocking the long-term resolution of that problem.

The best thing the United States could do to help the developing world today would be to get its own financial house in order and regain its status as a role model for developing countries. Take the lead among OECD countries to end ineffective ODA programs. Instead, encourage more trade and investment, for example by approving pending Free Trade Agreements and negotiating more.

Drastic cuts must be made to government spending at all levels in the U.S. in order eventually to reduce deficits to zero, thereby making more capital available to the private sector and spurring a renewed level of economic growth in the U.S. and globally. The U.S. has been the largest source of foreign direct investment in developing countries and the largest recipient of developing country exports. That is the best model for sustainable development—through economic growth.

Thank you very much and I look forward to your questions.

James M. Roberts is a research fellow for economic growth and freedom at The Heritage Foundation. He previously served as a Foreign Service Officer in the U.S. Department of State.

EXPLORING THE ISSUE

Does Spending on Foreign Aid Further U.S. National Interests?

Critical Thinking and Reflection

1. In a time of fiscal austerity, should the United States continue to allocate funding for foreign aid? If so, how should foreign aid spending be prioritized?
2. What types of foreign aid should the United States invest in? Should the focus be on developmental, geopolitical, humanitarian, or military goals? Are these goals mutually exclusive?
3. Should U.S. foreign aid be limited to humanitarian assistance in times of crisis or disaster?
4. As a tool of foreign policy, has foreign aid increased or decreased in importance in recent years? Explain your answer.

Is There Common Ground?

In the lively debate still raging over foreign aid, almost all participants can find common ground in the idea that sustained economic growth in the developing world is in the national interest of the United States. In addition, all generally agree that progress will require a focus on economic growth. However, there are still significant differences in opinion over whether the United States has the ability and responsibility to foster this development. Some argue that the most important enablers of economic growth are fundamentally in the hands of the developing countries themselves. Only these countries can create and sustain the effective, transparent government institutions, rule of law, and infrastructure that will foster the development of local entrepreneurs and make their economies attractive places for foreign investment. On the other hand, members of the international development community and advocates of U.S. foreign aid argue that many countries cannot achieve these goals on their own. Developing countries need a helping hand from abroad to foster the conditions that will enable economic growth to occur.

In addition, there is common ground to be found in the idea that some foreign aid is appropriate and some programs do work. As an example, even foreign aid critic James Roberts sees a role for disaster relief in U.S. foreign policy and is in favor of narrowly targeted aid efforts designed to achieve short-term, national security–related purposes. However, this approach leaves the process of economic development almost entirely in the hands of the private sector and the developing countries themselves. Advocates of development assistance argue that this approach is not adequate to meet developing countries' needs and that the world's wealthy countries have an obligation to do more.

Finally, even advocates of U.S. foreign aid are not likely to advocate that such spending should be funded by increasing the U.S. deficit. Especially as the United States

continues to face budgetary constraints, policymakers will need to weigh carefully which foreign aid programs deserve continued investment. Since results are important, a similar level of effort is necessary to enable assessments of effectiveness over time.

Additional Resources

Easterly, William. "The Utopian Nightmare." *Foreign Policy* 150 (September/October 2005): 58–64.

Easterly argues that expectations that foreign aid can contribute to utopian goals such as ending poverty worldwide are simply unrealistic. Such utopian goals generally do more harm than good. Instead, the international aid community should focus on the development of specific programs that work.

Millennium Challenge Corporation (MCC). *MCC: A Gateway to Opportunity*. Washington, DC: The Millennium Challenge Corporation, 2012.

This 2011 annual report of the Millennium Challenge Corporation explains the efforts of this development initiative that is intended to reward performance and foster development through economic growth. It explains the categories of investment and results achieved, as well as agreements with specific countries.

This useful primer provides data on key issues associated with foreign aid, such as different types of aid, which states give foreign aid, and why donor states give. It argues that strategic and political interests are the dominant motivation in the provision of foreign aid and best explain who provides aid to which states.

Sachs, Jeffrey D. "The Development Challenge." *Foreign Affairs* 84, no. 2 (March/April 2005): 78–90.

The author of this article argues that while the United States has repeatedly declared its support for economic development initiatives, its actual actions have fallen far short of its rhetoric. The article concludes by listing four steps that the United States could take to live up to its commitments, which would not only improve its reputation internationally but would also better serve U.S. national security interests.

Tarnoff, Curtm and Marian Leonardo Lawson. *Foreign Aid: An Introduction to U.S. Programs and Policy* (Washington, DC: Congressional Research Service, February 10, 2011).

This study provides useful and comprehensive data about U.S. foreign aid, to include a portrayal of trends over time. It also points out that since the terrorist attacks against the United States on September 11, 2001, U.S. foreign aid has increasingly come to be seen as one of the three pillars—along with defense and diplomacy—of U.S. national security strategy.

United Nations. *The Millennium Development Goals Report 2012*. New York: United Nations, June 2012.

This report outlines the eight development goals agreed upon by world leaders in September 2000 and reports on progress toward their achievement.

World Bank. *The World Development Report 2012: Gender Equality and Development*. Washington, DC: The World Bank, 2011.

The annual reports of the World Bank are a valuable source of data on where countries around the world stand with regard to economic development In addition, they focus on a theme related to development that varies from year to year The 2012 report focuses on the role of women in economic development, explaining the status of gender equality in a comparative context and making recommendations on the way ahead.

Internet References . . .

Center for Global Development

Steven Radelet's Working Paper No. 92, "A Primer on Foreign Aid, July 2006," is available at the this link.

www.cgdev.org/files/8846_file_WP92.pdf

Selected, Edited, and with Issue Framing Material by:
Suzanne Nielsen, *U.S. Military Academy*
and
Scott Handler, *U.S. Military Academy*

ISSUE

Should the United States Continue a Strategy of State Building in Afghanistan?

YES: **Paul D. Miller,** from "Finish the Job: How the War in Afghanistan Can Be Won," *Foreign Affairs* (January/February 2011)

NO: **Joshua Rovner and Austin Long,** from *Dominoes on the Durand Line? Overcoming Strategic Myths in Afghanistan and Pakistan* (Cato Institute, June 14, 2011)

Learning Outcomes

After reading this issue, you should be able to:

- Explain different perspectives on what U.S. national interests are at stake in Afghanistan and how these interests can best be furthered.
- Understand the arguments for and against a significant U.S. investment in state building in Afghanistan.
- Articulate the advantages and possible risks associated with an approach toward Afghanistan that is narrowly focused on counterterrorism operations.
- Acknowledge the complexity of the security situation in Central and South Asia, and discuss the ways in which security challenges in Afghanistan and Pakistan are interrelated.

ISSUE SUMMARY

YES: Paul D. Miller, an assistant professor at the National Defense University, argues that the United States and its allies have made major gains in Afghanistan since 2010 that would be put at risk by a precipitous withdrawal of coalition forces. The counterinsurgency campaign should be continued, bolstered by greater civilian investments in governance. This approach will enable Afghanistan to build the political institutions necessary for development and long-term stability and security.

NO: Joshua Rovner, an assistant professor at the U.S. Naval War College, and Austin Long, an assistant professor at Columbia University, argue that the underlying assumptions driving U.S. efforts at state building in Afghanistan are wrong. State building is not necessary to prevent the reemergence of terrorist safe havens, nor is it necessary to prevent instability in Afghanistan from adversely affecting the political stability of neighboring, nuclear-armed Pakistan. The United States should focus more narrowly on counterterrorism objectives. Such a strategy would more effectively protect vital U.S. national security interests at lower cost.

Afghanistan was the first focus of U.S. national security decision makers after the devastating terrorist attacks against the United States on September 11, 2001. The Taliban regime in Afghanistan had been providing Al Qaeda with a safe haven, which Al Qaeda could use to plan, prepare, and orchestrate the execution of terrorist attacks. In the aftermath of 9/11, the United States quickly identified Osama bin Laden and his Al Qaeda organization as prime suspects. The United States acted on this assessment by making a series of demands to the Taliban, which included the turning over of key Al Qaeda leaders and the elimination of all terrorist camps in Afghanistan. After the Taliban refused these demands, the United States—in partnership with local forces—invaded and quickly overthrew the Taliban regime. Despite the amazing rapidity of these developments, it gradually became clear that the overthrow of the Taliban did not mean an end to conflict in Afghanistan.

Now, over a decade later, policy debates continue over appropriate U.S. strategy in Afghanistan. Some argue that investments in state building are necessary because only a stable government capable of protecting itself from external threats and exercising governance within its borders offers the promise of a long-term, sustainable solution. Without the development of institutions capable of governing effectively, going after terrorists can be like playing a game of "whack a mole." A specific target may be destroyed, but the organization itself will survive and individual members will be replaced. An even worse scenario is that the use of force for counterterrorism purposes could alienate the local population—perhaps through collateral damage—and expand the pool of potential recruits for the organization being targeted. Only comprehensive efforts at state building, which offer members of the local population security and the prospect of a better future, can address the problem of terrorism at the level of root causes.

Despite the merits of the case for state building, even advocates of this approach acknowledge that it is a challenging, resource-intensive, and long-term endeavor. In the first decade of its operations, for example, the United States has lost almost 2,000 troops in combat and spent $500 billion in Afghanistan (Belasco, 2011). The challenges are especially great in that country, which is one of the world's least developed countries, with a recent past that is dominated by armed conflict. In addition, the decision to invest in state building abroad comes with significant opportunity costs for the intervening party or parties; the resources devoted to state building in another country cannot be invested toward other national purposes abroad or at home. In light of the costs incurred and the necessity of sustained commitment, opponents of continued state building have argued for a narrower view of the United States' strategic interests focused on counterterrorism. This perspective has become increasingly salient in the U.S. foreign and security policy-making circles as the United States and many of its allies and coalition partners in Afghanistan face serious fiscal challenges and are still struggling to recover from one of the most severe economic recessions in recent history.

Others argue that state building in Afghanistan is not just too expensive; it is also both infeasible and unnecessary. Among the reasons that it may be considered infeasible are the following: The lack of legitimacy and corruption that plague the current government in Afghanistan are too great, the needed security forces are too unreliable and too expensive to be sustained, and there is insufficient political will in the intervening countries to sustain the needed long-term commitment. Others point to the importance of regional dynamics, arguing that until the countries in its region—with a special focus on Pakistan—have a greater interest in Afghanistan's success than they do its failure, efforts at state building will fail.

These arguments about infeasibility are sometimes coupled with arguments about strategic necessity. It is simply not necessary for the United States to engage in state building abroad to protect its vital national interests. If the United States wants to prevent Al Qaeda or other international terrorist organizations from enjoying safe havens in Afghanistan, it is most cost effective to focus U.S. investments on special operations forces, intelligence, and local security force capacity since these have the greatest potential to make direct contributions to counterterrorism objectives. By contrast, much of the money invested in infrastructure, schools, and so on, for the purposes of state building may end up wasted or only inefficiently—if at all—contributing to combating terrorism. Ineffective state building efforts can actually be counterproductive if they fuel local corruption or even put resources directly into the hands of terrorists or other nefarious actors.

When considering the strategic choices facing the United States in the near term, it is also useful to take recent historical context and domestic politics into account. Today's decisions about Afghanistan cannot be fully divorced from popular views of the U.S. war in Iraq, which many Americans see as having come with significant costs that were not balanced by commensurate strategic gains. In addition, as of the fall of 2012, the United States has been in Afghanistan for well over a decade. Those who would advocate greater investments must explain how their proposals will be more successful than those that have already been tried. On the other hand, those arguing for a reduced commitment face other challenges. The United States, along with its North Atlantic Treaty Organization allies and other coalition partners, has made significant sacrifices in blood and treasure to enable the mission in Afghanistan to succeed. Though it may not be fully rational to focus on sunk costs, they also are difficult to ignore fully. Finally, as is to be expected in a democracy, arguments relating to the way ahead in Afghanistan are politically contentious. While the idea of state building has its detractors, so does the idea of engaging in counterterrorism operations with no associated efforts to deal with the underlying social, economic, or political problems that make it easier for terrorists to operate.

In "Finish the Job," Paul Miller argues that a focus on state building is still the appropriate approach to addressing U.S. national security concerns in Afghanistan. He points out that it is important to start with an accurate picture of Afghanistan in 2001, which was then the world's "most failed state." Those who do not appreciate the desperate situation of Afghanistan in 2001 often fail to see the progress that has been made. Anticipating the critique that U.S. and coalition partners have been operating in Afghanistan for over a decade with little to show for their efforts, Miller also argues that a counterinsurgency approach has only recently been adopted and already has shown results. If the international community were to make investments in building institutional capacity in the Afghan government that are commensurate with the investment already made in fighting insurgents and building security forces, the war in Afghanistan could yet be won.

In "Dominoes on the Durand," Joshua Rovner and Austin Long broaden the lens somewhat by arguing that the key U.S. national security interests in the region include preventing Pakistani nuclear materials from falling into dangerous hands as well as preventing international terrorist organizations from acquiring safe havens in the region. They argue that neither of these objectives requires the United States to engage in a futile, expensive state-building effort in Afghanistan. The United States should scale back its ambitions in Afghanistan, greatly reducing its force presence and overall investment. A more focused counterterrorism strategy in Afghanistan—in combination with effective diplomatic engagement with Pakistan—will more effectively protect a clear-eyed view of vital U.S. interests at lower cost.

Few Americans were against the initial invasion of Afghanistan following Al Qaeda's attacks on 9/11, but the past decade of war has been costly. State building is expensive in terms of both time and resources. Today's policymakers must decide whether the benefits of such an approach justify the cost.

YES ↵

Paul D. Miller

Finish the Job: How the War in Afghanistan Can Be Won

Pessimism abounds in Afghanistan. Violence, NATO casualties, corruption, drug production, and public disapproval in the United States are at record levels. Ahmed Rashid, a prominent Pakistani journalist and an expert on the region, declared the U.S. mission in Afghanistan a failure in his scathing 2008 book, *Descent Into Chaos*. Seth Jones, the leading U.S. scholar on the Taliban insurgency, has argued that the United States had an opening to make a difference in Afghanistan after 2001, but that it "squandered this extraordinary opportunity." U.S. Secretary of Defense Robert Gates attempted to manage expectations when he testified before the Senate Armed Services Committee in January 2009. "If we set ourselves the objective of creating some sort of Central Asian Valhalla over there, we will lose," he argued, "because nobody in the world has that kind of time, patience, and money." U.S. policymakers and the public increasingly doubt that the war can be won. These assessments are based on real and credible concerns about the rising insurgency, the drug trade, endemic corruption, and perennial government weakness.

Yet the stabilization and reconstruction effort in Afghanistan has gone better than is widely believed. The pessimists fail to understand how badly the Afghan state had failed in 2001 and thus are blind to how much it has improved in many areas—particularly in economic and political reconstruction. The pessimists are right to be worried about the rise of the Taliban insurgency and the weak rule of law, but they also tend to overstate the competence and scale of the insurgency.

Many analysts critical of the war effort have drawn misguided lessons from cartoonish and caricatured versions of Afghan history—comparing ISAF to the armies of Alexander the Great, William Elphinstone, or Boris Gromov—to conclude that the laws of history bar foreign militaries from accomplishing anything in the land of the Hindu Kush. They sound dire warnings about U.S. and NATO staying power after a nine-year-old war. But they are wrong on all counts. The insurgency did not pick up steam until late 2005, and ISAF, which started changing its posture and strategy in late 2006, arguably did not implement a coherent counterinsurgency campaign until 2009. It would be myopic and irresponsible to conclude that the international community should walk away from the mission due to a lack of adequate progress.

The greatest threat to long-term success in Afghanistan is not the Taliban, who are fairly weak compared to other insurgent movements around the world. It is the Afghan government's endemic weakness and the international community's failure to address it. Although the international community helped rebuild economic institutions and infrastructure and facilitated elections, it did not invest significantly in government ministries, the justice system, the army and the police, or local governance for the first five years of the intervention, which permitted the Taliban to regroup and challenge the nascent Afghan government.

If additional U.S. and NATO soldiers are matched by a comparable civilian surge, a continuing donor commitment, and a heightened focus on capacity development—increasing the capabilities and performance of civilian institutions of governance, including the ministries in Kabul, their provincial counterparts, and the legal system—the international community is likely to achieve its core goals and Afghanistan will have a genuine chance of becoming stable for the first time in a generation. Although serious challenges remain, victory is attainable—if the troops and their civilian counterparts are given time to complete their mission.

The World's Worst Country

In 2001, Afghanistan was the world's most failed state. The security environment was anarchic, large-scale fighting against the Taliban and al Qaeda continued until March 2002, and following the fall of the Taliban, 50,000–70,000 Northern Alliance militiamen became a poorly managed, largely unaccountable force deployed across the country. There was no professional army or police force, leaving warlords to wage mini wars against one another. The United Nations judged in early 2002 that "banditry continues as a lingering manifestation of the war economy." The drug trade, suppressed during the Taliban's last year in power, sprang back into existence as the poppy crop expanded almost tenfold—from 20,000 acres to 183,000 acres—between 2001 and 2002. The resurgence of opium production enriched a new set of elites and created a wealthy criminal class that was neither loyal to Kabul nor cooperative with international forces. . . .

With an anarchic security situation and a nonfunctional state, the Afghan economy had collapsed by the end of the Taliban's misrule. Afghans were the world's seventh-poorest people in 2001. The International Monetary Fund estimates that in 2002, GDP per capita was about $176 in current U.S. dollars: Afghans lived on about 48 cents per day, comparable to the poorest people in sub-Saharan Africa. Lacking a national currency, different factions issued their own bills for use within their fiefdoms. What little infrastructure the country once had was in ruins: little more than a tenth of the roads were paved, less than one-third of Afghans had access to sanitation, and only a fifth had clean water. Economic collapse led to a generation of lost human capital. A third or less of Afghans could read and write, and only roughly a quarter of school-aged children were enrolled in the country's nearly defunct educational system. In a country of approximately 25 million people, there was just one TV station, eight airplanes, 60 trained pilots, and fewer than 50,000 passenger cars. . . .

Somalia is often cited as the archetype of a failed state. It is not. Despite Somalia's infamous anarchy, Somalis are still relatively free from government oppression and have not experienced ethnic cleansing or genocide. The Afghans, by contrast, had the worst of all worlds under the Taliban. They had Somalian anarchy, Haitian poverty, Congolese institutions, Balkan fractiousness, and a North Korean–style government. In January 2001, *The Economist* awarded Afghanistan the title of the world's "worst country." Any judgments about the international community's success or failure in Afghanistan need to begin with this benchmark.

A Delicate Constitution

. . . The UN, with U.S. help, convened a conference in Bonn, Germany, to select an interim administration and outline a process for reconstruction. The resulting Bonn agreement became a road map for establishing and legitimizing a new Afghan government. . . .

The Afghan people s reaction to the constitution was overwhelmingly positive. One member of the *loya jirga* (grand council of elders) convened to ratify the document said after voting for its approval that it was "99 percent based on the will of the people." A group calling itself the National Democratic Front and claiming to represent 47 interest groups endorsed the new constitution, as did a tribal gathering in the borderlands of Paktia Province, illustrating the document's broad base of support among both urban politicos and rural dwellers. Qala-e Naw, a major radio station, rejoiced that Afghans would now enjoy the same rights as the rest of the world.

After the constitution was ratified, the international community funded and administered a voter registration drive and two elections: over eight million Afghans voted in the nation's first-ever presidential contest in October 2004, and 6.4 million voted for the nation's legislature in September 2005—Afghanistan's first freely elected legislature since 1973. In 2006, Freedom House upgraded the country to "partly free," and 76 percent of those Afghans surveyed said they were satisfied with democracy, according to the Asia Foundation. Afghans' enthusiastic embrace of voting, representative institutions, and majority rule undermined the arguments of critics who claimed that democracy was an alien transplant doomed to fail in inhospitable Afghan soil. But the success of the Bonn process was not a foregone conclusion. Similar UN-sponsored processes in postconflict countries have collapsed and led to renewed violence, including in Angola and Liberia in the 1990s. It succeeded in Afghanistan because of strong international engagement and support at every stage of the process.

Afghans continue to face challenges in their effort to institutionalize a process of peaceful political competition. The 2009 and 2010 elections were notoriously marred by fraud and low turnout. But it is important to note that power brokers, accustomed to enforcing their writ undemocratically, decided to manipulate the electoral system to serve their own interests rather than ignore it altogether, because they recognized that Afghans now embrace the new democratic constitution as the basis for their state's legitimacy. The international community must pressure the Afghan government to crack down on corruption and develop robust political parties. But to declare total failure is to ignore Afghanistan's political transformation.

Rebuilding Prosperity

IN RESPONSE to the economic and humanitarian emergency in Afghanistan in 2001, the international community undertook one of the largest and most ambitious relief, reconstruction, and development efforts in the world—eventually committing a total of $18.4 billion in aid to economic reconstruction, economic development, and humanitarian relief between 2001 and 2009. . . .

The result was an unheralded and dramatic success. Partly because of U.S. and international aid, Afghanistan experienced a post-Taliban economic boom. Real GDP grew by nearly 29 percent in 2002 alone—faster than West Germany in 1946—and averaged 15 percent annual licit growth from 2001 to 2006, making Afghanistan one of the fastest-growing economies in the world (it was still averaging 13.5 percent through 2009, after a drought in 2008). The pace of its growth was due in part to the low base from which it had started, but the rapid pace itself was an important achievement. Afghanistan had not grown significantly in more than two decades; the economic boom signaled a new era in Afghan life.

Between 2001 and 2009, almost every indicator of human development showed measurable improvement. By late 2008, 80 percent of the population had access to basic health services, up from eight percent in 2001. Also by 2008, Afghan children were being immunized against diphtheria, pertussis, and tetanus (DPT) at the same rate as children in the rest of the world and at a higher rate than in the rest of South Asia. The infant mortality rate fell by a third, and life expectancy inched upward. After the fall of the Taliban, school enrollment skyrocketed from 1.1 million students in 2001 to 5.7 million students in 2008—a third of whom were girls—promising to double or triple Afghanistan's literacy rate in a decade.

Meanwhile, infrastructure greatly improved with international help. The U.S. Agency for International Development (USAID) built 1,600 miles of roads, and the international community rebuilt three-quarters of the main highway from Herat to Kabul. In total, almost 33 percent of all roads in the country were paved by 2008, up from 13.3 percent in 2001. By 2008, Afghanistan had caught up to its regional and income cohorts in access to telecommunications—an astonishing feat. The cell-phone industry, nonexistent before 2001, had nearly eight million subscribers by the end of 2008. . . .

The impressive growth and improvement since 2001—stronger than in any postconflict state in which the UN has deployed a peace-building mission since the end of the Cold War—demonstrate that progress is achievable with robust resources and international attention. Aid dependency and a poorly diversified economy threaten Afghanistan's long-term economic stability, but the greater risk is that the country's recent progress will unravel unless security is greatly improved.

The UN's Blind Spot

. . . Because the United States and the UN could not confront the warlords directly without risking violence, they had to coax them into giving up their weapons by promising them a place in the new Afghan political order. The warlords thus made a successful entry into Afghan politics as governors, legislators, and cabinet ministers without ever facing prosecution or even a truth commission for alleged war crimes. In hindsight, nearly all scholars and commentators condemn the international community for allowing the warlords to retain power. Yet these same critics often deride the reverse strategy of building up a central government at the expense of local power brokers. After the fall of the Taliban, the international community attempted to navigate between these competing imperatives—disarming the warlords without unleashing a backlash and building a central government while respecting local authority. The result has been imperfect but better than permitting the warlords to retain their conventional military power, on the one hand, or risking violence by attempting to put them on trial, on the other.

Despite its success against the warlords, the international community failed to train enough new Afghan security forces or successfully contain the residual Taliban threat between 2001 and 2006. Early efforts to train Afghan police and reform the security sector had not achieved notable results by 2006. Washington had spent $4.4 billion on security assistance and had trained 36,000 soldiers and a comparable number of police officers in the first five years—too few to provide effective security. The police, moreover, were widely reported to be corrupt and

incompetent. At the same time, ISAF did not hold large swaths of territory or provide security to the vast majority of Afghans. Indeed, it did not have the mandate or the authorization to do so.

ISAF was relatively small in size, it was initially confined to Kabul, and it was hampered by restrictive rules of engagement and national caveats limiting where the soldiers were permitted to deploy or what kinds of operations they were allowed to engage in. (In 2003, the peacekeeping force had only 5,500 troops assigned to it.) Then, in 2005, ISAF was authorized to operate in the country's northern and western provinces, but it still numbered fewer than 10,000 troops, or four soldiers for every 10,000 Afghans (compared to approximately 42 soldiers per 10,000 civilians in the relatively successful UN-British operation in Sierra Leone in 2002). . . .

The Taliban were able to regroup and launch an insurgency because, effectively, nothing stood in their way. The Afghan government was still unable to offer services or resolve disputes, and there were too few international soldiers to secure the whole country. The state's institutional capacity remained weak, the rule of law was nonexistent, and the security services were still embryonic. "Weak governance is a common precondition of insurgencies," writes Jones, the Afghanistan expert; "Afghan insurgent groups took advantage of this anarchic situation."

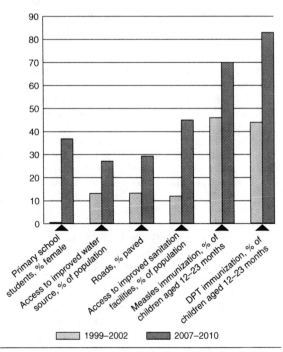

Development Indicators in Afghanistan

Sources: Central Statistics Organization of Afghanistan, World Bank, and World Health Organization.

Critics are right to argue that the rise of the insurgency is proof that the international state-building campaign had, as of 2006, failed to build a functioning Afghan state. But the intervention did not end in 2006. A U.S. National Security Council review of Afghan policy in late 2006 recognized the emerging challenges and called for substantially more security and development assistance. Following the review, U.S. funding for the Afghan security forces nearly quadrupled, from $1.9 billion in 2006 to $7.4 billion in 2007, and aggregate U.S. spending on security assistance increased fivefold. Starting in late 2007, entire district police units were sent to a training academy, and U.S. trainers were assigned to embed with each unit on graduation. In addition, the international community began experimenting with programs to enlist the aid of local, indigenous, and tribal security forces.

To staff the expanded training programs and provide security while the Afghan forces were coming up to speed, the United States more than quadrupled its military presence in Afghanistan between 2006 and 2010, from 22,100 troops to over 100,000—Washington's third-largest military deployment since Vietnam. Partner nations increased their troop deployments as well, from roughly 21,500 in early 2007 to 35,800 by the end of 2009. ISAF deployed nationwide in 2006, assuming responsibility for security assistance in the country's east and south for the first time. General Stanley McChrystal, who was then the commander of ISAF, also began in 2009 to change how U.S. and NATO troops were used. He sought to make the entirety of ISAF a part of the training and mentoring of the Afghan army and police and to focus on protecting the Afghan population. The moves collectively represented a huge shift in emphasis from a "light footprint" counterterrorism mission to a more robust, if still partial, counterinsurgency campaign. As a result, the United States nearly tripled the size of the Afghan army in three years, increasing it from 36,000 soldiers in 2006 to almost 100,000 by the end of 2009. It brought the Afghan police force up to its authorized strength of 82,000 and made incremental progress toward improving its capabilities.

Rising violence and the persistence of a Taliban safe haven in Pakistan have bred pessimism about the war and created a mystique about the resilience of the insurgency. Violence has indeed continued to escalate—insurgents initiated an average of 19 attacks per day in 2007, almost 30 per day in 2008, and 52 per day from January to August of 2009—but the spike in violence is a predictable effect of sending more troops into battle; there are more targets for the insurgents to attack. What matters is not the scale of the violence but the outcome of the battle. While ISAF has made impressive strides in its practice of unconventional warfare, the Taliban have not. The Taliban are not invincible superwarriors hardened by millennia of fighting and xenophobia; indeed, they are hardly even very competent insurgents compared to Nepal's Maoists, Sri Lanka's Tamil Tigers, or Colombia's FARC. They continue to espouse an unpopular extremist ideology and murder large numbers

of fellow Pashtun Muslims. Meanwhile, Washington's rumored recent expansion of its drone strikes will erode their safe haven in Pakistan. The single greatest resource the United States now needs is not more troops but more time.

The Governance Vacuum

IN ONE respect, the effort in Afghanistan has seriously faltered. The international community has largely stuck with a failing light-footprint approach toward Afghan governance and capacity development. Partly in reaction to the recent UN missions in Kosovo and East Timor, which were criticized for relying too heavily on experts from abroad, the UN secretary-general publicly and openly instructed UNAMA to "rely on as limited an international presence and on as many Afghan staff as possible." UN officials never considered whether the Afghans, whose human capital had been destroyed by war and depleted by emigration, were able to do the job.

Donors similarly neglected governance programs. They pledged a total of $1.2 billion for Afghan governance and rule-of-law programs between 2001 and 2006, or about $200 million per year, and only disbursed about half that amount. A substantial amount of this was dedicated to the 2004 and 2005 elections, leaving just a few hundred million dollars to train civil servants, judges, prosecutors, and lawyers; rebuild government offices and courthouses; and pay the international advisers and consultants to ministers and other government officials. Considering that Afghanistan was the weakest state in the world in 2001, these funds did not come close to meeting its needs. The international community was effectively asking Afghans with no shoes to lift themselves up by their bootstraps.

For example, a proposed Independent Administrative Reform and Civil Service Commission was supposed to lead efforts to streamline the bureaucracy, introduce a new pay and grade system, develop merit-based hiring and promotion criteria, and establish a civil service training institute. For this ambitious agenda, the Asian Development Bank gave $2.2 million starting in 2003, and the UN Development Program gave $500,000. A 2007 USAID review of capacity-development efforts in Afghanistan concluded that "capacity building has not been a primary objective of USAID projects" and that "what has occurred has been more ad hoc and 'spotty' rather than systematic and strategic." The review could identify only four ministries out of 25 that were "considered reasonably competent to carry out their primary responsibilities." The Afghan Research and Evaluation Unit, a nongovernmental organization, judged in late 2006 that public-administration reform had been "'cosmetic,' with superficial restructuring of ministries and an emphasis on higher pay rather than fundamental change." The Civil Service Commission did not open until January 2007, and after five years in power, the government could boast of only 7,500 civil servants hired under the new merit-based criteria in a government of 240,000 employees.

Similarly, the international community did not prioritize rebuilding the justice system or improving the rule of law. The U.S. Department of State's Bureau of International Narcotics and Law Enforcement Affairs and USAID did initiate a host of programs, but in practice they were too small to make a measurable difference in the worst justice system in the world. The Afghan government estimated that it would cost $600 million to implement its National Justice Sector Strategy, but donors had disbursed just $38 million in aid to the justice sector by the end of 2006. The UN secretary-general wrote that same year that "with approximately 1,500 judges and 2,000 prosecutors in the judicial system, demand for training far outstrips supply."

As a result of these shortcomings, Afghanistan ranked second worst in the world for the rule of law in 2006, after Somalia, according to the World Bank's governance indicators. Without the rule of law, corruption predictably exploded as the economy grew. As the political scientist Samuel Huntington noted long ago, modernization without strong institutions almost always yields corruption, and Afghanistan was no exception.

Corruption was increasingly fueled by the drug trade. The poppy crop had soared to 408,000 acres in 2006 and 477,000 in 2007, and Afghanistan was producing 82 percent of the world's poppy and 93 percent of the world's heroin by 2007, making the drug trade worth $4 billion—equivalent to half of Afghanistan's licit GDP. Because the Afghan government lacked strong institutions and the ability to enforce the rule of law, Afghanistan was becoming a lawless and corrupt narcostate.

When the crisis in governance became apparent with the rise of the Taliban insurgency in 2005 and 2006, the international community moved to bolster its governance programs. In dollar terms, the international community roughly doubled its training efforts in the Afghan civil administration and justice sectors, to $688 million, over the next three years, still a paltry figure relative to Afghanistan's needs. In 2007, USAID started the Capacity Development Program, a $219 million, five-year project to strengthen Afghan institutions such as the Ministries of Finance and Education and the Civil Service Commission. The program was a big improvement but still small in absolute terms. U.S. spending on rule-of-law programs doubled from 2006 to 2007 and nearly doubled again in 2008. The United States also doubled its much more substantial investment in counternarcotics programs—to $3.3 billion. The increased focus on governance and the rule of law spurred some institutional innovations in the Afghan government, but they have, to date, failed to markedly improve the quality of governance. Afghan President Hamid Karzai named an entirely new slate of justices to the Supreme Court in late 2006. The new court established a Regulation of Judicial Conduct, and the new justices began inspection tours of provincial courts to ensure their compliance with judicial standards. The Afghan government formed an anti-corruption unit in the attorney general's office in 2009 to investigate and prosecute cases of high-level corruption, but Afghanistan fell further on Transparency International's Corruption Perceptions Index, to 179th—second from the bottom—in 2009. According to a survey conducted by ABC News, the BBC, and the German television station ARD, the number of Afghans who believed the government was doing an excellent or good job fell from 80 percent in 2005 to 49 percent in 2008—most likely because their great expectations of 2001 remained unfulfilled.

The international community paid an enormous opportunity cost by failing to play a greater role and provide sufficient resources from the start. Most observers of Afghan governance focus on Karzai's policies, behavior, and fitness for office. But any other Afghan president would face a nearly insurmountable challenge trying to enact policy through an institutional apparatus that, for all intents and purposes, does not function. Others have focused on how centralized or decentralized, institutionalized or tribalized, the Afghan government should be. But that argument is moot. The international community's interest is in making governance effective, whatever it looks like, and that is what the international community failed to invest in building after 2001.

The Road to Victory

THE UNITED STATES is not yet winning the war in Afghanistan, but it is not losing as swiftly or as thoroughly as the current crisis of confidence would suggest. Although Afghanistan remains poor, violent, and poorly governed, it is richer, freer, and safer than it has been in a generation. The security situation is a major challenge, but the United States and its allies have moved since 2006 to adopt a much more aggressive military posture in response—and with the funding to match it.

The application of increased military resources and a coherent strategy almost certainly will have an effect on the Afghan battlefield if given enough time to succeed and backed by a complimentary civilian strategy. In particular, U.S. President Barack Obama should show the same flexibility toward his announced July 2011 withdrawal date that he showed toward his initial timeline for withdrawal from Iraq. He wisely announced that the withdrawal will only "begin" in July 2011, leaving open the door for a gradual and phased withdrawal. He should seize on that to give ISAF the time it needs, now that it finally, for the first time in nine years, has adequate resources.

The single greatest strategic threat is the weakness of the Afghan government. Efforts in recent years to increase the size and scope of governance-assistance efforts are a welcome gesture, but they are not enough. The Obama administration should push for a dramatically more ambitious capacity-development program, starting with a much larger civilian presence in the Afghan bureaucracy and court system. Washington should also recognize that it can choose to withdraw from Afghanistan quickly at high risk or slowly at low risk. The programs, budgets, and strategies that are now finally in place have only been operating for a few years; it is unlikely that there will be dramatic progress by July 2011. The Obama administration has calculated that some degree of withdrawal is necessary to pressure the Afghan government, but it should be wary lest a precipitous withdrawal lead to panic in Afghanistan, undoing a decade of careful gains.

If the international community had withdrawn from Afghanistan shortly after the initial round of elections in 2004–5, as it did in Cambodia, Haiti, and Liberia in the 1990s, the intervention would have failed. Governance had not improved, and most important, war had resumed. Remarkably, the international community did not seize on the completion of the Bonn process as a chance to declare victory and withdraw. Reflecting a realism and resilience evident in other recent operations—such as in Sierra Leone in 2002 and Iraq in 2007—international actors recognized

the emerging problems and attempted a midcourse correction. They did so in part because prior experiences in Afghanistan had demonstrated that success was possible. The same knowledge should help the United States and its partners overcome the current crisis of confidence.

The Afghan mission is still plagued with difficulties, in particular endemically weak institutions and a poor governance-assistance effort. But recent history has shown that, contrary to popular belief, outsiders can make a positive difference in Afghanistan if given the right time, resources, and leadership.

PAUL D. MILLER is an assistant professor of international security studies at the National Defense University. He previously served as a director for Afghanistan on the National Security Council staff.

Joshua Rovner and Austin Long    **NO**

Dominoes on the Durand Line?
Overcoming Strategic Myths in
Afghanistan and Pakistan

Introduction

Since the beginning of Operation Enduring Freedom, policymakers have emphasized two basic national security interests at stake in Afghanistan. The first is preventing al Qaeda and its Taliban allies from reestablishing a safe haven. The second is preventing the violence in Afghanistan from destabilizing Pakistan, thus putting its nuclear forces at risk and increasing the likelihood of nuclear terrorism. Coalition strategy is based on the assumptions that the only way to deny al Qaeda safe haven is by building a strong central Afghan state and that Pakistan's nuclear complex will become increasingly vulnerable to militant attacks if the Taliban succeeds in Afghanistan.

Both assumptions are wrong. The United States does not need to build a state in Afghanistan because the conditions that allowed al Qaeda safe haven in the 1990s have permanently changed. Moreover, the steps needed to help Pakistan secure its nuclear arsenal have nothing to do with the war in Afghanistan. Nonetheless, we continue to operate on the bases of these mistaken beliefs, and the result is that American strategy has become incoherent.

State Building Is Not Needed

State building has been fundamental to U.S. efforts since at least 2004. The logic is simple: failure to build a viable state that can exert control over the whole of the country will provide terrorists and insurgents a sanctuary from which to plot attacks against the United States and its allies. State building is also critical, the argument goes, because the United States cannot leave Afghanistan if it believes the government will quickly crumble thereafter. Success in the long term, we are told, is only possible if Kabul becomes legitimate in the eyes of the people and builds enough strength to tackle the Taliban anywhere in the country.

This argument is doctrinaire for large swaths of the U.S. foreign policy establishment. Policymakers have clung to the seductive logic of state building as the antidote to terrorist safe-havens. President Bush, who was

skeptical about state building before taking office, quickly changed gears in the aftermath of the 9/11 attacks. When asked about his previous doubts during the early days of the war in Afghanistan, Bush replied, "We've got to work for a stable Afghanistan so that her neighbors don't fear terrorist activity again coming out of that country."[1] The president never wavered from this basic position, and his critics argued that he should have done more to help build capacity in Kabul.

The Obama administration has also operated according to the belief that state building and counterterrorism are inseparable. The administration's recent National Security Strategy is quite clear: "In Afghanistan, we must deny al-Qaida a safe haven, deny the Taliban the ability to overthrow the government, and strengthen the capacity of Afghanistan's security forces and government so that they can take lead responsibility for Afghanistan's future."[2] At the same time, the administration has pledged to start withdrawing forces in 2011. Thus its strategy takes for granted that state building is necessary and assumes that it can be done relatively quickly.

But state building is a long, difficult, bloody affair. Political leaders in pre-modern societies are essentially gangsters who establish local control by running small protection rackets, using petty extortion to buy arms and rent mercenaries. As they carve out larger chunks of territory, they come into conflict with rival warlords. Those conflicts escalate into violent confrontation and war, which require higher taxes and more efficient organization. In Europe, the victors in this centuries-long evolutionary process sat atop organizations that resembled modern nation-states.[3] In Afghanistan, this process is still in its early days.

Trying to build someone else's state is even more difficult, and the United States has a decidedly mixed record in external state building.[4] Its most prominent success story, the decades-long postwar reconstruction of Germany and Japan, suggests that success requires a staggering investment of time and resources. Those successes also suggest that the process is most likely to work when new states are built upon existing social and political institutions.

In both Germany and Japan, U.S. officials reluctantly set aside plans for recrimination against thousands of fascist bureaucrats, instead co-opting their support in building new democratic governments.[5]

Unfortunately, the necessary ingredients for successful state building—time, money, and existing institutions— are in desperately short supply in Afghanistan. Public and congressional opposition to the war is rising in the United States, and the Obama administration has already announced it will scale back the U.S. commitment beginning next year. In addition, Afghanistan's political and economic institutions are extremely weak. The fledgling government has had enormous difficulty expanding control outside of Kabul. The judiciary, which is notoriously inefficient, competes in many places with a shadow Taliban court system.[6] Economic institutions remain fragile at best; witness the recent run on the Kabul Bank.[7] For all of these reasons, the U.S. desire to build a strong and legitimate government in Afghanistan is not practical.

The good news is that it is not necessary. The United States can achieve its most important objectives in Afghanistan without continuing its costly and quixotic statebuilding effort. As we describe in more detail below, U.S. forces can pursue al Qaeda and minimize the terrorist threat without establishing a government that can control most or all of the country's territory.

A state-building failure would not mean victory for al Qaeda or the Taliban. Even if the United States substantially reduces its ground forces in Afghanistan and the Kabul government remains weak and ineffectual, al Qaeda would not be able to recreate anything like the safe haven it once enjoyed. The original circumstances that made sanctuary possible no longer exist today. In the 1990s there was little domestic support for aggressive U.S. counterterrorism operations abroad, and the Clinton administration debated at length whether to strike large al Qaeda training camps. Today there would be little debate; indeed, the Obama administration would surely welcome the opportunity to conduct strikes against well-defined terrorist strongholds without having to cross over into Pakistan. The Afghan Taliban, which by now is very familiar with U.S. air power, has much to lose by inviting al Qaeda back.[8] As the Afghanistan Study Group aptly concludes, senior al Qaeda leaders "will likely have to remain in hiding for the rest of their lives, which means Al Qaeda will have to rely on clandestine cells instead of large encampments."[9]

The U.S. military has recently demonstrated the vulnerability of al Qaeda in Afghanistan. In the Korengal Valley of eastern Afghanistan, an area where the United States has withdrawn conventional forces, al Qaeda attempted to reestablish a training camp in 2010. It was subsequently struck by U.S. aircraft, resulting in the deaths of dozens of al Qaeda affiliates, including two senior leaders.[10] Some observers interpret this as demonstrating that al Qaeda will find sanctuary where U.S. conventional forces are absent, yet it actually demonstrates that U.S. intelligence collection and ability to strike are substantial, even in areas without conventional forces on the ground.

Nor will Afghan militants be eager to provide refuge for the Pakistani Taliban.[11] The reason is that not all safe havens are created equal. The Afghan Taliban enjoy some measure of sanctuary in Pakistan because Afghan militants receive support from the Pakistani Inter-Services Intelligence Directorate (ISI). Even al Qaeda enjoys a certain amount of safety there due to the limits of Pakistani willingness to allow U.S. operations on Pakistani territory. To be sure, the operation to kill Osama bin Laden shows that no sanctuary is absolute. But bin Laden was the highest of high-value targets, and the Obama administration acted only after months of painstaking intelligence work and policy deliberation. Moreover, al Qaeda operatives still residing in Pakistan may believe that they can wait out the United States before it leaves the region. Pakistani militants, on the other hand, are enemies of the Pakistani state, which is not going anywhere. If the Afghan Taliban succeeded in retaking part or all of Afghanistan, it would risk losing ISI support if it offered a substantial sanctuary to Pakistan's enemies. It is possible that some members of the Pakistani groups might find shelter there, but the Afghan militants would have a strong incentive to ensure that their numbers remained low enough to be plausibly deniable to the ISI.

And even if the Afghan militants are foolish enough to grant safe haven to substantial numbers of Pakistani militants, the protection they offer will be qualitatively different from the sanctuary currently enjoyed by Afghan militants in Pakistan. The sanctuary in Pakistan derives from the existence of a Pakistani state and, more importantly, a nuclear-armed Pakistani military.

Attacking Afghan militants on Pakistani soil without permission would be an act of war. Moreover, the United States receives Pakistan's help with intelligence collection along the border region and elsewhere. This means U.S. officials have large incentives to negotiate with the government before conducting operations in Pakistan. Because of the significant risks involved, the United States usually reserves unilateral actions for extraordinary cases. (Witness the lengthy debate that preceded the bin Laden mission and the visible nervousness of administration officials in photographs released by the White House shortly after it was over.) Drone strikes are only allowed in certain areas and ground force operations are apparently not allowed (or are so covert as to be invisible).[12] Paradoxically, Afghan militants have a fairly robust sanctuary from U.S. forces only because of the mixed interests of America's ally.

In contrast, who would stop the Pakistani military from acting in Afghanistan if its proxies harbored substantial numbers of Pakistani militants? If the United States withdrew from Afghanistan and the Kabul government collapsed, the answer is nobody. Pakistan could take covert or overt military action at will or could find new proxies. Indeed, the Taliban was created by ISI when its old proxies proved unable to secure Afghanistan.[13] The fact that ISI created the Taliban provides yet another reason to believe that few if any of the Afghan proxies of the ISI would shelter large numbers of Pakistan's enemies. To do so would put them between the devil and the deep blue sea, with the Pakistani military playing the part of the sea and the Tajiks, Uzbeks, and Hazaras of Afghanistan (the old Northern Alliance) in the role of the devil. These latter groups fought the Taliban before September 11, 2001, reportedly with aid from Russia, Iran, and India.[14] They would certainly fight on after a U.S. withdrawal in much the same way. Only ISI support enabled the Afghan Taliban to succeed in the 1990s; if Pakistan was actually fighting against them, they would be in serious trouble.

The upshot of this analysis is that state building is not necessary to succeed in Afghanistan. The decline of the central state will not lead to a domino effect in the region. Al Qaeda will not be able to recreate its old safe haven there even if the government collapses. Pakistani militants will not find reliable sanctuary either, regardless of what happens in Kabul. Rather than investing heavily in state building, the United States can achieve its interests by streamlining its counterterrorism campaign. It does not need to become mired in the bloody business of Afghanistan's political evolution.

Loose Talk about Loose Nukes

American leaders also claim that losing the war in Afghanistan will destabilize Pakistan, thus putting its nuclear forces at risk. According to the Obama administration, "The ability of extremists in Pakistan to undermine Afghanistan is proven, while insurgency in Afghanistan feeds instability in Pakistan. The threat that al Qaeda poses to the United States and our allies in Pakistan—including the possibility of extremists obtaining fissile material—is all too real."[15]

Prominent conservatives agree. An open letter to the president, signed by, among others, Sarah Palin and Robert Kagan, concludes that the "abandonment of Afghanistan would further destabilize the region, and put neighboring Pakistan and its nuclear arsenal at risk. All our efforts to support Islamabad's fight against the Taliban in Pakistan's tribal regions will founder if we do not match those achievements on the other side of that country's porous northwestern border."[16]

Both of these pronouncements echo the conventional wisdom that the war is intrinsically linked to the prevention of nuclear terrorism. Casual arguments along these lines are now commonplace, and they are almost never challenged. In reality, success or failure against the Afghanistan Taliban will not affect the security of Pakistan's nuclear arsenal. The issues are unrelated.

The logic behind the administration's concern is that militants will have a better chance of acquiring nuclear weapons if they operate from a secure foothold. The stronger the Taliban become in Afghanistan, the more dangerous they will become to Pakistan. And because political instability in Afghanistan is likely to spill across the border, the government in Islamabad will be less capable of stopping them.[17]

This logic is wrong. For the reasons discussed above, fear of a safe haven in Afghanistan is wildly exaggerated. Afghan militants may find some protection from U.S. forces by hiding in Pakistan, but Pakistani militants will find no similar refuge in an Afghanistan dominated by Islamic militants. The argument about a spillover effect is based on some unspecified notion about the causes of political instability; it imagines that Pakistani institutions will become weaker through some kind of cross-border osmosis. This modern version of the domino theory ignores the fact that the root causes of Pakistani instability are found in Pakistan, not across the border.

Nonetheless, recent attacks against Pakistan's military and nuclear complex have led to fresh concerns about the security of its technology and fissile material. In addition to the bombing of a bus full of workers from the Kahuta Research Laboratories in 2008, militants also launched rockets at suspected nuclear facilities. In the aftermath of the attacks, one observer concluded that a nuclear-armed Taliban "may not be as far-fetched as it might first appear."[18]

Yet closer examination of these attacks shows that the complex itself, much less the weapons, was never in any great danger. Two suicide bombings led to fears that facility defenses were vulnerable, but in both cases the outer perimeter held. In at least one case, the rest of the sprawling facility was immediately locked down when the attack happened.[19]

Rather than attacking facilities directly, militants could conceivably try to intercept weapons or fissile material in transit.[20] So far, none of the Pakistani groups have shown anything close to the sophistication and resources needed to pull off such an audacious attack. In any case, a safe haven far away in Afghanistan would not help militants seeking to mass forces inside Pakistan to intercept nuclear weapons.

A more realistic danger is that officials, scientists, or technicians in the Pakistani nuclear infrastructure will help al Qaeda covertly acquire nuclear material and technology. Among proliferation analysts, insider-outsider collusion is the scenario that appears to cause the most concern. The fact that A.Q. Khan, the father of the Pakistani nuclear program, was able to operate a semi-private proliferation network raises concerns that Pakistan still might be unable to control prominent officials within its own nuclear establishment. Moreover, clever officials may discover new ways of forging links with nonstate actors. In the 1990s, for example, senior Pakistani nuclear scientists founded the Umma-Tameer-e-Nau (UTN), a nongovernmental organization that provided cover for contacts between nuclear specialists and al Qaeda leaders.[21]

Other factors increase the risk of insideroutsider collusion. Rising anti-American sentiment within Pakistan might cause insiders to become radicals. Ominous trends in Pakistani public opinion could make it more difficult for the Pakistani government to reliably screen new hires. Analysts have speculated about creeping "Islamization" in the officer corps, which would also make it more likely that militant sympathizers could find their way into positions of authority in the nuclear establishment.[22] . . .

At this point it is worth reiterating that none of these problems has anything to do with the war in Afghanistan. Put simply, the United States does not need to fight in Afghanistan in order to keep nuclear weapons away from terrorists. There are better ways to reduce the risk of nuclear theft at relatively low cost. Increased technical assistance, along with quiet efforts to shore up Pakistan's recent organizational and personnel reforms, will go far to mitigate the danger of insider-outsider collusion. Diplomatic efforts on the subcontinent will also reduce the risk of crises, buying time for Pakistan to implement security reforms and prepare for contingencies. But given the undercurrent of anti-American sentiment in Pakistan which is fueled by the large U.S. military presence in the region, the United States must be careful to assist without provoking a hostile response. Overly intrusive measures and misguided rhetoric are likely to be counterproductive.

Above all, the United States must be patient. U.S. leaders typically fear the emergence of new nuclear powers because they are untested and possibly unreliable custodians of those weapons. They also worry that proliferation begets proliferation: one country's nuclear breakthrough will lead to local arms racing and a period of severe regional instability. Happily, the worst of these fears have never been realized, in part because of methodical diplomatic efforts to alleviate the concerns of emerging nuclear powers and their neighbors. U.S. efforts to facilitate better relations between India and Pakistan might be the most important element in securing Pakistan's arsenal. Routine diplomacy will buy time for Pakistan to implement and improve its security procedures by reducing the frequency of crises. A more low key and patient approach will also cut against the conspiracy theories that underpin extremist rhetoric, making insider-outsider collusion more unlikely.

The problem is that none of this will be done quickly, and the United States is under terrific pressure to change its strategic approach in the region. Of the challenges in U.S. strategy in South Asia, remaining patient might prove the hardest task of all.

Less Is More

The current U.S. strategy, a counterinsurgency and state-building hybrid, is based on weak assumptions. It is also costly in terms of blood and treasure. Between December 2009 and April 2011, 639 U.S. personnel were killed in Afghanistan.[23] Some will argue that this is a remarkably low number of fatal casualties, particularly when compared to other U.S. conflicts such as Vietnam. While true in a sense, this cost is still not trivial. Moreover, the combination of U.S. technologies from medical advances to precision firepower that enables this lower level of fatalities is incredibly expensive. Estimates indicate that each U.S. service member in Afghanistan costs between $500,000 and $1,200,000 annually.[24] With just under 100,000 troops in Afghanistan the bill will range between $50 billion and over $100 billion per year.[25] The United States is pursuing a costly strategy in Afghanistan that is unnecessary for securing vital U.S. interests in that country.

No matter how many troops the United States dispatches to Afghanistan, at least half of the problem remains across the border in Pakistan and is largely off limits. It is there, in Pakistan's tribal areas, that al Qaeda senior leadership has found sanctuary. Yet despite the limitations on sending troops to Pakistan, the United States has been able to disrupt al Qaeda with covert intelligence collection and drone strikes while seeking to bolster Pakistani security forces.

While U.S. strategy in Pakistan is not perfect, it is astronomically less expensive than the U.S. strategy in Afghanistan. If a similar strategy in Afghanistan, which we term the counterterrorism option, could prevent al Qaeda from enjoying safe haven, then it would be both cheaper and, as a result, more sustainable. The latter is becoming particularly important as the U.S. public becomes increasingly disillusioned with large-scale counterinsurgency in Afghanistan. A poll in July 2010 found that 76 percent of respondents thought the United States should begin to withdraw from Afghanistan in the summer of 2011 or sooner.[26] A March 2011 poll indicated that 73 percent of Americans thought that the United States should "withdraw a substantial number of U.S. combat forces from Afghanistan this summer" (although only 39 percent expected that Washington would do so).[27]

The counterterrorism option would require an ongoing U.S. presence in Afghanistan but at a much lower level than at present. U.S. conventional forces would begin to draw down in the summer of 2011 as per the president's announced timeline. By the end of 2012 the vast bulk of U.S. forces would be withdrawn. Special operations forces would remain in substantial numbers, with one set of special operators focused on targeting al Qaeda members seeking to return to Afghanistan. These operators would be based at airfields in the south and east of the country. They would be supported by a modest conventional force equivalent to a few battalions, principally for quick reaction. Another set of special operators, principally but not exclusively U.S. Army Special Forces, would continue to support local allies in the south, while U.S. advisers would continue to work with Afghan security forces. U.S. airpower would continue to provide transport and fire support to both U.S. and Afghan units.[28]

The total number of U.S. military personnel this counterterrorism option would require would be roughly 10,000–15,000. This would be supplemented by additional intelligence community personnel and contractors. While not cheap, this would be substantially less expensive in blood and treasure. On the latter, the price would likely be somewhere between $5 billion and $18 billion annually. As demonstrated by the previously noted strike in the Korengal Valley, this force would be at least as capable of collecting actionable intelligence as U.S. assets in Pakistan, Yemen, and Somalia, and thus able to conduct effective operations against al Qaeda.

Such a posture would be required both to conduct counterterrorism operations, the principal focus, but also to continue to support the government of Afghanistan and other local allies of the United States. Afghanistan is thus substantially different from both Yemen and Somalia and will require more resources than either. Unlike Yemen, where despite tribal revolt and political upheaval the government does not face a massive insurgency, Afghanistan will require a substantial number of U.S. assets. Unlike Somalia, the United States can neither conduct missions from friendly neighboring countries nor rely heavily on projecting power from offshore, as Afghanistan is landlocked with two of its major neighbors, Iran and Pakistan, having contentious relations with the United States.

To be clear: this posture would enable the Taliban to expand the areas it controls in Afghanistan. Yet even this expansion would be limited, as the Taliban lacks a major natural constituency outside of Pashtun regions. Indeed, many Hazaras, Uzbeks and Tajiks are more anti-Taliban than the United States. With continued support from the United States the central government would be able to retain control of at least half the country, including major cities such as Kabul and Kandahar City. This support should include financial rewards, which would reduce the incentive of local elites and central government figures to "bandwagon" with the Taliban.

This streamlined military approach to attacking al Qaeda, along with adroit and patient diplomacy with Pakistan to help it secure its nuclear complex, provides a practical, cost-effective strategy for achieving core U.S. interests on both sides of the Durand Line. Unlike the present strategy, it does not require open-ended and costly commitments to state building and counterinsurgency. It only requires limiting U.S. goals and setting aside ambitious hopes of using the American military to sow liberal ideals in South and Central Asia. In the long run, however, a less ambitious strategy offers the best chance of sustaining pressure on al Qaeda without wasting scarce resources or overtaxing expectations.

Notes

1. The President's News Conference, October 11, 2001. Cited in John T. Woolley and Gerhard Peters, "The American Presidency Project," Santa Barbara, CA, www.presidency.ucsb.edu/ws/?pid=73426.
2. The White House, "National Security Strategy," May 2010, p. 20, www.whitehouse.gov/sites/default/files/rss_viewer/national_security_strategy.pdf.
3. Charles Tilly, "War Making and State Making as Organized Crime," in *Bringing the State Back In*, ed. Peter Evans (Cambridge, UK: Cambridge University Press, 1985), pp. 169–87.
4. For criticism of contemporary external state-building efforts, see Justin Logan and Christopher Preble, "Fixing Failed States: A Dissenting View," in *Handbook on the Political Economy of War*, eds. Christopher J. Coyne and Rachel L. Mathers (Cheltenham, UK: Edward Elgar, 2011), pp. 379–96.
5. Jason Brownlee, "Can America Nation-Build?" *World Politics* 59, no. 22 (January 2007): 314–40.
6. Todd Pitman, "U.S. Forces Advance in Taliban Green Belt Stronghold," Associated Press, September 15, 2010.
7. Dexter Filkins, "Depositors Panic Over Bank Crisis in Afghanistan," *New York Times*, September 2, 2010.
8. The Afghan Taliban, while an imprecise term, here means the reconstituted former Taliban regime led by Mullah Omar, now known as the Quetta (or Karachi) Shura Taliban, the Haqqani Network, and to a lesser extent the Hizbl-Islami Gulbuddin (Islamic Party of Gulbuddin Hekmatyar).
9. Afghanistan Study Group, "A New Way Forward: Rethinking U.S. Strategy in Afghanistan," p. 5; www.afghanistanstudygroup.org/NewWayForward_report.pdf.
10. Matthew Rosenberg and Julian Barnes, "Al Qaeda Makes Afghan Comeback," *Wall Street Journal*, April 6, 2011.
11. Pakistani Taliban, like Afghan Taliban, is an imprecise term but here means the Tehrik-i-Taliban Pakistan led by Hakimullah Mehsud and its affiliates, most notably the Tehrik-e-Nafaz-e-Shariat-e-Mohammadi.
12. Eric Schmitt and Mark Mazetti, "In a First, U.S. Provides Pakistan with Drone Data," *New York Times*, May 13, 2009; "Gilani Denies Report about Balochistan Drone Attacks," *Dawn* (Pakistan), September 29, 2009; and Tim Reid, "Former CIA Agent's Hunt for Bin Laden in Pakistani Badlands," *Times* (UK), September 9, 2009.
13. Ahmed Rashid, *Taliban: Militant Islam, Oil and Fundamentalism in Central Asia* (New Haven, CT: Yale University Press, 2001).
14. Robyn Lim, "Russia Is Back in Kabul and in the 'Great Game,'" *New York Times*, November 29, 2001.
15. White House Interagency Policy Group, "White Paper on U.S. Policy toward Afghanistan and Pakistan," March 27, 2009; http://www.whitehouse.gov/assets/documents/afghanistan_pakistan_white_paper_final.pdf.
16. Foreign Policy Initiative, "Open Letter to the President," September 7, 2009; www.foreignpolicyi.org/node/11817.
17. Stephen Biddle, "Is It Worth It? The Difficult Case for War in Afghanistan," *The American*

Interest online (July–August 2009), www.the-american-interest.com/article.cfm?piece=617.

18. Lawrence Sellin, "Outside View: A Nuclear-Armed Taliban?" United Press International, September 9, 2009.

19. See Salman Masood, "Attack in Pakistani Garrison City Raises Anxiety About Safety of Nuclear Labs and Staff," *New York Times,* July 4, 2009; "Deadliest Attack on a Military Installation, at Least 70 Killed," *Daily Times* (Pakistan), August 22, 2008; and Vipin Narang, "Pakistan's Nukes are Safe. Maybe," *Foreign Policy* online, August 28, 2009, http://afpak.foreignpolicy.com/posts/2009/08/13/pakistans_nukes_are_safe_maybe_0.

20. Isambard Wilkinson, "US Concerned Taliban Will Snatch Pakistan's Nuclear Weapons," *Telegraph* (UK), May 4, 2009.

21. David Albright and Holly Higgins, "A Bomb for the Ummah," *Bulletin of the Atomic Scientist* 59, no. 2, (March/April 2003): 49–55; and Rolf Mowatt-Larssen, "Al Qaeda's Pursuit of Weapons of Mass Destruction," *Foreign Policy* online, January 25, 2010, http://www.foreignpolicy.com/articles/2010/01/25/al_qaedas_pursuit_of_weapons_of_mass_destruction?page=full

22. Sumit Ganguly, "Pakistan's Never-Ending Story," *Foreign Affairs* 79, no. 2 (March/April 2000): 6. On the history of Islamization in Pakistan, see Hassan Abbas, *Pakistan's Drift into Extremism: Allah, the Army, and America's War on Terror* (Armonk, NY: ME Sharpe, 2005).

23. Taken from http://icasualties.org/oef/.

24. See Christi Parsons and Julian Barnes, "Pricing an Afghan Troop Buildup Is No Simple Calculation," *Los Angeles Times,* November 23, 2009; and Todd Harrison, *Analysis of the FY 2011 Defense Budget* (Washington: Center for Strategic and Budgetary Assessments, 2010), p. 8.

25. For 2011 troop numbers, see Adam Entous and Julian Barnes, "U.S. Boosts Afghan Surge," *Wall Street Journal,* January 4, 2011.

26. Poll results can be found at www.washingtonpost.com/wp-srv/politics/polls/postpoll_07132010.html.

27. Poll results can be found at www.washingtonpost.com/wp-srv/politics/polls/postpoll_03142011.html.

28. For a much more detailed treatment of this counterterrorism force posture, see Austin Long, "Small is Beautiful: The Counterterrorism Option in Afghanistan," *Orbis* 54, no.2 (Spring 2010): 199–214.

JOSHUA ROVNER is an associate professor of strategy and policy at the U.S. Naval War College.

AUSTIN LONG is an assistant professor at the School of International and Public Affairs and a member of the Arnold A. Saltzman Institute of War and Peace Studies at Columbia University.

EXPLORING THE ISSUE

Should the United States Continue a Strategy of State Building in Afghanistan?

Critical Thinking and Reflection

1. Does the United States have vital national security interests in Afghanistan?
2. Does the United States possess the means needed, including economic resources, military power, and domestic political will, to pursue a state building approach?
3. Can state building efforts in Afghanistan improve prospects for economic and political development absent some changes within the Afghan government itself?
4. Will a strategy of state building best achieve U.S. national security objectives in Afghanistan?
5. Does a counterterrorism strategy provide greater strategic flexibility, both globally and in South Asia? What would be the greatest drawbacks of this approach?
6. How does Pakistan fit into the question of whether the United States should engage in state building in Afghanistan?
7. Is the existence of nuclear weapons in Pakistan reason enough to remain engaged in Afghanistan until it is capable of independently defeating internal security threats?

Is There Common Ground?

Both authors seem to agree that the United States must remain engaged in Afghanistan and the region for the foreseeable future. Both authors would probably also agree that state building undertaken by external powers is costly and has had a mixed record of success. Where they differ is on whether the United States should assume these costs in its approach to Afghanistan today. After more than a decade of involvement in Afghanistan, U.S. policymakers will have to come down on one side or the other of this debate. They will need to decide whether the United States has achieved all it reasonably can at the price it is willing to pay or whether a changed approach promises a better result.

There is also broad consensus that political stability and economic development in Afghanistan are desirable outcomes. However, there is less agreement as to whether and how external actors such as the United States can make these outcomes more likely.

Finally, domestic factors in the United States will be important in shaping the future options available to U.S. policymakers in their approach to Afghanistan. In a time of austerity, all national security decisions are likely to be subject to strict cost–benefit calculations. Even if a state building approach to Afghanistan is most likely to produce results that best serve U.S. national security interests over the long term, it may become increasingly difficult for policymakers to make long-term investments with high near-term costs.

Additional Resources

Bacevich, Andrew. *The Limits of Power: The End of American Exceptionalism.* New York: Metropolitan Books, 2008.

In this book, Dr. Bacevich argues that the United States has overused the military instrument of power in its foreign policy. He recommends a shift toward a more cautious and conservative approach to foreign affairs.

Belasco, Amy. *The Costs of Iraq, Afghanistan, and Other Global War on Terror Operations Since 9/11.* Washington, DC: Congressional Research Service, 29 March 2011.

This study attempts to capture comprehensively the costs associated with operations considered to be part of the "Global War on Terror" from fiscal year 2001 to fiscal year 2010.

Dobbins, James, Seth G. Jones, Keith Crane, and Beth Cole DeGrasse. *The Beginner's Guide to Nation-Building.* California: RAND, 2007.

This self-described guidebook to nation-building provides a doctrinal foundation for the conduct of such operations. Implicitly, it advocates for such military endeavors in support of national security objectives.

Frederick W. Kagan and Kimberley Kagan. "The Case for Continuing the Counterinsurgency Campaign in Afghanistan," *Foreign Affairs*, 16 December

2011. Retrieved from www.foreignaffairs.com/articles/136869/frederick-w-kagan-and-kimberly-kagan/the-case-for-continuing-the-counterinsurgency-campaign-in-afghan

The authors argue that a shift away from a large counterinsurgency effort in Afghanistan prior to securing the country would leave Afghanistan in worse shape than when U.S. forces invaded. This outcome would weaken the geopolitical position of the United States.

Hart, Michael. "West's Afghan Hopes Collide with Reality," *The National Interest* 118 (March/April 2012): 8–18.

This article approaches the war in Afghanistan from a realist perspective and critiques the ideas of state building and regime change that motivated the invasion. Hart points out that it will be the Afghans themselves who ultimately determine the fate of their country.

Yingling, Paul. "An Absence of Strategic Thinking," *Foreign Affairs,* 16 December 2011. Retrieved from www.foreignaffairs.com/articles/136882/paul-l-yingling/an-absence-of-strategic-thinking

Colonel Yingling argues that mistakes made early in the Afghanistan war have hindered later efforts at stability, and now domestic politics in the United States may matter more than events in Afghanistan.

Internet References . . .

Frederick W. Kagan and Kimberley Kagan. "The Case for Continuing the Counterinsurgency Campaign in Afghanistan"

The authors argue that a shift away from a large counterinsurgency effort in Afghanistan prior to securing the country would leave Afghanistan in worse shape than when U.S. forces invaded. This outcome would weaken the geopolitical position of the United States.

www.foreignaffairs.com/articles/136869/frederick-w-kagan-and-kimberly-kagan/the-case-for-continuing-the-counterinsurgency-campaign-in-afghan.

Paul Yingling's

"An Absence of Strategic Thinking"

Colonel Yingling argues that mistakes made early in the Afghanistan war have hindered later efforts at stability, and now domestic politics in the United States may matter more than events in Afghanistan.

www.foreignaffairs.com/articles/136882/paul-l-yingling/an-absence-of-strategic-thinking.

Unit III

UNIT

Regional and Bilateral Relations

*T*hough the United States is engaged throughout the world and it can be useful to think about its approach to foreign affairs in global terms, it can be equally useful for the makers of U.S. foreign policy to consider the characteristics of particular countries and regions as they weigh foreign policy options. After all, approaches that work well in one regional or country context may not work in others. For example, the United States has long pursued its security interests in Europe through membership in robust regional institutions—the foremost being the North Atlantic Treaty Organization (NATO). In East Asia, there is no one equivalent to NATO for a variety of political and historical reasons. Similarly, with regard to bilateral relations, the effectiveness of a particular foreign policy depends as much on the perspective and interests of the country concerned as it does on the intent of the United States.

These considerations suggest that for foreign policymakers to be as effective as possible, they should draw on experts about the countries and regions of concern. Relevant types of expertise include at least the following: domestic politics, economics, culture, language, demographics, security institutions, threat perceptions, and history. Trying to start from the inside out—in other words, trying to start from the perspective of the foreign actor or actors—may be the best approach in many cases, but demands a great amount of information. For a country like the United States that has worldwide interests, meeting these demands with well-informed and context-sensitive foreign policies is a constant challenge.

Selected, Edited, and with Issue Framing Material by:
Suzanne Nielsen, *U.S. Military Academy*
and
Scott Handler, *U.S. Military Academy*

ISSUE

Should the United States Use Military Force to Prevent Iran from Developing a Nuclear Weapon?

YES: **Matthew Kroenig**, from "Time to Attack Iran," *Foreign Affairs* (vol. 91, no. 1, pp. 76–86, January/February 2012)

NO: **Colin H. Kahl**, from "Not Time to Attack Iran," *Foreign Affairs* (March/April 2012)

Learning Outcomes

After reading this issue, you should be able to:

• Understand why states, such as Iran, might pursue nuclear weapons.
• Understand why the United States has an interest in preventing Iran from obtaining nuclear weapons.
• Be able to discuss how an Iran with nuclear weapons could impact regional security in the Middle East and the U.S. relationships with states in the region.
• Discuss the potential costs, benefits, and risks associated with a U.S. military strike intended to prevent Iran from obtaining nuclear weapons.
• Analyze the potential costs and challenges that the United States could face if Iran were to acquire nuclear weapons and the United States were to seek to deter their use.

ISSUE SUMMARY

YES: Matthew Kroenig, an assistant professor of government at Georgetown University, argues that the United States should carefully consider a military strike to destroy Iran's nuclear program. Though such an attack would risk negative political and economic consequences, it could succeed in convincing Iran to abandon its nuclear aspirations. If Iran succeeds in obtaining nuclear weapons, it will lead to nuclear proliferation across the Middle East and threaten vital U.S. interests in the region.

NO: Colin Kahl, an associate professor in the Security Studies Program at Georgetown University's Edmund A. Walsh School of Foreign Service, argues that a preventive war would be fundamentally unwise. Far from convincing Iran's leaders that the development of nuclear weapons is not in their interests, a military attack by the United States would instead make it more likely that Iran would become a nuclear weapons state over the longer term. In addition, a U.S. military attack would threaten the stability of a still-fragile global economy and risk igniting a broader conflict across the Middle East.

$\mathbf{A}$s the United States seeks to end its involvement in sustained wars in Iraq and Afghanistan and commits to a shift in focus to the Pacific region, it is faced with yet another dilemma which is pulling its attention back to the Middle East—the potential emergence of an Iran armed with nuclear weapons. Unlike the run-up to the 2003 U.S. invasion of Iraq, which was widely criticized for its anemic debate on the threat posed by a suspected Iraqi nuclear program, there have been lively discussions on what the United States should do about Iran. Policymakers, scholars, and pundits have offered a variety of views on the

feasibility of preventing Iran from acquiring nuclear weapons, the threat a nuclear Iran would pose to U.S. national interests, and the instability a nuclear Iran could cause in the Middle East.

Current tensions between the United States and Iran over the existence of a suspected Iranian nuclear weapons program are only the most recent manifestation of troubled relations between the two countries that go back decades. Both sides harbor grievances that have produced enduring enmity. On the Iranian side, these grievances date back to the U.S. role in the 1953 coup that overthrew an elected prime minister of Iran, Mohammed Mossadegh.

This event was followed by over two decades of U.S. support for the pro-Western but repressive regime of Mohammad Reza Pahlavi, the Shah of Iran from 1941 to 1979. Iranians also resent U.S. support for Iraq during the 1980–1988 Iran–Iraq War and repeated U.S. efforts to influence Iran through economic sanctions. On the U.S. side, views of Iran continue to be colored by events following the Iranian Revolution in 1979 that removed the pro-American Shah and ultimately enabled former Supreme Leader Ayatollah Khomeini to come to power. During this tumultuous period, the U.S. Embassy in Tehran was seized and U.S. embassy employees were held hostage by Iranian revolutionary groups for 444 days. In addition, the United States bristles at Iran's threats to impede the flow of oil through the Strait of Hormuz and Iranian hostility to the continued existence of the state of Israel. The United States also condemns Iran's links to dangerous proxy groups in the region, including Hezbollah and Hamas, as well as its history of supporting acts of terrorism abroad.

In addition to a history of troubled U.S.–Iranian relations, another important factor shaping the context of the current situation relates to regional dynamics. Tensions between Israel and Iran are particularly high, inflamed further by Iran's support for Hamas in the Palestinian territories and Hezbollah in Lebanon, as well as occasional rhetoric from Tehran that questions Israel's right to exist. In addition, Iran is unique among its neighbors in that its population is Persian rather than Arab. The majority of Iranians are Shi'ite Muslims and they are ruled by the only theocratic regime in the region. In combination with a history of conflict, these differences have contributed to tense relations between Iran and the Sunni-majority, Arab states of the Persian Gulf. Iran's strongest, long-standing ally in the region is Syria, which is now plagued by violent internal conflict.

A final important contextual factor that shapes perspectives on the existence of a possible Iranian nuclear weapons program is the Nuclear Non-Proliferation Treaty (NPT), which initially went into effect in 1970. The NPT was informed by two main ideas that are in tension with one another. The first idea is that nuclear technologies bring benefits, particularly with regard to energy production, that should be shared. The second idea, however, is that the proliferation of nuclear weapons poses a grave danger to international peace and security. As a reflection of these founding ideas, the treaty stipulates that the five nuclear weapons states party to the treaty—the United States, United Kingdom, France, Russia, and China—should share nuclear technologies dedicated to peaceful purposes while drawing down their arsenals, and all states should seek to prevent the proliferation of nuclear weapons to additional countries. Both the United States and Iran are parties to the treaty, with the United States signing on as one of the five recognized nuclear weapons states and Iran joining as a non-nuclear power. Today the NPT is the most widely embraced arms control treaty in existence with 190 parties. While the NPT has not succeeded

in preventing all nuclear weapons proliferation, the states that have since acquired nuclear weapons either never signed the treaty (India, Pakistan, and—as most suspect—Israel) or formally withdrew (North Korea).

The NPT is important to current debates about Iran and nuclear weapons in that it shapes the arguments being made on both sides. Iran has grounds, within the parameters of the NPT, to point out its right to develop indigenous nuclear capabilities for peaceful purposes. As of fall 2012, the leaders of Iran have emphasized that Iran's nuclear program is not dedicated to the production of weapons. On the other hand, those who question whether Iran is in compliance with the spirit of the NPT point out the following: a lack of transparency in Iran's activities; the fact that some Iranian nuclear activities seem directed at military purposes; and past Iranian failures to meet its commitments with regard to suspending the enrichment of uranium and other issues (IAEA, 2011).

Given that its suspected pursuit of nuclear weapons has already resulted in troubled diplomatic relations and economic sanctions, it is worth asking why Iran might be willing to bear these costs. There are at least two possible reasons. First, Iran could be seeking nuclear weapons as a way to tilt the regional balance of power in its favor and shape the behavior of its neighbors. Instead of looking to the West for protection, for example, states such as Iraq and Afghanistan could instead choose to defer to Iran. In addition, Iran's traditional regional adversaries, such as the Sunni-majority Arab states and Israel, might exercise more caution when challenging Iranian foreign policies. In addition to gaining influence and diplomatic leverage, a second reason Iran might pursue nuclear weapons is to ward off foreign threats. In recent years, the governments of several non-nuclear states—including Afghanistan, Iraq, and Libya—have been overthrown. These developments were the result of either foreign invasion or foreign support to domestic opposition groups. At the same time, states with nuclear weapons, such as North Korea and Pakistan, have experienced tense foreign relations without becoming the targets of military intervention. Iranian leaders may see the possession of nuclear weapons as the ultimate guarantor of regime stability and security.

Not all security studies scholars agree, however, that nuclear weapons would produce positive security benefits for Iran. It is also possible that Iran's possession of nuclear weapons would further alienate it from its neighbors and prolong the presence of the U.S. military in the region, developments Iran wishes to avoid (Lindsay, 2010). It is also possible that a nuclear-armed Iran could spark nuclear proliferation as its Arab neighbors decide that they need nuclear weapons to deter attack and prevent Iran from acquiring too much regional influence.

This background is useful in thinking through what the United States should do now. In the first of the two articles presented here, Matthew Kroenig argues that the United States should consider the employment of all means—to include a military strike—to prevent Iran from acquiring nuclear weapons. While recognizing the associated diplomatic and economic costs, he argues that an attack on Iran's nuclear program could succeed in delaying Iranian nuclear weapons development and perhaps even convince the regime's leaders that the pursuit of nuclear weapons is not in their best interest. An important driver behind his analysis is a forecast of the costs the United States would bear if Iran actually succeeded in deploying nuclear weapons. Kroenig argues that the United States would have to confront Iran with a strong deterrent posture in the region, which would be expensive and risky for a long time to come.

Cost calculations are also an important component of Colin Kahl's argument in the second article presented here, though he clearly disagrees with Kroenig and does not believe that cost calculations suggest that a military strike now would be beneficial. Hearkening back to the U.S. decision to invade Iraq in 2003, Kahl argues that it is easy to underestimate the costs and unpredictability of a preventive war. If policymakers were to heed Kroenig's advice, they would be repeating the errors of a decade ago when a different U.S. presidential administration decided to invade Iraq. There is still time for diplomacy to work, and the international community is likely to have adequate warning if the leadership in Iran takes the steps necessary to go beyond its current nuclear programs to the development of nuclear weapons. It is still in the best interest of the United States to avoid the risks to the global economy and to peace and security in the Middle East that a U.S. military strike on Iran would create.

YES

Matthew Kroenig

Time to Attack Iran

Why a Strike Is the Least Bad Option

In early October, U.S. officials accused Iranian operatives of planning to assassinate Saudi Arabia's ambassador to the United States on American soil. Iran denied the charges, but the episode has already managed to increase tensions between Washington and Tehran. Although the Obama administration has not publicly threatened to retaliate with military force, the allegations have underscored the real and growing risk that the two sides could go to war sometime soon—particularly over Iran's advancing nuclear program.

For several years now, starting long before this episode, American pundits and policymakers have been debating whether the United States should attack Iran and attempt to eliminate its nuclear facilities. Proponents of a strike have argued that the only thing worse than military action against Iran would be an Iran armed with nuclear weapons. Critics, meanwhile, have warned that such a raid would likely fail and, even if it succeeded, would spark a full-fledged war and a global economic crisis. They have urged the United States to rely on nonmilitary options, such as diplomacy, sanctions, and covert operations, to prevent Iran from acquiring a bomb. Fearing the costs of a bombing campaign, most critics maintain that if these other tactics fail to impede Tehran's progress, the United States should simply learn to live with a nuclear Iran.

But skeptics of military action fail to appreciate the true danger that a nuclear-armed Iran would pose to U.S. interests in the Middle East and beyond. And their grim forecasts assume that the cure would be worse than the disease—that is, that the consequences of a U.S. assault on Iran would be as bad as or worse than those of Iran achieving its nuclear ambitions. But that is a faulty assumption. The truth is that a military strike intended to destroy Iran's nuclear program, if managed carefully, could spare the region and the world a very real threat and dramatically improve the long-term national security of the United States.

Dangers of Deterrence

Years of international pressure have failed to halt Iran's attempt to build a nuclear program. The Stuxnet computer worm, which attacked control systems in Iranian nuclear facilities, temporarily disrupted Tehran's enrichment effort, but a report by the International Atomic Energy Agency this past May revealed that the targeted plants have fully recovered from the assault. And the latest IAEA findings on Iran, released in November, provided the most compelling evidence yet that the Islamic Republic has weathered sanctions and sabotage, allegedly testing nuclear triggering devices and redesigning its missiles to carry nuclear payloads. The Institute for Science and International Security, a nonprofit research institution, estimates that Iran could now produce its first nuclear weapon within six months of deciding to do so. Tehran's plans to move sensitive nuclear operations into more secure facilities over the course of the coming year could reduce the window for effective military action even further. If Iran expels IAEA inspectors, begins enriching its stockpiles of uranium to weapons-grade levels of 90 percent, or installs advanced centrifuges at its uranium-enrichment facility in Qom, the United States must strike immediately or forfeit its last opportunity to prevent Iran from joining the nuclear club.

Some states in the region are doubting U.S. resolve to stop the program and are shifting their allegiances to Tehran. Others have begun to discuss launching their own nuclear initiatives to counter a possible Iranian bomb. For those nations and the United States itself, the threat will only continue to grow as Tehran moves closer to its goal. A nuclear-armed Iran would immediately limit U.S. freedom of action in the Middle East. With atomic power behind it, Iran could threaten any U.S. political or military initiative in the Middle East with nuclear war, forcing Washington to think twice before acting in the region. Iran's regional rivals, such as Saudi Arabia, would likely decide to acquire their own nuclear arsenals, sparking an arms race. To constrain its geopolitical rivals, Iran could choose to spur proliferation by transferring nuclear technology to its allies—other countries and terrorist groups alike. Having the bomb would give Iran greater cover for conventional aggression and coercive diplomacy, and the battles between its terrorist proxies and Israel, for example, could escalate. And Iran and Israel lack nearly all the safeguards that helped the United States and the Soviet Union avoid a nuclear exchange during the Cold War—secure second-strike capabilities, clear lines of communication, long flight times for ballistic missiles from one country to the other, and experience managing nuclear arsenals. To be sure, a nuclear-armed Iran would not intentionally launch a suicidal nuclear war. But the volatile nuclear balance between Iran and Israel could easily spiral out of control as a crisis unfolds, resulting in a nuclear exchange between the two countries that could draw the United States in, as well.

These security threats would require Washington to contain Tehran. Yet deterrence would come at a heavy price. To keep the Iranian threat at bay, the United States would need to deploy naval and ground units and potentially nuclear weapons across the Middle East, keeping a large force in the area for decades to come. Alongside those troops, the United States would have to permanently deploy significant intelligence assets to monitor any attempts by Iran to transfer its nuclear technology. And it would also need to devote perhaps billions of dollars to improving its allies' capability to defend themselves. This might include helping Israel construct submarine-launched ballistic missiles and hardened ballistic missile silos to ensure that it can maintain a secure second-strike capability. Most of all, to make containment credible, the United States would need to extend its nuclear umbrella to its partners in the region, pledging to defend them with military force should Iran launch an attack.

In other words, to contain a nuclear Iran, the United States would need to make a substantial investment of political and military capital to the Middle East in the midst of an economic crisis and at a time when it is attempting to shift its forces out of the region. Deterrence would come with enormous economic and geopolitical costs and would have to remain in place as long as Iran remained hostile to U.S. interests, which could mean decades or longer. Given the instability of the region, this effort might still fail, resulting in a war far more costly and destructive than the one that critics of a preemptive strike on Iran now hope to avoid.

A Feasible Target

A nuclear Iran would impose a huge burden on the United States. But that does not necessarily mean that Washington should resort to military means. In deciding whether it should, the first question to answer is if an attack on Iran's nuclear program could even work. Doubters point out that the United States might not know the location of Iran's key facilities. Given Tehran's previous attempts to hide the construction of such stations, most notably the uranium-enrichment facilities in Natanz and Qom, it is possible that the regime already possesses nuclear assets that a bombing campaign might miss, which would leave Iran's program damaged but alive.

This scenario is possible, but not likely; indeed, such fears are probably overblown. U.S. intelligence agencies, the IAEA, and opposition groups within Iran have provided timely warning of Tehran's nuclear activities in the past—exposing, for example, Iran's secret construction at Natanz and Qom before those facilities ever became operational. Thus, although Tehran might again attempt

to build clandestine facilities, Washington has a very good chance of catching it before they go online. And given the amount of time it takes to construct and activate a nuclear facility, the scarcity of Iran's resources, and its failure to hide the facilities in Natanz and Qom successfully, it is unlikely that Tehran has any significant operational nuclear facilities still unknown to Western intelligence agencies.

Even if the United States managed to identify all of Iran's nuclear plants, however, actually destroying them could prove enormously difficult. Critics of a U.S. assault argue that Iran's nuclear facilities are dispersed across the country, buried deep underground and hardened against attack, and ringed with air defenses, making a raid complex and dangerous. In addition, they claim that Iran has purposefully placed its nuclear facilities near civilian populations, which would almost certainly come under fire in a U.S. raid, potentially leading to hundreds, if not thousands, of deaths.

These obstacles, however, would not prevent the United States from disabling or demolishing Iran's known nuclear facilities. A preventive operation would need to target the uranium-conversion plant at Isfahan, the heavy-water reactor at Arak, and various centrifuge-manufacturing sites near Natanz and Tehran, all of which are located aboveground and are highly vulnerable to air strikes. It would also have to hit the Natanz facility, which, although it is buried under reinforced concrete and ringed by air defenses, would not survive an attack from the U.S. military's new bunker-busting bomb, the 30,000-pound Massive Ordnance Penetrator, capable of penetrating up to 200 feet of reinforced concrete. The plant in Qom is built into the side of a mountain and thus represents a more challenging target. But the facility is not yet operational and still contains little nuclear equipment, so if the United States acted quickly, it would not need to destroy it.

Washington would also be able to limit civilian casualties in any campaign. Iran built its most critical nuclear plants, such as the one in Natanz, away from heavily populated areas. For those less important facilities that exist near civilian centers, such as the centrifuge-manufacturing sites, U.S. precision-guided missiles could pinpoint specific buildings while leaving their surroundings unscathed. The United States could reduce the collateral damage even further by striking at night or simply leaving those less important plants off its target list at little cost to the overall success of the mission. Although Iran would undoubtedly publicize any human suffering in the wake of a military action, the majority of the victims would be the military personnel, engineers, scientists, and technicians working at the facilities.

Setting the Right Redlines

The fact that the United States can likely set back or destroy Iran's nuclear program does not necessarily mean that it should. Such an attack could have potentially devastating consequences—for international security, the global economy, and Iranian domestic politics—all of which need to be accounted for.

To begin with, critics note, U.S. military action could easily spark a full-blown war. Iran might retaliate against U.S. troops or allies, launching missiles at military installations or civilian populations in the Gulf or perhaps even Europe. It could activate its proxies abroad, stirring sectarian tensions in Iraq, disrupting the Arab Spring, and ordering terrorist attacks against Israel and the United States. This could draw Israel or other states into the fighting and compel the United States to escalate the conflict in response. Powerful allies of Iran, including China and Russia, may attempt to economically and diplomatically isolate the United States. In the midst of such spiraling violence, neither side may see a clear path out of the battle, resulting in a long-lasting, devastating war, whose impact may critically damage the United States' standing in the Muslim world.

Those wary of a U.S. strike also point out that Iran could retaliate by attempting to close the Strait of Hormuz, the narrow access point to the Persian Gulf through which roughly 20 percent of the world's oil supply travels. And even if Iran did not threaten the strait, speculators, fearing possible supply disruptions, would bid up the price of oil, possibly triggering a wider economic crisis at an already fragile moment.

None of these outcomes is predetermined, however; indeed, the United States could do much to mitigate them. Tehran would certainly feel like it needed to respond to a U.S. attack, in order to reestablish deterrence and save face domestically. But it would also likely seek to calibrate its actions to avoid starting a conflict that could lead to the destruction of its military or the regime itself. In all likelihood, the Iranian leadership would resort to its worst forms of retaliation, such as closing the Strait of Hormuz or launching missiles at southern Europe, only if it felt that its very existence was threatened. A targeted U.S. operation need not threaten Tehran in such a fundamental way.

To make sure it doesn't and to reassure the Iranian regime, the United States could first make clear that it is interested only in destroying Iran's nuclear program, not in overthrowing the government. It could then identify certain forms of retaliation to which it would respond with devastating military action, such as attempting to close the Strait of Hormuz, conducting massive and sustained attacks on Gulf states and U.S. troops or ships, or launching terrorist attacks in the United States itself. Washington would then need to clearly articulate these "redlines" to Tehran during and after the attack to ensure that the message was not lost in battle. And it would need to accept the fact that it would have to absorb Iranian responses that fell short of these redlines without escalating the conflict. This might include accepting token missile strikes against U.S. bases and ships in the region—several salvos over the course of a few days that soon taper off—or the harassment

of commercial and U.S. naval vessels. To avoid the kind of casualties that could compel the White House to escalate the struggle, the United States would need to evacuate nonessential personnel from U.S. bases within range of Iranian missiles and ensure that its troops were safely in bunkers before Iran launched its response. Washington might also need to allow for stepped-up support to Iran's proxies in Afghanistan and Iraq and missile and terrorist attacks against Israel. In doing so, it could induce Iran to follow the path of Iraq and Syria, both of which refrained from starting a war after Israel struck their nuclear reactors in 1981 and 2007, respectively.

Even if Tehran did cross Washington's redlines, the United States could still manage the confrontation. At the outset of any such violation, it could target the Iranian weapons that it finds most threatening to prevent Tehran from deploying them. To de-escalate the situation quickly and prevent a wider regional war, the United States could also secure the agreement of its allies to avoid responding to an Iranian attack. This would keep other armies, particularly the Israel Defense Forces, out of the fray. Israel should prove willing to accept such an arrangement in exchange for a U.S. promise to eliminate the Iranian nuclear threat. Indeed, it struck a similar agreement with the United States during the Gulf War, when it refrained from responding to the launching of Scud missiles by Saddam Hussein.

Finally, the U.S. government could blunt the economic consequences of a strike. For example, it could offset any disruption of oil supplies by opening its Strategic Petroleum Reserve and quietly encouraging some Gulf states to increase their production in the run-up to the attack. Given that many oil-producing nations in the region, especially Saudi Arabia, have urged the United States to attack Iran, they would likely cooperate.

Washington could also reduce the political fallout of military action by building global support for it in advance. Many countries may still criticize the United States for using force, but some—the Arab states in particular—would privately thank Washington for eliminating the Iranian threat. By building such a consensus in the lead-up to an attack and taking the outlined steps to mitigate it once it began, the United States could avoid an international crisis and limit the scope of the conflict.

Any Time Is Good Time

Critics have another objection: even if the United States managed to eliminate Iran's nuclear facilities and mitigate the consequences, the effects might not last long. Sure enough, there is no guarantee that an assault would deter Iran from attempting to rebuild its plants; it may even harden Iran's resolve to acquire nuclear technology as a means of retaliating or protecting itself in the future. The United States might not have the wherewithal or the political capital to launch another raid, forcing it to rely on the same ineffective tools that it now uses to restrain

Iran's nuclear drive. If that happens, U.S. action will have only delayed the inevitable.

Yet according to the IAEA, Iran already appears fully committed to developing a nuclear weapons program and needs no further motivation from the United States. And it will not be able to simply resume its progress after its entire nuclear infrastructure is reduced to rubble. Indeed, such a devastating offensive could well force Iran to quit the nuclear game altogether, as Iraq did after its nuclear program was destroyed in the Gulf War and as Syria did after the 2007 Israeli strike. And even if Iran did try to reconstitute its nuclear program, it would be forced to contend with continued international pressure, greater difficulty in securing necessary nuclear materials on the international market, and the lurking possibility of subsequent attacks. Military action could, therefore, delay Iran's nuclear program by anywhere from a few years to a decade, and perhaps even indefinitely.

Skeptics might still counter that at best a strike would only buy time. But time is a valuable commodity. Countries often hope to delay worst-case scenarios as far into the future as possible in the hope that this might eliminate the threat altogether. Those countries whose nuclear facilities have been attacked—most recently Iraq and Syria— have proved unwilling or unable to restart their programs. Thus, what appears to be only a temporary setback to Iran could eventually become a game changer.

Yet another argument against military action against Iran is that it would embolden the hard-liners within Iran's government, helping them rally the population around the regime and eliminate any remaining reformists. This critique ignores the fact that the hard-liners are already firmly in control. The ruling regime has become so extreme that it has sidelined even those leaders once considered to be right-wingers, such as former President Ali Akbar Hashemi Rafsanjani, for their perceived softness. And Rafsanjani or the former presidential candidate Mir Hossein Mousavi would likely continue the nuclear program if he assumed power. An attack might actually create more openings for dissidents in the long term (after temporarily uniting Iran behind Ayatollah Ali Khamenei), giving them grounds for criticizing a government

that invited disaster. Even if a strike would strengthen Iran's hard-liners, the United States must not prioritize the outcomes of Iran's domestic political tussles over its vital national security interest in preventing Tehran from developing nuclear weapons.

Strike Now or Suffer Later

Attacking Iran is hardly an attractive prospect. But the United States can anticipate and reduce many of the feared consequences of such an attack. If it does so successfully, it can remove the incentive for other nations in the region to start their own atomic programs and, more broadly, strengthen global nonproliferation by demonstrating that it will use military force to prevent the spread of nuclear weapons. It can also head off a possible Israeli operation against Iran, which, given Israel's limited capability to mitigate a potential battle and inflict lasting damage, would likely result in far more devastating consequences and carry a far lower probability of success than a U.S. attack. Finally, a carefully managed U.S. attack would prove less risky than the prospect of containing a nuclear-armed Islamic Republic—a costly, decades-long proposition that would likely still result in grave national security threats. Indeed, attempting to manage a nuclear-armed Iran is not only a terrible option but the worst.

With the wars in Afghanistan and Iraq winding down and the United States facing economic hardship at home, Americans have little appetite for further strife. Yet Iran's rapid nuclear development will ultimately force the United States to choose between a conventional conflict and a possible nuclear war. Faced with that decision, the United States should conduct a surgical strike on Iran's nuclear facilities, absorb an inevitable round of retaliation, and then seek to quickly de-escalate the crisis. Addressing the threat now will spare the United States from confronting a far more dangerous situation in the future.

MATTHEW KROENIG is an assistant professor of government at Georgetown University and a Stanton Nuclear Security Fellow at the Council on Foreign Relations.

Colin H. Kahl

Not Time to Attack Iran

Why War Should Be a Last Resort

In "Time to Attack Iran" (January/February 2012), Matthew Kroenig takes a page out of the decade-old playbook used by advocates of the Iraq war. He portrays the threat of a nuclear-armed Iran as both grave and imminent, arguing that the United States has little choice but to attack Iran now before it is too late. Then, after offering the caveat that "attacking Iran is hardly an attractive prospect," he goes on to portray military action as preferable to other available alternatives and concludes that the United States can manage all the associated risks. Preventive war, according to Kroenig, is "the least bad option." But the lesson of Iraq, the last preventive war launched by the United States, is that Washington should not choose war when there are still other options, and it should not base its decision to attack on best-case analyses of how it hopes the conflict will turn out. A realistic assessment of Iran's nuclear progress and how a conflict would likely unfold leads one to a conclusion that is the opposite of Kroenig's: now is not the time to attack Iran.

Bad Timing

Kroenig argues that there is an urgent need to attack Iran's nuclear infrastructure soon, since Tehran could "produce its first nuclear weapon within six months of deciding to do so." Yet that last phrase is crucial. The International Atomic Energy Agency (IAEA) has documented Iranian efforts to achieve the capacity to develop nuclear weapons at some point, but there is no hard evidence that Supreme Leader Ayatollah Ali Khamenei has yet made the final decision to develop them.

In arguing for a six-month horizon, Kroenig also misleadingly conflates hypothetical timelines to produce weapons-grade uranium with the time actually required to construct a bomb. According to 2010 Senate testimony by James Cartwright, then vice chairman of the U.S. Joint Chiefs of Staff, and recent statements by the former heads of Israel's national intelligence and defense intelligence agencies, even if Iran could produce enough weapons-grade uranium for a bomb in six months, it would take it at least a year to produce a testable nuclear device and considerably longer to make a deliverable weapon. And David Albright, president of the Institute for Science and International Security (and the source of Kroenig's six-month

estimate), recently told Agence France-Presse that there is a "low probability" that the Iranians would actually develop a bomb over the next year even if they had the capability to do so. Because there is no evidence that Iran has built additional covert enrichment plants since the Natanz and Qom sites were outed in 2002 and 2009, respectively, any near-term move by Tehran to produce weapons-grade uranium would have to rely on its declared facilities. The IAEA would thus detect such activity with sufficient time for the international community to mount a forceful response. As a result, the Iranians are unlikely to commit to building nuclear weapons until they can do so much more quickly or out of sight, which could be years off.

Kroenig is also inconsistent about the timetable for an attack. In some places, he suggests that strikes should begin now, whereas in others, he argues that the United States should attack only if Iran takes certain actions—such as expelling IAEA inspectors, beginning the enrichment of weapons-grade uranium, or installing large numbers of advanced centrifuges, any one of which would signal that it had decided to build a bomb. Kroenig is likely right that these developments—and perhaps others, such as the discovery of new covert enrichment sites—would create a decision point for the use of force. But the Iranians have not taken these steps yet, and as Kroenig acknowledges, "Washington has a very good chance" of detecting them if they do.

Riding the Escalator

Kroenig's discussion of timing is not the only misleading part of his article; so is his contention that the United States could mitigate the "potentially devastating consequences" of a strike on Iran by carefully managing the escalation that would ensue. His picture of a clean, calibrated conflict is a mirage. Any war with Iran would be a messy and extraordinarily violent affair, with significant casualties and consequences.

According to Kroenig, Iran would not respond to a strike with its "worst forms of retaliation, such as closing the Strait of Hormuz or launching missiles at southern Europe" unless its leaders felt that the regime's "very existence was threatened." To mitigate this risk, he claims, the United States could "make clear that it is interested only in destroying Iran's nuclear program, not in overthrowing the government." But Iranian leaders have staked their domestic legitimacy on resisting international pressure to halt the nuclear program, and so they would inevitably view an attack on that program as an attack on the regime itself. Decades of hostility and perceived U.S. efforts to undermine the regime would reinforce this perception. And when combined with the emphasis on anti-Americanism in the ideology of the supreme leader and his hard-line advisers, as well as their general ignorance about what drives U.S. decision-making, this perception means that there is little prospect that Iranian leaders would believe that a U.S. strike had limited aims. Assuming the worst about Washington's intentions, Tehran is likely to overreact to even a surgical strike against its nuclear facilities.

Kroenig nevertheless believes that the United States could limit the prospects for escalation by warning Iran that crossing certain "redlines" would trigger a devastating U.S. counter-response. Ironically, Kroenig believes that a nuclear-armed Iran would be deeply irrational and prone to miscalculation yet somehow maintains that under the same leaders, Iran would make clear-eyed decisions in the immediate aftermath of a U.S. strike. But the two countries share no direct and reliable channels for communication, and the inevitable confusion brought on by a crisis would make signaling difficult and miscalculation likely.

To make matters worse, in the heat of battle, Iran would face powerful incentives to escalate. In the event of a conflict, both sides would come under significant pressure to stop the fighting due to the impact on international oil markets. Since this would limit the time the Iranians would have to reestablish deterrence, they might choose to launch a quick, all-out response, without care for redlines. Iranian fears that the United States could successfully disrupt its command-and-control infrastructure or preemptively destroy its ballistic missile arsenal could also tempt Iran to launch as many missiles as possible early in the war And the decentralized nature of Iran's Islamic Revolutionary Guard Corps, especially its navy, raises the prospect of unauthorized responses that could rapidly expand the fighting in the crowded waters of the Persian Gulf.

Controlling escalation would be no easier on the U.S. side. In the face of reprisals by Iranian proxies, "token missile strikes against U.S. bases and ships," or "the harassment of commercial and U.S. naval vessels," Kroenig says that Washington should turn the other cheek and constrain its own response to Iranian counterattacks. But this is much easier said than done. Just as Iran's likely expectation of a short war might encourage it to respond disproportionately early in the crisis, so the United States would also have incentives to move swiftly to destroy Iran's conventional forces and the infrastructure of the Revolutionary Guard Corps. And if the United States failed to do so, proxy attacks against U.S. civilian personnel in Lebanon or Iraq, the transfer of lethal rocket and portable air defense systems to Taliban fighters in Afghanistan, or missile strikes against U.S. facilities in the Gulf could cause significant U.S. casualties, creating irresistible political pressure in Washington to respond. Add to this the normal fog of war and the lack of reliable communications between the United States and Iran, and Washington would have a hard time determining whether Tehran's initial response to a strike was a one-off event or the prelude to a wider campaign. If it were the latter, a passive U.S. approach might motivate Iran to launch even more dangerous attacks—and this is a risk Washington may choose not to take. The sum total of these dynamics would make staying within Kroenig's proscribed limits exceedingly difficult.

Even if Iran did not escalate, purely defensive moves that would threaten U.S. personnel or international shipping in the Strait of Hormuz—the maritime chokepoint through which nearly 20 percent of the world's traded oil passes—would also create powerful incentives for Washington to preemptively target Iran's military. Of particular concern would be Iran's "anti-access/area-denial" capabilities, which are designed to prevent advanced navies from operating in the shallow waters of the Persian Gulf. These systems integrate coastal air defenses, shore-based long-range artillery and anti-ship cruise missiles, Kilo-class and midget submarines, remote-controlled boats and unmanned kamikaze aerial vehicles, and more than 1,000 small attack craft equipped with machine guns, multiple-launch rockets, anti-ship missiles, torpedoes, and rapid-mine-laying capabilities. The entire 120-mile-long strait sits along the Iranian coastline, within short reach of these systems. In the midst of a conflict, the threat to U.S. forces and the global economy posed by Iran's activating its air defenses, dispersing its missiles or naval forces, or moving its mines out of storage would be too great for the United States to ignore; the logic of preemption would compel Washington to escalate.

Some analysts, including Afshin Molavi and Michael Singh, believe that the Iranians are unlikely to attempt to close the strait due to the damage it would inflict on their own economy. But Tehran's saber rattling has already intensified in response to the prospect of Western sanctions on its oil industry. In the immediate aftermath of a U.S. strike on Iran's nuclear program, Iranian leaders might perceive that holding the strait at risk would encourage international pressure on Washington to end the fighting, possibly deterring U.S. escalation. In reality, it would more likely have the opposite effect, encouraging aggressive U.S. efforts to protect commercial shipping. The U.S. Navy is capable of keeping the strait open, but the mere threat of closure could send oil prices soaring, dealing a heavy blow to the fragile global economy. The measures that Kroenig advocates to mitigate this threat, such as opening up the U.S. Strategic Petroleum Reserve and urging Saudi Arabia to boost oil production, would be unlikely to suffice, especially since most Saudi crude passes through the strait.

Ultimately, if the United States and Iran go to war, there is no doubt that Washington will win in the narrow operational sense. Indeed, with the impressive array of U.S. naval and air forces already deployed in the Gulf, the United States could probably knock Iran's military capabilities back 20 years in a matter of weeks. But a U.S.-Iranian conflict would not be the clinical, tightly controlled, limited encounter that Kroenig predicts.

Spillover

Keeping other states in the region out of the fight would also prove more difficult than Kroenig suggests. Iran would presume Israeli complicity in a U.S. raid and would seek to drag Israel into the conflict in order to undermine potential support for the U.S. war effort among key Arab regimes. And although it is true, as Kroenig notes, that Israel remained on the sidelines during the 1990–91 Gulf War, the threat posed by Iran's missiles and proxies today is considerably greater than that posed by Iraq two decades ago. If Iranian-allied Hezbollah responded to the fighting by firing rockets at Israeli cities, Israel could launch an all-out war against Lebanon. Syrian President Bashar al-Assad might also try to use the moment to divert attention from the uprising in his country, launching his own assault on the Jewish state. Either scenario, or their combination, could lead to a wider war in the Levant.

Even in the Gulf, where U.S. partners are sometimes portrayed as passive, Iranian retaliation might draw Saudi Arabia and the United Arab Emirates into the conflict. The Saudis have taken a much more confrontational posture toward Iran in the past year, and Riyadh is unlikely to tolerate Iranian attacks against critical energy infrastructure. For its part, the UAE, the most hawkish state in the Gulf, might respond to missiles raining down on U.S. forces at its Al Dhafra Air Base by attempting to seize Abu Musa, Greater Tunb, and Lesser Tunb, three disputed Gulf islands currently occupied by Iran. A strike could also set off wider destabilizing effects. Although Kroenig is right that some Arab leaders would privately applaud a U.S. strike, many on the Arab street would reject it. Both Islamist extremists and embattled elites could use this opportunity to transform the Arab Spring's populist anti-regime narrative into a decidedly anti-American one. This would rebound to Iran's advantage just at the moment when political developments in the region, chief among them the resurgence of nationalism in the Arab world and the upheaval in Syria, are significantly undermining Iran's influence. A U.S. strike could easily shift regional sympathies back in Tehran's favor by allowing Iran to play the victim and, through its retaliation, resuscitate its status as the champion of the region's anti-Western resistance.

The Cost of Buying Time

Even if a U.S. strike went as well as Kroenig predicts, there is little guarantee that it would produce lasting results. Senior U.S. defense officials have repeatedly stated that an attack on Iran's nuclear facilities would stall Tehran's progress for only a few years. Kroenig argues that such a

delay could become permanent. "Those countries whose nuclear facilities have been attacked—most recently Iraq and Syria," he writes, "have proved unwilling or unable to restart their programs." In the case of Iraq, however, Saddam Hussein restarted his clandestine nuclear weapons program after the 1981 Israeli attack on the Osirak nuclear reactor, and it required the Gulf War and another decade of sanctions and intrusive inspections to eliminate it. Iran's program is also more advanced and dispersed than were Iraq's and Syria's, meaning it would be easier to reconstitute. A U.S. strike would damage key Iranian facilities, but it would do nothing to reverse the nuclear knowledge Iran has accumulated or its ability to eventually build new centrifuges.

A U.S. attack would also likely rally domestic Iranian support around nuclear hard-liners, increasing the odds that Iran would emerge from a strike even more committed to building a bomb. Kroenig downplays the "rally round the flag" risks by noting that hard-liners are already firmly in power and suggesting that an attack might produce increased internal criticism of the regime. But the nuclear program remains an enormous source of national pride for the majority of Iranians. To the extent that there is internal dissent over the program, it is a discussion about whether the country should acquire nuclear weapons or simply pursue civilian nuclear technology. By demonstrating the vulnerability of a non-nuclear-armed Iran, a U.S. attack would provide ammunition to hard-liners who argue for acquiring a nuclear deterrent. Kroenig suggests that the United States should essentially ignore "Iran's domestic political tussles" when pursuing "its vital national security interest in preventing Tehran from developing nuclear weapons." But influencing Iranian opinion about the strategic desirability of nuclear weapons might ultimately offer the only enduring way of keeping the Islamic Republic on a peaceful nuclear path.

Finally, if Iran did attempt to restart its nuclear program after an attack, it would be much more difficult for the United States to stop it. An assault would lead Iran to distance itself from the IAEA and perhaps to pull out of the Nuclear Non-proliferation Treaty altogether. Without inspectors on the ground, the international community would struggle to track or slow Tehran's efforts to rebuild its program.

Contain Yourself

Kroenig argues that "a nuclear-armed Iran would not intentionally launch a suicidal nuclear war" but still concludes that it is ultimately less risky to attack the Islamic Republic now than to attempt to contain it later. He warns that containment would entail a costly forward deployment of large numbers of U.S. forces on Iran's periphery for decades.

But the United States already has a large presence encircling Iran. Forty thousand U.S. troops are stationed in the Gulf, accompanied by strike aircraft, two aircraft carrier strike groups, two Aegis ballistic missile defense ships, and multiple Patriot antimissile systems. On Iran's eastern flank, Washington has another 90,000 troops deployed in Afghanistan and thousands more supporting the Afghan war in nearby Central Asian states. Kroenig claims that it would take much more to contain a nuclear-armed Iran. But U.S. forces in the Gulf already outnumber those in South Korea that are there to deter a nuclear-armed North. It is thus perfectly conceivable that the existing U.S. presence in the region, perhaps supplemented by a limited forward deployment of nuclear weapons and additional ballistic missile defenses, would be sufficient to deter a nuclear-armed Iran from aggression and blackmail.

To be sure, such a deterrence-and-containment strategy would be an extraordinarily complex and risky enterprise, and there is no doubt that prevention is preferable. Given the possible consequences of a nuclear-armed Iran, the price of failure would be very high. But Kroenig's approach would not solve the problem. By presenting the options as either a near-term strike or long-term containment, Kroenig falls into the same trap that advocates of the Iraq war fell into a decade ago: ignoring postwar scenarios. In reality, the strike that Kroenig recommends would likely be a prelude to containment, not a substitute for it.

Since a military raid would not permanently eliminate Iran's nuclear infrastructure, the United States would still need to construct an expensive, risky postwar containment regime to prevent Iran from reconstituting the program, much as it did in regard to Iraq after the Gulf War. The end result would be strikingly similar to the one that Kroenig criticizes, requiring Washington to maintain sufficient air, naval, and ground forces in the Persian Gulf to attack again at a moment's notice.

A strike carried out in the way Kroenig advocates— a unilateral preventive attack—would also make postwar containment more difficult and costly. Many countries would view such an operation as a breach of international law, shattering the consensus required to maintain an effective post-strike containment regime. The likelihood that the United States could "reduce the political fallout of military action by building global support for it in advance," as Kroenig suggests, would be extremely low absent clear evidence that Iran is dashing for a bomb. Without such evidence, Washington would be left to bear the costs of an attack and the resulting containment regime alone.

Finally, the surgical nature of Kroenig's proposed strike, aimed solely at Iran's nuclear program, would make postwar containment much harder. It would leave Tehran wounded and aggrieved but still capable of responding. Kroenig's recommended approach, then, would likely be just enough to ensure a costly, long-term conflict without actually compelling Iran to change its behavior.

The Options on the Table

In making the case for preventive war as the least bad option, Kroenig dismisses any prospect of finding a diplomatic solution to the U.S.-Iranian standoff. He concludes that the Obama administration's dual-track policy of engagement and pressure has failed to arrest Iran's march toward a bomb, leaving Washington with no other choice but to bomb Iran.

But this ignores the severe economic strain, isolation, and technical challenges that Iran is experiencing. After years of dismissing the economic effects of sanctions, senior Iranian officials now publicly complain about the intense pain the sanctions are producing. And facing the prospect of U.S. sanctions against Iran's central bank and European actions to halt Iranian oil imports, Tehran signaled in early January some willingness to return to the negotiating table. Washington must test this willingness and, in so doing, provide Iran with a clear strategic choice: address the concerns of the international community regarding its nuclear program and see its isolation lifted or stay on its current path and face substantially higher costs. In framing this choice, Washington must be able to assert that like-minded states are prepared to implement oil-related sanctions, and the Obama administration should continue to emphasize that all options, including military action, remain on the table.

Some will undoubtedly claim that highlighting the potential risks associated with war will lead the Iranians to conclude that the United States lacks the resolve to use force. But in authorizing the surge in Afghanistan, carrying out the raid that killed Osama bin Laden, and leading the NATO air campaign to oust Libya's Muammar al-Qaddafi, President Barack Obama has repeatedly shown that he is willing to accept risk and use force—both as part of a coalition and unilaterally—to defend U.S. interests. And as Martin Dempsey, chairman of the U.S. Joint Chiefs of Staff, told CNN late last December, the United States has a viable contingency plan for Iran if force is ultimately required. But given the high costs and inherent uncertainties of a strike, the United States should not rush to use force until all other options have been exhausted and the Iranian threat is not just growing but imminent. Until then, force is, and should remain, a last resort, not a first choice.

COLIN H. KAHL is an associate professor in the Security Studies Program at Georgetown University's Edmund A. Walsh School of Foreign Service and a Senior Fellow at the Center for a New American Security.

EXPLORING THE ISSUE

Should the United States Use Military Force to Prevent Iran from Developing a Nuclear Weapon?

Critical Thinking and Reflection

1. How might an Iran armed with nuclear weapons impact security and stability in the Middle East?
2. How might a nuclear-armed Iran affect U.S. interests and U.S. relations with Middle Eastern countries?
3. Is it feasible or desirable for the United States to use military force to prevent Iran from obtaining nuclear weapons? What are the potential costs and benefits of using military force?
4. If the United States were to use force against Iran, could the risk of escalation be mitigated?
5. How would a U.S. military strike on Iran impact on the global economy?

Is There Common Ground?

Both authors agree that it would be preferable for the United States and for regional peace and security in the Middle East if Iran did not become a nuclear weapons' state. Where they disagree is on the potential consequences that would follow. For Kroenig, the United States should be willing to bear the costs now of a military strike against Iran to prevent the future dangers that would arise if Iran develops nuclear weapons. In contrast, Kahl argues that there is still time for diplomacy and that a military strike would entail significant risks of escalation to a broader conflict.

It is worth noting that not all scholars see nuclear proliferation as dangerous to international peace and security (Sagan and Waltz, 2003). Foremost among the "nuclear optimists" is political scientist Kenneth Waltz who argues that nuclear arsenals can effectively raise the perceived costs of war and reinforce deterrence. The aggregate result of greater nuclear proliferation will be less war, not more. On the other side of this argument are "nuclear pessimists" such as political scientist Scott Sagan. According to pessimists, nuclear proliferation is dangerous because of the ever-present possibility of strategic miscalculation by states as well as the potential for organizational failures resulting in loss of control over nuclear materials or nuclear accidents. With regard to Iran, a commonly raised concern is that even if the Iranian state were deterred from using its nuclear weapons, its past support of international terrorism and relationships with proxy groups raise the possibility that nuclear materials could fall into the hands of nonstate actors that are not easily deterred.

It remains to be seen whether international tensions over Iran's suspected nuclear weapons program can be resolved with a compromise that avoids both armed conflict and a future in which Iran is a nuclear weapons' state. Certainly, a crisis atmosphere creates significant costs and risks for all parties concerned. The elements of a compromise might include improved transparency of Iran's nuclear programs combined with international reaffirmation of Iran's right to pursue nuclear technologies for peaceful purposes. Other issues that could become part of a package deal include, on the Western side: an end to economic sanctions against Iran, development assistance to Iran, U.S. pledges of noninterference in Iranian affairs, and an international push for renewed vigor in the Israeli–Palestinian peace process. With regard to Iran, it might put on the table: a willingness to embrace intrusive inspections of its nuclear facilities, recognition of Israel's right to exist, a pledge of noninterference with the flow of oil from the Persian Gulf, condemnation of state sponsorship of acts of terrorism, and a pledge not to meddle in the domestic affairs of neighboring Iraq or Afghanistan. None of these issues are subject to easy resolution, however, and progress has so far remained elusive.

Additional Resources

Gavin, Francis. "Same As It Ever Was: Nuclear Alarmism, Proliferation, and the Cold War," *International Security* 34, no. 3 (Winter 2009/2010): 7–37.

In this article, the author argues that that the costs of nonproliferation efforts are not usually calculated in a careful manner, making states prone to take actions in the service of nonproliferation that do more harm than good. In addition, the three most common fears about proliferation are often exaggerated. These fears are that rogue states cannot be relied upon to act rationally; that there will be a tipping point beyond which proliferation will become widespread; and that proliferation will make an act of nuclear terrorism more likely. A careful examination of the history of the nuclear world since 1945 suggests that these concerns are overblown.

IAEA Board of Governors, *Implementation of the NPT Safeguards Agreement and relevant provisions of Security Council resolutions in the Islamic Republic of Iran*. Vienna: International Atomic Energy Agency (IAEA), November 8, 2011.

The IAEA is charged with, among other things, providing nuclear inspectors to assess state compliance with international obligations. This report examines Iran's compliance with provisions of the NPT and decisions of the Security Council of the United Nations.

Kaplan, Robert D. *The Atlantic Monthly* 306, no. 2 (September 2012): 70–73.

This article reviews the ideas offered by former Secretary of State Henry Kissinger on the impact of nuclear weapons on international relations. Kissinger argues that the United States should take strong measures to seek to prevent Iran from becoming a nuclear weapons' state. However, if that fails, the United States can best keep the peace by demonstrating a credible willingness to use military force if necessary.

Lindsay, James and Ray Takeyh. "After Iran Gets the Bomb." *Foreign Affairs* 89, no. 2 (March/April 2010): 33–49.

The author of this article argues that the United States must continue to pressure Iran to not develop nuclear weapons. However, if this policy fails, the United States must then adopt a robust and comprehensive strategy in the Middle East to prevent catastrophic conflict.

Milani, Mohsen. "Tehran's Take." *Foreign Affairs* 88, no. 4 (July/August 2009): 46–62.

In this article, international affairs scholar Mohsen Milani explores why Iran might want nuclear weapons. He argues that the fundamental driver is strategic logic. Iran wishes to increase its influence in the Middle East while protecting itself from perceived threats posed by the United States.

Sagan, Scott and Kenneth Waltz. *The Spread of Nuclear Weapons: A Debate Renewed*. New York: W.W. Norton & Company, 2003.

The two scholars featured in this book debate the impact of nuclear proliferation on international peace and security. Professor Kenneth Waltz of Columbia University argues that more nuclear weapons in the world will diminish the desire of states to go to war. Offering an opposing view, Professor Scott Sagan of Stanford University contends that more nuclear weapons will decrease international stability and increase the risk of armed conflict.

Internet References . . .

Foreign Policy

Seeking to slow what the author perceives to be a rush to war, Yousaf Butt argues in this article that Iran has not yet violated international law and explores Iran's legal right to develop nuclear technology under the NPT.

www.foreignpolicy.com/articles/2012/01/19/stop_the_madness

Center for Strategic & International Studies

After presenting the threat perceptions of both Iran and the United States with regard to one another, this study suggests options the United States could pursue to prevent Iran from obtaining nuclear weapons.

http://csis.org/files/publication/100323_Options_todealwith_Iran.pdf

Foreign Policy

Stephen M. Walt provides a thorough critique of the article presented here by Matthew Kroenig. In addition to questioning many of Kroenig's assumptions, Walt also questions the feasibility and desirability of using military force to prevent Iran from acquiring nuclear weapons.

http://walt.foreignpolicy.com/posts/2011/12/21/the_worst_case_for_war_with_iran

Selected, Edited, and with Issue Framing Material by:
Suzanne Nielsen, *U.S. Military Academy*
and
Scott Handler, *U.S. Military Academy*

ISSUE

Is a Rising China a Threat to U.S. National Security?

YES: John J. Mearsheimer, from "The Gathering Storm: China's Challenge to US Power in Asia," *The Chinese Journal of International Politics* (2010)

NO: G. John Ikenberry, from "The Rise of China and the Future of the West; Can the Liberal System Survive?" *Foreign Affairs* (January/February 2008)

Learning Outcomes

After reading this issue, you should be able to:

• Discuss China's return to great power status.
• Identify potential development challenges that China still faces.
• Discuss various theoretical perspectives on whether a rising China poses a threat to U.S. interests.
• Identify and evaluate U.S. foreign policy options to deal with a rising China.

ISSUE SUMMARY

YES: John J. Mearsheimer, the R. Wendell Harrison Distinguished Service Professor of Political Science at the University of Chicago, posits that the United States will lose its position of preponderant power in the Asia-Pacific region as China gains in relative terms. The inevitable result of China's rise will be intense competition as China vies for regional hegemony and the United States seeks to prevent China from dominating East Asia.

NO: G. John Ikenberry, the Albert G. Milbank Professor of Politics and International Affairs at Princeton University, discusses China's rise and says that armed conflict between the United States and China is not inevitable. China's rise can occur peacefully as long as China continues to enjoy the benefits of participation in the Western liberal order of norms and institutions. The best approach that the United States can take to China's rise is to reaffirm its commitment to the vitality of this order.

In the fall of 2011, the administration of President Barack Obama announced a number of political, security, and economic initiatives that together were billed as constituting a "pivot" toward the Asia-Pacific region (Manyin et al., 2012). These initiatives demonstrate an appreciation among U.S. policymakers of the significance of Asia to U.S. national interests, though some observers argue that they reflect as much continuity as change. Ever since World War II, the importance of Asia to the United States has been evident in the U.S. actions that have included the stationing of troops in the region, the forging of bilateral alliances, participation in regional organizations, and even occasional wars to protect U.S. interests. While not responsible for originating this long-standing pattern of engagement, the rise of the People's Republic of China (PRC) to great power status has undoubtedly added a new dynamic. One of the most significant developments in international affairs over the past couple of decades, China's rise will inevitably impact the diplomatic, economic, and security interests of the United States in East Asia and beyond. In fact, this impact is arguably so great that the management of United States–China relations may be the most important test of the quality of contemporary U.S. foreign policy. Unsurprisingly, however, policymakers, analysts, and pundits disagree about what U.S. policies should look like and seek to do.

The return of China to great power status is a development of historic significance. After China's "Century of Humiliation" from the First Opium War in 1839 to the establishment of the PRC in 1949, China entered a period of internal turmoil, political repression, and failed economic policies. Chinese Communist leader Mao Zedong's ruthless and autocratic rule from 1949 to his death in 1976 left China hungry, poor, and behind technologically. Since Chinese leader Deng Xiaoping's economic reforms began in 1978, however, China has evolved into a country with a dynamic economy that is second in size only to that of the United States. With growth rates consistently above 9 percent, the world's largest cash reserve, a fifth of the world's population, and a massive export sector, China has positioned itself as a force to be reckoned with on the international stage.

In some easily quantifiable ways, China's *absolute* rise in power is undeniable. Most China watchers cite the growth of China's gross domestic product (GDP) as the best indicator. From $148 billion in 1978 to $7.3 trillion in 2011, China's GDP has increased by a factor of 50 in 33 years (The World Bank, 2012). Although China's military spending is somewhat opaque and therefore difficult to estimate, it has also increased. After two decades of steady growth, the U.S. Department of Defense estimates that the PRC's military-related spending was more than $160 billion in 2010 (Department of Defense, 2011). In 2011, China accounted for over 10 percent of the world economy representing an extraordinary increase since China's relative isolation in the Mao era (The World Bank, 2012).

Similarly, most agree that China has increased in power *relative* to the United States since the late 1970s. Though the United States has the largest economy in the world—at $15.1 trillion compared to China's $7 trillion—China's consistently high rate of economic growth has outpaced the U.S. average of 3 percent a year by a large margin over the past few decades. In terms of military power, the United States still possesses an unmatched ability to project military force worldwide. However, the PRC has made significant progress in modernizing its armed forces—particularly over the past decade—and developed important niche capabilities, particularly in support of anti-access and area-denial missions, that serve its national security strategy (Department of Defense, 2011).

Though the PRC's accomplishments in a number of areas are quite impressive, some question whether China can maintain its rapid pace of progress indefinitely. China faces an array of interrelated and deeply rooted problems that could challenge the ability of the PRC to continue to progress as rapidly as it has in the recent past. These problems include: social instability that stems from regional development disparities and rising income inequality; a vulnerable economic growth model that depends on exports to the global market; weak domestic consumption; vast environmental problems (including air and water pollution, resource depletion, droughts, and flooding) and related health issues; opaque decision-making processes and poor transparency in governance; a lack of expansion of political freedoms to match gains in wealth; demographic challenges, including a graying population whose work force will peak in the next decade; and scarcity in critical natural resources. Any one of these issues, on its own, could threaten China's economic miracle. A combination of several could result in insurmountable problems for the Chinese state.

Assuming for now that China continues its relative rise, the question of whether China will be a threat to U.S. national security still remains. According to political scientist Aaron Friedberg, three distinct groups support the proposition that China's rise poses a threat to U.S. national security (2005). The first group, the *realist pessimists,* sees states as embroiled in a perpetual and unavoidable conflict over finite resources. This competition is a zero-sum game in which one state's gain is another state's loss; only the strongest survive. Realist pessimists believe that militarily, politically, economically, and culturally the PRC will develop power in its region and in the world and seek to deny U.S. influence in a growing number of areas. As the PRC's foreign policy becomes more expansive and aggressive, it will bring the PRC into conflict with the United States.

A second group that sees a rising China as a threat consists of *neoconservatives.* Neoconservatives view regime type as a critical factor in determining state behavior internationally. Democratic states embrace liberal values including freedom of speech, assembly, and religion, and their behavior abroad is moderated by domestic constraints on the use of power and the requirement to be responsive to the public. Authoritarian states, on the other hand, do not have the same checks and balances and are therefore less prone to protect individual rights and more likely to engage in aggressive foreign policy. Because the PRC is ruled by an authoritarian regime, the PRC and the United States are destined for confrontation. The United States should therefore try to constrain the PRC and sustain U.S. dominance.

Finally, *liberal pessimists* also view a rising China as a threat to U.S. security. They argue that the pursuit of a democracy promotion agenda will necessarily bring the United States into conflict with China, an authoritarian state with a different concept of individual rights. Rhetoric from both sides will result in spiraling tensions. In addition, rather than facilitating cooperation, international institutions will be misused by the United States to attempt to thwart China and therefore become merely another source of tension and conflict.

In contrast to these perspectives, Friedberg also identifies two schools of thought that argue that a rising China will not necessarily pose a threat to the United States. The first, *realist optimists,* emphasizes that China's power is limited—especially in military terms, given that U.S. military spending is probably three to five times as large as that of the PRC. Realist optimists argue that the expansion of the PRC's aspirations will be slow and limited to understandable concerns over protecting vital imports and securing the state's sovereignty. Finally, realist optimists point to ample evidence of Chinese weakness, including the developmental challenges discussed above, as evidence that China's rise should not be assumed to be threatening.

The second group that sees a rising China as unthreatening is made up of *liberal optimists.* Members of this camp argue that international institutions such as the United Nations and World Trade Organization, as well as regional organizations, will help to constrain the behavior of both the United States and the PRC. Furthermore, they point to some of China's domestic reforms as evidence of a move toward a more open society. If these reforms continue, the prospects for conflict between the United States and the PRC will continue to decline over time.

The YES and NO selections are forceful articulations of two important positions in the above debate. In answering YES to the question of whether a rising China poses a threat to U.S. national security, political scientist John Mearsheimer takes the position of a realist pessimist. An increasingly powerful PRC will inevitably pursue an expanding set of ambitions that will increasingly cut against the interests of the United States. In response, the

United States should seek now to constrain rather than facilitate China's continued rise.

In answering NO, G. John Ikenberry presents what Friedberg calls the liberal optimist view. Ikenberry points out that the PRC has been a great beneficiary of the liberal international order that the United States helped to found. Most notably, the PRC's tremendous economic gains have been made possible in large part by its participation in international institutions and processes that facilitate free trade. The best approach the United States can take to a rising China is to commit itself to strengthening the liberal international order it did so much to create. In this way, the United States can help the PRC to see a future in which its interests are best served through constructive participation in this order rather than through an alternative strategy more likely to produce conflict.

YES

John J. Mearsheimer

The Gathering Storm: China's Challenge to US Power in Asia

The United States has been the most powerful state on the planet for many decades and has deployed robust military forces in the Asia-Pacific region since the early years of the Second World War. The American presence has had significant consequences for Australia and for the wider region. . . .

[T]he rise of China is having a significant effect on the global balance of power. In particular, the power gap between China and the United States is shrinking and in all likelihood 'US strategic primacy' in this region will be no more. This is not to say that the United States will disappear; in fact, its presence is likely to grow in response to China's rise. But the United States will no longer be the preponderant power in the Asia-Pacific region, as it has been since 1945.

. . . China's rise . . . is likely to lead to an intense security competition between China and the United States, with considerable potential for war. Moreover, most of China's neighbors, to include India, Japan, Singapore, South Korea, Russia, Vietnam—and Australia—will join with the United States to contain China's power. To put it bluntly: China cannot rise peacefully.

It is important to emphasize, however, that I am not arguing that Chinese behavior alone will drive the security competition that lies ahead. The United States is also likely to behave in aggressive ways, thus further increasing the prospects for trouble in the Asia-Pacific region.

Naturally, not everyone will agree with my assessment of the situation. Many believe that China can rise peacefully, that it is not inevitable that the United States and a powerful China will have confrontational relations. Of course, they assume that China will have peaceful intentions, and that welcome fact of life can help facilitate stability in this region, even though the underlying balance of power is expected to change dramatically.

The Case for China's Peaceful Rise

I examine here three key arguments that are often employed to support this optimistic prognosis. First, some claim that China can allay any fears about its rise by making it clear to its neighbors and the United States that it has peaceful intentions, that it will not use force to change

the balance of power. This perspective can be found in the [Australian] Defence White Paper, which states: 'The pace, scope and structure of China's military modernization have the potential to give its neighbors cause for concern if not carefully explained, and if China does not reach out to others to build confidence regarding its military plans'.[1] In essence, the belief here is that Beijing has the ability to signal its present and future intentions to Australia and other countries in compelling ways.

Unfortunately, states can never be certain about each other's intentions.[2] They cannot know with a high degree of certainty whether they are dealing with a revisionist state or a *status quo* power. For example, there is still no consensus among experts as to whether the Soviet Union was bent on dominating Eurasia during the Cold War. Nor is there a consensus on whether Imperial Germany was a highly aggressive state that was principally responsible for causing the First World War. The root of the problem is that unlike military capabilities, which we can see and count, intentions cannot be empirically verified. Intentions are in the minds of decision makers and they are especially difficult to discern. One might think that Chinese leaders can use words to explain their intentions. But talk is cheap and leaders have been known to lie to foreign audiences.[3] Thus, it is hard to know the intentions of China's present leaders, which is not to say that they are necessarily revisionist.

But even if one could determine China's intentions today, there is no way to know what they will be in the future. After all, it is impossible to identify who will be running the foreign policy of any country 5 or 10 years from now, much less whether they will have aggressive intentions. It cannot be emphasized enough that we face radical uncertainty when it comes to determining the future intentions of any country, China included.

A second line of argument is that a benign China can avoid confrontation by building defensive rather than offensive military forces. In other words, Beijing can signal that it is a *status quo* power by denying itself the capability to use force to alter the balance of power. After all, a country that has hardly any offensive capability cannot be a revisionist state, because it does not have the means to act aggressively. Not surprisingly, Chinese leaders often claim that their military is designed solely for defensive purposes.

Mearsheimer, John J. From *Chinese Journal of International Politics*, vol. 3, no. 4, 2010, pp. 381–391, 396. Copyright © 2010 by John J. Meirsheimer. Reprinted by permission of Oxford University Press via Rightslink.

For example, the *New York Times* recently reported in an important article on the Chinese navy that its leaders maintain that it is 'purely a self-defense force'.[4]

One problem with this approach is that it is difficult to distinguish between offensive and defensive military capabilities. Negotiators at the 1932 Disarmament Conference tried to make these distinctions and found themselves tied in knots trying to determine whether particular weapons like tanks and aircraft carriers are offensive or defensive in nature.[5] The basic problem is that the capabilities that states develop to defend themselves often have significant offensive potential.

Consider what China is doing today. It is building military forces that have significant power projection capability, and as the Defence White Paper tells us, China's 'military modernization will be increasingly characterized by the development of power projection capabilities'.[6] For example, the Chinese are building naval forces that can project power out to the so-called 'Second Island Chain' in the Western Pacific. And they also say that they are planning to build a 'blue water navy' that can operate in the Arabian Sea and the Indian Ocean. For understandable reasons, they want to be able to protect their sea lanes and not have to depend on the American navy to handle that mission for them. Although they do not have that capability yet, as Robert Kaplan points out in a recent article in *Foreign Affairs*, 'China's naval leaders are displaying the aggressive philosophy of the turn-of-the-twentieth-century US naval strategist Alfred Thayer Mahan, who argued for sea control and the decisive battle'.[7]

Of course, most Chinese leaders think that their navy is defensively oriented, even though it has considerable offensive capability and will have much more in the future. Indeed, they refer to their naval strategy as 'Far Sea Defense'.[8] As Kaplan's comments indicate, it seems almost certain that as the Chinese navy grows in size and capability, none of China's neighbors, including Australia, will consider it to be defensively oriented. They will instead view it as a formidable offensive force. Thus, anyone looking to determine China's future intentions by observing its military is likely to conclude that Beijing is bent on aggression.

Finally, some maintain that China's recent behavior toward its neighbors, which has not been aggressive in any meaningful way, is a reliable indicator of how China will act in the decades ahead. The central problem with this argument is that past behavior is usually not a reliable indicator of future behavior because leaders come and go and some are more hawkish than others. Also, circumstances at home and abroad can change in ways that make the use of military force more or less attractive.

The Chinese case is illustrative in this regard. Beijing does not possess a formidable military today and it is certainly in no position to pick a fight with the United States. This is not to say that China is a paper tiger, but it does not have the capability to cause much trouble, even in the Asia-Pacific region. However, that situation is expected to

change markedly over time, in which case China will have significant offensive capability. Then, we will see how committed it is to the *status quo*. But right now we cannot tell much about China's future behavior, because it has such limited capability to act aggressively.

What all of this tells us is that there is no good way to define what China's intentions will be down the road or to predict its future behavior based on its recent foreign policies. It does seem clear, however, that China will eventually have a military with significant offensive potential.

The Not-So-Benign United States

Up to now, I have been concerned with how an American or an Australian might assess China's future behavior. But to fully understand how China's rise will affect stability in the Asia-Pacific region, we must also consider what Chinese leaders can explain about future American behavior, by looking at its intentions, capabilities, and present behavior.

There is obviously no way China's leaders can know who will be in charge of American foreign policy in the years ahead, much less what their intentions toward China will be. But they do know that all of America's post-Cold War presidents, including Barack Obama, have stated that they are committed to maintaining American primacy.[9] And that means Washington is likely to go to considerable lengths to prevent China from becoming too powerful.

Regarding capabilities, the United States spends nearly as much money on defense as all the other countries in the world combined.[10] Moreover, because the American military is designed to fight all around the globe, it has abundant power projection assets. Much of that capability is either located in the Asia-Pacific region or can be moved there quickly should the need arise. China cannot help but see that the United States has formidable military forces in its neighborhood that are designed in good part for offensive purposes.[11] Surely, when Washington moves aircraft carriers into the Taiwan Straits—as it did in 1996—or when it redeploys submarines to the Western Pacific, China sees these naval assets as offensive, not defensive in nature.

This is not to deny that most Americans, like most Chinese, think that their military is a defensive instrument; but that is not the way it looks when you are at the other end of the rifle barrel.[12] Thus, anyone in China seeking to gauge American intentions by assessing its military capabilities is likely to think it is a revisionist state, not a *status quo* power.

Lastly, there is the matter of America's recent behavior and what that might tell us about future US actions. As I said earlier, past actions are usually not a reliable indicator of future behavior, because circumstances change and new leaders sometimes think differently about foreign policy than their predecessors. But if Chinese leaders try to gauge how the United States is likely to act down the road by looking at its recent foreign policy, they will almost certainly conclude that it is a war-like and dangerous country. After all, America has been at war for 14 of the 21 years since the Cold War ended. That is two out of every three years. And remember that the Obama administration is apparently contemplating a new war against Iran.

One might argue that this is all true, but the United States has not threatened to attack China. The problem with this argument is that American leaders from both the Democratic and Republican parties have made it clear that they believe the United States, to quote Madeleine Albright, is the 'indispensable nation' and therefore it has both the right and the responsibility to police the entire globe.[13] Furthermore, most Chinese are well aware of how the United States took advantage of a weak China by pushing forward the infamous 'Open Door' policy in the early twentieth century. Chinese officials also know that the United States and China fought a bloody war in Korea between 1950 and 1953. It is not surprising that the *Economist* recently reported that, 'A retired Chinese admiral likened the American navy to a man with a criminal record "wandering just outside the gate of a family home"'.[14] It seems that this is a case where we should be thankful that countries usually do not pay much attention to a potential rival's past behavior when trying to determine its future intentions.

What all of this tells us is that the future security environment in the Asia-Pacific region will revolve around China and the United States, and each of those great powers will have a military with significant offensive capability and unknowable intentions.

There is one other factor that matters greatly for future Sino–American relations. There is no centralized authority that states can turn to for help if a dangerous aggressor threatens them. There is no night watchman in the international system, which means that states have to rely mainly on themselves to ensure their survival.[15] Thus, the core question that any leader has to ask him or herself is this: what is the best way to maximize my country's security in a world where another state might have significant offensive military capability as well as offensive intentions, and where there is no higher body I can turn to for help if that other state threatens my country? This question—more than any other—will motivate American as well as Chinese leaders in the years ahead, as it has in the past.

The Pursuit of Regional Hegemony

I believe there is a straightforward answer to this question and that all great powers know it and act accordingly.[16] The best way for any state to ensure its survival is to be much more powerful than all the other states in the system, because the weaker states are unlikely to attack it for fear they will be soundly defeated. No country in the Western Hemisphere, for example, would dare strike the United States because it is so powerful relative to all its neighbors.

To be more specific, the ideal situation for any great power is to be the hegemon in the system, because its survival then would almost be guaranteed. A hegemon is a country that is so powerful that it dominates all the other states. In other words, no other state has the military wherewithal to put up a serious fight against it. In essence, a hegemon is the only great power in the system.

When people talk about hegemony these days, they are usually referring to the United States, which they describe as a global hegemon. I do not like this terminology, however, because it is virtually impossible for any state—including the United States—to achieve global hegemony. The main obstacle to world domination is the difficulty of projecting power over huge distances, especially across enormous bodies of water like the Atlantic and Pacific Oceans.

The best outcome that a great power can hope for is to achieve regional hegemony, and possibly control another region that is close by and easily accessible over land. The United States, which dominates the Western Hemisphere, is the only regional hegemon in modern history. Five other great powers have tried to dominate their region—Napoleonic France, Imperial Germany, Imperial Japan, Nazi Germany, and the Soviet Union—but none have succeeded.

The United States, it should be emphasized, did not become a hegemon in the Western Hemisphere by accident. When it gained its independence in 1783, it was a weak country comprised of 13 states running up and down the Atlantic seaboard. Over the course of the next 115 years, American policymakers worked unrelentingly in pursuit of regional hegemony. They expanded America's boundaries from the Atlantic to the Pacific Ocean as part of a policy commonly referred to as 'Manifest Destiny'. Indeed, the United States was an expansionist power of the first order. Henry Cabot Lodge put the point well when he noted that the United States had a 'record of conquest, colonization, and territorial expansion unequalled by any people in the nineteenth century'.[17] Or I might add the twentieth century.

But America's leaders in the nineteenth century were not just concerned with turning the United States into a powerful territorial state. They were also determined to push the European great powers out of the Western Hemisphere, and make it clear to them that they were not welcome back. This policy, which is still in effect today, is known as the 'Monroe Doctrine'. By 1898, the last European empire in the Americas had collapsed and the United States had become a regional hegemon.

States that achieve regional hegemony have a further aim: they seek to prevent great powers in other geographical regions from duplicating their feat. A regional hegemon, in other words, does not want peer competitors. The United States, for example, played a key role in preventing Imperial Japan, Imperial Germany, Nazi Germany, and the Soviet Union from gaining regional supremacy. Regional hegemons attempt to check aspiring hegemons in other regions, because they fear that a rival great power that dominates its own region will be an especially powerful foe that is essentially free to roam around the globe and cause trouble in their backyard. Regional hegemons prefer that there be at least two great powers located together in other regions, because their proximity will force them to concentrate their attention on each other rather than the distant hegemon. Furthermore, if a potential hegemon emerges among them, the other great powers in that region might be able to contain it by themselves, allowing the distant hegemon to remain safely on the sidelines.

The bottom line is that for sound strategic reasons the United States labored for more than a century to gain regional hegemony, and after achieving that goal, it has made sure that no other great power dominated either Asia or Europe the way it dominates the Western Hemisphere.

Imitating Uncle Sam

What does America's past behavior tell us about the rise of China? In particular, how should we expect China to conduct itself, as it grows more powerful? And how should we expect the United States and China's neighbors to react to a strong China?

I expect China to act the way the United States has acted over its long history. Specifically, I believe that China will try to dominate the Asia-Pacific region much as the United States dominates the Western Hemisphere. For good strategic reasons, China will seek to maximize the power gap between itself and potentially dangerous neighbors like India, Japan, and Russia. China will want to make sure that it is so powerful that no state in Asia has the wherewithal to threaten it. It is unlikely that China will pursue military superiority so that it can go on the warpath and conquer other countries in the region, although that is always a possibility. Instead, it is more likely that Beijing will want to dictate the boundaries of acceptable behavior to neighboring countries, much the way the United States makes it clear to other states in the Americas that it is the boss. Gaining regional hegemony, I might add, is probably the only way that China will get Taiwan back.

A much more powerful China can also be expected to try to push the United States out of the Asia-Pacific region, much the way the United States pushed the European great powers out of the Western Hemisphere in the 19th century. We should expect China to come up with its own version of the Monroe Doctrine, as Imperial Japan did in the 1930s. In fact, we are already seeing inklings of that policy. Consider that in March, Chinese officials told two high-ranking American policymakers that the United States was no longer allowed to interfere in the South China Sea, which China views as a 'core interest' like Taiwan and Tibet.[18] And it seems that China feels the same way about the Yellow Sea. In late July 2010, the United States and South Korean navies conducted joint naval exercises in response to North Korea's alleged sinking of a South Korean naval vessel. Those naval maneuvers were originally planned to take place in the Yellow Sea, which is adjacent to the Chinese coastline, but vigorous protests from China forced the Obama administration to move them further east into the Sea of Japan.[19]

These ambitious goals make good strategic sense for China. Beijing should want a militarily weak Japan and Russia as its neighbors, just as the United States prefers a militarily weak Canada and Mexico on its borders. No state in its right mind should want other powerful states located in its region. All Chinese surely remember what happened in the last century when Japan was powerful and China was weak. Furthermore, why would a powerful China accept US military forces operating in its backyard? American policymakers, after all, express outrage whenever distant great powers send military forces into the Western Hemisphere. Those foreign forces are invariably seen as a potential threat to American security. The same logic should apply to China. Why would China feel safe with US forces deployed on its doorstep? Following the logic of the Monroe Doctrine, would not China's security be better served by pushing the American military out of the Asia-Pacific region?

Why should we expect China to act any differently than the United States over the course of its history? Are they more principled than the Americans? More ethical? Are they less nationalistic than the Americans? Less concerned about their survival? They are none of these things, of course, which is why China is likely to imitate the United States and attempt to become a regional hegemon.

And what is the likely American response if China attempts to dominate Asia? It is crystal clear from the historical record that the United States does not tolerate peer competitors. As it demonstrated over the course of the 20th century, it is determined to remain the world's only regional hegemon. Therefore, the United States can be expected to go to great lengths to contain China and ultimately weaken it to the point where it is no longer a threat to rule the roost in Asia. In essence, the United States is likely to act toward China similar to the way it behaved toward the Soviet Union during the Cold War.

China's neighbors in the Asia-Pacific region are certain to fear its rise as well, and they too will do whatever they can to prevent it from achieving regional hegemony. Indeed, there is already substantial evidence that countries like India, Japan, and Russia, as well as smaller powers like Singapore, South Korea, and Vietnam, are worried about China's ascendancy and are looking for ways to contain it. India and Japan, for example, signed a 'Joint Security Declaration' in October 2008, in good part because they are worried about China's growing power.[20] India and the United States, which had testy relations at best during the Cold War, have become good friends over the past decade, in large part because they both fear China. In July 2010, the Obama administration, which is filled with people who preach to the world about the importance of human rights, announced that it was resuming relations with Indonesia's elite special forces, despite their rich history of human rights abuses. The reason for this shift was that Washington wants Indonesia on its side as China grows more powerful, and as the *New York Times* reported, Indonesian officials 'dropped hints that the group might explore building ties with the Chinese military if the ban remained'.[21]

Singapore, which sits astride the critically important Straits of Malacca and worries about China's growing power, badly wants to upgrade its already close ties with the United States. Toward that end, it built a deep-water pier at its new Changi Naval Base so that the US Navy could operate an aircraft carrier out of Singapore if the need arose.[22] And the recent decision by Japan to allow the US Marines to remain on Okinawa was driven in part by Tokyo's concerns about China's growing assertiveness in the region and the related need to keep the American security umbrella firmly in place over Japan.[23] Most of China's neighbors will eventually join an American-led balancing coalition designed to check China's rise, much the way Britain, France, Germany, Italy, Japan, and even China, joined forces with the United States to contain the Soviet Union during the Cold War.[24]

. . . The picture I have painted of what is likely to happen if China continues its impressive economic growth is not a pretty one. Indeed, it is downright depressing. I wish that I could tell a more optimistic story about the prospects for peace in the Asia-Pacific region. But the fact is that international politics is a nasty and dangerous business and no amount of good will can ameliorate the intense security competition that sets in when an aspiring hegemon appears in Eurasia. And there is little doubt that there is one on the horizon.

Notes

1. *Ibid.*, p. 34.
2. Dale C. Copeland, *The Origins of Major War* (Ithaca: Cornell University Press, 2000), Chapter 1; Thomas Hobbes, *Leviathan*, ed. C. B. Macpherson (Harmondsworth: Penguin, 1985), pp. 94–99, 131, 169–70, 194; John J. Mearsheimer, *The Tragedy of Great Power Politics* (New York: Norton, 2001), Chapter 2.
3. John J. Mearsheimer, *Why Leaders Lie: The Truth about Lying in International Politics* (New York: Oxford University Press, 2011).
4. Edward Wong, 'Chinese Military Seeks to Extend its Naval Power', *New York Times*, April 23, 2010.
5. Marion W. Boggs, *Attempts to Define and Limit "Aggressive" Armament in Diplomacy and Strategy* (Columbia: University of Missouri, 1941); Keir A. Lieber, *War and the Engineers: The Primacy of Politics over Technology* (Ithaca: Cornell University Press, 2008), pp. 12–13, 35–7.
6. Department of Defence, Australian Government, *Defending Australia in the Asia Pacific Century*, p. 34.
7. Robert D. Kaplan, 'The Geography of Chinese Power', *Foreign Affairs*, Vol. 89, No. 3 (2010), p. 34.
8. Edward Wong, 'Chinese Military'.
9. In April 2010, the Australian journalist, Kerry O'Brien asked President Obama, 'How hard is it going to be to for Americans to adjust in a mature way to the increasing prospect that you can't be number one forever?' Obama replied: 'I actually think that America can be number one for a very very long time but we think that there can be a whole host of countries that are prospering and doing well. Here's one way to think about it. The Chinese standard of living and industrial output per capita is about where the United States was back in 1910, I mean they've got a lot of catching up to do'. Transcript of 'Face to Face with Obama', *The 7:30 Report*, Australian Broadcasting Corporation, April 14, 2010.
10. The United States accounted for 43 percent of worldwide spending on defense in 2009, according to the *SIPRI Yearbook 2010: Armaments, Disarmament and International Security, Summary* (Oxford: Oxford University Press, 2010), p. 11.
11. Toshi Yoshihara, 'Chinese Missile Strategy and the US Naval Presence in Japan: The Operational View from Beijing', *Naval War College Review*, Vol. 63, No. 3 (2010), pp. 39–62.
12. This phenomenon where the measures a state takes to increase its own security decrease the security of other states is commonly referred to as the 'security dilemma'. See Charles L. Glaser, 'The Security Dilemma Revisited', *World Politics*, Vol. 50, No. 1 (1997), pp. 171–201; John H. Herz, 'Idealist Internationalism and the Security Dilemma', *World Politics*, Vol. 2, No. 2 (1950), pp. 157–80; Robert Jervis, 'Cooperation under the Security Dilemma', *World Politics*, Vol. 30, No. 2 (1978), pp. 167–214.
13. Secretary of State Albright said on February 19, 1998 that, 'If we have to use force, it is because we are America. We are the indispensable nation. We stand tall. We see further than other countries into the future'.
14. 'Naked Aggression', *Economist*, March 14, 2009, p. 45.
15. Kenneth N. Waltz, *Theory of International Politics* (Reading: Addison-Wesley, 1979), pp. 91, 107, 111.
16. John J. Mearsheimer, *Tragedy of Great Power Politics*, Chapter 2.
17. *Ibid.*, p. 238.
18. Edward Wong, 'Chinese Military'.
19. Chico Harlan, 'South Korea and US Send Message to North Korea with Drills in Sea of Japan', *Washington Post*, July 26, 2010; Peter Lee, 'South Korea Reels as US Backpedals', *Asia Times online*, July 24, 2010; Ben Richardson and Bill Austin, 'US–South Korea Drills to Avoid Yellow Sea amid China Concern', *Bloomberg Businessweek*, October 13, 2010; Michael Sainsbury, 'Don't

Interfere with Us: China Warns US to Keep its Nose Out', *The Australian*, August 6, 2010.

20. David Brewster, 'The India–Japan Security Relationship: An Enduring Security Partnership', *Asian Security*, Vol. 6, No. 2 (2010), pp. 95–120.

21. Elisabeth Bumiller and Norimitsu Onishi, 'US Lifts Ban on Indonesian Special Forces Unit', *New York Times*, July 22, 2010. Also see Robert Dreyfuss, 'Containing China is A Fool's Errand. Yet Obama's Deal with Indonesian Thugs is Aimed at Exactly That', *The Nation*, July 23, 2010; John Pomfret, 'US Continues Effort to Counter China's Influence in Asia', *Washington Post*, July 23, 2010.

22. 'Singapore Changi Naval Base', www.globalsecurity .org/military/facility/singapore.htm, accessed on October 20, 2010.

23. Blaine Harden, 'Japanese Prime Minister Yukio Hatoyama Resigns', *Washington Post*, June 2, 2007; 'Japan Agrees to Accept Okinawa Base', www.upi.com/Top_News/US/2010/05/23/ Japan-agrees-to-accept-Okinawa-base/ UPI-72831274623169/, accessed on May 23, 2010.

24. For more evidence of Asian countries beginning to balance against China, see Andrew Jacobs, 'China Warns US to Stay Out of Islands Dispute', *New York Times*, July 26, 2010; Jay Solomon, Yuka Hayashi, and Jason Dean, 'As China Swaggers, Neighbors Embrace US', *Wall Street Journal*, May 25, 2010.

JOHN J. MEARSHEIMER is the R. Wendell Harrison Distinguished Service Professor of Political Science and the co-director of the program on international security policy at the University of Chicago.

G. John Ikenberry

 **NO**

The Rise of China and the Future of the West; Can the Liberal System Survive?

The rise of China will undoubtedly be one of the great dramas of the twenty-first century. China's extraordinary economic growth and active diplomacy are already transforming East Asia, and future decades will see even greater increases in Chinese power and influence. But exactly how this drama will play out is an open question. Will China overthrow the existing order or become a part of it? And what, if anything, can the United States do to maintain its position as China rises?

Some observers believe that the American era is coming to an end, as the Western-oriented world order is replaced by one increasingly dominated by the East. The historian Niall Ferguson has written that the bloody twentieth century witnessed "the descent of the West" and "a reorientation of the world" toward the East. Realists go on to note that as China gets more powerful and the United States' position erodes, two things are likely to happen: China will try to use its growing influence to reshape the rules and institutions of the international system to better serve its interests, and other states in the system—especially the declining hegemon—will start to see China as a growing security threat. The result of these developments, they predict, will be tension, distrust, and conflict, the typical features of a power transition. In this view, the drama of China's rise will feature an increasingly powerful China and a declining United States locked in an epic battle over the rules and leadership of the international system. And as the world's largest country emerges not from within but outside the established post-World War II international order, it is a drama that will end with the grand ascendance of China and the onset of an Asian-centered world order.

That course, however, is not inevitable. The rise of China does not have to trigger a wrenching hegemonic transition. The U.S.-Chinese power transition can be very different from those of the past because China faces an international order that is fundamentally different from those that past rising states confronted. China does not just face the United States; it faces a Western-centered system that is open, integrated, and rule-based, with wide and deep political foundations. The nuclear revolution, meanwhile, has made war among great powers unlikely—eliminating the major tool that rising powers have used

to overturn international systems defended by declining hegemonic states. Today's Western order, in short, is hard to overturn and easy to join.

This unusually durable and expansive order is itself the product of farsighted U.S. leadership. After World War II, the United States did not simply establish itself as the leading world power. It led in the creation of universal institutions that not only invited global membership but also brought democracies and market societies closer together. It built an order that facilitated the participation and integration of both established great powers and newly independent states. (It is often forgotten that this postwar order was designed in large part to reintegrate the defeated Axis states and the beleaguered Allied states into a unified international system.) Today, China can gain full access to and thrive within this system. And if it does, China will rise, but the Western order—if managed properly—will live on.

As it faces an ascendant China, the United States should remember that its leadership of the Western order allows it to shape the environment in which China will make critical strategic choices. If it wants to preserve this leadership, Washington must work to strengthen the rules and institutions that underpin that order—making it even easier to join and harder to overturn. U.S. grand strategy should be built around the motto "The road to the East runs through the West." It must sink the roots of this order as deeply as possible, giving China greater incentives for integration than for opposition and increasing the chances that the system will survive even after U.S. relative power has declined.

The United States' "unipolar moment" will inevitably end. If the defining struggle of the twenty-first century is between China and the United States, China will have the advantage. If the defining struggle is between China and a revived Western system, the West will triumph.

Transitional Anxieties

China is well on its way to becoming a formidable global power. The size of its economy has quadrupled since the launch of market reforms in the late 1970s and, by some estimates, will double again over the next decade. It has become one of the world's major manufacturing centers and consumes roughly a third of the global supply of iron, steel, and coal. It has accumulated massive foreign reserves, worth more than $1 trillion at the end of 2006. Chinas military spending has increased at an inflation-adjusted rate of over 18 percent a year, and its diplomacy has extended its reach not just in Asia but also in Africa, Latin America, and the Middle East. Indeed, whereas the Soviet Union rivaled the United States as a military competitor only, China is emerging as both a military and an economic rival—heralding a profound shift in the distribution of global power.

Power transitions are a recurring problem in international relations. As scholars such as Paul Kennedy and Robert Gilpin have described it, world politics has been marked by a succession of powerful states rising up to organize the international system. A powerful state can create and enforce the rules and institutions of a stable global order in which to pursue its interests and security. But nothing lasts forever: long-term changes in the distribution of power give rise to new challenger states, who set off a struggle over the terms of that international order. Rising states want to translate their newly acquired power into greater authority in the global system—to reshape the rules and institutions in accordance with their own interests. Declining states, in turn, fear their loss of control and worry about the security implications of their weakened position.

These moments are fraught with danger. When a state occupies a commanding position in the international system, neither it nor weaker states have an incentive to change the existing order. But when the power of a challenger state grows and the power of the leading state weakens, a strategic rivalry ensues, and conflict—perhaps leading to war—becomes likely. The danger of power transitions is captured most dramatically in the case of late-nineteenth-century Germany. In 1870, the United Kingdom had a three-to-one advantage in economic power over Germany and a significant military advantage as well; by 1903, Germany had pulled ahead in terms of both economic and military power. As Germany unified and grew, so, too, did its dissatisfactions and demands, and as it grew more powerful, it increasingly appeared as a threat to other great powers in Europe, and security competition began. In the strategic realignments that followed, France, Russia, and the United Kingdom, formerly enemies, banded together to confront an emerging Germany. The result was a European war. Many observers see this dynamic emerging in U.S.-Chinese relations. "If China continues its impressive economic growth over the next few decades," the realist scholar John Mearsheimer has written, "the United States and China are likely to engage in an intense security competition with considerable potential for war."

But not all power transitions generate war or overturn the old order. In the early decades of the twentieth century, the United Kingdom ceded authority to the United States without great conflict or even a rupture in relations. From the late 1940s to the early 1990s, Japan's economy grew from the equivalent of five percent of U.S. GDP to the equivalent of over 60 percent of U.S. GDP, and yet Japan never challenged the existing international order.

Clearly, there are different types of power transitions. Some states have seen their economic and geopolitical power grow dramatically and have still accommodated themselves to the existing order. Others have risen up and sought to change it. Some power transitions have led to the breakdown of the old order and the establishment of a new international hierarchy. Others have brought about only limited adjustments in the regional and global system.

A variety of factors determine the way in which power transitions unfold. The nature of the rising state's regime and the degree of its dissatisfaction with the old order are critical: at the end of the nineteenth century, the United States, a liberal country an ocean away from Europe, was better able to embrace the British-centered international order than Germany was. But even more decisive is the character of the international order itself—for it is the nature of the international order that shapes a rising state's choice between challenging that order and integrating into it.

Open Order

The postwar Western order is historically unique. Any international order dominated by a powerful state is based on a mix of coercion and consent, but the U.S.-led order is distinctive in that it has been more liberal than imperial—and so unusually accessible, legitimate, and durable. Its rules and institutions are rooted in, and thus reinforced by, the evolving global forces of democracy and capitalism. It is expansive, with a wide and widening array of participants and stakeholders. It is capable of generating tremendous economic growth and power while also signaling restraint—all of which make it hard to overturn and easy to join.

It was the explicit intention of the Western order's architects in the 1940s to make that order integrative and expansive. Before the Cold War split the world into competing camps, Franklin Roosevelt sought to create a one-world system managed by cooperative great powers that would rebuild war-ravaged Europe, integrate the defeated states, and establish mechanisms for security cooperation and expansive economic growth. In fact, it was Roosevelt who urged—over the opposition of Winston Churchill—that China be included as a permanent member of the UN Security Council. The then Australian ambassador to the United States wrote in his diary after his first meeting with Roosevelt during the war, "He said that he had numerous discussions with Winston about China and that he felt that Winston was 40 years behind the times on China and he continually referred to the Chinese as 'Chinks' and 'Chinamen' and he felt that this was very dangerous. He wanted to keep China as a friend because in 40 or 50 years' time China might easily become a very powerful military nation."

Over the next half century, the United States used the system of rules and institutions it had built to good effect. West Germany was bound to its democratic Western European neighbors through the European Coal and Steel Community (and, later, the European Community) and to the United States through the Atlantic security pact; Japan was bound to the United States through an alliance partnership and expanding economic ties. The Bretton Woods meeting in 1944 laid down the monetary and trade rules that facilitated the opening and subsequent flourishing of the world economy—an astonishing achievement given the ravages of war and the competing interests of the great powers. Additional agreements between the United States, Western Europe, and Japan solidified the open and multilateral character of the postwar world economy. After the onset of the Cold War, the Marshall Plan in Europe and the 1951 security-pact between the United States and Japan further integrated the defeated Axis powers into the Western order.

In the final days of the Cold War, this system once again proved remarkably successful. As the Soviet Union declined, the Western order offered a set of rules and institutions that provided Soviet leaders with both reassurances and points of access—effectively encouraging them to become a part of the system. Moreover, the shared leadership of the order ensured accommodation of the Soviet Union. As the Reagan administration pursued a hard-line policy toward Moscow, the Europeans pursued detente and engagement. For every hard-line "push," there was a moderating "pull," allowing Mikhail Gorbachev to pursue high-risk reforms. On the eve of German unification, the fact that a united Germany would be embedded in European and Atlantic institutions—rather than becoming an independent great power—helped reassure Gorbachev that neither German nor Western intentions were hostile. After the Cold War, the Western order once again managed the integration of a new wave of countries, this time from the formerly communist world. Three particular features of the Western order have been critical to this success and longevity.

First, unlike the imperial systems of the past, the Western order is built around rules and norms of nondiscrimination and market openness, creating conditions for rising states to advance their expanding economic and political goals within it. Across history, international orders have varied widely in terms of whether the material benefits that are generated accrue disproportionately to the leading state or are widely shared. In the Western system, the barriers to economic participation are low, and the potential benefits are high. China has already discovered the massive economic returns that are possible by operating within this open-market system.

Second is the coalition-based character of its leadership. Past orders have tended to be dominated by one state.

The stakeholders of the current Western order include a coalition of powers arrayed around the United States—an important distinction. These leading states, most of them advanced liberal democracies, do not always agree, but they are engaged in a continuous process of give-and-take over economics, politics, and security. Power transitions are typically seen as being played out between two countries, a rising state and a declining hegemon, and the order falls as soon as the power balance shifts. But in the current order, the larger aggregation of democratic capitalist states—and the resulting accumulation of geopolitical power—shifts the balance in the order's favor.

Third, the postwar Western order has an unusually dense, encompassing, and broadly endorsed system of rules and institutions. Whatever its shortcomings, it is more open and rule-based than any previous order. State sovereignty and the rule of law are not just norms enshrined in the United Nations Charter. They are part of the deep operating logic of the order. To be sure, these norms are evolving, and the United States itself has historically been ambivalent about binding itself to international law and institutions—and at no time more so than today. But the overall system is dense with multilateral rules and institutions—global and regional, economic, political, and security-related. These represent one of the great breakthroughs of the postwar era. They have laid the basis for unprecedented levels of cooperation and shared authority over the global system.

The incentives these features create for China to integrate into the liberal international order are reinforced by the changed nature of the international economic environment—especially the new interdependence driven by technology. The most farsighted Chinese leaders understand that globalization has changed the game and that China accordingly needs strong, prosperous partners around the world. From the United States' perspective, a healthy Chinese economy is vital to the United States and the rest of the world. Technology and the global economic revolution have created a logic of economic relations that is different from the past—making the political and institutional logic of the current order all the more powerful.

Accommodating the Rise

The most important benefit of these features today is that they give the Western order a remarkable capacity to accommodate rising powers. New entrants into the system have ways of gaining status and authority and opportunities to play a role in governing the order. The fact that the United States, China, and other great powers have nuclear weapons also limits the ability of a rising power to overturn the existing order. In the age of nuclear deterrence, great-power war is, thankfully, no longer a mechanism of historical change. War-driven change has been abolished as a historical process.

The Western order's strong framework of rules and institutions is already starting to facilitate Chinese integration. At first, China embraced certain rules and institutions for defensive purposes: protecting its sovereignty and economic interests while seeking to reassure other states of its peaceful intentions by getting involved in regional and global groupings. But as the scholar Marc Lanteigne argues, "What separates China from other states, and indeed previous global powers, is that not only is it 'growing up' within a milieu of international institutions far more developed than ever before, but more importantly, it is doing so while making active use of these institutions to promote the country's development of global power status." China, in short, is increasingly working within, rather than outside of, the Western order.

China is already a permanent member of the UN Security Council, a legacy of Roosevelt's determination to build the universal body around diverse great-power leadership. This gives China the same authority and advantages of "great-power exceptionalism" as the other permanent members. The existing global trading system is also valuable to China, and increasingly so. Chinese economic interests are quite congruent with the current global economic system—a system that is open and loosely institutionalized and that China has enthusiastically embraced and thrived in. State power today is ultimately based on sustained economic growth, and China is well aware that no major state can modernize without integrating into the globalized capitalist system; if a country wants to be a world power, it has no choice but to join the World Trade Organization (WTO). The road to global power, in effect, runs through the Western order and its multilateral economic institutions.

China not only needs continued access to the global capitalist system; it also wants the protections that the system's rules and institutions provide. The WTO's multilateral trade principles and dispute-settlement mechanisms, for example, offer China tools to defend against the threats of discrimination and protectionism that rising economic powers often confront. The evolution of China's policy suggests that Chinese leaders recognize these advantages: as Beijing's growing commitment to economic liberalization has increased the foreign investment and trade China has enjoyed, so has Beijing increasingly embraced global trade rules. It is possible that as China comes to champion the WTO, the support of the more mature Western economies for the WTO will wane. But it is more likely that both the rising and the declining countries will find value in the quasi-legal mechanisms that allow conflicts to be settled or at least diffused.

The existing international economic institutions also offer opportunities for new powers to rise up through their hierarchies. In the International Monetary Fund and the World Bank, governance is based on economic shares, which growing countries can translate into greater institutional voice. To be sure, the process of adjustment has been slow. The United States and Europe still dominate the IMF. Washington has a 17 percent voting share (down from 30 percent)—a controlling amount, because 85 per-

cent approval is needed for action—and the European Union has a major say in the appointment of ten of the 24 members of the board. But there are growing pressures, notably the need for resources and the need to maintain relevance, that will likely persuade the Western states to admit China into the inner circle of these economic governance institutions. The IMF's existing shareholders, for example, see a bigger role for rising developing countries as necessary to renew the institution and get it through its current crisis of mission. At the IMF's meeting in Singapore in September 2006, they agreed on reforms that will give China, Mexico, South Korea, and Turkey a greater voice.

As China sheds its status as a developing country (and therefore as a client of these institutions), it will increasingly be able to act as a patron and stakeholder instead. Leadership in these organizations is not simply a reflection of economic size (the United States has retained its voting share in the IMF even as its economic weight has declined); nonetheless, incremental advancement within them will create important opportunities for China.

Power Shift and Peaceful Change

Seen in this light, the rise of China need not lead to a volcanic struggle with the United States over global rules and leadership. The Western order has the potential to turn the coming power shift into a peaceful change on terms favorable to the United States. But that will only happen if the United States sets about strengthening the existing order. Today, with Washington preoccupied with terrorism and war in the Middle East, rebuilding Western rules and institutions might to some seem to be of only marginal relevance. Many Bush administration officials have been outright hostile to the multilateral, rule-based system that the United States has shaped and led. Such hostility is foolish and dangerous. China will become powerful: it is already on the rise, and the United States' most powerful strategic weapon is the ability to decide what sort of international order will be in place to receive it.

The United States must reinvest in the Western order, reinforcing the features of that order that encourage engagement, integration, and restraint. The more this order binds together capitalist democratic states in deeply rooted institutions; the more open, consensual, and rule-based it is; and the more widely spread its benefits, the more likely it will be that rising powers can and will secure their interests through integration and accommodation rather than through war. And if the Western system offers rules and institutions that benefit the full range of states—rising and falling, weak and strong, emerging and mature—its dominance as an international order is all but certain.

The first thing the United States must do is reestablish itself as the foremost supporter of the global system of governance that underpins the Western order. Doing so will first of all facilitate the kind of collective problem solving that makes all countries better off. At the same time, when other countries see the United States using its power to strengthen existing rules and institutions, that power is rendered more legitimate—and U.S. authority is strengthened. Countries within the West become more inclined to work with, rather than resist, U.S. power, which reinforces the centrality and dominance of the West itself.

Renewing Western rules and institutions will require, among other things, updating the old bargains that underpinned key postwar security pacts. The strategic understanding behind both NATO and Washington's East Asian alliances is that the United States will work with its allies to provide security and bring them in on decisions over the use of force, and U.S. allies, in return, will operate within the U.S.-led Western order. Security cooperation in the West remains extensive today, but with the main security threats less obvious than they were during the Cold War, the purposes and responsibilities of these alliances are under dispute. Accordingly, the United States needs to reaffirm the political value of these alliances—recognizing that they are part of a wider Western institutional architecture that allows states to do business with one another.

The United States should also renew its support for wide-ranging multilateral institutions. On the economic front, this would include building on the agreements and architecture of the WTO, including pursuing efforts to conclude the current Doha Round of trade talks, which seeks to extend market opportunities and trade liberalization to developing countries. The WTO is at a critical stage. The basic standard of nondiscrimination is at risk thanks to the proliferation of bilateral and regional trade agreements. Meanwhile, there are growing doubts over whether the WTO can in fact carry out trade liberalization, particularly in agriculture, that benefits developing countries. These issues may seem narrow, but the fundamental character of the liberal international order—its commitment to universal rules of openness that spread gains widely—is at stake. Similar doubts haunt a host of other multilateral agreements—on global warming and nuclear nonproliferation, among others—and they thus also demand renewed U.S. leadership.

The strategy here is not simply to ensure that the Western order is open and rule-based. It is also to make sure that the order does not fragment into an array of bilateral and "minilateral" arrangements, causing the United States to find itself tied to only a few key states in various regions. Under such a scenario, China would have an opportunity to build its own set of bilateral and "minilateral" pacts. As a result, the world would be broken into competing U.S. and Chinese spheres. The more security and economic relations are multilateral and all-encompassing, the more the global system retains its coherence.

In addition to maintaining the openness and durability of the order, the United States must redouble its efforts to integrate rising developing countries into key global institutions. Bringing emerging countries into the governance of the international order will give it new life. The United States and Europe must find room at the table

not only for China but also for countries such as Brazil, India, and South Africa. A Goldman Sachs report on the so-called BRICs (Brazil, Russia, India, and China) noted that by 2050 these countries' economies could together be larger than those of the original G-6 countries (Germany, France, Italy, Japan, the United Kingdom, and the United States) combined. Each international institution presents its own challenges. The UN Security Council is perhaps the hardest to deal with, but its reform would also bring the greatest returns. Less formal bodies—the so-called G-20 and various other intergovernmental networks—can provide alternative avenues for voice and representation.

The Triumph of the Liberal Order

The key thing for U.S. leaders to remember is that it may be possible for China to overtake the United States alone, but it is much less likely that China will ever manage to overtake the Western order. In terms of economic weight, for example, China will surpass the United States as the largest state in the global system sometime around 2020. (Because of its population, China needs a level of productivity only one-fifth that of the United States to become the world's biggest economy.) But when the economic capacity of the Western system as a whole is considered, China's economic advances look much less significant; the Chinese economy will be much smaller than the combined economies of the Organization for Economic Cooperation and Development far into the future. This is even truer of military might: China cannot hope to come anywhere close to total OECD military expenditures anytime soon. The capitalist democratic world is a powerful constituency for the preservation—and, indeed, extension—of the existing international order. If China intends to rise up and challenge the existing order, it has a much more daunting task than simply confronting the United States.

The "unipolar moment" will eventually pass. U.S. dominance will eventually end. U.S. grand strategy, accordingly, should be driven by one key question: What kind of international order would the United States like to see in place when it is less powerful?

This might be called the neo-Rawlsian question of the current era. The political philosopher John Rawls argued that political institutions should be conceived behind a "veil of ignorance"—that is, the architects should design institutions as if they do not know precisely where they will be within a socioeconomic system. The result would be a system that safeguards a person's interests regardless of whether he is rich or poor, weak or strong. The United States needs to take that approach to its leadership of the international order today. It must put in place institutions and fortify rules that will safeguard its interests regardless of where exactly in the hierarchy it is or how exactly power is distributed in 10, 50, or 100 years.

Fortunately, such an order is in place already. The task now is to make it so expansive and so institutionalized that

China has no choice but to become a full-fledged member of it. The United States cannot thwart China's rise, but it can help ensure that China's power is exercised within the rules and institutions that the United States and its partners have crafted over the last century, rules and institutions that can protect the interests of all states in the more crowded world of the future. The United States' global position may be weakening, but the international system the United States leads can remain the dominant order of the twenty-first century.

G. John Ikenberry is the Albert G. Milbank Professor of Politics and International Affairs at Princeton University in the Department of Politics and the Woodrow Wilson School of Public and International Affairs.

EXPLORING THE ISSUE

Is a Rising China a Threat to U.S. National Security?

Critical Thinking and Reflection

1. Is the People's Republic of China (PRC) best seen as a strategic partner of the United States? Or, is the PRC instead a strategic competitor? Explain.
2. Where do the national interests of the United States and the PRC align? Where are they in competition? Over what issues, if any, does the possibility of armed conflict arise?
3. What theoretical perspectives support the view that China's rise will pose a threat to U.S. national security? Are these perspectives persuasive? Why or why not?
4. Will the PRC's conception of its national interests inevitably expand as its material capabilities grow? Why or why not?
5. If China is a threat to U.S. national security, what U.S. policies would best address this threat?
6. If China is not a threat to U.S. national security, what policies toward China should the United States adopt?

Is There Common Ground?

The relationship between the United States and the PRC may be the most important bilateral relationship of the twenty-first century. If this relationship is dominated by conflict, it will have potentially significant security, economic, and even environmental implications for the Asia-Pacific region and beyond. Experts on both sides of the issue debated here agree that the PRC–United States relationship should not be ignored.

Even if China does not appear to pose a threat now or in the near future to U.S. national security, history is full of unexpected developments. Prudent policymakers do not hope for the best; instead, they use diplomatic, informational, military, and economic tools in order to try to influence other states in ways that serve their country's interests. With respect to China and the United States, the financial and trade interdependence that has developed since 1978 helps provide incentive to both sides to foster each other's success. This may be a useful foundation on which policymakers on both sides can continue to build.

Given the tremendous combined power represented by the United States and China, there is enormous potential for this bilateral relationship to achieve things no other partnership can in the international community. Together, these two countries account for over 1/3 of the world's economic activity and almost a quarter of the world's population. However, whether both countries can overcome competing national interests and achieve such cooperation remains to be seen.

Additional Resources

Christensen, Thomas. "Fostering Stability or Creating a Monster? The Rise of China and U.S. Policy toward East Asia." *International Security* 31, no. 1 (Summer 2006): 81–126.

In this article, the author examines U.S. foreign policy toward China, exploring whether both countries can gain from positive developments in United States–China relations or whether one side's gains are best seen as the other side's loss.

Fravel, M. Taylor. "China's Search for Military Power." *The Washington Quarterly* 31 (Summer 2008): 125–141.

This article explores China's national strategic goals through the lens of Chinese military doctrine.

Friedberg, Aaron. "The Future of U.S.-China Relations: Is Conflict Inevitable?" *International Security* 30, no. 2 (Fall 2005): 7–45.

A useful survey of theoretical perspectives on the rise of China, this article explores what they suggest about the potential for future Sino-U.S. conflict.

Manyin, Mark E., et al. *Pivot to the Pacific? The Obama Administration's "Rebalancing" Toward Asia*. Washington, DC: Congressional Research Service, March 28, 2012.

This study examines the Obama Administration's intensified focus on the Asia-Pacific in historic terms and seeks to identify associated issues that members of Congress should consider.

Office of the Secretary of Defense. *Military and Security Developments Involving the People's Republic of China, 2011.* Washington, DC: Department of Defense, 2011.

This document is an annual comprehensive report from the Secretary of Defense to the U.S. Congress that details Chinese strategy and force modernization, the military balance across the Taiwan Strait, and the PRC-U.S. military relationship.

Overholt, William H. "Reassessing China: Awaiting Xi Jinping." *The Washington Quarterly* 35, no. 2 (Spring 2012): 121–137.

The year 2012 is a year of change in China's political and party leadership. This article examines the uncertainties surrounding this transition.

Subramanian, Arvind. "The Inevitable Superpower: Why China's Dominance is a Sure Thing." *Foreign Affairs* 90, no. 5 (September/October 2011): 66–78.

This article argues that by 2030 China will have supplanted the United States as the world's dominant power and that U.S. policy will have little impact on this outcome.

Zheng, Bijian. "China's 'Peaceful Rise' to Great Power Status." *Foreign Affairs* 84, no. 5 (September/October 2005): 18–24.

This article argues that China will continue to rise to great power status in a peaceful manner and will not make a bid for hegemony.

Internet References . . .

Foreign Policy

This online commentary argues that the military threat that China poses to the United States is overblown and will not materialize any time in the near future. He cites the vast disparity between U.S. and Chinese military capabilities, military spending, ability and willingness to project power, and demographic trends to show that although future conflict is possible, alarmists have overestimated the China threat.

www.foreignpolicy.com/articles/2010/02/22/think_again_chinas_military

The World Bank

2012 data in the World Bank can be found at the following link.

http://data.worldbank.org/

Should the United States Play the Leading Role in Revitalizing the Israeli-Palestinian Peace Process? by Nielsen and Handler

135

Selected, Edited, and with Issue Framing Material by:
Suzanne Nielsen, *U.S. Military Academy*
and
Scott Handler, *U.S. Military Academy*

ISSUE

Should the United States Play the Leading Role in Revitalizing the Israeli–Palestinian Peace Process?

YES: Daniel Kurtzer, from "Reviving the Peace Process," *The National Interest* (2012)

NO: Salman Shaikh, from *The "Peace Process" is Dead; What's Next?* (Brookings Institution, 2011)

Learning Outcomes
After reading this issue, you should be able to: • Appreciate the complexity of the relationship between the United States and Israel.   • Understand the main areas of contention between the Israelis and the Palestinians.   • Describe the various attempts at peace that have been made in the past and understand why they failed.   • Explain how the "special relationship" between Israel and the United States could affect the ability of the United States to reenergize the peace process.   • Discuss how other actors might play a larger role in the peace process.

ISSUE SUMMARY

YES: Daniel Kurtzer, a professor of Middle Eastern Studies at Princeton University and a former U.S. ambassador to Egypt and Israel, lays out needed elements of a U.S. approach with the aim of reviving a seemingly moribund peace process between the Israelis and Palestinians. He argues that if the United States leaves the Israelis and Palestinians to come to terms on their own, the result will be more conflict. Despite extraordinary challenges, the United States should act like a world leader and push the parties to negotiate a comprehensive peace.

NO: Salman Shaikh, the director of the Brookings Institution Doha Center, contends that the United States is not an honest broker and lacks the will to mediate a fair agreement. He also asserts that the Middle East Quartet—made up of the United States, Russia, the European Union (EU), and the United Nations (UN) Secretary General—has become ineffective. A new, broader coalition of states will need to play a role if peace is to be achieved.

The Israeli–Palestinian conflict has proven to be one of the most intractable in recent history. Almost every U.S. administration since the creation of Israel in 1948 has played a role in trying to bring the warring sides together, and some contend that the United States must continue to take the leading role in any peace process. Some argue that the United States must lead the peace effort due to the strong ties it has had with Israel since the early years of the Cold War when Israel was seen as an important U.S. ally against Soviet encroachment in the Middle East. It was President John F. Kennedy who first explicitly articulated, in a meeting with Israeli Prime Minister Golda Meir, that a "special relationship" existed between the two countries.

Some advocates of U.S. leadership in the peace progress argue that this "special relationship"—along with the three billion dollars in annual aid the United States provides to Israel—should enable the United States to bring Israel to the negotiating table to discuss key issues including borders, the status of Jerusalem, and a solution for Palestinian refugees.

Others agree that the United States must take a leading role in reactivating the peace process, but not solely because of historically strong U.S. relations with Israel. Instead, the United States must lead because no other player has enough military, economic, or political clout to influence both sides. Some scholars assert that although the United States did not initiate the most successful breakthroughs in peacemaking between Arabs and Israelis, including the 1978 Camp David Accords and the 1993 Oslo Accords, U.S. participation is nevertheless required for the successful conclusion of such agreements because of U.S. power and its important role in the Middle East (Peleg and Scham, 2010). Even some Palestinian leaders who believe that the United States is biased in favor of Israel nevertheless concede that U.S. leadership is critical. In 2010, for example, Palestinian Ambassador to the UN Riyad Mansour stated that strong U.S. leadership would contribute greatly to restarting the Israeli–Palestinian peace process (Miller, 2011).

A third perspective, which still advocates the necessity of U.S. leadership, emphasizes that others also need to become constructively involved. This is the position of Rory Miller, Director of the Middle East and Mediterranean Studies Program at King's College London, who argues that "Europe will always play second fiddle to the United States in the Middle East—regardless of how effective or ineffective the U.S. president happens to be" (Miller, 2011). However, he also points out that the EU holds significant influence in the region and must play a larger role in the process. As the leading donor to the Palestinian Authority—the governing authority in the Palestinian territories established after the Oslo Accords in 1993—the EU can do more to assist the Palestinians in state building. Miller believes that the creation of a strong state that allows for economic growth could place the Palestinians in a better position for peacemaking.

A contrasting view is that it is precisely because of its close ties with Israel that the United States should not take the leading role in the peace process. Some argue that these ties prevent the United States from pushing Israel to take critical steps toward peace. As an example, despite its stated opposition to such activities, the United States has not succeeded in getting the Israeli government to prevent the building of new Jewish settlements in the West Bank. Because the United States is incapable of serving as an honest broker, the burden of reactivating the peace process should be shared among other regional and international actors. Marina Ottoway, a Middle East analyst with the Carnegie Endowment for International Peace, argues what is really needed is a multilateral approach that includes important states from within the region. The United States can assist, but "the Arab countries must take upon themselves the main burden of moving their initiative from an idea to an agreement" (Ottoway, 2008).

Another perspective, which similarly starts from the idea that the United States has not proven itself to be an honest broker and instead acts as "Israel's attorney," argues for a new paradigm to govern negotiations. While the United States has in the past sought to be a mediator, its inability or unwillingness to be an honest broker has been detrimental to this role. As a new way ahead, Asaf Siniver of Birmingham University suggests that arbitration may yield more favorable results. Arbitration refers to a process where a panel of arbitrators, selected by parties to the dispute, is charged to find solutions. The scope of discussion is agreed upon by the parties, so there is consensus as to what topics are discussed; any resolution is usually founded on past agreements and international conventions. Arbitration is legally binding, although there are no mechanisms, other than the commitment of the parties to the dispute, to implement or enforce the decisions (Siniver, 2011).

Over the years many attempts have been undertaken to resolve the Israeli–Palestinian conflict, but it was not until the signing of the Oslo Accords between the Palestinians and Israelis in 1993 that real progress was made. Though a step forward, the Accords were not able to reach their goal of a final resolution of the conflict within 5 years due to problems with the structure of the agreement and implementation challenges. The United States nevertheless continued to push for a peace settlement. In July 2000, President Bill Clinton brought the Israelis and Palestinians together in an effort to revive the stalled Oslo Accords. This attempt ended in failure and the conflict continued in September 2000 with the beginning of a new Palestinian uprising—the *Al Aqsa Intifada*—in the West Bank and Gaza Strip. As violence and hostilities escalated on both sides, with suicide bombings by Palestinians in Israel and retaliatory attacks by Israelis in the Palestinian territories, a flurry of diplomatic activities began in March 2002 to coax the parties back to the negotiating table.

Regional players began to take the initiative in advancing options. The Arab League, led by Saudi Arabia, developed the Arab Peace Initiative calling for Israel to withdraw to the borders that had existed before the Six-Day War in 1967 and recognize a Palestinian state in all of the West Bank and Gaza Strip. In return, Israel would receive full recognition from the 22 Arab States represented in the Arab League. Israel was skeptical of this offer and, after a spate of suicide bombings in Israel and a large Israeli military operation in the West Bank, the plan was shelved (Podeh, 2007). In 2007, the plan was reaffirmed by the Arab League, but Israel rejected this offer on the grounds that it only demanded concessions from the Israelis and none from the Palestinians (Ben-Meir, 2008). From Israel's perspective, agreeing to withdraw to the 1967 borders would set the boundaries of the Palestinian state prior to any negotiations when it should be one of the subjects to be discussed.

In another attempt to resuscitate the Israeli–Palestinian peace process, the Middle East Quartet drafted a plan dubbed the "Road Map" in 2002. The goal was to obtain a comprehensive settlement by 2005. The Quartet, which included the UN, EU, Russia, and the United States, was designed to include players who had leverage with one or both parties to the conflict and had significant interests in the Middle East. Each member of the Quartet brought strengths to this arrangement, which was described by UN envoy Terje Rod-Larsen "as the perfect marriage of U.S. power, EU money, and UN legitimacy" (Elgindy, 2012).

Unfortunately, even before the end of 2003 the Road Map collapsed in a new outbreak of violence. In addition, the Quartet lost legitimacy as the United States wielded unequal power and was perceived as dominating the group (Elgindy, 2012).

In 2011, the President of the Palestinian Authority, Mahmoud Abbas, rejected internationally facilitated, bilateral negotiations with Israel completely and brought the question of Palestinian statehood to the UN. Frustrated with the lack of progress and perceived intransigence on the Israeli side, President Abbas made a speech at the UN General Assembly calling for the creation of a Palestinian state on the basis of the June 4, 1967 borders and appealing for Palestine to be offered full UN membership (Herzog, 2011). Although this bid was unsuccessful, when considered in conjunction with Israel's non-negotiated withdrawal from Gaza in 2005, it suggests that each side of the conflict may turn increasingly to unilateral actions in the absence of a settlement.

Daniel Kurtzer, a former ambassador to both Egypt and Israel, recognizes the challenges but nevertheless takes the YES position, arguing that the United States must still play the leading role in the peace process. Kurtzer argues that without immediate U.S. involvement to resume negotiations and support a comprehensive peace, the situation will deteriorate quickly. The United States must invest in diplomatic engagement because peace in the region is a U.S. national security interest. Additionally, Kurtzer argues that if the United States believes itself to be a world power, then it must act like one and take a leading role to solve this challenging crisis.

In the NO selection, Salman Shaikh, director of the Doha Brookings Institution, asserts that the United States can no longer hold the key leadership role because it lacks both the will and the ability to be even-handed in the peace process. Although he argues for a broader group of international actors to engage, he believes that the Quartet is not a viable option. Rather, Arab states, Turkey, and the EU—in coordination with China and India—could facilitate a more effective process. As a first step, these players should support the Palestinian bid to be a nonmember state with observer status at the UN. A new approach to the peace process is urgently needed. If one is not adopted, Shaikh cautions, violence will ensue.

YES ⤶

Daniel Kurtzer

Reviving the Peace Process

As the end of 2011 approached, the Obama administration appeared positioned to have presided over three definitive foreign-policy outcomes in the broader Middle East for which it could claim substantial credit. The death of Osama bin Laden, while not bringing the war against al-Qaeda to an end, surely closed an important chapter in the longterm struggle against militant Islam. Others will rise to take bin Laden's place at the top of the al-Qaeda hierarchy, but his death leaves a void in that organization that will be hard to fill.

The death of Muammar el-Qaddafi similarly brings to a close the sometimes odd but almost always violent struggle between the United States and Libya. Washington played an important role in Qaddafi's downfall and thus helped set the stage for the transition that will follow. Libya may or may not move toward democracy, but at least it is free of one of the world's most mercurial, brutal and enduring dictators.

Finally, the withdrawal of U.S. combat troops from Iraq looks to bring about a new stage in the nearly ten-year war. There is already a healthy debate about the purposes, costs and outcomes of this war, one which helped bankrupt our treasury in pursuit of objectives that even the Bush administration had trouble defining. But with that chapter's conclusion, 2012 will usher in an opportunity for Iraq to make its own way, absent American forces on the ground.

Against this backdrop of successes, two issues stand apart. Iran remains intent on developing nuclear-weapons capability, and no combination of U.S. and international efforts—diplomacy, sanctions or threats—has led Iran to change its policy. The Middle East peace process, the subject of this essay, also stands apart. Described early and often by President Obama as one of the signature issues of his administration, the peace process has achieved neither a definitive end nor a tentative beginning. Rather, it is stuck.

The recent decision by the Palestinian Authority (PA) to seek reconciliation with Hamas and gain membership status in the UN reflects two important perceptions on the part of Palestinians—first, that serious negotiations with an Israeli government led by Benjamin Netanyahu are not possible; and, second, that the Obama administration cannot or will not exercise enough pressure on Israel to stop settlement activity, the Palestinians' precondition for resumed negotiations. They may also view prospects of a two-state solution as diminishing rapidly.

For its part, the Netanyahu government in Israel has tried to portray itself as willing to talk, and the prime minister has repeatedly called for negotiations without preconditions. But the actual behavior of the Israeli government raises suspicions about that claim. The ten-month moratorium on new housing starts to which Israel agreed in 2009–10 did not stop the pace of ongoing construction in the territories. New housing projects beyond the Green Line have been announced regularly since 2010 and have accelerated recently in response to Palestinian diplomatic successes in UNESCO and elsewhere. Even when direct talks took place in September 2010, Netanyahu reportedly did not bring substance to the table. Israelis, like Palestinians, may have concluded that prospects for a two-state settlement are fading.

All this raises two fundamental questions: Are we at the cusp of a new phase in the long-running Arab-Israeli conflict, in which the two-state paradigm no longer motivates Palestinians and Israelis to seek a peace settlement? Have the diplomatic efforts of the Obama administration contributed to this possibility by failing to bring American diplomatic power to bear in the process?

The Arab-Israeli conflict has passed through three broad phases since the establishment of the state of Israel in 1948. The first phase was marked by the success of Zionism in creating the state and by the dispersion of Palestinians as a result of the 1947–49 conflict. The second phase began in June 1967, marked by the defeat of Arab armies in the Six-Day War, Israel's occupation and settlement of the West Bank, Gaza and the Golan Heights, and the reemergence of the Palestinians at the center stage of the conflict. Today, we are living in the third phase, in which Israelis and Palestinians have been trying to reach a conflict-ending settlement through negotiations leading to a two-state outcome. The Madrid Conference in 1991, the Oslo accords in 1993 and the "road map for peace" process launched in 2003 have been directed at defining the modalities and substance of a peace settlement.

The Madrid Conference, the first breakthrough, launched parallel bilateral and multilateral peace talks. For the first time, Israel conducted bilateral peace negotiations with each of its neighbors. And for the first time, Arabs from the rest of the region sat with Israel to discuss transnational issues such as water, the environment and economic development. The Madrid talks proceeded in fits and starts but did not accomplish much substantively.

The Oslo accords resolved what appeared to be the most important lacuna of Madrid, namely, defining the role of the Palestine Liberation Organization, which had been left out of Madrid, and thereby giving Palestinian decision making the definitiveness it had previously lacked. In 1993, Israel and the PLO agreed on mutual recognition, a process of negotiations and a timetable designed to culminate in Palestinian statehood by May 1999. But things didn't quite turn out that way. Negotiations proceeded almost endlessly but without conclusive results. Bad behavior by both sides created an atmosphere of distrust: Palestinian violence and terrorism never really stopped, nor did Israeli settlement activities. Palestinian leader Yasir Arafat found it difficult to overcome his persona as a revolutionary leader and embrace the core concessions and trade-offs required for success. Israeli prime minister Ehud Barak did reach beyond the political constraints of Israeli society to put forward far-reaching ideas, but even they fell short of the minimum requirements of the Palestinians. For its part, the Clinton administration tried hard to keep the process going but ultimately failed to deal with the two fundamental requirements of success: stopping the bad behavior of both sides and defining the substantive trade-offs required for a deal.

The road map was developed by the Bush administration and the so-called quartet of Middle East peacemakers (the United Nations, United States, European Union and Russia). Its aim was to correct some of the weaknesses of Oslo by aligning a three-stage process of negotiations with changes in the parties' behavior. The two sides committed themselves to fulfilling certain responsibilities: for Israel, this meant a complete settlements freeze and increasing Palestinian mobility in the territories; for the Palestinians, it meant cracking down on terrorist infrastructure and accelerating the statebuilding process. The road map required mutually reinforcing actions from each side in parallel and sequentially. But this process also collapsed, primarily under the weight of Palestinian terrorism that the PA, under Yasir Arafat, could not or would not police.

In a last-gasp effort by the Bush administration to salvage the two-state solution, the Annapolis Conference was held in 2007, leading to intensive direct negotiations during 2008. To the surprise of everyone, these proved to be the most serious and far-reaching negotiations to date. Former prime minister Ehud Olmert, in his recently published memoir, details how close the parties came to bridging the gaps between them even on the most contentious issues of borders, settlements, Jerusalem and refugees. Some of what Olmert has written has been confirmed in the leaked "Palestine Papers" that provide insight into internal Palestinian deliberations on the core issues. And former secretary of state Condoleezza Rice confirms Olmert's assertions in her own just-published autobiography. Indeed, it can be argued that the only element missing in the Annapolis process to help the parties bridge the final gaps was a robust American role. Rice traveled constantly in search of the finish line but never got the backing of the White House to bring serious enough American influence to bear on the negotiations.

Many believed the Obama administration would provide that final missing puzzle piece. Here was a White House that inherited a negotiating process that had produced significant progress. Here was a president who proclaimed at the outset that he valued peace in the Middle East as a U.S. national-security interest, not as a favor being done for the parties. Obama appointed a senior, experienced negotiator, George Mitchell, to carry the ball. And then the administration proceeded to fumble. Instead of a comprehensive peace strategy, Washington tried confidence-building measures, including the quest for a complete settlements freeze. The new Israeli prime minister, Benjamin Netanyahu, wouldn't bite. The White House tried proximity talks, direct talks and, most recently, quartet-led talks designed to lead to further negotiations. Not only did the tactics not work, but the administration also was revealed to have little stomach for the rough-and-tumble of actually trying to advance the peacemaking process. Confronted with opposition to its ideas, Washington invariably retreated.

The result is that the processes and progress of the past are now in doubt. The search for peace is in a state of acute crisis, with many analysts arguing the basic paradigm of peacemaking is dead. But in the Middle East, as a friend once pointed out, dead is not really dead until it is dead and buried. The question is whether the peace process is merely dead, or dead and buried.

There is no simple answer to the question of why this phase of peacemaking has defied resolution or definitiveness over the years. It has not been for lack of interest. Since 1991, leaders in the region have reiterated time and again their commitment to peace, even if their actions did not measure up to their words. It has not been for lack of vision. Even if policy makers could not reach a negotiated settlement, private individuals showed how it could be done. The Geneva Initiative and the Ayalon-Nusseibeh Agreement demonstrated that reasonable people on both sides could visualize a peace deal.

And failure has not been for lack of imperative. The Arab-Israeli conflict is not the most violent or dangerous conflict globally, perhaps not even in the top tier of dangerous conflicts. But it has become a chronic, enduring and open wound, susceptible to dangerous infection that generates fever throughout the region. On the Arab side, the conflict played no role in the first days of the Arab Spring; since then, it has become a rallying cry for disaffected Arab masses that get no fulfillment of basic needs and thus call on governments to deal with this emotional need at the very least. On the Israeli side, the persistence of the conflict raises the specter of demographic change that could call into question either Israel's Jewish character or its democratic character if it continues to deny equal rights to a population under occupation.

If we are thus at the cusp of what may be a new stage in the Arab-Israeli conflict—one that turns the page and ends the chapter of negotiations leading to a two-state solution—what might a new phase look like? Palestinian president Mahmoud Abbas, in a May 2011 op-ed piece in the *New York Times*, argued that "Palestinian national unity is a key step" in preserving the chance for a just end to the conflict—a reference to the long-sought but elusive goal of reconciliation between the PA and Hamas. He added, "Palestine's admission to the United Nations would pave the way for the internationalization of the conflict as a legal matter, not only a political one." Does either element of Abbas's vision of peacemaking hold out a possibility of success?

I met with senior Hamas officials in Damascus in October 2010, and I heard no flexibility with respect to their stated opposition to any conclusive peace with Israel. Hamas has told many interlocutors that it would accept a state in the West Bank and Gaza provided Israel withdraws from Jerusalem and allows the right of return for Palestinian refugees. Yet, this "acceptance" does not mean that Hamas would recognize Israel or declare an end to the conflict. To be fair, I suppose it should not be expected that Hamas would change its long-standing ideology in a meeting with foreign nonofficials, especially since Western officials refuse even to meet with representatives of the organization. But this stated position belies Abbas's argument that national unity will help move the peace process forward.

Regarding Abbas's second point, it is true that membership of Palestine in the United Nations would give the Palestinians standing to bring cases on their own before such global legal organs as the International Court of Justice and the International Criminal Court. Palestine could tie up Israel constantly with cases involving settlements, occupation practices, unilateral Israeli actions in building infrastructure and roads, and so on. Over time, Palestinian successes in these legal forums would create a presumptive case for a larger political assault on Israel as an apartheid state.

But Palestinian standing as a state is a two-way street, for Israel would also be able to bring Palestinians and the Palestinian state before the bar of international justice regarding ongoing terrorism, rocket fire and the like. While this legal process could achieve some measure of punitive damage, it is hard to see how it moves either party closer to a settlement. Abbas's emerging vision of this new phase in the peace process is thus not very compelling, for it is a road that leads inexorably to a dead end of mutual recriminations and legal maneuvers.

Although Netanyahu has been somewhat less clear about how he envisages a next phase, the elements of the approach he is following appear equally unconvincing of his ultimate desire for a serious peace process with Palestinians. In a seminal speech at Bar-Ilan University in June 2009, Netanyahu coupled his willingness to accept a demilitarized Palestinian state next to Israel with a key demand: "I have already stressed the first principle—recognition. Palestinians must clearly and unambiguously recognize Israel as the state of the Jewish people."

This is a challenging precondition from the leader of a state that has, until now, been unable to define its own character in a constitution. The creation of Israel surely fulfills the Zionist vision of Jewish self-determination and independence in the historical homeland of the Jewish people, but does that require others to recognize the character of the state as a precondition for negotiations? When I served as U.S. ambassador to Israel, then prime minister Ariel Sharon often expressed the same sentiment as Netanyahu regarding Arab acceptance of Israel's right to exist as a Jewish state, but he cast it as an outcome of the peace process rather than as a precondition for negotiations.

In the course of just three days this past September, we were given additional insight into how the Palestinian and Israeli leaders see the period ahead. In their speeches to the United Nations General Assembly, Abbas and Netanyahu delivered spirited expositions of their respective positions. Abbas explained why it was time for the United Nations to accept Palestine as a full member state, and Netanyahu explained why Israel rejected this move. The diametrically opposed Palestinian and Israeli narratives of the conflict were on full view. Both sides point to exile from their homeland as refugees. Both are victims who have suffered at the hands of the other. Both seek recognition of the legitimacy of their historical experience. Both place a high value on the justice of their cause. Both are acutely insecure and have deep security needs. Both are attached to the (same) land. Both see themselves as nations with ties to ethnic brethren internationally. And both place a high value on the concept of national unity, although both are anything but unified internally.

In exposing their competing and complementary narratives so clearly, the two protagonists set aside any pretense of trying to rebuild the bridges of dialogue and understanding that had been constructed during two decades of face-to-face Israeli-Palestinian negotiations. Reflecting how far apart these parties had grown, that same week the international quartet limited itself to calling for "a preparatory meeting between the parties to agree [to] an agenda and method of proceeding in the negotiation"—in other words, a meeting to produce agreement on how to hold another meeting.

If anyone expected the United States to reassert the centrality of the two-state solution and of direct negotiations as the means to achieve that outcome, President Obama's UN speech was something else entirely. He delivered a spirited defense of Israel, and he spared no words in defining the security and legitimacy dilemmas that Israel faces. After a tour d'horizon of many conflict environments, Obama stressed that "peace is hard. Peace is hard." Peace, he said, will not come through UN resolutions. But in a twist away from the expected insistence on resumption of talks based, for example, on the agenda he set forth last May—starting with borders and security—Obama said: "Deadlock will only be broken when each side learns to stand in the other's shoes; each side can see the world through the other's eyes. That's what we should be encouraging. That's what we should be promoting."

In other words, the president was saying that the future of this conflict will be defined by the ability of the two sides to cope with their national narratives. It is unclear what happens when Israelis understand how Palestinians see the world and vice versa. The question is whether, by that time, there will be anything left to negotiate.

Yogi Berra once advised, sagaciously, that when you arrive at a fork in the road, take it. For the United States, the policy choice ahead is binary: Do we pull the plug on the life-support system of the peace process that we constructed in 1991, let this phase of Arab-Israeli interaction die a peaceful death, and try to develop a different paradigm for resolving the conflict? Or do we persist, maintaining the same goal of a two-state solution and essentially the same process of arriving at peace through bilateral negotiations? I don't see merit in a third option of waiting it out, living with the status quo, allowing the conflict to "ripen" and choosing a different time for negotiations. There is no such thing as a status quo in conflict situations: things either improve or get worse. This conflict—if left to develop on its own and subject to the machinations of those on both sides who are intent upon disrupting any resolution effort—will get much worse, much faster than anyone can anticipate.

To suggest that the United States activate an ambitious peace strategy now, however, runs against the grain of what I have come to call the prevailing "Washington consensus." At every meeting, working group or seminar in Washington at which the peace process is the topic, the discussion produces a chorus of the following sentiments: "It is too hard." "Let it ripen until the parties are hurting more." "The leaders are too weak or too ideologically opposed to peace." "The United States cannot want peace more than the parties themselves." "It is really up to the parties to get serious about peace." "What if we fail?"

These are serious questions and observations. Yes, it is hard, but America can do hard diplomacy and succeed, as it has in the past. This conflict needs no more ripening; it is already overripe for resolution, and the idea of a mutually hurting stalemate—the centerpiece of the ripeness theory—has already applied to this conflict for years. Yes, leadership in the region is a problem, and even brilliant U.S. diplomacy will not offer a complete substitute; however, U.S. diplomatic strength can get the political juices in the region flowing, producing debates within the two societies as to whether leadership changes are required in order to move forward. Yes, we cannot want peace more than the parties do, but that is not the point: peace in the region is a U.S. national-security interest, and we should pursue that interest vigorously. As to the question of possible failure—well, that is not a serious question. All policies run the risk of failure, but no policy or strategy should be avoided simply because it may fail. A strong and determined U.S. policy will give our diplomats material to work with even if the parties do not immediately agree to what we are trying to accomplish.

One of the most serious questions posed is why Israel should take risks during this period of uncertainty in the Arab world. When its treaties with both Egypt and Jordan are coming under pressure from angry Arab publics, shouldn't Israel hunker down and weather the storm? Israel faces serious security threats today as it has throughout its history. In addition to the potentially existential threat posed by a nuclear-armed Iran, Israel faces a very well-armed and hostile pair of nonstate actors—Hezbollah and Hamas (and other militant Islamist bedfellows in Gaza).

Despite these real concerns, it is hard to see how Israel's security situation improves by passively awaiting the results of political change elsewhere. To be sure, Israel would need to approach negotiations today with extra care, given the enhanced risks associated with territorial withdrawals in an age of advanced rocketry, but Israel could gain potential political advantage by neutralizing, or at least dealing seriously with, the core issues at the heart of its long-running conflict with the Arabs. Indeed, this would be a moment when the United States and others would be more sympathetic to Israel's security requirements in the context of peace negotiations, and thus a moment when Israel could gain some advantage by negotiating now, not postponing talks.

Even if the "Washington consensus" of naysayers and Israel's reluctance can be overcome or circumvented, two key questions remain: Should the United States wait to activate peace diplomacy until after the 2012 election? And why should the president divert attention from pressing issues at home to focus attention on the Arab-Israeli issue?

Indeed, President Obama's speech to the UN could be read as the political manifesto for his reelection campaign: focusing on the problems Israel faces and the support his administration has given to Israel's vital security requirements. Clearly, this will sit well with the pro-Israel community in the United States that has raised questions about Obama's commitment to Israel, and it has already lowered the temperature in the sometimes heated relationship that Obama has had with Netanyahu. However, as noted above, the Middle East does not take a break from conflict just because we are having an election. By postponing action now, the administration may find itself immersed in a real crisis, perhaps a violent crisis, even during the election campaign itself. Recall that Hamas's escalation of attacks against Israel and Israel's war against Hamas took place at the end of 2008, just after our last presidential election.

As to the president's priorities, Obama himself, early in his tenure, elevated the issue of Arab-Israeli peace to near the top of his agenda. He has already invested political capital and presidential time on the issue. Ignoring it now, when the conflict-resolution process is in crisis, will undercut the very importance that the president previously attributed to it. Why should attacks from Republican opponents and a segment of the pro-Israel community that will not vote for him anyway deter President Obama from exercising leadership on this issue at a time of crisis in the negotiations? Indeed, a robust peace strategy now—constructed to be fair and reasonable—will allow the president to justify having devoted time and energy to this issue during his first term.

The only serious option, therefore, for a United States that sees itself as a leading world power is to act like a world power and lead. In the peace process, this would mean unveiling a comprehensive strategy now—right now, when everyone else is drifting further and further apart. Such a strategy should encompass at least four elements:

First, we should develop a set of parameters on all the key issues which would then become the starting point and terms of reference for negotiations. These parameters should be developed on the basis of where the two sides left off negotiations in 2008. In laying them out, Washington would explain that we intend to play an active role in helping to build bridges and overcome gaps between the parties. The negotiations would be bilateral, but we would accompany the talks closely so as to keep edging them forward.

Is it possible for the United States to develop parameters that will not drive the parties further apart? Since we know where the parties left off in 2008, we know how far the leaders then were prepared to go. These starting points would be harder to accept for Prime Minister Netanyahu, who was not in office then, than for President Abbas, who was. The U.S. intention would not be to create a political crisis in Israel, but Washington should be aware that such a crisis could erupt over the parameters. To the extent that they are crafted artfully and fairly, the United States needs to be prepared to defend these parameters in a sustained manner, even if a political crisis intervenes in Israel.

Second, Washington should encourage more ambitious state-building efforts by the Palestinians. The PA should be expected to do more to create the institutions of statehood. Under Abbas and Prime Minister Salam Fayyad, the PA has undertaken some reforms, especially in the security area. But more can be done. In the context of a serious negotiating environment, Palestinians can be asked to take more significant steps against those who commit acts of violence against Israel and those who operate outside the purview of the national authority.

Next, the United States should reiterate the need for the two sides to meet the commitments they agreed to in the road map, especially within the context of a comprehensive strategy for peacemaking. America needs to be ready to monitor the performance of the parties, hold them accountable for the failure to fulfill their commitments and exact consequences for road-map violations.

Last, Washington should press Arabs to activate the Arab Peace Initiative now. It is not enough for the Arabs to promise recognition, security and peace for Israel at the conclusion of the peace process; Arabs should be asked to start processes of reconciliation in parallel with peace negotiations. This is not far-fetched. In 1992, most Arab states agreed to participate with Israel in multilateral negotiations. Subsequently, most Arab states participated with Israel in four regional economic summits, designed to build private-public business and trade partnerships. As Israelis and Palestinians commit to the challenging work of negotiating peace, Arabs should be expected to play an affirmative role in demonstrating that peace yields tangible rewards for everyone in the region.

Even if elements of this strategy are not accepted by both parties, it remains a sustainable one that need not and should not be abandoned at the first sign of opposition. Until now, our diplomats have been working with discrete tactical approaches—a settlements freeze, proximity talks, direct talks—but without terms of reference, and the administration has backed away early when the tactics have not worked. But the strength of a comprehensive strategy should give the United States the confidence not to accept "no" as an answer. Even if the strategy does not work immediately, it will give Washington significant diplomatic maneuvering space for a long period ahead, as well as significant political benefits in our international diplomacy.

A report card on the administration's handling of the peace process until today would probably say: "Too many erratic beginnings; lacked a definitive outcome." It is unrealistic to believe that a definitive outcome can be achieved before our next election, but it is not too late to craft a wise beginning—a strong, reasonable and sustainable peace strategy that forms the basis of the next phase of Middle East peacemaking.

DANIEL KURTZER is the S. Daniel Abraham Professor in Middle Eastern Policy Studies at Princeton University. His previous career as a Foreign Service Officer included service as the U.S. Ambassador to Egypt and as the U.S. Ambassador to Israel.

Salman Shaikh

 **NO**

The "Peace Process" is Dead; What's Next?

Recent events at the United Nations confirmed what has been blindingly obvious for months: the Israeli-Palestinian "peace process" is dead. Furthermore, with elections scheduled in the United States, Palestine, and perhaps Israel in the next twelve months, it is hard to imagine that any meaningful negotiations can overcome the political realities in each country. As a result, the United States will come under increasing pressure to relinquish its decades-old monopoly on peacemaking, particularly at a time when its influence and reputation in the Middle East is deeply threatened. Under such scenarios, the obvious question that is raised is what could be next?

If we had any doubt about where the "peace process" is headed, the much-anticipated appearances of Mahmoud Abbas and Benjamin Netanyahu at the UN made clear the cold reality of where we are. Both stressed the historical grievances and deep-seated existential fears that have made the conflict between their peoples so intractable. At times, it seemed that each was making closing arguments in a courtroom drama rather than preparing for hard bargaining and historical compromises. President Obama had spoken before them in a vain attempt to discourage the Palestinian bid and urge direct talks. On the latter, no one, not even Obama himself, really believed this was a possibility.

With domestic considerations high on their agendas, all three leaders spoke as much to their audiences at home as they did to each other. Yet, in the long run, it will be the audiences in the volatile Middle East that will matter. This fact is something Abbas understood and Obama got horribly wrong.

For weeks, Abbas endured unrelenting American and Israeli pressure to abandon his bid for UN membership. He had also been coordinating with the Arab states on what looked to be the more realistic goal of upgrading Palestine to a non-member observer state of the UN. In the end, Abbas chose—and chose alone—to take the most difficult route, through the Security Council for full membership of the world body.

Abbas's address in the General Assembly has already entered Palestinian folklore for its defiance and courage. He proclaimed that "Palestine is reborn," yet it was also Abbas himself who had been born again as the leader of the Palestinian people. Indeed, he has wrested the Palestinian cause from the grasp of other regional powers and made it his own. The baton first raised by Yasser Arafat in the same hall in 1974 has been handed to Abbas.

Yet, in taking on the mantle, Abbas has made clear that there will be no negotiations until certain conditions are met, in particular the end of all Israeli construction in the occupied West Bank, including East Jerusalem. Furthermore, he has directly challenged the U.S. monopoly on peacemaking, otherwise known as the "peace process." Abu Mazen's patience finally ran out for the endless incrementalism that characterized the "process" and which seemed to place conditions solely on the Palestinians, while Israel continued to take Palestinian land and Netanyahu played for time. Abbas's deep disappointment with Obama personally led him to believe that the United States neither has the will nor the ability to act as the even-handed broker that the situation requires. Rather than trust an unreliable U.S. peacebroker, Abbas has chosen to internationalize the dispute by taking it to the UN, thereby leveling the playing field for future negotiations.

Meanwhile, Netanyahu evoked his country's deep existential fears that have driven him personally and politically. In doing so, he reminded the audience at the UN and perhaps more importantly, the Israelis themselves of the unique vulnerabilities that their country faces. While he proclaimed his readiness to start negotiations without preconditions, Netanyahu's dismissal of Abbas's call to halt settlement building and his insistence that Palestinians recognize Israel as the Jewish state will not bring Abbas back to the negotiating table—a fact Netanyahu already knew. In any case, the Israeli Prime Minister's main audience was neither the Palestinians nor the UN—the "house of many lies"—but rather the Israelis and U.S. presidential candidates that will face their electorate in just over a year.

As the Palestinian and Israeli leaders spoke at the UN, the Middle East Quartet—United States, Russia, the European Union and the UN Secretary-General - was meeting to hammer out their much-anticipated statement to urge negotiations—or, more likely, to stop the Palestinian bid that would undermine their efforts. Over the years, the U.S.-led Quartet has developed a habit of only producing statements when the United States is in need of one.

The latest Quartet statement should be its last. Building on the body's reputation of putting forth deadlines recognized by no one, it proposed timelines for negotiations yet offered no substance that could push the Israelis and Palestinians back to the negotiating table. Even by the standards of the past few years, this was "peace processing" gone wild. What had preceded the announcement were spirited discussions on the "terms of references" for future negotiations, including borders, security, and Israel's insistence on being recognized as a Jewish state. However, time ran out without the Quartet's members agreeing even on the most basic positions. Most disturbingly, and for the first time in Obama's presidency, there was no reference to Israeli settlement construction. The obvious question remains: how can the Quartet convince Abbas and Netanyahu what is good for them when they themselves cannot agree on the basic conditions for peacemaking?

For Obama and his administration, one can only feel disappointment. The president did the right thing by taking on the critical job of attempting to broker Israeli-Palestinian peace from day one. In doing so, however, he raised the mistrust of Israelis and their supporters at home, something from which he has yet to recover. Today, there is a growing realization that the United States cannot be the only leader of Palestinian-Israeli negotiations. At the UN, Arabs, Europeans, and those from the newly emerging powers such as Brazil, India, Russia and China speak openly about the diminished credibility of the United States. More deeply, its perceived weakness on this issue is seen as symptomatic of the general decline in U.S. power in global affairs. There is also concern that there currently is no effective mechanism to manage fires that may be ignited in the region as a result of the breakdown in relations between Israelis and Palestinians, let alone make peace.

With negotiations dead and not likely to be revived any time soon, a fresh approach to Arab- Israeli peace making is urgently needed. The internationally agreed-upon goal of two states, Israel and Palestine, is fading and urgently requires new management. The U.S. monopoly (yet not necessarily its leadership) of peacemaking is over. The drive for Arab-Israeli peace needs to include a broader range of international actors, including the Arab states, Europe and Turkey and for them to coordinate with such new world powers as China and India. Rather than obsessing over stopping it, the current action at the UN can be turned in to an opportunity where such a coalition comes together. The current situation may in fact be bringing these players together, with France and key

Arab states already leading the talk in the corridors of the UN.

A great deal has already been written about Abbas's gambit at the UN for full membership, and much more will be written about the different scenarios that could play out in the UN Security Council and the General Assembly in the weeks ahead. By challenging the U.S.-led "peace process" paradigm, Abbas may have already achieved his objectives, regardless of whether he can achieve full UN membership for Palestine now. For now, Abbas has chosen confrontation with the United States, but this need not be the future.

Abbas can be instrumental in constructing a new paradigm at the UN that the United States and the rest of the international community should support. Sixty-one years after Resolution 181, a new UN General Assembly resolution that again sets the goal of a new Palestinian state alongside Israel is necessary. Abbas should be offered, and he should accept, Palestine as a non-member state with observer status at the UN. The new UN resolution enabling the upgrade in status should also enshrine in international law commonly known parameters on the core issues of the borders of a future Palestinian state with Israel, Palestinian refugees and Jerusalem. In addition, it should recognize Israel's security concerns and demand a complete halt to all Israeli settlement building. Such a resolution would bind all Palestinians and Arab countries to the internationally agreed-upon goal of two states and once again offer Israelis a historic opportunity to choose peace and an end to their conflict with the Palestinians. Such a resolution would offer the basis for future direct negotiations between Israel and Palestine. With events on the ground threatening to re-ignite violence, there is no time to lose.

SALMAN SHAIKH is director of the Brookings Institution Doha Center and fellow at the Saban Center for Middle East Policy. He has held posts at the United Nations and the Office of Her Highness Sheikha Mozah Bint Nasser Al Missned in Qatar.

EXPLORING THE ISSUE

Should the United States Play the Leading Role in Revitalizing the Israeli–Palestinian Peace Process?

Critical Thinking and Reflection

1. Does the close U.S. relationship with Israel hamper the ability of the United States to deal effectively with the Palestinians? Does a U.S. bias in favor of Israel exacerbate relations between Israel and the Palestinians?
2. Can other actors such as the Quartet or the EU be more effective than the United States in getting the peace process restarted? Do they have the influence and leverage to do so?
3. What can be done to help the Israelis and Palestinians find a solution to the most contentious issues: borders, Jerusalem, and refugees? What are some possible solutions to these issues? Who can help the two parties achieve these solutions, and through what means?
4. Do you agree with the argument that the United States acts as "Israel's attorney"? If so, what factors influence this bias in favor of Israel? How can the United States become a more objective player? If not, why has such a perception developed and how can the United States overcome it?

Is There Common Ground?

The debate rages on as to what role the United States should play in the peace process. But there is general agreement that the United States must be involved in some capacity if a resolution to the Israeli–Palestinian conflict is to be achieved. This is affirmed by the historical record, which indicates that although the United States does not always initiate the process, its participation has been a critical enabler to the conclusion of the major agreements that have been reached.

At the heart of the issue of whether the United States should take the leading role in reactivating the peace process is the perception that the United States lacks objectivity with regard to Israel. Under President George W. Bush, the United States tacitly supported Israel's settlements in the West Bank. Although many held out hope that President Barack Obama would reverse this support and therefore be more successful in rejuvenating the peace process, this has not occurred. In addition, members of both political parties continue to seek political advantage by pledging their support for Israel and its security. The perception that the United States disregards Palestinian interests has heightened a search for other players who could lead a peace process. However, there may be no real replacement for sustained and tough diplomacy by the United States.

The historical record also illustrates that the peace process has progressed most when the United States genuinely considered both parties' interests. This suggests that to make progress in the future, the United States must strive to act as an honest broker and be willing to leverage the prestige of the Office of the President at the appropriate stage of negotiations. A resolution of the Israeli–Palestinian conflict would benefit the countries of the Middle East and further U.S. interests in the region. Without a solution, violence will continue to the detriment of both regional players and the international community.

Additional Resources

Ben-Meir, Alon. "Reconciling the Arab Initiative with Israel's Core Requirements for Peace." *International Journal on World Peace* 25, no. 4 (December 2008): 75–113.

The author lays out the key principles of the Arab Peace Initiative and explores Israel's reservations about the plan. He also explains that the main difference between the Road Map and the Arab Peace Initiative is that the Peace Initiative is advanced by those involved in the dispute

Elgindy, C. Khaled. "The Middle East Quartet: A Post-Mortem (excerpts)." *Journal of Palestine Studies* 41, no. 3 (Spring 2012): 235–240.

These published excerpts of a Brookings Institution analysis paper review the weaknesses of the Middle East Quartet. The author makes the point that while the Quartet was multilateral in form, it became a tool of American foreign policy in its operations. Additionally, the divergent aims of the Quartet's participants detracted from the group's ability to get the peace process on track.

Miller, Rory. "Europe's Palestine Problem." *Foreign Affairs* 90, no. 5 (September/October 2011): 8–12.

This article advances the argument that the EU should use the power that it has as the largest donor to the Palestinian Authority to play a larger, more beneficial role in the peace process.

Peleg, Ilan, and Paul Scham. "Historical Breakthroughs in the Arab-Israeli Negotiations Lessons for the Future." *Middle East Journal* 64, no. 2 (Spring 2012): 215–233.

The authors explore past negotiations and isolate six conditions that they find to be crucial to diplomatic breakthroughs. These conditions include an intense U.S. role in the peace process and direct U.S. presidential leadership.

Podeh, Elie. "The Peace Initiative: A Missed Opportunity?" *Palestine-Israel Journal of Politics, Economics & Culture* 14, no. 4 (2007): 5–11.

This article explores the Arab Peace Initiative, which was advanced by Saudi Arabia in 2002 and reaffirmed by the Arab League in 2007. The author examines why various groups in Israel rejected the proposal and argues that this rejection constitutes a missed opportunity for peace.

Siniver, Asaf. "Change Nobody Believes In: Obama and the Israeli-Palestinian Conflict." *Diplomacy & Statecraft* 22, no. 4 (2011): 678–695.

This article argues that the United States has proven that it is incapable of being an impartial mediator in the Israeli–Palestinian peace process. Because of this, the peace process should shift to a model of arbitration where key decisions are in the hands of a broader array of actors selected by both parties.

Internet References . . .

Washington Institute for Near East Policy

This analysis paper details the extraordinary challenges that would have to be overcome to bridge the gap between the Israelis and Palestinians on the issues of borders and territory.

www.washingtoninstitute.org/templateC04
.php?CID=357

Washington Institute for Near East Policy

In this study, the author lays out the areas of agreement and disagreement between the United States and Israel with regard to the peace process

www.washingtoninstitute.org/templateC04
.php?CID=345

Carnegie Endowment for International Peace

This article contends that the United States should support regional initiatives and encourage Arab states to take the lead in promoting peace in the region.

http://carnegieendowment.org/2008/12/18/
sharing-burden-in-middle-east/1l93

Selected, Edited, and with Issue Framing Material by:
Suzanne Nielsen, *U.S. Military Academy*
and
Scott Handler, *U.S. Military Academy*

ISSUE

Should the United States Cut Foreign Aid to Pakistan?

YES: **Stephen D. Krasner,** from "Talking Tough to Pakistan: How to End Islamabad's Defiance," *Foreign Affairs* (January/February 2012)

NO: **Jeffrey Goldberg and Marc Ambinder,** from "The Ally From Hell," *The Atlantic* (December 2011)

Learning Outcomes

After reading this issue, you should be able to:

- Understand the potential sources of tension in U.S.–Pakistani relations.
- Examine the role that foreign assistance to Pakistan plays in furthering U.S. goals in South Asia.
- Assess challenges in defining and prioritizing U.S. national security objectives that seek to foster near-term counterterrorism cooperation as well as long-term regional stability.
- Analyze the regional implications of a suspension of U.S. aid to Pakistan.
- Discuss alternative ways to develop a more productive U.S.–Pakistani relationship.

ISSUE SUMMARY

YES: Stephen D. Krasner, professor of international relations at Stanford University, argues that the billions of dollars in aid that the United States has provided to Pakistan over the past decade has done nothing to induce the critical cooperation needed from Islamabad to combat terrorism, address growing anti-American sentiment, and stop nuclear proliferation. He argues that the only way to get Islamabad to act will be with credible threats to suspend U.S. aid and isolate Pakistan internationally.

NO: Jeffery Goldberg, a national correspondent at *The Atlantic,* and Marc Ambinder, a contributing editor for *The Atlantic,* recognize the tensions in the U.S.–Pakistani relationship but argue that instead of abandoning it, the United States must recast this relationship to address mutual interests. Both parties remain concerned about the security of Pakistan's nuclear arsenal, though perhaps for different reasons, and understand how critical Pakistan's survival is for regional stability. Continued engagement, not isolation, is the more prudent policy.

Shortly after the May 2011 U.S. raid on a compound in Abbottabad, Pakistan, that killed Al Qaeda leader Osama bin Laden, members of Congress began to question the utility and value of continuing U.S. military and economic aid to that country. Amid allegations that the Pakistani government may have been complicit in sheltering the terrorist leader, it seemed reasonable to question the approximately $20 billion in aid the United States had provided to Pakistan over the past decade. This high figure was in part the result of a significant increase in U.S. aid after the terrorist attacks against the United States on September 11, 2001. In the wake of these attacks, Pakistan rapidly became an essential partner in the U.S. response to Al Qaeda and its ally, the Afghan Taliban, by enabling the flow of logistics to the U.S. military in Afghanistan and by locating and arresting key terrorist leaders and

insurgents in Pakistan. However, the fact that Osama bin Laden had found sanctuary for at least several years in a small city near Pakistan's capital—a city that is also home to Pakistan's elite military academy and a major military base—suggested to some that the Pakistani government was either duplicitous in concealing bin Laden's presence from the United States or incompetent in its efforts to locate the world's most wanted terrorist.

During the year that followed this watershed event, United States–Pakistan relations were further strained by additional incidents that included: a November 2011 North Atlantic Treaty Organization (NATO) military engagement along the Afghanistan–Pakistan border that resulted in the inadvertent deaths of 24 Pakistani soldiers; accusations by senior U.S. officials that Pakistan was supporting Pakistan-based insurgents fighting U.S. forces in Afghanistan; and allegations by senior Pakistani officials that U.S.

actions, such as drone strikes in the Northwest Frontier Province, were regularly violating Pakistan's sovereignty. These developments only served to heighten mutual mistrust. On the U.S. side, Senator Frank Lautenberg framed the issue in stark terms when he said, "The United States provides billions of dollars in aid to Pakistan. Before we send another dime, we need to know whether Pakistan truly stands with us in the fight against terrorism. Until Congress and the American public are assured that the Pakistani government is not shielding terrorists, financial aid to Pakistan should be suspended" (Lautenberg, 2011). Pakistan has its own reasons to be suspicious of the United States as a strategic partner, including the unpredictability of U.S. aid in the face of shifting U.S. foreign policy objectives and priorities. A sense that the United States is unreliable is a significant reason why Pakistan's cooperation is sometimes less than robust.

An additional critical underlying reason for distrust is the divergent and, at times, competing national security priorities of the United States and Pakistan. To the United States, Pakistan should do more to help achieve the critical objectives of dismantling terrorist networks and weakening Afghan militants fighting against American troops in Afghanistan. To Pakistan, however, the United States is a fair-weather ally intent on using Pakistan to achieve U.S. objectives without addressing Pakistan's legitimate security concerns with its neighbor and rival on the subcontinent, India. The United States, whose intense involvement in the region is likely to be transitory, should not expect Pakistan to forgo its long-term interests in Afghanistan entirely, especially while Pakistan believes that India still poses an existential threat to its existence.

Pakistan's concerns about U.S. reliability have a long heritage, as U.S. aid to Pakistan has waxed and waned over the past 50 years with changing U.S. foreign policy priorities. Throughout this period, the United States has viewed South Asia in light of its global security interests and never shared Pakistan's perception of India as a threat. In the 1960s, the United States attempted to ratchet down tensions in South Asia by suspending aid to Pakistan after the second of what was to become four wars between India and Pakistan. During the 1980s, against the backdrop of the Cold War, the United States dramatically increased its assistance to Pakistan to counter the Soviets in Afghanistan. During this conflict, U.S. aid focused heavily on military assistance, which unintentionally strengthened Pakistan's military and intelligence agencies at the expense of its civilian institutions. In the 1990s, the pendulum swung back again as the United States reduced aid due to concerns over Pakistan's nuclear weapons program.

After 9/11, there was another dramatic expansion of U.S. military and civilian assistance to Pakistan in exchange for support for U.S.-led counterterrorism efforts and the war in Afghanistan. U.S. aid to Pakistan rose from roughly $36 million in 2000 to more than $2 billion in 2001, including $600 million provided in an emergency cash transfer in September 2001. Since then, Pakistan has received approximately $3 billion annually. In 2010, Pakistan placed second among top U.S.-aid recipients, after Afghanistan and ahead of Israel (Epstein and Kronstadt, 2011).

However, Pakistan's importance to the United States extends beyond immediate post 9/11–security concerns. It is in the long-term interest of the United States to see a stable and prosperous Pakistan with strong civilian governance institutions capable of exercising responsible control over its nuclear arsenal and willing to consider the pursuit of peaceful relations with India. Unfortunately, Pakistan today is beset by many political, economic, and social challenges. Plagued by a history of political instability, it is a developing country with an estimated per capita gross domestic product (GDP) of less than $3,000, which places it 136th in global rankings. The government dedicates less than 3 percent of GDP to education, the country's energy infrastructure is inadequate to meet current demands, and the health sector is unable to provide basic health services to the population (Epstein and Kronstadt, 2011). Pakistani society is also characterized by the existence of multiple separatist, sectarian, and terrorist groups that conduct politically motivated, armed attacks on a near daily basis.

As the United States seeks to end its combat involvement in Afghanistan and increasingly focuses on domestic fiscal concerns, it is likely that U.S. aid to Pakistan will decrease from its current levels. In 2009, the United States was already looking to refocus its aid to spend more on economic development and less on security assistance with the passage of the Enhanced Partnership with Pakistan Act, better known as the Kerry-Lugar-Bergman bill. This bill not only authorized $1.5 billion annually over 5 years for a broad range of nonmilitary initiatives, including education, health care, and infrastructure development, but also made U.S. security assistance contingent on Pakistani cooperation. Unfortunately, Pakistan viewed these conditions as impinging on its sovereignty and this negative perception diminished the positive impact of the new U.S. focus on development.

Unfortunately, the fallout from the bin Laden operation has further damaged U.S.–Pakistani relations. Given some Pakistanis' fears that an important goal of the U.S. government is to denuclearize Pakistan, there is intense alarm in some circles in Pakistan about the U.S. capability this raid demonstrated to conduct operations on Pakistani soil without detection. The American public, on the other hand, is not particularly sensitive to these concerns and instead is inclined to see bin Laden's presence in Pakistan as evidence of Pakistani duplicity. Particularly in light of the political salience of the U.S. budget deficit, many question whether U.S. largesse to Pakistan has been misused.

Looking ahead, the future of U.S. aid to Pakistan is likely to remain a topic of debate. Sharing Senator Lautenberg's concerns, some on both sides of the aisle in American politics are arguing for a suspension of all assistance. Others argue that over the long term, U.S. national interests are best promoted through continued engagement with Pakistan. As

Senator Lindsey Graham noted in response to calls in Congress to hold Pakistan accountable for its alleged harboring of bin Laden, "For those who want to cut off aid to Pakistan, I understand your frustration, but at the end of the day, if you want to create a failed state in Pakistan, one of the best things to do is sever relationships. It is not in our national security interest to let this one event destroy what is a difficult partnership but a partnership nonetheless" (Goldberg and Ambinder, 2011).

In the following selections, the authors present competing sides in this debate. In the YES selection, Professor Stephen Krasner argues that current U.S. aid policy is not working because it rewards Pakistan for poor behavior. To incentivize full Pakistani cooperation, the United States needs to be able to credibly threaten to adopt a policy of "malign neglect" or even "active isolation." The first of these options would entail cutting off military and civilian assistance and escalating unilateral U.S. military action in Pakistani territory; the latter would go further by labeling Pakistan a state sponsor of terrorism and levying sanctions for such behavior. Only after Pakistan changes its current behavior to meet U.S. demands should the United States resume aid efforts.

In the NO selection, journalists Jeffery Goldberg and Marc Ambinder do not advocate for a particular aid policy toward Pakistan, but rather note the detrimental and destabilizing effects that a suspension of U.S. aid and engagement could have on Pakistan and the region. Cutting aid to Pakistan's civilian government could lead to the collapse of a state armed with nuclear weapons and facilitate the rise of radical Islamist groups seeking to fill the resulting void. By focusing U.S. assistance programs too intensely on short-term counterterrorism interests, the United States deepens Pakistani distrust and risks undermining long-term American security and foreign policy interests in the region.

YES ↵

Stephen D. Krasner

Talking Tough to Pakistan: How to End Islamabad's Defiance

Late last month, after a NATO engagement in Pakistan went wrong and left 25 Pakistani troops dead, the West scrambled to get its story straight. Anders Fogh Rasmussen, NATO's secretary-general, quickly called the battle a "tragic unintended accident." The White House waffled; President Barack Obama later expressed regret over the incident but did not apologize. Islamabad, meanwhile, castigated the United States for violating its sovereignty, closed the Torkham border crossing, and announced it would sit out the recent Bonn conference on Afghanistan.

Whether the attack was entirely unintended or a pointed provocation, the Pakistani reaction offered yet further proof that current U.S. policy toward Pakistan has failed.

On November 28, White House Press Secretary Jay Carney noted that the relationship with Pakistan "continues to be an important cooperative relationship" but added that it "is also very complicated." In fact, the relationship is not cooperative, and U.S. policy is not complicated. It is incoherent. As I recently wrote in the January/February issue of Foreign Affairs (below), Pakistan does not heed even overt U.S. threats and censure, because Washington has time and again backed down from them, believing that Pakistan's policies, though unhelpful, could get much worse. Only by credibly threatening to end all assistance to Islamabad can Washington convince Pakistan's leaders that genuine cooperation is in their best interest.

***

On September 22, 2011, Admiral Mike Mullen, then chairman of the U.S. Joint Chiefs of Staff, made his last official appearance before the Senate Armed Services Committee. In his speech, he bluntly criticized Pakistan, telling the committee that "extremist organizations serving as proxies for the government of Pakistan are attacking Afghan troops and civilians as well as U.S. soldiers." The Haqqani network, he said, "is, in many ways, a strategic arm of Pakistan's Inter-Services Intelligence Agency [ISI]." In 2011 alone, Mullen continued, the network had been responsible for a June attack on the Intercontinental Hotel in Kabul, a September truck-bomb attack in Wardak Province that wounded 77 U.S. soldiers, and a September attack on the U.S. embassy in Kabul.

These observations did not, however, lead Mullen to the obvious conclusion: Pakistan should be treated as a hostile power. And within days, military officials began walking back his remarks, claiming that Mullen had meant to say only that Islamabad gives broad support to the Haqqani network, not that it gives specific direction. Meanwhile, unnamed U.S. government officials asserted that he had overstated the case. Mullen's testimony, for all the attention it received, did not signify a new U.S. strategy toward Pakistan.

Yet such a shift is badly needed. For decades, the United States has sought to buy Pakistani cooperation with aid: $20 billion worth since 9/11 alone. This money has been matched with plenty of praise. At his first press conference in Islamabad following his 2007 appointment as chairman of the Joint Chiefs, Mullen called Pakistan "a steadfast and historic ally." In 2008, then Secretary of State Condoleezza Rice even said that she "fully believed" that Pakistan "does not in any way want to be associated with terrorist elements and is indeed fighting to root them out wherever [Pakistani officials] find them." Meanwhile, U.S. leaders have spent an outsized amount of face time with their Pakistani counterparts. As secretary of state, Hillary Clinton has made four trips to Pakistan, compared with two to India and three to Japan. Mullen made more than 20 visits to Pakistan.

To be sure, Mullen was not the first U.S. official to publicly point the finger at Islamabad, nor will he be the last. In 2008, the CIA blamed Pakistan's ISI for aiding the bombing of the Indian embassy in Kabul. In July 2011, two months after U.S. Navy SEALS raided Osama bin Laden's compound near the prestigious Pakistan Military Academy, Admiral James Winnefeld, vice chair of the Joint Chiefs, told the Senate Armed Services Committee, "Pakistan is a very, very difficult partner, and we all know that." And in an October press conference with Afghan President Hamid Karzai, Clinton noted that the Obama administration intended to "push the Pakistanis very hard," adding, "they can either be helping or hindering."

Washington's tactic—criticism coupled with continued assistance—has not been effectual. Threats and censure go unheeded in Pakistan because Islamabad's leaders do not fear the United States. This is because the United States has so often demonstrated a fear of Pakistan, believing that although Pakistan's policies have been unhelpful, they could get much worse. Washington seems to have concluded that if it actually disengaged and as a result Islamabad halted all its cooperation in Afghanistan, then U.S. counterinsurgency efforts there would be doomed. Even more problematic, the thinking goes, without external support, the already shaky Pakistani state would falter. A total collapse could precipitate a radical Islamist takeover, worsening Pakistani relations with the U.S.-backed Karzai regime in Afghanistan and escalating tensions, perhaps even precipitating a nuclear war, between Pakistan and India.

Weighing of Deeds

The U.S.-Pakistani relationship has produced a few modest successes. Pakistan has generally allowed NATO to transport supplies through its territory to Afghanistan. It has helped capture some senior al Qaeda officials, including Khalid Sheik Mohammed, the 9/11 mastermind. It has permitted the United States to launch drone strikes from bases in Baluchistan.

Yet these accomplishments pale in comparison to the ways in which Pakistan has proved uncooperative. The country is the world's worst nuclear proliferator, having sold technology to Iran, Libya, and North Korea through the A. Q. Khan network. Although Islamabad has attacked those terrorist groups, such as al Qaeda and the Pakistani Taliban, that target its institutions, it actively supports others, such as the Haqqani network, the Afghan Taliban, and Hezb-i-Islami, that attack coalition troops and Afghan officials or conspire against India. Pakistan also hampers U.S. efforts to deal with those groups; although many Pakistani officials privately support the drone program, for example, they publicly exaggerate the resulting civilian deaths. Meanwhile, they refuse to give the United States permission to conduct commando raids in Pakistan, swearing that they will defend Pakistani sovereignty at all costs.

A case in point was the raid that killed bin Laden. Rather than embrace the move, Pakistani officials reacted with fury. The police arrested a group of Pakistani citizens who were suspected of having helped the United States collect intelligence prior to the operation and delayed U.S. interrogations of bin Laden's three wives for more than a week. Lieutenant General Ahmed Shuja Pasha, head of the ISI, condemned the U.S. raid before a special session of parliament, and the government passed a resolution pledging to revisit its relationship with the United States. Of course, the operation was embarrassing for the Pakistani military, since it showed the armed forces to be either complicit in harboring bin Laden or so incompetent that they could not find him under their own noses. But Pakistan could easily have saved face by publicly depicting the operation as a cooperative venture.

The fact that Pakistan distanced itself from the raid speaks to another major problem in the relationship: despite the billions of dollars the United States has given Pakistan, public opinion there remains adamantly anti-American. In a 2010 Pew survey of 21 countries, those Pakistanis polled had among the lowest favorability ratings of the United States: 17 percent. The next year, another Pew survey found that 63 percent of the population disapproved of the raid that killed bin Laden, and 55 percent thought it was a bad thing that he had died.

Washington's current strategy toward Islamabad, in short, is not working. Any gains the United States has bought with its aid and engagement have come at an extremely high price and have been more than offset by Pakistan's nuclear proliferation and its support for the groups that attack Americans, Afghans, Indians, and others.

Rational Choice

It is tempting to believe that Pakistan's lack of cooperation results from its weakness as a state. One version of this argument is that much of Pakistan's civilian and military leadership might actually want to be more aligned with the United States but is prevented from being so by powerful hard-line Islamist factions. Its advocates point to the fact that pubic officials shrank from condemning the bodyguard who in January 2011 shot Salman Taseer, the governor of Punjab, who had spoken out against Pakistan's blasphemy law. Similar silence followed the March assassination of Shahbaz Bhatti, the minorities minister and only Christian in the cabinet, who had also urged reforming the law. Presumably, the politicians held their tongues out of fear of reprisal. Another explanation of the weakness of the Pakistani state is that the extremists in the government and the military who support militants offer that support despite their superiors' objections. For example, the May 2011 terrorist attack on Pakistan's naval air base Mehran, which the top military brass condemned, was later suspected to have been conducted with help from someone on the inside.

Still, there is a much more straightforward explanation for Pakistan's behavior. Its policies are a fully rational response to the conception of the country's national interest held by its leaders, especially those in the military. Pakistan's fundamental goal is to defend itself against its rival, India. Islamabad deliberately uses nuclear proliferation and deterrence, terrorism, and its prickly relationship with the United States to achieve this objective.

Pakistan's nuclear strategy is to project a credible threat of first use against India. The country has a growing nuclear arsenal, a stockpile of short-range missiles to carry warheads, and plans for rapid weapons dispersion should India invade. So far, the strategy has worked; although Pakistan has supported numerous attacks on Indian soil, India has not retaliated.

Transnational terrorism, Pakistanis believe, has also served to constrain and humiliate India. As early as the 1960s, Pakistani strategists concluded that terrorism could help offset India's superior conventional military strength. They were right. Pakistani militant activity in Kashmir has led India to send hundreds of thousands of troops into the province—as many as 500,000 during a particularly tense moment with Pakistan in 2002. Better that India sends its troops to battle terrorists on its own territory, the Pakistani thinking goes, than march them across the border. Further, the 2008 Mumbai attack, which penetrated the heart of India, was a particularly embarrassing episode; the failure to prevent it, and the feeble response to it, demonstrated the ineffectuality of India's security forces.

Pakistan's double game with the United States has been effective, too. After 9/11, Pakistan's leaders could hardly resist pressure from Washington to cooperate. But they were also loath to lose influence with the insurgents in Afghanistan, which they believed gave Pakistan strategic depth against India. So Islamabad decided to have things both ways: cooperating with Washington enough to make itself useful but obstructing the coalition's plans enough to make it nearly impossible to end the Afghan insurgency. This has been an impressive accomplishment.

Caring by Neglecting

As Mullen's comments attest, U.S. officials do recognize the flaws in their country's current approach to Pakistan. Yet instead of making radical changes to that policy, Washington continues to muddle through, working with Pakistan where possible, attempting to convince its leaders that they should focus on internal, rather than external, threats, and hoping for the best. For their part, commentators mostly call for marginal changes, such as engaging the Pakistani military more closely on the drone program and making the program more transparent, opening U.S. textile markets to Pakistani trade, helping Pakistan address its energy deficit, focusing on a peaceful resolution of the Kashmir dispute, and developing closer ties to civilian officials. Many of these suggestions seem to be based on the idea that if millions of dollars in U.S. aid has not been enough to buy Pakistani support, perhaps extra deal sweeteners will be.

The one significant policy change since 2008 has been the retargeting of aid to civilians. Under the Obama administration, total assistance has increased by 48 percent, and a much higher percentage of it is economic rather than security related: 45 percent in 2010 as opposed to 24 percent in 2008. The Enhanced Partnership With Pakistan Act of 2009, which committed $7.5 billion to Pakistan over five years, conditioned disbursements on Pakistan's behavior, including cooperation on counterterrorism and the holding of democratic elections.

Despite Pakistan's ongoing problematic behavior, however, aid has continued to flow. Clinton even certified in March 2011 that Pakistan had made a "sustained commitment" to combating terrorist groups. Actions such as this have undermined American credibility when it comes to pressuring Pakistan to live up to its side of the bargain. The United States has shown that the sticks that come with its carrots are hollow.

The only way the United States can actually get what it wants out of Pakistan is to make credible threats to retaliate if Pakistan does not comply with U.S. demands and offer rewards only in return for cooperative actions taken. U.S. officials should tell their Pakistani counterparts in no uncertain terms that they must start playing ball or face malign neglect at best and, if necessary, active isolation. Malign neglect would mean ending all U.S. assistance, military and civilian; severing intelligence cooperation; continuing and possibly escalating U.S. drone strikes; initiating cross-border special operations raids; and strengthening U.S. ties with India. Active isolation would include, in addition, declaring Pakistan a state sponsor of terrorism, imposing sanctions, and pressuring China and Saudi Arabia to cut off their support, as well.

Of course, the United States' new "redlines" would be believable only if it is clear to Pakistan that the United States would be better off acting on them than backing down. (And the more believable they are, the less likely the United State will have to carry them out.) So what would make the threats credible?

First, the United States must make clear that if it ended its assistance to Pakistan, Pakistan would not be able to retaliate. The United States could continue its drone strikes, perhaps using the stealth versions of them that it is currently developing. It could suppress Pakistani air defenses, possibly with electronic jammers, so as to limit military deaths and collateral damage. And even if Pakistan shot down some drones, it could not destroy them all. The United States might even be able to conduct some Special Forces raids, which would be of such short duration and against such specific targets that Pakistan would not be able to retaliate with conventional forces. Pakistan might attempt to launch strikes against NATO and Afghan forces in Afghanistan, but its military would risk embarrassing defeat if those campaigns did not go well. Pakistan might threaten to cut off its intelligence cooperation, but that cooperation has never really extended to sharing information on the Afghan Taliban, one of the United States' main concerns in Afghanistan. Moreover, if Pakistan started tolerating or abetting al Qaeda on its own soil, the country would be even more at risk. Al Qaeda could turn against the state and attempt to unseat the government. And the United States would surely begin striking Pakistan even more aggressively if al Qaeda found haven there.

Second, the United States must show that it can neutralize one of Pakistan's trump cards: its role in the war in Afghanistan. Washington must therefore develop a strategy for Afghanistan that works without Pakistan's help. That means a plan that does not require transporting personnel or materiel through Pakistan. Nearly 60 percent of the NATO supplies sent into Afghanistan are already routed through the north, through Russia and Central Asia. The U.S. military is hoping to increase that number to 75 percent. Without Pakistan, therefore, the coalition could still support a substantial force in Afghanistan, but not one as big as the current one of 131,000 troops. The basic objective of that force would necessarily be counterterrorism, not counterinsurgency. Counterterrorism is less personnel- and resource-intensive because it aims only to prevent the country from becoming a haven for Islamist extremists, not to transform it into a well-functioning democracy. Given the Obama administration's current plans to withdraw 24,000 U.S. troops by the summer of 2012, with many more to follow, such a strategy is already inescapable.

Finally, Washington must shed its fear that its withdrawal of aid or open antagonism could lead to the Pakistani state's collapse, a radical Islamist takeover, or nuclear war. Pakistanis, not Americans, have always determined their political future. Even substantial U.S. investments in the civilian state and the economy, for example, have not led to their improvement or to gains in stability. With or without U.S. aid to Pakistan, the Pakistani military will remain the most respected institution in the country. In a 2011 Pew poll of Pakistanis, 79 percent of respondents said that the military was having a good influence on the country's direction, compared with 20 percent who said that the national government was.

As for the possibility of an Islamist takeover, the country's current power centers have a strong interest in maintaining control and so will do whatever they can to keep it—whatever Washington's policy is. It is worth remembering that Pakistan has already proved itself able to take out the terrorist networks that threaten its own institutions, as it did in the Swat Valley and the district of Buner in 2009. Moreover, government by radical Islamists has not proved to be a popular choice among Pakistanis. In the last general election, the Muttahida Majlis-e-Amal, a coalition of Islamist parties, won only seven out of 340 seats in the National Assembly.

The possibility that nuclear weapons could wind up in the hands of terrorists is a serious risk, of course, but not one that the United States could easily mitigate whatever its policy in the region. Pakistan's nuclear posture, which involves rapid dispersion, a first-strike capability, and the use of tactical weapons, increases the chances of the central government's losing control. Even so, Pakistan will not alter that posture because it is so effective in deterring India. Meanwhile, previous U.S. efforts to help tighten Pakistan's command-and-control systems have been hampered by mutual distrust. Any new such efforts would be, too. Finally, since India has both a first- and a second-strike capability, Pakistan would not likely strike India first in the event of a crisis. In any case, even if things did escalate, there is not much that the United States, or anyone else, could do—good relations or not.

From a U.S. perspective, then, there is no reason to think that malign neglect or active isolation would make Pakistan's behavior or problems any worse.

Heads I Win, Tails You Lose

Even as the United States threatens disengagement, it should emphasize that it would still prefer a productive relationship. But it should also make clear that the choice is Pakistan's: if the country ends its support for terrorism; works in earnest with the United States to degrade al Qaeda, the Taliban, and the Haqqani network; and stops its subversion in Afghanistan, the United States will offer generous rewards. It could provide larger assistance programs, both civilian and military; open U.S. markets to Pakistani exports; and support political arrangements in Kabul that would reduce Islamabad's fear of India's influence. In other words, it is only after Pakistan complies with its demands that the United States should offer many of the policy proposals now on the table. And even then, these rewards should not necessarily be targeted toward changing Pakistan's regional calculus; they should be offered purely as payment for Pakistan's cooperation on the United States' most important policies in the region.

A combination of credible threats and future promises offers the best hope of convincing Islamabad that it would be better off cooperating with the United States. In essence, Pakistan would be offered a choice between the situation of Iran and that of Indonesia, two large Islamic states that have chosen very different paths. It could be either a pariah state surrounded by hostile neighbors and with dim economic prospects or a country with access to international markets, support from the United States and Europe, and some possibility of détente with its neighbors. The Indonesian path would lead to increased economic growth, an empowered middle class, strengthened civil-society groups, and a stronger economic and social foundation for a more robust democracy at some point in the future. Since it would not directly threaten the military's position, the Indonesian model should appeal to both pillars of the Pakistani state. And even if Islamabad's cooperation is not forthcoming, the United States is better off treating Pakistan as a hostile power than continuing to spend and get nothing in return.

Implicit in the remarks Mullen made to the Senate was the argument that Washington must get tough with Pakistan. He was right. A whole variety of gentle forms of persuasion have been tried and failed. The only option left is a drastic one. The irony is that this approach won't benefit just the United States: the whole region, including Pakistan, could quickly find itself better off.

STEPHEN D. KRASNER is the Graham H. Stuart Professor of International Studies and the deputy director of the Freeman Spogli Institute (FSI) at Stanford University, where he is also a fellow of the Hoover Institution. He previously served as the Director of Policy Planning at the U.S. State Department.

Jeffrey Goldberg and Marc Ambinder    **NO**

The Ally From Hell

Shortly after American Navy Seals raided the Pakistani city of Abbottabad in May and killed Osama bin Laden, General Ashfaq Kayani, the Pakistani chief of army staff, spoke with Khalid Kidwai, the retired lieutenant general in charge of securing Pakistan's nuclear arsenal. Kidwai, who commands a security apparatus called the Strategic Plans Division (SPD), had been expecting Kayani's call.

General Kayani, the most powerful man in a country that has only a simulacrum of civilian leadership, had been busy in the tense days that followed the bin Laden raid: he had to assure his American funders (U.S. taxpayers provide more than $2 billion in annual subsidies to the Pakistani military) that the army had no prior knowledge of bin Laden's hideout, located less than a mile from Pakistan's preeminent military academy; and at the same time he had to subdue the uproar within his ranks over what was seen as a flagrant violation of Pakistan's sovereignty by an arrogant Barack Obama. But he was also anxious about the safety of Pakistan's nuclear weapons, and he found time to express this worry to General Kidwai.

. . . Much of the world, of course, is anxious about the security of Pakistan's nuclear weapons, and for good reason: Pakistan is an unstable and violent country located at the epicenter of global jihadism, and it has been the foremost supplier of nuclear technology to such rogue states as Iran and North Korea. It is perfectly sensible to believe that Pakistan might not be the safest place on Earth to warehouse 100 or more nuclear weapons. These weapons are stored on bases and in facilities spread across the country (possibly including one within several miles of Abbottabad, a city that, in addition to having hosted Osama bin Laden, is home to many partisans of the jihadist group Harakat-ul-Mujahideen). Western leaders have stated that a paramount goal of their counterterrorism efforts is to keep nuclear weapons out of the hands of jihadists.

"The single biggest threat to U.S. security, both short-term, medium-term, and long-term, would be the possibility of a terrorist organization obtaining a nuclear weapon," President Obama said last year at an international nuclear-security meeting in Washington. Al-Qaeda, Obama said, is "trying to secure a nuclear weapon—a weapon of mass destruction that they have no compunction at using."

Pakistan would be an obvious place for a jihadist organization to seek a nuclear weapon or fissile material: it is the only Muslim-majority state, out of the 50 or so in the world, to have successfully developed nuclear weapons; its central government is of limited competence and has serious trouble projecting its authority into many corners of its territory (on occasion it has difficulty maintaining order even in the country's largest city, Karachi); Pakistan's military and security services are infiltrated by an unknown number of jihadist sympathizers; and many jihadist organizations are headquartered there already.

"There are three threats," says Graham Allison, an expert on nuclear weapons who directs the Belfer Center for Science and International Affairs at Harvard. The first is "a terrorist theft of a nuclear weapon, which they take to Mumbai or New York for a nuclear 9/11. The second is a transfer of a nuclear weapon to a state like Iran. The third is a takeover of nuclear weapons by a militant group during a period of instability or splintering of the state." Pakistani leaders have argued forcefully that the country's nuclear weapons are secure. In times of relative quiet between Pakistan and India (the country that would be the target of a Pakistani nuclear attack), Pakistani officials claim that their weapons are "de-mated"—meaning that the warheads are kept separate from their fissile cores and their delivery systems. This makes stealing, or launching, a complete nuclear weapon far more difficult. Over the past several years, as Pakistan has suffered an eruption of jihadist terrorism, its officials have spent a great deal of time defending the safety of their nuclear program. . . .

Current officials of the Pakistani government are even more adamant on the issue. In an interview this summer in Islamabad, a senior official of the Inter-Services Intelligence directorate (ISI), the Pakistani military's spy agency, told *The Atlantic* that American fears about the safety of Pakistan's nuclear weapons were entirely unfounded. "Of all the things in the world to worry about, the issue you should worry about the least is the safety of our nuclear program," the official said. "It is completely secure." He went on to say, "It is in our interest to keep our bases safe as well. You must trust us that we have maximum and impenetrable security. No one with ill intent can get near our strategic assets."

Like many statements made by Pakistan's current leaders, this one contained large elements of deceit. At least six facilities widely believed to be associated with Pakistan's nuclear program have already been targeted by militants. In November 2007, a suicide bomber attacked a bus carrying workers to the Sargodha air base, which is believed to house nuclear weapons; the following month, a school bus was attacked outside Kamra air base, which may also serve as a nuclear storage site; in August 2008, Pakistani Taliban suicide bombers attacked what experts believe to be the country's main nuclear-weapons-assembly depot in Wah cantonment. If jihadists are looking to raid a nuclear facility, they have a wide selection of targets: Pakistan is very secretive about the locations of its nuclear facilities, but satellite imagery and other sources suggest that there are at least 15 sites across Pakistan at which jihadists could find warheads or other nuclear materials. . . .

Some American intelligence experts question Pakistan's nuclear vigilance. Thomas Fingar, a former chairman of the National Intelligence Council and deputy director of national intelligence under President George W. Bush, said it is logical that any nuclear-weapons state would budget the resources necessary to protect its arsenal—but that "we do not know that this is the case in Pakistan." The key concern, Fingar says, is that "we do not know if what the military has done is adequate to protect the weapons from insider threats, or if key military units have been penetrated by extremists. We hope the weapons are safe, but we may be whistling past the graveyard."

There is evidence to suggest that neither the Pakistani army, nor the SPD itself, considers jihadism the most immediate threat to the security of its nuclear weapons; indeed, General Kayani's worry, as expressed to General Kidwai after Abbottabad, was focused on the United States. According to sources in Pakistan, General Kayani believes that the U.S. has designs on the Pakistani nuclear program, and that the Abbottabad raid suggested that the U.S. has developed the technical means to stage simultaneous raids on Pakistan's nuclear facilities.

In their conversations, General Kidwai assured General Kayani that the counterintelligence branch of the SPD remained focused on rooting out American and Indian spies from the Pakistani nuclear-weapons complex, and on foiling other American espionage methods. . . .

Nuclear-weapons components are sometimes moved by helicopter and sometimes moved over roads. And instead of moving nuclear material in armored, well-defended convoys, the SPD prefers to move material by subterfuge, in civilian-style vehicles without noticeable defenses, in the regular flow of traffic. According to both Pakistani and American sources, vans with a modest security profile are sometimes the preferred conveyance. And according to a senior U.S. intelligence official, the Pakistanis have begun using this low-security method to transfer not merely the "de-mated" component nuclear parts but "mated" nuclear weapons. . . .

What this means, in essence, is this: In a country that is home to the harshest variants of Muslim fundamentalism, and to the headquarters of the organizations that espouse these extremist ideologies, including al-Qaeda, the Haqqani network, and Lashkar-e-Taiba (which conducted the devastating terror attacks on Mumbai three years ago that killed nearly 200 civilians), nuclear bombs capable of destroying entire cities are transported in delivery vans on congested and dangerous roads. And Pakistani and American sources say that since the raid on Abbottabad, the Pakistanis have provoked anxiety inside the Pentagon by increasing the pace of these movements. In other words, the Pakistani government is willing to make its nuclear weapons more vulnerable to theft by jihadists simply to hide them from the United States, the country that funds much of its military budget.

The nuclear shell game played by Pakistan is one more manifestation of the slow-burning war between the U.S. and Pakistan. The national-security interests of the two countries are often in almost perfect opposition, but neither Pakistan nor the U.S. has historically been able or willing to admit that they are locked in conflict, because they are also dependent on each other in crucial ways: the Pakistani military still relies on American funding and American-built weapons systems, and the Obama administration, in turn, believes Pakistani cooperation is crucial to the achievement of its main goal of defeating the "al-Qaeda core," the organization now led by bin Laden's former deputy, Ayman al-Zawahiri. The U.S. also moves much of the material for its forces in Afghanistan through Pakistan, and must cross Pakistani airspace to fly from Arabian Sea–based aircraft carriers to Afghanistan. (In perhaps the most bizarre expression of this dysfunctional relationship, Osama bin Laden's body was flown out of Pakistan by the American invasion force, which did not seek Pakistani permission and was prepared to take Pakistani anti-aircraft fire—but then, hours later, bin Laden's body was flown back over Pakistan on a regularly routed American military flight between Bagram Air Base in Afghanistan and the aircraft carrier *Carl Vinson*, in the Arabian Sea.)

Public pronouncements to the contrary, very few figures in the highest ranks of the American and Pakistani governments suffer from the illusion that their countries are anything but adversaries, whose national-security interests clash radically and, it seems, permanently. Pakistani leaders obsess about what they view as the existential threat posed by nuclear-armed India, a country that is now a strategic ally of the United States. Pakistani policy makers *The Atlantic* interviewed in Islamabad and Rawalpindi this summer uniformly believe that India is bent on drawing Afghanistan into an alliance against Pakistan. (Pervez Musharraf said the same thing during an interview in Washington.) Many of Pakistan's leaders have long believed that the Taliban, and Taliban-like groups, are the most potent defenders of their interests in Afghanistan. . . .

While the hostility and distrust have increased of late, the relationship between the two countries has been shot through with rage, resentment, and pretense for years. The relationship has survived as long as it has only because both countries have chosen to pretend to believe the lies they tell each other.

Pakistan's lies, in particular, have been abundant. The Pakistani government has willfully misled the U.S. for more than 20 years about its support for terrorist organizations, and it willfully misleads the American government when it asserts, against the evidence, that "rogue elements" within the ISI are responsible for the acts of terrorism against India and U.S. forces in Afghanistan. Most American officials are at this late stage convinced that there are no "rogue elements" of any size or importance in the ISI; there are only the ISI and the ISI assets that the ISI (with increasing implausibility) denies having. (The ISI's S Wing, the branch of the service that runs anti-India activities, among other things, is said to have a very potent "alumni association," in the words of Stephen P. Cohen, a leading American scholar of Pakistan based at the Brookings Institution.) A particular challenge the ISI poses is that while it funds and protects various jihadist groups, these groups often pick their own targets and the timing of their attacks. The ISI has worked for years against American interests—not only against American interests in Afghanistan, but against the American interest in defeating particular jihadist networks, even while it was also working *with* the Americans against *other* jihadist organizations. . . .

The American lies about this tormented relationship are of a different sort. The U.S. government has lied to itself, and to its citizens, about the nature and actions of successive Pakistani governments. Pakistani behavior over the past 20 years has rendered the State Department's list of state sponsors of terrorism effectively meaningless. The U.S. currently names four countries as state sponsors of terror: Sudan, Iran, Syria, and Cuba. American civilian and military officials have for years made the case, publicly and privately, that Pakistan is a state sponsor of terrorism—yet it has never been listed as such. In the last 12 months of the presidency of George H. W. Bush, for example, Secretary of State James Baker wrote a letter to the Pakistani prime minister, Nawaz Sharif, accusing Pakistan of supporting Muslim terrorists in Indian-administered Kashmir, as well as Sikh terrorists operating inside India. "We have information indicating that [the ISI] and others intend to continue to provide material support to groups that have engaged in terrorism," the letter read. At this same time, a talking-points memo read to Pakistani leaders by Nicholas Platt, who was then the American ambassador to Pakistan, asserted, "Our information is certain." The memo went on: "Please consider the serious consequences [to] our relationship if this support continues. If this situation persists, the Secretary of State may find himself required by law to place Pakistan on the state sponsors of terrorism list."

The Baker threat caused a crisis inside the Pakistani government. In his book *Pakistan: Between Mosque and Military*, Husain Haqqani, the current Pakistani ambassador to Washington, writes that Javed Nasir, who was the ISI chief during this episode, told Prime Minister Sharif, "We

have been covering our tracks so far and will cover them even better in the future." The crisis was resolved, temporarily, when Nasir was removed as ISI chief the following year.

Similar crises have erupted with depressing frequency. . . .

According to a secret 2006 U.S. National Intelligence Estimate on Afghanistan, "Available evidence strongly suggests that [the ISI] maintains an active and ongoing relationship with certain elements of the Taliban." A 2008 National Intelligence Estimate concluded that the ISI was providing "intelligence and financial support to insurgent groups—especially the Jalaluddin Haqqani network out of Miram Shah, North Waziristan—to conduct attacks against Afghan government, [International Security Assistance Force], and Indian targets." By late 2006, according to the intelligence historian Matthew Aid, who documents the dysfunctional relationship between the ISI and the CIA in his forthcoming book, *Intel Wars*, the U.S. had reliable intelligence indicating that Jalaluddin Haqqani and another pro-Taliban Afghan warlord, Gulbuddin Hekmatyar, were being given financial assistance by the ISI (which of course receives substantial financial assistance from the United States). . . .

Meanwhile American generals, briefing Congress and officials of the Bush and Obama administrations, gave repeated assurances that they had developed the sort of personal relationships with Pakistani military leaders that would lead to a more productive alliance. Admiral Michael Mullen, who stepped down as chairman of the Joint Chiefs of Staff in late September, invested a great deal of time in his relationship with General Kayani. But eventually Mullen's patience was exhausted; days before his retirement, Mullen finally broke with Kayani, publicly accusing the Pakistani army of supporting America's enemies in Afghanistan. In his final appearance before the Senate Armed Services Committee, on September 22, Mullen said that ISI-supported operatives of the Haqqani network had conducted a recent attack on the American Embassy in Kabul. "The Haqqani network acts as a veritable arm of Pakistan's Inter-Services Intelligence agency," he said. . . .

What really worries American strategic thinkers is . . . the long-term stability and coherence of the Pakistani state itself. Stephen P. Cohen, the Brookings Institution scholar, says that if Pakistan were not in possession of nuclear weapons, the problem would not be nearly the same. Pakistan without nuclear weapons, he says, would be the equivalent of "Nigeria without oil"—a much lower foreign-policy priority.

American strategists like Cohen argue that the U.S. must maintain its association with a nuclear Pakistan over the long term for three main reasons. The first is that an unstable and friendless Pakistan would be more apt to take precipitous action against India; the second is that nuclear material, or a warhead, could go missing; the third, longer-term worry is that the Pakistani state itself could implode. "One of the negative changes we've seen is that Pakistan is losing its coherence as a state," Cohen said. "Its economy has failed, its politics have failed, and its army either fails or looks the other way. There are no good options." Few experts believe that Pakistan is in imminent danger of complete collapse—but the trends, as Cohen notes, are wholly negative. The government is widely considered to be among the world's most corrupt. (President Asif Ali Zardari is himself informally known as "Mr. 10 Percent.") Last year, Pakistan's inflation rate hit a high of 15 percent, and the real unemployment rate was 34 percent. Some 60 percent of Pakistanis survive on less than $2 a day. Nearly a quarter of the government budget goes to the military. . . .

The policy goals of the Obama administration are focused not on Pakistan's nuclear program, but rather on the terrorist groups based there. "Our core goal is to disrupt, dismantle, and eventually defeat al-Qaeda," one senior administration official says. "This is a very clarifying way to think about what we are doing and why cooperation with Pakistan is important."

This narrow focus has led to some achievements—not only the bin Laden raid, which was obviously accomplished without the cooperation of the ISI, but also the capture or killing (with the ISI's help) of several other al-Qaeda figures over the years. This focus on al-Qaeda may have sidelined other tactical priorities (such as trying to disrupt and defeat Pakistani groups providing assistance to the Afghan Taliban) and has led to some uncomfortable trade-offs. When asked why the U.S. doesn't target the factories located on Pakistani territory that produce the improvised explosive devices deployed by the Taliban against American troops inside Afghanistan, the same senior Obama-administration official said: "What we want to do, above all else, is not lose progress on the core goal" of defeating al-Qaeda, a goal that calls for continuing to cooperate with, and to fund, the ISI. So: the U.S. funds the ISI; the ISI funds the Haqqani network; and the Haqqani network kills American soldiers.

Another senior administration official, when presented with this formula, said: "It's not as simple as that. We've identified a core interest, and we wouldn't have been able to make as much progress as we've made, without Pakistan. A lot of the assistance we provide them is focused on specific counterterrorism issues. This is not just cutting a check." Money, of course, is fungible—funds earmarked for fighting al-Qaeda can end up supporting the Haqqani network, which is fighting the United States. But, the senior official said, "we have demonstrated that we will impose restrictions on assistance, and withhold assistance for a time, if the Pakistanis aren't cooperating with us"—a reference to a recent decision by the administration to temporarily hold back $800 million in reimbursements for counterterror activities and other military aid.

To Stephen P. Cohen, the Pakistan analyst at Brookings, the administration's singular focus on al-Qaeda means that American policy makers are not focused on larger issues. The rationale for continued, even heightened,

engagement with Pakistan, he said, is that the country is "too nuclear to fail." The arguments made by the administration about the importance of focusing on al-Qaeda at the expense of focusing on Pakistan per se remind Cohen of arguments from the Cold War. "It's the same line I heard 20 years ago in the State Department," he says. "The program was to get the Soviets out of Afghanistan. We privileged one goal over another. In Pakistan we have several goals, but we are ignoring the Pakistani nuclear-weapons program, ignoring India-Pakistan relations, ignoring the country's growing societal degradation. We have to have a better policy than keeping our fingers crossed."

Few policy makers believe that cutting aid to Islamabad is practical, especially while American troops in Afghanistan depend on supplies trucked through Pakistan. Even Admiral Mullen, who has been disillusioned by the behavior of Pakistan's ruling generals, argued before the Senate Armed Services Committee just prior to his retirement that the U.S. must not give up on its relationship with Pakistan. "Now is not the time to disengage from Pakistan; we must, instead, reframe our relationship," he said. "A flawed and strained engagement with Pakistan is better than disengagement." . . .

This should motivate American policy makers to devise a new approach, while remaining focused on the most important goal: keeping Pakistan's nuclear arsenal secure and holstered.

"South Asia remains the most dangerous nuclear-confrontation zone in the world, and these are not issues we can solve unilaterally," says Toby Dalton, the deputy director of the Nuclear Policy Program at the Carnegie Endowment for International Peace and a former Department of Energy representative at the U.S. Embassy in Islamabad. "We share a common goal with Pakistan, in preventing nuclear war and preventing terrorists from gaining access to a nuclear weapon. We have to work with them on nuclear security and have meaningful technical exchanges on best practices. This has to continue."

The United States must, for its own security, keep watch over Pakistan's nuclear program—and that's more easily done if we remain engaged with the Pakistani government. The U.S. must also be able to receive information from the ISI about al-Qaeda, even if such information is provided sporadically. And the U.S. will simply not find a way out of Afghanistan if Pakistan becomes an open enemy. Pakistan, for its part, can afford to lose neither America's direct financial support, nor the help America provides with international lending agencies. Nor can Pakistan's military afford to lose its access to American weapons systems, and to the trainers attached to them. Economically, Pakistan cannot afford to be isolated by America in the way the U.S. isolates countries it considers sponsors of terrorism. Its neighbor Iran is an object lesson in this regard. For all these reasons, Pakistan and America remain locked in a hostile embrace.

There is no escaping this vexed relationship—and little evidence to suggest that it will soon improve. But the

American officials in closest contact with the Pakistanis—
Admiral Mullen being the notable exception—still seem
predisposed to optimism, apparently embracing the belief
that Islamabad will change through tough love. A senior U.S. intelligence official told us that General David
Petraeus, the new director of the CIA, says he believes he
can rebuild relations with the ISI, because he has "a good
personal relationship with these guys."

Jeffery Goldberg is a correspondent for *The Atlantic* and
a recipient of the National Magazine Award for Reporting.
He is also the author of *Prisoners: A Story of Friendship and
Terror.*

Marc Ambinder is editor-at-large of *The Week* and a contributing editor at *GQ* and at *The Atlantic*. He is also a former
White House correspondent for the *National Journal*.

EXPLORING THE ISSUE

Should the United States Cut Foreign Aid to Pakistan?

Critical Thinking and Reflection

1. What do the United States and Pakistan each seek to gain from their relationship with one another? Are these national interests compatible?
2. Does the United States need Pakistan more than Pakistan needs the United States? Or is the reverse true? Explain your position.
3. What are some of the reasons that Pakistan may not cooperate fully in the achievement of U.S. national security objectives in Afghanistan and in U.S. counterterrorism efforts?
4. What should the goals of American foreign aid to Pakistan be? Should the United States prioritize short-term or long-term interests as it establishes these goals?
5. What is the role of Pakistan's nuclear arsenal in shaping U.S. decisions to provide foreign aid to that country? What should it be?

Is There Common Ground?

In assessing the options available, it is important to consider whether a strained relationship with Pakistan is better than no relationship at all and whether changes in U.S. foreign policy can foster a more productive partnership. The extreme positions are fairly clear: on the one hand, the United States could engage in what Stephen Krasner calls "active isolation" and accept that Pakistan is more adversary than partner; on the other, the United States can continue to label Pakistan a strategic partner and ignore Pakistani behavior that belies that image. There is probably common ground in the idea that neither extreme is desirable. While Krasner argues that the United States should acquire the ability to credibly threaten active isolation, for example, actually having to implement that policy is another matter. The real goal of advocates on both sides of the issue is to enhance cooperation.

A second important issue relates to how aid is used. Here again there is common ground in that advocates on all sides seek transparency. Those who believe that economic development assistance should take priority over short-term security goals argue that this transparency can best be achieved by assisting in the development of Pakistan's civilian institutions of governance. However, those who argue that only narrowly targeted security assistance is likely to support U.S. national security objectives are also concerned that any aid provided is used for the intended purpose.

Finally, while tensions seem likely to persist, there is broad agreement that a stable and democratic Pakistan would be beneficial to U.S. interests in the region. However, whether the United States can really do much to affect the likelihood of this outcome remains an open question. With discussions of disengagement once again clouding U.S.–Pakistani relations, as they did in the 1990s, the way ahead is likely to be challenging.

Additional Resources

Epstein, Susan B., and K. Alan Kronstadt. *Pakistan: U.S. Foreign Assistance.* Washington, DC: Congressional Research Service, June 7, 2011.

Internet References . . .

Center for American Progress

The authors of this study contend that any aid program must have a long-term focus and be centered on economic and political development. The United States must realize that the shifts it would like to see in Pakistan's national strategy, especially vis-à-vis militant groups, may not be feasible in the short term but will become more likely if Pakistan succeeds in adopting and sustaining governance and economic reforms.

**www.americanprogress.org/issues/2011/07/pdf/
pakistan_aid.pdf**

Foreign Affairs

This article contends that instead of cutting aid to Pakistan, the United States must increase its assistance and better focus it on the civilian sector. This refocusing will help Pakistan to better manage internal civil–military relations that have overly privileged the military since Pakistan's independence.

**www.foreignaffairs.com/articles/136412/
c-christine-fair/doubling-down-on-civilian-
engagement-in-pakistan**

TimesReporter

Lindsey Graham cited in "Congress May Dock Pakistan Aid Over Osama bin Laden" is available at this link.

**www.timesreporter.com/news/x294379337/Congress-
may-dock-Pakistan-aid-over-bin-Laden**

Lautenberg Press Office

"Appropriations Committee Member Lautenberg Questions Pakistan Aid in Wake of Bin Laden Raid," is available at this link.

**http://lautenberg.senate.gov/newsroom/record.
cfm?id=332658**

The New York Times Online

This article contends that corruption in Pakistan's civilian bureaucracy and, a misplaced U.S. focus on big-impact projects, rather than locally tailored ones, have led to the failures of U.S. aid thus far. The author goes on to offer that the promotion of free trade may work better than aid programs.

**www.nytimes.com/2011/05/02/world/asia/02pakistan.
html?_r=1**

The New Yorker Online

This article discusses the unforeseen consequences of U.S. military aid to Pakistan. The author contends that Pakistan has diverted aid to its nuclear weapons program and continues to divert aid today to fund radical Islamist organizations.

**www.newyorker.com/reporting/2011/05/16/
110516fa_fact_wright**

Carnegie Endowment for International Peace

This study argues that the main beneficiary of U.S. aid is the Pakistani military, which cooperates with the United States just enough to assure that aid flows continue. The author argues that an assistance package that shifts the focus from military assistance to a focus on economic development and democratic institution building would be in the best interest of both countries.

**http://carnegieendowment.org/files/pakistan
_aid2011.pdf**

Unit IV

UNIT

U.S. Economic Concerns

*I*n today's globalized world, a country's interactions with the outside world are increasingly important to its economic competitiveness, growth, and prosperity. For the U.S. government, this makes economics a matter of foreign as well as domestic policy and raises a host of interesting questions. How can U.S. trade interests be best served? Should the United States be concerned with fair trade as well as free trade? Is it possible for other countries, for example, to advantage their industries through unfair currency manipulation practices? How do private flows of capital around the world affect U.S. interests? Does the government have a role to play in fostering U.S. competitiveness in foreign markets and attracting foreign capital to the United States? These questions are politically salient, since economic exchange creates winners and losers who can be expected to mobilize around their interests.

There are also security implications associated with U.S. economic relations with the rest of the world. While economic exchange can create a mutually beneficial interdependence that leads to cooperation between states and leaves everyone better off, it can also create dependencies that may be leveraged by one side against the other in a crisis—or even contribute to conflict. Those who focus on the first of these outcomes might advocate that the United States continue to promote the development of international institutions that facilitate an open trading system. Others, who are more concerned about dangerous dependencies, might advocate policies that protect U.S. markets and promote the development of domestic industries, moving the United States closer to self-sufficiency in strategic sectors. The issues presented in this unit speak to these debates.

Selected, Edited, and with Issue Framing Material by:
Suzanne Nielsen, *U.S. Military Academy*
and
Scott Handler, *U.S. Military Academy*

ISSUE

Is Free Trade Good for the United States?

YES: Daniel J. Ikenson and Scott Lincicome, from "Beyond Exports: A Better Case for Free Trade," *Free Trade Bulletin* (January 31, 2011)

NO: Michael Lind, from "The Cost of Free Trade," *The American Prospect* (December 1, 2011)

Learning Outcomes
After reading this issue, you should be able to: • Understand the concept of gains from trade. • Recognize that some people gain from free trade, while others are hurt by it. • Discuss how trade policy can be used to help mitigate resource transition costs. • Understand the concept of rent-seeking behavior and explain how it relates to trade policy. • Discuss how trade policy can influence economic growth.

ISSUE SUMMARY

YES: Daniel J. Ikenson, director of Cato's Herbert A. Stiefel Center for Trade Policy Studies, and Scott Lincicome, international trade attorney with the law firm of White & Case, LLP, argue that the most principled case for free trade is a moral one: voluntary economic exchange is inherently fair, benefits both parties, and allocates scarce resources more efficiently than a system under which government dictates or limits choices. In addition, countries that are more open to the global economy grow faster and achieve higher incomes than those that are relatively closed.

NO: Michael Lind, policy director and co-founder of the Economic Growth Program at the New America Foundation, argues that any resurgence of American manufacturing will occur when U.S. trade policy favors the growth of U.S. exports rather than free trade. Existing U.S. free trade policies have fostered the off-shoring of manufacturing jobs as corporations respond to tax subsidies, lower environmental and labor regulatory standards, currency manipulation practices, and strategic industrial policies of U.S. trading partners.

The debate over whether or not free trade is good for the United States is an emotional one because trade decisions help create winners and losers in society. However, the ferocity of this debate ebbs and flows with the overall strength of the economy. From the beginning of President Ronald Reagan's administration in 1981 through the recession that began in late 2008, American presidents from both political parties sought to promote free trade. Though it was Republican President George H.W. Bush who negotiated the North American Free Trade Agreement (NAFTA) between the United States, Canada, and Mexico in 1992, it was President Bill Clinton of the Democratic Party who completed the agreement and obtained Senate ratification in 1993. President Clinton also led American efforts to transform the General Agreement on Tariffs and Trade into the stronger World Trade Organization in 1995. Clinton's successor, President George W. Bush, continued

to promote free trade through multiple bilateral agreements after assuming office in 2001. It was not until 2008, and the onset of recession, that trade promotion appeared to stall as a foreign policy priority. As of early October 2012, full recovery remains elusive as the U.S. economy continues to see flat growth and unemployment remains at levels consistently above 8 percent. Owing their rise in part to economic hardship, populist movements on the left and the right—embodied by the Occupy Movement and the Tea Party, respectively—have brought a vitriolic debate over free trade back into the public eye.

In order to assess arguments for and against free trade, it is useful to start with the economic theories that explain expected gains from trade. Adam Smith first articulated the fundamental economic efficiency case for free trade in *An Inquiry into the Nature and Causes of the Wealth of Nations*, which was published in 1776. In this book, Smith explained the cost advantages associated with production for large markets using the concept of economies of scale. As the number of items produced increased, the cost per item could be reduced. David Ricardo extended this argument by developing the concept of comparative advantage in 1817 in his *On the Principles of Political Economy and Taxation*. According to Ricardo, every country has something at which it can be more cost efficient at producing than another country. If all countries produce according to their comparative advantages and then engage in free trade, all can be better off.

The works of Smith and Ricardo responded to a set of trade policies persisting from feudal Europe, which were known as mercantilism. Mercantilism encouraged exports and discouraged imports to develop a positive flow of revenue into national treasuries. At the same time, however, these trade policies also implicitly taxed domestic consumers by causing artificially elevated prices for domestically manufactured goods. The dominance of mercantilist policies in early industrial Europe was in part a legacy of its class structure. The political elites owned the nonlabor factors of production, which were land and capital. Since the financial gains associated with the policies of the mercantilists accrued to landowners and capitalists, these political elites benefitted, whereas the consumers—who were primarily laborers—bore the costs. This history has modern analogs, since the trade policies of different countries are often still shaped as much by the relative political power of various groups as they are by pure economic logic.

In addition to the concepts of economies of scale and comparative advantage, the pro-free trade position rests on the idea that individuals are best suited to make decisions about their own welfare since they hold the most in-depth knowledge of their own circumstances. Since individuals consider their own budgetary constraints when choosing what goods or services to purchase, the product's price will affect the individual's consumption choices based upon the laws of supply and demand. All else remaining equal, as the price of a product increases, individuals will choose to consume less. These signals help producers to make rational decisions, while the competition of producers with one another tends to produce competition, efficiency, and economic growth.

Government restrictions on free trade can impede the market signals received by producers, affect the ability of individual consumers to make their own choices, and lower consumer welfare. As an example, when governments impose trade restrictions that limit the import of foreign goods, these restrictions reduce availability and drive domestic prices upward in the protected markets. Free trade, on the other hand, maximizes efficiency and competition and has the potential to leave all consumers better off. From the perspective of the U.S. economy as a whole, there is a strong case for free trade. This may help to explain why Presidents of both parties, who have the country as a whole as their constituencies, tend to favor free trade.

However, free trade also has distributional implications, which are politically salient. Critics of free trade generally rest their arguments on one of three main issues: transition costs, market failures, and social justice. The transition cost argument assumes that one cannot easily transfer factors of production—land, labor, and capital—from one sector of the economy to another. For this reason, no efficiency gains from free trade may be realized. If domestic producers are pushed out of the market by foreign competition, their land, labor, and capital may simply remain idle. The more specific those resources are to particular uses, the more difficult it is to employ them in new sectors (Lind, 2011). Some opponents of free trade argue for trade restrictions on the basis that they will ease needed transitions. This is one of the principal arguments often made when policies are considered that will protect the U.S. manufacturing sector from foreign competition. The basic argument is that cheaper imports in products such as automobiles, for example, could threaten the vitality of domestic productive resources. Without government protection, factories will close and workers will be laid off. Since it is not easy to convert auto factories—land and capital—and auto workers—labor—to other productive uses, these resources may remain idle for a substantial period of time. While proponents of free trade may appreciate the costs of transition, they still resist protectionist policies because once such policies are enacted they can be difficult to roll back. Over time, this can further contribute to a loss of competitiveness in domestic industries that now have a lesser incentive to try and keep up.

A second major critique of free trade rests on the concept of market failure. Proponents of the market failure critique support trade restrictions in response to variations in environmental and safety standards between developed and developing countries. These critics argue that the production of goods will move overseas if other countries have lower environmental standards and allow companies to pollute more freely. Without having to incorporate pollution costs, companies can produce their goods cheaper in countries with lax regulations, leading to the offshoring of production and the disadvantaging of domestic producers (Battacharya et al., 1999). This is the line of argument that was used for over 15 years to prevent Mexican trucking companies from entering the United States. Protected industries in the United States claimed that Mexico's lower emissions and safety standards would have given Mexican logistics firms an unfair advantage in the United States.

Finally, the social justice critique of free trade focuses on variations in labor standards between countries. The basic argument is that many companies in developing countries do not pay their workers a just wage; therefore, it is not possible for American businesses to compete with these producers. Other countries may fail to create and enforce occupational safety standards, allow firms to use child labor, or turn a blind eye when employers use coercive means to obtain workforce participation (Mathews, 2009).

All of these behaviors are seen as sources of social injustice. Domestic producers should be protected against such unfair practices, which also have the potential to violate basic human rights.

The YES and NO selections wade into these debates. In the YES selection, Daniel Ikenson and Scott Lincicome claim that free trade is fair trade and good for the United States. They argue that trade barriers result in the diversion of productive resources to achieve political ends. Consumers pay taxes that are unfair in order to subsidize the special interests that succeed in enlisting the weight of the government on their side. Based on the economic logic of gains from trade, Ikenson and Lincicome argue that when government authorities decide what goods consumers should choose, they reduce total welfare. At their core, trade barriers represent the triumph of coercion and politics over free choice and economics.

In contrast, Michael Lind focuses on China as he answers NO to whether free trade is in the best interest of the United States. He relies largely on the transition cost concern, arguing that restrictive trade policies against China that will reduce the number of manufacturing jobs lost in the United States are justified. He also suggests that free trade is not in the best interest of the United States because China does not reciprocate. Since China practices mercantilist trade policies, the United States should also follow a mercantilist policy that would hurt China even if it hurts the United States as well.

YES

Daniel J. Ikenson and Scott Lincicome

Beyond Exports: A Better
Case for Free Trade

Introduction

The 112th Congress begins its term amid renewed optimism about prospects for U.S. trade liberalization. Big labor's stranglehold over the congressional trade agenda was broken with the election in November. The U.S. government finally appears willing to end its disgraceful ban on Mexican trucks. And in his State of the Union address, President Obama implored Congress to pass the trade agreement with South Korea as soon as possible, and articulated his commitment to bringing the other two pending bilateral agreements, as well as the Transpacific Partnership negotiations and the Doha Round, to successful conclusions.

After four years of stasis on the trade front, the new environment is a welcome change. Removing barriers to trade—in both directions—is essential to sustained economic recovery and long-term growth.

But how long will this window of opportunity remain ajar? Despite trade's benefits, American sentiment toward it is lukewarm in the best of times, and always vulnerable to manipulation by politicians and media charlatans looking to blame foreigners for domestic shortcomings. Before the end of this year, the 2012 presidential election campaigns will be in high gear—and trade has been a particularly dirty word in stump speeches and political debates in the past. Indeed, one of the reasons for the energetic trade policy push in 2011 is that the political environment next year is expected to be less hospitable to trade initiatives.

The fact that public opinion about trade is so malleable and arguments for restricting it so resonant at times speaks to a failure of free trade's proponents to make their compelling message stick. It is sad but true that so many Americans need to be reminded of the benefits of being free to choose how and with whom to conduct commerce. But in an atmosphere where demagogues peddle myths to mislead the public into believing that it is preferable for government to limit their choices and direct their resources to chosen ends, it is crucial that the case for free trade be made more clearly, comprehensively, and consistently than it has been in the past.

Thus, in addition to securing the immediate goal of concluding and passing trade liberalizing agreements in 2011, advocates of trade in Congress, the administration,

the business community, think tanks, academia, and among the general public should update their arguments and invest in the process of winning the trade debate once and for all. Some of the most compelling arguments for free trade have been only modestly summoned or absent from the discussion for too long.

Message Matters

Most Americans enjoy the fruits of international trade and globalization every day: driving to work in vehicles containing at least some foreign content, relying on smart phones assembled abroad from parts made in multiple countries (including the United States), having more to save or spend because retailers pass on cost savings made possible by their access to thousands of foreign producers, designing and selling products that would never have been commercially viable without access to the cost efficiencies afforded by transnational production and supply chains, enjoying fresh imported produce that was once unavailable out of season, depositing bigger paychecks on account of their employers' growing sales to customers abroad, and enjoying salaries and benefits provided by employers that happen to be foreign-owned companies.

Nevertheless, public opinion polls routinely find tepid support among Americans for free trade. Regardless of the prevailing economic conditions; how the questions are phrased; or whether the subject is attitudes toward free trade, trade agreements, or the impact of trade on the U.S. economy, most polls typically find that fewer than half of all Americans view trade favorably, and that skeptical views have become more prevalent in recent years.

Some of that skepticism can be attributed to the perpetuation of myths about how unfair foreign trade practices have destroyed the U.S. manufacturing sector or about how the trade deficit reflects a failure of trade policy and constitutes a drag on economic growth—the staple arguments of most protectionists.[1] However, we free trade advocates need to bear some of the responsibility for not winning Americans' hearts and minds. In a Cato Institute study published nearly two years ago, the authors of this paper asserted: "Pro-trade advocates have failed to make a convincing and durable case for why free trade is superior to the alternatives. The factual arguments are compelling, but tend to get lost on a public that is more susceptible to depictions of worst-case scenarios and the ill-conceived bromides that follow. The scholarship is there, but we need better salesmanship."[2]

The Stock Pro-Trade Message Contains the Seeds of Its Own Destruction

Despite the window of opportunity to move the trade agenda forward this year, it is fair to say that trade skeptics have the upper hand in the battle over messaging. After all, trade's proponents are intent on getting so much accomplished in 2011 because it is assumed that in 2012—an election year—the trade agenda will again be radioactive on Capitol Hill. But why shouldn't campaigning politicians in both major political parties feel comfortable explaining the benefits of trade in the face of constituent skepticism?

One explanation for the resonance of anti-trade sentiment is that it is easier to whip up public opinion by playing to stereotypes and characterizing trade as a zero sum game between "us" (Americans) and "them" (foreigners) than it is to explain the process by which economic value is created and how free trade facilitates that process. Theirs is a black and white message. Once the public's mind has been filled with images of shuttered factories and unemployed workers—regardless of the real cause of those conditions—it becomes more difficult to convey the truth about how Americans benefit from trade and how much poorer we would be without it.

But that hurdle can be overcome. The solution requires more than rationalization; it requires introspection, then change. Many of trade's most vocal and active proponents in government and the private sector have relied too heavily and for too long on a faulty marketing strategy, which posits that more trade and more trade agreements mean more export opportunities, and more exports mean more economic growth and more jobs.[3] The political appeal of that message is obvious, and there is nothing dishonest about it. Exports do contribute to economic growth, which is essential to job creation.

However, that message invites the following retort: if exports help grow the economy and create jobs, then imports must shrink the economy and cost jobs. In failing to explain why that conclusion about imports is wrong, trade proponents have yielded the floor to trade skeptics, who have been more than happy to manufacture talking points about the "deleterious" impact of imports on the U.S. economy.[4] Most of those talking points are misleading or plain wrong, but there has been inadequate effort to correct the record. As a result, too many Americans accept the mercantilist fallacy that exports are good, imports are bad, and the trade account is a scoreboard.

The pervasive view that exports are good and imports are bad is a central misconception upon which rests the belief that trade negotiations and "reciprocity" are essential to trade liberalization.[5] Under this formulation, an optimal trade agreement, from the perspective of U.S. negotiators, is one that maximizes U.S. access to foreign markets and minimizes foreign access to U.S. markets. An agreement requiring large cuts to U.S. tariffs, which would thus deliver significant benefits to consumers, would not pass political muster unless it could be demonstrated that even larger export benefits were to be had. This misguided premise that imports are the cost of exports and should be minimized lies at the root of public skepticism about trade. Ironically, it is also a prominent feature of the favored pro-trade argument. . . .

Likewise, the business community—in its efforts to promote trade—tends to fixate on the export potential of this or that agreement.[6] Of course that is important information to disseminate. But in ignoring or downplaying the primary benefits of trade to consumers—that is, greater access to imports—the business community's message reinforces false impressions that trade only benefits rich corporations at the expense of working Americans.

Of the "Top Ten Reasons Trade is Good for America," a list extracted from a recent letter to Congress from a coalition of businesses and posted on the website of the U.S. Chamber of Commerce, only one made reference to imports.[7] If proponents want to avoid the perennial disruptions to the trade agenda caused by the perceived need to tiptoe around the electoral calendar, we will need better selling points. We must articulate a more resonant message, so that the benefits of trade need not be rationalized or couched in defensive rhetoric.

A More Compelling Case for Free Trade

The case for free trade is much broader than the one that trumpets only export potential. And it is more elegant. The most principled case is a moral one: voluntary economic exchange is inherently fair, benefits both parties, and allocates scarce resources more efficiently than a system under which government dictates or limits choices. Moreover, government intervention in voluntary economic exchange on behalf of some citizens necessarily comes at the expense of others and is inherently unfair, inefficient, and subverts the rule of law. At their core, trade barriers are the triumph of coercion and politics over free choice and economics. Trade barriers are the result of productive resources being diverted to achieve political ends and, in the process, taxing unsuspecting consumers to line the pockets of the special interests that succeeded in enlisting the weight of the government on their side.

Protectionism is akin to earmarks, but it comes out of the hides of American families and businesses instead of the general treasury. Policymakers on the right should support free trade because it is consistent with their principled opposition to higher taxes on American businesses and consumers and to big government telling people how and where they should spend their money. A vote for free trade is a vote to cut taxes and to get government out of the business of picking winners and losers in the market. Policymakers on the left should support free trade because it is consistent with their opposition to corporate welfare and regressive taxation.

Beyond the moral case for free trade, when people are free to buy from, sell to, and invest with one another as they choose, they can achieve far more than when governments attempt to control their decisions. Widening the circle of people with whom we transact brings benefits to consumers in the form of lower prices, greater variety, and better quality, and it allows companies to reap the benefits of innovation, specialization, and economies of scale that larger markets afford. Free markets are essential to prosperity, and expanding free markets as much as possible enhances that prosperity.

When goods, services, and capital flow freely across U.S. borders, Americans can take full advantage of the opportunities of the international marketplace. They can buy the best or least expensive goods and services the world has to offer, they can sell to the most promising markets, they can choose among the best investment opportunities, and they can tap into the worldwide pool of labor and capital. Study after study has shown that countries that are more open to the global economy grow faster and achieve higher incomes than those that are relatively closed.[8]

Retorting Some Common Myths

In the bright light of these broader free trade arguments, it becomes clear that those seeking to restrict trade are trying to commit an offense. They are attempting to enlist the force of government—via higher taxes, more regulation, or corporate welfare—to prevent individuals from engaging in consensual, mutually beneficial exchange. And they should be forced to explain themselves in terms of the harm they would inflict on others through state coercion. Regrettably, that never happens.

Instead, those seeking protection claim immunity from the logic and equity of those moral and economic parameters, preferring to invoke claims of exceptional circumstances, labeling those opposed to their agenda as unpatriotic, or playing on fears about the consequences of exercising one's rights to trade. Of course free trade is ideal in theory, they will say, but reality demands special consideration in our case. Or, of course individuals should be free to choose with whom they transact, but their expressed preferences for imports imperil their jobs and America's future.

Trade skepticism is rooted in fear, which thrives on the propagation and acceptance of recycled myths. Thus, in making the case for free trade, proponents must be better prepared to refute the plausible-sounding fallacies about imports, trade deficits, and zero-sum games that have been allowed to linger for too long.[9]

The allegation that imports have destroyed the U.S. manufacturing sector persists despite the wealth of evidence to the contrary. U.S. manufacturing took its lumps during the recent recession (as did all other sectors of the economy), but by all credible metrics it has been thriving for decades. In fact, U.S. factories account for more manufacturing value-added than the factories of any other country in the world.[10]

If imports detract from growth and reduce the number of jobs in the economy, then why does import value tend to rise when the economy is expanding and adding jobs and fall when the economy is contracting and shedding jobs?[11] Imports are vital to economic growth. U.S. producers account for the majority of imports. More than 55 percent of what Americans purchase from abroad is classified as industrial supplies or capital goods—inputs used in manufacturing and other value-added activities, such as the construction and transportation industries.[12]

By limiting Americans' access to imports, production costs and other business costs would be higher, necessitating higher prices, lower wages, and other cost savings to make enterprises profitable. Consumers, businesses, and government would have less purchasing power, which would curtail economic growth and hurt U.S. companies trying to compete abroad, thus reducing exports. In fact, export sales would be even more difficult to come by, as foreigners, deprived of their sales to Americans, would have fewer dollars to spend on U.S. goods.

Contrary to some assertions, imports actually support jobs in U.S. manufacturing and in many other sectors of the economy. In addition to the imported intermediate goods that keep U.S. companies competitive and able to provide jobs, a significant percentage of U.S. imports are final goods that were simply assembled abroad from components produced, designs engineered, and ideas hatched in the United States. Without access to lower-cost labor in places like China, products like Apple's iPod, iPhone, and iPad might never have been commercially viable.[13] These ubiquitous products—which have spawned the creation of new industries producing dozens of accessory items (think docking stations and apps)—might have been too expensive to produce for mass consumption had all of the manufacturing and assembling been required to occur in the United States. Instead of $300–$400 iPhones, the devices might have retailed for double or triple that price and their consumer potential never realized.

The example of the iPhone production and supply chain also reveals the absurdity of hand wringing over trade deficits. The alleged U.S. high-tech trade deficit with China is simply a function of antiquated trade flow accounting that has failed to keep up with the reality of globalization. Even though each iPhone imported from China registers as a $179 import (the full cost of its production), only $6.50 of that amount represents the cost of Chinese inputs.[14] The bottom line is that each iPhone imported from China supports U.S. employment up and down the supply chain, from Apple's designers and engineers to independent component manufacturers to logistics providers, truckers, port workers, and retail employees. And misguided policies designed to "fix" the trade deficit would imperil this wealth-creating process. The arguments of trade's critics remain valid only to those who fail to examine the facts about our modern global economy. Illuminating those facts is the burden of free trade advocates.

Conclusion

In order to win the hearts and minds of a skeptical American public, trade advocates need to broaden their arguments to include more than just happy talk about potential export growth. The case for free trade is more compelling than that. In light of the arguments above, we conclude with the five most compelling reasons free trade is good for America.

1. Free trade is fair trade. Trade occurs between individuals, not countries. This voluntary economic exchange is inherently fair, benefits both parties, and allocates scarce resources more efficiently than a system under which government dictates or limits choices. It is thus morally imperative that Americans have the freedom to engage in commerce with whomever they choose.[15]
2. Free trade is appealing across the political spectrum. Free trade is consistent with the imperative of smaller government (lower taxes and fewer restrictions), greater transparency (fewer backroom deals—think Mexican truck ban), opposition to corporate welfare, and opposition to regressive taxation.
3. Free trade is just the extension of free markets across national borders. Widening the circle of people with whom we transact brings benefits to consumers in the form of lower prices, greater variety, and better quality, and it allows companies to reap the benefits of innovation, specialization, and economies of scale that larger markets afford. Free markets are essential to prosperity, and expanding free markets as much as possible enhances that prosperity.
4. Free trade creates prosperity and supports rising living standards. Study after study has shown that countries that are more open to the global economy grow faster and achieve higher incomes than those that are relatively closed. When goods, services, and capital flow freely across U.S. borders, Americans can take full advantage of the opportunities of the international marketplace. They can buy the best or least expensive goods and services the world has to offer; they can sell to the most promising markets; they can choose among the best investment opportunities; and they can tap into the worldwide pool of labor and capital.
5. Free trade is essential to America's continued prosperity. As the world's leading producer of goods and services, the United States needs to ensure that production and supply chains remain open in both directions so that foreigners can sell intermediate goods to U.S. producers and final goods to U.S. consumers, and so they can earn U.S. dollars with which they can consume U.S. products and services and invest in the United States.

Notes

1. For a refutation of these myths that malign trade, see Daniel Ikenson and Scott Lincicome, "Audaciously Hopeful: How President Obama Can Help Restore to Pro-Trade Consensus," Cato Institute Trade Policy Analysis no. 39, April 28, 2009, p. 12.
2. Ibid., p.3.
3. See, e.g., Scott Linicome, http://lincicome.blogspot.com/2010/01/potus-trade-pitch-misses-plate.html.
4. See, e.g., Economic Policy Institute, www.epi.org/publications/entry/bp171/.
5. For a discussion of the perils of insisting on reciprocity, see Scott Lincicome, http://lincicome.blogspot.com/2010/02/perils-of-reciprocal-trade-policy.html. For a comprehensive analysis of the costs and benefits of reciprocity and the costs and benefits of unilateral trade liberalization, see Daniel Ikenson, "Leading the Way: How U.S. Trade Policy Can Overcome Doha's Failings," Cato Institute Trade Policy Analysis no. 33, June 19, 2006.
6. See, e.g., *Washington Post*, www.washingtonpost.com/wp-dyn/content/article/2011/01/20/AR2011012007089.html.
7. ChamberPost, www.chamberpost.com/2011/01/top-ten-reasons-trade-is-good-for-america.html?utm_source=feedburner&utm_medium=feed&utm_campaign=Feed:+Chamberpost+(The+ChamberPost).
8. See, e.g., David Dollar and Aart Kraay, "Trade, Growth, and Poverty," World Bank, Development Research Group, June 2001, or Council of Economic Advisers, "The History and Future of International Trade."
9. See, e.g., Public Citizen, www.citizen.org/documents/SOTU.pdf.
10. For a comprehensive treatment of this subject, see Daniel Ikenson, "Thriving in a Global Economy: The Truth about U.S. Manufacturing and Trade, Cato Institute Trade Policy Analysis no. 35, August 28, 2007. See also *The American*, http://blog.american.com/?p=25164.
11. Cato Institute, www.cato-at-liberty.org/media-feeds-americas-skepticism-about-trade/#more-20197.
12. Blogspot, http://1.bp.blogspot.com/_otfwl2zc6Qc/TQWl8UsaCuI/AAAAAAAAOuA/LkdxeTbfABI/s1600/imports.jpg.
13. For a comprehensive treatment of this subject, see Daniel Ikenson, "Made on Earth: How Global Economic Integration Renders Trade Policy Obsolete," Cato Institute Trade Policy Analysis

no. 42, December 2, 2009. For a shorter analysis and updated statistics, see http://lincicome.blogspot.com/2010/01/explaining-ipads-stunning-price.html.

14. See Cato Institute, www.cato-at-liberty.org/lies-damned-lies-and-trade-statistics/.

15. Of course, certain exceptions, such as those based on valid national security concerns, should apply. As Milton Friedman stated, "it cannot be denied that on occasion [national security] might justify the maintenance of otherwise uneconomical productive facilities." However, more often than not, anti-trade policies based on national security, such as unilateral sanctions or steel tariffs, have proven to be ineffectual or unnecessary.

DANIEL J. IKENSON is the director of the Cato Institute's Herbert A. Stiefel Center for Trade Policy Studies. Previously, he was the director of international trade planning for an international accounting and business advisory firm.

SCOTT LINCICOME is an international trade attorney with the law firm of White & Case, LLP. Previously, he was a research assistant with the Cato Institute's Center for Trade Policy Studies.

Michael Lind

 **NO**

The Cost of Free Trade

Any renaissance of American manufacturing must begin by fundamentally reversing our trade policies—both in general and in particular toward China. Over the past two decades, leading U.S. manufacturers, both the venerable (like General Electric) and the new (like Apple), have offshored millions of jobs—by one recent estimate, 2.9 million—to China to take advantage of the cheap labor, generous state subsidies, and low currency valuation that are linchpins of China's mercantilist development strategy. Other factors, including increasingly automated production, have also taken a toll on America's manufacturing workforce, but it's the mass exodus of American production to China and, more recently, the rise of indigenous, state-subsidized Chinese production that have decimated American industry and reduced the incomes of American workers.

The United States government did not have to stand idly by while the nation's industrial base was disassembled. It could have preserved and promoted key industries and supply networks by creating favorable credit policies, tax incentives, local content rules, and tariffs to punish currency manipulation from countries like China. For that matter, the U.S. could have created more flexible trade rules when it helped to craft the World Trade Organization.

There was considerable support, particularly within the Democratic Party, for these kinds of policies—yet no such policy was ever put into place, for trade divides the Democrats more than any other issue. The division is peculiar: It splits Democratic presidents into two people, the candidate and the elected official.

In 2008, candidate Barack Obama, campaigning in Ohio, vowed: "I voted against CAFTA [the Central American Free Trade Agreement], never supported NAFTA [the North American Free Trade Agreement], and will not support NAFTA–style trade agreements in the future. While NAFTA gave broad rights to investors, it paid only lip service to the rights of labor and the importance of environmental protection."

Now the Obama administration has won Congress's support for trade deals with South Korea, Colombia, and Panama that are difficult to distinguish from CAFTA and NAFTA (though a provision in the Korean deal increases the number of American-assembled cars that can be sold there). In addition, the administration is hosting talks intended to promote a trans-Pacific partnership in trade with a variety of countries on both sides of the Pacific.

By reversing himself on trade, the president is following the example set by Bill Clinton. Clinton, too, sounded like a trade hawk in his 1992 campaign, in which he promised to crack down on unfair Japanese trade practices. By the end of his two terms, however, he was boasting of his record in passing NAFTA and legislation granting permanent normalized trade status to China.

In a January 2000 piece titled "Expanding Trade, Projecting Values: Why I'll Fight to Make China's Trade Status Permanent" that was published in *The New Democrat*, the newsletter of the Democratic Leadership Council, Clinton asserted that establishing normalized trade relations with China would boost American exports there and that increased trade would foster China's democratization: "We want a prosperous China open to American exports; whose people have access to ideas and information; and that upholds the rule of law at home and plays by global rules of the road on everything from nuclear nonproliferation to human rights to trade. . . . It will open a growing market to American workers, farmers, and businesses. And more than any other step we can take right now, it will encourage China to choose reform, openness, and integration with the world."

None of Clinton's confident predictions have been borne out.

China remains a repressive authoritarian state engaged in dealings with abusive regimes around the world. In the first decade of the 21st century, the proportion of industrial production undertaken by state-controlled companies grew instead of shrinking. The flood of American exports to the China market never materialized. Instead, the flood of Chinese imports swelled. The U.S. trade deficit between 1976 and 2010 added up to more than $7 trillion; of that, more than 70 percent was accumulated after 2000. In 2006, just before the crash that began the Great Recession, the U.S. trade deficit had grown to 6 percent of U.S. gross domestic product (GDP). Between 1998 and 2008, the U.S. merchandise trade deficit with China alone rose 470 percent.

The top five U.S. exports to China between 2005 and 2010 were oilseeds and grains (mainly soybeans), waste and scrap, semiconductors and other electronic components, aerospace and aircraft parts, and resin, synthetic rubber, and synthetic fibers. Two of these export sectors depend heavily on U.S. government support—Defense Department procurement, in the case of aircraft parts, and federal farm subsidies, in the case of agricultural exports.

While manufacturing as a share of employment declined in all nations with advanced industrial economies (OECD) countries from around a quarter in 1970 to an average of 16 percent in 2008, it declined least in countries with export trade surpluses like Germany (19 percent in 2008) and most in countries running large merchandise trade deficits like the U.S. (9.5 percent in 2008).

If ever a policy has been discredited by its results, it is the American trade policy of Democratic presidents Obama and Clinton, which is indistinguishable from that of Republican presidents Ronald Reagan, George H.W. Bush, and George W. Bush. Yet every president asserts that the next feeble and unbalanced trade treaty or two will turn America into an export powerhouse of the kind that it has not been for the past 30 years.

What explains this disconnect between rhetoric and reality? Economic interest groups that have profited from the offshoring of industry to China—multinational corporations and their investors, importers and retailers like Wal-Mart—support the status quo. The Wall Street wing of the Democratic Party—personified by Clinton Treasury Secretary Robert Rubin and his protégé, Obama Treasury Secretary Timothy Geithner—has worked hard to ensure that Democratic presidents promote such trade deals, over the objections of the labor movement and many (at times, most) Democratic members of Congress. Meanwhile, the decline of American domestic manufacturing and its workforce has reduced the numbers and influence of the major constituencies for an alternative trade policy.

But there is more to America's perverse and unsuccessful trade policy than interest-group pressure. The belief that greater liberalization of trade and investment must invariably benefit the American economy in the long run, no matter its short-term costs in terms of crippled industries and lost jobs, has become an article of faith for America's bipartisan establishment for more than 50 years.

It was not always thus. Before World War II, the United States was one of the most protectionist nations in the world. University academic faculties generally reflect the interests of the businessmen who serve as regents, so it should come as no surprise that economics was taught differently in different parts of the United States in the 19th century. In the commodity-exporting South and the commercial Northeast, economists preached free trade. The center of protectionist economics was the newly industrializing Mid-Atlantic and Midwest, where the internationally famous economist Henry Carey was one of many who championed Kentucky Senator Henry Clay's American System, which was inspired by Alexander Hamilton's earlier support for federal promotion of infant industries. (Hamilton, it should be noted, preferred subsidies to tariffs.)

In 1881, in order to promote protectionism, a Philadelphia industrialist named Joseph Wharton founded the first business school in the U.S. Wharton viewed free trade as a "fungus . . . which healthy political organisms can hardly afford to tolerate." In his deed of gift to the Wharton School of Finance and Economy at the University of Pennsylvania, the industrialist specified that the school should teach "how by craft in commerce one nation may take the substance of a rival and maintain for itself virtual monopoly of the most profitable and civilizing industries; how by suitable tariff legislation a nation may thwart such designs." He made his gift conditional: "The right and duty of national self-protection must be firmly asserted and demonstrated."

Unlike the Republicans, the party of manufacturing, the Democrats with their base among Southern and Western agrarians—eager to export their crops and to purchase manufactured goods at the lowest possible price—had usually favored free trade and low tariffs. But Republicans dominated national government from 1865 through 1932, promoting protectionist policies. By contrast, the one major Democratic president during this period, Woodrow Wilson, entertained a utopian vision of a global free market policed by a system of collective security. His congressional ally (and later Franklin Roosevelt's secretary of state) Cordell Hull of Tennessee declared in his 1948 memoirs that he had long believed "unhampered trade dovetailed with peace." Hull had reversed cause and effect: Military rivals do not engage in free trade, but that does not mean that free trade will end military rivalries.

Twenty years later, campaigning for the presidency in the depths of the Depression and in a nation more industrialized than it had been in Wilson's time, Franklin Roosevelt insisted that he supported protection for American industries where it was necessary. But Roosevelt fiercely attacked Herbert Hoover for his support of the 1930 Smoot-Hawley tariff legislation, and the accusation that Hoover wrecked the world economy by signing the tariff became part of Democratic partisan mythology.

Economists from Milton Friedman on the right to Paul Krugman on the left have dismissed the idea that the tariff significantly worsened the Depression in America or that foreign retaliation against the tariff caused global trade to collapse. U.S. exports were no more than 7 percent of gross national product (GNP) in 1929. Between 1929 and 1931, U.S. exports fell by 1.5 percent of GNP, while U.S. GNP declined by ten times as much—by 15 percent. The volume of world trade shrank by two-thirds from the last quarter in 1929 to the first quarter in 1933. The global collapse in trade that came after the passage of the tariff was the result of a sudden, universal drop in demand, not of retaliation against American protectionism. A similar collapse in trade occurred in 2008–2009 at the beginning of the Great Recession, in the absence of tariff wars.

But the myth of Smoot-Hawley wouldn't die. During his 1993 debate with Ross Perot about the pending NAFTA legislation, Vice President Al Gore handed Perot a framed picture of Senator Reed Smoot and Representative Willis Hawley, asserting that the tariff bill that bore their name "was one of the principal causes, many economists say the principal cause, of the Great Depression in this country and around the world."

Gore was merely invoking what had become holy writ among America's internationalist policy elites who had directed national policy ever since World War II and who lived in fear that the U.S. would revert to its prewar isolationism and protectionism. In the same way that "Munich"—British Prime Minister Neville Chamberlain's agreement with Hitler in 1938—was invoked by the American foreign-policy establishment as a symbol of appeasement, so Smoot-Hawley became a symbol of the protectionist economic strategy that the now-hegemonic U.S. had repudiated.

The fear that actions taken to protect American industries from foreign competition, even in retaliation against unfair foreign practices, would lead to trade wars and global discord wasn't the only pillar buttressing the cult of free trade. In 1934, the New Deal Congress passed the Reciprocal Trade Agreements Act, which transferred the right to set tariffs from Congress to the president as a way to guard against parochial trade policies. When the act was passed, no one anticipated that, in slightly more than a decade, the U.S. would be the dominant power in a war-ruined world and the leader of a four-decade struggle against the Soviet Union. Thanks to the Cold War, presidents began using their power as trade negotiators to give other countries access to American consumer markets in return for supporting American military or diplomatic policies.

As Alfred E. Eckes Jr. notes in *Opening America's Market: U.S. Foreign Trade Policy Since 1776*, the limits on foreign aid imposed by American public opinion prompted American foreign-policy officials to opt for what Eckes calls a policy of "trade, not aid." In the decades following World War II, the U.S. so dominated the global economy that policy-makers gave little if any thought to the prospect that free trade might ultimately undermine America's manufacturing prowess. In an unpublished page for his memoirs, President Harry Truman wrote: "American labor can now produce so much more than low-priced foreign labor in a given day's work that our workingmen need no longer fear, as they were justified in fearing in the past, the competition of foreign workers." In December 1946, the State Department instructed its officials to help the countries in which they were stationed to export to the U.S.: "In general, a Foreign Service officer should give the same attention to serving United States importers as he would give to United States exporters."

In 1953, a commission on trade headed by Daniel W. Bell, Roosevelt's former budget director, proposed to increase imports of manufactured goods even if that led to unemployment for an estimated 60,000 to 90,000 American workers: "In cases where choice must be made between injury to the national interest and hardship to an industry, the industry [should] be helped to make adjustments by means other than excluding imports—such as

through extension of unemployment insurance, assistance in retraining workers, diversification of production, and conversion to other lines." President Dwight Eisenhower argued that measures "which tend to drive away an ally as dependable as Great Britain . . . do much more harm in the long run to our security than would be done by permitting a U.S. industry to suffer from British competition."

Not content just to help Cold War allies prosper, the U.S. in the 1960s also sought to use access to the American market to drive development in the post-colonial world. In 1963, President John F. Kennedy called on the U.S. and its allies to open "our markets to the developing countries of Africa, Asia, and Latin America." Kennedy warned an AFL-CIO convention in Miami that protection of U.S. industry risked "driving potential trading partners into the arms of the Soviets." In March 1964, a Johnson administration task force on foreign economic policy, anticipating the rhetoric of 1990s New Democrats, called for a "war on poverty—worldwide. . . . The whole country would be the gainer if, over time, we could shift resources away from textiles, shoes and other unsophisticated manufactures into more advanced items where we have a comparative advantage . . . [such as] capital, scientific and technological research, skilled and educated labor."

One of the few government officials who dissented from the prevailing orthodoxy was George Humphrey, Eisenhower's secretary of the Treasury. A veteran of the mining industry, Humphrey declared at a 1954 cabinet meeting, according to another participant, "We were protectionists by history and had been living under a greatly lowered schedule of tariffs in a false sense of security because the world was not in competition. That has changed now, and the great wave of competition from plants we had built for other nations [is] going to bring vast unemployment to our country." Humphrey's cautions went totally unheeded, however.

Today, in challenging a powerful bipartisan consensus supported by Rooseveltian liberal internationalism and Reaganite conservatism and buttressed by academic dogma and historical mythology, progressive critics of the conventional wisdom about trade and investment have failed to speak with a single voice. Indeed, some progressive alternatives to free trade end up reinforcing the assumptions of the orthodoxy that they are meant to supplant.

It is tempting, for instance, for the center-left to invoke international economic competitiveness as a rationale for doing things that progressives want to do anyway, like investing in schools and infrastructure. But the unstated assumption behind the rhetoric of competitiveness is that countries like China are outdoing the U.S. in manufacturing because their educational system or their infrastructure is superior to that of the U.S. In reality, Chinese mercantilism, like that of Japan, South Korea, and other Asian mercantilist countries, is based chiefly on currency manipulation and state-directed credit to targeted export industries and infrastructure. As long as countries manipulate their currencies and subsidize their industries, no amount of investment in American education and infrastructure is likely to improve America's trade balance and reignite American manufacturing.

A similar criticism can be made of progressives who confine their critique to calling for higher labor and environmental standards in our trading partners in order to "level the playing field." Corporate decisions about off-shoring have as much to do with state capitalist subsidies as they do with poorly paid workers. Germany and Japan, where wages are comparable to those in the U.S., continue to run chronic merchandise trade surpluses for reasons having nothing to do with low-wage workforces and everything to do with those nations' strategic industrial policies and the structure and governance of their corporate and financial sectors.

The progressive case for rethinking America's failed trade policies is weakened the most by those on the center-left who accept the premise that the U.S. must give up traditional industries to other countries and specialize in this or that "industry of the future." These new industries are sometimes identified as "knowledge industries," like product design and software writing, or with "green technologies," like solar and wind power. But history shows that countries like the U.S. in the 19th century or China today may begin by manufacturing products invented elsewhere but soon develop their own native classes of inventors and entrepreneurs, along with native bankers to finance them. China is accelerating this process by compelling U.S. and European companies that hope to market their goods there to share their advanced, proprietary technology with their Chinese corporate counterparts.

Within the U.S., it would be absurd to create factories capable of manufacturing only renewable—energy products, instead of a broader range of manufactured items. Solar panels, for example, depend on the generalist industry of glass manufacturing. Finally, such new industries as renewable technologies are no more likely to remain in the U.S. than the old industries, confronted as they are by subsidized Chinese competition.

Nothing Lasts Forever, and in time, the post-1945 American approach to trade will change. The driver of change may ultimately be strategic military and diplomatic retrenchment, as the American-dominated unipolar system gives way to a messier multipolar order. It may have made sense during the Cold War for the U.S. to have tolerated our allies' mercantilism in order to keep them in the anti-Soviet alliance. But if, in the next few decades, China surpasses the U.S. as the largest economy, it would be absurd to argue that the world's second-largest

economy would have a moral duty to set an example of economic liberalism by unilaterally opening its market to subsidized exports from the world's largest economy. By that time, emerging powers like India and Brazil as well as China may have begun rewriting the rules of world trade on their own. The result is unlikely to be a global economic order of which Cordell Hull would have approved.

In the meantime, proponents of action against foreign mercantilism and for an industrial policy that promotes American manufacturing might take heart from the statements and actions of some Democrats in Congress. Senators and representatives from the industrial states like Sherrod Brown of Ohio continue to champion the beleaguered manufacturing sector, while Senator Charles Schumer of New York speaks for many in Congress in threatening retaliation against Chinese currency manipulation. Congressional Democrats have set forth a "Make It in America" agenda including crackdowns on mercantilist trading practices abroad as well as advocating investments in infrastructure, energy, and education at home. The message appeals to Republican voters as well, to judge from the criticisms of Chinese mercantilism by Mitt Romney. What is more, Congress enacted Buy American rules in the 2009 stimulus bill, despite a chorus of disapproval by the media and policy establishment. The Obama administration bailed out General Motors and Chrysler and, responding to a petition from the Steelworkers Union, imposed temporary tariffs on Chinese steel pipes and tires. This October, the Senate passed a bill enabling the president to impose tariffs on Chinese imports unless China allows the yuan to appreciate (though House Speaker John Boehner has made clear he's disinclined to let it come to a vote in his chamber).

But similar temporary tariffs or quotas imposed by presidents from Reagan to George W. Bush have served only as an occasional counterpoint to the long-term process of offshoring productive industry from the United States. Washington has declined to develop anything resembling a national industrial and trade strategy, though such things are routine among most of the nations we trade with. The Great Recession and the ongoing erosion of domestic manufacturing may cause many to rethink the conventional wisdom about American trade policy—but there's no guarantee this will actually happen.

MICHAEL LIND is a co-founder of the New America Foundation in Washington, D.C., where he currently serves as the Policy Director of the Economic Growth Program.

EXPLORING THE ISSUE

Is Free Trade Good for the United States?

Critical Thinking and Reflection

1. In what ways can free trade benefit economic growth?
2. Should the United States accept the inefficiencies and reduced economic growth that come from restricted and managed trade as the price U.S. society has to pay in order to reduce inequality and the uncertainty of economic outcomes for individuals in society?
3. Does it make sense for a country to restrict foreign trade in a time of recession? Why or why not?
4. Are trade restrictions an effective way to manage the creative destruction associated with open market systems? What are the advantages and disadvantages of such restrictions? What alternative policy options exist?

Is There Common Ground?

Across the political spectrum in the United States, there is generally broad agreement that free markets best produce economic growth and gains in individual welfare over time. However, there is less agreement about international trade policies. Even if the goal is to preserve a free market economy in the United States, what trade policies will best serve that end? Is the fairness of other countries' trade practices important, and should the United States only embrace free trade with countries that reciprocate fully? Or is free trade in the best interests of the United States no matter what other countries do? Even when the ends of policy are broadly accepted, vigorous debates about the appropriate means are still possible.

In addition, there is broad agreement that free trade will cause the need for domestic economic adjustments over time. In essence, this is nothing more than the "creative destruction" that is at the heart of capitalism itself. But varying views exist about the appropriate U.S. government response. Should the United States protect infant industries in order to give them a chance to become competitive? Should it protect ailing industries to ease the needed transition? Others argue for the need for protection for a variety of national security purposes. While some of these arguments have merit, policymakers also need to take into account the fact that policies gain constituencies once they are enacted and can be difficult to phase out. Those who would like the government to adopt trade restrictions to buffer the costs of transition or to serve other social purposes would be wise to consider alternative approaches that may also serve these ends.

Additional Resources

Bergsten, C. Fred. "Commentary: The Move Towards Free Trade Zones." *Economic Review* 76, no. 6 (1991): 27–36.

The author argues that using free trade zones as a substitute for true multilateral trade negotiations distracts the trade discussion from a worldwide liberal trade agenda.

Bhagwati, Jagdish. *In Defense of Globalization.* New York: Oxford University Press, 2004.

This book makes a compelling argument that a liberalized global trade regime can serve as a powerful force for social justice and worldwide economic growth.

Irwin, Douglas A. *Free Trade Under Fire*, 3rd ed. Princeton, NJ: Princeton University Press, 2009.

This book provides a systematic dismantling of the most common protectionist arguments.

Krugman, Paul. "Is Free Trade Passe?" *The Journal of Economic Perspectives* 1, no. 2 (1987): 131–144.

In this article, economist Paul Krugman presents a compelling catalog of both the advantages and disadvantages of free trade.

Krugman, Paul. "The Move Toward Free Trade Zones." *Economic Review* 76, no. 6 (1991): 5–26.

This article argues that the focus on free trade zones, though successful in practice, has introduced negative side effects that distort trade advantages within and outside of the trade zones. The geopolitical impact of these trading blocs may undermine more general multilateral trade negotiations.

Stiglitz, Joseph E. and Andrew Charlton. *Fair Trade for All: How Trade Can Promote Development.* New York: Oxford University Press, 2005.

This stunning critique of the current global trading system focuses on how lesser developed countries are coerced into liberalized trade agreements that disadvantage them.

Internet References . . .

United Nations Environmental Programme

This is a case study on Bangladesh's shrimp farming industry titled, *Environmental Impacts of Trade Liberalization and Policies for the Sustainable Management of Natural Resources: A Case Study on Bangladesh's Shrimp Farming Industry.*

www.unep.ch/etu/etp/acts/capbld/rdone/ bangladesh.pdf

United Nations

This paper by Tomy Mathews, "Enhancing the Global Linkages of Cooperatives: The Fairtrade Option," was presented at the United Nations Expert Group Meeting on "Cooperatives in world in Crisis," New York, April 28–30, 2009.

www.un.org/esa/socdev/egms/docs/2009/ cooperatives/Tomy.pdf

Selected, Edited, and with Issue Framing Material by:
Suzanne Nielsen, *U.S. Military Academy*
and
Scott Handler, *U.S. Military Academy*

ISSUE

Should the United States Eliminate Its Dependence on Foreign Oil?

YES: Clifford Krauss and Eric Lipton, from "The Energy Rush; U.S. Inches Toward Goal of Energy Independence," *The New York Times* (March 22, 2012)

NO: Paul Roberts, from "The Seven Myths of Energy Independence: Why Forging a Sustainable Energy Future Is Dependent on Foreign Oil," *Mother Jones* (May/June 2008)

Learning Outcomes
After reading this issue, you should be able to: • Discuss the history of the political debate about energy independence in the United States.   • Distinguish energy independence from energy security.   • Discuss the argument that energy independence would further U.S. national security.   • Assess the ability of the United States to end its use of foreign oil.   • Discuss the viability of alternative forms of energy to replace oil.

ISSUE SUMMARY

YES: Clifford Krauss and Eric Lipton, correspondents with *The New York Times*, argue that eliminating U.S. dependence on foreign oil is feasible and should be a strategic priority for the United States. Recent technological advances that enable the expanded use of U.S. oil reserves and reduce the energy consumption of consumer goods make it possible for the United States to produce enough energy domestically to meet its needs.

NO: Paul Roberts, a freelance journalist, argues that the idea that the United States can obtain independence from foreign oil is an illusion that distracts politicians from the more practical long-term goal of energy security. Energy security is the pursuit of energy sources that are "reliable and reasonably affordable, that can be deployed quickly and easily, yet are also safe and politically and environmentally sustainable." To obtain energy security, the United States should continue to draw on both domestic and foreign energy sources.

The debate in the United States over the pursuit of energy independence began almost four decades ago. In response to the Organization of Petroleum Exporting Countries (OPEC) oil embargo in 1973, President Richard Nixon declared that energy independence had become a vital national security concern. Despite continued rhetorical support for this goal from every one of Nixon's successors as President, U.S. oil imports increased from 35 percent in 1973 to 60 percent in the late 2000s. They subsequently dropped to 45 percent by 2011, but this was largely due to declining demand caused by the 2009 recession (Mullaney, 2012). In the 2012 election year, the debate continued through the campaign speeches given by incumbent Democratic President Barack Obama and his Republican challenger, Governor Mitt Romney. While both candidates recommended different policy solutions,

both argued that achieving independence from foreign oil was achievable. While the debate remains lively, in some sense both sides are backing an untested proposition since many policies that could promote the achievement of energy independence have not been implemented due to other, overriding domestic and national security concerns.

Energy independence is defined here as the ability of the United States to produce all of its oil needs domestically. Oil drives, literally, much of what powers industrialized society because the economy largely relies upon oil, in the form of gasoline and diesel fuel, to move goods to domestic and foreign markets and workers to and from their jobs. As of 2010, oil was used to meet over 90 percent of U.S. transportation requirements (U.S. Energy Information Administration, 2010). Yet, uncertainty exists about the size of existing global oil reserves and the ability of these reserves to meet expanding global demand for oil

(Jordan et al., 2009). Developing countries, such as China and India, are rapidly increasing their use of oil as they industrialize, placing upward pressure on oil prices. As their economies grow, domestic producers in these countries require more oil to transport goods to market and consumers need more oil to fuel the cars they are increasingly able to afford. Given these factors, "most oil economists agree that the global economy will run through the remaining deposits of easy oil much faster [than in the past] . . ., resulting in abruptly higher and unpredictable price levels" (Doran, 2008).

Efforts are being made to meet this growing demand through exploration and the development of new oil fields and methods of extraction. Yet, oil remains a relatively inelastic good in the short term, meaning that there are no close substitutes available now to replace its use. Despite ongoing research, a viable alternative to oil has not yet been found to fuel the transportation sector. In addition to the difficulty of finding short-term substitutes, there is also concern about sufficient availability of oil over the longer term. While new fields and production methods allow for greater oil production, costs of production are increasing because much of this oil is harder to exploit because it is located deeper and/or further off-shore. Many of the newly discovered fields also contain oil that is of lesser quality, and therefore requires more complex refining to bring it to market (Campbell and Laherrere, 1998).

In addition to the demand-side pressures on the global oil market that stem from economic growth in emerging economies, geopolitical developments can also increase the economic and security costs to the United States of foreign oil dependence. Most recently, political turmoil in the Middle East in the wake of the Arab Spring and international tensions over a potential Iranian nuclear weapons program have placed further upward pressure on oil prices and created new uncertainties about supply. Especially in a global oil market made tighter by increases in demand, a disruption in the flow of oil from the Persian Gulf could have a significant economic impact. Though the dynamics would be different than those that created by the supply-side shocks that arose from the Arab–Israeli War of 1973 and the Iranian Revolution in 1979, the resulting negative impact of new instability in the oil market could be significant. In the 1970s, oil shortages in select countries contributed to periods of painfully high inflation, high interest rates, and several years of recession (Hubbard and O'Brien, 2010). Some analysts fear that the impact of a new energy crisis now could be even more extreme.

Advocates of breaking U.S. dependence on foreign oil argue that oil imports from the Persian Gulf and other unstable regions create an "American dependence on foreign oil [that] at current levels . . . [constitutes] a grave security and economic risk" (Hakes, 2008). From a security perspective, energy independence advocates argue that U.S. reliance on volatile and unfriendly countries for oil fosters political instability and strengthens U.S. adversaries.

For example, oil exports may provide resources that give hostile governments the ability to remain in power and enable states like Iran to fund violent proxy groups abroad like Hamas or Hezbollah that may contribute to political instability. From an economic perspective, U.S. reliance on foreign oil is a risk since potential adversaries could use this dependence to gain leverage against the United States. If, for example, countries were to use oil today as a weapon by withholding its flow to the world market—like OPEC did in the 1970s—the United States could face high inflation and reduced economic activity caused by higher oil prices. Given its slow recovery from the 2009 recession, such a development could push the United States into another recession. Instead of accepting these risks, if the United States were to further develop domestic oil sources, the United States would lessen its dependence on potential future adversaries. It is with this logic in mind that Governor Sarah Palin's 2008 campaign slogan, "Drill, baby, drill," which advocated access to all reserves in the United States—including those containing oil that requires more refining and those that are in environmentally sensitive areas—still resonates with some (Doran, 2008).

As an alternative to breaking foreign dependence on oil by developing and extracting more oil from domestic sources, some insist that the United States should focus on transitioning to domestically generated alternative sources of energy. This group of proponents, which includes former oilman T. Boone Pickens, wants to shift the American energy infrastructure toward one based largely on natural gas and augmented by wind. Pickens estimates that "building new wind generation facilities, conserving energy, and increasing the use of our natural gas resources [could] replace more than one-third of our foreign oil imports in ten years." He also makes an economic argument to support his push away from oil, claiming that developing the vast natural gas reserves in the United States and building a natural gas-based infrastructure would generate jobs at home, while enabling the use of a relatively secure energy source to fuel U.S. homes and industry. As a further benefit, the United States could also generate revenue by exporting excess domestic production (Pickens, 2012).

Critics of energy independence question the feasibility of rejecting foreign oil and trying to rely solely on domestic sources, and they also question whether the benefits of attaining energy independence would outweigh the costs. They argue that to sustain economic growth and improve living standards, the United States will require continued access to oil from all possible sources. As long as other countries continue to produce oil at relatively low costs compared to the cost to produce a barrel of U.S. oil—and as long as they maintain large reserves—Saudi Arabia and other major producers will remain dominant (Cordesman and Al-Rodhan, 2006). Rather than resisting this practical reality, the United States should encourage the production of a relatively stable supply of petroleum into the near future. Over the long term, the United States should work with OPEC countries and other major producers to prolong the production value of their remaining reserves, while focusing U.S. industries on the production of oil-based products such as gasoline, plastics, and chemicals for domestic and export markets.

Critics of the pursuit of energy independence also believe the United States should recognize the global nature of the market for oil and act accordingly. It is incorrect to believe that "oil markets are structurally fragmented so that the ramifications of disruptions are localized, rather than felt globally, and that by arranging regional supply agreements, a nation can immunize itself against a disruption elsewhere in the world" (Griffin, 2009). In reality, any disruption to the oil supply affects the price consumers in every country must pay. Focusing on independence from foreign oil distracts the U.S. government from the policies it really needs that would supplement the workings of the global oil market rather than work fruitlessly against it. Such policies would support research and development on alternative energy sources and facilitate the construction of the distribution infrastructure needed for U.S. consumers and industry to use these new forms of energy.

In addressing the question of whether or not the United States should pursue energy independence by eliminating U.S. dependence on foreign oil, Clifford Krauss and Eric Lipton say YES. They argue that the United States does not have to worry about domestic oil depletion. This is due to supply-side and demand-side technological improvements. On the supply side, fears about oil depletion have been overblown because the oil industry has found, due to new technological advances, new reserves and ways to extract more from existing reserves. On the demand side, the domestic demand for oil has decreased because consumer goods and automobile manufacturers have developed much more energy-efficient products. Kraus and Lipton believe that continued supply- and demand-side technological advances will allow the United States to become energy independent.

In countering with a NO answer, Paul Roberts says that the United States should not make the elimination of dependence on foreign oil a strategic priority. Instead, the real goal of U.S. policy should be energy security. Roberts discusses seven myths and addresses each one to explain how the United States should build a strategy that enables access to reliable, accessible, and safe energy from a wide variety of sources—at home and abroad.

YES ↵

Clifford Krauss and Eric Lipton

The Energy Rush; U.S. Inches Toward Goal of Energy Independence

The desolate stretch of West Texas desert known as the Permian Basin is still the lonely domain of scurrying road-runners by day and howling coyotes by night. But the roar of scores of new oil rigs and the distinctive acrid fumes of drilling equipment are unmistakable signs that crude is gushing again.

And not just here. Across the country, the oil and gas industry is vastly increasing production, reversing two decades of decline. Using new technology and spurred by rising oil prices since the mid-2000s, the industry is extracting millions of barrels more a week, from the deepest waters of the Gulf of Mexico to the prairies of North Dakota.

At the same time, Americans are pumping significantly less gasoline. While that is partly a result of the recession and higher gasoline prices, people are also driving fewer miles and replacing older cars with more fuel-efficient vehicles at a greater clip, federal data show.

Taken together, the increasing production and declining consumption have unexpectedly brought the United States markedly closer to a goal that has tantalized presidents since Richard Nixon: independence from foreign energy sources, a milestone that could reconfigure American foreign policy, the economy and more. In 2011, the country imported just 45 percent of the liquid fuels it used, down from a record high of 60 percent in 2005.

"There is no question that many national security policy makers will believe they have much more flexibility and will think about the world differently if the United States is importing a lot less oil," said Michael A. Levi, an energy and environmental senior fellow at the Council on Foreign Relations. "For decades, consumption rose, production fell and imports increased, and now every one of those trends is going the other way."

How the country made this turnabout is a story of industry-friendly policies started by President Bush and largely continued by President Obama—many over the objections of environmental advocates—as well as technological advances that have allowed the extraction of oil and gas once considered too difficult and too expensive to reach. But mainly it is a story of the complex economics of energy, which sometimes seems to operate by its own rules of supply and demand.

With gasoline prices now approaching record highs and politicians mud-wrestling about the causes and solutions, the effects of the longer-term rise in production can be difficult to see.

Simple economics suggests that if the nation is producing more energy, prices should be falling. But crude oil—and gasoline and diesel made from it—are global commodities whose prices are affected by factors around the world. Supply disruptions in Africa, the political stand-off with Iran and rising demand from a recovering world economy all are contributing to the current spike in global oil prices, offsetting the impact of the increased domestic supply.

But the domestic trends are unmistakable. Not only has the United States reduced oil imports from members of the Organization of the Petroleum Exporting Countries by more than 20 percent in the last three years, it has become a net exporter of refined petroleum products like gasoline for the first time since the Truman presidency. The natural gas industry, which less than a decade ago feared running out of domestic gas, is suddenly dealing with a glut so vast that import facilities are applying for licenses to export gas to Europe and Asia.

National oil production, which declined steadily to 4.95 million barrels a day in 2008 from 9.6 million in 1970, has risen over the last four years to nearly 5.7 million barrels a day. The Energy Department projects that daily output could reach nearly seven million barrels by 2020. Some experts think it could eventually hit 10 million barrels—which would put the United States in the same league as Saudi Arabia.

This surge is hardly without consequences. Some areas of intense drilling activity, including northeastern Utah and central Wyoming, have experienced air quality problems. The drilling technique called hydraulic fracturing, or fracking, which uses highly pressurized water, sand and chemical lubricants that help force more oil and gas from rock formations, has also been blamed for wastewater problems. Wildlife experts also warn that expanded drilling is threatening habitats of rare or endangered species.

Greater energy independence is "a prize that has long been eyed by oil insiders and policy strategists that can bring many economic and national security benefits," said Jay Hakes, a senior official at the Energy Department during the Clinton administration. "But we will have to work through the environmental issues, which are a definite challenge."

The increased production of fossil fuels is a far cry from the energy plans President Obama articulated as a candidate in 2008. Then, he promoted policies to help combat global warming, including vast investments in renewable energy and a cap-and-trade system for carbon emissions that would have discouraged the use of fossil fuels.

More recently, with gasoline prices rising and another election looming, Mr. Obama has struck a different chord. He has opened new federal lands and waters to drilling, trumpeted increases in oil and gas production and de-emphasized the challenges of climate change. On Thursday, he said he supported expedited construction of the southern portion of the proposed Keystone XL oil pipeline from Canada.

Mr. Obama's current policy has alarmed many environmental advocates who say he has failed to adequately address the environmental threats of expanded drilling and the use of fossil fuels. He also has not silenced critics, including Republicans and oil executives, who accuse him of preventing drilling on millions of acres off the Atlantic and Pacific Coasts and on federal land, unduly delaying the decision on the full Keystone project and diverting scarce federal resources to pie-in-the-sky alternative energy programs.

Just as the production increase was largely driven by rising oil prices, the trend could reverse if the global economy were to slow. Even so, much of the industry is thrilled at the prospects.

"To not be concerned with where our oil is going to come from is probably the biggest home run for the country in a hundred years," said Scott D. Sheffield, chief executive of Pioneer Natural Resources, which is operating in West Texas. "It sort of reminds me of the industrial revolution in coal, which allowed us to have some of the cheapest energy in the world and drove our economy in the late 1800s and 1900s."

The Foundation Is Laid

For as long as roughnecks have worked the Permian Basin—made famous during World War II as the fuel pump that powered the Allies—they have mostly focused on relatively shallow zones of easily accessible, oil-soaked sandstone and silt. But after 80 years of pumping, those regions were running dry.

So in 2003, Jim Henry, a West Texas oilman, tried a bold experiment. Borrowing an idea from a fellow engineer, his team at Henry Petroleum drilled deep into a hard limestone formation using a refinement of fracking. By blasting millions of gallons of water into the limestone, they created tiny fissures that allowed oil to break free, a technique that had previously been successful in extracting gas from shale.

The test produced 150 barrels of oil a day, three times more than normal. "We knew we had the biggest discovery in over 50 years in the Permian Basin," Mr. Henry recalled.

There was just one problem: At $30 a barrel, the price of oil was about half of what was needed to make drilling that deep really profitable.

So the renaissance of the Permian—and the domestic oil industry—would have to wait.

But the drillers in Texas had important allies in Washington. President Bush grew up in Midland and spent 11 years as a West Texas oilman, albeit without much success, before entering politics. Vice President Dick Cheney had been chief executive of the oil field contractor Halliburton. The Bush administration worked from the start on finding ways to unlock the nation's energy reserves and reverse decades of declining output, with Mr. Cheney leading a White House energy task force that met in secret with top oil executives.

"Ramping up production was a high priority," said Gale Norton, a member of the task force and the secretary of the Interior at the time. "We hated being at the mercy of other countries, and we were determined to change that."

The task force's work helped produce the Energy Policy Act of 2005, which set rules that contributed to the current surge. It prohibited the Environmental Protection Agency from regulating fracking under the Safe Drinking Water Act, eliminating a potential impediment to wide use of the technique. The legislation also offered the industry billions of dollars in new tax breaks to help independent producers recoup some drilling costs even when a well came up dry.

Separately, the Interior Department was granted the power to issue drilling permits on millions of acres of federal lands without extensive environmental impact studies for individual projects, addressing industry complaints about the glacial pace of approvals. That new power has been used at least 8,400 times, mostly in Wyoming, Utah and New Mexico, representing a quarter of all permits issued on federal land in the last six federal fiscal years.

The Bush administration also opened large swaths of the Gulf of Mexico and the waters off Alaska to exploration, granting lease deals that required companies to pay only a tiny share of their profits to the government.

These measures primed the pump for the burst in drilling that began once oil prices started rising sharply in 2005 and 2006. With the world economy humming—and China, India and other developing nations posting astonishing growth—demand for oil began outpacing the easily accessible supplies.

By 2008, daily global oil consumption surged to 86 million barrels, up nearly 20 percent from the decade before. In July of that year, the price of oil reached its highest level since World War II, topping $145 a barrel (equivalent to more than $151 a barrel in today's dollars).

Oil reserves once too difficult and expensive to extract—including Mr. Henry's limestone fields—had become more attractive.

If money was the motivation, fracking became the favored means of extraction.

While fracking itself had been around for years, natural gas drillers in the 1980s and 1990s began combining high-pressure fracking with drilling wells horizontally, not just vertically. They found it unlocked gas from layers of shale previously seen as near worthless.

By 2001, fracking took off around Fort Worth and Dallas, eventually reaching under schools, airports and inner-city neighborhoods. Companies began buying drilling rights across vast shale fields in a variety of states. By 2008, the country was awash in natural gas.

Fracking for oil, which is made of larger molecules than natural gas, took longer to develop. But eventually, it opened new oil fields in North Dakota, South Texas, Kansas, Wyoming, Colorado and, most recently, Ohio.

Meanwhile, technological advances were making deeper oil drilling possible in the Gulf of Mexico. New imaging and seismic technology allowed engineers to predict the location and size of reservoirs once obscured by thick layers of salt. And drill bits made of superstrong alloys were developed to withstand the hot temperatures and high pressures deep under the seabed.

As the industry's confidence—and profits—grew, so did criticism. Amid concerns about global warming and gasoline prices that averaged a record $4.11 a gallon in July 2008 ($4.30 in today's dollars), President Obama campaigned on a pledge to shift toward renewable energy and away from fossil fuels.

His administration initially canceled some oil and gas leases on federal land awarded during the Bush administration and required more environmental review. But in a world where crucial oil suppliers like Venezuela and Libya were unstable and high energy prices could be a drag on a weak economy, he soon acted to promote more drilling. Despite a drilling hiatus after the 2010 explosion of the Deepwater Horizon in the Gulf of Mexico, which killed 11 rig workers and spilled millions of barrels of crude oil into the ocean, he has proposed expansion of oil production both on land and offshore. He is now moving toward approving drilling off the coast of Alaska.

"Our dependence on foreign oil is down because of policies put in place by our administration, but also our predecessor's administration," Mr. Obama said during a campaign appearance in March, a few weeks after opening 38 million more acres in the gulf for oil and gas exploration. "And whoever succeeds me is going to have to keep it up."

An American Oil Boom

The last time the Permian Basin oil fields enjoyed a boom—nearly three decades ago—Rolls-Royce opened a showroom in the desert, Champagne was poured from cowboy boots, and the local airport could not accommodate all the Learjets taking off for Las Vegas on weekends.

But when crude prices fell in the mid-1980s, oil companies pulled out and the Rolls dealership was replaced by a tortilla factory. The only thriving business was done by bankruptcy lawyers and auctioneers helping to unload used Ferraris, empty homes and useless rigs.

"One day we were rolling in oil," recalled Jim Foreman, the general manager of the Midland BMW dealership, "and the next day geologists were flipping burgers at McDonald's."

The burger-flipping days are definitely over. Today, more than 475 rigs—roughly a quarter of all rigs operating in the United States—are smashing through tight rocks across the Permian in West Texas and southeastern New Mexico. Those areas are already producing nearly a million barrels a day, or 17 percent more than two years ago. By decade's end, that daily total could easily double, oil executives say, roughly equaling the total output of Nigeria.

"We're having a revolution," said G. Steven Farris, chief executive of Apache Corporation, one of the basin's most active producers. "And we're just scratching the surface."

It is a revolution that is returning investments to the United States. Over several decades, Pioneer Natural Resources had taken roughly $1 billion earned in Texas oil fields and drilled in Africa, South America and elsewhere. But in the last five years, the company sold $2 billion of overseas assets and reinvested in Texas shale fields.

"Political risk was increasing internationally," said Mr. Sheffield, Pioneer's chief executive, and domestically, he was encouraged to see "the shale technology progressing."

Pioneer's rising fortunes can be seen on a 10,000-acre field known as the Giddings Estate, a forsaken stretch inhabited by straggly coyotes, rabbits, rattlesnakes and cows that forage for grass between the sagebrush. When Pioneer bought it in 2005, the field's hundred mostly broken-down wells were producing a total of 50 barrels a day. "It was a diamond in the rough," said Robert Hillger, who manages it for Pioneer.

Mr. Hillger and his colleagues have brought an array of new tools to bear at Giddings. Computer programs simulate well designs, minimizing trial and error. Advanced fiber optics allow senior engineers and geologists at headquarters more than 300 miles away to monitor progress and remotely direct the drill bit. Subterranean microphones help identify fissures in the rock to plan subsequent drilling.

Today, the Giddings field is pumping 7,000 barrels a day, and Pioneer expects to hit 25,000 barrels a day by 2017.

The newfound wealth is spreading beyond the fields. In nearby towns, petroleum companies are buying so many pickup trucks that dealers are leasing parking lots the size of city blocks to stock their inventory. Housing is in such short supply that drillers are importing contractors from Houston and hotels are leased out before they are even built.

Two new office buildings are going up in Midland, a city of just over 110,000 people, the first in 30 years, while the total value of downtown real estate has jumped 50 percent since 2008. With virtually no unemployment, restaurants cannot find enough servers. Local truck drivers are making six-figure salaries.

"Anybody who comes in with a driver's license and a Social Security card, I'll give him a chance," said Rusty Allred, owner of Rusty's Oilfield Service Company.

If there is a loser in this boom, it is the environment. Water experts say aquifers in the desert area could run dry if fracking continues expanding, and oil executives concede they need to reduce water consumption. Yet environmental concerns, from polluted air to greenhouse gas emissions, have gained little traction in the Permian Basin or other outposts of the energy expansion.

On the front lines in opposition is Jay Lininger, a 36-year-old ecologist who drives through the Permian in an old Toyota Tacoma with a hard hat tilted on his head and a federal land map at the ready.

A former national park firefighter, he says he is now battling a wildfire of a different sort—the oil industry.

Nationally, environmentalists have challenged drilling with mixed results. Efforts to stop or slow fracking have succeeded in New York State and some localities in other states, but it is spreading across the country.

In the Permian, Mr. Lininger said, few people openly object to the foul-smelling air of the oil fields. Ranchers are more than happy to sell what water they have to the oil companies for fracking.

Mr. Lininger and his group are trying to slow the expansion of drilling by appealing to the United States Fish and Wildlife Service to protect several animal species, including the five-inch dunes sagebrush lizard.

"It's a pathetic little lizard in an ugly desert, but life needs to be protected," he said. "Every day we burn fossil fuel makes it harder for our planet to recover from our energy addiction."

Mr. Lininger said the oil and ranching industries had already destroyed or fragmented 40 percent of the lizard's habitat, and 60 percent of what is left is under lease for oil and gas development.

The wildlife agency proposed listing the lizard as endangered in 2010 and was expected to decide last December, but Congressional representatives from the oil patch won a delay. Oil companies are working on a voluntary program to locate new drilling so it will not disturb the lizard habitat.

But for Mr. Lininger's group, the Center for Biological Diversity, that is far from sufficient.

Brendan Cummings, senior counsel of the center, said protecting the lizard was part of a broader effort to keep drilling from harming animals, including polar bears, walruses and bowhead whales in the Alaskan Arctic and dwarf sea horses and sea turtles in the Gulf of Mexico.

"When you are dealing with fossil fuels, things will always go wrong," Mr. Cummings said. "There will always be spills, there will always be pollution. Those impacts compound the fragmentation that occurs and render these habitats into sacrifice areas."

A Turn Toward Efficiency

If the Permian Basin exemplifies the rise in production, car-obsessed San Diego is a prime example of the other big factor in the decline in the nation's reliance on foreign oil.

Just since 2007, consumption of all liquid fuels in the United States, including diesel, jet fuel and heating oil, has dropped by about 9 percent, according to the Energy Department. Gasoline use fell 6 to 12 percent, estimated Tom Kloza, chief oil analyst at the Oil Price Information Service.

Although Southern California's love affair with muscle cars and the open road persists, driving habits have changed in subtle but important ways.

Take Tory Girten, who works as an emergency medical technician and part-time lifeguard in the San Diego area. He switched from driving a Ford minivan to a decidedly smaller and more fuel-efficient Dodge Caliber. Fed up with high gasoline prices, he also moved twice recently to be closer to the city center, cutting his daily commute considerably—a hint of the shift taking place in certain metropolitan areas as city centers become more popular while growth in far-out suburbs slows.

"I would rather pay a little more monthly for rent than for just filling up my tank with gas," he said, after pulling into a local gas station to fill up.

Mr. Girten is one of millions of Americans who have downsized. S.U.V.'s accounted for 18 percent of new-car sales in 2002, but only 7 percent in 2010.

The surge in gasoline prices nationwide—they are already at a record level for this time of year—has contributed to the shift toward more fuel-efficient cars. But a bigger factor is rising federal fuel economy standards. After a long freeze, the miles-per-gallon mandate has been increased several times in recent years, with the Obama administration now pushing automakers to hit 54.5 m.p.g. by 2025.

As Americans replace their older cars—they have bought an average of 1.25 million new cars and light trucks a month this year—new technologies mean they usually end up with a more efficient vehicle, even if they buy a model of similar size and power.

California has long pushed further and faster toward efficiency than the rest of the country. It has combated often severe air pollution by mandating cleaner-burning cars, including all-electric vehicles, and prodded Washington to increase the fuel efficiency standards.

Thousands of school buses, trash trucks, tractor-trailers and street sweepers and public transit buses in the state run on natural gas, which is cheaper than gasoline and burns more cleanly. That switch cuts the consumption of foreign oil, as does the corn-based ethanol that is now mixed into gasoline as a result of federal mandates.

Longer-term social and economic factors are also reducing miles driven—like the rise in Internet shopping and telecommuting and the tendency of baby boomers to drive less as they age. The recession has also contributed, as job losses have meant fewer daily commutes and falling home prices have allowed some people to afford to move closer to work.

The trend of lower consumption, when combined with higher energy production, has profound implications, said Bill White, former deputy energy secretary in the Clinton administration and former mayor of Houston.

"Energy independence has always been a race between depletion and technologies to produce more and use energy more efficiently," he said. "Depletion was winning for decades, and now technology is starting to overtake its lead."

CLIFFORD KRAUSS is a correspondent for the *New York Times*. Previously, he worked as a foreign correspondent for *The Wall Street Journal* and was the Edward R. Murrow fellow at the Council on Foreign Relations.

ERIC LIPTON is a correspondent for the *New York Times*. Previously, he worked at *The Washington Post* and *The Hartford Courant*.

Paul Roberts  **NO**

The Seven Myths of Energy Independence: Why Forging a Sustainable Energy Future Is Dependent on Foreign Oil

Myth #1
Energy Independence Is Good

On February 1, 2006, Prince Turki al-Faisal, Saudi Arabia's ambassador to Washington, arrived at the White House in a state of agitation. The night before, in his State of the Union address, President Bush had declared the United States to be "addicted to oil, which is often imported from unstable parts of the world." He had announced plans to "break this addiction" by developing alternatives—including a multibillion-dollar subsidized ramp-up of biofuels—and had boldly stated that by 2025, America could cut imports from Gulf states by three-quarters and "make our dependence on Middle Eastern oil a thing of the past." "I was taken aback," Prince Faisal later told cnn, "and I raised this point with government officials."

Two years on, anyone who's been to a gas station or a grocery store knows the prince had very little to worry about. Despite supposedly bold initiatives such as last year's Energy Independence and Security Act, America is no freer from foreign oil: Since 2006, imports have remained steady at about 13 million barrels every day, while the price for each of those barrels has jumped by $30. And though federal efforts to encourage biofuel production have significantly boosted output, our heavily subsidized ethanol refiners now use so much corn (closing in on a third of the total crop) that prices for all grains have soared, sparking inflation here at home and food riots abroad.

Okay, so maybe ethanol's critics are right, and turning food into fuel isn't the smartest way to wean ourselves from imported oil. But the deeper lesson here isn't that Washington backed the wrong weapon in the war for energy independence, but that most policymakers—and Americans generally—still think "energy independence" is a goal we can, or should, achieve. Nine in ten voters say the country is too dependent on foreign crude. Every major presidential hopeful formulated some kind of strategy for energy liberation (Rudy Giuliani unveiled his at a NASCAR race), and between 2001 and 2006 the number of media references to "energy independence" jumped by a factor of eight.

And on the surface, the argument seems solid. Imported oil, some 60 percent of the oil we use, exposes our economy and politics to stresses halfway around the world (bin Laden calls it "the umbilical cord and lifeline of the crusader community"). It also increases our already massive trade imbalance, which must be corrected by ever-greater federal borrowing, and funnels tens of billions of dollars to the likes of Saudi Arabia, Russia, and Venezuela—countries that are unfriendly and, in some cases, actively anti-American. What's not to like about energy independence?

In a word, everything. Despite its immense appeal, energy independence is a nonstarter—a populist charade masquerading as energy strategy that's no more likely to succeed (and could be even more damaging) than it was when Nixon declared war on foreign oil in the 1970s. Not only have we no realistic substitute for the oceans of oil we import, but many of the crash programs being touted as a way to quickly develop oil replacements—"clean coal," for example, or biofuels—come at a substantial environmental and political cost. And even if we had good alternatives ready to deploy—a fleet of superefficient cars, say, or refineries churning out gobs of cheap hydrogen for fuel cells—we'd need decades, and great volumes of energy, including oil, to replace all the cars, pipelines, refineries, and other bits of the old oil infrastructure—and thus decades in which we'd depend on oil from our friends in Riyadh, Moscow, and Caracas. Paradoxically, to build the energy economy that we want, we're going to lean heavily on the energy economy that we have.

None of which is exactly news. Thoughtful observers have been trying to debunk energy independence since Nixon's time. And yet the dream refuses to die, in no small part because it offers political cover for a whole range of controversial initiatives. Ethanol refiners wave the banner of independence as they lobby Congress for massive subsidies. Likewise for electric utilities and coal producers as they push for clean coal and a nuclear renaissance. And it shouldn't surprise that some of the loudest proponents of energy liberation support plans to open the Arctic National Wildlife Refuge and other off-limits areas to oil drilling—despite the fact that such moves would, at best, cut imports by a few percentage points. In the doublespeak of today's energy lexicon, says Julia Bovey of the Natural Resources Defense Council, "'energy independence' has become code for 'drill it all.'"

Yet it isn't only the hacks for old energy and Archer Daniels Midland who are to blame. Some proponents of good alternatives like solar and wind have also harped on fears of foreign oil to advance their own sectors—even though many of these technologies are decades away from being meaningful oil replacements.

Put another way, the "debate" over energy independence is not only disingenuous, it's also a major distraction from the much more crucial question—namely, how we're going to build a secure and sustainable energy system. Because what America should be striving for isn't energy independence, but energy security—that is, access to energy sources that are reliable and reasonably affordable, that can be deployed quickly and easily, yet are also safe and politically and environmentally sustainable. And let's not sugarcoat it. Achieving real, lasting energy security is going to be extraordinarily hard, not only because of the scale of the endeavor, but because many of our assumptions about energy—about the speed with which new technologies can be rolled out, for example, or the role of markets—are woefully exaggerated. High oil prices alone won't cure this ill: We're burning more oil now than we were when crude sold for $25 a barrel. Nor will Silicon Valley utopianism: Thus far, most of the venture capital and innovation is flowing into status quo technologies such as biofuels. And while Americans have a proud history of inventing ourselves out of trouble, today's energy challenge is fundamentally different. Nearly every major energy innovation of the last century—from our cars to transmission lines—was itself built with cheap energy. By contrast, the next energy system will have to contend with larger populations and be constructed using far fewer resources and more expensive energy.

So it's hardly surprising that policymakers shy away from energy security and opt instead for the soothing platitudes of energy independence. But here's the rub: We don't have a choice. Energy security is nonnegotiable, a precondition for all security, like water or food or defense. Without it, we have no economy, no progress, no future. And to get it, we'll not only have to abandon the chimera of independence once and for all, but become the very thing that many of us have been taught to dread—unrepentant energy globalists.

Myth #2
Ethanol Will Set Us Free

What's wrong with energy independence? Let's start with the sheer physical enormity of replacing imports. Even if we limit the discussion to oil (and America buys boatloads of foreign natural gas, electricity, and even coal), the job is far more daunting than many liberationists—or environmentalists—want to believe.

If we distilled our entire corn crop into ethanol, the fuel produced would displace less than a sixth of the gasoline we currently guzzle, and other candidates, like hydrogen, are even more marginal. The challenge isn't simply quantity, but quality. Oil dominates the energy economy, and especially the transportation sector (which is 95 percent dependent on crude), in part because no other fuel offers the same combination of massive energy density and ease of handling. As author Richard Heinberg has observed, enough energy is contained in a single gallon of gasoline to replace 240 hours of human labor—considerably more than oil's likely rivals.

And because oil is relatively easy to produce, the energy "investment" needed to exploit that massive energy content is small. On average, an oil company burns the energy equivalent of 1 gallon of oil to produce 20 gallons of oil. In other words, oil's energy return on energy invested is quite high. By contrast, the return for oil's declared alternatives is quite low. For example, hydrogen, once considered a natural successor to oil, is so tricky to refine and handle that, by one study, a gallon of hydrogen contains nearly 25 percent less energy than was consumed producing it. As for ethanol's energy return, scientists are debating whether it's slightly positive or altogether negative.

Oil's qualities were unbeatable when it cost[s] $25 a barrel, and even at $100, it still has a critical advantage. Because it was generated ages ago and left for us in deep underground reservoirs, oil exists more or less in a state of economic isolation; that is, oil can be produced—pumped from the ground and refined—without directly impinging on other pieces of the world economy. By contrast, many of oil's competitors are intimately linked to that larger economy, in the sense that to make more of an alternative (ethanol, say) is to have less of something else (food, sustainably arable land).

Granted, oil's advantages will ultimately prove illusory due to its huge environmental costs and finite supply. But oil's decline won't, by itself, make alternatives any less problematic. Higher oil prices do encourage alternatives to expand, but in a world of finite resources, these expansions can come at substantial cost. Because good U.S. farmland is already scarce, every additional acre of corn for ethanol is an acre unavailable for soybeans, or wheat, whose prices then also rise—a ripple effect that affects meat, milk, soft drinks. . . . And for the record, to make enough corn ethanol to replace all our gasoline, we'd need to plant 71 percent of our farmland with fuel crops.

To be fair, ethanol can be produced in a way that is less disruptive to the food economy. Cellulosic ethanol, for example, is made from wood chips, crop detritus, and other organic waste. And in Brazil they make ethanol from sugarcane—a process a third as energy intensive as corn ethanol's. But cellulosic ethanol, though quite promising, is not yet commercial, while Brazilian ethanol is, well,

Brazilian: It's effectively barred from our market by a 54 cents per gallon tariff, which U.S. lawmakers defend on the grounds of energy independence, but which coincidently leaves corn ethanol, with its massive federal subsidy, as pretty much the only game in town. So much corn is now going to biofuel that the food and energy markets are effectively linked, an unprecedented coupling that not only disrupts global food security but also undermines corn ethanol's usefulness as an oil replacement.

The ripple effect of energy alternatives isn't confined to the economic sphere. As eager farmers have expanded their corn crops (U.S. farmers planted more acres in 2007 than anytime since World War II), they've tilled land not suited for intensive agriculture, exacerbating erosion and other environmental problems. Corn is also the most chemically intensive commercial grain crop; runoff attributable to the ethanol boom is causing oceanic dead zones and pesticide-laden groundwater.

Ethanol is an easy target, but the sad truth is that all of the ballyhooed alternatives carry at least some environmental or other external costs. Wind requires vast amounts of land; solar-cell manufacturing is chemically intensive. Nuclear energy is steeped in safety and security concerns. And although the United States could fuel its entire car fleet with a synthetic gasoline made from abundant coal, syngas is even more ecologically challenged than oil. Industry likes to trumpet potential technologies to capture and sequester coal's carbon dioxide, but the federal government has cut research funding. And as Severin Borenstein, an economist at the University of California-Berkeley, points out, even if we do find climate-friendly ways to turn coal into fuel, that's only one end of the process: "We're still going to be burning that fuel in cars and thus releasing all that CO_2 out the tailpipe."

Such problems drive home a critical flaw in the paradigm of energy independence—namely, that energy isn't a zero-sum game anymore. We can no longer look at the energy economy as a constellation of discrete sectors that can be manipulated separately; everything is tied together, which means that fixing a problem in one part of the system all but invariably creates a new problem, or a whole series of problems, somewhere else.

Myth #3
Conservation Is a "Personal Virtue"

By now it should be clear not only that energy independence is prohibitively costly, but that the saner objective—energy security—won't be met through some frantic search for a fuel to replace oil, but by finding ways to do without liquid fuel, most probably through massive increases in energy efficiency.

This isn't a popular idea with Dick Cheney, who before 9/11 famously said that "conservation may be a sign of personal virtue, but it is not a sufficient basis for a sound, comprehensive energy policy." Nor among traditional energy players, who desperately want to find something to sell us if oil becomes untenable—and don't really care if that something is hydrogen or ethanol or pig manure. But for the rest of us, the logic of conservation is pretty hard to argue with. Better energy efficiency is one of the fastest ways to reduce not only energy use, but pollution and greenhouse gas emissions: According to a new study by McKinsey & Company, if the United States aggressively adopted more efficient cars, factories, homes, and other infrastructure, our CO_2 emissions could be 28 percent below 2005 levels by 2030. And saving energy is almost always cheaper than making it: There is far more oil to be "found" in Detroit by designing more fuel-efficient cars than could ever be pumped out of ANWR. And because transportation is the biggest user of oil—accounting for 7 of every 10 barrels we burn—any significant reduction in the sector's appetite has massive ramifications. Even the relatively unambitious 2007 energy bill, which raises fuel-economy standards from 25 mpg to 35 mpg by 2020, would save 3.6 million barrels a day by 2030. And if we persuaded carmakers to switch to plug-in hybrids, we could cut our oil demand by a staggering 9 million barrels a day, about 70 percent of our current imports.

Such a shift would impose massive new demand on an electric grid already struggling to meet need, but plug-in hybrids actually stretch the grid's existing capacity. Charged up at night, when power demand (and thus prices) are low, plug-in hybrids exploit the grid's large volume of unused (and, until now, unusable) capacity. Such "load balancing" would let power companies run their plants around the clock (vastly more cost-effective than idling plants at night and revving them up at dawn); as important, it would substantially boost the grid's overall output. According to the Department of Energy, with such load balancing, America's existing power system could meet current power demands and generate enough additional electricity to run almost three-quarters of its car and light-truck fleet. That alone would be enough to drop oil consumption by 6.5 million barrels a day, or nearly a third of America's current demand.

Granted, this switch to electric-powered cars wouldn't be free. Seventy percent of America's electricity is made from high-carbon fuels like natural gas and especially coal, which is why the power sector emits 40 percent of all U.S. carbon emissions. Just 8.4 percent comes from renewable sources, and most of that is environmentally dubious hydroelectric; wind, solar, geothermal, and biomass together supply 2.4 percent, and despite rapid growth, their share of the power market will remain small for decades. Even so, an electric or plug-in hybrid fleet is still probably the most environmentally plausible path away from oil. Why? Because kilowatt for kilowatt, turning fossil fuels into electricity in massive centralized power plants and then putting that juice into car batteries is more efficient than burning fossil fuels directly in internal combustion engines, and thus generates fewer CO_2 emissions per mile traveled. (Our existing fleet generates a third of America's CO_2 emissions.) The DOE found that replacing three-quarters of the U.S. fleet with plug-in hybrids would cut vehicle CO_2 emissions by 27 percent nationwide—40 percent or more if the country's power system were upgraded to match California's low-carbon grid. And once the new fleet is in place, there is nothing stopping us from upgrading our power sources to truly renewable systems.

Myth #4
We Can Go It Alone

Given America's reliance on imported oil, it seems safe to assume that if we succeeded in getting such dramatic reductions, whatever sacrifices we'd made would be more than compensated for by our new immunity to the nastiness of world oil markets. Let Saudi Arabia cut its production. Let Hugo Chávez sell his oil to China. Such maneuvers no longer matter to Fortress America.

And yet, no country can really hope to improve its energy security by acting alone. True, cutting our own oil use would bring great things here at home, everything from cleaner air and water to lower noise pollution. But we'd be surprised by how little our domestic reductions changed the rest of the world—or improved our overall energy security.

The first problem, once again, is the small-planet nature of energy. America may be the biggest user of oil, but the price we pay is determined by global demand, and demand is being driven largely by booming Asia, which is only too happy to burn any barrel we manage to conserve or replace. Second, any shift to alternatives or better efficiency will take years and perhaps decades to implement. The U.S. car fleet, for example, turns over at a rate of just eight percent a year. That's as fast as consumers can afford to buy new cars and manufacturers can afford to make them, which means that—even in a fantasy scenario where the cars were already designed, the factories retooled, and the workers retrained—it would still take 12 years to deploy a greener fleet.

Most forecasts fail to acknowledge how slowly such changes could actually occur. Sure, if the United States could cut its oil consumption overnight by 9 million barrels, or 6.5 million barrels, or even 3.6 million barrels, it would have a staggering impact on oil prices. But barring a global depression, demand won't ever drop so rapidly; instead, our demand reductions will be incremental and thus effectively canceled out by the expected demand growth in other, less efficiency-minded countries like China. Berkeley's Borenstein, for example, estimates that the 3.6 million barrels the United States would save by 2030 under the 2007 energy bill will be more than offset by growth in demand elsewhere. Put another way, we could all squeeze into smaller cars and still be paying $4 for a gallon of gasoline.

To be sure, energy security isn't defined solely by cheap energy, and in fact, a great many enviros and energy wonks like oil at $100 a barrel, as it seems to be the only thing keeping more of us from buying Hummers. But high prices are killing our other energy-security objectives. High prices mean that money is still flowing into rogue states. High oil prices also imply tight oil markets, prone to massive price swings that are painful for consumers and make it virtually impossible for companies and governments to forecast their future energy costs—and so correctly gauge how much to invest in next-generation energy technologies. And no matter how clean and carbon free the United States becomes, if China and India are still burning massive volumes of oil we haven't done much to improve long-term security of any kind.

The only way to achieve real energy security is to reengineer not just our energy economy but that of the entire world. Oil prices won't fall, evil regimes won't be bankrupt, and sustainability won't be possible—until global oil demand is slowed. And outside of an economic meltdown, the only way it can be is if the tools we deploy to improve our own security can be somehow exported to other countries, and especially developing countries.

Energy globalism doesn't mean that every new energy gadget or fuel we invent has to work in Beijing or Burkina Faso. It does, however, suggest that our current energy strategy, tailored primarily to our own markets and our own technical capabilities, will be next to useless in an energy economy that is increasingly global—and that at least some of our energy investments should be compatible with regions where natural resources are strained, governments are poor, and consumers don't have access to home-equity lines of credit.

Myth #5
Some Geek in Silicon Valley Will Fix the Problem

So, what kinds of technologies would qualify under this more global strategy? Although corn and even cane ethanol are dubious—arable land in most of the developing world is already far too scarce—cellulosic ethanol has definite potential. Plug-in hybrids are probably too expensive for most Third World consumers, but have possibilities in the megacities of Asia and Latin America.

In the near term, however, the most practical energy export will be efficiency. China is so woefully inefficient that its economy uses 4.5 times as much energy as the United States for every dollar of output. This disparity explains why China is the world's second-biggest energy guzzler, but also why selling China more efficient technologies—cars, to be sure, but also better designs for houses, buildings, and industrial processes—could have a huge impact on global energy use and emissions.

As a bonus, such exports would likely be highly profitable. Japan, whose economy is nine times as energy efficient as China's, sees enormous economic and diplomatic opportunities selling its expertise to the Chinese, and America could tap into those opportunities as well—provided technologies with export potential get the kind of R&D support they need. Yet this isn't assured. You may have read that the volume of venture capital flowing into energy-technology companies is at a record high. But much of this capital is flowing into known technologies with rapid and assured payoffs—such as corn ethanol—instead of more speculative, but potentially more useful, technologies like cellulosic ethanol.

Once upon a time, America compensated for investor reluctance with gobs of federal money. But though President Bush routinely promises to spend more on alternative energy, little new money has appeared; federal spending on solar research, for example, is well short of that in the Clinton years, and the $148 million Bush pledged for solar back in 2006 was, in inflation-adjusted terms, less than half of what we spent annually in the 1970s. Other technologies suffer as well. Senator Richard Lugar, an Indiana Republican who has long argued for a global approach to energy security, notes that despite Bush's stated support for cellulosic ethanol, the Energy Department's "glacial implementation" of R&D loan guarantees has turned off potential investors. "The project is moving forward," Lugar says, "but critical time was lost."

Myth #6
Cut Demand and the Rest Will Follow

Given America's tectonic pace toward energy security, the time has come for tough love. Most credible proposals call for some kind of energy or carbon tax. Such a tax would have two critical effects. It would keep the cost of oil high and thus discourage demand, as it has in Europe, and it would generate substantial revenues that could be used to fund research into alternatives, for example, or tax credits and other incentives to invest in the new energy technologies.

To be sure, higher fuel taxes, never popular with voters, would be even less so with gasoline prices already so high. Indeed, many energy wonks are still bitter that President Bush didn't advocate for a fuel tax or other demand-reduction measures in the aftermath of 9/11, when oil prices were relatively low and Americans were in the mood for sacrifice. Bush "could have gotten any set of energy measures passed after 9/11 if he had had an open and honest dialogue with America about how bad things were," says Edward Morse, an energy market analyst and former State Department energy official.

Instead, Bush urged Americans to . . . go shopping. Seven years later, with oil prices soaring and the economy hurting, swaying the electorate will take a politician who is politically courageous, extraordinarily articulate—and willing to dispense with the sweet nothings of energy independence.

And higher energy taxes are just the first dose of bitter medicine America needs to swallow if it wants real energy security. For no matter how aggressively the United States cuts oil demand both at home and abroad, it will be years and perhaps decades before any meaningful decline. The 12-year fleet-replacement scenario outlined above, for example, assumes that efficient new cars are being mass-produced worldwide and that adequate new volumes of electricity can be brought online as the fleet expands—assumptions that at present are wildly invalid. A more reasonable timetable is probably on the order of 20 years.

During this transition away from oil, we will still need lots and lots (and lots) of oil to fuel what remains of the oil-burning fleet. If over those 20 years global oil demand were to fall from the current 86 million barrels a day to, say, 40 million barrels a day, we'd still need an average of 63 million barrels a day, for a total of 459 billion barrels, or almost half as much oil as we've used since the dawn of humankind.

And here we come to two key points. First, because the transition will require so much old energy, we may get only one chance: If we find ourselves in 2028 having backed the wrong clusters of technologies or policies, and are still too dependent on oil, there may not be enough crude left in the ground to fuel a second try. Second, even if we do back the right technologies, the United States and the world's other big importers will still need far too much oil to avoid dealing with countries like Iran, Saudi Arabia, and Russia—no matter how abhorrent we find their politics.

In one of the many paradoxes of the new energy order, more energy security means less energy independence.

Myth #7
Once Bush Is Gone, Change Will Come

No presidential candidate has indicated he or she will raise energy taxes or sit down in oil talks with Tehran. All have ties to a self-interested energy sector, be it coal, ethanol, or nukes. And even after the election, energy security is so complex and requires such hard choices that any president, and most members of Congress, will be sorely tempted to skirt the issue in the tried and true manner, by pushing for a far more palatable "energy independence." As Senator Lugar so choicely put it, "The president will have advisers who will be whispering cautions about the risks of committing the prestige of any administration to aggressive energy goals. Those advisers will say with some credibility that a president can appear forward-looking on energy with a few carefully chosen initiatives and occasional optimistic rhetoric promoting alternative sources. They will say that the voting public's overwhelming energy concern is high prices for gasoline and home heating, and that as long as the president appears attentive to those concerns they can cover their political bases without asking for sacrifices or risking the possible failure of a more controversial energy policy."

Lugar, a veteran pol, is no doubt correct about the pressures the next president will face. What we can only hope is that by the time he or she is chosen, the signals from an overheating energy economy will have reached a point where platitudes no longer suffice—where it is possible to embark on a "controversial energy policy," to ask voters to make sacrifices, and above all, to push America, the champion of globalization, out of a posture of self-absorption and into a stance that is genuinely and sustainably global—at which point the Saudi ambassador really would have something to worry about.

Paul Roberts is a freelance journalist who writes about the interplay of economics, technology, and the natural world.

EXPLORING THE ISSUE

Should the United States Eliminate Its Dependence on Foreign Oil?

Critical Thinking and Reflection

1. What distinguishes energy independence from energy security?
2. What impact would legislation that promotes independence from foreign oil have on domestic economic growth and development?
3. Will a strategy of energy independence or energy security better foster investment into the development and use of alternative energy sources?
4. Describe some public policies that could promote independence from foreign oil for the United States. Describe some public policies that could promote energy security for the United States. Discuss the commonalities and differences between the policies that would promote these two different strategies.

Is There Common Ground?

Most people agree that policies that would help reduce energy costs for Americans and leave the United States less vulnerable to other countries would be in the best interest of the United States. The difficult question remains whether a strategy of energy independence that would allow the United States to be completely free of the need to import oil from other states is realistic, prudent, or truly sustainable.

Both those in favor of and those against the pursuit of energy independence note the importance of investing in energy research and development. However, some favor investment in the extraction of more domestic oil, whereas others would like to see more investment in alternative energy sources. Over the past three decades, the dominant focus of research and development funding in the United States has been on the development of new extraction methods and the identification of new reserves. In fact, funding for research on alternative, renewable energy sources was three times greater in 1979 than it has been during this period. The need for greater attention to alternative energy source development may be another potential source of common ground for both proponents and critics of energy independence.

If market prices for oil keep rising, then this may make "policy choices for secure energy much easier . . . [by stimulating] production of non-OPEC conventional and nonconventional oil substitutes" (Griffin, 2009). Such policies could further both energy independence and energy security, as these two ideas are not diametrically opposed. Shifting the energy sector toward a nonoil-based infrastructure over the long term could allow for the gradual substitution of oil for other energy sources, once they are developed, and prove that they can also enable economic growth and improvements in standards of living. Whether the United States will be able to take a proactive approach to this transition, or whether it will merely react through disparate and inefficient responses to energy crises, remains to be seen.

Additional Resources

Cordesman, Anthony H. and Khalid R. Al-Rodhan. *The Global Oil Market: Risks and Uncertainties.* Washington, DC: Center for Strategic and International Studies Press, 2006.

Griffin, James M. *A Smart Energy Policy: An Economist's Rx for Balancing Cheap, Clean, and Secure Energy.* New Haven, CT: Yale University Press, 2009.

Hakes, Jay. *Declaration of Energy Independence: How Freedom from Foreign Oil Can Improve National Security, Our Economy, and the Environment.* Hoboken: John Wiley and Sons, Inc., 2008.

This author argues that energy independence is a prudent strategic objective for the United States, yet each presidential administration has impeded the goal through contrary energy policies. The book explains how energy independence can still save the United States from its impending energy crisis by outlining seven economic and political ways that America can produce and use energy more efficiently and break its dependence on foreign oil.

Jordan, Amos A., William J. Taylor, Jr., Michael J. Meese, and Suzanne C. Nielsen. *American National Security*, 6th ed. Baltimore, MD: Johns Hopkins University Press, 2009.

Simmons, Matthew R. *Twilight in the Desert: The Coming Saudi Oil Shock and the World Economy.* Hoboken: John Wiley & Sons, Inc., 2005.

Internet References . . .

The Oil Crisis

This article describes the current energy crisis, indicating that, based upon geological and oil discovery trends, the supply of conventional oil will not keep up with the demand for oil within the next decade.

**www.oilcrisis.com/_archive/
ScientificAmerican199803/EndOfCheapOil.htm**

The Financial Times

This article examines whether energy independence is more viable for the United States now than in past years. The author argues that the benefits of self-sufficiency include importing less oil, improving the United States' current account deficit, and mitigating OPEC's power.

**www.ft.com/cms/s/65bfd07a-03b3-11e1-bbc5-
00144feabdc0**

The American Interest

This article examines the difficulties associated with decreasing supplies of relatively cheap, easily accessible, and viscous oil sources in the face of rapidly growing consumer demand. The author suggests that the increasing costs of extracting the remaining oil will push consumers to accept and adopt alternative energy technologies.

**www.the-american-interest.com/article.
cfm?piece=446**

Reuters

This article examines oil price spikes and the physical availability of oil and concludes that energy independence is not a feasible strategy due to the global nature of the oil market.

**www.reuters.com/article/2011/11/30/
column-us-exports-energy-
independence-idUSL5E7MU6OT20111130**

USA Today Online

Tim Mullaney's "U.S. Energy Independence is no Longer a Pipe Dream," is available at this link.

**www.usatoday.com/money/industries/
energy/story/2012-05-15/1A-COV-ENERGY-
INDEPENDENCE/54977254/1**

Pickens Plan

T. Boone Pickens' piece, "The Plan," is available at this link.

www.pickensplan.com/theplan

U.S. Energy Information Administration

"Primary Energy Consumption by Source and Sector, 2010" is available at this link.

**www.eia.gov/totalenergy/data/annual/
pecss_diagram.cfm**

Unit V

UNIT

The United States and International Rules, Norms, Laws, and Institutions

A central feature that distinguishes international politics from domestic politics is the existence of anarchy in the international system, where there is no higher authority above the state. Within individual countries, governments create order by promulgating known laws, establishing mechanisms to judge violations of those laws, and providing enforcers to punish transgressors. Since there is no government for the world as a whole, states sometimes seek to establish international institutions to perform some of these functions. While international institutions may be helpful in the promulgation of known rules and be able to facilitate information sharing to assess violations, they lack the power of enforcement.

Despite their lack of independent enforcement capability, the United States has actively promoted international institutions to encourage cooperation among states and to reshape the world politically, economically, and militarily. American leaders after World War II, for example, helped create the United Nations, the World Bank, the International Monetary Fund, the General Agreement on Tariffs and Trade (now the World Trade Organization), and the North Atlantic Treaty Organization. In the twenty-first century, significant transnational concerns—including state failure, war crimes, and other grievous human rights abuses, climate change, organized crime, and terrorism—point to the need for expanded international cooperation. The issues in this section address the collective action problems associated with some of these transnational challenges and present options for addressing them.

Selected, Edited, and with Issue Framing Material by:
Suzanne Nielsen, *U.S. Military Academy*
and
Scott Handler, *U.S. Military Academy*

ISSUE

Should the United States Join the International Criminal Court?

YES: Julia Martinez Vivancos, from "Why the International Criminal Court Is in the United States' National Interest," *American NGO Coalition for the ICC* (August 2010)

NO: Brett D. Schaefer and Steven Groves, from "The U.S. Should Not Join the International Criminal Court," *The Heritage Foundation Backgrounder* (August 2009)

Learning Outcomes

After reading this issue, you should be able to:

- Explain why the International Criminal Court (ICC) was created.
- Explain the importance of the U.S. decision to sign, but not ratify, the Rome Statute in 2000.
- Discuss what led to the U.S. decision to withdraw as a signatory to the Rome Statute in 2002.
- Understand the perspective of the administration of President Barack Obama on the ICC.
- Understand why the United States has not yet joined the ICC.

ISSUE SUMMARY

YES: Julia Martinez Vivancos, a researcher for the American Non-Governmental Organizations Coalition for the International Criminal Court, urges the United States to join the International Criminal Court (ICC) without further delay. The ICC is compatible with America's values and, by becoming a member, the United States can improve its tarnished international image and enhance its ability to employ soft power in international affairs.

NO: Brett D. Schaefer and Steven Groves, fellows at The Heritage Foundation, maintain that the ICC violates known international laws when it prosecutes and punishes citizens of countries that have not joined the ICC. They also declare that too many of the cases brought before the ICC are politically motivated and only complicate relations among states.

In an ideal world, society would not need laws; individuals would understand and abide by cultural norms that govern behavior while simultaneously respecting the rights of others. Yet, as political philosophers have long pointed out, human beings are not perfect and there are many disadvantages to living in a lawless society. For this reason, those countries that are considered to be well-governed are characterized by a rule of law that includes a relatively stable body of law, police forces, lawyers (prosecutors and defenders), judges, and a prison system. Though the specifics vary across national contexts, where the rule of law exists, the citizens have an expectation that justice will be done.

Due to the existence of anarchy in the international system—with anarchy defined as the absence of a higher sovereign authority above states—criminal law has traditionally fallen within the sovereign domain of individual states. But as the world continues to globalize, the significance of state borders is diminishing. Individuals around the globe are more aware than ever before of developments in other states, and behavior in one state can increasingly impact outcomes in others. The war crimes tribunals following World War II represent an important milestone, as they involved holding individuals directly responsible for crimes against humanity—regardless of whether they were abiding by domestic law. Since this time, efforts to establish individual criminal responsibility for violations of human rights based upon international standards have continued. As consensus grew about the need to stop crimes against humanity in the wake of the multiple genocides that took place during the twentieth century, it was nevertheless still a complex task to determine who would have the duty and right to prosecute and enforce punishment.

"Recognizing that such grave crimes threaten the peace, security, and well-being of the world," over

160 countries attempted to address these concerns in 1998 during discussions to create the International Criminal Court (ICC) through the Rome Statute (United Nations, 1998). The Rome Statute focused the prosecutorial jurisdiction of the ICC on "genocide, crimes against humanity, war crimes, and the crime of aggression" (United Nations, 1998). The subsequent adoption of the Rome Statute by over 120 states led to the establishment of a permanent standing body to prosecute such crimes. Several important states have refused to join the ICC, however, including China, Iraq, Israel, and the United States (Coalition for the ICC, 2012).

Given its historic support for the idea of individual accountability for crimes against humanity, the failure of the United States to join the ICC may at first appear surprising. After World War II, the United States championed the creation of and led the Nuremberg Tribunal. As noted above, the resulting Nuremberg trials were the first to hold individuals responsible for committing crimes against humanity based on international law. The reasoning was that since "crimes against international law are committed by men, not by abstract entities . . . only by punishing individuals who commit such crimes can the provisions of international law be enforced" (Nuremberg, 1946). The United States also led the effort to establish the International Military Tribunal for the Far East in January 1946, which used the legal precedence established at Nuremberg to hold Japanese individuals responsible for war crimes (Shaw, 2008).

Though the United States is a past advocate for such efforts, before the ICC only the United Nations Security Council (UNSC), through its resolution mechanism, could convene international tribunals to prosecute war crimes. Although such UNSC Resolutions were rare after the Nuremburg and the Far East Tribunals, the International Criminal Tribunal for the Former Yugoslavia and the International Criminal Tribunal for Rwanda, which were also supported by the United States, were the products of such resolutions (Shaw, 2008).

Despite past support for similar efforts, as noted above, the United States chose not to become a party to the Rome Statute. Though actively involved, U.S. negotiators failed to secure key provisions of interest relating to the rules, authority, and jurisdiction of the ICC. Just prior to leaving office, President Bill Clinton signed the Rome Statute on December 31, 2000, stating that "a properly constituted and structured International Criminal Court would make a profound contribution in deterring egregious human rights abuses worldwide." Despite this rhetorical support, however, Clinton refused to submit the Statute to the Senate for ratification because he held "concerns about significant flaws in the treaty" (Clinton, 2000). Even President Clinton's symbolic support, however, vanished during the presidency of his successor, George W. Bush. Officially withdrawing the U.S. signature on May 6, 2002, President Bush thereby relieved the United States "of the obligations imposed on signatories" (AMICC, 2011).

At the heart of U.S. concerns about the Rome Statute and the ICC are three issues: extent of jurisdiction, the uncontrolled power of the prosecutor, and the limited due process rights of defendants. Turning first to the issue of jurisdiction, Article 12 of the Statute decrees that the ICC's jurisdiction extends beyond the citizens of member states. Citizens of non-member states may also be held accountable for alleged crimes committed on the territory of a member state if that member state is unwilling or unable to investigate and prosecute the alleged crime (United Nations, 1998). Since the U.S. armed forces serve around the globe, the United States is concerned that its service members could be subject to politically motivated prosecutions. Critics of this concern argue that U.S. military personnel are usually protected by Status of Forces Agreements (SOFAs) with host nations that "address how the domestic laws of the foreign jurisdiction shall be applied to U.S. personnel." Under most SOFAs, the U.S. government retains "the right to exercise all criminal and disciplinary jurisdiction for violations of the laws of the foreign nation while the individual is present in that country" (Mason, 2011). Nevertheless, U.S. concerns over the ICC's jurisdiction persist.

Second, the United States has reservations about the selection procedures for and authority granted to the ICC's prosecutor. According to Article 42 of the Rome Statute, the chief prosecutor is selected by winning an absolute majority of a secret ballot by members of the Assembly of State Parties (United Nations, 1998). The United States is concerned about the politicization of this potential selection, given that most state parties are not U.S. allies. Additionally, Article 15 grants the chief prosecutor self-initiating prosecutorial power. This means that the prosecutor can initiate investigations without the approval of any member nation or the UNSC, creating fear among non-member states "that a malevolent prosecutor could initiate cases to pursue political ends" (Feinstein, 2009). Critics of this reasoning argue that the self-initiating power of the prosecutor is what gives the ICC its autonomy and prevents international power politics from influencing prosecutorial decisions. However, this argument has not alleviated U.S. concerns over what it sees as unchecked power.

Third and finally, the United States worries that any U.S. citizen standing before the ICC will not have the same rights and due process protections they are afforded under the U.S. Constitution. While Article 67 of the Rome Statute lists the rights of the accused, this list does not explicitly guarantee a "trial by jury" as required by the Sixth Amendment of the U.S. Constitution. The Statute also fails to enumerate the level of proof, such as beyond a reasonable doubt, which must be established for a suspect to be found guilty of an alleged crime. This may violate the due process clause of the Fifth Amendment (Feinstein, 2009).

President George W. Bush felt so strongly about these concerns that he not only withdrew the U.S. signature from the treaty, but he also sought legislation from Congress to protect U.S. service members from the ICC's reach.

Congress passed and President Bush signed the American Service-Members' Protection Act (ASPA) in August 2002, which declared, "Members of the Armed Forces of the United States should be free from the risk of prosecution by the International Criminal Court, especially when they are stationed or deployed around the world to protect the vital national interests of the United States" (U.S. Department of State, 2003). The ASPA sought to achieve this goal by threatening to withdraw U.S. forces and ending financial and military aid to any state that refused to agree to exclude U.S. military personnel from the ICC's jurisdiction.

Though the United States has still not become a member, official U.S. rhetoric toward the ICC has softened since 2002. In 2006, Senator John McCain and former Senator Bob Dole acknowledged a role for ICC in an OpEd about the crisis in Darfur. They wrote that it was important to hold Sudanese leaders accountable for conducting genocide and crimes against humanity, and went on to say that "the International Criminal Court has [the] jurisdiction to prosecute [such] war crimes" (McCain and Dole, 2006). Since taking office in 2009, President Barack Obama has pledged to assist the ICC with holding individuals responsible for Darfur and with the capture of a rebel leader in Uganda, Joseph Kony, who created an army of child soldiers and sex slaves.

In the YES article for this debate about whether or not the United States should join the ICC, Julia Martinez Vivancos presents the case for why the United States should sign and ratify the Rome Statute. First, the ICC is completely compatible with American values and with the importance the United States places on the rule of law. Second, becoming a member of the ICC also serves U.S. interests. The United States can use the ICC as a venue in which it can provide moral leadership in continuing to develop international law, regaining the mantle it held following Nuremberg.

In contrast, Brett D. Schaefer and Steven Groves answer NO to the debate question and adamantly maintain that the United States should continue to refuse to join the ICC. The ICC is not only flawed due to the nearly unlimited authority granted to its head prosecutor, but it also actively works against the goals of other international institutions such as the UN. Furthermore, the inclusion of the ambiguous term "crime of aggression" within the ICC's mandate exposes the United States to the political agendas of ICC prosecutors and other members.

YES

Julia Martinez Vivancos

Why the International Criminal Court Is in the United States' National Interest

Traditional opponents of the International Criminal Court (ICC) have argued that the Court is undemocratic, undermines sovereignty and damages the interests of the United States. However, in the last National Security Strategy report, President Obama recognized the Court's importance to the emphasis of his foreign policy on multilateral relations. It is now time for those who oppose the Court in Congress and in American public to take a second look of the ICC. The purpose of this paper is twofold. First, it will analyze how the ICC embodies some of the main American values and interests. Second, it will demonstrate that by welcoming the ICC, the US will fortify its global image and therefore sustain its moral leadership in the world and thus its soft power.

The NSS: ICC as Part of Multilateral Approach to Foreign Policy

Since assuming the presidency, President Obama has taken a series of steps to return the US to multilateral engagement. This shift in American foreign policy is reflected in the National Security Strategy (NSS) report released over his signature which specifically mentions the need of *sustaining broad cooperation on key global challenges*. The Obama administration has made a strategic calculation that working within international institutions is preferable to marginalizing them. International institutions are essential and unavoidable for dealing with all major international problems. In addition to that, international institutions are potential vehicles for legitimating American leadership. This idea is also contained in the NSS which advocates for *strengthening institutions and mechanisms for cooperation.*

The NSS specifically mentions the ICC. It recognizes that supporting the Court is not only a moral imperative, but a pragmatic national security one as well. The end of impunity and the promotion of justice are stabilizing forces in international affairs. Recognizing this, the NSS states that those who intentionally target innocent civilians must be held accountable. Here is an acknowledgement that justice, of course, is only one element of foreign policy, but it is an important one. Historically, America has led efforts of the international community to bring justice to victims of atrocious crimes. America should continue to support institutions and prosecutions that advance this important interest and it should fully embrace the ICC as an expression of its values and interests.

American Values and Interests and the ICC

Traditional arguments by American opponents of the ICC have failed the test of reality. The ICC is compatible with the world envisioned by the US—a democratic and just world—because the ICC embodies some of the most relevant American values and interests.

Democracy

The ICC is a democratic organization; its structure and governance, as well as the nature of most of its members, demonstrate this. Moreover, the ICC also helps to promote democracy around the world.

Membership. Most of the Court's member states are democratic and the vast majority of them are also allies of the US. Only a few non-democratic states have ratified the Rome Statute. This is not surprising. On the one hand, governments lacking democratic legitimacy are more likely to commit atrocities as a means to keep power. Thus, repressive governments would not want to ratify the Statute out of the fear of prosecution. On the other hand, the ICC is a positive attraction for democratic governments as a proof of their commitment to the rule of law and due process. Joining the ICC is also an expression, which democracy makes possible, of the outrage of peoples and governments over atrocities. The ICC has, therefore, become an association of predominantly democratic and free states. The US should work closely with the ICC and with its major allies in the Court as part of its renewed multilateral approach to international affairs and so as to promote democracy.

ICC officials. A criminal justice system that is honest, fair and effective is one of America's most important institutions. It is equally important for the ICC to ensure the professionalism, effectiveness and independence of its officials, judges and prosecutor. To this end, ICC officials have specific functions and limitations and as well they are subject to strict control mechanisms to prevent misconduct.

The 18 judges of the ICC are accomplished legal experts and practitioners, all from democratic countries. As in the US, judicial independence and impartiality are two of the main principles of the ICC judiciary. The Rome Statute establishes certain measures to protect judges from improper influences from outside the ICC. Judges are elected to the Court by the Assembly of States Parties (ASP). They serve nine-year terms and are not generally eligible for re-election. All judges must be nationals of states parties to the Rome Statute, and no two judges may be nationals of the same state. They must be persons of high moral character, impartiality and integrity who possess the qualifications required in their respective States for appointment to the highest judicial offices. Through processes similar to the impeachment process in the US system, the ASP can remove judges of the ICC from office if they are found to have committed serious misconduct. The removal of a judge must be recommended to the ASP by two-thirds majority of the other judges and two-thirds of the States Parties must vote to approve his or her removal. Judges could also be disqualified from any case in which his or her impartiality might be doubted.

The first prosecutor, Luis Moreno-Ocampo, is an Argentine lawyer and former Harvard visiting professor who has won worldwide recognition for his work in battling corruption in several countries and prosecuting human rights abuses committed by Argentina's former military regime. The Rome Statute provides that the Office of the Prosecutor shall act independently. No member of the Office may seek or act on instructions from any external source, such as states, international organizations, non-governmental organizations or individuals. Any person being investigated or prosecuted may request the disqualification of a prosecutor from any case in which his or her impartiality might reasonably be doubted on any ground. The Appeals Chamber would decide on his or her disqualification. In addition, the ICC Prosecutor may be removed from office by an absolute majority of the States Parties if he or she is found to have committed serious misconduct or a serious breach of his or her duties or is unable to exercise his or her functions. This is similar to what happens in the US where each federal prosecutor is subjected, by law, to removal by the President.

Promotion of democracy by the ICC. The ICC is not only an agent of the international community, determined to prevent the commission of human rights atrocities. Also, for many individual states, joining the Court gives them another way to protect their citizens against atrocities. In this way, the ICC contributes to the promotion of democracy. It is certainly the case that democratic institutions constitute a formidable barrier to the commission of atrocities. That barrier is strengthened when a country ratifies the ICC, thereby making its citizens and people on its territory vulnerable to international prosecution for the commission of such crimes. The ICC helps to promote democracy in two specific ways.

First, the ICC enables ratifying states to warn anti-democratic actors that any resort to atrocities will result in a potential ICC prosecution. The Court has a state-building rather than an interventionist character. The ICC can coordinate legal assistance with a government that struggles to maintain law and order. Second, ratification is a courageous act by which a country publicly pledges itself to the prevention of atrocities. By ratifying the Rome Statute, a State Party gives itself an added incentive to uphold the democratic institutions that make atrocities far less likely.

The promotion of democracy is a central US interest. As the recent NSS clearly states, the US supports the expansion of democracy and human rights abroad because governments that respect these values are more just, peaceful, and legitimate. The US also does so because their success fosters an international environment that supports America's national interests. Political systems that protect universal rights are ultimately more stable, successful, and secure. Since one of the most positive effects of the Court's work is promoting democracy, the US should work closely with the ICC.

Rule of Law

Historically, the US has led in promoting the rule of law worldwide and, specifically, in the development of international criminal justice. The ICC is the current culmination of this process and a key piece in the present international system of criminal justice. US support and cooperation with the ICC will serve the American role in promoting the rule of law.

From Nuremberg to the ICC. The US was the main force in promoting the Nuremberg tribunals and continually supported the trials. After Nuremberg, the UN recognized the need for a permanent international court to deal with atrocities of the kind committed during World War II but the Cold War made the establishment of an international criminal court politically unrealistic. The idea was revived in 1989 and the work on drafting a statute began. However, before the statute was finished, the events in Rwanda and Yugoslavia compelled the international community to establish two ad hoc tribunals to try atrocities committed during these two conflicts. Pursuing the idea that those atrocities must be punished, the US strongly supported the creation of these two criminal tribunals. Their work further highlighted the need for a permanent international criminal court. Such a court would allow the international community to initiate prosecutions of future atrocities without having to start from scratch each time. After years of negotiations, the General Assembly convened a conference in Rome in June 1998, with the aim of finalizing a treaty to create such a court. On July 17, 1998, the Rome Statute of the International Criminal Court was adopted.

The ICC is the culmination of the process initiated in Nuremberg in 1948 by the US and other countries.

If the US wants to maintain international credibility in its pursuit of the global rule of law it needs to be sure that its current position carries forward the legacy of Nuremberg.

Filling the gaps: the principle of complementarity. According to the United Nations Charter, each nation, including the US, should be able to deal with its own internal issues and exercise its sovereignty in the most effective and responsible way. A responsible exercise of a country's sovereignty includes a judicial response when atrocities occur. The US is thus working to strengthen national justice systems so that every country could fairly and effectively address its own internal problems. This is exactly the main goal of the ICC. The ICC is a final option that is only available when domestic courts and procedures cannot deal with atrocities. This is referred to as the principle of complementarity.

Thus, the ICC is complementary to other courts. First, the ICC encourages national governments to strengthen their own enforcement of international atrocity law. However, when national jurisdictions are unable or unwilling to investigate atrocities, the ICC may take jurisdiction. Secondly, the ICC coexists with other national and international tribunals that deal with atrocity crimes, just as the gacaca courts in Rwanda work national in parallel with the UN International Criminal Tribunal for Rwanda (ICTR).

The Court itself does respect national sovereignty, including US sovereignty, because it does not have universal jurisdiction. The ICC can hear cases involving only four categories of crimes: genocide, crimes against humanity, war crimes and crimes of aggression. Even within these categories, the ICC can only take cases that involve severe and grave abuses. Furthermore, unless it is responding to a Security Council referral or a voluntary submission by a country, the Court can only consider cases if the events took place on the territory of a State Party or if the accused is a national of a State Party. In addition, the ICC cannot intervene if a nation investigates an allegation in good faith, even if it declines to prosecute.

The central purpose of the ICC is to try genocide, war crimes, crimes against humanity and crimes of aggression. The Court aims to end impunity for international atrocities. The further mission of the Court is to deter these crimes and thus to protect individuals from them. The US will continue to work to strengthen national criminal systems. However, this is not enough. Sometimes, national jurisdictions are not prepared or willing to deal effectively with atrocities. This is why the ICC is still necessary to promote the rule of law. The US is not a State Party to the Rome Statute but has a long history of cooperation with other nations in promoting the rule of law. This is why the limited US engagement with the ICC has been so disappointing. If the US really wants to promote the rule of law around the world, it should actively support the ICC since this Court fills the gaps where the other mechanisms fail, through the principle of complementarity.

Justice

America is a nation that strongly believes in law and justice, not only in order to bring justice to the victims but also to assure procedural guarantees for the defendants. The US criminal justice system upholds a defendant's rights to a fair and regular trial and also has laws in place to ensure that criminals are not abused or cruelly punished. Bringing justice to victims is the central purpose of the ICC. However, the Court recognizes that it is equally important to protect the rights of the accused during prosecution and trial, just as the US does.

The Rome Statute provides extensive protections to persons being investigated and those eventually accused of crimes. It gives broad rights to persons under investigation by the Court. These rights include the right to remain silent, the right to speedy trial, the right not to be subject to arbitrary arrest or detention and the right to have legal counsel provided when he or she cannot afford it, among others. After charges have been confirmed, the Statute expands upon the rights already mentioned. It provides that the accused has to be tried without undue delay, will have adequate time and facilities for the preparation of defense, and will have, free of cost, an interpreter and translation as necessary for the defense.

Defendants at the ICC enjoy all the due process rights of defendants in US courts except trial by jury. However, as it has been pointed out numerous times, the Bill of Rights has some limitations. First, if the crime is committed by military servicemembers, the US military courts-martial do not provide jury trials. Secondly, there is nothing new about Americans being subject to foreign laws when they commit the crime outside the US. Moreover, the US has also extradited Americans for trials in countries which do not use juries and has strongly supported the International Criminal Tribunal for the former Yugoslavia (ICTY) and ICTR, neither of which provides for trials by jury.

The ICC perfectly embodies the principle of justice in which America strongly believes. The Court offers to the defendant all rights that the US criminal justice system recognizes to the accused, except trial by jury. The misconception that the Court lacks enough protections for the defendant should not prevent the US from supporting actively the ICC.

Development of International Law

As mentioned above, America is a nation that strongly believes in the importance of law both . . . domestically and internationally. The ICC boosts the prestige and importance of international law. It helps to remind the international community that, despite the legal maneuvers and atrocious practices of dictatorial regimes, violations of the most fundamental rights remain forbidden and punishable under international law.

The Rome Statute is regarded as one of the most important multilateral instruments negotiated in the last decade of the twentieth century. The Statute codifies international law, for the purpose of the ICC, regarding genocides, war crimes, crimes against humanity and crimes of aggression. During the negotiations for the Rome Statute, in which the US was an active participant, momentum developed to write a treaty that further improved international protection against atrocities. Building upon the statutes and judicial decisions of the Tribunals for Rwanda and the Balkans, the Rome Statute consolidates and develops international criminal law in four particular areas, for the purpose of the ICC:

- The Statute spells out with greater precision prohibitions against sexual crimes.
- It extends war crimes provisions to internal as well as international conflicts.
- It does not require that an international conflict takes place to consider crimes against humanity.
- It refuses immunity based on official capacity.

These developments represent significant advances in the protection against atrocities. They also represent American contributions to international law as well as implementation of US national interests in international action against atrocities.

The Power of Example: Coherence and Consistency

US power has been unrivaled in many dimensions: the hard power of military strength, the economic power that stems from the world's largest economy, the soft power that comes from being associated with the promotion and protection of human rights. This is no longer the case. Military superiority is not always enough to ensure national safety and social and economic development worldwide. American economic power is no longer as exceptional as it used to be due to the growth of economies such as China and Brazil. But probably it is the American reputation as a moral leader which has been harmed the most in the last decade. In order to once again attract nations and peoples to its values, the US needs to rethink the face it presents to the world and recover its status as a moral leader.

Not being part of the ICC damages the US position in international relations, creating conflict with allies and causing disassociation from . . . some of the most important American values and interests—democracy, rule of law, justice and development of international law. If the US fortifies its standing by acting coherently and consistently, it will sustain a key source of its strength and leadership in the world.

The ICC has matured independently and responsibly while the US has, until recently, remained officially outside, and sometimes even manifestly opposed the Court. Now, it is time for the US to participate actively in the ICC and renew its own moral leadership. The ICC embodies values of justice and democracy that the US support for a just and democratic world. The US has led the long process of creating an international system of criminal justice that would end impunity, and the ICC is a major step forward and a culmination of this process. The Obama administration should expand and deepen the renewed engagement with the Court which it has begun cautiously.

Conclusion

The Obama administration has understood and begun to act on the perception that America needs to rethink its position toward the ICC. Law is, of course, only one element of foreign policy, but it is a powerful one. By appealing to principle, the US can better persuade. By acquiring legitimacy, the US actions take on a new authority. By delivering justice, America can win hearts and minds. If the US embraces the ICC, the US would better defend its values and interests. As a result, America will have the opportunity to cultivate trust and trustworthiness at the international level, to foster a circle of fairness and legitimacy in the global enforcement of human rights, and thus to promote the twin goals of justice and peace.

Julia Martinez Vivancos is a researcher at the American Non-Governmental Organizations Coalition for the International Criminal Court.

Brett D. Schaefer and Steven Groves  **NO**

The U.S. Should Not Join the International Criminal Court

Persistent Barriers to U.S. Ratification

. . . ICC supporters have called for the Obama Administration to re-sign the Rome Statute, reverse protective measures secured during the Bush Administration (Article 98 agreements), and fully embrace the ICC. Indeed, the Obama Administration may be considering some or all of those actions.[1] However, the ICC's flaws advise caution and concern, particularly in how the ICC could affect national sovereignty and politically precarious situations around the globe.

When it decided to un-sign the Rome Statute, the Bush Administration voiced five concerns regarding the Rome Statute.[2] These critical concerns have not been addressed.

The ICC's Unchecked Power. The U.S. system of government is based on the principle that power must be checked by other power or it will be abused and misused. With this in mind, the Founding Fathers divided the national government into three branches, giving each the means to influence and restrain excesses of the other branches. For instance, Congress confirms and can impeach federal judges and has the sole authority to authorize spending, the President nominates judges and can veto legislation, and the courts can nullify laws passed by Congress and overturn presidential actions if it judges them unconstitutional.

The ICC lacks robust checks on its authority, despite strong efforts by U.S. delegates to insert them during the treaty negotiations. The court is an independent treaty body. In theory, the states that have ratified the Rome Statute and accepted the court's authority control the ICC. In practice, the role of the Assembly of State Parties is limited. The judges themselves settle any dispute over the court's "judicial functions." The prosecutor can initiate an investigation on his own authority, and the ICC judges determine whether the investigation may proceed. The U.N. Security Council can delay an investigation for a year—a delay that can be renewed—but it cannot stop an investigation. As Grossman noted:

> Under the UN Charter, the UN Security Council has primary responsibility for maintaining international peace and security. But the Rome Treaty removes this existing system of checks and balances, and places enormous unchecked power in the hands of the ICC prosecutor and judges. The treaty created a

self-initiating prosecutor, answerable to no state or institution other than the Court itself.[3]

The Challenges to the Security Council's Authority. The Rome Statute empowers the ICC to investigate, prosecute, and punish individuals for the as yet undefined crime of "aggression." This directly challenges the authority and prerogatives of the U.N. Security Council, which the U.N. Charter gives "primary responsibility for the maintenance of international peace and security" and which is the only U.N. institution empowered to determine when a nation has committed an act of aggression. Yet, the Rome Statute "empowers the court to decide on this matter and lets the prosecutor investigate and prosecute this undefined crime" free of any oversight from the Security Council.[4]

A Threat to National Sovereignty. A bedrock principle of the international system is that treaties and the judgments and decisions of treaty organizations cannot be imposed on states without their consent. In certain circumstances, the ICC claims the authority to detain and try U.S. military personnel, U.S. officials, and other U.S. nationals even though the U.S. has not ratified the Rome Statute and has declared that it does not consider itself bound by its signature on the treaty. As Grossman noted, "While sovereign nations have the authority to try non-citizens who have committed crimes against their citizens or in their territory, the United States has never recognized the right of an international organization to do so absent consent or a U.N. Security Council mandate."[5]

As such, the Rome Statute violates international law as it has been traditionally understood by empowering the ICC to prosecute and punish the nationals of countries that are not party to it. In fact, Article 34 of the Vienna Convention on the Law of Treaties unequivocally states: "A treaty does not create either obligations or rights for a third State without its consent."[6]

Protestations by ICC proponents that the court would seek such prosecutions only if a country is unwilling or unable to prosecute those accused of crimes within the court's jurisdiction—the principle of complementarity—are insufficient to alleviate sovereignty concerns. As Casey and Rivkin note:

> [C]omplementarity applies only if the state in question handles the particular case at issue in a manner consistent with the ICC's understanding of the applicable legal norms. If the court concludes

that a state has been unwilling or unable to prosecute one of its citizens or government officials because it does not consider the questioned conduct unlawful, based on its own interpretation of the relevant international legal requirements, the court can proceed with an investigation.[7]

For example, the Obama Administration recently declared that no employee of the Central Intelligence Agency (CIA) who engaged in the use of "enhanced interrogation techniques" on detainees would be criminally prosecuted.[8] That decision was presumably the result of an analysis of U.S. law, legal advice provided to the CIA by Justice Department lawyers, and the particular actions of the interrogators. Yet if the U.S. were a party to the Rome Statute, the Administration's announced decision not to prosecute would fulfill a prerequisite for possible prosecution by the ICC under the principle of complementarity. That is, because the U.S. has no plans to prosecute its operatives for acts that many in the international community consider torture, the ICC prosecutor would be empowered (and possibly compelled) to pursue charges against the interrogators.

Erosion of Fundamental Elements of the U.N. Charter. The ICC's jurisdiction over war crimes, crimes against humanity, genocide, and aggression directly involves the court in fundamental issues traditionally reserved to sovereign states, such as when a state can lawfully use armed force to defend itself, its citizens, or its interests; how and to what extent armed force may be applied; and the point at which particular actions constitute serious crimes. Blurring the lines of authority and responsibility in these decisions has serious consequences. As Grossman notes, "with the ICC prosecutor and judges presuming to sit in judgment of the security decisions of States without their assent, the ICC could have a chilling effect on the willingness of States to project power in defense of their moral and security interests."[9] The ability to project power must be protected, not only for America's own national security interests, but also for those individuals threatened by genocide and despotism who can only be protected through the use of force.

Complications to Military Cooperation Between the U.S. and Its Allies. The treaty creates an obligation to hand over U.S. nationals to the court, regardless of U.S. objections, absent a competing obligation such as that created through an Article 98 agreement. The United States has a unique role and responsibility in preserving international peace and security. At any given time, U.S. forces are located in approximately 100 nations around the world, standing ready to defend the interests of the U.S. and its allies, engaging in peacekeeping and humanitarian operations, conducting military exercises, or protecting U.S. interests through military intervention. The worldwide extension of U.S. armed forces is internationally unique. The U.S. must ensure that its soldiers and government officials are not exposed to politically motivated investigations and prosecutions.

Ongoing Causes for Concern

Supporters of U.S. ratification of the Rome Statute often dismiss these concerns as unjustified, disproved by the ICC's conduct during its first seven years in operation, or as insufficient to overcome the need for an international court to hold perpetrators of serious crimes to account.[10] Considering the other options that exist or could be created to fill the ICC's role of holding perpetrators of war crimes, crimes against humanity, genocide, and aggression to account, the benefits from joining such a flawed institution do not justify the risks.

Furthermore, based on the ICC's record and the trend in international legal norms, they are being disingenuous in dismissing concerns about overpoliticization of the ICC, its impact on diplomatic initiatives and sovereign decisions on the use of force, its expansive claim of jurisdiction over the citizens of non-states parties, and incompatibility with U.S. legal norms and traditions. A number of specific risks are obvious.

Politicization of the Court. Unscrupulous individuals and groups and nations seeking to influence foreign policy and security decisions of other nations have and will continue to seek to misuse the ICC for politically motivated purposes. Without appropriate checks and balances to prevent its misuse, the ICC represents a dangerous temptation for those with political axes to grind. The prosecutor's *proprio motu* authority to initiate an investigation based solely on his own authority or on information provided by a government, a nongovernmental organization (NGO), or individuals[11] is an open invitation for political manipulation.

One example is the multitude of complaints submitted to the ICC urging the court to indict Bush Administration officials for alleged crimes in Iraq and Afghanistan. The Office of the Prosecutor received more than 240 communications alleging crimes related to the situation in Iraq. Thus far, the prosecutor has demonstrated considerable restraint, declining to pursue these cases for various reasons, including that the ICC does not have "jurisdiction with respect to actions of non-State Party nationals on the territory of Iraq," which is also not a party to the Rome Statute.[12]

All current ICC cases were referred to the ICC by the governments of the territories in which the alleged crimes occurred or by the Security Council. Comparatively speaking, these cases are low-hanging fruit—situations clearly envisioned to be within the authority of the court by all states. Even so, they have not been without controversy, as demonstrated by the AU reaction to the arrest warrant for President Bashir and attempts to have the Security Council defer the case.[13]

However, the ICC's brief track record is no assurance that future cases will be similarly resolved, especially given the increasing appetite for lodging charges with the ICC.[14] A far more significant test will arise if the prosecutor decides to investigate (and the court's pre-trial chamber authorizes) a case involving a non-ICC party without a Security Council referral or against the objections of the government of the involved territory.

This could arise from the prosecutor's monitoring of the situation in Palestine.[15] Even though Israel is not a party to the Rome Statute, the ICC prosecutor is exploring a request by the Palestinian National Authority to prosecute Israeli commanders for alleged war crimes committed during the recent actions in Gaza.[16] The request is supported by 200 complaints from individuals and NGOs alleging war crimes by the Israeli military and civilian leaders related to military actions in Gaza.[17]

Palestinian lawyers maintain that the Palestinian National Authority can request ICC jurisdiction as the de facto sovereign even though it is not an internationally recognized state. By countenancing Palestine's claims, the ICC prosecutor has enabled pressure to be applied to Israel over alleged war crimes, while ignoring Hamas's incitement of the military action and its commission of war crimes against Israeli civilians. Furthermore, by seemingly recognizing Palestine as a sovereign entity, the prosecutor's action has arguably created a pathway for Palestinian statehood without first reaching a comprehensive peace deal with Israel. This determination is an inherently political issue beyond the ICC's authority, yet the prosecutor has yet to reject the possibility that the ICC may open a case on the situation.

Alternatively, the prosecutor could raise ire by making a legal judgment call on a crime under the court's jurisdiction that lacks a firm, universal interpretation, such as:

- "Committing outrages upon personal dignity, in particular humiliating and degrading treatment"[18];
- "Intentionally launching an attack in the knowledge that such attack will cause incidental loss of life or injury to civilians or damage to civilian objects or widespread, long-term and severe damage to the natural environment which would be clearly excessive in relation to the concrete and direct overall military advantage anticipated"[19]; or
- Using weapons "which are of a nature to cause superfluous injury or unnecessary suffering or which are inherently indiscriminate in violation of the international law of armed conflict."[20]

In each of these cases, a reasonable conclusion could be made to determine whether a crime was committed. For instance, many human rights groups allege outrages on personal dignity and "humiliating and degrading treatment" were committed at the detention facility at Guantanamo Bay, Cuba. The U.S. disputes these claims. Excessive use of force has been alleged in Israel's attacks in Gaza, while others insist Israel demonstrated forbearance and consideration in trying to prevent civilian casualties.[21] There is also an ongoing international effort to ban landmines and cluster munitions. If the ICC member states agree to add them to the annex of banned weapons, it could lead to a confrontation over their use by non-party states, such as the U.S., which opposes banning these weapons. These are merely some scenarios in which politicization could become an issue for the ICC.

Disruption of Diplomatic Efforts. ICC decisions to pursue investigations and indictments can upset delicate diplomatic situations. Although the U.N. Security Council has been largely deadlocked over placing strong sanctions on the government of Sudan for its complicity in the terrible crimes in Darfur, it did pass a resolution in 2005 referring the situation in Darfur to the ICC. In summer 2008, the ICC announced that it would seek an indictment against Sudanese President Omar al-Bashir for his involvement in crimes committed in Darfur. On March 4, 2009, a warrant was issued for his arrest.[22]

Issuing the arrest warrant for Bashir was certainly justified. His government has indisputably supported the janjaweed militias that have perpetrated massive human rights abuses that rise to the level of crimes against humanity. His complicity in the crimes demands that he be held to account. Regrettably, the decision to refer the case to the ICC and the subsequent decision to issue an arrest warrant for the sitting Sudanese head of state have aggravated the situation in Darfur and may put more innocent people at risk.

In response to his indictment, Bashir promptly expelled vital humanitarian NGOs from Sudan.[23] Bashir may ultimately decide he has nothing to lose and increase his support of the janjaweed, encouraging them to escalate their attacks, even against aid workers and U.N. and AU peacekeepers serving in the African Union/UN Hybrid operation in Darfur (UNAMID). It could also undermine the 2005 peace agreement meant to reconcile the 20-year north–south civil war, which left more than 2 million dead.

Moreover, the decision to seek the arrest of Bashir, cheered by ICC supporters, may actually hurt the court in the long run. African countries, which would bear the most immediate consequences of a more chaotic Sudan, have called on the Security Council to defer the Bashir prosecution. Sudan's neighbors may be forced to choose between arresting Bashir, which could spark conflict with Sudan, or ignoring the court's arrest warrant. Indeed, all AU members except for Botswana announced in July 2009 that they would not cooperate with the ICC in this instance. South Africa subsequently announced that it would honor the ICC warrant in August 2009.[24] Whether the AU decision will have broader ramifications for the court's relationship with African governments remains to be seen. Some African ICC parties have mentioned withdrawing from the Rome Statute.

The desire to see Bashir face justice for his role in the crimes committed in Darfur is understandable and should not be abandoned. However, premature efforts to bring

Bashir to justice may be counterproductive. The priority in Sudan is to reduce the violence, stop the atrocities, restore peace and security, reconstitute refugees, and set the region on a path to avoid a return to conflict. This requires strong action by the AU and the international community, including economic and diplomatic sanctions designed to bring maximum pressure to bear on Bashir and his allies. It may require military intervention. Once this is achieved, justice can be pursued by the Sudanese themselves through their courts, through an ad hoc tribunal, or even through the ICC.

In another situation, the Ugandan government referred alleged crimes committed by the Lord's Resistance Army in northern Uganda to the court in 2004 in hopes of "engaging the western powers who had ignored the situation in northern Uganda"[25] and pressuring the LRA to negotiate a peace. Regrettably, the LRA has responded by announcing that it will not agree to peace talks until the ICC arrest warrants are withdrawn. If Uganda could resolve its long festering conflict with the LRA by agreeing not to prosecute its leader, it would have no ability to call off the ICC prosecution. Thus, the ICC's involvement could be a real impediment to peace in Uganda, assuming the LRA would abide by an agreement.[26]

The desire to address tragedies such as those in Darfur and Uganda is as laudable as the international community's unwillingness or inability to act is frustrating. The perpetrators of war crimes, genocide, and crimes against humanity should be held to account, but ICC investigation and arrest warrants cannot substitute for decisive action to stop the perpetrators and resolve such situations. Because the vast majority of the court's discretion lies within the Office of the Prosecutor, there is little opportunity to resolve disputes, conflicts, or sensitive political issues diplomatically after a case is brought to the ICC.

Furthermore, the ICC prosecutor and judges are unlikely ever to be held accountable if their decisions lead to greater carnage in Darfur or prolong the conflict in Uganda. They are free to act without considering the potential consequences. Others are not so lucky.

The long-term implications of supporting the ICC, which has become a wild card in a foreign and security policy, are significant, and they emphasize the need for the ICC to keep its distance from political issues.

The Undefined Crime of Aggression. It would be irresponsible for the U.S. to expose its military personnel and civilian officials to a court that has yet to define the very crimes over which it claims jurisdiction. Yet that is the situation the U.S. would face if it ratified the Rome Statute. The Statute includes the crime of aggression as one of its enumerated crimes, but the crime has yet to be defined, despite a special working group that has been debating the issue for more than five years.

For instance, some argue that any military action conducted without Security Council authorization violates international law and is, therefore, an act of aggression that could warrant an ICC indictment. The U.S. has been the aggressor in several recent military actions, including military invasions of the sovereign territories of Afghanistan and Iraq, albeit with the U.N. Security Council's blessing in the case of Afghanistan. U.S. forces bombed Serbia in 1999 and launched dozens of cruise missiles at targets in Afghanistan and the Sudan in 1998 without explicit Security Council authorization. While charges of aggression are unlikely to be brought against U.S. officials *ex post facto* for military actions in Iraq and elsewhere—certainly not for actions before July 2002 as limited by the Rome Statute—submitting to the jurisdiction of an international court that judges undefined crimes would be highly irresponsible and an open invitation to levy such charges against U.S. officials in future conflicts.

If the U.S. becomes an ICC party, every decision by the U.S. to use force, every civilian death resulting from U.S. military action and every allegedly abused detainee could conceivably give cause to America's enemies to file charges against U.S. soldiers and officials. Indeed, any U.S. "failure" to prosecute a high-ranking U.S. official in such instances would give a cause of action at the ICC. For example, the principle of complementarity will not prevent a politicized prosecutor from bringing charges against a sitting U.S. President or Secretary of Defense. That is, the U.S. Department of Justice is unlikely to file criminal charges against such officials for their decisions involving the use of military force. This decision not to prosecute would be a prerequisite for the ICC taking up the case.

At best, the U.S. would find itself defending its military and civilian officials against frivolous and politically motivated charges submitted to the ICC prosecutor. At worst, international political pressure could compel the ICC's prosecutor to file charges against current or former U.S. officials. Until the crime of aggression is defined, U.S. membership in the ICC is premature. . . .

Conclusion

While the International Criminal Court represents an admirable desire to hold war criminals accountable for their terrible crimes, the court is flawed notionally and operationally. The ICC has not overcome many of the problems plaguing the ad hoc tribunals established for Yugoslavia and Rwanda. It remains slow and inefficient. Worse, unlike ad hoc tribunals, it includes a drive to justify its budget and existence in perpetuity rather than simply completing a finite mission.

Its broad autonomy and jurisdiction invite politically motivated indictments. Its inflexibility can impede political resolution of problems, and its insulation from political considerations can complicate diplomatic efforts. Efforts to use the court to apply pressure to inherently political issues and supersede the foreign policy prerogatives of sovereign nations—such as the prosecutor's decision to consider Israel's actions in Gaza—undermine the court's credibility and threaten its future as a useful tool for holding accountable the perpetrators of genocide, war crimes, and crimes against humanity.

President Clinton considered the ICC's flaws serious enough to recommend against U.S. ratification of the Rome Statute unless they were resolved, and President Bush concurred. These issues remain unresolved and continue to pose serious challenges to U.S. sovereignty and its national interests. Unless the serious flaws are addressed fully, President Obama should similarly hold the ICC at arm's length. To protect its own interests and to advance the notion of a properly instituted international criminal court, the U.S. should continue to insist that it is not bound by the Rome Statute and does not recognize the ICC's authority over U.S. persons and should exercise great care when deciding to support the court's actions.

Notes

1. Kralev, "U.S. Warms to Global Court."
2. Grossman, "American Foreign Policy and the International Criminal Court."
3. *Ibid.*
4. *Ibid.*
5. *Ibid.*
6. Vienna Convention on the Law of Treaties.
7. Casey and Rivkin, "Making Law," p. 48.
8. Siobhan Gorman and Evan Perez, "CIA Memos Released; Immunity for Harsh Tactics," *The Wall Street Journal,* April 17, 2009, at http://online.wsj.com/article/SB123990682923525977.html (August 3, 2009).
9. Grossman, "American Foreign Policy and the International Criminal Court."
10. For example, see American Society of International Law, "U.S. Policy Toward the International Criminal Court."
11. Rome Statute of the International Criminal Court, Art. 15.
12. Luis Moreno-Ocampo, Chief Prosecutor, International Criminal Court, letter, February 9, 2006, at www2.icc-cpi.int/NR/rdonlyres/04D143C8-19FB-466C-AB77-4CDB2FDEBEF7/143682/OTP_letter_to_senders_re_Iraq_9_February_2006.pdf (August 3, 2009).
13. Article 16 of the Rome Statute allows the U.N. Security Council to defer an ICC investigation or prosecution for a renewable period of 12 months, "No investigation or prosecution may be commenced or proceeded with under this Statute for a period of 12 months after the Security Council, in a resolution adopted under Chapter VII of the Charter of the United Nations, has requested the Court to that effect; that request may be renewed by the Council under the same conditions." See also James Sturcke, "UN Extends Darfur Peacekeeping Mandate in Last-Minute Vote," *The Guardian,* August 1, 2008, at www.guardian.co.uk/world/2008/aug/01/unitednations.sudan (August 3, 2009).
14. American Society of International Law, "U.S. Policy Toward the International Criminal Court," p. 18, and International Criminal Court, Office of the Prosecutor, "Communications, Referrals and Preliminary Analysis," at www2.icc-cpi.int/Menus/ICC/Structure+of+the+Court/Office+of+the+Prosecutor/Comm+and+Ref (August 3, 2009).
15. Catherine Philip and James Hinder, "Prosecutor Looks at Ways to Out Israeli Officers on Trial for Gaza 'War Crimes,'" *The Times,* February 2, 2009, at www.timesonline.co.uk/tol/news/world/middle_east/article5636069.ece (August 3, 2009).
16. International Criminal Court, Office of the Prosecutor, "Visit of the Palestinian National Authority Minister of Foreign Affairs, Mr. Riad al-Malki, and Minister of Justice, Mr. Ali Khashan, to the Prosecutor of the ICC (13 February 2009)," at www2.icc-cpi.int/NR/rdonlyres/4CC08515-D0BA-454D-A594-446F30289EF2/280140/ICCOTP20090213Palestinerev.pdf (August 3, 2009), and Sebastian Rotella, "International Criminal Court to Consider Gaza Investigation," *Los Angeles Times,* February 5, 2009, at http://articles.latimes.com/2009/feb/05/world/fg-court-palestinians5 (August 3, 2009).
17. International Criminal Court, Office of the Prosecutor, "Visit of the Minister of Justice of the Palestinian National Authority, Mr. Ali Khashan, to the ICC (22 January 2009)," at www.icc-cpi.int/en_menus/icc/press%20and%20media/press%20releases/press%20releases%20(2010)/Pages/icc%20vice_president%20meets%20with%20the%20minister%20of%20justice%20of%20montenegro.aspx (August 3, 2009).
18. Rome Statute of the International Criminal Court, Art. 8(2)(c)(ii).
19. *Ibid.,* Art. 8(2)(b)(iv).
20. *Ibid.,* Art. 8(2)(b)(xx). Likely candidates are landmines and cluster munitions, which are targets for bans under international treaty and are used by the U.S.
21. Alan M. Dershowitz, "Israel's Policy Is Perfectly 'Proportionate,'" *The Wall Street Journal,* January 2, 2009, at http://online.wsj.com/article/SB123085925621747981.html?mod=googlenews_wsj (August 3, 2009).
22. Press release, "ICC Issues a Warrant of Arrest for Omar Al Bashir, President of Sudan," International Criminal Court, March 4, 2009, at http://www.icc-cpi.int/en_menus/icc/situations%20and%20cases/situations/situation%20icc%200205/press%20

releases/Pages/icc%20issues%20a%20warrant%20 of%20arrest%20for%20omar%20al%20bashir_%20 president%20of%20sudan.aspx Issues a Warrant of Arrest for (August 3, 2009).

23. Xan Rice and Tania Branigan, "Sudanese President Expels Aid Agencies," *The Guardian,* March 5, 2009, at www.guardian.co.uk/world/2009/mar/05/ sudan-aid-agencies-expelled (August 3, 2009).

24. Republic of South Africa, Department of Foreign Affairs, "Notes following the Briefing of Department International Relations and Cooperation's Director-General, Ayanda Ntsaluba," updated August 3, 2009, at www.dfa.gov.za/docs/ speeches/2009/ntsa0731.html (August 7, 2009).

25. Payam Akhavan, "Uganda: ICC Warrants Not Stopping Peace Search—Expert," interview by Rosebell Kagumire, *The Monitor* (Kampala, Uganda), at http://allafrica.com/stories/200710280004 .html (August 3, 2009).

26. The LRA is notoriously unpredictable and intransigent, and there is no guarantee that its leaders would abide by a peace agreement.

BRETT D. SCHAEFER is the Jay Kingham Fellow in International Regulatory Affairs at The Heritage Foundation's Margaret Thatcher Center for Freedom. He previously worked in the Pentagon as an assistant for International Criminal Court policy.

STEVEN GROVES is the Bernard and Barbara Lomas Senior Research Fellow in the Margaret Thatcher Center for Freedom at The Heritage Foundation. Previously, he was senior counsel to the U.S. Senate Permanent Subcommittee on Investigations and an associate at Boise, Schiller & Flexner LLP.

EXPLORING THE ISSUE

Should the United States Join the International Criminal Court?

Critical Thinking and Reflection

1. Would the American people support a decision by the U.S. government to join the ICC? Why or why not?
2. In what ways could membership in the ICC support U.S. national interests? In what ways could joining the ICC harm U.S. national interests?
3. Is the ICC's chief prosecutor "impartial"? Define impartiality.
4. How could states perceive prosecutorial actions as being political rather than legal in nature? Discuss how members of the ICC can address and mitigate this concern.
5. Does absence of the United States from the ICC's membership do more harm to the United States or to the ICC? Explain.

Is There Common Ground?

A recent international drive to bring Ugandan rebel leader Joseph Kony to justice has revealed how difficult this task can be. The leader of the Lord's Resistance Army, Kony has led a vicious campaign of ethnic cleansing in Uganda, the Democratic Republic of Congo, the Central African Republic, and South Sudan. He has also abducted tens of thousands of children and turned them into child soldiers and sex slaves. These activities resulted in Kony's indictment as a war criminal by the ICC in 2005. Though President Barack Obama dispatched a contingent of soldiers in 2011 to train, advise, and provvide intelligence to African forces to help them capture Kony and bring him to trial, as of October 2012 Kony remains at large.

While they do not suggest that bringing war criminals to account is easy, President Obama's actions in this case do reveal the possible existence of common ground. Despite not being a member of the ICC, and lingering concerns about jurisdiction, the authority of the chief prosecutor, and rights of the accused, the United States appears willing to recognize that the ICC can play a constructive role in some situations. When this occurs, it is possible that the United States can help the ICC enforce its arrest warrants and bring accused criminals to trial. In addition, there may be broad agreement that some mechanism is needed to hold the perpetrators of grievous crimes against humanity accountable, even if the United States does not agree with how the ICC was set up to fulfill that role.

The United States has a long history of leading efforts to expand international law to hold individuals responsible for heinous crimes committed during conflict. The vehicle for expanding justice provided by the creation of the ICC provides the United States with another opportunity to be a leader in helping the international community to continue to develop international law as it relates to individual criminal accountability. As long as the United States remains outside of the organization, its ability to lead is diminished. However, this does not mean that the United States should just sign the treaty. Because the United States commits to treaties that it will fulfill, it must agree with their basic provisions. Instead, the United States should continue to exhibit the norms of behavior that it wants to establish and work closely with the ICC, bilaterally and through the United Nations Security Council, to establish a working relationship and level of trust with the organization. This approach may allow the United States and the ICC members to find a way to meet both their needs and develop a pathway toward eventual U.S. membership.

Additional Resources

Elsea, Jennifer K. *U.S. Policy Regarding the International Criminal Court*. Washington, DC: Congressional Research Service, 2006.

This report describes the position of the U.S. government toward the ICC, and specifically enumerates the main objections that the United States has against the ICC.

Feinstein, Lee. *Means to an End: U.S. Interest in the International Criminal Court*. Washington, DC: Brookings Institution Press, 2009.

Mason, R. Chuck. *Status of Forces Agreement (SOFA): What Is It, and How Has It Been Utilized?* Washington, DC: Congressional Research Service, 2011.

Mayerfeld, Jamie. "Who Shall Be Judge? The United States, the International Criminal Court, and the Global Enforcement of Human Rights." *Human Rights Quarterly* 25, no. 1 (2003): 93–129.

This article examines unilateral and multilateral approaches to developing the rule of law. The author analyzes whether collective enforcement or unilateral efforts are best suited to succeed in prosecuting human rights violations.

Shaw, Malcolm N. *International Law*. Cambridge: Cambridge University Press, 2008.

Internet References . . .

U.S. Department of State

This page outlines the American Service-Members' Protection Act.

www.state.gov/t/pm/rls/othr/misc/23425.htm

The American Non-Governmental Organizations Coalition for the International Criminal Court

This fact sheet details the U.S. government's actions related to the International Criminal Court.

www.amicc.org/docs/US%20Chronology.pdf

Bill Clinton Statement

President Bill Clinton's "Statement by U.S. President Bill Clinton, Authorizing the U.S. Signing of the Rome Statute of the International Criminal Court" is available at this link.

www.iccnow.org/documents/ USClintonSigning31Dec00.pdf

Coalition for the International Criminal Court

This website represents the views of over 2,500 civil society organizations from more than 150 different countries that support the strengthening of the International Criminal Court. The site's document library contains audio-visual resources to enhance viewers' understanding of current cases, as well as potential cases the ICC is considering.

www.iccnow.org/

Coalition for the International Criminal Court

The "History of the ICC" is available at this link.

www.iccnow.org/?mod=icchistory

Coalition for the International Criminal Court

This official website of the ICC describes the Court's structure, history, and current cases, and also provides information on past activities.

www.icc-cpi.int/Menus/ICC?lan=en-GB

The Washington Post

John McCain and Robert Dole's "Rescue Darfur Now" is available at this link.

www.washingtonpost.com/wp-dyn/content/article/ 2006/09/08/AR2006090801664.html.

Yale Law School

The Avalon Project site houses documents in law and history, including this piece, *Judgment of the International Military Tribunal.*

http://avalon.law.yale.edu/subject_menus/judcont.asp

United Nations

The Rome Statute is the foundational document that established the International Criminal Court and is essential reading. It defines key terms such as genocide, crimes against humanity, and war crimes. The Rome Statute also describes the operations of and funding for the ICC, as well as other procedural matters.

http://untreaty.un.org/cod/icc/statute/romefra.htm

Selected, Edited, and with Issue Framing Material by:
Suzanne Nielsen, *U.S. Military Academy*
and
Scott Handler, *U.S. Military Academy*

ISSUE

Should the United States Intervene Militarily in the Absence of a Direct Threat to U.S. National Interests?

YES: Nikolas K. Gvosdev and Ray Takeyh, from "Decline of Western Realism," *The National Interest* (January/February 2012)

NO: John J. Mearsheimer, from "Imperial by Design," *The National Interest* (January/February 2011)

Learning Outcomes

After reading this issue, you should be able to:

- Discuss the possible considerations that guide decisions to intervene militarily abroad.
- Explain competing views about how national interests are best conceived.
- Understand how international relations theory can be used to explain foreign policy decisions.
- Discuss the possible motivations for future U.S. military interventions.

ISSUE SUMMARY

YES: According to Nikolas Gvosdev, senior editor of *The National Interest* and professor of national security studies at the U.S. Naval War College, and Ray Takeyh, senior fellow for Middle Eastern studies at the Council on Foreign Relations, American actions in Libya in 2011 suggest a decreasing need to justify military interventions in security terms. Instead, U.S. ideals may be a sufficient basis for future U.S. military interventions in cases where U.S. policymakers believe that the post-intervention successor government will be no worse than the pre-intervention regime.

NO: John Mearsheimer, professor of political science at the University of Chicago, argues that military interventions will fail when there is no threat to America's core national security interests. Instead of engaging in misadventures in far-flung corners of the globe, the United States should focus its power against the rising threat of China.

In 2011, a revolution began in Libya when parts of the population in eastern Libya took to the streets. In the spirit of the "Arab Spring," which had been sweeping across North Africa over the past year, participants in this popular uprising demanded the end of the regime of Libyan President Muammar Qadhafi. As the violence escalated, demands for international intervention to stop the killing grew—to include U.S. allies in Europe and the Persian Gulf. In response, the United States agreed to participate in a military intervention in Libya to prevent a pending humanitarian crisis. With authorization from a United Nations Security Council Resolution (UNSCR), the international coalition established a "no-fly zone" in order to protect the civilian population from air attacks by the Libyan government (United Nations, 2011). The Libyan rebels, who received training and equipment support from the intervening coalition, captured President Qadhafi and killed him on October 20, 2011. After taking over the country, the leaders of the rebel forces were recognized as the acting government by the United Nations (UN) on October 23, 2012.

From the perspective of U.S. foreign policy and the debate question being examined here, the interesting thing about this case is that President Barack Obama never claimed that the Libyan situation posed a direct threat to the United States. In fact, Secretary of Defense Robert Gates, a senior member of the Obama administration, was on record as having said that he did not think that Libya or the situation there was "a vital interest of the United States" (Hilsenrath, 2011). Nevertheless, while no one claimed that vital U.S. interests were at imminent risk, President Obama did argue that developments in Libya would affect the United States. As he explained, non-intervention would have resulted in "a massacre that would have reverberated across the region and stained the conscience of the world . . . [therefore, i]t was not in our national interest to let that happen" (Obama, 2011). So, while the situation in Libya did not represent a direct threat, it did represent a legitimate concern. In the judgment of President Obama, a limited use of American military power was an appropriate component of the U.S. response.

In making this case, President Obama touched on two important matters of debate. The first, which will never be subject to final resolution, is over the definition of U.S. national interests. Some argue that national interests are best defined in material terms and confined to factors that affect U.S. physical security, economic prosperity, and the democratic system of government that enable the U.S. way of life. Others, however, argue that the values of the United States—including the universal claim in the Declaration of Independence that every individual has the right to "life, liberty, and the pursuit of happiness"—are inextricably intertwined with the country's material interests. Since these are inseparable, the protection of U.S. national interests also requires the protection of U.S. values. Exactly what can be done to further these interests in any given case is a matter for political judgment. The second debate is over the conditions under which it is appropriate to employ U.S. military power. Though the debate goes back to the founding of the United States, an important post–Vietnam War effort to set rules that limit the use of force remains the Weinberger Doctrine, which was originally articulated by Secretary of Defense Caspar Weinberger in 1985. Among the conditions he set were that the United States only ought to use force as a last resort, when vital national interests were at stake, and where there was a clear intent to win (Weinberger, 1985). Underlying Weinberger's argument is an assessment that military action is costly and risky, and therefore ought not to be undertaken lightly. Though others were quick to debate Weinberger's restrictive formulation, it continues to resonate with those who favor a restrained role for the United States military abroad.

Since the end of the Cold War in the early 1990s, these domestic debates have also been influenced by a larger one taking place on the international stage. In her work, scholar Martha Finnemore examines the construction of an international norm of humanitarian intervention and examines how this norm influences state behavior. In defining humanitarian intervention, she argues that it occurs when "no obvious national interest is at stake for the states bearing the burden of the military intervention" (Finnemore, 1996). Many of the early post–Cold War military interventions in which the United States participated, to include those in Somalia and Bosnia, are a reflection of this emerging norm and also contributed to its weight. This process has been further encouraged by international organizations, especially the UN, which has grappled with defining its role and that of other states

when people are preyed on by their own governments or caught in a cycle of endemic civil conflict. Previous interpretations of the concept of sovereignty, which dates back to the Peace of Westphalia in 1648, suggested that what goes on within one state's borders is not a matter of concern for other states. As more people came to be killed by their own governments and in civil conflict than by wars among states, this approach came to be seen as increasingly inadequate. As a result, in 2005 the UN articulated a new outlook called the "Responsibility to Protect" (R2P). R2P argues that sovereignty is a responsibility, not just a right. When a state fails to live up to its responsibility to protect its population from genocide, war crimes, ethnic cleansing, and crimes against humanity, the international community may intervene—with force if necessary (United Nations, 2005). The record of the United States in this area is mixed. While the United States intervened during the 1990s in Somalia, Bosnia, and Kosovo, it did not intervene to stop genocide in Rwanda in 1994.

Many arguments about the appropriateness of military intervention can be traced back to the two primary schools of thought in international relations, realism and liberalism. To a realist, the lawless nature of relations among states means that states are constantly embroiled in a struggle for survival. Even if they are not currently fighting one another, war remains an ever-present possibility. With this view of the international system in mind, it is easy to understand the realist perspective on what constitutes the national interest. The father of modern political realism, Hans Morgenthau (2006[1948]), famously equated interest with power, and claimed that this "is an objective category that is universally valid" (Morgenthau, (2006[1948]). The concept of sovereignty holds value for realists because whatever the flaws of individual states may be, sovereignty at least limits conflict among them. If states were involved constantly in one another's affairs, war would be endless. In addition, a state that intervened in another's affairs, particularly when its security was not at stake, would merely be dissipating its power and making itself weaker vis-à-vis other threats. A final realist argument against intervention is a practical one: since states are motivated most by the pursuit of power, they will not necessarily devote the resources to humanitarian interventions that success would require. In sum, humanitarian interventions are unwise and, over the long term, more likely to do harm than good.

Theorists from the liberal school of international relations are likely to take a different view on the nature of the international system, the concept of national interest, and the appropriateness of humanitarian intervention. While liberals agree that there is no authority over states in the international system, they are more inclined to see the possibilities for cooperation as well as conflict. In addition, their core values differ. Whereas realists see the core value as state security, liberals instead focus on the liberty and autonomy of the individuals within states. This leads liberals to take a different view of sovereignty than realists.

Sovereignty is of value because, as U.S. President Woodrow Wilson so famously argued in his "Fourteen Points," it allows people to exercise the self-determination that is their basic right (Wilson, 1918). However, the value of sovereignty is conditional; it depends on the legitimacy of the state concerned and the extent to which it upholds the liberty, autonomy, and welfare of its citizens. When states fail in these tasks, or even actively prey upon their populations, humanitarian intervention may be appropriate.

The next two articles represent the continuation of a long-standing debate over whether the United States should intervene militarily even when not confronted with a direct threat. Though they recognize the possible pitfalls, national security analysts Nikolas Gvosdev and Ray Takeyh suggest that the answer is YES. In their view, good foreign policy is responsive to the nature of the times. In this post–Cold War period, it may be appropriate for the United States to use military force for humanitarian purposes even when its direct security interests are not at stake.

In contrast, political scientist John Mearsheimer argues in the NO article that the largely unchanging structure of the international system necessitates a more realist approach to U.S. military interventions abroad. Mearsheimer suggests that American military interventions since the end of the Cold War have distracted the United States from a real potential concern, namely a rising China whose actions could threaten U.S. vital interests in Asia.

YES ↵

Nikolas K. Gvosdev and Ray Takeyh

Decline of Western Realism

When Operation Odyssey Dawn commenced in the skies over Libya on March 19, 2011, it represented a major turnaround in U.S. policy. Only nine months earlier, U.S. ambassador Gene Cretz had characterized the regime as a "strategic ally" of the United States due to Libyan cooperation on counterterrorism and nonproliferation issues. . . . Now Libya found itself on the receiving end of conventional U.S. military power for repressing a civilian population agitating for governmental change. Considerations that over the past sixty years might have stayed the hand of an earlier president—fears about regime change leading to a hostile government taking power in an oil-rich and geostrategic Middle Eastern state, or concerns about the potential debilitating costs of intervention—were set aside. And while Muammar el-Qaddafi's distant past as an international renegade and sponsor of terrorism was invoked by Barack Obama, there was little effort to portray twenty-first-century Libya as a looming security threat to the United States. Indeed, given the more recent history of Libyan-American rapprochement, including Qaddafi's active cooperation with the West in the struggle against al-Qaeda, such an attempt would have rung hollow. Instead, the Obama team embraced Qaddafi's treatment of his population as the central rationale for the operation.

This marks a fundamental break with past American emphasis on serious threats to U.S. national security as the prime motivation for action, especially armed intervention. In making the case for war against Saddam Hussein in 2003, the Bush administration highlighted the Iraqi tyrant's abuse of his citizens and his war crimes against Iran and the Kurds. But the case for invading Iraq rested not so much on humanitarian concerns as on displacing a volatile actor who threatened core American security interests. Saddam's suspected depositories of unconventional weapons and his ties to terrorists became the central rallying cries of the proponents of coercive regime change, while humanitarian impulses to liberate an oppressed population were a secondary justification. In the case of Libya, however, no such national-security arguments were seriously proffered in support of the necessity for military action. The Obama administration never suggested that its intervention was designed to redeem any critical national interests; as a matter of fact, outgoing defense secretary Robert Gates loudly and repeatedly proclaimed that there were no vital interests at stake in Libya.

Moreover, the Libya operation took place against a backdrop of regional ferment that already had claimed the political lives of two close U.S. partners, Egypt's Hosni Mubarak and Tunisia's Zine el-Abidine Ben Ali. . . . Saddam Hussein had been an avowed enemy of the United States, which lent a certain geopolitical logic to George W. Bush's invasion. But now Washington was demonstrating a willingness to side "with the street" against regimes that were pro-American. . . . Are we witnessing a subtle paradigm shift, where governments' treatment of their citizens, as opposed to their geopolitical conduct, is more important as a factor for U.S. policy? . . . [H]as America entered a postrealist phase in its foreign policy, where it believes that it is possible to promote U.S. values at minimal cost to U.S. interests?

If these questions can be answered in the affirmative, then America could stand at the threshold of a new foreign-policy era dominated by a twenty-first-century iteration of Wilsonism—the widespread application of American power on behalf of humanitarian ideals even when it risks compromising key interests. . . .

For decades, the specter of an Iran "lost" after the overthrow of the shah has hung over America's Middle East policy. Washington saw how a revolution initially defined by calls for democracy and liberalization ended up ushering in an Islamic Republic bitterly hostile to U.S. interests. . . .

While experiments with democracy could be tolerated in some parts of the world because vital U.S. interests were not at stake, there was no room for error in the Middle East during the Cold War. In January 1980, Jimmy Carter made it explicit that the United States would respond, by military means if necessary, to any "grave threat to the free movement of Middle East oil" to the Western world.

In the years following the rise of Ayatollah Ruhollah Khomeini, a generation of hereditary monarchs and authoritarian presidents throughout the Middle East convinced Washington that, as much as their illiberal regimes might offend American democratic sensibilities, the alternatives would be worse—whether revolutionary regimes more inclined to side with the Soviet Union or Islamists convinced that America was indeed the Great Satan. The "Reagan Corollary" to the so-called "Carter Doctrine," announced in October 1981, more explicitly committed the United States to preserving the internal stability of Western partners in the region, beginning with Saudi Arabia and its ruling House of Saud. . . .

So the Middle Eastern imperatives of geology and geography conspired to disabuse American officialdom of any Wilsonian impulses to push for democracy and human rights. The region's oil was necessary for the free world's economic vitality, and its strategic outposts were needed for the containment of the Soviet and Iranian menaces. The constellation of conservative monarchies and presidential dictatorships was important in subduing the radical clients of the Soviet Union; Saudi Arabia's embrace of the mantle of the defenders of Islam was essential in negating Iran's theocratic rage, while Saddam Hussein proved indispensible in checking Iran's ambitions. And when Hussein himself sought to reorder the region's politics more to his liking with his invasion of Kuwait in 1990, the United States assembled an international coalition that ejected him from his conquest and crushed his military. . . .

The collapse of the Soviet Union in 1991 did not fundamentally alter the trajectory of U.S. policy. Replacing the "Red Menace" was now the "Green Crescent"—fears that militantly anti-Western Islamist groups were on the march. When Algeria's Islamists seemed on the verge of taking control of a key North African state after the results of the first round of elections in 1991, the West acquiesced in the Algerian military's January 1992 decision to cancel further balloting. In Egypt, the most populous state in the Arab world, a terror campaign by Al Gamaa al-Islamiyya to bring down the government by targeting police and foreign tourists reinforced the belief that the regime of Hosni Mubarak must get America's unconditional support or Egypt could be "lost" to a hostile ideology. . . .

[T]he Clinton team focused on isolating the so-called "backlash states" that "seek to advance their agenda through terror, intolerance and coercion." This propelled the United States to prevent the potential resurgence of Iraq, to prolong the policy of coercing Iran, and to continue to isolate bad actors such as Libya and Yemen. All this necessitated partnerships with authoritarian monarchs and presidents and militated against any "third wave of democratization" in the Middle East to complement developments in Eastern Europe and Latin America. But the Clinton administration was also uneasy about accepting the cold dictates of realism that rated interests over values. Hence, continued support for autocrats was justified by arguments that governments in the region lacked the skills to engineer transitions to democracy. That is why the U.S. government, working with private-sector democracy initiatives, began to churn out programs to train judges, publish guides on voting procedures and extend financial support for ngos that pledged their commitment to liberal values (but which commanded very little popular support). Still, one heard little sustained public criticism about Egypt's deformed politics, Saudi support for inflammatory Islam or a Persian Gulf order comfortable with its autocratic ways.

Indeed, when Sheikh Hamad bin Khalifa al-Thani removed his father and took control of Qatar in 1995, this coup d'état was quietly hailed as the possible beginning of a generational transfer of power in the Middle East that would bring younger, more liberal leaders to power. These expectations were heightened when Bashar al-Assad succeeded his father Hafez as president in Syria in 2000 and quickly dropped hints about "reform." This "Damascus Spring," when liberal-leaning discussion groups sprang up in the capital, proved short-lived. But these assumptions helped define a strategy of accepting the status quo for the foreseeable future while training a group of democracy activists and waiting for the next generation of supposedly more liberal leaders to take power.

It was perhaps inevitable that the tragedies of 9/11 would jolt the Washington establishment and call into question the value of America's long-standing relationships with regional despots. Indeed, the argument was soon advanced that the United States was being imperiled by the lack of democracy in the region, which nurtured a dysfunctional political culture serving as a feeding ground for organizations such as al-Qaeda. The approach embraced by previous administrations was explicitly rejected; the United States could not wait for generational change to "drain the swamp" through gradual reform and liberalization. Speaking in Cairo in 2005, Secretary of State Condoleezza Rice bluntly commented that "for sixty years, my country, the United States, pursued stability at the expense of democracy in this region here in the Middle East—and we achieved neither." . . .

In the past, concerns about costs to U.S. interests had always acted as a brake on American interventions unrelated to national interests. Large-scale interventions, particularly using conventional military forces to achieve forcible regime change, were expensive and risky. Reagan's Grenada operation and George H. W. Bush's Panama incursion were the exceptions, not the rule. The limitations of the Cold War also meant that large swaths of the world were effectively "off-limits" for U.S. action. . . .

But the 1999 Kosovo operation marked a critical turning point in how Washington conceptualized the risks and opportunities of intervention. In contrast to the first Gulf War, which occurred with the concurrence of Moscow and Beijing, this action lacked their support. But opposition to military intervention in the former Yugoslavia wasn't sufficient to prevent it from occurring. And the operation took place in a part of Europe that only ten years earlier would have been deemed a no-go area for nato forces. The apparent ease of the campaign—an air war that was nearly casualty free for the allies and produced a capitulation and transition without need of ground forces—also changed the intervention calculus in Washington, displacing the failed legacy of Vietnam with a belief that a "shock and awe" campaign could produce dramatic on-the-ground transformations.

There was near unanimity in Washington that Saddam Hussein, as Scowcroft noted, was

a menace. . . . We will all be better off when he is gone.

But there were very different ways to prosecute the war. An invasion designed to decapitate the regime and ensure that Iraq was disarmed would look very different from a campaign aimed at reconstructing the country in the image of postwar Germany or Japan. So the subsidiary theme of the invasion was that removing Hussein would not be enough; a prospective democratic government in Baghdad would establish an inclusive polity that would be accountable at home and align itself with U.S. security interests abroad, including concluding a peace treaty with Israel and aggressively containing Iran and Syria.

In some of his most eloquent speeches, George W. Bush cast aside the assertion that the Arab masses were ill equipped for self-determination and democratic accountability. But he also cautiously emphasized that America would safeguard its interests while redeeming its ideals. The assumption was that, starting in a reformed Iraq, an empowered Arab citizenry would choose leaders focused on fixing broken economies, addressing institutional decay and the consequences of the region's demographic bulge—rather than striving to thwart U.S. security interests. To be sure, the process would be unsteady and sometimes tumultuous, but in the end large areas of a new Middle East would be governed by popularly elected regimes that would freely choose to join a U.S.-led global order as opposed to plotting against its norms.

The first part of the Iraq invasion fulfilled the promise of Kosovo: Saddam Hussein was removed quickly with few coalition casualties. But securing the democratic peace in Iraq proved far more elusive, reawakening the ghost of Vietnam as more soldiers were killed and wounded and as costs kept rising (to a cumulative total of $1 trillion). And Iraqi elections have overwhelmingly empowered ethnosectarian parties whose leaders did not play out the role scripted for them by Washington. None of the grandiose expectations of American officials were fulfilled. . . .

Elsewhere the picture was similar. The 2005 Cedar Revolution in Lebanon initially brought to the fore a pro-Western coalition of parties but ended up strengthening Hezbollah's hold on the country. The Bush administration's flirtation with the proposition that promoting democracy advances American security in the Middle East came to a sudden end with the results of the January 2006 elections in the Palestinian territories. There was an air of unease about the entire situation, as the radical Islamist group, Hamas, seemed poised to undo the political hegemony of Fatah. In previous decades, Washington might have called for postponement of the elections or acquiesced to their rigging by Fatah to produce a more desirable government. However, the Bush administration had invested so much in its democratic advocacy that it almost had no choice but to watch the ballots being cast and hope for the best.

When it was over, Hamas won seventy-four out of 132 parliamentary seats and claimed the post of premiership. In due course, Palestinian unity would fall apart, and Hamas would confine itself to Gaza, from which it would periodically launch missile attacks against Israel. Not for the first time, the Middle East escaped Washington's preferred template and confronted the United States with choices and decisions that it had hoped to avert.

In the aftermath of the Palestinian elections, the Bush administration's democratic enterprise limped along, devoid of ambition or any clear agenda. Coercive pressure for reforms in places such as Egypt or Saudi Arabia was abandoned. The administration returned to "practical" issues—stabilizing Iraq, resuming the Israeli-Palestinian peace process and attempting to restrain Iran's ambitions. The Bush team fell back on the earlier paradigm of relying on hereditary monarchs and authoritarian presidents to deliver stability in the region. The league of despots proved as useful to the Bush administration as it did to its predecessors. In a sense, realism seemed to have overwhelmed the ideological convulsions of post-9/11 Washington.

The second half of the Bush administration focused its efforts not on forcible regime change but on regime rehabilitation followed by gradual liberalizing amelioration: cultivating liberalizing autocrats who could retain control over the process and keep U.S. security interests intact but who would lay the groundwork for an eventual democratic transition. . . .

The U.S.-Libya relationship became the incubator of this approach after Qaddafi renounced state support for terror activities, ended Libya's embryonic mass-destruction weapons program and aligned Libya with Western interests. This laid the basis for Tripoli's rapprochement with Washington, a policy that enjoyed strong bipartisan support in the U.S. Congress. . . .

In dealing with hereditary politics in the Middle East, the United States held out hope that the Taiwan scenario (the passage of power from an autocratic father to a more liberalizing son) might be duplicated in the region—especially when it came to two sons, Seif al-Islam el-Qaddafi and Gamal Mubarak, who were seen as liberalizing "heirs-in-waiting" to take over Libya and Egypt from their elderly fathers. Having younger, Western-educated sons take control from aging parents seemed the best way to encourage democratization in the Middle East.

For its first two years, the Obama administration continued to adhere to this script. Then a university-educated fruit seller in Tunisia immolated himself, and everything changed.

The Arab Spring was bound to present the United States with stark choices. Suddenly a regional revolt in the name of democracy and accountability confronted pliable American allies who sought to cloak their repressive tendencies in the name of resisting Islamic radicalism. Mubarak, Qaddafi and others threatened by revolts from below had assumed that close cooperation with America's security agenda for the Middle East would buy their regimes a certain degree of immunity from U.S. criticism and pressure. They were wrong.

Initially, many expected the Obama team to embrace the two-track approach undertaken by earlier administrations in other parts of the world, particularly in East Asia during the 1980s: up-front backing for an embattled leader to take whatever steps were needed to secure his regime and restore order with a promise to initiate reforms over the long term. . . . But when Obama's special envoy to Egypt, Frank Wisner, expressed support for the old approach, his remarks were repudiated in Washington, and Obama abruptly changed course to push for Mubarak's complete and immediate removal.

Realist voices in the administration raised all the traditional cautionary flags. But they were brushed aside. In Egypt, the notion that any post-Mubarak government would be less sensitive to core U.S. interests was seen as a condition that Washington would have to live with; in earlier times it was considered an eventuality to be crushed. The concerns that Libya might disintegrate as a nation-state, facilitating the rise of Islamist militants in ungoverned spaces, were set aside for the benefit of preventing a feared humanitarian crisis. Certainly, by the end of 2011, political figures and movements that the United States worked hard for decades to keep away from the levers of power—the Muslim Brotherhood in Egypt, members of the Libyan Islamic Fighting Group, Libyan Islamists, Rachid al-Ghannouchi in Tunisia—were all playing roles in the postdictator political arena. . . .

Undoubtedly the death of Osama bin Laden, the successful elimination of other key al-Qaeda leaders and operatives, and the belief that al-Qaeda was "losing its struggle for relevance" in the region, to quote from Obama's May 2011 address at the State Department, contributed to the assessment that backing revolutionary ferment in the Arab world would not automatically hand power over to an implacable foe of the United States. Obama has expressed his optimism that successor regimes will not seek to alter fundamentally their countries' ongoing cooperation with the United States, particularly in continuing efforts to combat terrorism and broker a lasting Middle East peace settlement. . . . But it remains a big question whether Islamists will undergo a democratic transformation and eventually create moderate governments. . . .

Indeed, there has been a real shift in American attitudes, a willingness to take the risks of losing short-term security advantages in favor of encouraging long-term societal change. To be sure, such a paradigm shift is not categorical or complete. America's foreign policy is never without its inconsistencies and contradictions. Washington continues to cater to Saudi sensibilities, and it looked askance as Riyadh marched into Bahrain to buttress its Sunni satrap through continued repression of the majority Shia population. The fact that the Gulf monarchies demonstrated limited appetite for viable political reforms has not elicited loud American objections. The need for Gulf oil and military bases and the common cause of contain-

ing a recalcitrant Iran continue to overwhelm Washington's democratic penchants . Nonetheless, a new tendency has fractured America's long-held realism in the Middle East. How these states conduct their internal affairs and treat their citizens will be taken into account as the United States determines its alliances, shifts its loyalties and considers its interests. No country has ever conducted its policy solely on the basis of humanitarian considerations, but, given the events of the past year, they are poised to exercise more influence over decision making than ever before.

A foreign-policy doctrine must be suited for its times, tailored to exploit available opportunities, and flexible enough to take advantage of sudden and subtle shifts in the international system. Many critics allege that realism is hardly suitable for the changing regional landscape confronting Washington today, that America needs a foreign policy based on values, and that embracing and encouraging rapid political change throughout the Middle East is both necessary and desirable.

But what is to be done if change must be nudged or forced? The 2003 Iraq War vindicated many realist objections, but the apparent success of the 2011 Libya operation—which ended up deposing Qaddafi from power without the loss of a single American life and without any serious rupture in U.S. relations with other powers—begs the question as to whether the Obama administration wants to enter a postrealist era where the old trade-offs between pursuing American ideals and securing U.S. interests are no longer relevant.

In the past, debates over the advisability of intervention were driven by two considerations: the potential cost of the proposed action and the likelihood that it would precipitate a clash with another major power. . . . The Arab Spring could offer the United States a template for future limited interventions that could uphold American values without exacting much cost in return.

One of the factors that may be driving the administration's confidence that a new era of interventionism is warranted comes from the reality that so-called "rogue regimes" around the world are under a new set of pressures. In the 1990s, regimes from Iran to Cuba found relief from unilateral U.S. sanctions and pressure by turning to European states that were willing to continue engagement. The Europeans embraced a policy of critical dialogue, which stressed that through diplomatic discussions and economic incentives rogue regimes could be persuaded to modify their behavior. The proponents of such an outlook argued that even rogue states contain factions of moderates and pragmatists that serve as potential interlocutors. From this perspective, an inclusive approach was designed to empower the pragmatists and diminish the standing of the hard-liners. Clever despots could exploit the divergence between the United States and Europe, as punitive U.S. measures were frequently undermined by a European policy of commerce and dialogue. Meanwhile, U.S. pressure on Europe, manifested primarily through the imposition of secondary sanctions on European firms doing business in places such as Tehran and Havana, often backfired.

During the first years of the Bush administration, transatlantic ties were aggravated over a whole host of issues, ranging from climate change to the Iraq invasion. In particular, the United States and several of its key allies in Europe, especially Germany and France, saw the Middle East from vastly different perspectives. Yet during the latter part of the Bush presidency, the first signs of convergence began to emerge. Once the allies put the divisive issue of Iraq behind them, they found much common ground. Washington accepted the need for international coalitions to deal with regional problems, and a new generation of European leaders such as France's Nicolas Sarkozy began to see that financial incentives and soothing words were unlikely to temper hardened ideologues.

What the Arab Spring has demonstrated is that many autocratic regimes around the world are particularly vulnerable to protest movements that originate in concerns about poor economic prospects. The despots of anemic economies cannot pay off their revolting masses if sanctions prevent them from selling their commodities or raising loans once easily available from Paris or London. Over the last several years, European governments began to place a greater emphasis on values over business interests, imposing stronger economic sanctions on illiberal regimes even when European economic interests could be negatively affected. While traditional concerns of statecraft—among them access to energy and security cooperation—remain key motives for both American and European policy in the Middle East, the question of how governments in the region treat their populations is gaining traction as a point which must be given equal consideration. The emergence of a broad transatlantic consensus makes it harder for other power centers to wholeheartedly oppose all interventions.

Thus, there is a growing perception that concerted opposition to any new humanitarian interventions will be limited. Certainly, while other great power ssuch as China, India or Russia may not join the effort, just as they abstained from the Security Council vote that authorized the Libya no-fly zone, it is not entirely clear that Beijing, New Delhi or Moscow would risk frayed relations with the West in order to prevent such operations from going forward in areas of the world where they do not have fundamental interests. This outlook may be summarized as: let the Western countries expend their blood and treasure if they wish. A Beijing, for instance, that still remains preoccupied with domestic economic growth and stability will not be handing out blanket security commitments to authoritarian governments around the world with any sort of guarantee that is equivalent to nato's famed Article 5. Of course, there will be exceptions involving countries in their immediate neighborhood. Russia, for example, might assent to a nato mission in Libya but be much more hostile to an intervention in Central Asia seeking to displace a pro-Russian government.

But what of the times when Russian and Chinese opposition in the Security Council has seemingly torpedoed calls for intervention or otherwise watered down its provisions? To some extent, this has served as a convenient excuse when the Western powers themselves have been unsure or unwilling to get involved, such as in Darfur. But as we have seen in recent years, when the United States is particularly committed to action, these countries begin to give ground, allowing for an opening wedge to emerge that could serve as justification for intervention.

In addition, China has discovered that it can retain and perhaps expand its influence even after an intervention creates a supposedly "pro-Western" government. China has much greater access to the Iraqi oil industry in the wake of the U.S. invasion than it did during the days of Saddam Hussein. Beijing counts on the attractiveness of its terms for economic engagement; governments unable or unwilling to meet Western criteria have found in China an alternative partner for economic development. An interesting test will be whether, despite early criticisms of Beijing for its lack of support for intervention against Qaddafi, a new Libyan government ends up turning to China for the same reason that has led so many other states in Africa and Latin America to do so in the recent past: the country's no-strings-attached aid and development policies. If this happens, it would further diminish China's appetite for trying to directly challenge U.S. interventions around the world.

Finally, there is the ongoing revolution in military affairs—particularly the emergence of new technologies such as unmanned drones and advances in cyberwarfare—that hold out the promise of low-cost interventions that do not require a large conventional force. The Libya operation is estimated to have cost only $1 billion, a trifle compared to what has been spent in Iraq and Afghanistan. The Obama national-security team has embraced Libya as a useful example in these times of budget austerity for facilitating U.S. values and interests around the world. . . .

Instead of relying upon large concentrations of ground forces to deliver knockout blows, the belief is that a combination of air power and special-forces units allows for small, light-footprint, rapid-strike missions that take out an opposing regime.

If, in order to alleviate concerns about costs, the United States in the future will be forgoing large-scale interventions in favor of covert actions and small-scale special military operations, then it suggests that a postrealist approach will focus on taking steps that are likely to produce a satisfactory outcome rather than guarantee an optimal one.

If the current situation holds—that no durable anti-American coalition is emerging to put checks on the exercise of U.S. power around the globe—then the postrealist view may gain greater traction. The strictures of the Cold War imposed a certain discipline on the process of deciding whether and when to intervene militarily in a given conflict. Intervention in some states was ruled out for reasons of geography—in the case of close proximity to the Soviet Union, for instance. Security considerations governed other situations. There was a reluctance to take action against a reasonably pro-Western, authoritarian regime for fear that it might be replaced by a pro-Soviet successor. None of these considerations is weighing on the minds of policy makers today.

Instead, if an intervention can be sold to policy makers as quick and inexpensive, with little likelihood that other major powers will significantly raise the cost of action, the propensity for intervention rises. In addition, if policy makers believe that the successor government is likely to be no worse than, or even better than, the status quo, then the path to intervention is cleared. After laboring for several years to wind down the Bush legacy in international affairs, the Obama team may be prepared to start implementing this new approach.

NIKOLAS K. GVOSDEV is a professor of national security studies at the U.S. Naval War College. Previously, he was the senior editor of *The National Interest* and a senior fellow for strategic studies at The Nixon Center.

RAY TAKEYH is a senior fellow for Middle Eastern studies at the Council on Foreign Relations and an adjunct professor at the Center for Security Studies at Georgetown University.

John J. Mearsheimer  **NO**

Imperial by Design

In the first years after the Cold War ended, many Americans had a profound sense of optimism about the future of international politics. . . .

The basis of all this good feeling was laid out at the time in two famous articles by prominent neoconservatives. In 1989, Francis Fukuyama argued in "The End of History?" that Western liberal democracy had won a decisive victory over communism and fascism and should be seen as the "final form of human government."[1] One consequence of this "ideological evolution," he argued, was that large-scale conflict between the great powers was "passing from the scene," although "the vast bulk of the Third World remains very much mired in history, and will be a terrain of conflict for many years to come." Nevertheless, liberal democracy and peace would eventually come to the Third World as well, because the sands of time were pushing inexorably in that direction.

One year later, Charles Krauthammer emphasized in "The Unipolar Moment" that the United States had emerged from the Cold War as by far the most powerful country on the planet.[2] He urged American leaders not to be reticent about using that power "to lead a unipolar world, unashamedly laying down the rules of world order and being prepared to enforce them." Krauthammer's advice fit neatly with Fukuyama's vision of the future: the United States should take the lead in bringing democracy to less developed countries the world over. . . .

U.S. grand strategy has followed this basic prescription for the past twenty years, mainly because most policy makers inside the Beltway have agreed with the thrust of Fukuyama's and Krauthammer's early analyses.

The results, however, have been disastrous. The United States has been at war for a startling two out of every three years since 1989, and there is no end in sight. . . .

[T]he United States is now engaged in protracted wars in Afghanistan and Iraq that have so far cost well over a trillion dollars and resulted in around forty-seven thousand American casualties. The pain and suffering inflicted on Iraq has been enormous. Since the war began in March 2003, more than one hundred thousand Iraqi civilians have been killed, roughly 2 million Iraqis have left the country and 1.7 million more have been internally displaced. Moreover, the American military is not going to win either one of these conflicts. . . .

The unpleasant truth is that the United States is in a world of trouble today on the foreign-policy front, and this state of affairs is only likely to get worse in the next few years, as Afghanistan and Iraq unravel and the blame game escalates to poisonous levels. . . .

This regrettable situation raises the obvious questions of what went wrong? And can America right its course? . . .

Washington has always had a choice in how to approach grand strategy. One popular option among some libertarians is *isolationism*. This approach is based on the assumption that there is no region outside the Western Hemisphere that is strategically important enough to justify expending American blood and treasure. Isolationists believe that the United States is remarkably secure because it is separated from all of the world's great powers by two giant moats—the Atlantic and Pacific Oceans—and on top of that it has had nuclear weapons—the ultimate deterrent—since 1945. . . . American policy makers have come to believe the country should be militarily involved on the world stage. Yet though no mainstream politician would dare advocate isolationism at this point, the rationale for this grand strategy shows just how safe the United States is. This means, among other things, that it will always be a challenge to motivate the U.S. public to want to run the world and especially to fight wars of choice in distant places.

Offshore balancing, which was America's traditional grand strategy for most of its history, is but another option. Predicated on the belief that there are three regions of the world that are strategically important to the United States—Europe, Northeast Asia and the Persian Gulf—it sees the United States' principle goal as making sure no country dominates any of these areas as it dominates the Western Hemisphere. This is to ensure that dangerous rivals in other regions are forced to concentrate their attention on great powers in their own backyards rather than be free to interfere in America's. The best way to achieve that end is to rely on local powers to counter aspiring regional hegemons and otherwise keep U.S. military forces over the horizon. But if that proves impossible, American troops come from offshore to help do the job, and then leave once the potential hegemon is checked.

Selective engagement also assumes that Europe, Northeast Asia and the Persian Gulf are the only areas of the world where the United States should be willing to deploy its military might. It is a more ambitious strategy than offshore balancing in that it calls for permanently stationing U.S. troops in those regions to help maintain peace. For selective engagers, it is not enough just to thwart aspiring

Mearsheimer, John J. From *The National Interest*, January/February 2011, pp. 16–34. Copyright © 2011 by National Interest. Reprinted by permission.

hegemons. It is also necessary to prevent war in those key regions, either because upheaval will damage our economy or because we will eventually get dragged into the fight in any case. . . .

The root cause of America's troubles is that it adopted a flawed grand strategy after the Cold War. From the Clinton administration on, the United States rejected all these other avenues, instead pursuing *global dominance*, or what might alternatively be called global hegemony, which was not just doomed to fail, but likely to backfire in dangerous ways if it relied too heavily on military force to achieve its ambitious agenda.

Global dominance has two broad objectives: maintaining American primacy, which means making sure that the United States remains the most powerful state in the international system; and spreading democracy across the globe, in effect, making the world over in America's image. The underlying belief is that new liberal democracies will be peacefully inclined and pro-American, so the more the better. . . . With global dominance, no serious attempt is made to prioritize U.S. interests, because they are virtually limitless.

This grand strategy is "imperial" at its core; its proponents believe that the United States has the right as well as the responsibility to interfere in the politics of other countries. One would think that such arrogance might alienate other states, but most American policy makers of the early nineties and beyond were confident that would not happen, instead believing that other countries—save for so-called rogue states like Iran and North Korea—would see the United States as a benign hegemon serving their own interests.

There is, however, an important disagreement among global dominators about how best to achieve their strategy's goals. On one side are the neoconservatives, who believe that the United States can rely heavily on armed force to dominate and transform the globe, and that it can usually act unilaterally because American power is so great. Indeed, they tend to be openly contemptuous of Washington's traditional allies as well as international institutions. . . . Neoconservatives see spreading democracy as a relatively easy task. For them, the key to success is removing the reigning tyrant; once that is done, there is little need to engage in protracted nation building.

On the other side are the liberal imperialists, who are certainly willing to use the American military to do social engineering. But they are less confident than the neoconservatives about what can be achieved with force alone. Therefore, liberal imperialists believe that running the world requires the United States to work closely with allies and international institutions. Although they think that democracy has widespread appeal, liberal imperialists are usually less sanguine than the neoconservatives about the ease of exporting it to other states. . . .

Bill Clinton was the first president to govern exclusively in the post–Cold War world, and his administration pursued global dominance from start to finish. Yet Clinton's foreign-policy team was comprised of liberal imperialists; so, although the president and his lieutenants made clear that they were bent on ruling the world . . . they employed military force reluctantly and prudently. They may have been gung ho about pushing the unipolar moment onward and upward, but for all their enthusiasm, even these democracy promoters soon saw that nation building was no easy task. . . .

By early 1998, the neoconservatives were pressuring Clinton to use military force to remove Saddam Hussein. The president endorsed the long-term goal of ousting the Iraqi leader, but he refused to go to war to make that happen. The United States under Bill Clinton was, as Richard Haass put it, a "reluctant sheriff." . . .

[G]iven the American public's natural reluctance to engage in foreign adventures, by the 2000 presidential campaign, many were unhappy with even this cautious liberal imperialism. George W. Bush tried to capitalize on this sentiment by criticizing Clinton's foreign policy as overzealous—and as it turns out, ironically, especially for doing too much nation building. The Republican candidate called for the United States to scale back its goals and concentrate on reinvigorating its traditional Cold War alliances. The main threat facing the United States, he argued, was a rising China; terrorism was paid little attention. In effect, Bush was calling for a grand strategy of selective engagement. Not surprisingly, his opponent, Vice President Al Gore, called for pursuing global dominance, albeit in a multilateral guise.

When Bush won, it appeared that the United States was about to adopt a less ambitious grand strategy. But that did not happen because the new Bush administration drastically altered its approach to the world after 9/11.

There was never any question that Washington would treat terrorism as its main threat after that horrific day. . . . Over the course of the next year, Bush turned away from selective engagement and embraced global dominance. Unlike his predecessor in the White House, however, he adopted the neoconservative formula for ruling the world. And that meant relying primarily on the unilateral use of American military force. From the early days of Afghanistan onward, America was to enter the age of the "Bush Doctrine," which was all about using the U.S. military to bring about regime change across the Muslim and Arab world. . . .

By pursuing this extraordinary scheme to transform an entire region at the point of a gun, President Bush adopted a radical grand strategy that has no parallel in American history. It was also a dismal failure. . . .

With the attacks on the World Trade Center and the Pentagon, the Bush administration all of a sudden was forced to think seriously about terrorism. Unfortunately, the president . . . misread what the country was dealing with in two important ways: greatly exaggerating the threat's severity, and failing to understand why al-Qaeda was so enraged at the United States. These mistakes led the administration to adopt policies that made the problem worse, not better.

In the aftermath of 9/11, terrorism was described as an existential threat. President Bush emphasized that virtually every terrorist group on the planet—including those that had no beef with Washington—was our enemy and had to be eliminated if we hoped to win what became known as the global war on terror (gwot). The administration also maintained that states like Iran, Iraq and Syria were not only actively supporting terrorist organizations but were also likely to provide terrorists with weapons of mass destruction (wmd). Thus, it was imperative for the United States to target these rogue states if it hoped to win the gwot. . . . Indeed, Bush said that any country which "continues to harbor or support terrorism will be regarded by the United States as a hostile regime." . . .

This assessment of America's terrorism problem was flawed on every count. It was threat inflation of the highest order. It made no sense to declare war against groups that were not trying to harm the United States. . . . In addition, there was no alliance between the so-called rogue states and al-Qaeda. In fact, Iran and Syria cooperated with Washington after 9/11 to help quash Osama bin Laden and his cohorts. Although the Bush administration and the neoconservatives repeatedly asserted that there was a genuine connection between Saddam Hussein and al-Qaeda, they never produced evidence to back up their claim for the simple reason that it did not exist.

The fact is that states have strong incentives to distrust terrorist groups, in part because they might turn on them someday, but also because countries cannot control what terrorist organizations do, and they may do something that gets their patrons into serious trouble. This is why there is hardly any chance that a rogue state will give a nuclear weapon to terrorists. That regime's leaders could never be sure that they would not be blamed and punished for a terrorist group's actions. Nor could they be certain that the United States or Israel would not incinerate them if either country merely suspected that they had provided terrorists with the ability to carry out a wmd attack. A nuclear handoff, therefore, is not a serious threat. . . .

This conspicuous threat inflation has hurt the American effort to neutralize al-Qaeda. By foolishly widening the scope of the terrorism problem, Washington has ended up picking fights with terrorist groups and countries that otherwise had no interest in attacking the United States, and in some cases were willing to help us thwart al-Qaeda. Enlarging the target set has also led American policy makers to take their eyes off our main adversary. Furthermore, defining the terrorist threat so broadly . . . has led U.S. leaders to wage war all around the globe and to think of this struggle as lasting for generations. This is exactly the wrong formula for dealing with our terrorism problem. We should instead focus our attention wholly on al-Qaeda and any other group that targets the United States, and we should treat the threat as a law-enforcement problem rather than a military one that requires us to engage in largescale wars the world over. . . .

To deal effectively with terrorism, it is imperative to understand what motivates al-Qaeda to target the United States in the first place. One also wants to know why large numbers of people in the Arab and Muslim world are so angry with America that they support, or at least sympathize with, these types of terrorist groups. Simply put, why do they hate us?

There are two possible answers to this question. One possibility is that al-Qaeda and its supporters loathe us because of who we are; in other words, this is a clash of civilizations that has arisen because these extremists hate Western values in general and liberal democracy in particular. Alternatively, these groups may hate us because they are furious with our Middle East policies. There is an abundance of survey data and anecdotal evidence that shows the second answer is the right one. Anger and hatred toward the United States among Arabs and Muslims is largely driven by Washington's policies, not by any deep-seated antipathy toward the West.[3] The policies that have generated the most anti-Americanism include Washington's support for Israel's treatment of the Palestinians; the presence of American troops in Saudi Arabia after the 1991 Gulf War; U.S. support for repressive regimes in countries like Egypt; American sanctions on Baghdad after the First Gulf War . . .; and the U.S. invasion and occupation of Iraq. . . .

Given American military might and the belief that democracy was sweeping the globe, the Bush administration and its supporters reasoned that it would be relatively easy to remake the Arab and Muslim world in America's image. They were wrong, of course, for the Bush administration failed to understand the limits of what American military power could do to transform the Middle East.

The faulty assumption that America could perform social engineering through its indomitable military might . . . found its roots in Afghanistan.

By December 2001, it appeared that the U.S. military had won a quick and stunning victory against the Taliban and installed a friendly regime in Kabul that would be able to govern the country effectively for the foreseeable future. Very importantly, the war was won with a combination of American airpower, local allies and small Special Forces units. How easy it seemed to deliver that country its freedom. There was no need for a large-scale invasion, so when the fighting ended, the United States did not look like an occupier. Nor did it seem likely to become one, because Hamid Karzai was expected to keep order in Afghanistan without much U.S. help.

The perception of a stunning triumph in Afghanistan was significant because leaders rarely initiate wars unless they think that they can win quick and decisive victories. The prospect of fighting a protracted conflict makes policy makers gun-shy, not just because the costs are invariably high, but also because it is hard to tell how long wars will come to an end. But by early 2002, it seemed that the United States had found a blueprint for winning wars in the developing world quickly and decisively, thus eliminating the need for a protracted occupation. It appeared that the American military could exit a country soon after toppling its regime and installing a new leader, and move on to the next target. It looked like the neoconservatives had been vindicated. . . .

And with this hubris firmly in place, America attacked Iraq on March 19, 2003. Within a few months, it looked like the "Afghan model" had proved its worth again. Saddam was in hiding and President Bush landed on the USS *Abraham Lincoln* with a big banner in the background that announced: "Mission Accomplished." . . .

It all turned out to be a mirage, of course, as Iraq quickly became a deadly quagmire with Afghanistan following suit a few years later.

Indeed, what initially appeared to be a dazzling victory in Afghanistan was not. There was little chance that the United States would avoid a protracted occupation, since we faced two insurmountable problems. While it was relatively easy to topple the Taliban from power, it was not possible for the American military and its allies to decisively defeat that foe. When cornered and facing imminent destruction, Taliban fighters melted away into the countryside or across the border into Pakistan, where they could regroup and eventually come back to fight another day. . . .

Furthermore, the Karzai government was doomed to fail, not just because its leader was put in power by Washington, and not just because Afghanistan has always had a weak central government, but also because Karzai and his associates are incompetent and corrupt. This meant that there would be no central authority to govern the country and check the Taliban when it came back to life. And that meant the United States would have to do the heavy lifting. American troops would have to occupy the country and fight the Taliban, and they would have to do so in support of a fragile government with little legitimacy outside of Kabul. . . .

If more evidence is needed that the "Afghan model" does not work as advertised, Iraq provides it. . . . Not only did Baghdad have few well-established political institutions and a weak civil society, the removal of Saddam was certain to unleash powerful centrifugal forces that would lead to a bloody civil war in the absence of a large American presence. In particular, the politically strong Sunnis were sure to resist losing power to the more numerous Shia, who would benefit the most from the U.S. invasion. There were also profound differences among various Shia groups, and the Kurds did not even want to be ruled by Baghdad. . . . All of this meant that a protracted American occupation would be necessary to keep the country from tearing itself apart. . . .

There is no question that it is possible to defeat an insurgency, but it is almost never quick or easy, and there is no single formula for success. As [*U.S Army Field Manual 3–24*] (*FM 3–24*) warns, "Political and military leaders and planners should never underestimate its scale and complexity." . . . What makes the enterprise so difficult is that

victory usually . . . demands nation building . . . because it is essential to fix the political and social problems that caused the insurgency in the first place; otherwise, it is likely to spring back to life. So even if it was a sure bet that the United States could succeed at counterinsurgency with the right people and doctrine, it would still take many years to achieve decisive results. . . .

It is hard to believe that any policy maker or student of international affairs could have believed that democracy would spring forth quickly and easily once tyrants like Saddam Hussein were toppled. After all, it is clear from the historical record that imposing democracy on another country is an especially difficult task that usually fails.[4]

The United States in particular has a rich history of trying and failing to impose democracy on other countries. New York University professors Bruce Bueno de Mesquita and George Downs report in the *Los Angeles Times* that:

> Between World War II and the present, the United States intervened more than 35 times in developing countries around the world. . . . In only one case—Colombia after the American decision in 1989 to engage in the war on drugs—did a full-fledged, stable democracy . . . emerge within 10 years. That's a success rate of less than 3%.

. . . None of this is to say that it is impossible for the United States to impose democracy abroad. But successes are the exception rather than the rule, and as is the case with democratization in general, externally led attempts to implant such a governing structure usually occur in countries with a particular set of internal characteristics.

It helps greatly if the target state has high levels of ethnic and religious homogeneity, a strong central government, reasonably high levels of prosperity and some experience with democracy. The cases of post–World War II Germany and Japan, which are often held up as evidence that the United States can export democracy to the Middle East, fit these criteria. But those examples are highly unusual, which is why the United States has failed so often in its freedom-spreading quest. . . .

The United States needs a new grand strategy. Global dominance is a prescription for endless trouble—especially in its neoconservative variant. Unfortunately, the Obama administration is populated from top to bottom with liberal imperialists who remain committed to trying to govern the world, albeit with less emphasis on big-stick diplomacy and more emphasis on working with allies and international institutions. . . .

The Obama team's thinking was clearly laid out in Secretary of State Hillary Clinton's speech to the Council on Foreign Relations this past September. . . . Clinton said:

> I think the world is counting on us today as it has in the past. When old adversaries need an honest broker or fundamental freedoms need a champion, people turn to us. When the earth shakes

or rivers overflow their banks, when pandemics rage or simmering tensions burst into violence, the world looks to us. . . .

President Obama is making a serious mistake heading down this road. He should instead return to the grand strategy of offshore balancing, which has served this country well for most of its history and offers the best formula for dealing with the threats facing America. . . .

In general terms, the United States should concentrate on making sure that no state dominates Northeast Asia, Europe or the Persian Gulf, and that it remains the world's only regional hegemon. This is the best way to ensure American primacy. We should build a robust military to intervene in those areas, but it should be stationed offshore or back in the United States. In the event a potential hegemon comes on the scene in one of those regions, Washington should rely on local forces to counter it and only come onshore to join the fight when it appears that they cannot do the job themselves. Once the potential hegemon is checked, American troops should go back over the horizon.

Offshore balancing does not mean that the United States should ignore the rest of the world. But it should maintain a substantially lower profile outside of Northeast Asia, Europe and the Gulf, and it should rely on diplomacy and economic statecraft, not military force, to protect its interests in areas of little strategic importance. Washington should also get out of the business of trying to spread democracy around the globe, and more generally acting as if we have the right and the responsibility to interfere in the domestic politics of other countries. . . .

Washington relied on Iraq to contain Iran during the 1980s, and kept the rapid-deployment force—which was built to intervene in the Gulf if the local balance of power collapsed—at the ready should it be needed. This was smart policy.

After Iraq invaded Kuwait in August 1990, the United States, once again acting as an offshore balancer, moved large numbers of troops into Saudi Arabia to liberate Kuwait. After the war was won and victory was consolidated, those troops should have been pulled out of the region. But that did not happen. Rather, Bill Clinton adopted a policy of dual containment—checking both Iran and Iraq instead of letting them check one another. And lest we forget, the resulting presence of U.S. forces in Saudi Arabia was one of the main reasons that Osama bin Laden declared war on the United States. The Bush administration simply made a bad situation even worse.

Sending the U.S. military into countries in the Arab and Muslim world is helping to cause our terrorism problem, not solve it. The best way to fix this situation is to . . . pull all American troops out of Afghanistan and Iraq, then deploy them over the horizon as part of an offshore-balancing strategy. To be sure, the terrorist challenge

would not completely disappear if the United States went back to offshore balancing, but it would be an important step forward. . . .

Offshore balancing costs considerably less money than does global dominance, allowing America to better prepare for the true threats it faces. This is in good part because this strategy avoids occupying and governing countries in the developing world and therefore does not require large armies trained for counterinsurgency. Global dominators naturally think that the United States is destined to fight more wars like Afghanistan and Iraq, making it essential that we do counterinsurgency right the next time. This is foolish thinking, as both of those undertakings were unnecessary and unwinnable. Washington should go to great lengths to avoid similar future conflicts, which would allow for sharp reductions in the size of the army and marine corps. . . .

The overarching goal, however, should be to take a big slice out of the defense budget to help reduce our soaring deficit and pay for important domestic programs. Offshore balancing is simply the best grand strategy for dealing with al-Qaeda. . . .

It is time for the United States to show greater restraint and deal with the threats it faces in smarter and more discerning ways. That means putting an end to America's pursuit of global dominance and going back to the time-honored strategy of offshore balancing.

Notes

1. Francis Fukuyama, "The End of History?" *The National Interest* (Summer 1989).
2. Charles Krauthammer, "The Unipolar Moment," *Foreign Affairs* 70, no. 1 (1990/1991).
3. Office of the Under Secretary of Defense for Acquisition, Technology, and Logistics, *Report of the Defense Science Board Task Force on Strategic Communication* (Washington, DC: Government Printing Office, September 2004); John Zogby and James Zogby, "Impressions of America 2004: How Arabs View America; How Arabs Learn about America" (Washington, DC: Zogby International, 2004).
4. Andrew Enterline and J. Michael Greig, "The History of Imposed Democracy and the Future of Iraq and Afghanistan," *Foreign Policy Analysis* 4, no. 4 (October 2008). In an examination of forty-three cases of imposed democratic regimes between 1800 and 1994, it was found that 63 percent failed.

JOHN J. MEARSHEIMER is the R. Wendell Harrison Distinguished Service Professor of Political Science and the co-director of the program on international security policy at the University of Chicago.

EXPLORING THE ISSUE

Should the United States Intervene Militarily in the Absence of a Direct Threat to U.S. National Interests?

Critical Thinking and Reflection

1. Is there a tension between the preservation of American power and the promotion of American values? If so, how should these imperatives be balanced?
2. Is humanitarian intervention in America's national interest? Explain.
3. What costs are acceptable when the United States undertakes a military intervention that does not directly increase U.S. security or economic prosperity?
4. Has there been a fundamental change in the international environment such that U.S. military intervention for humanitarian purposes is more appropriate now than it has been in the past?

Is There Common Ground?

Views about military intervention are not cleanly demarcated across the political spectrum in the United States. Both Republicans and Democrats claim that their policies are "realistic," whether or not they agree with realist international relations theory. There are also different schools of thought within each party. For example, the Republican Party includes neoconservatives who argue that the United States should use military power to foster democratic development in other countries. However, the Republican Party also includes libertarian thinkers, some of whom come close to embracing isolationism and tend to argue against the use of the U.S. armed forces abroad unless absolutely necessary. The Democratic Party contains similar divisions, with some members more willing to embrace military interventions for humanitarian purposes and others who are more skeptical of the utility of force.

The articles presented here suggest that debates over future American military interventions will be as much about cost as they are about values. While some proponents of intervention will support their arguments based on humanitarian grounds, the expenses—economic, human, and reputational—of the conflicts in Iraq and Afghanistan will likely temper enthusiasm for future interventions that are not seen to directly affect American national interests. However, if an administration believes that the costs of intervening in a conflict will be relatively low, it remains possible that the United States will intervene militarily even when the conflict does not pose a major threat to U.S. national interests.

It is clear that costs were relevant to President Barack Obama when he decided to support military intervention in Libya with participation by the U.S. armed forces. However, the Libyan operation also shows that both the costs and benefits associated with such operations are likely to remain unpredictable. This was recently made evident once again on September 11, 2012, when an Al-Qaeda affiliated group attacked the American Consulate in Benghazi, Libya, and killed the U.S. ambassador and three other embassy personnel. This incident inevitably calls into question the wisdom of the international community's military intervention, since it casts additional doubt on whether Libya's future will be better than its past. Lingering instability in Libya also feeds into hesitation to embark on military intervention in other cases of deadly conflict. As of October 2012, for example, there have been many more deaths in Syria's internal conflict than there had been in Libya when the no-fly zone was established, yet the United Nations has been beset with gridlock as it tries to prevent a humanitarian crisis there. Debates over the wisdom and effectiveness of military interventions for humanitarian purposes are likely to continue for some time to come.

Additional Resources

Finnemore, Martha. "Constructing Norms of Humanitarian Intervention." In *The Culture of National Security: Norms and Identity in World Politics.* Ed. Peter J. Katzenstein, pp. 153–185. New York: Columbia University Press, 1996.

Mearsheimer, John. *The Tragedy of Great Power Politics.* New York: W.W. Norton, 2001.

In this book, John Mearsheimer puts forward the theoretical argument for "offensive realism," which suggests that there is no natural limit to a state's pursuit of power. Mearsheimer concludes that the United States should focus its attention on the possible rise of China in Asia.

Should the United States Intervene Militarily in the Absence of a Direct Threat to U.S. National Interests? by Nielsen and Handler

225

Morgenthau, Hans J. *Politics among Nations: The Struggle for Power and Peace.* Eds. Kenneth W. Thompson and W. David Clinton, 7th Ed. New York: McGraw-Hill, 2006 [1948].

Weinberger, Caspar. "The Uses of Military Power," *Defense '85* (January 1985): 2–11.

Internet References . . .

Foreign Policy

"View From the Top: Nine of the World's Top International Relations Scholars Weigh in on the Ivory Tower Survey", is available at this link.

www.foreignpolicy.com/articles/2012/01/03/view_from_the_top?page=0,2

The Wall Street Journal

Jon Hilsenrath's "Gates Says Libya Not Vital National Interest" is available at this link.

http://online.wsj.com/article/SB10001424052748704308904576226704261420430.html

Royal United States Services Institute

This think tank report suggests the Libyan intervention is unlikely to be a model for future interventions. The authors argue that the peculiarities of the political circumstances surrounding the Libyan campaign are unlikely to be replicated or have implications for the concept of Responsibility to Protect.

www.rusi.org/downloads/assets/WHR_1-12.pdf

The Whitehouse.gov Website

The address to the nation by President Barack H. Obama highlights the President's remarks on Libya.

www.whitehouse.gov/photos-and-video/video/2011/03/28/president-obama-s-speech-libya#transcript

United Nations

This web page outlines discussions and outcomes of the 2005 United Nations General Assembly World Summit.

www.un.org/en/preventgenocide/adviser/pdf/World%20Summit%20Outcome%20Document.pdf#page=30

United Nations

This website focuses on the Security Council Resolutions expressed within the United Nations Organization.

www.un.org/Docs/sc/unsc_resolutions11.htm

Yale Law School

Woodrow Wilson's "The Fourteen Points" address to U.S. Congress, in 1918, can be found here within The Avalon Project collection.

http://avalon.law.yale.edu/20th_century/wilson14.asp

Selected, Edited, and with Issue Framing Material by:
Suzanne Nielsen, *U.S. Military Academy*
and
Scott Handler, *U.S. Military Academy*

ISSUE

Are U.S. Diplomatic Efforts Needed to Create a Binding International Climate-Change Treaty?

YES: **Ruth Greenspan Bell**, from "What to Do About Climate Change," *Foreign Affairs* (May/June 2006)

NO: **Bjørn Lomborg**, "The Emperor's New Climate-Change Agreement," *Project Syndicate* (January 2012)

Learning Outcomes

After reading this issue, you should be able to:

- Explain what climate change is and why it has become an international concern.
- Understand the relationship of greenhouse gases, specifically carbon dioxide, to climate change.
- Discuss what a "commons" problem is and how climate change poses such a challenge.
- Discuss the results to date of international diplomatic efforts to address climate change.
- Describe the role technological solutions may play in curbing climate change.

ISSUE SUMMARY

YES: Ruth Greenspan Bell, director of International Institutional Development and Environmental Assistance at Resources for the Future, argues for the value of international climate change treaties but points out that the problem in achieving binding agreements has been overreach. Instead of trying for large commitments, concerned parties should pursue smaller initiatives that gradually reduce emissions while strengthening relevant international norms and institutions.

NO: Bjørn Lomborg, head of the Copenhagen Consensus Center and adjunct professor at Copenhagen Business School, believes the answer lies not in international agreements or institutions, but in harnessing market forces to change behaviors. Long-term sustainable progress in reducing greenhouse gas emissions will only be achieved through the development of green energy alternatives that can compete with fossil fuels.

Climate scientists have documented the presence of climate change for over two decades, and the leaders of most countries now acknowledge that climate change poses significant international challenges. Scientists from around the world reported through a United Nations Intergovernmental Panel on Climate Change (IPCC) assessment that the evidence that the earth and its climate system are changing is "unequivocal" (IPCC, 2007). According to the U.S. Global Change Research Program, global temperatures have increased over the past 50 years (USGCRP, 2009). Along with the growing recognition that climate change is occurring, a general consensus has developed that the change is anthropogenic—that is, human activities, largely through the use of fossil fuels, have contributed the most to increases in greenhouse gas (GHG) emissions. Carbon dioxide (CO_2), while not the most potent of the GHGs, poses the greatest climate change threat due to the sheer volume of CO_2 created by human activity. If the rate of global economic development continues unchanged without commensurate efforts to mitigate GHG emissions, CO_2 concentrations are expected to almost double by the end of the twenty-first century, contributing to an estimated 7.2 degrees Fahrenheit increase in global temperatures (IPCC, 2007).

Along with increases in the planet's temperature, climate change is expected to cause other potentially devastating global developments. These include higher sea levels, dramatic shifts in precipitation patterns, and greater threats to human health in the form of heat stress, water-borne illnesses, and the spread of certain diseases. The exact magnitude of these phenomena and the potential damage they may cause are difficult to quantify, but the scientific community has achieved general consensus that anthropogenic climate change is placing communities at risk from extreme events and disasters (IPCC, 2012).

Because CO_2 emissions readily disperse into the atmosphere with no concern for geographical or political boundaries, industrial activities and the use of fossil fuels in one country can negatively impact the climate and environmental conditions in other countries. Due to this fact, the IPCC believes that no single country can address these challenges on its own. It will take immediate international collaboration to address these concerns and mitigate the most extreme impacts of climate change (IPCC, 2007). Yet, the history of climate change negotiations to date has been one of bold declarations followed by minimal action.

Several European countries first initiated international efforts to address climate change in 1990. At that time, the United States and the Soviet Union strongly resisted entering into any obligation to reduce their CO_2 emissions. Two years of international negotiations resulted in the signing of the United Nations Framework Convention on Climate Change (UNFCCC) in 1992. At the insistence of the United States, the Convention documented the intent of 40 industrialized countries to reduce their CO_2 emissions but contained no binding commitments to do so (UNFCCC, 1992). Since the UNFCCC went into effect in 1994, seventeen subsequent Conferences of the Parties (COPs) have been held. With one exception, the Kyoto Protocol of 1997, the parties have made no binding commitments to reduce their CO_2 emissions.

The Kyoto Protocol, which has now been ratified by 191 countries, commits member countries to reduce their CO_2 emissions to specified levels by 2012. However, the United States never ratified the Kyoto Protocol, and Canada, which did ratify the Protocol, withdrew in 2011 after acknowledging it would not meet its reduction targets. The Kyoto Protocol expires in 2012 with no replacement agreement. Despite the intent of the Protocol, global CO_2 emissions have increased every year since it went into effect. The one exception is 2009, with the decline largely attributed to that year's global economic downturn (IEA, 2011).

Other than the Kyoto Protocol, the UNFCCC has not succeeded in obligating its members to reduce CO_2 emissions and slow the increase in atmospheric concentrations of GHGs. The 2009 COP in Copenhagen, Denmark, was expected to be the definitive conference to replace the Kyoto Protocol with a substantive, binding climate change agreement. To the disappointment of many, the United States, China, Brazil, India, and South Africa held side negotiations that scuttled efforts for a binding agreement. Instead, the Copenhagen COP ended with a non-binding accord that committed $30 billion to short-term mitigation efforts, established reporting and transparency standards, and noted that global warming must be limited to two degrees Celsius (Copenhagen Climate Change Accord, 2009). At the 2010 COP in Cancun, Mexico, the parties acknowledged that in order to limit global temperature increases to 2 degrees, CO_2 emissions would have to be cut in half by 2050. Yet, no new reduction pledges were made, and the parties recognized that even if all current non-binding pledges were met, emissions would increase by 20 percent by 2050 (Climate Action Tracker, 2012).

Facing the expiration of the Kyoto Protocol, the 2011 COP in Durban, South Africa, resulted in a commitment by European Union members to extend their Kyoto commitments another five years and an agreement by all parties to negotiate a new binding agreement by 2015.

This lack of progress on an international treaty in the face of increasing international concern about anthropogenic climate change and the long-term threat it poses appears puzzling. Why would countries fail to cooperate to solve a problem that they openly acknowledge is a serious danger to the international community? The principal explanation for this lack of progress is that climate change represents a global "commons" problem, as described originally by ecologist Garrett Hardin. A commons problem arises when multiple parties, each acting rationally from a short-term, individual perspective, deplete a shared resource even though it harms all parties' long-term needs for access to that resource. To illuminate this problem, Hardin gives an example in which the shared resource is a pasture where ranchers may let their cattle graze. It is in each resident's self-interest to place as many cattle as she can upon the commons since she does not bear the entire cost of using the land. Yet, as all ranchers do this, the pasture becomes overgrazed and barren, ultimately harming each individual's long-term interests. Despite this negative outcome, each rancher does not want to be the only one to limit her use of the pasture if others continue to use it to the same extent (Hardin, 1968). The planet's atmosphere and climate similarly serve as a common resource shared by all countries. Although emissions of CO_2 damage that resource incrementally, the activities that produce the emissions benefit the originating country and it does not bear all the costs. No country wants to limit its own economic development and improvements in its living standards unless other countries take similar actions to protect the commons.

Therefore, although all countries contribute to climate change to some degree, the benefits of stabilizing atmospheric CO_2 levels and the costs of reducing emissions are not evenly distributed. Developed countries expect developing countries to agree to reduce equally their CO_2 emissions, but developing countries argue that their per capita emissions are significantly lower already and they have the right to continue producing emissions in order to achieve their economic development goals. At the same time, large industrialized countries argue that they will realize no near-term, measurable benefits to justify the economic costs of emission reductions. In addition, they cannot afford the costs to mitigate effects created by others and have little power in the international system to push for stricter emission standards. Uncertainties about the exact costs of climate change and when or where these costs might appear hinder every country's ability to determine whether the benefits will outweigh the costs of any particular agreement. Additionally, the decades-long lag time to experience the negative effects of climate change removes the sense of urgency that could spur public demand for international action.

Given this combination of factors, are U.S. diplomatic efforts required to create binding climate change agreements and reduce greenhouse gas emissions? In the article for the YES position, Ruth Greenspan Bell maintains that binding agreements and subsequent domestic regulations are needed to shape the markets and to force development of the technologies that will be the actual tools of emission reduction. Bell advocates starting with small agreements that the parties know that they can commit to instead of broad, all-encompassing agreements. These small yet increasingly ambitious agreements will reinforce international norms that favor emissions controls and cause countries to develop the domestic policies needed to enable them to meet their climate change commitments.

Bjørn Lomborg's article for the NO position, on the other hand, represents a market-based approach. He believes that international institutions are incapable of developing binding, substantive commitments to address climate change. All that has resulted from the UNFCCC, Lomborg asserts, is an illusion of progress and a massive amount of misspent effort. Instead of seeking binding agreements, countries like the United States should focus on developing cheap alternative energy sources that can compete with fossil fuels. Countries will not sign binding agreements that are not in their interests, regardless of the exhortations of fellow parties to the agreement. Consequently, only technological advances can create the cheaper alternatives which will then allow market forces to drive emission reductions. International agreements are not a viable option.

YES

Ruth Greenspan Bell

What to Do About Climate Change

The Heat Is On

. . . Curbing greenhouse gas emissions, a problem that took many years to develop, will be a prolonged and messy process. But two actions are called for now. The first is to revise the assumptions behind currently proposed fixes, namely emissions-trading regimes, which by themselves actually do too little to cap pollution. The second is to devise strategies customized to the needs and means of the governments that must implement them, distinguishing developed countries from developing ones. . . .

The Gas on Emissions

Current proposals for curbing carbon dioxide emissions start with the reasonable assumption that the first step toward fighting climate change is to make the issue a priority. And so over the past three decades, the standard response to global environmental threats has been to draft international agreements. There are now some 900 environmental treaties on the books. Unfortunately, few have achieved any genuine reductions in pollution. Under the UN Framework Convention on Climate Change, which entered into force in 1994, and its controversial Kyoto Protocol, which entered into force after Russia ratified it in 2005, some industrialized nations agreed to reduce greenhouse gas emissions between 2008 and 2012 to levels below those of 1990. It has yet to be seen whether these commitments will yield any significant results. . . .

The generally accepted plan takes an approach with essentially two drivers—one based on economic incentives, the other on technological ones. The first driver, now enshrined in the Kyoto Protocol, is a sophisticated global system for trading greenhouse gas emissions modeled on the successful U.S. "cap-and-trade" system designed to control the release of sulfur dioxide (which produces acid rain). Relying on a trading system assumes that the opportunity to profit from reducing greenhouse gas emissions will motivate industrial emitters, wherever they are located, to change the way they operate power plants and factories. Implicit in this assumption is the belief that advanced technology will help emitters change their ways, because technology can always help solve complex problems. . . .

The problem with this setup is that it is anyone's guess whether such trading can work on a global scale. . . .

It is highly unlikely that anything approximating the rigor of the U.S. system can be devised to control climate change worldwide. Enforcement has long been the Achilles' heel of international environmental agreements, largely because countries submit to international oversight, which they see as a threat to their sovereignty, only with the greatest reluctance. Although some progress was made on the issue of noncompliance at a recent meeting of the parties to the Kyoto Protocol, the enforcement plan that came out of it assumes that countries will not risk being shut out of participating in the agreement's flexible trading mechanisms. Even if a more rigorous compliance regime could be instituted, obtaining accurate measurements of actual emissions would be difficult.

Much of the discussion, meanwhile, has centered on how to refine the existing trading mechanisms rather than on the most difficult but most important issue: how to set and enforce caps on greenhouse gas emissions. It is the commitment to make steady reductions in harmful emissions that will make or break the overall scheme. Caps have never worked without serious compliance efforts backed up by old-fashioned penalties against laggards and cheaters. But countries that have been slow to control even significant local pollution are now being asked to perform the far more complicated task of managing greenhouse gases so that they can sell reductions in emissions on a global marketplace. Global trading is no magic remedy. Reducing emissions worldwide requires exactly the same attention to conventional regulatory processes as does effective domestic regulation.

Moreover, global trading itself is unusual. U.S.-style emissions trading has never been done on a global scale or even outside the United States. Countries that must be part of the solution, such as China and India, have at best achieved a handful of highly orchestrated domestic trades between carefully selected polluters. Few of these countries can actually cap pollution; many do not have the skills to manage or enforce complex intangible property rights concerning goods such as polluted air escaping from a factory.

So what will motivate industrial plants that are currently free to pollute to clean up their act? This is where technology is supposed to come into play. Under Joint Implementation, outsiders with the economic incentive to control emissions of carbon dioxide are expected to provide the appropriate technology. But even if the lucky manager of a firm being offered, say, free equipment to capture emissions understands that he is being given something of value, he might not have the incentive to pay for running and maintaining the equipment. If anything, experience shows that he is unlikely to turn it on without the watchful eye of disinterested enforcement bodies looking on. Evidence from China demonstrates that even plants equipped with superior pollution equipment do not run those controls when doing so proves inconvenient.

No wonder some observers are now questioning whether trading mechanisms can contribute to a reliable reduction of greenhouse gas emissions. India's Center for Science and the Environment (CSE) recently examined two deals for carbon dioxide pursuant to the CDM that involved Indian companies and European governments, the latter seeking to gain credits to meet their Kyoto targets. The CSE cast serious doubt on these deals' efficacy. It concluded that certain conditions for the transactions had not been met, despite being specified in the deals' design document; that it was impossible to determine whether the transactions met other standards, because their terms were not transparent; and that Indian authorities seemed to have approved the projects not on their merit, but on the basis of the prestige of the consultant who validated them. The CSE questioned whether these transactions could honestly be said to achieve the CDM objectives or India's pollution-reduction goals.

Starting Small

For the developing world and much of the former Soviet bloc, where Westerners will inevitably look for emissions credits, achieving steady reductions in emissions will require fundamental reform. Trading and technology are great policy tools, but they must be part of a larger program whose core objective is the systematic reduction of greenhouse gas emissions.

The first steps toward the effective enforcement of high environmental standards should be to adjust expectations on all sides and encourage developing countries to set goals they can meet, as a preliminary move toward developing a more rigorous regime. Achievable caps would not be very ambitious at first. But setting them could help mobilize governments and get them moving in the right direction, helping them gain real experience in managing greenhouse gas emissions. With some practice and success under their belts, governments would then be in a position to tighten the caps.

For any such effort to succeed, environmental regulation will have to become a priority in the developing world; that means making a serious commitment to achieving whatever caps on greenhouse gas emissions that are deemed appropriate. In a handful of countries, regulation is working; in too many others, it is not. Effective environmental regulation will require close cooperation between those leaders who are concerned about the perils

of greenhouse gases and those governments whose cooperation is needed to reduce emissions.

Many laws and ministries have been created in the developing world since the 1972 UN Conference on the Human Environment, in Stockholm. But it is still a challenge to turn current regulations from lifeless words into effective practices—a goal that can be attained with skilled regulators and support from the highest levels of government. Many of the officials tasked with protecting the environment lack the clout of their counterparts in industry and finance ministries. Heading an environment ministry should no longer be a consolation prize for members of small political parties in coalition governments; environment ministers should be invited to sit at the grown-ups' table. . . .

All Aboard

Another important task is to help developing countries gain appropriate regulatory skills by providing them with training and equipment. Countries without strong experience need assistance to build effective monitoring, inspection, and enforcement practices. Sporadic efforts have been made to help some states in the former Soviet bloc develop regulatory capacity. But the help has not been consistent or systematic. Development assistance efforts have often tried, unsuccessfully, to import Western economic practices into the law, traditions, and culture of the developing world.

A better approach would be to devise practices and institute reforms that are customized to each country's particular circumstances. Take the role of law. Western reformers often assume that enacting a law will produce its objective. But in China, for example, where the strength of personal relationships has guided business and other significant interactions for millennia, relying on legal obligations is very new. In addition to helping the Chinese develop a new legal ethic, reformers must also consider enforcing environmental standards in ways more consistent with local culture, such as through the naming and shaming of polluting plants. (Of course, it helps to be alert to other driving motivations, as the Chinese leaders' commitment to cleaning up Beijing for the 2008 Olympics demonstrates.) Enforcement through locally appropriate measures would breed demand for other enforcement tools, and at that point the developing world might turn to North America and western Europe for additional compliance methods and techniques.

Implicit in the hope for such progress is the importance of public opinion. Where the government fails to act or to enforce laws, the public can be a force for reform. Citizen groups were an important factor in jump-starting environmental protection in the United States. Non-governmental organizations (NGOS) around the world, including in developing countries, are starting to flex their muscles and push governments toward greater compliance. In the new democracies of central and eastern

Europe, NGOS are demanding that their governments disclose more data on the environment. In India, NGOS delivered a one-two punch that ultimately won a commitment to improve local air quality: one NGO brought a lawsuit before the Indian Supreme Court; another published information describing how air pollution in New Delhi endangers the city's residents. Their success prompted lawsuits in Pakistan, Bangladesh, and other neighboring countries. In China, a public interest group is seeking damages for pollution victims. Public participation is also critical in countries with strong enforcement bodies, because no government has the resources to stop all noncompliance. The right to bring a suit is particularly useful when governments are inactive. Philippine law, for example, allows citizens to bring polluters to justice when official enforcement agencies do not.

Sometimes the private sector will be motivated to take the initiative. A small number of multinational corporations, General Electric and Shell among them, are putting their own environmental best-practices plans into action at plants worldwide—a move that could embolden local regulators and pressure local companies to improve their habits.

Building the capacity to deliver verifiable reductions of greenhouse gases is tedious work. But with persist-ence, political will, and some help, regulatory skills can be improved. Internal pressure can speed the way and supplement governments' scarce enforcement resources. The overall objective should be to develop a culture of strict environmental compliance that will ensure that promises of emissions reductions will be met. Focusing on capping emissions requires steadiness of purpose, imperviousness to the siren song of short-term interests, and the willingness to commit significant resources. But it is a realistic and effective strategy for fighting a problem that reaches deep into every economy. Harnessing the magic of the market and enlisting technology may become significant tools in combating climate change, but they will not work on their own. And like climate change itself, this sobering truth is best faced sooner rather than later.

Ruth Greenspan Bell is a public policy scholar at the Woodrow Wilson Center for Scholars. Previously, she was a senior fellow at the World Resources Institute and the director of international institutional development and environmental assistance at Resources for the Future.

Bjørn Lomborg    **NO**

The Emperor's New Climate-Change Agreement

Copenhagen—Dressing up failure as victory has been integral to climate-change negotiations since they started 20 years ago. The latest round of talks in Durban, South Africa, in December was no exception.

Climate negotiations have been in virtual limbo ever since the catastrophic and humiliating Copenhagen summit in 2009, where vertiginous expectations collided with hard political reality. So as negotiators—and a handful of government ministers—arrived in Durban, expectations could not have been lower.

Yet, by the end of the talks, the European Union's climate commissioner, Connie Hedegaard, was being applauded in the media for achieving a "breakthrough" that had "salvaged Durban," and, most significantly, for achieving the holy grail of climate negotiations, a "legally binding treaty." According to British climate minister Chris Huhne, the results showed that the United Nations climate-change negotiation system "really works and can produce results."

Sure, the agreement would come into effect only in 2020—which sounds oddly complacent when environmentalists and political leaders warned ahead of the Copenhagen conference that we had just six months or 50 days to solve the climate problem. But, as the British newspaper *The Guardian* assured readers, this was a breakthrough, because developing countries, including India and China, were, for the first time, "agreeing to be legally bound to curb their greenhouse gases." And, just as importantly, the US was making the same promise.

Let's take a look at the actual agreement reached in Durban that generated all that congratulatory backslapping. It won't take long: the document runs to two pages, contains no commitments to cut emissions, and outlines no policies to implement the undefined cuts. There is simply a promise "to launch a process to develop a protocol, another legal instrument, or an agreed outcome with legal force."

An agreement to launch a legal process. That is what everyone got so worked up about? And, again, the negotiators merely promised to set themselves a deadline of 2015 to finish setting up this legal process, which would enter into force five years hence.

Just a few days later, the Indian environment minister, Shrimati Jayanthi Natarajan, stressed that there was no legally binding treaty: "India cannot agree to a legally binding agreement for emissions reduction at this stage of our development. . . . I must clarify that [Durban] does not imply that India has to take binding commitments to reduce its emissions in absolute terms in 2020."

India was not alone. The day after the Durban conference, Canada officially withdrew from the Kyoto Protocol, which Russia and Japan have already declined to extend, leaving only the EU's member states and a few other countries committed to further reductions.

Hollow victories have been central to climate negotiations since they began. The Durban agreement uncannily echoes the agreement reached in Bali in 2007 "to launch a comprehensive process to enable the full, effective, and sustained implementation of the [UN Climate] Convention through long-term cooperative action." According to that deal—which was, of course, much celebrated at the time—a legal treaty was supposed to be ready for the 2009 Copenhagen meeting.

In Kyoto in 1997, the treaty was acclaimed as "a milestone in the history of climate protection," and President Bill Clinton declared that "the United States has reached an historic agreement with other nations of the world to take unprecedented action to address global warming."

Of course, the treaty had already been rejected in the US Senate by a 95-0 vote, and thus was dead on arrival. This, and lax interpretations of emissions in the years following Kyoto, meant that more emissions occurred under the protocol than had been expected to occur in its absence according to research undertaken by the economists Christoph Böhringer and Carsten Vogt.

Even at the start of global climate-change negotiations in Rio de Janeiro in 1992, the aim of putting the planet "on a course to address the critical issue of global warming" soon went awry. Rich countries fell 12% short of their promise to cut emissions to 1990 levels by 2000.

For 20 years, climate negotiators have repeatedly celebrated deals that haven't panned out. Worse, for all practical purposes, the promises that have been made have had no impact on global CO_2 emissions. They have only provided false hope that we have addressed climate change and allowed us to push it to the back burner for another few years. So, before we get too excited celebrating the "breakthrough" of Durban, we would do well to reflect on a two-decade history of flogging a dead horse.

We will never reduce emissions significantly until we manage to make green energy cheaper than fossil fuels.

We must focus sharply on research and development to drive down alternative energy prices over coming decades.

The first step toward doing that is to end our collective suspension of disbelief when it comes to climate-change negotiations. We need to see through the hype and self-serving political spin. We owe it to the future to do better.

BJØRN LOMBORG is the director of the Copenhagen Consensus Center, an adjunct professor at Copenhagen Business School, and the former director of the Environmental Assessment Institute.

EXPLORING THE ISSUE

Are U.S. Diplomatic Efforts Needed to Create a Binding International Climate-Change Treaty?

Critical Thinking and Reflection

1. Why would a state sign a climate change treaty if it lacks the technical means to implement the agreed upon reductions in CO_2 emissions?
2. Given the presence of a fully developed infrastructure based around fossil fuels and the delayed onset of problems created by climate change, what short- to medium-term approaches can help stimulate the development of alternative energy technologies to help mitigate the long-term effects of climate change?
3. How have domestic politics in the United States influenced international negotiations related to climate change?
4. While the United States has yet to sign any binding commitments to reduce CO_2 emissions, how has U.S. participation in the UNFCCC and international discussion about climate change influenced American domestic policy making?
5. What are the opportunities and challenges for countries that try to achieve emissions reductions solely through technological advances and market-based mechanisms? Explain.

Is There Common Ground?

While Ruth Greenspan Bell and Bjørn Lomborg disagree on whether international institutions or market forces will be most effective in mitigating climate change, they both identify technological innovation as the key to any successful climate change policy. Bell sees technology as an effective tool for helping to solve emissions problems and believes it is best deployed in support of a programmed reduction in emissions. In Lomborg's view, the incentives created by markets to develop new technologies are the only mechanisms to able to move the world away from its dependence on fossil fuels.

The small steps that Bell advocates be driven by international commitments may be as much as existing technologies can support. She acknowledges that building the global capacity to deliver verifiable reductions in CO_2 will be a protracted process, and that pollution-abatement systems will play a part. She also notes that some of the key polluting countries are currently unable to either measure or manage intangibles such as polluted air escaping from a factory. Therefore, technology may be more central to the program her article promotes than is apparent at first glance.

Similarly, Lomborg's call for research and development could benefit from the collaboration and direction inherent in the international agreements that Bell sees as possible. While states have failed to commit to reducing their emissions in any meaningful way, as Lomborg sharply documents in his article, they might succeed in jointly cultivating the alternative energy sources he prizes.

Sometimes the existence of international institutions influences behavioral norms of states even when states do not sign binding agreements. On a global scale, such an institution focused on climate change may help drive technical innovation by producing a demand where none before existed.

Additional Resources

Axelrod, Regina, David Leonard Downie, Norman J. Vig, Eds. *The Global Environment: Institutions, Law and Policy,* 2nd ed. Washington, DC: CQ Press, 2005.

This edited volume examines the international institutions and regimes that focus on environmental issues, the environmental policies they produce, and the limitations and controversies associated with their work. The "Global Climate Change Policy: Making Progress or Spinning Wheels?" chapter directly addresses climate change as a foreign policy issue.

Chasek, Pamela S., David L. Downie, and Janet Welsh Brown. *Global Environmental Politics,* 4th ed. Cambridge: Westview Press, 2006.

This primer on global environmental politics provides the foundational concepts for understanding how environmental regimes form, the behaviors of specific environmental regimes, and the limits of these regimes.

Hardin, Garrett J. The Tragedy of the Commons. *Science* 162 (1968): 1243–1248.

UN Intergovernmental Panel on Climate Change (IPCC). *Managing Risks of Extreme Events and*

Disasters to Advance Climate Change Adaptation. A Special Report of Working Groups I and II of the IPCC. New York: Cambridge University Press, 2012.

Internet References . . .

Climate Action Tracker

This site is an independent science-based assessment that tracks climate and emissions, and provided an up-to-date assessment of individual national pledges to reduce greenhouse gas emissions.

www.climateactiontracker.org/

United Nations Framework Convention on Climate Change

"Decision-/CP.15" *The Copenhagen Climate Change Accord* is available at this link.

http://unfccc.int/files/meetings/cop_15/application/ pdf/cop15_cph_auv.pdf

United Nations Framework Convention on Climate Change

The Kyoto Protocol is an international agreement linked to the United Nations Framework Convention on Climate Change.

http://unfccc.int/key_documents/kyoto_protocol/ items/6445.php

International Energy Agency (IEA)

CO$_2$ Emissions from Fuel Combustion: Highlights, 2011 Edition. This document is available at this link.

www.iea.org/co2highlights/co2highlights.pdf

United Nations Framework Convention on Climate Change

The official website of the UNFCCC, this online resource provides all the documents and party statements from the previous 17 Conferences of the Parties to the UNFCCC. The original Convention document, the 2007 Bali Road Map, and the 2011 Cancun Agreement are attempts to achieve international collaboration without binding agreements.

http://unfccc.int

UN Intergovernmental Panel on Climate Change (IPCC)

Climate Change 2007: Synthesis Report is available at this link.

www.ipcc.ch/pdf/assessment-report/ar4/syr/ ar4_syr.pdf

U.S. Global Change Research Program (USGCRP)

Global Climate Change Impacts in the United States: 2009 Highlights is available at this link.

http://library.globalchange.gov/products/ assessments/2009-national-climate-assessment

Unit VI

UNIT

Domestic Influences on U.S. Foreign Policy

T he question of why a state chooses the foreign policy it adopts is a fundamental one to students of international affairs. Some international relations theorists first look to the international system or to regional dynamics for the answer. At times, this is appropriate; sometimes a state's foreign policy choice is best understood as a response to opportunities or threats external to that state. At other times, however, this may be misleading. The leaders of other countries may choose their foreign policies based on domestic political imperatives, and events in the international system may be almost irrelevant. In any given case, it is useful to evaluate both the potential domestic as well as international sources of states' foreign policy choices.

With regard to the United States, it is always useful to consider the possible domestic sources of foreign policy when trying to understand U.S. actions abroad. Domestic influences can include the characteristics of U.S. political institutions, the nature of the foreign policy process, the influence of particular personalities, the role of ideology, American political culture, the role of the media, and the involvement of special interest groups. Under what conditions will these domestic factors drive U.S. foreign policy, and when will international events and developments play the more important role? Though many scholars have done useful research in this area, more remains to be done.

Selected, Edited, and with Issue Framing Material by:
Suzanne Nielsen, *U.S. Military Academy*
and
Scott Handler, *U.S. Military Academy*

ISSUE

Is Congress Still Relevant in U.S. Foreign Policy making?

YES: James M. Lindsay, from "The Shifting Pendulum of Power: Executive–Legislative Relations on American Foreign Policy," in *The Domestic Sources of American Foreign Policy: Insights and Evidence,* 6th ed. (July 2012)

NO: Norman J. Ornstein and Thomas E. Mann, from "When Congress Checks Out," *Foreign Affairs* (December 2006)

Learning Outcomes
After reading this issue, you should be able to: • Describe the constitutional powers of Congress with respect to American foreign policy.   • Discuss patterns of congressional activism in American foreign policy in the modern era.   • Understand how political and institutional factors may influence congressional assertiveness in the realm of foreign policy.   • Discuss how congressional oversight can influence American foreign policy.   • Assess the potential positive and negative consequences of congressional assertiveness in American foreign policy.

ISSUE SUMMARY

YES: James M. Lindsay, the director of Studies at the Council on Foreign Relations, argues that Congress still is relevant, but that congressional involvement in foreign policy ebbs and flows based on the perceived threat to America and on the success of the President's foreign policy initiatives. Congress will tend to defer to the President when the perceived threat is high or when the President's policies are successful. When these two conditions are not present, Congress is more likely to become actively involved in American foreign policy.

NO: Norman J. Ornstein, a resident scholar at the American Enterprise Institute, and Thomas E. Mann, a senior fellow in Governance Studies at the Brookings Institution, claim that Congress no longer fulfills its constitutional responsibility to monitor the President's execution of foreign and national security policy. One important reason for this lack of oversight is that fewer and fewer members value Congress as an institution and focus on protecting its prerogatives.

Although the U.S. Constitution gives Congress numerous prerogatives with regard to foreign policy, there is considerable debate over whether or not Congress is sufficiently assertive in exercising them. Critics of Congress argue that its members have ignored their basic foreign policy obligations. Because individual members do not have strong incentives to invest in most foreign policy matters, and because they may take a political risk when challenging the President on national security-related issues, members often chose to defer to the executive branch. In addition, in an era in which many individual Congressmen are popular but Congress as an institution is not, there may not be a sense of institutional identity within Congress sufficient to motivate members to protect the prerogatives of their branch of government against potential encroachments by the executive. As a result, the executive branch is too often left unchecked.

If this assertion of congressional passivity is correct, it seems contrary to the Constitution's intent. Seeking to prevent a concentration of power that they saw as dangerous to liberty, the drafters of the Constitution deliberately dispersed control over foreign policy throughout the branches of the national government. Although the Constitution gives the role of "Commander-in-Chief" and the power to negotiate treaties to the executive, it also gives Congress many explicit prerogatives. These include the powers to "provide for the common Defense"; "regulate Commerce with foreign Nations"; "declare War"; "raise and support Armies"; "provide and maintain a

Navy"; and "make Rules for the Government and Regulation of the land and naval Forces." The Constitution also states that the Senate must advise the President and grant its consent on all treaties with foreign governments. Far from envisioning Congress as a lesser player, the Constitution appears to have intended Congress to be a necessary and active participant in American foreign policy making.

Despite these intentions, some argue that congressional assertiveness in foreign affairs has declined. This case is easiest to support when it comes to the war power. For at least the first 150 years of the country's history, it was fairly clear that Congress and the President shared responsibility for the country's decisions to go to war. Although Presidents James Polk, Abraham Lincoln, William McKinley, Woodrow Wilson, and Franklin Roosevelt all pushed the limits of their constitutional prerogatives during wartime, Congress retained an active role in war policy and on other matters of foreign policy. President Harry Truman's decision to declare the Korean War a "police action" that did not require a declaration of war, however, is often considered a turning point. It established a precedent that Presidents could decide to send forces into combat without explicit congressional approval (Fisher, 1995). Congress has not declared war in more than 70 years, yet Presidents have continued to send troops abroad to fight.

Those concerned about whether Congress is fulfilling its role adequately have often criticized its performance on domestic as well as foreign policy issues. However, charges of congressional passivity in the area of foreign policy have persisted longer and have echoed more loudly than similar charges about the lack of congressional influence in other matters. More than four decades ago, political scientist Aaron Wildavsky first articulated his "two presidencies" thesis, which asserts that the President has more discretion in international affairs than on domestic matters (Wildavsky, 1975). Wildavsky argued that technological changes following World War II had allowed Presidents to gain greater control over foreign policy information and to act more quickly than their counterparts in Congress. This dominance over information and decision-making processes made it difficult for Congress to challenge the President's foreign policy initiatives effectively. Other scholars have extended this narrative of presidential dominance in the face of congressional impotence by arguing that the executive branch in the United States has become an "Imperial Presidency" (Schlesinger, 1974; Rudalevige, 2005). Though these concerns were raised with particular vehemence during the presidential administrations of Richard M. Nixon and George W. Bush, claims that Congress does not adequately constrain the executive branch extend beyond individual administrations. Legal scholar Louis Fisher, speaking about foreign policy since the Truman administration, voices a strong version of this concern when he argues, "we have what the framers thought they had put behind them: a monarchy. Checks and balances? Try to find them" (Fisher, 2002).

Though the war power is usually at the center of concerns over whether Congress is meeting its responsibilities, other scholars emphasize that the power to issue formal declarations of war is not the only prerogative that Congress has relating to foreign policy. Indeed, Congress still is active in foreign policy making in many ways (Lindsay 1994; Howell and Pevehouse 2007). Congress passes legislation that affects the substance of foreign policy and even requires that certain processes are followed as foreign policy is formulated. Congress also grants or withholds funds to shape national security institutions and to influence vital national security programs. Congress can also exert some influence on policies, institutions, and programs through its power to confirm presidential appointees. Finally, Congress uses its oversight authorities to monitor the implementation of foreign policy. Indeed, the powers of legislation, appropriation, confirmation, and oversight are critical in enabling members of Congress to exert significant influence on U.S. foreign and national security policy. While the President may have plenty of room to take the initiative in foreign affairs, the support of Congress is often important to any policy's prospects for long-term success.

Though views differ as to whether changes in the role of Congress in foreign policy making are a cause for concern, another source of debate is over the factors that explain these trends. Some scholars look to partisan behavior as having great explanatory value. One proposition here is that congressional assertiveness and relevance depend heavily on the party of the President and the parties holding the majorities in both houses on Capitol Hill. Congress will be least assertive when the President is of the same party as the majorities in both houses of Congress. When the President is of a different party than the majorities in both houses, Congress is more likely to take an active role (Howell and Pevehouse, 2007). If this view is correct, the relative influence of Congress is likely to vary in a cyclical fashion with the changing political fortunes of the two political parties. Others, such as Wildavsky cited above, are more inclined to point to other trends such as the influence of technology and the growth of the executive branch. To the extent that this explanation has merit, and absent countervailing developments, the ability of Congress to assert itself over certain forms of foreign policy might simply continue to decline over time.

The two articles presented here wade into these debates. In answering YES to whether Congress is still relevant to U.S. foreign policy making, political scientist James Lindsay argues its relative levels of involvement are best explained by the intensity of perceived threats to the United States and the success of the President's foreign policy initiatives. He claims that Congress is more likely to defer to the President when the perceived threat is high and when the President's policies are successful. He supports his argument by providing examples of congressional assertiveness and deference during the modern era. Although Lindsay agrees that the period from 2001 until

2006 was marked by low levels of congressional assertiveness in foreign policy, he sees this period of deference as a natural consequence of the sense of threat that resulted from the terrorist attacks of September 11, 2001. Lindsay believes that Congress still can, and will, play a vital role in U.S. foreign policy, though he believes that the dictates of politics will affect the degree of congressional assertiveness over time.

In taking the NO position, authors Norman J. Ornstein and Thomas E. Mann claim that members of Congress have failed to fulfill their constitutional responsibilities to monitor the President's execution of foreign wars and antiterrorist initiatives. With a focus on the period between 2001 and 2006, they cite a number of statistics showing that Congress spends less time in Washington conducting its oversight role. They argue that this lack of oversight stems from a lack of congressional appetite for involvement in foreign affairs as well as the lack of a strong institutional identity. They also look to partisanship as having explanatory value, suggesting that members of Congress from the Republican Party acted more as "field lieutenants in the President's army rather than as an independent branch of government." However, they believe that a mere change in partisan control will not address the underlying problem. Ornstein and Mann believe that a greater sense of institutional identity among members of Congress is really the key, and they conclude by outlining a number of institutional and structural changes that they think will help.

YES

James M. Lindsay

The Shifting Pendulum of Power: Executive–Legislative Relations on American Foreign Policy

In 2002, Congress looked to have surrendered its constitutional role in foreign-policy making to the White House. After voting nearly unanimously a year earlier to attack Afghanistan for harboring the plotters behind the 9/11 attacks, many lawmakers were privately questioning President George W. Bush's handling of the war on terrorism and especially his mounting push to overthrow Saddam Hussein. But few lawmakers aired their criticisms publicly. When President Bush asked Congress to give him authority to wage war on Iraq, Congress quibbled with some of the language of the draft resolution. Nonetheless, the revised bill, which the House and Senate passed overwhelmingly, amounted to a blank check that the president could cash as he saw fit. When asked why congressional Democrats had not done more to oppose a resolution so many thought unwise or premature, Senate Majority Leader Tom Daschle (D-S.D.) replied, "The bottom line is . . . we want to move on."[1] Congress's eagerness to delegate its war power to the president drew the ire of Senator Robert Byrd (D-W.Va.), a veteran of five decades of service on Capitol Hill. "How have we gotten to this low point in the history of Congress? Are we too feeble to resist the demand of a president who is determined to bend the collective will of Congress to his will?"[2]

Five years later, however, Congress recovered its voice on foreign policy. In January 2007, President Bush unveiled a proposal to send 21,500 additional U.S. troops to Iraq in a bid to stop escalating sectarian violence there. Rather than applauding the president, members of Congress from both parties assailed the plan and his overall handling of the Iraq War. Senator Russell D. Feingold (D-Wis.) accused the administration of committing "quite possibly the greatest foreign policy mistake in the history of our nation."[3] Senator Chuck Hagel (R-Neb.), a decorated Vietnam War veteran, called the troop increase proposal "a dangerous foreign policy blunder."[4] Members in both the House and Senate rushed to submit bills to limit the president's ability to send more troops to Iraq. Senator Olympia Snowe (R-Maine) captured the new mood on Capitol Hill: "Now is the time for the Congress to make its voice heard on a policy that has such significant implications for the nation, the Middle East, and the world."[5]

Congress's resurgent interest in foreign policy carried over into Barack Obama's presidency. Stiff congressional opposition forced him to abandon his plans to close down the prison at Guantánamo Bay that held foreign terrorists and to start a nation-wide program to reduce the emission of greenhouse gases. His effort to win Senate approval of the New START Treaty, which lowered the limit on the number of strategic nuclear warheads that Russia and United States could deploy, met strong Republican opposition. Unlike the case with the initial military actions in Afghanistan and Iraq, his decision to launch Operation Odyssey Dawn, the military operation intended to protect Libyan civilians from the Muammar Qaddafi's military forces, drew sharp criticism on Capitol Hill. Some members of Congress lambasted him for moving too slowly, while others complained that he had overstepped his constitutional authorities.

The change in the tone of executive–legislative relations between the beginning of the decade and end of it was dramatic. It was not, however, unprecedented. The pendulum of power on foreign policy has swung back and forth between Congress and the president many times over the course of American history. The reason does not lie in the Constitution. Its formal allocation of foreign policy powers, which gives important authorities to both Congress and the president, has not changed since it was drafted. Rather, the answer lies in politics. How aggressively Congress exercises its foreign policy powers turns on two critical questions: Does the country see itself as threatened or secure? Are the president's policies working or not? Times of peace favor congressional activism, while times of war favor congressional deference. Successful presidents have more followers than failed ones do. . . .

Does it matter whether Congress exercises its foreign policy powers? The answer to this question lies in the eyes of the beholder. Americans can and do disagree over what constitutes the "national interest" and which policies will do the most to achieve them. What is certain, though, is that the balance of power between the two ends of Pennsylvania Avenue will continue to ebb and flow with the political tides.

The Constitution and Foreign Policy

Ask most Americans who makes foreign policy in the United States and their immediate answer is the president. And to a point they are right. But even a cursory reading of the Constitution makes clear that Congress also possesses extensive powers to shape foreign policy. Article 1, section 8, assigns Congress the power to "provide for the common Defence," "To regulate Commerce with foreign Nations," "To define and punish Piracies and Felonies committed on the high Seas," "To declare War," "To raise and support Armies," "To provide and maintain a Navy," and "To make Rules for the Government and Regulation of the land and naval Forces." Article 2, section 2, specifies that the Senate must give its advice and consent to all treaties and ambassadorial appointments. And Congress's more general powers to appropriate all government funds and to confirm cabinet officials provide additional means to influence foreign policy.

These powers can have great consequence. To begin with, they enable Congress—or, in the case of the treaty power, the Senate—to specify the substance of American foreign policy. The most popular vehicle for doing so is the appropriations power, which, while not unlimited in scope, is nonetheless quite broad. (The Supreme Court has never struck down any use of the appropriations power as an unconstitutional infringement on the president's authority to conduct foreign policy.) Dollars are policy in Washington, D.C., and the president generally cannot spend money unless Congress appropriates it. Thus, by deciding to fund some ventures and not others, Congress can steer the course of U.S. defense and foreign policy. Congress can also specify the substance of foreign policy by regulating foreign commerce. One notable instance in which it used its trade power this way was a 1986 bill that placed sanctions on South Africa in order to pressure Pretoria to end its policy of apartheid. The Senate's treaty power can have similar effects. When the Senate rejected the Treaty of Versailles after World War I, it blocked U.S. membership in the League of Nations and preserved the traditional U.S. policy of avoiding entangling alliances.

Congress's power to establish and direct the business of the federal bureaucracy (e.g., to provide and maintain a navy) also enables it to influence foreign policy by changing the procedures that the executive branch must follow in making decisions. The premise underlying such procedural legislation is that changing the rules governing how the executive branch makes decisions will change the decisions it makes. In trade policy, for example, U.S. law requires the White House to consult with a wide range of consumer, industry, and labor groups whenever it is negotiating an international trade agreement. The law's sponsors calculated that including these groups in decision making would make it more likely that U.S. trade policy would reflect U.S. economic interests. Likewise, over the years, Congress has directed the State Department to set up special offices to handle issues such as democracy, counterterrorism, and

trafficking in persons. In each instance, the idea was that the executive branch would be more likely to address the issue in question if someone in the bureaucracy had clear responsibility for it.

Congress's broader powers to hold hearings, conduct investigations, and debate issues also give it the ability to *indirectly* shape the course of foreign policy. What is said—and what is not said—on Capitol Hill influences public opinion. That in turn helps determine how much leeway presidents have to act. A Congress that applauds a president's proposals makes it all but certain that the public will rally behind the White House. Conversely, a Congress that condemns presidential initiatives fuels public skepticism and forces the White House to pay a higher—and possibly unacceptable—political price to get its way.

The overarching lesson here is that when it comes to foreign affairs, Congress and the president *both* can claim ample constitutional authority. The two branches are, in Richard Neustadt's oft-repeated formulation, "separated institutions *sharing* power."[6] . . .

To say that Congress *can* put its mark on foreign policy, however, is not the same as saying that it *will* do so. To understand why congressional activism and influence on foreign policy varies over time, it is necessary to leave the realm of law and enter the realm of politics.

Politics and Foreign Policy

The explanation for why Congress's say in foreign policy ebbs and flows lies first in an observation that the famed French commentator on American life Alexis de Tocqueville made more than 150 years ago. Surprised to find that the pre–Civil War Congress played a major role in foreign policy, he speculated that congressional activism stemmed from the country's isolation from external threat. "If the Union's existence were constantly menaced, and if its great interests were continually interwoven with those of other powerful nations, one would see the prestige of the executive growing, because of what was expected from it and of what it did."[7]

Why might perceptions of threat affect how Congress behaves? When Americans believe they face few external threats—or think that international engagement could itself produce a threat—they see less merit in deferring to the White House on foreign policy and more merit to congressional activism. Debate and disagreement are not likely to pose significant costs; after all, the country is secure. But when Americans believe the country faces an external threat, they quickly convert to the need for strong presidential leadership. Congressional dissent that was previously acceptable suddenly looks to be unhelpful meddling at best and unpatriotic at worst. Members of Congress are themselves likely to feel the same shifting sentiments toward the wisdom of deferring to the president as well as profoundly aware that being on the wrong side of that shift could hurt them come the next election.

A second factor shaping executive–legislative interactions on foreign policy is how well the president's policies are faring. Presidents who succeed find themselves surrounded by admirers; presidents who don't find themselves targeted by critics. The reason is easy to understand. It is difficult to argue with success. When things go well for a White House, friends on Capitol Hill applaud and critics bite their tongues. But when policies fail, critics step up their attacks and friends worry about their own political futures. That is precisely what happened to President George W. Bush in 2006 and 2007; as the death toll of U.S. soldiers in Iraq mounted, so too did domestic criticism of his policies. The statement that President Kennedy made when he took responsibility for the disastrous U.S. effort to foment Castro's overthrow by landing Cuban exiles at the Bay of Pigs in 1961 captures the underlying political reality: "Victory has a hundred fathers and defeat is an orphan."[8]

Throughout American history, power over foreign policy has flowed back and forth between the two ends of Pennsylvania Avenue according to these two basic dynamics. . . .

As Americans became convinced in the late 1940s that hostile communist states threatened the United States and the rest of the free world, they increasingly came to agree on two basic ideas: the United States needed to resist communist expansion, and achieving this goal demanded strong presidential leadership. Most members of Congress shared these two basic beliefs (and helped promote them); those who disagreed risked punishment at the polls. The process became self-reinforcing. As more lawmakers stepped to the sidelines on defense and foreign policy over the course of the 1950s, others saw it as increasingly futile, not to mention dangerous politically, to continue to speak out. By 1960, the "imperial presidency," the flip side of a deferential Congress, was in full bloom.[9] As one senator complained in 1965, members of Congress were responding to even the most far-reaching presidential decisions on foreign affairs by "stumbling over each other to see who can say 'yea' the quickest and loudest."[10]

The era of congressional deference to an imperial president came to a crashing halt when public opinion soured on the Vietnam War. Many Americans became convinced that communist revolutions in the Third World posed no direct threat to core U.S. security interests and that the United States could find a way to co-exist peacefully with the Soviet Union. With the public more willing to question administration policies, so too were members of Congress. Many lawmakers had substantive disagreements with the White House over what America's vital interests were and how best to advance them. Moreover, members of Congress had less to fear politically by the early 1970s in challenging the White House than they had only a few years earlier. Indeed, many lawmakers calculated that challenging the president's foreign policies could actually help at the ballot box by enabling them to stake out positions that their constituents favored. The result was a surge in congressional activism. Presidents Carter and Reagan received far less cooperation from Capitol Hill than Presidents Eisenhower and Kennedy did. . . .

The Fall of the Berlin Wall

The end of the Cold War accelerated the trend toward greater congressional activism that Vietnam triggered. With the Soviet Union relegated to the ash heap of history, most Americans looked abroad and saw no threat of similar magnitude on the horizon. When asked to name the most important problem facing the United States, polls in the 1990s rarely found that more than 5 percent of Americans named a foreign policy issue. That was a steep drop from the upward of 50 percent who named a foreign policy issue during the height of the Cold War. Moreover, many Americans had trouble identifying any foreign policy issue that worried them. One 1998 poll asked people to name "two or three of the biggest foreign-policy problems facing the United States today." The most common response by far, at 21 percent, was "don't know."[11]

These public attitudes meant that members of Congress who challenged the White House on foreign policy ran almost no electoral risks. With the public not caring enough to punish them for any excesses, lawmakers went busily about challenging Bill Clinton's foreign policy. In April 1999, for instance, during the Kosovo War, the House refused to vote to support the bombing. Not to be outdone, the Senate voted down the Comprehensive Test Ban Treaty in October 1999 even though President Clinton and sixty-two senators had asked that it be withdrawn from consideration.[12] . . .

The Deferential Congress Returns

Congress's assertiveness in the first post–Cold War decade rested on the public's belief that what happened outside America's borders mattered little for their lives. September 11 punctured that illusion and ended America's decade-long "holiday from history."[13] Foreign policy suddenly became a top priority with the public. Not surprisingly, the pendulum of power swung sharply back toward the White House. . . .

Members of Congress similarly rallied behind the president. Three days after the attack, all but one member of Congress voted to give the president open-ended authority to retaliate against those responsible, authorizing him "to use all necessary and appropriate force against those nations, organizations, or persons he determines planned, authorized, committed, or aided the terrorist attacks that occurred on September 11, 2001, or harbored such organizations or persons." In short, Congress effectively declared war and left it up to President Bush to decide who the enemy was.

Over the next few months, Congress reversed key policy stands that administration officials said interfered with its conduct of the war on terrorism. For several years, conservative legislators had blocked a bipartisan plan to pay much of the outstanding U.S. dues to the United Nations. President Bush argued that these back dues hindered his efforts to assemble a multinational coalition to prosecute the war on terrorism, so Congress appropriated the long-delayed funds without opposition. Congress did something else that had been unthinkable only a month earlier—it allowed President Bush to lift the sanctions that the United States had imposed on Pakistan to protest General Pervez Musharraf's seizure of power in 1999. When President Bush proposed increasing defense spending by $38 billion in 2003—a sum equal to Great Britain's entire military budget and three-quarters of China's—Congress quickly voted to appropriate the funds. Lawmakers' enthusiasm for the spending increase was not diminished by the fact that most of the new money went to fund defense programs that had been on the drawing boards before September 11 rather than to meet the needs of the war on terrorism. . . .

The willingness of members of Congress to defer to President Bush on foreign policy after 9/11 stemmed in good part from a basic principled motive—the crisis demanded less "second guessing" of the White House. But lawmakers who might have preferred different policies quickly understood that discretion was the greater part of valor. They worried that if they challenged a popular wartime president, they risked being accused of playing politics with national security. This was not an idle fear. When Senate Majority Leader Tom Daschle (D-S.D.) said in February 2002 that the Bush administration's efforts to expand the war lacked "a clear direction," Republican leaders questioned his patriotism. One went as far as to accuse him of "giving aid and comfort to our enemies," which happens to be the legal definition of treason.[14]

Party reputations reinforced Congress's instinct to defer to the White House. Because President Bush was a Republican, challenges to his foreign policy stewardship would more likely come from congressional Democrats than congressional Republicans. But Democrats had a problem in trying to criticize a popular Republican president on foreign policy—most Americans lacked confidence in their ability to handle national security issues. Ever since the Vietnam War, Americans had given Republicans far higher marks than Democrats on defense and foreign policy. In times of peace and prosperity, like the 1990s, these perceptions did not create insurmountable obstacles for Democrats. In a wartime context, however, they left Democrats such as Daschle, who offered even mild criticisms of the White House, open to charges of being unpatriotic.

A desire not to give the Republicans a campaign issue, perhaps more than agreement on the substance, explains why many Democrats embraced President Bush's call in the fall of 2002 for a resolution authorizing him to wage war on Iraq. Leading congressional Democrats privately believed the request was both premature and unwise.[15] Most of America's traditional allies publicly opposed the White House's policy of regime change in Iraq. Moreover, while few lawmakers doubted that the U.S. military could capture Baghdad, most feared that the ouster of Saddam Hussein could have tremendous unintended and undesirable consequences. Finally, in asking Congress to act, President Bush said he had not made up his mind whether to wage war

against Iraq. Lawmakers knew, however, that the war power was a use-it-and-lose-it authority. Once they gave President Bush authority to wage war, he could exercise it as he saw fit, even if most members of Congress (or most Americans) thought the circumstances no longer warranted it. . . .

In the end, political calculations trumped. Congress did something unprecedented in American history—it authorized a war against another country before the United States itself had been attacked and even before the president had publicly made up his mind to wage war.

Congress Regains Its Voice

Four years after Congress authorized the invasion of Iraq, many Democrats and more than a few Republicans wished they could take back their votes. The speedy U.S. conquest of Baghdad had given way to a protracted and bloody occupation. By the start of 2007, more than 3,000 U.S. troops had died, and many times that had been wounded. Rather than forging a new democracy, Iraq looked to be spiraling into a civil war. With the death toll mounting and the prospects for a stable Iraq, let alone a democratic one, receding, George W. Bush discovered what Lyndon Johnson learned more than three decades earlier on Vietnam—the fact that members of Congress defer to the White House on the takeoff in foreign policy does not mean they will be deferential when it crashes.

A major blow to the Bush White House came when Democrats retook control of both houses of Congress in the 2006 midterm elections. No one doubted that the Republicans' stunning defeat reflected the public's unhappiness with the war in Iraq. Empowered by their status as the new majority party, Democrats held hearings and pursued investigations critical of the Bush administration. Even more troubling for the White House, the once solid Republican support for Bush's policies began to crack. The defections partly reflected doubts that the president's policies would work. "I've gone along with the president on this, and I bought into his dream," remarked Senator George V. Voinovich (R-Ohio), "and at this stage of the game, I don't think it's going to happen."[16] But Republican dissatisfaction also reflected political calculations. Representative Ray LaHood (R-Ill.) put the White House's problem bluntly: "People are worried about their political skins."[17]

In seeking to regain a say in foreign policy, members of Congress quickly discovered that authority once given away is hard to reclaim. Because Congress had approved the FY 2007 defense budget in 2006, the Bush administration already had sufficient funds to finance the major new policy initiative it unveiled in January 2007: the dispatch of 21,500 additional U.S. troops to Iraq. That funding decision could be reversed only if Congress passed a new funding bill by a veto-proof majority. And that Congress failed to do. In May 2007, President Bush vetoed a bill that would have begun the withdrawal of U.S. troops from Iraq. Congressional leaders subsequently acknowledged that while they could pass symbolic, non-binding resolutions criticizing the administration's Iraq policy, they lacked the votes needed to override the president's veto.

Barack Obama learned that Capitol Hill could be equally unwelcoming to a Democratic president. On his third day in office, he fulfilled one of his campaign promises by ordering the closure of the U.S. prison at Guantánamo Bay, Cuba, which housed foreign fighters captured in the war on terror. However, fierce congressional criticism ultimately forced him to reverse his decision. Obama had also campaigned on a promise to establish a so-called cap-and-trade-system for curtailing the emission of the greenhouse gases driving climate change. The House passed the legislation needed to start the program, but the Senate refused to act on it. After a year of fruitless efforts to spur Senate action, Obama acknowledged politically reality and abandoned the cap-and-trade initiative.

Another of Obama's foreign policy priorities was negotiating a new arms control agreement with Russia to succeed the START Treaty, which expired in December 2009. Obama and Russian President Dmitri Medvedev eventually signed the New START Treaty in April 2010. The White House anticipated rapid Senate approval. After all, a who's who of military leaders and foreign policy luminaries, including former Republican secretaries of state Henry Kissinger, James Baker, Lawrence Eagleburger, and Colin Powell as well as Republican national security adviser Brent Scowcroft, endorsed the agreement. Instead, a group of Senate Republicans, led by Senate Minority Leader Mitch McConnell (R-Ky.) and Senate Minority Whip Sen. Jon Kyl (R-Ariz.), fought to kill the treaty. The Senate approved it in the end, but only after a protracted White House lobbying effort. The administration's legislative push included promising something that many of the treaty's critics wanted: a commitment to spend billions of dollars modernizing the U.S. nuclear weapons arsenal.

Obama's decision to launch Operation Odyssey Dawn, the military operation to protect Libyan civilians from the Muammar Qaddafi's military forces, also faced congressional opposition. Some lawmakers criticized Obama for acting too slowly and ineffectively to topple the Libyan dictator. However, far more lawmakers argued that by attacking a country that had not attacked the United States or even threatened to, Obama had usurped Congress's war power. The White House argued that the 1973 War Powers Resolution gave the president the authority to use military force for up to ninety days without prior congressional authorization. When the military operations continued past the ninety-day mark, the House of Representatives voted overwhelmingly not to authorize continued airstrikes against Libya. Meanwhile, the White House continued with the airstrikes but carefully limited U.S. air operations and repeatedly refused to consider sending U.S. ground troops to Libya in order to avoid antagonizing Congress further.

The surge in Iraq and Operation Odyssey Dawn show that a more assertive Congress does not necessarily get its way. When presidents are intent on exercising their constitutional authorities—and willing to pay the price for doing so—they may carry the day. This is most likely to happen in situations in which presidents can act *until* Congress stops them. This was precisely the case with Bush in Iraq and Obama in Libya. With the federal courts historically reluctant to intervene in disputes between the White House and Congress over decisions to use military force, Congress could impose its will only by passing a law with enough support that it would withstand the inevitable presidential veto. As Iraq shows, that is enormously difficult to do. Conversely, the advantage shifts to Congress when the Constitution or existing legislation bars the president from acting *unless* he gets congressional approval. In these situations, the difficulties in assembling congressional majorities work against the president, witness the failure of the effort to create a cap-and-trade system.

Although a more assertive Congress may not win a showdown with the White House, its willingness to resist presidential initiatives can still shape foreign policy. Presidents worry about how they spend their time, energy, and political capital. They may decide against pursuing policies that Congress is likely to oppose because they are not confident they will win or they judge that the political costs of winning are too high. For example, the fierce resistance Senate Republicans put up against the START Treaty persuaded the Obama administration not to ask the Senate to vote on an even more controversial arms control agreement, the Comprehensive Test Ban Treaty. As a result, Congress influences foreign policy not just by what it does, but what it can persuade the White House not to do.

Conclusion

The framers of the Constitution created a political system that gives Congress substantial powers to shape the course of American foreign policy. Congress's willingness to exercise those powers has ebbed and flowed over time according to the vicissitudes of politics. When Americans are at peace and believe themselves secure, congressional assertiveness grows. When Americans find themselves at war or fear great peril, congressional deference to the president comes to the fore. At the same time, how much deference the president can expect from Capitol Hill depends on whether presidential policies are seen to be succeeding. Successful presidents can push Congress to the sidelines, while struggling presidents see their policies challenged on Capitol Hill.

Is there any reason to believe that America's foreign policy is better served by an assertive Congress or deferential one? This question is easy to ask and impossible to answer. No objective standard exists for judging the proper balance between activism and deference. The temptation is always to judge Congress in light of whether one likes what the president wants to do. As one Reagan administration official commented, "I have been a 'strong president man' when in the executive branch and a 'strong Congress man' when out of the government in political opposition."[18] That answer hardly satisfies those who have different partisan preferences.

What is clear is that activist and deferential congresses pose different mixes of costs and benefits. Although congressional activism usually looks unhelpful from the vantage point of the White House, it has several merits. For the same reason that an upcoming test encourages students to study, the possibility that Congress might step into the fray encourages administration officials to think through their policy proposals more carefully. Members of Congress also bring different views to bear on policy debates, views that can provide a useful scrub for administration proposals. When Capitol Hill is more hawkish than the White House, congressional activism strengthens the president's hand overseas. And congressional debate helps to legitimate foreign policy with the public. This latter virtue should not be underestimated; the success of the United States abroad ultimately depends on the willingness of Americans to accept the sacrifices asked of them.

But if congressional activism can be helpful, it can also be harmful. At a minimum, it makes an already cumbersome decision-making process even more so. More people need to be consulted, and more opportunities to derail a policy are created. Such inefficiency is not inherently disastrous—after all, the maxim "he who hesitates is lost" has its counterpoint in "decide in haste, repent at leisure." It does, however, increase the burdens on the time and energy of executive branch officials, potentially keeping them from other duties, and it can strain relations with allies that don't understand why Washington is so slow in acting. At its worst, congressional activism may render U.S. foreign policy incoherent as members of Congress push issues they do not fully understand and pursue narrow interests rather than national ones.

A deferential Congress avoids these problems but can easily create others. Presidents unburdened by congressional second-guessing find it easier to exploit the advantages of "decision, activity, secrecy, and dispatch" that Alexander Hamilton long ago hailed as the great virtues of the presidency.[19] But presidents and their advisers are not infallible. They can choose unwisely, and the lack of domestic checks can tempt them to overreach. President George W. Bush's critics would offer up his handling of the Iraq War as a case in point. But he was hardly the only American president to find his foreign policy plans go awry. It was the imperial presidency, after all, that gave America the Bay of Pigs and the Vietnam War.

A decade after 9/11, the political winds on foreign policy blew briskly in the direction of Capitol Hill. How long the new period of congressional assertiveness lasts and how far Congress will go to put its mark on foreign policy depends on events abroad and the consequences of White House policies. Only one thing is for certain: the pendulum of power will continue to swing back and forth between the two ends of Pennsylvania Avenue.

Notes

1. Quoted in Frank Rich, "It's the War, Stupid," *New York Times*, October 12, 2002.

2. Robert C. Byrd, "Congress Must Resist the Rush to War," *New York Times*, October 10, 2002.

3. Quoted in Thom Shanker and David S. Cloud, "Bush's Plan for Iraq Runs into Opposition," *New York Times*, January 12, 2007.

4. Shanker and Cloud, "Bush's Plan for Iraq Runs into Opposition."

5. Quoted in Carl Hulse, "Measure in Senate Urges No Troop Rise in Iraq," *New York Times*, January 18, 2007.

6. Richard E. Neustadt, *Presidential Power and the Modern Presidents: The Politics of Leadership from Roosevelt to Reagan* (New York: Free Press, 1990), 29.

7. Alexis de Tocqueville, *Democracy in America* (New York: Anchor Books, 1969), 126.

8. Quoted in Arthur M. Schlesinger Jr., *A Thousand Days* (Boston: Houghton Mifflin, 1965), 289–90.

9. Arthur M. Schlesinger Jr., *The Imperial Presidency* (Boston: Houghton Mifflin, 1973).

10. Quoted in James L. Sundquist, *The Decline and Resurgence of Congress* (Washington, D.C.: Brookings Institution, 1981), 125.

11. John E. Reilly, "Americans and the World: A Survey at Century's End," *Foreign Policy* 114 (Spring 1999): 111.

12. Charles Krauthammer, "The Hundred Days," *Time*, December 31, 2001, 156.

13. Representative Tom Davis (R-Va.), quoted in Helen Dewar, "Lott Calls Daschle Divisive," *Washington Post*, March 1, 2002.

14. See Elizabeth Drew, "War Games in the Senate," *New York Review of Books*, December 5, 2002, 66–68.

15. Quoted in Michael Abramowitz and Jonathan Weisman, "Bush's Iraq Plan Meets Skepticism on Capitol Hill," *Washington Post*, January 12, 2007.

16. Quoted in David Rogers, "Groundwork for a War Debate," *Wall Street Journal*, January 17, 2007.

17. Quoted in Rogers, "Groundwork for a War Debate."

18. John Lehman, *Making War: The 200-Year-Old Battle between the President and Congress over How America Goes to War* (New York: Scribner, 1992), xii.

19. Alexander Hamilton, "Federalist No. 70," in Alexander Hamilton, James Madison, and John Jay, *The Federalist Papers*, ed. Garry Wills (New York: Bantam Books, 1982), 356.

JAMES M. LINDSAY is the senior vice president, director of studies, and Maurice R. Greenberg chair at the Council on Foreign Relations. Previously, he was the director for global issues and multilateral affairs on the staff of the National Security Council.

Norman J. Ornstein and Thomas E. Mann    **NO**

When Congress Checks Out

Failing Oversight

The making of sound U.S. foreign policy depends on a vigorous, deliberative, and often combative process that involves both the executive and the legislative branches. The country's Founding Fathers gave each branch both exclusive and overlapping powers in the realm of foreign policy, according to each one's comparative advantage—inviting them, as the constitutional scholar Edwin Corwin has put it, "to struggle for the privilege of directing American foreign policy."

One of Congress' key roles is oversight: making sure that the laws it writes are faithfully executed and vetting the military and diplomatic activities of the executive. Congressional oversight is meant to keep mistakes from happening or from spiraling out of control; it helps draw out lessons from catastrophes in order to prevent them, or others like them, from recurring. Good oversight cuts waste, punishes fraud or scandal, and keeps policymakers on their toes. The task is not easy. Examining a department or agency, its personnel, and its implementation policies is time-consuming. Investigating possible scandals can easily lapse into a partisan exercise that ignores broad policy issues for the sake of cheap publicity.

The two of us began our immersion in Congress 37 years ago, participating in events such as the Senate Foreign Relations Committee's extended hearings on the Vietnam War. Throughout most of our time in Washington, tough oversight of the executive was common, whether or not different parties controlled the White House and Congress. It could be a messy and contentious process, and it often embarrassed the administration and its party. But it also helped prevent errors from turning into disasters and kept administrations more sensitive to the ramifications of their actions and inactions.

In the past six years, however, congressional oversight of the executive across a range of policies, but especially on foreign and national security policy, has virtually collapsed. The few exceptions, such as the tension-packed Senate hearings on the prison scandal at Abu Ghraib in 2004, only prove the rule. With little or no midcourse corrections in decision-making and implementation, policy has been largely adrift. Occasionally—as during the aftermath of Hurricane Katrina last year—the results have been disastrous.

Off Kilter

In October 2005, Representative John Dingell (D-Mich.) reached the 50-year mark for service in the House. Through seven presidents, much of the time as the chair of the Energy and Commerce Committee, often as the chair of its vaunted Oversight and Investigations Subcommittee, Dingell oversaw the executive branch to make sure it acted without bias or malfeasance. He did not shrink from making presidents, Democrat and Republican alike, uncomfortable. At times, even colleagues winced when he grilled bureaucrats. But the result was better execution of policy.

Dingell is now a unique figure on Capitol Hill, but he was not always alone. To be sure, the failure to ask tough questions of the military or challenge wartime decisions is neither new to Congress nor limited to Republicans. There has never been a golden era of congressional oversight. More often than not, oversight of foreign policy has taken the form of "fire alarm" hearings, responding to scandals or crises, rather than of "police patrols," designed to prevent problems before they occur. But at one time there was more robust give-and-take, even when the country was at war or when the president and the majority in Congress belonged to the same party. . . .

Vigorous oversight was the norm until the end of the twentieth century. During the Korean War, a special committee chaired by then Senator Lyndon Johnson strongly criticized the Truman administration. According to the historian Bruce Schulman, it also "reduced waste, improved the efficiency of wartime agencies and reaffirmed the patriotism of administration officials—no trivial matter when [Senator Joseph] McCarthy and his allies saw every small mishap as evidence of disloyalty and subversion." In the 1970s, there were the Church committee investigations of intelligence failures and secret illegal surveillance. In the 1980s, joint congressional committees scrutinized the Iran-contra affair. In the 1990s, authorizing committees and appropriations committees in both houses reviewed military operations in Kosovo. When the Republicans took control of Congress under President Bill Clinton, overall oversight declined. (Joel Aberbach, a political scientist at the University of California, Los Angeles, has found that the overall number of oversight hearings in the House— excluding the appropriations committees—dropped from 782 during the first six months of 1983 to 287 during the first six months of 1997. The falloff in the Senate between 1983 and 1997 is just as striking: from 429 to 175.) But there were still some visible and aggressive investigations, albeit often driven by an obsession with scandal.

But since George W. Bush has become president, oversight has all but disappeared. From homeland security to the conduct of the Iraq war, from allegations of torture at Abu Ghraib to the surveillance of domestic telephone calls by the National Security Agency (NSA), Congress has mostly ignored its responsibilities. The same is true of less publicized issues involving the United States and the rest of the world, including U.S. relations with trading partners and rivals, allies and adversaries. The year-and-a-half hiatus in the Republicans' control of the Senate, which came after 9/11 and during a nationwide surge in patriotism, did not noticeably reverse that pattern.

The numbers are striking. Examining reports of the House Government Reform Committee, the journalist Susan Milligan found just 37 hearings described as "oversight" in 2003–4, during the 108th Congress, down from 135 in 1993–94, during the last Congress dominated by Democrats. The House Energy and Commerce Committee produced 117 pages of activity reports on oversight during the 1993–94 cycle, compared with 24 pages during 2003–4. In the mid-1990s, the Republican Congress took 140 hours of testimony on whether President Clinton had used his Christmas mailing list to find potential campaign donors; in 2004–5, House Republicans took 12 hours of testimony on Abu Ghraib.

When committees do hold hearings, they tend to focus on routine budget review. Charles Stevenson, a longtime Senate staffer, has noted that "the Senate Armed Services Committee held no hearings specifically on operations in Afghanistan in 2003 and 2004, and only nine on Iraq [excluding the prisoner-abuse matter] in that two year period—less than 10 percent of its total hearings. The House Armed Services Committee held only one hearing on Afghanistan in 2003 and 18 on Iraq during 2003–2004—less than 14 percent of its total number of hearings. The Senate Foreign Relations Committee spent 19 percent of its time on those two countries." Such hearings, moreover, suffer from "stovepiping"—the practice of looking only at matters and people within one's narrow jurisdiction—which prevents Congress from taking a comprehensive view of certain policies. Only one Senate Foreign Relations Committee hearing involved a senior military officer, and only two saw witnesses from the Department of Defense.

Anybody Home?

Foreign policy has dominated the attention of Americans since 9/11, and especially since the Iraq war began. Major issues have included the formulation and execution of terrorism policy, the invasion of Afghanistan, prewar intelligence, the invasion of Iraq, the conduct of the Iraq war and its aftermath, the NSA's surveillance program, reform of the intelligence apparatus, homeland security, the treatment of detainees, and U.S. borders and immigration. And yet, Congress has failed to ask how policies in these areas have been carried out, how faithfully laws have been executed, how reasonably taxpayer dollars have been spent, how well the executive branch has stayed within its constitutional bounds, and how vigorously malfeasance or nonfeasance by public agencies and private contractors has been handled.

Lapses have been especially apparent on issues relating to homeland security. The Department of Homeland Security (DHS) has been beset by a series of management problems, a lack of consistent focus, and a failure to sort out its numerous responsibilities—all problems that were utterly predictable. From its inception, the department has been a near revolving door when it comes to its top management team, has had major problems integrating agencies, and has had a less-than-stellar record creating an integrated information-management system for the department, not to mention coordinating its computers with those at the FBI.

What are the causes of these problems? Poor planning and faulty execution. Even prior to 9/11, the Hart-Rudman commission, which was set up to review U.S. national security needs for the twenty-first century, had recommended the creation of a new department bringing together agencies and bureaus tasked with combating terrorist threats and responding to domestic attacks and natural catastrophes. It was a powerful idea but a complex task, and determining what the department should look like and do called for much debate. Yet these questions were never debated. After vehemently resisting the creation of such a body for almost nine months, in 2002 President Bush made a dramatic turnaround virtually overnight and unveiled a far more sweeping plan, which had been secretly hatched by several key administration aides. There was no deliberative process to question the extent of the reorganization and its breakneck pace. Absent, too, was any talk of starting with a new department of border security and moving incrementally to something grander. When the DHS bill came to Congress, it sparked only one serious controversy: Would civil service protections for the DHS' 170,000 employees be eliminated? That question became a major campaign issue in the 2002 elections, while important questions about what the DHS should be and do were ignored. The DHS that was eventually created was much larger than the Hart-Rudman commission had envisioned: it had to integrate 22 preexisting entities—the largest reorganization in the history of the federal government. It was still reeling from the job when Katrina struck in August 2005, and so rather than operate as the centerpiece of a federal response to the crisis, as foreseen, the bloated bureaucracy was unable to figure out what to do for days, its inaction compounding the tragedy.

Congress' failure to oversee the DHS has been crushing. Realistically, only Congress can prod such a massive department and determine whether when mad cow disease strikes or self-initiated Minutemen patrol the border, the Animal and Plant Health Inspection Service or the Citizenship and Immigration Services (formerly the Immigration and Naturalization Service), both part of the DHS, are able to manage the problems. The same is true of the Federal Emergency Management Agency (FEMA), which lost its robust independent status when it was subsumed in the DHS; it has been roiling with confusion ever since.

For three years after the creation of the department, Congress did nothing to ensure that the preexisting functions of its 22 components were well maintained while new ones were added. The House only reluctantly and belatedly created the Select Committee on Homeland Security and gave it no legislative jurisdiction or control over the DHS' budget or activities. Knowing the committee's relative powerlessness, top officials at the DHS have treated it with indifference or contempt.

More generally, there has been no serious oversight of the DHS in either house. Perversely, the problem has been compounded by the incessant demands of the 88 congressional committees and subcommittees that, eager for political cachet and cover, have sought to grab a piece of homeland security jurisdiction by demanding that top DHS officials testify before them. The agency's top managers have spent a lot of time at Congress but almost none seriously examining the DHS' functions and performance. One result was the abject failure of the DHS and FEMA to handle the aftermath of Hurricane Katrina.

A Killer Blind Spot

Thursday, August 3, 2006, was a remarkable day in Congress. The Senate Armed Services Committee held an oversight hearing on Iraq featuring three star witnesses: General John Abizaid, the commander of U.S. Central Command; General Peter Pace, the chairman of the Joint Chiefs of Staff; and Defense Secretary Donald Rumsfeld. The hearing led the evening news, with footage of General Abizaid, echoed by General Pace, warning about the danger of a civil war in Iraq. Senator John McCain (R-Ariz.) asked both generals if they had foreseen that possibility a year earlier; both said no. Senator Hillary Clinton (D-N.Y.) recited to Secretary Rumsfeld a litany of failures over the past three years; his first response was "Oh my goodness."

The frank and pessimistic admissions by two top generals and the tense moment of theater between Senator Clinton and Secretary Rumsfeld were striking indeed. But even more striking was the fact of the oversight hearing itself. Secretary Rumsfeld, when asked to testify, first brushed off the request, changing his mind only after Senator Clinton turned his refusal into a major public issue.

Oversight failures in regard to the Iraq war go back to before the beginning of the war. On June 15 of this year, the House of Representatives convened a debate over the war—which Democrats called a sham—to consider a nonbinding resolution about whether to stay the course or

cut and run. It was the first formal discussion of the U.S. military role in Iraq since Congress voted to authorize the use of force in October 2002. And that was not much to brag about. As Thomas Ricks writes in *Fiasco: The American Military Adventure in Iraq*, "When the House debate began there was just one reporter in the press gallery. At their most intense points, the debates in both the House and Senate attracted fewer than 10 percent of each body's members." Unlike during the lead-up to the Persian Gulf War in 1990–91, there was little sustained discussion before the Iraq war. As Ricks puts it, "There were many failures in the American system that led to the war, but the failures in Congress were at once perhaps the most important and the least noticed." He adds, "There was little follow-up investigation or oversight. There were, for example, no hearings with returning division commanders."

Congress has also done little about the Bush administration's lack of any plan for the post–Saddam Hussein regime, its quashing of the State Department's planning, and its stunning failure to provide adequate armor to all U.S. troops. One senator said of the equipment problem, "There really is no excuse for this. Many in the military thought this would be a short conflict, and they did not want to lay out large sums of money for vehicles that would soon be superfluous. Some of the Pentagon officials said that there was only one manufacturer of the appropriate body armor, and the pipeline got clogged. If we had ridden herd on them regularly and publicly, it would have been different." . . .

Contempt of Congress

Since Congress has shown little appetite for any serious oversight or for using the power of the purse or pointed public hearings to call the executive branch to account, executive agencies that once viewed Congress with at least some trepidation now regard it with contempt.

In March 2003, the Senate Foreign Relations Committee slated a hearing to examine the postinvasion planning for Iraq, with retired Lieutenant General Jay Garner, the first U.S. civilian administrator of Iraq, as the star witness. Garner canceled at the last minute, prompting the committee's chair, Richard Lugar (R-Ind.), to call the event a "fiasco." "He was not able to come to the [Senate] Dirksen Building, but could brief [reporters] in the Pentagon," Lugar told the *National Journal*. "On the face of it, it was ridiculous." A senator on the Senate Armed Services Committee told us that Chair John Warner (R-Va.) was apoplectic when Garner also stood up his committee. Last January, an hour into a Senate Appropriations Subcommittee hearing on mine safety, Chair Arlen Specter (R.-Pa.) asked the administration's top two mine-safety officials to stay for another hour to answer more questions. It was a routine request, but the two said they were too busy and, despite another more pointed appeal from Specter, abruptly rose and exited through a back door. Relating the incident, *The Washington Post's* Ruth Marcus reported that the Bush administration "thinks of congressional oversight as if it were a trip to the dentist, to be undertaken reluctantly and gotten over with as quickly as possible. Most astonishingly, it reserves the right simply to ignore congressional dictates that it has decided intrude too much on executive branch power."

Consider, too, the Senate Armed Services Committee hearing in May 2004 on torture at the Abu Ghraib prison, a crucial test for the Defense Department and the U.S. military. During Senator McCain's tough questioning about who was responsible, Rumsfeld said that the military brass with him had prepared a chart showing the chain of command. When one of the generals said they had forgotten to bring it, Rumsfeld said, "Oh my."

Meanwhile, the Bush administration has aggressively asserted its executive power and displayed a strong aversion to sharing information with Congress and the public. In early 2001, the president issued an executive order granting former presidents, vice presidents, or their representatives the right to block the release of documents "reflecting military, diplomatic, or national security secrets, Presidential communications, legal advice, legal work, or the deliberative processes of the President and the President's advisors." (The order also directed the Justice Department to litigate on behalf of any such blocks.) The Bush administration has also refused to respond to requests for information under the Freedom of Information Act. In an October 2001 directive (planned well before 9/11), Attorney General John Ashcroft announced a departure from the Clinton administration's standard. Eschewing the "foreseeable harm" standard—which required agencies to release records under the Freedom of Information Act as long as there was no foreseeable harm in doing so—Ashcroft adopted a "sound legal basis" standard that allows agencies to withhold information if they have *any* legal basis to do so.

In addition to resisting congressional and public access to information, the Bush administration has substantially increased the number of documents it classifies and decreased the number it declassifies, blocked the release of documents and briefs requested as part of congressional investigations of the terrorist attacks, refused a House committee request for the numbers that were adjusted to reflect the undercounting in the 2000 census, invoked executive privilege in denying Congress access to information concerning the FBI's misuse of organized-crime informants in Boston, refused to share information on missile defense with the Senate subcommittee that oversees the project, delayed sending to Congress full cost estimates of the Medicare drug bill before it was signed into law, denied the Senate Homeland Security and Governmental Affairs Committee information about undisclosed meetings between Enron executives and top administration officials, and restricted Congress' access to environmental records. The administration has also engaged in many battles—with Congress and in the courts—over what information on the handling

of terrorist detainees and enemy combatants it has to release. The NSA surveillance initiatives were shared with a bipartisan group of only eight top party and committee members—all of whom were sworn to secrecy and could reveal nothing to their colleagues—rather than with the full congressional intelligence committees. Members of both parties have been quite open with us about the dismissive attitude, indeed the contempt, with which President Bush and Vice President Dick Cheney have greeted requests for information. National security briefings were often considered a complete waste of time; reading the morning newspaper was much more informative. Senator Dianne Feinstein (D-Calif.) said, "The briefings go on . . . but we could be anybody in those briefings. . . . It doesn't matter what we think."

This behavior is entirely consistent with the Bush administration's view of executive prerogatives. At times, it has been difficult to discern the administration's motivations for denying information to Congress and the public. But avoiding political embarrassment must have factored into some of these decisions. As former Senator Daniel Patrick Moynihan (D-N.Y.) has argued, the net effect of avoiding transparency in executive decision-making may have done the country more harm than good.

President Bush has arguably been stonewalling in the hope of leaving a stronger executive behind. But that ambition cannot explain the behavior of Congress, which has been strikingly supine. Minority Democrats often demanded information with gusto. But without support from the majority, they had little chance of prevailing in battles with the executive or in getting media attention. Some Republican senators, such as McCain, Maine's Susan Collins, South Carolina's Lindsey Graham, and Iowa's Chuck Grassley, and Republican representatives, such as Indiana's Dan Burton and Connecticut's Christopher Shays, fought for the release of critical information, but they seldom had the support of their party's leadership or their colleagues. Even their exceptional efforts have had limited success.

An Ailing Body

Why has Congress abandoned oversight when it is most needed? The most logical explanation, which has been confirmed by comments we have heard from many members of Congress, is that the body now lacks a strong institutional identity. Members of the majority party, including congressional leaders, act as field lieutenants in the president's army rather than as members of an independent branch of government. Serious oversight almost inevitably means criticism of performance, and this Republican Congress has shied away from criticizing its own White House.

The weakening of Congress' institutional identity probably began in the 1980s, when the insurgent Republican Newt Gingrich, of Georgia, campaigned to nationalize congressional politics, turning elections from individual referendums on incumbents into national referendums on what he claimed was a corrupt Congress long misled by Democrats. Candidates for congressional seats who picked up on that rhetoric and won in the November 1994 Republican sweep of the midterm elections settled into Congress with little regard for it as an institution. (This was not so, ironically, of Gingrich who, as Speaker of the House, was a staunch congressionalist.) Instead of arriving in Washington excited at the chance of belonging to the storied institution, the new lawmakers saw public service as a dirty job that someone had to do. Since 1994, most new members of Congress have left their families at home in the districts, and many have declared limits on their own terms.

Members of Congress have ratcheted down the amount of time they spend in Washington, which has led to a sharp decline in the number of days Congress is in session and the number of committee meetings that are held. When Congress is in session, both the floor and the committees are sparsely and intermittently attended, as members rush away from Capitol Hill whenever they can to make fundraising phone calls. During a typical week when Congress is in session, no votes occur before 6:30 PM on Tuesday or after noon on Thursday, leaving little time for extended oversight hearings or other related activities.

Close voting margins have also contributed to the problem, as members of Congress have focused more on holding (or overturning) slender majorities than on broad matters of governance. When Bush became president and the Republicans secured control of the House and the Senate, Republican congressional leaders reacted reflexively as members of his team, eager to advance his agenda and avoid any turmoil. (As he was leaving Congress in the fall of 2005, House Majority Leader Tom DeLay, of Texas, said that when the president and the congressional majority are of the same party, "You don't need the [oversight] hearings.") Ideological polarization combined with near parity between the parties raised the stakes of majority control, weakening the institutional incentives that the founders had designed to ensure vigorous congressional oversight of the executive.

In recent months, spurred by revelations about the NSA surveillance program, the Supreme Court's ruling in *Hamdan v. Rumsfeld* (which scuttled the executive branch's efforts to try suspected terrorists before military commissions), Bush's defiant signing of presidential statements, and the growing unpopularity of the president and his conduct of the Iraq war, Congress has shown small signs that it may be steeling its backbone. The Senate Intelligence Committee voted to demand that the administration notify it of surveillance activity and intelligence operations. After the *Hamdan* decision, Congress also vowed to set new rules for the treatment of detainees. Senator Specter, who has stood out for his willingness to fulfill Congress' role, told *USA Today* in June, "If you ask me if I still feel like a lonely voice, I would say that I feel like a member of a small chorus."

But it is far from obvious that the chorus will grow. In the final weeks of the 109th Congress, efforts to craft serious legislative remedies to problems with the administration's detainee and surveillance policies played second fiddle to the congressional leadership's focus on framing these issues for the upcoming midterm elections. Were the House or the Senate to fall to the Democrats, they would certainly usher in aggressive challenges to executive actions, including requests for information, subpoenas for committee appearances, and frequent constitutional confrontations. Less obvious is how serious, informed, and constructive Democrat-led congressional oversight of the executive would be under a divided government and whether such oversight would translate into wiser policy and more effective implementation. (The record of the Republican Congress under Clinton is not encouraging.) It is also far from clear that reinvigorated congressional oversight would extend into whatever government emerges in the 2008 elections.

Although fixing the oversight problem is an urgent goal in and of itself, it is also part of a larger challenge: to mend the broken legislative branch and restore a healthy balance to U.S. democracy. At a minimum, oversight demands an aroused public willing to hold its elected representatives accountable and even to toss majority parties out of power when they underperform. That, in turn, means having enough competitive seats to permit more frequent changes of party control on Capitol Hill. Reforming campaign finance and redistricting would be a good place to start. Congress' composition should also be changed; having fewer ideological zealots and partisan warriors and more institutionalists would go a long way toward toughening congressional oversight of the executive. As the *Washington Post* columnist David Broder has put it, "We need an infusion of men and women committed to Congress as an institution—to engaging with each other seriously enough to search out and find areas of agreement and to join hands with each other to insist on the rights and prerogatives of the nation's legislature, not make it simply an echo chamber of presidential politics." Institutionalists need to be encouraged and rewarded, by the public and the press.

More specifically, better oversight will require a commitment by Congress to do more sustained legislative work. Changing the congressional schedule is a necessary step. Congress has radically cut back on the time devoted to a panoply of traditional legislative activities, including by reducing the number of days spent in session and the number of overall committee meetings and hearings held. The current 109th Congress is slated to have the smallest number of days in session in our lifetimes, with fewer than 100 in 2006. In the 1960s and 1970s, Congress held an average of 5,372 committee and subcommittee meetings every two years; in the 1980s and 1990s, the average was 4,793; and in 2003–4, it was 2,135.

The best reform would be to require Congress to hold sessions five days a week for a minimum of 26 weeks a year, with members spending two weeks on, in Washington, and two weeks off, in their home districts. Members of

Congress should not be distracted by permanent campaigning; accordingly, fundraising in the capital should be banned when the legislature is in session.

Congress also needs to overhaul its appropriations and authorization processes. In the past, much of the best oversight came from the House and Senate Appropriations Committees. But their activities have deteriorated, as the drive to earmark funds for particular projects in states or districts has replaced the desire to see that taxpayer dollars are spent wisely. Earmark reform would be a step toward revitalizing those committees. The authorization process, in which agencies and programs have to be reapproved every few years, has virtually collapsed in recent years. Leaders of the majority party should commit to reinstating annual or biannual authorizations for major programs. Exacting standards should be expected of the House and Senate majorities that are elected in November. Congressional leaders of both parties should be pushed to pledge that changes will be implemented when the new Congress is organized in January 2007. Meanwhile, Congress has plenty of urgent issues to oversee: whether the adminis-

tration's plans for an eventual withdrawal from Iraq are appropriate, how to handle a possible confrontation with Iran over its nuclear weapons capacity, and how to deal with the global threat of radical Islamism. If Congress falters again, the chances of policy lapses, mismanagement, corruption, and mistakes borne of arrogance or stubbornness happening will be even higher—and too high for Americans to tolerate.

NORMAN J. ORNSTEIN is a resident scholar at the American Enterprise Institute. As a senior counselor to the Continuity of Government Commission, he led a working group of scholars and practitioners who helped shape the McCain-Feingold campaign finance reform law.

THOMAS E. MANN is the W. Averell Harriman Chair and senior fellow in governance studies at Brookings Institution. Previously, he was the director of governmental studies at Brookings and the executive director of the American Political Science Association.

EXPLORING THE ISSUE

Is Congress Still Relevant in U.S. Foreign Policy making?

Critical Thinking and Reflection

1. What foreign policy powers does the Constitution grant to Congress? What foreign policy powers does the Constitution grant to the President? How has the relative power of each of these two institutions changed over time?
2. In what ways have members of Congress been influential in shaping American foreign policy? What are the limits of congressional influence in foreign affairs today?
3. Does congressional assertiveness in the area of foreign policy guarantee that Congress will also be influential? Why, or why not? Are there institutional changes that would lead to greater congressional assertiveness in American foreign policy?
4. How does congressional oversight contribute to accountability and transparency? Does aggressive congressional oversight help or hurt public confidence in American institutions and policies?
5. Will congressional assertiveness lead to more effective U.S. foreign policy? In what ways can Congress contribute? In what ways might congressional involvement hinder or detract from good policy?

Is There Common Ground?

There seems to be general agreement among most scholars that the exclusive control of Congress over the war power has diminished. However, to make a balanced assessment of the role of Congress in foreign policymaking, it is necessary to examine more than just the power to declare war. Both articles presented here recognize that answering the question of whether or not Congress is still relevant in foreign policy making requires the use of a broader lens. If and when members of Congress choose to use them, congressional powers of oversight, appropriations, legislation, and confirmation still provide Congress with the ability to play a significant role in American foreign policy making.

There is also common ground to be found in the idea that congressional assertiveness alone does not guarantee congressional influence. Greater congressional activism also does not guarantee that the resulting U.S. foreign policies will be more effective. If the making of foreign policy becomes just one more arena for intense partisan competition, congressional assertiveness may contribute to paralysis in U.S. foreign policy and do more harm than good. However, Congress can also play a constructive role to the extent its scrutiny and involvement fosters better-considered policy options and choices. Congress can also use its powers to increase the accountability and transparency of U.S. government departments and agencies, with additional beneficial effects.

Additional Resources

_____. *Defending Congress and the Constitution.* Lawrence: University of Kansas Press, 2011.

This book highlights past legislative accomplishments, but also criticizes the current Congress for not defending the power of the purse and the power to declare war. The author argues that inaction by members of Congress undermines the U.S. system of checks and balances.

Fisher, Louis. "Dose of Law and Realism for Presidential Studies." *Presidential Studies Quarterly* 32, no. 4 (December 2002): 672–692.

_____. "The Law: Scholarly Support for Presidential Wars." *Presidential Studies Quarterly* 35, no. 3 (September 2005): 590-607.

Hinckley, Barbara. *Less Than Meets the Eye: Foreign Policy Making and the Myth of the Assertive Congress.* Chicago: University of Chicago Press, 1994.

This book examines congressional voting behavior relating to major military actions, foreign aid authorizations, and select key controversies. The author finds that Congress more often than not votes with the President, and has done so consistently during the modern era.

Howell, William, and Jon Pevehouse. *While Dangers Gather: Congressional Checks on Presidential War Powers.* Princeton: Princeton University Press, 2007.

The authors provide evidence showing that presidents are systematically less likely to use military force when their partisan opponents have control of Congress. They also argue that Congress often exercises influence through public posturing with the media and during the oversight process rather than through bold legislative action.

Lindsay, James. "Congress and Foreign Policy: Why the Hill Matters." *Political Science Quarterly* 107, no. 4 (1992): 607–628.

This article examines the ways in which Congress can influence foreign policy outcomes beyond the legislative process. The author argues that Congress can have substantial influence on the foreign policy process through indirect means such as creating anticipated reactions in the White House, changing the structure of American national security organizations, and raising political costs to the President through political grandstanding.

Rudalevige, Andrew. *The New Imperial Presidency: Renewing Presidential Power after Watergate.* Ann Arbor: University of Michigan Press, 2005.

Schlesinger, Arthur M. *The Imperial Presidency.* Boston: Houghton Mifflin, 1973.

Wildavsky, Aaron. "The Two Presidencies," *Trans-Action* 4, no. 2 (December 1966), reprinted in *Perspectives on the Presidency.* Ed. Aaron Wildavsky. Boston: Little, Brown and Company, 1975.

This seminal article on presidential power, published in 1966, lays out the thesis that there are "two presidencies"—one focused on foreign affairs and defense and one focused domestically. The author argues that presidents are able to wield more power and meet with greater success in the realm of foreign policy.

Internet References . . .

Council on Foreign Relations

This paper examines the roles played by the President, Congress, and the Supreme Court in U.S. detention policies in the years after the terrorist attacks of September 11, 2001. It also reviews the constitutional powers and political factors that shape U.S. policies at Guantanamo Bay.

www.cfr.org/terrorism-and-the-law/judging-guantanamo-court-congress-white-house/p11025

Foreign Policy

This article highlights an increase in congressional oversight of the U.S. war in Afghanistan. It also criticizes Congress for not taking a more active oversight role earlier in the U.S. intervention.

www.foreignpolicy.com/articles/2011/02/14/congressional_oversight

The Miami Herald

This article identifies several of the political obstacles that President Barack Obama faced as he tried to close the U.S. detention facilities at Guantanamo Bay. The author argues that Congress played a significant role in preventing President Obama from closing the facility.

www.mcclatchydc.com/2012/01/09/135179/congress-rule-keep-obama-from.html

Selected, Edited, and with Issue Framing Material by:
Suzanne Nielsen, *U.S. Military Academy*
and
Scott Handler, *U.S. Military Academy*

ISSUE

Does the President Have Too Much Power in Decision Making About the Use of American Military Power Abroad?

YES: **Robert J. Delahunty**, from "War Powers Irresolution: The Obama Administration and the Libyan Intervention," *Engage* (September 2011)

NO: **Congressional Research Service**, from "Overview of United States Activities in Libya," *White House Report to Congress* (June 2011)

Learning Outcomes

After reading this issue, you should be able to:

- Describe the constitutional authorities of the president and Congress relating to the use of force.
- Understand the War Powers Resolution of 1973 and the constraints it seeks to impose on presidential authority.
- Discuss tensions between the president and Congress regarding the use of military force, especially in the years since the War Powers Resolution became law.
- Discuss the impact that international organizations may have on presidential decision making regarding the use of force.

ISSUE SUMMARY

YES: Robert J. Delahunty, an associate professor at the University of St. Thomas School of Law, argues that the Obama Administration's military intervention in Libya exceeded the president's constitutional authorities and constituted a violation of the War Powers Resolution. The administration's argument that U.S. actions in Libya fall short of what the War Powers Resolution considers "hostilities" lacks credibility.

NO: Congressional Research Service, in its report to Congress on U.S. involvement in Libya, contends that its actions were limited in nature, part of a broader international coalition, and consistent with United Nations Security Council resolutions. Moreover, contrary to claims otherwise, the administration consulted extensively with Congress regarding its actions in Libya.

The establishment of limits on the power of government is one of the defining features of the U.S. Constitution. The framers, concerned to prevent any one branch from becoming dominant, carefully divided power among the three branches and instituted a system of checks and balances to guard against possible encroachments. Decision making regarding the use of force is no exception. While Article II establishes the president as the commander in chief of the armed forces, Congress has the power to declare war, raise and maintain an army and a navy, and maintain appropriate funds for national defense. Given this arrangement, tensions between the two branches over matters of foreign and security policy are inevitable. However, from the framers' perspective, these tensions are desirable. The decision to go to war is a weighty one,

with implications for the health of democracy at home as well as the protection of U.S. national interests against international threats. Such decisions should require the democratic deliberation that the Constitution appears to require.

Particularly in the latter half of the twentieth century, the power of the presidency has evolved; some suggest that the balance has shifted too far in the president's direction. As discussed in the previous issue, many scholars see the Korean War as a turning point. When President Harry Truman argued that U.S. involvement in that conflict did not require an explicit congressional declaration of war, he set a precedent for future presidents. The U.S. war in Vietnam followed less than two decades later. During this extended and costly conflict, which became increasingly unpopular at home, the administration of President

Richard Nixon came to be seen by many as acting on an expansive interpretation of executive power with regard to the conduct of the war and in other policy areas. Some scholars even warned of the emergence of an "Imperial Presidency" in which an increasingly dominant president threatened the checks and balances originally established in the Constitution (Schlesinger, 1973 [2004]).

As one of its responses to these concerns, Congress passed the War Powers Resolution in 1973 over President Nixon's veto. Aimed at limiting presidential authority, the War Powers Resolution requires the president to consult Congress before committing U.S. forces abroad. In what is probably its most controversial provision (Section 4(a)(1)), this law also requires the president to withdraw troops 60 days after the commencement of hostilities unless Congress has issued a declaration of war. Since this bill became law, presidents of both parties have questioned the constitutionality of the War Powers Resolution (Grimmett, 2012). Critics of the War Powers Resolution argue that while consultation with Congress is appropriate, the specific provisions of this law overly constrain the president's constitutional authority as commander in chief, do not adequately recognize the need to defer to the president in times of crisis, and do not represent an appropriate approach to the use of force given the complex challenges posed by today's dynamic international security environment.

Those who advocate for a robust view of presidential authority emphasize that decisions regarding the use of military force are influenced by a host of considerations. In recent decades, for example, support from key international organizations—such as the United Nations (UN) and North Atlantic Treaty Organization (NATO)—has served as an increasingly significant consideration as presidents have decided whether to commit U.S. troops abroad. In fact, since the War Powers Resolution was passed, some presidents seemed more eager to seek international consensus and legitimacy than to obtain congressional approval for the use of force. While technically international endorsement does not substitute for domestic political processes, it can be politically relevant. International organizations such as the UN and NATO recognize that member countries will still be governed by ratification processes within their own governments when deciding whether to participate in multilateral military operations. Therefore, there is little basis for an argument that suggests that UN endorsement is a legal substitute for congressional approval. Politically, however, presidents have been able to leverage the international commitments of the United States to their advantage when arguing for appropriateness of a particular decision to use force abroad.

Further pushing this point, legal scholar John Kavanagh argues that the UN's collective security arrangement has almost made the power of Congress to declare war obsolete. Moreover, Kavanagh argues that the War Powers Resolution has ultimately failed to serve as a significant check to presidential power, in large part due to the ambiguous wording of the resolution and the reluctance of Congress to challenge the President (1997). But, he goes on to argue, this does not represent a significant break with past practices because presidents have long tended to receive substantial deference from Congress during wartime. From 1798 to 1983, the U.S. military has been deployed abroad in more than 210 instances, yet Congress only declared war five times (Kavanagh, 1997). Do these facts represent appropriate congressional deference to the president? Or, do they suggest that Congress has failed to fulfill its responsibilities? These interpretations remain a matter for debate.

Some scholars have suggested that two presidencies exist—one devoted to domestic affairs and one to foreign affairs. Originally offering this thesis in 1966, political scientist Aaron Wildavsky argues that presidents wield more power and are more successful in accomplishing their policy objectives in the realm of foreign policy and defense than they are in purely domestic matters (Wildavsky, 1975). The implication is that presidential power is more likely to trump that of Congress when it comes to issues related to international affairs. Other scholars have examined Wildavsky's "two presidencies" thesis more recently and found it to still be relevant. Presidents maintain first-mover, informational, and electoral advantages that posture them to be more influential in foreign policy than Congress. Furthermore, members of Congress are incentivized to focus more of their time and efforts on domestic issues, thereby further fueling a tendency to cede primacy in foreign affairs to the president (Canes-Wrone et al., 2008).

As mentioned above in relation to the Nixon administration, some scholars—including noted historian Arthur Schlesinger—maintain that the actions of successive administrations in the arena of foreign policy over the past 50 years have transformed the executive branch into an "Imperial Presidency" (Schlesinger, 1973 [2004]). More so than on domestic policy questions, where pressures from interest groups as well as the incentives of members of Congress tend to be stronger, presidents have exceeded their constitutional authority in matters of foreign policy. Critics argue that the failure by presidents to accept the constitutionality of the War Powers Resolution is just one example of an increasing tendency of presidents to exercise authorities beyond those envisioned by the drafters of the Constitution, with problematic implications for the long-term health of the system of checks and balances that the Constitution sought to create.

The U.S. intervention in Libya in 2011 provides a rich case study in presidential decision making over the use of force. In February 2011, the Libyan people began public demonstrations, demanding reforms from the regime of their ruler, President Muammar Qadhafi. However, Qadhafi's forces quickly retaliated and used force to suppress the dissidents. On March 17, 2011, the UN passed Security Council Resolution 1973, which called for an immediate cease fire. By the end of March 2011, a NATO-led coalition had established a no-fly zone and initiated offensive operations to enforce the UN resolution. Though President Barack Obama committed U.S. forces in support of this operation, Congress did not declare war. Eventually, the commitment of U.S. forces exceeded the 60-day time limit specified under the War Powers Resolution, and no explicit congressional approval was forthcoming. Although the Obama Administration argued its actions were consistent with the provisions of the War Powers Resolution and necessary in order to stop the crimes against humanity being committed by the Qadhafi regime, critics contended that the President had exceeded his constitutional and statutory authorities (Ackerman, 2011).

The YES and NO selections address the question of whether the President has acquired too much authority to use military force abroad by using this Libyan intervention as a case study. In the YES selection, law professor Robert Delahunty takes issue with the argument articulated by the Justice Department's Office of Legal Counsel in this case, which claims that because U.S. involvement in Libya was of a limited nature and short in duration, congressional authorization was unnecessary. Delahunty points out that the declaration of war clause in Article I of the Constitution draws no such distinctions; small wars require the approval of Congress as much as large ones do. Delahunty also argues that the Obama Administration violated the War Powers Resolution, to include the 60-day termination provision. By mid-June 2011, the Obama Administration should have either sought congressional approval for continued military operations in Libya or withdrawn U.S. troops. Neither of these actions occurred.

The NO selection, which argues that the President has not acquired too much authority, is provided by the Obama Administration. In its report to Congress on the U.S. role in Libya, the Administration contends that its actions were limited in nature, part of a broader international coalition, and consistent with UN Security Council resolutions. Moreover, it states that far from ignoring Congress, the Obama Administration consulted extensively with members of Congress regarding its actions. From March to June 2011, members of the Administration testified at 10 congressional hearings and participated in over 30 briefings to members of Congress and their staffs. Finally, the report argues that although intervention was necessary to stop the killing being done by the Qadhafi regime, U.S. military involvement was subordinate to a NATO operation and limited in scope. Overall, the report portrays this military intervention as a judicious use of U.S. power toward important ends that should not be seen as an overreach of presidential power relating to the use of force.

YES ↵

Robert J. Delahunty

War Powers Irresolution: The Obama Administration and the Libyan Intervention

The U.S. military intervention in Libya . . . has brought two fundamental and recurrent constitutional questions to the fore. The first is whether the President can initiate a war, admittedly not in national self-defense or for the protection of U.S. persons or property abroad, without prior approval from Congress. The second is whether the provisions of the War Powers Resolution[1] that require disengagement if the President has not obtained congressional sanction within two months of beginning such a war are constitutional.

Both questions have been prominent in public policy debates from the Vietnam War up to the 2008 presidential election and after. Political leaders, legal scholars, and activists in the Democratic Party over four decades have denounced what they see as the pretensions of an "Imperial Presidency" bent on aggression and conquest, and called for the restoration of what they contend are Congress' original powers over war policy.[2] Moreover, before assuming their current offices, the President, the Vice-President, and the Secretary of State had all emphatically stated views on the matter that reflected the dominant opinion within their party. I shall discuss and analyze in Part I the Administration's legal position on the President's war powers. Then in Part II, I will consider the Administration's stance on the War Powers Resolution.

I. The Justice Department's Opinion

On April 1, 2011, the Office of Legal Counsel (OLC) of the Department of Justice issued an opinion defending the legality of President Obama's attack on Libya.[3] OLC's main argument for concluding that the President needed no antecedent declaration of war or other specific congressional authorization was, in substance, that the Libyan intervention would turn out to be a small, short war. Affirming that the President "had constitutional authority, as Commander in Chief and Chief Executive and pursuant to his foreign affairs powers, to direct . . . limited military operations abroad, even without prior specific congressional approval,"[4] OLC "acknowledged one possible constitutionally-based limit on this presidential authority"—"a planned military engagement that constitutes a 'war' within the meaning of the Declaration of War Clause."[5] The purported constitutional distinction turned on "whether the military operations that the President anticipated ordering would be sufficiently extensive in 'nature, scope, and duration' to constitute a 'war' requiring specific congressional approval."[6]

OLC's distinction between small, short wars that the President may begin unilaterally and large, long wars that require prior congressional approval has no foundation in the Constitution's text. The Declaration of War Clause says simply that Congress has the power "To declare War, grant Letters of Marque and Reprisal, and make Rules concerning Captures on Land and Water."[7] Nothing in the clause explicitly differentiates between "small" and "large" wars. Dr. Samuel Johnson's *English Dictionary,* which provides evidence of how the term would have been understood in the Founding period, defines "war" as "[t]he exercise of violence under sovereign command against withstanders."[8] That definition covers wars both large and small. . . .

The text and background of the Declare War Clause, therefore, do not support OLC's position. . . . [T]he U.S. intervention in Libya is by no means a "measure short of war." As President Obama and other NATO leaders have repeatedly insisted, the Allies' overriding war aim is regime change—to bring down Colonel Muammar Gaddafi's government.[9] Further, despite official disclaimers, NATO forces have obviously been seeking to "decapitate" the Libyan regime by targeting Gaddafi and other senior figures in his government.[10] The costs of the operation as of mid-May to the U.S. alone are $750 million—and climbing.[11] The President's original claim to members of Congress that his intervention would be successful in "days, not weeks" has been falsified by events[12]: the President now acknowledges that there is no end in sight.[13] On June 1, 2011, NATO announced the extension of the Libyan campaign for at least a further ninety days, and some reports indicate that NATO may be mulling the introduction of ground troops into Libya. Any candid evaluation of the "scope" of the conflict should also take into account that Libyan-sponsored terrorists may attack Western cities or civilians (as Libya has done in the past). And although the President thought the Libyan operation to be too "small" to require Congress' approval beforehand, he also considered it sufficiently "large" to require a sign-off from the UN Security Council before he went forward.

The President and his senior colleagues have also held inconsistent positions on the question of presidential war powers. In a 2007 interview with *The Boston Globe*, then-candidate Obama stated, "The President does not have power under the Constitution to unilaterally authorize a military attack in a situation that does not involve stopping an actual or imminent threat to the nation."[14]

Then-candidate Hillary Clinton told the *Globe*, "[T]he Constitution requires Congress to authorize war. I do not believe that the President can take military action—including any kind of strategic bombing—against Iran without congressional authorization."[15]

Vice President Joe Biden stated in 2007 (in the context of a possible U.S. attack on Iran):

> I was chairman of the Judiciary Committee for 17 years . . . I teach separation of powers in constitutional law. This is something I know. So I got together and brought a group of constitutional scholars together to write a piece that I'm gonna deliver to the whole United States Senate, pointing out the president has no constitutional authority to take this nation to war against a country of 70 million people unless we're attacked or unless there is proof that we are about to be attacked. And if he does . . . I will move to impeach him. . . . I would lead an effort to impeach him.[16]

II. The War Powers Resolution

The War Powers Resolution (WPR) was enacted over President Richard Nixon's veto in 1973 by a Democrat-controlled Congress in the depths of Vietnam and Watergate.[17] Since then, the WPR has remained a venerated talisman for anti-war advocates whenever a war looms. Presidents, however, invariably see things Nixon's way. Since Nixon's veto, "every President has taken the position that [the WPR] is an unconstitutional infringement by the Congress on the President's authority as Commander in Chief."[18]

The WPR states that the President's "constitutional powers . . . as Commander-in-Chief" to introduce U.S. armed forces into actual or threatened hostilities are exercised "only" pursuant to (1) a declaration of war; (2) specific statutory authorization; or (3) a national emergency created by an attack on the U.S. or its armed forces. It requires the President to "consult" with Congress "in every possible instance" before troops are introduced into hostile situations. Section 4(a) requires the President to report to Congress when (in the absence of a declaration of war) armed forces are deployed (1) into actual or threatened hostilities; (2) "into the territory, airspace or waters of a foreign nation, while equipped for combat . . ."; or (3) in numbers which "substantially enlarge" U.S. armed forces equipped for combat who were already in a foreign nation. The heart of the WPR is section 5(b), which requires the President, within sixty days of filing (or being obligated to file) a report under section 4(a)(1), to "terminate any use of United States Armed Forces" that was subject to the reporting requirement unless Congress in the interval has declared war, enacted a "specific authorization" for the deployment, extended the sixty-day period, or been unable to meet because of an attack on the U.S. The sixty-day period may be extended by an additional thirty days "if the President determines and certifies to the Congress in writing that *unavoidable military necessity requires the continued use of such armed forces in the course of bringing about a prompt removal of such forces*" (emphasis added).

The executive branch has frequently objected to the sixty/ninety-day limit as unconstitutional. In his veto message, President Nixon objected that under this framework, "[n]o overt Congressional action would be required to cut off [the President's] powers—they would disappear automatically unless the Congress extended them." Arguing that this enabled Congress to increase its policy-making role through mere inaction, Nixon maintained that "the proper way for Congress to make known its will on such foreign policy questions is through a positive action, with full debate on the merits of the issue and with each member taking full responsibility of casting a yes or no vote."[19]

In a similar vein, Monroe Leigh, Legal Counsel to the State Department in the Ford Administration, argued that the sixty/ninety-day framework imposed an unconstitutional straitjacket on the President's power:

> The question inevitably arises: If the president has an independent constitutional power to order troop movements in the first place, how can a statute of Congress override or limit the exercise of that power? . . . [A] statute cannot constitutionally limit the President's discretion when to commit and when to withdraw armed forces from hostilities.[20]

These objections do not exhaust the possible constitutional arguments against WPR § 5(b). Critics can also appeal to constitutional structure, which assigns the federal branches very different responsibilities with respect to foreign affairs.[21] Section 5(b) impairs the President's effectiveness in conducting diplomatic negotiations (which the Constitution entrusts solely to the executive) because the ability to make credible threats of force is important to successful diplomacy. In the Libyan situation, for instance, the U.S., its NATO partners, its Russian and Chinese rivals, the Arab League, and Libya itself were and are engaged in strategic interactions premised on certain assumptions about U.S. intentions, resolve, and capabilities. Thus, Britain and France might not have intervened militarily but for the expectation of continuing U.S. involvement; likewise, the Libyan rebels might have surrendered by now but for the hope of more substantial U.S. support. If foreign actors come to expect the U.S. to begin withdrawing its forces after two months unless the President managed to persuade Congress to extend that period, our prospective partners' willingness to co-operate with us would be diminished, while our enemies' resolve to resist us would likely be strengthened.

But the WPR has survived intact despite all efforts to repeal or amend it. President Clinton supported a 1995 effort to eliminate the sixty-day withdrawal provisions, and Senator Majority Leader Dole's 1995 proposal to repeal most of the WPR even became the subject of a hearing. But Congress has consistently declined to act. The continuing vitality of the WPR as statutory law therefore cannot be doubted. Both the Authorization for the Use of Military Force (2001) and the Authorization for the Use of Force Against Iraq Resolution (2002) explicitly referenced it. Indeed, on March 21, 2011, President Obama himself reported to Congress on the start of military operations in Libya "consistent with the War Powers Resolution."

With the expiration of the sixty-day period, therefore, the President faced a seemingly inescapable choice: either discontinue operations in Libya as the WPR requires; or declare the WPR's withdrawal provisions to be unconstitutional. Instead, he did neither. In his May 20, 2011 letter to Congress, the President wrote:

> On March 21, I reported to the Congress that the United States, pursuant to a request from the Arab League and authorization by the United Nations Security Council, had acted 2 days earlier to prevent a humanitarian catastrophe by deploying U.S. forces to protect the people of Libya from the Qaddafi regime. As you know, over these last 2 months, the U.S. role in this operation to enforce U.N. Security Council Resolution 1973 has become more limited, yet remains important. . . . Since April 4, U.S. participation has consisted of: (1) non-kinetic support to the NATO-led operation, including intelligence, logistical support, and search and rescue assistance; (2) aircraft that have assisted in the suppression and destruction of air defenses in support of the no-fly zone; and (3) since April 23, precision strikes by unmanned aerial vehicles against a limited set of clearly defined targets in support of the NATO-led coalition's efforts. While we are no longer in the lead, U.S. support for the NATO-based coalition remains crucial to assuring the success of international efforts to protect civilians from the actions of the Qaddafi regime. . . .

> Congressional action in support of the mission would underline the U.S. commitment to this remarkable international effort. Such a Resolution is also important in the context of our constitutional framework, as it would demonstrate a unity of purpose among the political branches on this important national security matter. It has always been my view that it is better to take military action, even in limited actions such as this, with Congressional engagement, consultation, and support.[22]

The President's statement does not reflect any willingness to comply with the WPR's withdrawal requirement. It does not actually mention the WPR or in any way acknowledge that the WPR might apply to the Libyan intervention. Instead, it defies that law—though not so as to draw attention to that defiance. Section 5(b) states, in terms that are excruciatingly clear, that if the President wishes to continue a deployment into hostilities after the sixty-day period has run, he must advise Congress that "*unavoidable military necessity requires the continued use of such armed forces in the course of bringing about a prompt removal of such forces.*" But rather than claiming that additional time is needed as an "unavoidable military necessity" before the "prompt removal" of our forces, the President explicitly affirmed that our forces will continue operations indefinitely ("U.S. support . . . remains crucial"). In speeches and press conferences after May 20, the President remained adamant on the goal of regime change in Libya and saw no discernible end to U.S. military participation in the NATO campaign until after Gaddafi's fall.

Two principled courses of action were open to the President. If he considered the WPR constitutional, he should have ordered U.S. forces to stand down immediately in Libya, as the statute required. (Since there were no U.S. troops on the ground and at risk in Libya, there was no apparent need to wait an additional thirty days.) If he considered the WPR unconstitutional (as his predecessors in office had), he should have laid out his arguments, declined to order a stand-down, and accepted the legal and political consequences of his decision. Instead, in a message that did not contain any legal reasoning, he did neither. He stated that it would be "better" for him to have "Congressional engagement, consultation, and support"—and then did not mention an Act of Congress designed to ensure that Presidents in his position would engage Congress, consult with it, and seek its support.

In his 2007 *Boston Globe* interview, Obama was asked if "the Constitution empower[s] the president to disregard a congressional statute limiting the deployment of troops"? He answered:

> No, the President does not have that power. To date, several Congresses have imposed limitations on the number of US troops deployed in

a given situation. As President, I will not assert a constitutional authority to deploy troops in a manner contrary to an express limit imposed by Congress and adopted into law.[23]

In mid-June, just before the end of the WPR's ninety-day period for ceasing operations in Libya, the Administration submitted a report to Congress with less than a paragraph of legal reasoning supporting the continuation of conflict without congressional authorization. Here is that reasoning in full (emphasis added):

> The President is of the view that the current U.S. military operations in Libya are consistent with the War Powers Resolution and do not under that law require further congressional authorization, *because U.S. military operations are distinct from the kind of "hostilities" contemplated by the Resolution's 60 day termination provision.* U.S. forces are playing a constrained and supporting role in a multinational coalition, whose operations are both legitimated by and limited to the terms of a United Nations Security Council Resolution that authorizes the use of force solely to protect civilians and civilian populated areas under attack or threat of attack and to enforce a no-fly zone and an arms embargo. U.S. operations do not involve sustained fighting or active exchanges of fire with hostile troops, nor do they involve the presence of U.S. ground troops, U.S. casualties or a serious threat thereof, or any significant chance of escalation into a conflict characterized by those factors.[24]

So the WPR does not apply because the U.S. is not engaging in "hostilities" in Libya. Colonel Gaddafi and other targets of U.S. drone attacks would surely be confounded by this assertion. So might the U.S. military personnel who have been drawing combat pay since April for their service in the President's Libyan intervention.[25]

The Administration's attempt to downplay the extent of U.S. military actions in Libya in its mid-June Report to Congress was undercut some two weeks later when the U.S. Air Force confirmed that since NATO's Operation Unified Protection Protector (OUP) took over from the American-led Operation Odyssey Dawn on March 31, the U.S. military has flown hundreds of strike sorties. Previously, Washington had claimed it was mostly providing intelligence, surveillance and reconnaissance (ISR) and tanker support to NATO forces operating over Libya. "U.S. aircraft continue to fly support [ISR and refueling] missions, as well as strike sorties under NATO tasking," AFRICOM [Africa Command] spokeswoman Nicole Dalrymple said in an emailed statement. "As of today, and since March 31, the U.S. has flown a total of 3,475 sorties in support of OUP. Of these, 801 were strike sorties, 132 of which actually dropped ordnance."[26]

Consider some of the consequences of the Obama Administration's understanding of "hostilities." Actions like President Nixon's bombing of Cambodia—the very type of operation one might have thought the framers of the WPR intended to cover—might be excluded (no U.S. ground troops; no exchanges of fire; no serious risks of U.S. casualties or of escalation). The same would seem to be true of actions similar to President Kennedy's Bay of Pigs operation; President Reagan's mining the harbor in Managua, Nicaragua; or the U.S. "no-fly zone" in Iraq, maintained by Presidents George H.W. Bush and Clinton. And what if the US were to impose a naval arms embargo tomorrow on Cuba—would this conduct not constitute "hostilities" under the law?

Future Presidents using advanced or even current types of weaponry against other nations will also not be engaging in "hostilities" in this Administration's judgment. Presidents could engage in major, covert cyber wars—say, destroying Iranian nuclear facilities by using the Stuxnet computer worm—without introducing U.S. ground troops, engaging in active exchanges of fire, risking U.S. casualties, or even causing a significant chance of escalation.[27] They could use extra-terrestrial lasers or unmanned drones to strike at North Korea. They could even drop a nuclear weapon on Caracas if Hugo Chavez refused to relinquish power: again, no "hostilities."

The Administration attempts to argue *both* that the U.S. is not engaging in "hostilities" in Libya *and* that our military participation in the NATO campaign is indispensable for its success. The Report states:

> The United States is providing unique assets and capabilities that other NATO and coalition nations either do not possess or possess in very limited numbers—such as suppression of enemy air defense (SEAD); unmanned aerial systems; aerial refueling; and intelligence, surveillance, and reconnaissance (ISR) support. These unique assets are critical to the successful execution and sustainment of NATO's ability [to conduct military operations in Libya.][28]

How, one might ask, can the U.S. *not* be engaged in the ongoing "hostilities" in Libya, even though we insist that our military efforts are critical to NATO's success? The Administration is trying to talk law out of one side of its mouth, and diplomacy out of the other. The result is incoherence.

Conclusion

The Libyan intervention is rich in ironies. Three former Senators now at the helm in the Executive branch—Obama, Biden, and Clinton—have all discarded, without explanation or apology, their earlier, seemingly well-considered views on the constitutional allocation of the war powers between Congress and the President. The party that enacted the War Powers Resolution and championed it for decades thereafter, now in possession of the White House, blithely disregards it. And the Administration hardly lifts a finger to win congressional authorization for its Libyan adventure, even though it courted the Arab League assiduously and would not have dared to strike a blow at Libya without the Security Council's permission.

What explains these shifts? We are seeing a contradiction emerge between two policy imperatives. One imperative, codified in the WPR, is to oppose making wars that protect U.S. national security and promote U.S. interests. The newer, contrary imperative is to support humanitarian wars that uphold the international human rights of oppressed peoples. These imperatives led, respectively, to opposition to wars in Vietnam and Iraq, and to support for wars in Kosovo and, now, Libya.[29] The WPR is a substantial legal obstacle to pursuing wars of either kind: hence supporters of humanitarian wars can neither wholly accept it nor wholly reject it. Indeed, the WPR is a more serious obstacle to wars of humanitarian intervention, because the political costs to the President of "selling" such wars to Congress within two months are much higher. The public understands the arguments for what may be wars of necessity; it has little appetite for what are clearly wars of choice.

Notes

1. 50 U.S.C. 1541–48.

2. Thus, in a July 30, 1998 Senate speech, then-Senator Biden argued:

   [T]he "monarchist" view of the war power has become the prevalent view at the other end of Pennsylvania Avenue, and it does not matter whether it is a Democratic President or a Republican President. And the original framework of the war power clause envisioned by the Founding Fathers, I think, has been greatly undermined over the last several decades. Cong. Rec. 105th Cong. (1998).

3. *See Re:* Authority to Use Military Force in Libya, 35 Op. Off. Legal Counsel 1 (2001) [hereinafter OLC Opinion] (written by Caroline D. Krass, Principal Deputy Attorney General).

4. *Id.* at 6.

5. *Id.* at 8.

6. *Id.* at 10.

7. U.S. Const., art. I, § 8, cl. 11.

8. Johnson's English Dictionary, as Improved by Todd, and Abridged by Chalmers 1008 (1835) (entry for "war").

9. On NATO's war aims and tactics, see David Rieff, *Saints Go Marching In,* Nat'l Int., June 21, 2011, *available at* http://nationalinterest.org/article/saints-go-marching-5442.

10. *See* Josh Rogin, *Exclusive: Top US Admiral Admits We Are Trying to Kill Qaddafi,* Foreign Pol'y, June 24, 2011, *available at* http://thecable.foreignpolicy.com/posts/2011/06/24/exclusive__top__admiral__admits__we__are__trying__to__kill__qaddafi. The killing of a head of state (or other high-ranking government functionary) has been long regarded as an act of war. The assassination in July 1914 by suspected Serbian agents of the Archduke Franz Ferdinand, heir to the Austro-Hungarian throne, precipitated the First World War. Austria-Hungary, defending its harsh ultimatum to Serbia in a Letter of Explanation Transmitted to the Various European Powers (July 23, 1914), stated that "the sentiments of all civilized nations . . . cannot permit regicide to become a weapon that can be employed with impunity in political strife."

11. *Gates Puts Cost of Libya Mission at $750 Million,* N.Y. Times, May 12, 2011, *available at* www.nytimes.com/2011/05/13/world/africa/13gates.html?. The Administration subsequently revised that figure downward (to $715.9 million as of June 3), but estimated a cost of about $1.1 billion through September 30. *See* United States Activities in Libya 13-4 (2011) (report submitted to Congress), *available at* www.foreignpolicy.com/files/fp_uploaded_documents/110615_United_States_Activities_in_Libya_—_6_15_11.pdf.

12. Jake Tapper, Obama: *U.S. Involvement in Libya Would Last 'Days, Not Weeks,'* ABC News, Mar. 18, 2001, available at http://abcnews.go.com/International/libya-crisis-obama-moammar-gaddafi-ultimatum/.

13. In a press conference on May 25, the President said: "[U]ltimately this is going to be a slow, steady process in which we're able to wear down the regime forces and change the political calculations of the Qaddafi regime to the point where they finally realize that they're not going to control this country." Barack Obama, President of the United States, remarks with Prime Minister Cameron of the United Kingdom in Joint Press Conference in London, United Kingdom (May 25, 2011).

14. Charlie Savage, *Barack Obama's Q&A,* Boston Globe, Dec. 20, 2007, *available at* www.boston.com/news/politics/2008/specials/CandidateQA/ObamaQA/?page=full.

15. Charlie Savage, *Hillary Clinton Q&A,* Boston Globe, Dec. 20, 2007, *available at* www.boston.com/news/politics/2008/specials/CandidateQA/ClintonQA/?page=full.

16. *Quoted in* Monte Kuligowski, *Per the War Powers Resolution (and His Own Words), Obama Should Be Impeached,* RenewAmerica.com, Apr. 8, 2011, *available at* www.renewamerica.com/columns/kuligowski/110408; *see also* Adam Leech, *Biden: Impeachment If Bush Bombs Iran,* Seacoastonline.com, Nov. 29, 2007, *available at* http://www.seacoastonline.com/articles/20071129-NEWS-71129018?cid=sitesearch

17. The War Powers Resolution was one of several "framework" statutes enacted in the 1970s to constrain executive power, chiefly in the national security area. The "framework" has not endured: the statutes have proven to be ineffective, if indeed they have not become dead letters. See Eric A. Posner & Adrian Vermeule, The Executive Unbound: After the Madisonian Republic 85–9 (2010). On the War Powers Resolution in particular, see Major Geoffrey S. Corn, *Clinton, Kosovo, and the Final Destruction of the War Powers Resolution,* 42 Wm. & Mary L. Rev. 1149, 1151–2 (2001) ("Looking back over this period, it is indisputable that the central component of the War Powers Resolution— the requirement that the President obtain express congressional authorization to conduct such operations—has been virtually meaningless. In fact, it is probably only a slight exaggeration to state that the most significant effect of the War Powers Resolution has been to provide separation of powers scholars with an interesting subject to analyze and debate. Analysis of the actual operation of the Resolution in relation to these various combat operations reveals a consistent pattern of executive side-stepping, legislative acquiescence, and judicial abstention.").

18. Richard F. Grimmett, Cong. Research Serv., War Powers Resolution: Presidential Compliance 3 (2011).

19. President Nixon's Statement Vetoing the War Powers Resolution (Oct. 24, 1973).

20. Monroe Leigh, *A Modest Proposal for Moderating the War Powers Controversy,* 11 Geo. Mason U. L. Rev. 195, 198 (1988/9).

21. For a skillful elaboration of this point, see W. Michael Reisman, *War Powers: The Operational Code of Compliance,* 83 Am. J. Int'l L. 777, 784–5 (1989).

22. *President Obama's Letter About Efforts in Libya,* N.Y. Times, May 20, 2011, *available at* www.nytimes.com/2011/05/21/world/Africa/21libya-text.html?.

23. *See Barack Obama's Q&A, supra* note 34.

24. Report, *supra* note 31, at 25.

25. "The Defense Department decided in April to pay an extra $225 a month in 'imminent danger pay' to service members who fly planes over Libya or serve on ships within 110 nautical miles of its shores. That means the Pentagon has decided that troops in those places are 'subject to the threat of physical harm or imminent danger because of civil insurrection, civil war, terrorism or wartime conditions.' " See David A. Fahrenholdt, *Obama's Negation of 'Hostilities' in Libya Draws Criticism,* Wash. Post, June 20, 2011, *available at* www.washingtonpost.com/politics/obamas-negation-of-hostilities-in-libya-draws-criticism/2011/06/20.

26. Dave Majumdart, *AFRICOM: AF, Navy Still Flying Libya Missions,* Air Force Times, June 30, 2011, *available at* www.airforcetimes.com/news/2011/06/defense-africom-air-force-navy-flying-libya-missions.

27. The Pentagon has recently concluded that cyber attacks *would* be acts of war. *See* Siobhan Gorman & Julian E. Barnes, *Cyber Combat: Act of War,* Wall St. J., May 31, 2011, at A1.

28. Report, *supra* note 31, at 12.

29. The growing strength of the second imperative seems explicable if the U.S. is withdrawing from its role as global hegemon, and is increasingly following, rather than trying to lead, the international community.

Robert J. Delahunty is an associate professor at the University of St. Thomas School of Law. Previously, he was the deputy general counsel at the White House Office of Homeland Security.

Congressional Research Service    **NO**

Overview of United States Activities in Libya

In his address to the nation on Libya on March 28, 2011, President Obama presented a comprehensive explanation for why he authorized military action as part of an international coalition to protect the people of Libya and to enforce U.N. Security Council Resolution (UNSCR) 1973.

In the intervening weeks and months, coalition efforts have been effective in protecting the Libyan population. The regime has suffered numerous defeats, cities and towns across Libya have been liberated from brutal sieges, strong sanctions are in place, and the regime is encountering serious difficulties raising revenues through oil sales or other means. All these actions and outcomes are consistent with UNSCR 1973.

As the President explained, much was at stake when Qadhafi began attacking his people and threatened to show "no mercy" to the city of Benghazi and its population of 700,000:

> "In this particular country—Libya—at this particular moment, we were faced with the prospect of violence on a horrific scale. We had a unique ability to stop that violence: an international mandate for action, a broad coalition prepared to join us, the support of Arab countries, and a plea for help from the Libyan people themselves. We also had the ability to stop Qaddafi's forces in their tracks without putting American troops on the ground."

The United States and its international partners acted decisively and with unprecedented speed to mobilize a broad coalition, secure an international mandate to protect civilians, stop an advancing army, prevent a massacre, and establish a no-fly zone. In contrast, the war in Bosnia raged for nearly two years before the first NATO military operations took place, and three years before NATO began ground strikes to protect the civilian population.

The President authorized these actions for several reasons of national interest:

- To limit the spread of violence and instability in a region pivotal to our security interests, particularly while it is undergoing sensitive transitions;

- To prevent an imminent humanitarian catastrophe; and
- To show the people of the Middle East and North Africa that America stands with them at a time of momentous transition.

Beyond the specific military objectives, the President has stated that Qadhafi has lost all legitimacy to rule and must step down. His brutal behavior against his own population has been catalogued by a United Nations Commission of Inquiry and has resulted in a request for arrest warrants by the Prosecutor of the International Criminal Court for crimes against humanity.

Moreover, the Libyan government's actions posed a significant threat to regional peace and security. As the President noted in his March 21 report to Congress, the Qadhafi regime's "illegitimate use of force" was "forcing many [civilians] to flee to neighboring countries, thereby destabilizing the peace and security of the region." "Left unaddressed," the President further noted, "the growing instability in Libya could ignite wider instability in the Middle East, with dangerous consequences to the national security interests of the United States." The risk of regional destabilization was also recognized by the UN Security Council, which determined in Resolution 1973 that the situation in Libya was "a threat to international peace and security." Indeed, as Secretary of Defense Robert Gates testified to Congress on March 31, "it continues to be in our national interest to prevent Qadhafi from visiting further depredations on his own people, destabilizing his neighbors, and setting back the progress the people of the Middle East have made. . . ."

Further, the longstanding U.S. commitment to maintaining the credibility of the United Nations Security Council and the effectiveness of its actions to promote international peace and security were at stake in Libya once the Council took action to impose a no-fly zone and to authorize all necessary measures to protect civilians and civilian populated areas under threat of attack, particularly after Qadhafi's forces ignored the UNSC's call for a cease fire and for the cessation of attacks on civilians.

As President Obama noted in his March 28 speech, without military action to stop Qadhafi's repression, "[t]he

Published by *Congressional Research Service (CRS)*, June 15, 2011.

writ of the United Nations Security Council would have been shown to be little more than empty words, crippling that institution's future credibility to uphold global peace and security." . . .

Political and Military Objectives and Means

The President has honored his commitment to focus the preponderance of our military effort on the front end of operations in Libya, using our unique assets to destroy key regime military targets and air defense capabilities in order to establish a no-fly zone and enable protection of civilians as part of the enforcement of UNSCR 1973. These actions set the conditions so that, after a limited time, command of these operations transferred to NATO. Since that April 4 transition, U.S. military involvement has been limited to a supporting role, enabling our allies and partners to ensure the safety of Libyan civilians. On the political front, the United States, with its partners in the coalition, has also continued to employ other elements of national power to support efforts to bring stability to Libya and allow the Libyan people to reclaim their future. As Secretary of State Hillary Clinton testified to Congress on March 1, "The stakes are high. And this is an unfolding example of using the combined assets of diplomacy, development and defense to protect our interests and advance our values."

The crisis began when the Libyan people took to the streets in February to demand reforms and stand up for their human rights. Qadhafi's security forces responded with extreme violence. Fighter jets and helicopter gunships attacked people who had no means to defend themselves. There were reports of government agents raiding homes and hospitals to round up or kill wounded protestors, and of indiscriminate killings, arbitrary arrests, and torture as Qadhafi's forces began a full-scale assault on cities that were standing up against his rule. For these reasons, the International Criminal Court Prosecutor has requested arrest warrants for crimes against humanity for Qadhafi, his son Saif al-Islam, and one of his intelligence chiefs. The Prosecutor also recently announced that he has found increasing evidence that Qadhafi was personally involved in ordering mass rapes of Libyan women as part of his campaign of terror.

The President responded to the growing violence in Libya on February 25 when he issued Executive Order 13566, which imposed significant economic sanctions on Qadhafi, his government, and close associates. The Executive Order imposed a general freeze on all assets of the Government of Libya that are in the United States or are in the possession or control of U.S. persons anywhere in the world. The President authorized the Treasury Department, in consultation with the State Department, to publicly designate for sanctions on additional senior Libyan government officials, those responsible for human rights abuses related to political repression in Libya, and those

who provide material financial support for individuals and entities whose assets are frozen. To date, we have frozen over $37 billion pursuant to E.O. 13566. We strongly support Senate Bill 1180 that was introduced by Senators Johnson, Shelby, Kerry, McCain, Levin and Lieberman on June 13. This legislation would make frozen assets available for humanitarian relief purposes to and for the benefit of the Libyan people.

Also on February 25, the Secretary of State approved a policy to revoke the visas held by these officials, others responsible for human rights violations in Libya, and their immediate family members. The Secretary of State also suspended the very limited military cooperation we have had with Libya, including pending sales of spare military equipment.

On February 26, the U.N. Security Council also responded to this violence by unanimously adopting Resolution 1970, which demanded an end to the violence, referred the situation in Libya to the International Criminal Court, imposed a travel ban on, and froze the assets of Qadhafi, and members of his family and inner circle.

Rather than respond to the international community's demand for an end to the violence, Qadhafi's forces continued their brutal assault against the Libyan people. On March 1, the U.S. Senate passed a resolution that "condemn[ed] the gross and systematic violations of human rights in Libya, including violent attacks on protestors" and urged that the United Nations take action to protect civilians in Libya from attack, including by imposing a no-fly zone.

The people of Libya appealed to the world for help. The Gulf Cooperation Council and the Arab League called for the establishment of a no-fly zone. Acting with partners in NATO, the Arab World and the African members of the Security Council, the United States pushed for the passage of U.N. Security Council Resolution 1973 on March 17. The resolution demanded an immediate ceasefire in Libya, including an end to the current attacks against civilians; imposed a ban on all flights in the country's airspace; authorized the use of all necessary measures to protect civilians; and tightened sanctions on the Qadhafi regime and entities it owns or controls, including the National Oil Corporation and its subsidiaries. As his troops continued pushing toward Benghazi, a city of nearly 700,000 people, Qadhafi again defied the international community, declaring, "We will have no mercy and no pity."

At that moment, as the President explained in his speech to the nation on March 28: "We knew that if we waited one more day, Benghazi could suffer a massacre that would have reverberated across the region and stained the conscience of the world." Stopping a potential humanitarian disaster became a question of hours, not days. The costs of inaction would have been profound. Thousands of civilians would very likely have been slaughtered, a ruthless dictator would have been triumphant precisely at a time when people across the region are challenging decades of repression, and key U.S. allies, including Egypt and Tunisia, would have been threatened by instability on their borders during a critical point in their own transitions toward a more promising future.

Consequently, the President directed U.S. departments and agencies to rapidly help establish a no-fly zone, stop Qadhafi's forces from advancing on Benghazi, expand the coalition, and respond to the humanitarian crisis in Libya.

The President made clear that our military objective, supported by a coalition of allies and partners, would be to protect civilians and enforce the terms of the resolution, requiring:

- That all attacks against civilians must stop;
- That Qaddafi stop his troops from advancing on Benghazi, pull them back from Ajdabiya, Misrata, and Zawiya and other cities, and establish water, electricity and gas supplies to all areas; and
- That humanitarian assistance be allowed to reach the people of Libya.

Establishing these conditions would pave the way for a genuine political transition—of which Qadhafi's departure is a critical component. To bring about this objective, along with the international community, the United States responded to this crisis by developing, implementing, and monitoring sanctions and freezing billions in Government of Libya assets, building a broad international coalition focused on escalating diplomatic pressure on Qadhafi and increasing his isolation, and initiating and sustaining political support for military operations. This operation was launched just over a month after the first significant protests in Libya, nine days after Gaddafi began using airpower against civilians—and, most importantly, before Qadhafi was able to overrun Benghazi with "no mercy" as he pledged he would do.

To lend perspective on how rapidly this military and diplomatic response came together, when people were being brutalized in Bosnia in the 1990s, it took the international community two years to intervene with air power to protect civilians and a year to defend the people of Kosovo. It took the United States and its coalition partners 31 days to prevent a slaughter in Libya.

The United States has also helped the international effort to provide humanitarian relief to the people of Libya, providing almost $81 million to help those in need inside Libya and those who have fled the violence. These funds help evacuate and repatriate third-country nationals, care for refugees on Libya's borders, and deliver food and medicine. With U.S. government funding, four non-governmental organizations (NGOs), four U.N. agencies, and two international organizations are actively providing assistance inside Libya. The international community has already contributed, "committed[,]" or pledged $245 million. The U.S. government has also provided military in-kind assistance valued at nearly $1.1 million, pertaining to the transport of 1,158 Egyptians from Tunisia to Egypt via U.S. C-130 aircraft.

An international coalition of NATO and Arab allies continues to pursue the limited military mission to enforce U.N. Security Council Resolutions 1970 and 1973 and protect the Libyan people. At the onset of military operations, the United States leveraged its unique military capabilities to halt the regime's offensive actions and degrade its air defense systems before turning over full command and control responsibility to a NATO-led coalition on March 31. Since that time:

- Three-quarters of the over 10,000 sorties flown in Libya have now been by non-U.S. coalition partners, a share that has increased over time.
- All 20 ships enforcing the arms embargo are European or Canadian.
- The overwhelming majority of strike sorties are now being flown by our European allies while American strikes are limited to the suppression of enemy air defense and occasional strikes by unmanned Predator UAVs against a specific set of targets, all within the UN authorization, in order to minimize collateral damage in urban areas.
- The United States provides nearly 70 percent of the coalition's intelligence capabilities and a majority of its refueling assets, enabling coalition aircraft to stay in the air longer and undertake more strikes.

Politically, U.S. leadership continues to play an important role in maintaining and expanding this international consensus that Qadhafi must step down, sending an unambiguous message to the regime. We continue working with the international community to enhance the capabilities of the Libyan opposition and increase the ability to achieve political transition. After many meetings with senior opposition members in Washington and abroad, combined with daily interactions with the U.S. mission in Benghazi, we have stated that the TNC has demonstrated itself to be the legitimate interlocutor of the Libyan people, in contrast to the Qadhafi regime that has lost all legitimacy to rule.

The TNC has recently expanded to include representatives from across the country as it aims to become a truly representative body. It has committed itself to promoting a democratic transition, and to adhering to international standards and human rights. We continue working to facilitate greater political, financial, and non-lethal support, to include up to $25 million in medical supplies, rations, and personal protective gear. Perhaps most important is determining an expedient way to unfreeze Libyan government assets to meet pressing humanitarian needs in a manner that is consistent with domestic legal requirements and UNSCRs 1970 and 1973. This is an area where the assistance of Congress is most needed and could become a linchpin in the success of our strategy.

At no point has the United States acted alone, instead helping to mobilize the international community for collective actions, and creating the conditions for others to work toward our mutual objectives and to share the costs of these efforts. The NATO-led coalition has made its dedication to sustaining this momentum clear, recently deciding to extend Operation Unified Protector for another 90 days after June 27th. At the June 8 meeting of NATO Defense Ministers, NATO reaffirmed the April 14th statement of Foreign Ministers that operations would continue

> "until all attacks and threats against civilians and civilian populated areas have stopped . . . until the regime has pulled back all its forces—including its snipers and its mercenaries—away from civilian centers and back to their bases. And until there is a credible and verifiable ceasefire, paving the way for a genuine political transition and respecting the legitimate aspirations of the people of Libya."

As the coalition continues its effort to protect Libya's civilian population, we are likewise escalating the political, diplomatic, and financial pressure on Qadhafi. The results of this effort are most tangibly demonstrated in the list of former officials who have now abandoned him, which continues to grow. His foreign ministers, an interior minister, ambassadors to the United States and the United Nations, a central bank governor, an oil minister, five Generals, and his labor minister have defected as well. And we have again begun to see brave protestors taking to the streets of Tripoli as well as uprisings in the key cities of Zawiyah and Zlitan . . . . **U.S. Support to NATO Mission**

Acting under U.N. Security Council Resolution 1973, and as part of a multilateral coalition with broad international support, Operation ODYSSEY DAWN (OOD) was launched on March 19, 2011, to protect the Libyan people from Qadhafi's forces. Responsibility for leading and conducting this mission—now called Operation UNIFIED PROTECTOR (OUP)—transitioned on March 31 to an integrated NATO command, with all operations fully under NATO by April 4. The focus of OUP is to protect civilians and civilian-populated areas under attack or threat of attack. The mission continues to concentrate on three elements: enforcement of a naval arms embargo, enforcement of a no-fly zone, and actions to protect civilians from attack or the threat of attack.

The Department of Defense is providing forces to NATO in support of OUP. U.S. armed forces now provide unique capabilities to augment and support NATO and coalition partner contributions. These capabilities include the following: electronic warfare assistance; aerial refueling; strategic lift capability; personnel recovery and search and rescue, intelligence, surveillance and reconnaissance support; and an alert strike package. The United States is also augmenting the NATO Peacetime Establishments at the three NATO Headquarters with a number of additional U.S. military personnel. The additional strike assets described above are on continuous stand-by alert status to augment NATO and coalition forces if their capacity or capability were to be deemed inadequate by Supreme Allied Commander Europe (SACEUR) and those assets were subsequently authorized for use by the U.S. Secretary of Defense. . . .

As President Obama has clearly stated, our contributions do not include deploying U.S. military ground forces into Libya, with the exception of personnel recovery operations as may be necessary. . . .

The United States is providing unique assets and capabilities that other NATO and coalition nations either do not possess or posses in very limited numbers—such as suppression of enemy air defense (SEAD); unmanned aerial systems; aerial refueling; and intelligence, surveillance, and reconnaissance (ISR) support. These unique assets and capabilities are critical to the successful execution and sustainment of NATO's ability to protect Libyan civilians and civilian populated areas from attack or the threat of attack and NATO's ability to enforce the no-fly zone and arms embargo. They enable the Operation UNIFIED PROTECTOR (OUP) commander to find, fix, track, target, and destroy regime forces threatening and attacking civilians and civilian populated areas.

Consequences of U.S. Not Participating in NATO Operations

If the United States military were to cease its participation in the NATO operation, it would seriously degrade the coalition's ability to execute and sustain its operation designed to protect Libyan civilians and to enforce the no-fly zone and the arms embargo, as authorized under UNSCR 1973. Cessation of U.S. military activities in support of OUP would also significantly increase the level of risk for the remaining Allied and coalition forces conducting the operation, which in turn would likely lead to the withdrawal of other NATO and coalition nation participation in the operation. Furthermore, if NATO had to terminate the operation before the recently agreed 90-day extension (to September 27) because it did not possess the assets and capabilities required to conduct or sustain the operation, then NATO's credibility would be damaged with significant consequences for U.S., European, and global security. . . .

Legal Analysis and Administration Support for Bipartisan Resolution

Given the important U.S. interests served by U.S. military operations in Libya and the limited nature, scope and duration of the anticipated actions, the President had constitutional authority, as Commander in Chief and Chief Executive and pursuant to his foreign affairs powers, to direct such limited military operations abroad. The President is of the view that the current U.S. military operations in Libya are consistent with the War Powers Resolution and do not under that law require further congressional authorization, because U.S. military operations are distinct from the kind of "hostilities" contemplated by the Resolution's 60 day termination provision. U.S. forces are playing a constrained and supporting role in a multinational coalition, whose operations are both legitimated by and limited

Does the President Have Too Much Power in Decision-making About the Use of American Military Power Abroad? by Nielsen and Handler

269

to the terms of a United Nations Security Council Resolution that authorizes the use of force solely to protect civilians and civilian populated areas under attack or threat of attack and to enforce a no-fly zone and an arms embargo. U.S. operations do not involve sustained fighting or active exchanges of fire with hostile forces, nor do they involve the presence of U.S. ground troops, U.S. casualties or a serious threat thereof, or any significant chance of escalation into a conflict characterized by those factors. . . .

Congressional Consultation

The Administration has consulted extensively with Congress about U.S. engagement in Libya. Since March 1, the Administration has:

- testified at over 10 hearings that included a substantial discussion of Libya;
- participated in over 30 Member and/or staff briefings, including the March 18 Presidential meeting with Congressional Leadership, Committee Chairs and Ranking Members; all three requested "All Members Briefings" (two requested by the Senate, one by the House); and all requested "All Staff Briefings;"
- conducted dozens of calls with individual Members; and

- provided 32 status updates via e-mail to over 1,600 Congressional staff. . . .

In addition, the Intelligence Community has provided and continues to provide frequent classified written intelligence products on Libya and regular Libya intelligence update briefings to Members and Committees, numbering in the dozens of such briefings since March 1. . . .

USAID/DCHA (with AA Nancy Lindborg, DAA Mark Ward, D/OFDA Mark Bartolini, or DD/OFDA Carol Chan) and State/PRM (with PDAS David Robinson or Kelly Clements) held regular conference calls with Congressional staff to provide briefing updates on humanitarian assistance to Libya and its borders with Egypt and Tunisia.

Beginning February 28 through June 14 there were 16 conference calls held—initially twice weekly, then weekly, and now periodically as needed. . . .

THE CONGRESSIONAL RESEARCH SERVICE (CRS) works exclusively for the United States Congress, providing policy and legal analysis to committees and Members of both the House and Senate, regardless of party affiliation. As a legislative branch agency within the Library of Congress, CRS has been a valued and respected resource on Capitol Hill for nearly a century.

EXPLORING THE ISSUE

Does the President Have Too Much Power in Decision Making About the Use of American Military Power Abroad?

Critical Thinking and Reflection

1. Is the War Powers Resolution unconstitutional, or is it a legitimate, necessary check on presidential power? On what grounds do presidents continue to claim that it is unconstitutional? If it were to be amended, in what ways should its provisions be altered?
2. How effective is the War Powers Resolution in bringing about presidential consultation with Congress on the use of force?
3. Did President Barack Obama act in accordance with the War Powers Resolution when the United States became involved in Libya in early 2011? What else could Congress or the president have done to ensure greater consultation regarding military intervention in Libya?
4. How do international organizations such as the UN and NATO impact presidential decision making on the use of force?

Is There Common Ground?

The U.S. system of checks and balances remains a defining feature of the American system of government. In "Federalist No. 51," James Madison wrote in 1788 that "each department must have a will of its own," but went on to warn against "a gradual concentration of the several powers in the same department." While the War Powers Resolution may represent an attempt to check presidential power in accordance with the spirit of the U.S. system of checks and balances, it also raises a host of practical questions regarding the use of force. These questions become even more complex when viewed in a broader international context and against the backdrop of the evolution of the power of the presidency over time.

Few would argue against the value of consultation between the president and Congress when it comes to committing U.S. forces abroad. However, what the nature of this consultation should be is a matter for debate. The War Powers Resolution is widely viewed as an imperfect effort to force such consultations. However, there is less agreement over what might work better. Could a few minor revisions to the War Powers Resolution make it more effective? Or is the law flawed beyond repair? Given the hesitation that both the President and Congress have shown with regard to subjecting this law to an explicit constitutional test, the question is likely to remain an open one for some time to come.

Additional Resources

Canes-Wrone, Brandice, William G. Howell, and David E. Lewis. "Toward a Broader Understanding of Presidential Power: A Reevaluation of the Two Presidencies Theory." *Journal of Politics* 70, no. 1 (2008): 1–16.

This article provides an updated look at political scientist Aaron Wildavsky's "two presidencies" thesis. These authors agree that presidents exert more influence in foreign policy than domestic policy and further suggest that members of Congress may have incentives to delegate responsibility for foreign affairs to the president.

Grimmett, Richard F. *War Powers Resolution: Presidential Compliance.* Washington, DC: Congressional Research Service, August 30, 2012.

This report recounts how presidents have interpreted the War Powers Resolution over the past four decades, highlighting a number of U.S. military interventions in the post-Vietnam era that lacked congressional authorization and did not conform to the provisions of this law.

Kavanagh, John J. "U.S. Powers and the United Nations Security Council." *Boston College International and Comparative Law Review* 20, no. 1 (1997): 159–186.

This essay argues that collective security arrangements under the United Nations have tended to supersede congressional authorities outlined in the War Powers Resolution and make the latter obsolete.

Schlesinger, Arthur. *The Imperial Presidency.* New York: Houghton Mifflin, 1973 [2004].

Through the use of case studies, Schlesinger charts the expansion of presidential power over time and argues that presidents have increasingly exceeded